T0238892

Lecture Notes in Computer Science   9633

Commenced Publication in 1973
Founding and Former Series Editors:
Gerhard Goos, Juris Hartmanis, and Jan van Leeuwen

Advanced Research in Computing and Software Science

Subline of Lecture Notes in Computer Science

More information about this series at http://www.springer.com/series/7407

Perdita Stevens · Andrzej Wąsowski (Eds.)

Fundamental Approaches to Software Engineering

19th International Conference, FASE 2016
Held as Part of the European Joint Conferences
on Theory and Practice of Software, ETAPS 2016
Eindhoven, The Netherlands, April 2–8, 2016
Proceedings

 Springer

Editors
Perdita Stevens
University of Edinburgh
Edinburgh
UK

Andrzej Wąsowski
IT University of Copenhagen
Copenhagen
Denmark

ISSN 0302-9743   ISSN 1611-3349   (electronic)
Lecture Notes in Computer Science
ISBN 978-3-662-49664-0   ISBN 978-3-662-49665-7   (eBook)
DOI 10.1007/978-3-662-49665-7

Library of Congress Control Number: 2016932867

LNCS Sublibrary: SL1 – Theoretical Computer Science and General Issues

Printed on acid-free paper

This Springer imprint is published by Springer Nature
The registered company is Springer-Verlag GmbH Berlin Heidelberg

ETAPS Foreword

Welcome to the proceedings of ETAPS 2016, which was held in Eindhoven, located in "the world's smartest region," also known as the Dutch Silicon Valley. Since ETAPS' second edition held in Amsterdam (1999), ETAPS returned to The Netherlands this year.

ETAPS 2016 was the 19th instance of the European Joint Conferences on Theory and Practice of Software. ETAPS is an annual federated conference established in 1998, consisting of five constituting conferences (ESOP, FASE, FoSSaCS, TACAS, and POST) this year. Each conference has its own Programme Committee and its own Steering Committee. The conferences cover various aspects of software systems, ranging from theoretical computer science to foundations to programming language developments, analysis tools, formal approaches to software engineering, and security. Organizing these conferences in a coherent, highly synchronized conference program, enables attendees to participate in an exciting event, having the possibility to meet many researchers working in different directions in the field, and to easily attend the talks of various conferences. Before and after the main conference, numerous satellite workshops took place and attracted many researchers from all over the globe.

The ETAPS conferences received 474 submissions in total, 143 of which were accepted, yielding an overall acceptance rate of 30.2%. I thank all authors for their interest in ETAPS, all reviewers for their peer-reviewing efforts, the Program Committee members for their contributions, and in particular the program co-chairs for their hard work in running this intensive process. Last but not least, my congratulations to all the authors of the accepted papers!

ETAPS 2016 was greatly enriched by the unifying invited speakers Andrew Gordon (MSR Cambridge and University of Edinburgh, UK), and Rupak Majumdar (MPI Kaiserslautern, Germany), as well as the conference-specific invited speakers (ESOP) Cristina Lopes (University of California at Irvine, USA), (FASE) Oscar Nierstrasz (University of Bern, Switzerland), and (POST) Vitaly Shmatikov (University of Texas at Austin, USA). Invited tutorials were organized by Lenore Zuck (Chicago) and were provided by Grigore Rosu (University of Illinois at Urbana-Champaign, USA) on software verification and Peter Ryan (University of Luxembourg, Luxembourg) on security. My sincere thanks to all these speakers for their inspiring and interesting talks!

ETAPS 2016 took place in Eindhoven, The Netherlands. It was organized by the Department of Computer Science of the Eindhoven University of Technology. It was further supported by the following associations and societies: ETAPS e.V., EATCS (European Association for Theoretical Computer Science), EAPLS (European Association for Programming Languages and Systems), and EASST (European Association of Software Science and Technology). The local organization team consisted of Mark van den Brand, Jan Friso Groote (general chair), Margje Mommers, Erik Scheffers, Julien Schmaltz, Erik de Vink, Anton Wijs, Tim Willemse, and Hans Zantema.

The overall planning for ETAPS is the main responsibility of the Steering Committee, and in particular of its Executive Board. The ETAPS Steering Committee consists of an Executive Board and representatives of the individual ETAPS conferences, as well as representatives of EATCS, EAPLS, and EASST. The Executive Board consists of Gilles Barthe (Madrid), Holger Hermanns (Saarbrücken), Joost-Pieter Katoen (chair, Aachen and Twente), Gerald Lüttgen (Bamberg), Vladimiro Sassone (Southampton), and Tarmo Uustalu (Tallinn). Other members of the Steering Committee are: Parosh Abdulla (Uppsala), David Basin (Zurich), Giuseppe Castagna (Paris), Marsha Chechik (Toronto), Javier Esparza (Munich), Jan Friso Groote (Eindhoven), Reiko Heckel (Leicester), Marieke Huisman (Twente), Bart Jacobs (Nijmegen), Paul Klint (Amsterdam), Jens Knoop (Vienna), Kim G. Larsen (Aalborg), Axel Legay (Rennes), Christof Löding (Aachen), Matteo Maffei (Saarbrücken), Pasquale Malacaria (London), Tiziana Margaria (Limerick), Andrzej Murawski (Warwick), Catuscia Palamidessi (Palaiseau), Frank Piessens (Leuven), Jean-Francois Raskin (Brussels), Mark Ryan (Birmingham), Julia Rubin (Massachussetts), Don Sannella (Edinburgh), Perdita Stevens (Edinburgh), Gabriele Taentzer (Marburg), Peter Thiemann (Freiburg), Luca Vigano (London), Igor Walukiewicz (Bordeaux), Andrzej Wąsowski (Copenhagen), and Hongseok Yang (Oxford).

I sincerely thank all ETAPS Steering Committee members for all their work in making the 19th edition of ETAPS a success. Moreover, thanks to all speakers, attendees, organizers of the satellite workshops, and Springer for their support. Finally, a big thanks to Jan Friso and his local organization team for all their enormous efforts enabling ETAPS to take place in Eindhoven!

January 2016   Joost-Pieter Katoen
                                                                  ETAPS SC Chair
                                                                  ETAPS e.V. President

Preface

This book contains the proceedings of FASE 2016, the 19th International Conference on Fundamental Approaches to Software Engineering, held in Eindhoven in April 2016, as part of the annual European Joint Conferences on Theory and Practice of Software (ETAPS 2016).

As usual for FASE, the contributions combine the development of conceptual and methodological advances with their formal foundations, tool support, and evaluation on realistic or pragmatic cases. As a result the volume contains regular research papers, long tool papers, and a short tool demo paper. It is also complemented by a controversial but very interesting essay from our keynote speaker, Oscar Nierstrasz. We hope that the community will find this volume engaging and worth reading.

The contributions included have been carefully selected. We received 108 abstract submissions, from which 90 full-paper submissions materialised. All were reviewed by experts in the field, and after intense discussion, only 24 were accepted, giving an acceptance rate of only 27%. We thank all the authors for their hard work and willingness to contribute, and all the Programme Committee members and external reviewers who invested time in the selection process.

This year, FASE has experimented with a double-blind review process. The authors were asked not to disclose their identity in the papers submitted for review. The reviewers were thus able to read and discuss the papers while avoiding unintended bias caused by author names, affiliations, and other potential influencing factors. The survey of authors' preferences indicates that the authors find this feature of the process valuable, and worth the additional effort of anonymising the papers. We thank the many people who filled in our surveys on the subject. FASE is likely to experiment more with the idea in the future. The community is encouraged to contact the Steering Committee members if they would like to comment.

January 2016

Perdita Stevens
Andrzej Wąsowski

Organization

Programme Committee

Sagar Chaki	Carnegie Mellon University, USA
Nancy Day	University of Waterloo, Canada
Ewen Denney	SGT/NASA Ames, USA
Juergen Dingel	Queen's University, Canada
Stéphane Ducasse	Inria Lille Nord Europe, France
Alexander Egyed	Johannes Kepler University, Austria
Bernd Fischer	Stellenbosch University, South Africa
Milos Gligoric	University of Illinois at Urbana-Champaign, USA
Stefania Gnesi	ISTI-CNR, Italy
Marieke Huisman	University of Twente, The Netherlands
Valerie Issarny	Inria, France
Marta Kwiatkowska	University of Oxford, UK
Barbara König	Universität Duisburg-Essen, Germany
Axel Legay	IRISA/Inria, Rennes, France
Martin Leucker	University of Lübeck, Germany
Fabrizio Pastore	University of Luxembourg
Julia Rubin	Massachusetts Institute of Technology, USA
Bernhard Rumpe	RWTH Aachen University, Germany
Ina Schaefer	Technische Universität Braunschweig, Germany
Perdita Stevens	University of Edinburgh, UK
Marielle I.A. Stoelinga	University of Twente, The Netherlands
Gabriele Taentzer	Philipps-Universität Marburg, Germany
Mohammad Torabi Dashti	ETH Zurich, Switzerland
Andrzej Wąsowski	IT University of Copenhagen, Denmark
Martin Wirsing	Ludwig-Maximilians-Universität München, Germany
Yingfei Xiong	Peking University, China

Additional Reviewers

Arendt, Thorsten	Botterweck, Goetz
Autili, Marco	Britz, Arina
Basset, Nicolas	Calinescu, Radu
Beohar, Harsh	Cito, Jürgen
Bertram, Vincent	Darabi, Saeed
Biondi, Fabrizio	Decker, Normann
Blom, Stefan	Demuth, Andreas

Dong, Wei
Eikermann, Robert
Fahrenberg, Uli
Fantechi, Alessandro
Ferrari, Alessio
Fischer, Stefan
Gerhold, Marcus
Golas, Ulrike
Gordon, Michael
Greene, Gillian
Guarnieri, Marco
Guck, Dennis
Harder, Jannis
Heim, Robert
Hermerschmidt, Lars
Hildebrandt, Thomas
Huang, Xiaowei
Hölldobler, Katrin
Ismail, Azlan
Itzhaky, Shachar
Jiang, Jiajun
Kerstan, Henning
Kim, Chang Hwan Peter
Knapp, Alexander
Knaust, Alexander
Kolassa, Carsten
Kowal, Matthias
Kretchmer, Roland
Kumar, Rajesh
Kuraj, Ivan
Küpper, Sebastian
Lachmann, Remo
Linsbauer, Lukas
Lity, Sascha
Markin, Grigory
Mazzanti, Franco
Meijer, Jeroen
Meis, Rene
Milios, Dimitrios
Mir Seyed Nazari, Pedram
Moreira, Alvaro
Mostowski, Wojciech
Naddeo, Marco

Nagarajan, Vijay
Nieke, Michael
Noll, Thomas
Oortwijn, Wytse
Paoletti, Nicola
Plotnikov, Dimitri
Poll, Erik
Priefer, Dennis
Qu, Hongyang
Quilbeuf, Jean
Raco, Deni
Rensink, Arend
Roth, Alexander
Saha, Ripon
Scheffel, Torben
Schmitz, Malte
Schrammel, Peter
Schulze, Christoph
Schulze, Sandro
Schumann, Johann
Seidl, Christoph
Selim, Gehan M.K.
Semini, Laura
Shafiei, Nastaran
Sirjani, Marjan
Spagnolo, Giorgio Oronzo
Strüber, Daniel
Stückrath, Jan
Stümpel, Annette
Svoreňová, Mária
Thoma, Daniel
Thorn, Johannes
Tiezzi, Francesco
Traonouez, Louis-Marie
Tribastone, Mirco
Tsankov, Petar
Vallecillo, Antonio
van Dijk, Tom
von Wenckstern, Michael
Wille, David
Yu, Ingrid Chie
Zufferey, Damien

Contents

Analysis and Bug Triaging

Probabilistic and Stochastic Systems

Proof and Theorem Proving

Verification

Keynote Paper

The Death of Object-Oriented Programming

Oscar Nierstrasz[✉]

Software Composition Group, University of Bern, Bern, Switzerland
oscar@inf.unibe.ch
http://scg.unibe.ch/

Abstract. Modern software systems are increasingly long-lived. In order
to gracefully evolve these systems as they address new requirements,
developers need to navigate effectively between domain concepts and
the code that addresses those domains. One of the original promises
of object-orientation was that the same object-oriented models would
be used throughout requirements analysis, design and implementation.
Software systems today however are commonly constructed from a heterogeneous "language soup" of mainstream code and dedicated DSLs
addressing a variety of application and technical domains. Has object-
oriented programming outlived its purpose?

In this essay we argue that we need to rethink the original goals of
object-orientation and their relevance for modern software development.
We propose as a driving maxim, *"Programming is Modeling,"* and explore
what this implies for programming languages, tools and environments. In
particular, we argue that: (1) source code should serve not only to specify
an implementation of a software system, but should encode a queryable
and manipulable model of the application and technical domains concerned; (2) IDEs should exploit these domain models to enable inexpensive browsing, querying and analysis by developers; and (3) barriers
between the code base, the running application, and the software ecosystem at large need to be broken down, and their connections exploited
and monitored to support developers in comprehension and evolution
tasks.

1 Introduction

Is object-oriented programming dying?

The code of real software systems is structured around a number of interacting and overlapping technical and application domains. As we shall see, this
fact is not well supported by mainstream languages and development environments. Although object-oriented software development made early promises to
close the gaps between analysis, design and implementation by offering a unifying object-oriented modeling paradigm for these activities, we still struggle to
navigate between these worlds. Do the emergence of domain-specific languages
(DSLs) and model-driven development (MDD) prove that object-orientation has
failed?

In this essay we explore some of the symptoms of this apparent failure, and
argue that we need to be bolder in interpreting the vision of object-orientation.

© Springer-Verlag Berlin Heidelberg 2016
P. Stevens and A. Wąsowski (Eds.): FASE 2016, LNCS 9633, pp. 3–10, 2016.
DOI: 10.1007/978-3-662-49665-7_1

We propose the slogan "Programming is Modeling" and identify a number of challenges this leads us to.

Let us briefly summarize the key symptoms:

There Exists a Large Gap Between Models and Code. In an ideal world, requirements and domain models are clearly visible in the implementation of a software system. In reality, most mainstream programming languages seem to be ill-equipped to represent domain concepts in a concise way, leading to a proliferation of DSLs. Internal DSLs, for example, "fluent interfaces" that exploit the syntax of a host language, are often less fluent and readable than they should be. External DSLs (*i.e.* with their own dedicated syntax) can lead to a "soup" of heterogeneous code that is hard to navigate, understand, and analyse.

MDD represents another important trend, in which high-level models are typically transformed to implementations, but such "model compilers" tend to pay off only in well-understood domains where changes in requirements can be well-expressed by corresponding changes to models.

Mainstream IDEs are Glorified Text Editors. Although software developers spend much of their time reading and analyzing code, mainstream IDEs mostly treat source code as text. In general, the IDE is not aware of application or technical domain concepts, and does not help the developer to formulate domain-specific queries or custom analyses, such as: *Where is this feature implemented? Will this change impact the system architecture? Who is an expert on this part of the code?* Similarly classical development tools belonging to the IDE are unaware of the application domain. A classical example is the interactive debugger, which offers a uniform interface to debugging based on the run-time stack, without any knowledge of the underlying application domain. Although popular IDEs offer plugin architectures that allow third-party developers to integrate new tools into the IDE, the barrier to building such tools remains relatively high, and the application domain models of the underlying code base remain relatively inaccessible.

Programming Languages and Tools Live in a Closed World. Mainstream programming languages assume the world is closed and frozen. Static type systems, for example, assume that the type of an entity is fixed and will never change or evolve. When a type changes, the entire world must change with it. In reality, complex software systems have to cope with evolving and possibly inconsistent entities. Another symptom is the strict divide between "compile time" and "run time" in mainstream programming. For example, it is not possible to navigate seamlessly from a feature of a running system to the code that implements it. Finally, we see that developers often resort to web search engines and dedicated Q&A fora to answer questions that the IDE cannot. We need to acknowledge that code lives within a much larger ecosystem than the current code base.

In this essay we argue that we should revisit the object-oriented paradigm to address these issues by adopting the maxim that "Programming is Modeling." We further propose a number of research challenges along the following lines:

1. *Bring models closer to code* by expressing queryable and manipulable domain models directly in source code;
2. *Exploit domain models in the IDE* to enable custom analyses by developers;
3. *Link the code to its ecosystem* and monitor them both to steer their evolution.

Caveat: we apologize in advance for referencing only little of the vast amount of relevant related work.[1]

2   Bring Models Closer to Code

When we develop and evolve code, we need to comprehend the relationships between requirements that refer to domain models, and the underlying code that realizes those requirements. Ideally we want to see domain concepts directly in the code. We therefore argue that *a program should not just serve to specify an implementation of a set of requirements, but it should encode domain models suitable for querying and analysis.*

This, we believe, was one of the early promises of object-oriented programming as expressed in the 1980s. Nowadays, however, complex software systems are implemented as a soup of mainstream and domain-specific languages. DSLs can be used to address either technical or application domains. Typically several DSLs are needed to address a complex application. Despite the availability of many dedicated DSLs, important aspects of a software system may not be explicitly modeled at all. Notoriously, architectural constraints are implemented with the help of frameworks and architectural styles, but rarely represented explicitly or checked as the system evolves.

Introducing ever more DSLs is not a solution. Having many external DSLs complicates program comprehension and makes it difficult for tools to reason about the relationships between them.[2]

Internal (or embedded) DSLs are hard to achieve because (1) the syntax of many mainstream object-oriented languages does not support well the design of truly fluent interfaces (with some notable exceptions, such as Smalltalk, Ruby, Scala, ...), and (2) design methods emphasize the development of "fluent interfaces," so they can be hard to achieve *post hoc*.

We think that many of these problems have their roots in a *fundamental misunderstanding of the object-oriented paradigm.* While the imperative programming paradigm can be summarized as *programs = algorithms + data structures*, object-oriented programming is often explained (following Alan Kay [8][p 78]) as *programs = objects + messages*. While this is not incorrect, it is a mechanistic interpretation that misses the key point.

In our view, the object-oriented paradigm is better expressed as: *"design your own paradigm" (i.e. programming is modeling).* A well-designed object-oriented

---

[1] A representative selection of related work can be found in the research plan of our SNSF project, "Agile Software Analysis": http://scg.unibe.ch/research/snf16.

[2] Coping with this complexity is one of the goals of the GEMOC initiative [6]. See http://gemoc.org.

system consists of objects representing exactly the domain abstractions that are needed for your application and suitable operations over them (if you like, a many-sorted algebra). Code can be separated into the objects (or "components") representing domain concepts, and *scripts* that configure them [1].

We therefore posit as a challenge to *revive object-oriented programming by viewing OO languages as modeling languages, not just implementation languages.* Rather than viewing DSLs and MDD as the competition, we should encourage the use of OO languages as modeling tools, and even as language workbenches for developing embedded DSLs.[3]

3 Exploit Domain Models in the IDE

Although developers are known to spend much of their development time reading and analyzing code, mainstream IDEs do not do a good job of supporting program comprehension. IDEs are basically glorified text editors.

Developers need custom analyses to answer the questions that arise during typical development tasks [7,16]. Building a dedicated analysis tool is expensive, even using a plugin architecture such as that of Eclipse. Dedicated analysis platforms like Moose [12] and Rascal [9] reduce the cost of custom queries, but they rely on the existence of a queryable model of the target software.

As we have seen in the previous section, even though we would like to see programs as models, they are not in a form useful for querying and analysis, so we need to do extra work to extract these models and work with them.

We see two important challenges. The first is *"Agile Model Extraction"*, *i.e.* the ability to efficiently extract models from source code. This is not just a problem of parsing heterogeneous code and linking concepts encoded in different languages (*e.g.* Java, SQL, XML), but also of recognizing concepts coming from numerous and intertwined domain models. We are experimenting with approximate parsing technology, inexpensive heuristics, and other techniques [10,13] to quickly and cheaply extract models from heterogeneous source code.

The second challenge is *"Context-Aware Tooling"*, *i.e.* the ability to cheaply construct dedicated, custom analyses and tools that close the gap between IDEs and application software. The key idea is, once we have access to the underlying domain model of code (whether it is offered by the underlying infrastructure or obtained by Agile Model Extraction), to make it easy to exploit that model in tools used by developers to produce code, browse and query it, analyze it and debug it. On the one hand, generic core functionality is needed for querying and navigating models. On the other hand, tools and environments need to be aware of the context of the domain model of the code under study so they can adapt themselves accordingly.

An example is the "moldable debugger" which, instead of presenting only a generic stack-based interface to the run-time environment, is aware of relevant domain concepts, such as notifications in an event-driven system, or grammar

---

[3] See, for example, Helvetia, a workbench for integrating DSLs into the IDE and toolchain of the host language [15].

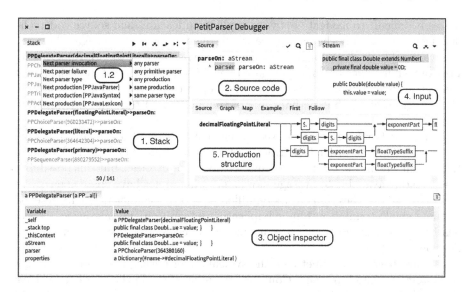

Fig. 1. A domain-specific debugger for PetitParser. The debugging view displays relevant information for debugging parsers ((4) Input, (5) Production structure). Each widget loads relevant debugging operations (1, 2, 4).

rules in a parser [4]. In Fig. 1 we see a screenshot of a domain-specific debugger for *PetitParser*, a parser combinator framework for Pharo Smalltalk [14]. Each widget of the debugger is context-sensitive and loads the appropriate debugging operations for the current context. The debugger is aware of a grammar's production rules and is capable, for example, of stepping to the next production or the next parser failure, rather than simply to the next expression, statement or method. Custom visualizations are also loaded to display the production structure in a suitable way. Custom debuggers can be defined in a straightforward way by leveraging the explicit representation of the underlying application domain.

The same principles have been applied to the "moldable inspector," a context-aware tool for querying and exploring an object space [5]. Domain-specific views are automatically loaded depending on the entities being inspected. As with the moldable debugger, custom views are commonly expressed with just a few lines of code.

In the long run we envision a development environment in which we are not forced to extract models from code, but in which the code is actually a model that we can interact with, query and analyze.

4   Link the Code to Its Ecosystem

Conventional software systems are trapped behind a number of artificial barriers. The most obvious is the barrier between the source code and the running application. This is manifested in the usual program/compile/run cycle. This makes it difficult to navigate between application features and source code. The debugger is classically the only place where the developer can navigate between the two worlds. It does not have to be that way, as seen in the Morphic framework of Self, in which one may navigate freely between user interface widgets and the source code related to them [11]. (This is just one dramatic manifestation of "live programming", but perhaps one of the most important ones for program comprehension.)

A second barrier is that between a current version of a system and other related versions. In order to extract useful information about the evolution of the system, one must resort to "mining software repositories", but this possibility is not readily available to average developers who do not have spare capacity to carry out such studies. Furthermore, different versions cannot normally co-exist within a single running system, complicating integration and migration. (There has been much interesting research but not much is available for mainstream development.)

A third barrier exists between the system under development and the larger ecosystem of related software. Countless research efforts in the past decade have shown that, by mining the ecosystem, much useful knowledge can be gleaned about common coding practices, bugs and bug fixes, and so on. Unfortunately this information is not readily accessible to developers, so they often turn instead to question and answer fora.

We see two main challenges, namely *"Ecosystem Mining"* and *"Evolutionary Monitoring."* By mining software ecosystems and offering platforms to analyze them [2], we hope to automatically discover intelligence relevant to a given project. Examples are opportunities for code reuse, automatically-generated and evolving documentation, and usage information than can influence maintainers of libraries and frameworks.

Evolutionary monitoring refers to steering the evolution of a software system by monitoring stakeholder needs. An example of this is *architectural monitoring* [3] which formalizes architectural constraints and monitors conformance as the application evolves. Other examples include tracking the needs of stakeholders (*i.e.* both developers and users) to determine chronic pain points and opportunities for improvements; tracking technical debt to assess priorities for reengineering and replacement; and monitoring technical trends, especially with respect to relevent technical debt.

In the long run, we envision a development environment that integrates not just the current code base and the running application, enabling easy navigation between them, but also knowledge mined from the evolution of the software under development as well as from the software ecosystem at large. The development environment should support active monitoring of the target system as well as the ecosystem to identify and assess opportunities for code improvements.

5   Conclusion

Object-oriented programming has fulfilled many of its promises. Software systems today are longer-lived and more amenable to change and extension than ever. Nevertheless we observe that object orientation is slowly dying, with the introduction of ever more complex and heterogeneous systems.

We propose to rejuvenate object-oriented programming and let ourselves be guided by the maxim that "programming is modeling." We need programming languages, tools and environments that enable models to be directly expressed in code in such a way that they can be queried, manipulated and analyzed.

Acknowledgments. We thank Mircea Lungu for his comments on an early draft of this essay. We also gratefully acknowledge the financial support of the Swiss National Science Foundation for the project "Agile Software Analysis" (SNSF project No. 200020-162352, Jan 1, 2016 - Dec. 30, 2018), and its predecessor, "Agile Software Assessment" (SNSF project No. 200020-144126/1, Jan 1, 2013 - Dec. 30, 2015).

References

1. Achermann, F., Nierstrasz, O.: Applications = components + scripts—a tour of piccola. In: Aksit, M. (ed.) Software Architectures and Component Technology, pp. 261–292. Kluwer, Alphen aan den Rijn (2001)
2. Caracciolo, A., Chiş, A., Spasojević, B., Lungu, M.: Pangea: a workbench for statically analyzing multi-language software corpora. In: 2014 IEEE 14th International Working Conference on Source Code Analysis and Manipulation (SCAM), pp. 71–76. IEEE, September 2014
3. Caracciolo, A., Lungu, M., Nierstrasz, O.: A unified approach to architecture conformance checking. In: Proceedings of the 12th Working IEEE/IFIP Conference on Software Architecture (WICSA), pp. 41–50. ACM Pres, May 2015
4. Chiş, A., Denker, M., Gîrba, T., Nierstrasz, O.: Practical domain-specific debuggers using the moldable debugger framework. Comput. Lang. Syst. Struct. **44**(Part A), 89–113 (2015). Special issue on the 6th and 7th International Conference on Software Language Engineering (SLE 2013 and SLE 2014)
5. Chiş, A., Gîrba, T., Nierstrasz, O., Syrel, A.: The moldable inspector. In: Proceedings of the ACM International Symposium on New Ideas, New Paradigms, and Reflections on Programming and Software. ACM, New York (2015) (Onward! 2015, page to appear)
6. Combemale, B., Deantoni, J., Baudry, B., France, R.B., Jézéquel, J.-M., Gray, J.: Globalizing modeling languages. Computer **47**(6), 68–71 (2014)
7. Fritz, T., Murphy, G.C.: Using information fragments to answer the questions developers ask. In: Proceedings of the 32nd ACM/IEEE International Conference on Software Engineering, vol. 1, ICSE 2010, pp. 175–184. ACM, New York (2010)
8. Kay, A.C.: The early history of Smalltalk. In: ACM SIGPLAN Notices, vol. 28, pp. 69–95. ACM Press, March 1993
9. Klint, P., van der Storm, T., Vinju, J.: RASCAL: A domain specific language for source code analysis and manipulation. In: Ninth IEEE International Working Conference on Source Code Analysis and Manipulation, SCAM 2009, pp. 168–177 (2009)
10. Kurš, J., Lungu, M., Nierstrasz, O.: Bounded seas. Comput. Lang. Syst. Struct. **44**(Part A), 114–140 (2015). Special issue on the 6th and 7th International Conference on SoftwareLanguage Engineering (SLE 2013 and SLE 2014)

11. Maloney, J.H., Smith, R.B.: Directness and liveness in the morphic user interface construction environment. In: Proceedings of the 8th Annual ACM Symposium on User Interface and Software Technology, UIST 1995, pp. 21–28. ACM, New York (1995)
12. Nierstrasz, O., Ducasse, S., Gîrba, T.: The story of Moose: an agile reengineering environment. In: Proceedings of the European Software Engineering Conference (ESEC/FSE 2005), pp. 1–10. ACM Press, New York, September 2005 (invited paper)
13. Nierstrasz, O., Kurš, J.: Parsing for agile modeling. Sci. Comput. Program. **97**(Part 1), 150–156 (2015)
14. Renggli, L., Ducasse, S., Gîrba, T., Nierstrasz, O.: Practical dynamic grammars for dynamic languages. In: 4th Workshop on Dynamic Languages and Applications (DYLA 2010), Malaga, Spain, pp. 1–4, June 2010
15. Renggli, L., Gîrba, T., Nierstrasz, O.: Embedding languages without breaking tools. In: D'Hondt, T. (ed.) ECOOP 2010. LNCS, vol. 6183, pp. 380–404. Springer, Heidelberg (2010)
16. Sillito, J., Murphy, G.C., De Volder, K.: Asking and answering questions during a programming change task. IEEE Trans. Softw. Eng. **34**, 434–451 (2008)

Concurrent and Distributed Systems

Automated Choreography Repair

Samik Basu[1(✉)] and Tevfik Bultan[2]

[1] Iowa State University, Ames, USA
sbasu@iastate.edu
[2] University of California at Santa Barbara, Santa Barbara, USA
bultan@cs.ucsb.edu

Abstract. Choreography analysis is a crucial problem in concurrent and distributed system development. A choreography specifies the desired ordering of message exchanges among the components of a system. The realizability of a choreography amounts to determining the existence of components whose communication behavior conforms to the given choreography. The realizability problem has been shown to be decidable. In this paper, we investigate the repairability of un-realizable choreographies, where the goal is to identify a set of changes to a given un-realizable choreography that will make it realizable. We present a technique for automatically repairing un-realizable choreographies and provide formal guarantees of correctness and termination. We demonstrate the viability of our technique by applying it to several representative unrealizable choreographies from Singularity OS channel contracts and Web services.

1 Introduction

Choreography specifications are used in a variety of domains including coordination of software in service-oriented computing [18], specification of process interactions in Singularity OS [11], and specification of communication behavior among processes in distributed programs [2]. Choreographies describe desired message exchange sequences among components, programs or processes (we will refer to them as *peers*) of a distributed system. The choreography realizability problem is determining whether one can construct peers whose interaction behavior conforms to the given choreography. As an example, consider the choreography over two peers P_1 and P_2 shown in Fig. 1(a) where edges represent messages sent from one peer to another. This choreography describes a simple file transfer protocol [9] where P_1 is the client asking for the file transfer and P_2 is the file server. First, the client sends a message to the server to request that the server starts the transfer. When the transfer is finished, the server sends the "Transfer Finished" message and the protocol terminates. However, the client may decide to cancel the transfer before hearing back from the server by sending a "Cancel Transfer" message in which case the server responds with "Transfer Finished" message, which, again, terminates the protocol.

This work is partially supported by NSF grants CCF 1116836, CCF 1555780 and CCF 1117708.

© Springer-Verlag Berlin Heidelberg 2016
P. Stevens and A. Wąsowski (Eds.): FASE 2016, LNCS 9633, pp. 13–30, 2016.
DOI: 10.1007/978-3-662-49665-7_2

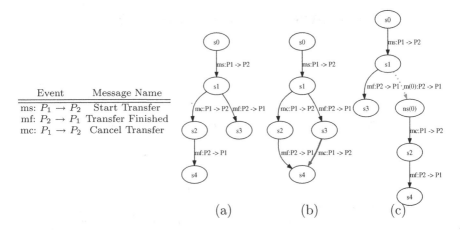

Event	Message Name
ms: $P_1 \rightarrow P_2$	Start Transfer
mf: $P_2 \rightarrow P_1$	Transfer Finished
mc: $P_1 \rightarrow P_2$	Cancel Transfer

(a)   (b)   (c)

Fig. 1. (a) Un-realizable choreography [9]; Repair by (b) relaxation, (c) restriction (Color figure online).

Figure 3(a) presents the projection of the choreography onto the participating peers resulting in the corresponding peer behaviors (send actions are denoted by "!" and receive actions are denoted by "?"). The distributed system that consists of the peer specifications shown in Fig. 3(a) can generate the message sequence:

$$ms^{P_1 \rightarrow P_2}, mf^{P_2 \rightarrow P_1}, mc^{P_1 \rightarrow P_2} \tag{1}$$

This sequence corresponds to the case where the server sends a "Transfer Finished" message (mf), but before consuming that message, the client sends the cancellation request message (mc). The sequence moves the server to an undefined (error) configuration, where the server does not know whether the file was transferred completely to the client before the client sent the cancellation request. In terms of the choreography specification shown in Fig. 1(a), the message sequence given above is not covered by the choreography, but any implementation of this choreography that uses asynchronous message passing will generate the message sequence: (1), violating the choreography specification. Hence, the choreography specification shown in Fig. 1(a) is un-realizable.

Problem Statement. This brings up the question: *when a choreography is determined to be un-realizable, is it possible to automatically repair the choreography such that the repaired version is realizable?* We will refer to this problem as the *choreography repairability problem*. Its importance stems from the fact that automation in repairing choreography will allow faster development of distributed systems with formal guarantees of correctness.

Our Solution. Our choreography repair technique analyzes and eliminates the cause of violation of the condition for choreography realizability. In [4], we have proved that choreography $\mathcal{C}$ is realizable if and only if its behavior (i.e., the set of message sequences generated by $\mathcal{C}$, denoted as $\mathcal{L}(\mathcal{C})$) is identical to the behavior of $\mathcal{I}_1^{\mathcal{C}}$ (denoted as $\mathcal{L}(\mathcal{I}_1^{\mathcal{C}})$), where $\mathcal{I}_1^{\mathcal{C}}$ is the asynchronous system in which each

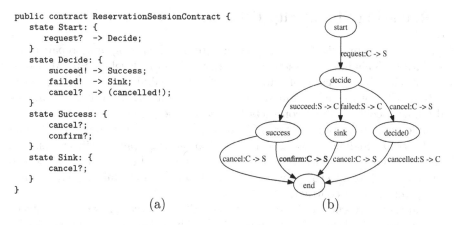

```
public contract ReservationSessionContract {
    state Start: {
        request?  -> Decide;
    }
    state Decide: {
        succeed! -> Success;
        failed!  -> Sink;
        cancel?  -> (cancelled!);
    }
    state Success: {
        cancel?;
        confirm?;
    }
    state Sink: {
        cancel?;
    }
}
```

(a)   (b)

Fig. 2. (a) Channel contract for ReservationSession and (b) the corresponding state machine

participating peer has at most one pending message at any point of time, and is obtained from the projection of C. We present two types of choreography repair mechanisms that eliminate the differences between $\mathcal{L}(C)$ and $\mathcal{L}(\mathcal{I}_1^C)$:

1. *Relaxation.* The choreography C is changed to C' such that $\mathcal{L}(C) \subseteq \mathcal{L}(C')$, i.e., new behavior is added to C, such that $\mathcal{L}(C') = \mathcal{L}(\mathcal{I}_1^{C'})$.
2. *Restriction.* The choreography C is changed to C' such that $\mathcal{L}(C) = \mathcal{L}(C \downarrow_c) = \mathcal{L}(\mathcal{I}_1^{C'} \downarrow_c) \subseteq \mathcal{L}(\mathcal{I}_1^C)$, where $\downarrow_c$ denotes the behavior projected on the messages in C. This change implies that some behavior of $\mathcal{I}_1^C$ is disallowed in $\mathcal{I}_1^{C'}$. This is achieved by adding extra synchronization messages in C'. When these extra messages are projected away, the repaired choreography C' specifies exactly the same sequences of messages specified by the un-realizable choreography C.

For example, the choreography in Fig. 1(a) is changed to the one in Fig. 1(b) via relaxation, by adding new behavior (blue bold-edge), which makes the latter realizable. This is because the sequence that made C un-realizable (see sequence (1) above) is now included in the repaired version C'. On the other hand, Fig. 1(c) demonstrates repair via restriction, by adding synchronization messages from state s_1 to $ns(0)$ (red dotted-edges); this repair also makes the resulting choreography realizable. In this case, the sequence in (1) is not possible in $\mathcal{I}_1^{C'}$.

Contribution. We present a formal characterization of choreography repairability. To the best of our knowledge, this is the first time such a characterization has been presented. We present a sound and complete algorithm for choreography repair based on this characterization. We also discuss its application by demonstrating automated repair of several unrealizable choreographies. Although choreography examples we use in this paper consist of two-party choreographies, the formal model and the repair algorithm we present are general and handle multi-party choreographies.

2   Repairing Singularity OS Channel Contracts

We motivate the practical applicability of automated choreography repair using Singularity OS channel contracts. Singularity OS [16] is developed by Microsoft research with the objective of improving OS dependability by ensuring process isolation. The processes in Singularity OS communicate over FIFO channels and follow specific channel contracts (choreographies in our case); that specify allowable communication patterns between processes (client and server). The Singularity OS channel contracts correspond to choreography specifications. One problem is to determine whether one can implement a client and a server whose interaction conforms to the given channel contract, i.e., determining realizability of the given channel contract.

Figure 2(a) presents a channel contract called reservation session contract (where message declarations are omitted for brevity). The contract specifies four explicit states and the message sequences from the perspective of the server. For instance, the contract specifies that the state changes from "Start" to "Decide" when the server receives a message "request" from the client. From the state "Decide", there are three choices: the server sends the message "succeed" to the client resulting in the state update to "Success"; the server responds to the client with message "failed" leading to the state "Sink"; the client sends "cancel" followed by the server sending "cancelled" message. Figure 2(b) presents the state machine for this contract (C represents the client and S represents the server).

The Singularity Design Note 5 [16] states that the client and server processes that are verified to conform to a given channel contract (i.e., that implement the projection of the channel contract correctly) are guaranteed to interact without any deadlocks. However, in [17], the authors demonstrated that this claim is incorrect since the channel contract itself can be un-realizable, in which case the processes implemented based on the projection of the contract can deadlock. One of the examples demonstrating this problem is the reservation session contract from Singularity OS shown above. Due to asynchronous communication, the client and server can move out-of-sync and deadlock. Consider the scenario where the client sends a "cancel" message and waits for the "cancelled" message from the server, while the server sends a "failed" message and consumes the "cancel" message from the client. This sequence of interactions leads to a deadlock. In fact there are no client and server processes that can conform to this contract without deadlock while interacting via FIFO channels (as required by the Singularity OS), i.e., the choreography specified by this channel contract is un-realizable.

The automated choreography repair technique we present in this paper is directly applicable to Singularity OS channel contracts. Using our technique we can repair un-realizable channel contracts, and ensure deadlock free implementation of repaired contracts. We will discuss the application of our automated choreography repair technique to the reservation contract in Sect. 5.

3   Choreography Realizability

We proceed by presenting an overview of the existing results [4] on choreography realizability, which forms the basis of our automated choreography repair strategy.

Peers. The behavior $\mathcal{B}$ of a peer P is a finite state machine (M, T, t_0, δ) where M is the union of input (M^{in}) and output (M^{out}) message sets, T is the finite set of states, $t_0 \in T$ is the initial state, and $\delta \subseteq T \times (M \cup \{\epsilon\}) \times T$ is the transition relation. A transition $\tau \in \delta$ can be one of the following three types: (1) a send-transition of the form $(t_1, !m_1, t_2)$ which sends out a message $m_1 \in M^{\text{out}}$, (2) a receive-transition of the form $(t_1, ?m_2, t_2)$ which consumes a message $m_2 \in M^{\text{in}}$ from peer's input queue, and (3) an ϵ-transition of the form (t_1, ϵ, t_2). We write $t \xrightarrow{a} t'$ to denote that $(t, a, t') \in \delta$. Figure 3(a) illustrates the behavior of peers P_1 and P_2; states in P_i are denoted by a tuple (P_i:"state-name").

System. Given a set of peers $\mathcal{P} = \{P_1, \ldots, P_n\}$ with $\mathcal{B}_i = (M_i, T_i, t_{0i}, \delta_i)$ denoting the behavior of P_i and $M_i = M_i^{\text{in}} \cup M_i^{\text{out}}$ such that $\forall i : M_i^{\text{in}} \cap M_i^{\text{out}} = \emptyset$, and $\forall i, j : i \neq j \Rightarrow M_i^{\text{in}} \cap M_j^{\text{in}} = M_i^{\text{out}} \cap M_j^{\text{out}} = \emptyset$. A system behavior or simply a system over $\mathcal{P}$ is denoted by a (possibly infinite state) state machine $\mathcal{I} = (\mathcal{P}, S, s_0, M, \Delta)$ where $\mathcal{P}$ is the set of peers, S is the set of states in the

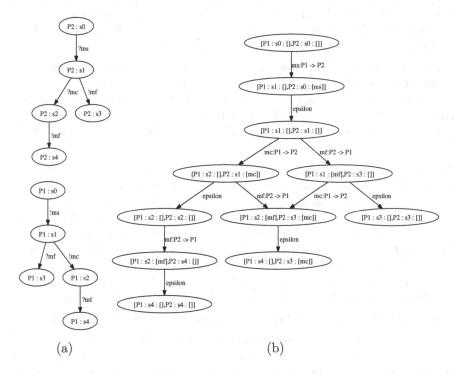

(a)   (b)

Fig. 3. (a) Projected peers $\mathcal{P}_1$ and $\mathcal{P}_2$ for Fig. 1(a); (b) System behavior

system and each state $s = (Q_1, t_1, Q_2, t_2, \ldots Q_n, t_n)$ in the system is described by the local states (t_is) of the peers in $\mathcal{P}$ along with the contents of their queues (Q_is). $s_0 \in S$ is the start state, where none of the peers have any pending messages in their queue to consume. The set M contains the set of all messages that are being exchanged by the participating peers.

Finally, the transition relation Δ is described as follows. The send actions are non-blocking, i.e., when a peer P_i sends a message m to a peer P_j (denoted by $m^{P_i \to P_j}$), the message gets appended to the tail of the queue associated to P_j. We refer to the queue as the receive queue of P_j. The receive actions are blocking, i.e., a peer can only consume a message if it is present at the head of its receive queue; on consumption of the message, it is removed from the head of the queue. Only the send actions are observable in the system as these actions involve two entities: the sender sending the message and the receive queue of the receiver. All other actions are local to one peer and, therefore, unobservable (ϵ-transitions). We will use the functions $\texttt{lSt}(.,.)$ and $\texttt{lQu}(.,.)$ to obtain local state and queue of a peer from a state in the system, i.e., for $s = (Q_1, t_1, Q_2, t_2, \ldots Q_n, t_n) \in S$, $\texttt{lSt}(s, P_1) = t_1$ and $\texttt{lQu}(s, P_1) = Q_1$.

K-bounded System. A k-bounded system (denoted by $\mathcal{I}_k$) is a system where the length of message queue for any peer is at most k. In any k-bounded system, the send actions can block if the receive queue of the receiver peer is full. Any k-bounded system is finite state as long as the behaviors of the participating peers are finite state. Figure 3(b) illustrates the system $\mathcal{I}_1$ obtained from the communicating peers P_1 and P_2 of Fig. 3(a). Note that initially P_1 is at the local state $P_1 : s_1$ with an empty receive queue denoted by [ ].

Choreography Specification. A choreography specification is a finite state machine $\mathcal{C} = (\mathcal{P}, S^C, s_0^C, L, \Delta^c)$ where $\mathcal{P}$ is a finite set of peers, S^C is a finite set of states, $s_0^C \in C$ is the initial state, L is a finite set of message labels and, finally, $\Delta^c \subseteq S^C \times \mathcal{P} \times L \times \mathcal{P} \times S^C$ is the transition relation. A transition of the form $(s_i^C, P, m, P', s_j^C) \in \Delta^c$ represents the sending of message m from P to P' ($P, P' \in \mathcal{P}$).

Peer Projection. The projection of a choreography $\mathcal{C}$ on one of the peers P, is obtained from $\mathcal{C}$ by performing the following updates to the state machine describing $\mathcal{C}$. (a) If a transition label is $m^{P \to P'}$ then replace it with $!m$; (b) if a transition label is $m^{P' \to P}$ then replace it with $?m$; (c) otherwise, replace transition label with ϵ. The system obtained from the asynchronous communication of the projected peers of $\mathcal{C}$ is denoted by $\mathcal{I}^{\mathcal{C}}$; $\mathcal{I}_1^{\mathcal{C}}$ being the corresponding 1-bounded system. The language of a choreography or a system is described in terms of a set of sequences of send actions of the form $m^{P \to P'}$; the concatenation of ϵ to any sequence results in the sequence itself. The language is denoted by $\mathcal{L}(.)$.

Theorem 1 (Realizability [4]). $\mathcal{C}$ *is language realizable* $\Leftrightarrow [\mathcal{L}(\mathcal{C}) = \mathcal{L}(\mathcal{I}_1^{\mathcal{C}})]$

This theorem states that a choreography is realizable if and only if the set of sequences of send actions of a choreography is identical to the set of sequences of send actions of the 1-bounded system where the participating peers are generated from the (determinized) projection of the choreography under consideration.

Figure 3(b) presents the behavior of the system $\mathcal{I}_1^{\mathcal{C}}$ for the choreography specification $\mathcal{C}$ shown in Fig. 1(a), where epsilon-labeled transitions denote consumption of messages and other transitions denote sending of messages. The choreography $\mathcal{C}$ is un-realizable because it does not include a specific send sequence that is possible in $\mathcal{I}_1^{\mathcal{C}}$ (Fig. 3(b)) (Sequence (1) discussed in Sect. 1).

4   Choreography Repair

Types of Repair. In this paper, we present two alternative techniques for repairing un-realizable choreographies. One is based on adding new behaviors (in terms of sends) to $\mathcal{C}$, which we call *relaxation*. The other is based on adding constraints that do not alter allowed sequences of sends in $\mathcal{C}$ but restrict the behavior in $\mathcal{I}_1^{\mathcal{C}}$. We call this approach *restriction*. The techniques will be based on the observation that from Theorem 1 and from the nature of asynchrony, it follows: $\mathcal{L}(\mathcal{C}) \neq \mathcal{L}(\mathcal{I}_1^{\mathcal{C}}) \Rightarrow \mathcal{L}(\mathcal{C}) \subset \mathcal{L}(\mathcal{I}_1^{\mathcal{C}})$.

State Relationships Between $\mathcal{I}_1^{\mathcal{C}}$ and $\mathcal{C}$. Before we describe the repair techniques, we first discuss the structure of the $\mathcal{I}_1^{\mathcal{C}}$, which is crucial for understanding our approach. If a state in $\mathcal{C}$ is represented as $s^{\mathcal{C}}$, then the corresponding state in the peer P is a tuple denoted by $P : s^{\mathcal{C}}$. Proceeding further, if s is a state in $\mathcal{I}_1^{\mathcal{C}}$, then $s = (Q_1, t_1, \ldots, Q_n, t_n)$, where n is the number of peers and t_i is of the form $P_i : s_i^{\mathcal{C}}$. Note that, the local states of each peer in s may have been obtained from different states $s_i^{\mathcal{C}}$ in $\mathcal{C}$.

Consider for example, the second state of the system in Fig. 3(b)–P_1 is at a state $P_1 : s_1$ obtained from the state s_1 in $\mathcal{C}$ and P_2 is at a state $P_2 : s_0$ obtained from the state s_0 in $\mathcal{C}$. Using the notations introduced in Sect. 3, $\mathtt{lSt}((P_1 : s_1 : [\,], P_2 : s_0 : [ms]), P_1) = P_1 : s_1$; $\mathtt{lQu}((P_1 : s_1 : [\,], P_2 : s_0 : [ms]), P_2) = [ms]$.

4.1   Differences Between $\mathcal{C}$ and $\mathcal{I}_1^{\mathcal{C}}$

In order to apply relaxation or restriction, it is important to identify at least one difference between $\mathcal{C}$ and $\mathcal{I}_1^{\mathcal{C}}$ in terms of sequences of send actions. We know that for un-realizable $\mathcal{C}$, $\mathcal{L}(\mathcal{C}) \subset \mathcal{L}(\mathcal{I}_1^{\mathcal{C}})$. Therefore, there exists at least one send sequence in $\mathcal{I}_1^{\mathcal{C}}$ which is absent in $\mathcal{C}$.

Consider that there exists a path in $\mathcal{I}_1^{\mathcal{C}}$ in the form

$$s_1 \xrightarrow{\; m_1^{P_1 \to P_1'} \;} s_2 \xrightarrow{\; m_2^{P_2 \to P_2'} \;} s_3 \to \ldots s_i \xrightarrow{\; m_i^{P_i \to P_i'} \;} s_{i+1} \qquad (2)$$

which generates the following sequence of send actions $m_1^{P_1 \to P_1'}, m_2^{P_2 \to P_2'}, \ldots,$ $m_i^{P_i \to P_i'}$. Assume that, none of the paths in $\mathcal{C}$ allow the above send sequence. However, there exists a path in $\mathcal{C}$ which replicates the above sequence till $m_{i-1}^{P_{i-1} \to P_{i-1}'}$. Let such a path be denoted by

$$t_1 \xrightarrow{m_1^{P_1 \to P_1'}} t_2 \xrightarrow{m_2^{P_2 \to P_2'}} t_3 \to \ldots t_{i-1} \xrightarrow{m_{i-1}^{P_{i-1} \to P_{i-1}'}} t_i \qquad (3)$$

where t_i does not have any outgoing transition labeled by $m_i^{P_i \to P_i'}$. In summary, one of the differences between the send sequences present in $\mathcal{C}$ and $\mathcal{I}_1^{\mathcal{C}}$ is due to the presence of send action $m_i^{P_i \to P_i'}$ at s_i and absence of the same at t_i. For instance, going back to the example in Fig. 3, the difference between $\mathcal{C}$ and $\mathcal{I}_1^{\mathcal{C}}$ is due to $ms^{P_1 \to P_2}, mf^{P_2 \to P_1}, mc^{P_1 \to P_2}$, in which case s_i is equal to $(P_1 : s_1 : [mf], P_2 : s_3 : [])$ in $\mathcal{I}_1^{\mathcal{C}}$ and t_i is equal to s_3 in $\mathcal{C}$. The cause of the difference between the behaviors can be explained in one of the two ways:

Independent Branches. The choreography specification includes a branching behavior involving sends from at least two peers in two different branches. The sender peers follow different paths in the branches. This is the case in Fig. 1(a).

Independent Sequences. The choreography specification includes a path where there are two messages sent by two different peers and the sender of the second message does not depend on the first message. This situation can be illustrated using the following choreography specification: $t_0 \xrightarrow{m^{P_1 \to P_2}} t_1 \xrightarrow{m^{P_3 \to P_4}} t_2$. The first and second transitions correspond to send actions of P_1 and P_3, which can occur in any order in the corresponding system and therefore, this choreography, therefore, cannot be realized. We will refer to the path as independent sequences and the transitions as *independent transitions*.

The objective of repair via relaxation or restriction is to alter the behavior of $\mathcal{C}$ proceeding from t_i such that the above causes of differences can be eliminated.

4.2   Repair by Relaxation

As noted before, relaxing $\mathcal{C}$ corresponds to adding new behaviors to $\mathcal{C}$. Specifically, adding a new behavior from state t_i (in path (3) above) implies adding a transition from t_i to some t_i' with transition label $m_i^{P_i \to P_i'}$. The addition of such a new transition obviously results in a new choreography specification, say $\mathcal{C}'$. We will denote relaxation of $\mathcal{C}$ to $\mathcal{C}'$ as $\mathcal{C} \nearrow \mathcal{C}'$. Note that, the following holds: $\mathcal{C} \nearrow \mathcal{C}' \Rightarrow \mathcal{L}(\mathcal{C}) \subseteq \mathcal{L}(\mathcal{C}')$.

While adding a new transition from t_i to a state (say t_i') eliminates the difference due to the send action $m_i^{P_i \to P_i'}$, the important next step is to identify a suitable t_i'. There are two possibilities: we can either assign t_i' to some existing state in $\mathcal{C}$ or generate a new state. Careful selection of one of the two choices is important because it impacts the termination of the repair mechanism. Using the form of the system path shown in (2), let $\mathtt{1St}(s_i, P_i) = P_i : c_i$; $\mathtt{1St}(s_{i+1}, P_i) = P_i : c_{i+1}$; $\mathtt{1Qu}(s_i, P_i) = Q_i$; $\mathtt{1Qu}(s_{i+1}, P_i) = Q_{i+1}$. In the above, $Q_i = Q_{i+1}$ because the peer P_i does not consume any messages at this transition.

Case 1. Consider that the receive queue Q_i of the peer P_i is non-empty, implying that there is one pending message to be consumed (recall that the $\mathcal{I}_1^{\mathcal{C}}$ is 1-bounded system with each receive queue capacity being 1). In other words, some peer (say, R) has sent the message (say m) to P_i and P_i has not encountered any receive action along the choreography path it has taken resulting in system path shown in (2).

This case corresponds to the situation described as *independent branching* (see above), when peer P_i is moving along a choreography specification path π and the other peer R is moving along a different path π' of the choreography specification, resulting in the path shown in (2). Furthermore, R has sent m to P_i which resides un-consumed in the receive queue of P_i.

Case 1a. Let there be a transition in the behavior of peer P_i at state $P_i : c_{i+1}$, where it can consume the message in its queue: $P_i : c_{i+1} \xrightarrow{?m} P_i : c'_i$. That is, the choreography specification includes $c_{i+1} \xrightarrow{m^{R \to P_i}} c'_i$ along the path π. Therefore, both of the paths under consideration, π and π', have the send action $m^{R \to P_i}$. In π, $m_i^{P_i \to P'_i}$ is followed by $m^{R \to P_i}$. In π', $m^{R \to P_i}$ is not followed by $m_i^{P_i \to P'_i}$.

In this case, the relaxation adds $t_i \xrightarrow{m_i^{P_i \to P'_i}} t'_i$ in the choreography specification and sets t'_i to c'_i.

Case 1b. On the other hand, if there exists no transition in the behavior of peer P_i starting from state $P_i : c_{i+1}$ where it can consume the message in its queue, then the following repair is done.

Case 1b-i. If $P_i : c_{i+1}$ belongs to a cycle then in the newly added transition $t_i \xrightarrow{m_i^{P_i \to P'_i}} t'_i$, t'_i is set to a newly generated state, which replicates the choreography specification starting from c_{i+1}. Note that, the repair does not assign t'_i to c_{i+1}. This is because such assignment will result in unnecessary over-relaxation of choreography specification due to the presence in $m^{R \to P_i}$ in path π' and its possible absence in the cycle which is part of the path π. We will discuss below this scenario using the example in Fig. 4.

Case 1b-ii. If P_i at $P_i : c_{i+1}$ cannot consume the pending message and $P_i : c_{i+1}$ does not belong to any cycle, then t'_i is set to a newly generated state. The addition of the new transition removes the identified difference between the choreography and the system.

For instance, in Fig. 3(b), the path in $\mathcal{I}_1^{\mathcal{C}}$ that is absent in $\mathcal{C}$ (Fig. 1(a)) has the sequence $ms^{P_1 \to P_2}$, $mf^{P_2 \to P_1}$, $mc^{P_1 \to P_2}$. Note that, we are considering only the send actions and the transitions are considered with zero or more occurrences of ϵ followed by a send action. The path in $\mathcal{C}$ that replicates most of this sequence is $s_0 \xrightarrow{ms^{P_1 \to P_2}} s_1 \xrightarrow{mf^{P_2 \to P_1}} s_3$. Therefore, for repair by relaxation, our objective is to add a transition with send action $mc^{P_1 \to P_2}$ from the choreography state s_3. From the system, we know that the peer P_1 at the state $P_1 : s_2$ can consume the message m_f in its receive queue and move to a state in $P_1 : s_4$ (see Fig. 3). Therefore, the transition added from s_3 has the destination state s_4. The result of this repair by relaxation is the choreography specification presented in Fig. 1(b). This illustrates the **Case 1a** of repair by relaxation.

Figure 4 illustrates the applications of **Case 1b-i** and **1a**. The local states of the peers participating in the system transitions are presented in bold-font.

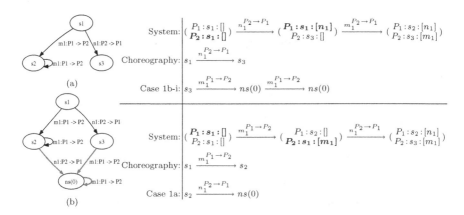

Fig. 4. Example illustrating application of Case 1b-ii and 1a of relaxation

In the first step, the difference between the system transition sequence and the choreography sequence is repaired following the Case 1b-i. $P_1 : s_2$ does not have a transition where it consumes the pending message n_1, and $P_1 : s_2$ belongs to a cycle. Therefore, a new state $ns(0)$ replicating s_2 is generated as part of the repair strategy instead of adding the transition $m_1^{P_1 \to P_2}$ from s_3 to s_2.

Case 2. Now consider that the receive queue Q_i of the peer P_i is empty, implying that there is no pending message to be consumed. Unlike the previous case, in this situation, the difference between $\mathcal{I}_1^C$ and $\mathcal{C}$ (represented by paths (2) and (3) in Sect. 4.1) is *not necessarily* due to independent branches, when two peers move along two different paths of the choreography specification.

Instead the peers may be moving along the same path of the choreography specification, and the latter has imposed an "un-realizable" ordering of send actions involving $m_i^{P_i \to P_i'}$. In other words, it is not possible to "stop" P_i from sending the message m_i from its projected behavior when the choreography specification reaches t_i, however t_i does not have $m_i^{P_i \to P_i'}$. This corresponds to the case of independent sequences (see above).

Recall that, the choreography specification state is t_i from where there is no matching $m_i^{P_i \to P_i'}$ event. We check whether there exists a path from $P_i : t_i$ (i.e., local state of P_i obtained from projection at t_i) to $P_i : t_i$ in the peer P_i via a sequence of transitions such that after a sequence of ϵ-transitions, there is a $!m_i$ transition followed by some other sequence of transitions.

Case 2a. If the check is successful, then we can infer that t_i is part of a loop and it contains independent transitions, which cause un-realizability.

Case 2a-i. Then we identify the first intermediate state $P_i : t$ in this loop, which has an outgoing transition over some other output action. In this case, a new transition $t_i \xrightarrow{m_i^{P_i \to P_i'}} t_i'$ with t_i' set to t is added to replicate the behavior in $\mathcal{I}_1^C$.

Case 2a-ii. If no such intermediate state exists, then $t_i \xrightarrow{\ m_i^{P_i \to P_i'}\ } t_i'$ with t_i' set to t_i (self-loop) is added.

In either case, the permutations of pairs of independent transitions that were identified as the difference between $\mathcal{C}$ and $\mathcal{I}_1^{\mathcal{C}}$ are added and nothing else.

Case 2b. On the other hand, if the check is unsuccessful, then we can infer that t_i is not part of a loop.

Case 2b-i. We find out whether $P : c_{i+1}$ (local state of the sender at s_{i+1}) has a path to $P : t_i$ (t_i being the choreography state that cannot replicate the behavior of the system from s_i). If such path exists in the behavior of P_i, we infer that P_i moves along a path different from $t_1, t_2, \ldots, t_i$ (see path 3) in choreography but the path has the ability to join at t_i. In this case, we add a new transition labeled with $t_i \xrightarrow{\ m_i^{P_i \to P_i'}\ } c_{i+1}$ to remove the difference between the choreography and corresponding the system.

Case 2b-ii. If the condition in Case 2b-i fails, then we find out the choreography state reachable from c_{i+1} (the choreography state corresponding the senders local state at s_{i+1}) via the action $m_{i-1}^{P_{i-1} \to P_{i-1}'}$. If such a state is t, then this implies that the choreography path extending from c_{i+1} allows $m_{i-1}^{P_{i-1} \to P_{i-1}'}$ after $m_i^{P_i \to P_i'}$, while the choreography path along $t_1, t_2, \ldots, t_i$ (see path 3) does not allow $m_i^{P_i \to P_i'}$ after $m_{i-1}^{P_{i-1} \to P_{i-1}'}$. The repair in this case is similar to Case 1a and amounts to adding $t_i \xrightarrow{\ m_i^{P_i \to P_i'}\ } t$. On the other hand, if no such choreography state t exists, then a new state is generated and a transition over $m_i^{P_i \to P_i'}$ is added from t_i to this newly generated state.

Figure 5 illustrates the application of Case 2 of relaxation.

4.3   Repair by Restriction

The objective of restriction, unlike relaxation, is to constrain the behavior of the system $\mathcal{I}_1^{\mathcal{C}}$. In other words, going back to paths (3) and (2) in Sect. 4.1, restriction implies disallowing the transition $s_i \xrightarrow{\ m_i^{P_i \to P_i'}\ } s_{i+1}$ in $\mathcal{I}_1^{\mathcal{C}}$ i.e., introducing restriction to disallow the transition $c_i \xrightarrow{\ m_i^{P_i \to P_i'}\ } c_i'$ in $\mathcal{C}$ from happening at the system state s_i, where $\mathrm{1St}(s_i, P_i) = P_i : c_i$ and $\mathrm{1St}(s_{i+1}, P_i) = P_i : c_{i+1}$. The restriction of transition $c_i \xrightarrow{\ m_i^{P_i \to P_i'}\ } c_i'$ is achieved by adding a new intermediate state between c_i and c_i'.

Case 1. Let t_i have a transition to t where some peer P sends a message m to P' and P is different from P_i, the sender peer of the message m_i. We verify whether the transition $c_i \xrightarrow{\ m_i^{P_i \to P_i'}\ } c_{i+1}$ is reachable from t.

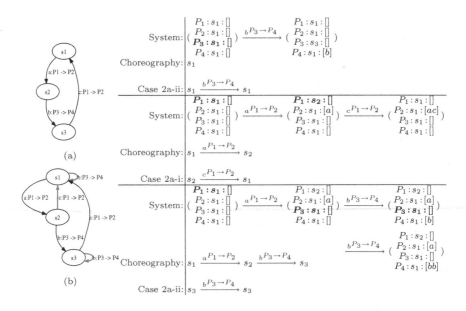

Fig. 5. Example illustrating application of Case 2a of Relaxation

If the verification is successful, this corresponds to the case of unrealizability due to *independent transitions*. The repair, in this case, results from the addition of an intermediate state between t_i and t such that $t_i \xrightarrow{m^{P \to P'}} ns \xrightarrow{nm^{P' \to P_i}} t$, where nm is a new message and ns is a new state. Addition of such transitions will disallow the $m_i^{P_i \to P_i'}$ at the system state s_i.

Case 2. However, if there is no transition from the state t_i or the transition is labeled with a send action performed by the same peer P_i, then it corresponds to the case of unrealizability due to *independent branches*. In this case, we identify the sender peer P_{i-1} for the transition from t_{i-1} to t_i. The restriction is achieved by introducing an intermediate state between c_i and c_{i+1} as follows: $c_i \xrightarrow{nm^{P_{i-1} \to P_i}} ns \xrightarrow{m_i^{P_i \to P_i'}} c_{i+1}$, where nm and ns are newly added message and newly added state, respectively.

These newly added messages and transitions in the choreography can be viewed as an extra step which forces the peer P_i to come in sync with some other peer (P' in Case 1a above and P in Case 1b and 2 above) before sending the message m_i. We refer to such extra step as the *synchronization step*.

We will denote restriction of $\mathcal{C}$ to generate $\mathcal{C}'$ as $\mathcal{C} \setminus \mathcal{C}'$. It is immediate that

$$\mathcal{C} \setminus \mathcal{C}' \Rightarrow \mathcal{L}(\mathcal{C}' \downarrow_\mathcal{C}) = \mathcal{L}(\mathcal{C}') \wedge \mathcal{L}(\mathcal{I}_1^{\mathcal{C}'} \downarrow_\mathcal{C}) \subseteq \mathcal{L}(\mathcal{I}_1^\mathcal{C}) \tag{4}$$

The operation $'.'\downarrow_\mathcal{C}$ extracts the behavior with respect to actions present in $\mathcal{C}$. The restriction does not alter the behavior of the choreography in terms of the actions in $\mathcal{C}$ but restricts the behavior of the corresponding system in terms

Algorithm 1. Repair($\mathcal{C}$, inputRepairMechanism)	
1: Compute $\mathcal{I}_1^{\mathcal{C}}$	
2: **if** $\mathcal{L}(\mathcal{C}) = \mathcal{L}(\mathcal{I}_1^{\mathcal{C}})$ return $\mathcal{C}$	▷ $\mathcal{C}$ is realizable
3: Find a difference between $\mathcal{C}$ and $\mathcal{I}_1^{\mathcal{C}}$	▷ Sect. 4.1
4: Apply $\mathcal{C}$ inputRepairMechanism $\mathcal{C}'$	▷ Sects. 4.2, 4.3
5: GOTO Line 1 with $\mathcal{C}$ assigned to $\mathcal{C}'$	▷ Iterate

of the actions in $\mathcal{C}$. Figure 1(c) presents the result of applying restriction based repair of the choreography in Fig. 1(a). There exists a path in the system where it reaches the state $P_1 : s_1 : [mf], P_2 : s_3 : []$ via the send sequence $ms^{P_1 \to P_2}$, $mf^{P_2 \to P_1}$; from this state, the system is capable of producing $mc^{P_1 \to P_2}$ (see Fig. 3). The choreography via the same sequence of sends reaches the state s_3. Therefore, the restriction is achieved by following the Case 2 above resulting in a repaired choreography in Fig. 1(c).

4.4 Iterative Algorithm

It is necessary to apply the relaxation or the restriction iteratively till a realizable choreography is obtained and all differences between the choreography and the corresponding 1-bounded system behavior have been resolved. In Algorithm 1 the input parameter "inputRepairMechanism" is either set to $\nearrow$ (relaxation) or $\searrow$ (restriction). Figures 4 and 5 illustrate the application of Algorithm 1.

Theorem 2 (Correctness). *The algorithm* REPAIR *is guaranteed to terminate and produce a repaired (i.e., realizable) choreography.*

Proof Sketch. The algorithm iterates as long as there is a difference between the choreography $\mathcal{C}$ and the interaction behavior of the corresponding system $\mathcal{I}_1^{\mathcal{C}}$. To address the difference, the algorithm introduces new states as part of the repair process. The number of such introduction of new states depends directly on the number of independent branches and independent transitions (that cause un-realizability of the choreography). The number of independencies are bounded by the number of branches and the maximum length of a path (with one unfolding) in the choreography, which ensures the boundedness in the introduction of new states. This, in turn, ensures that all possible causes of choreography un-realizability is removed within finite number of steps. □

5 Case Studies

We have implemented Algorithm 1 and used it to repair several un-realizable choreographies that were reported earlier [7,17]. Our implementation obtains repaired versions of these un-realizable choreographies within a second.

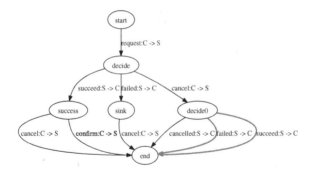

Fig. 6. ReservationSession contract repaired by relaxation

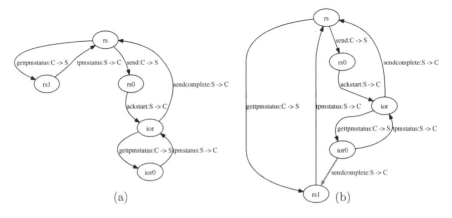

Fig. 7. (a) TpmContract specification, (b) repaired.

Recall that the Singularity OS reservation contract (see Sect. 2) is un-realizable. Figure 6 presents a repaired version by adding new message exchanges. Another un-realizable contract is TpmContract (Fig. 7(a)). In Fig. 7(b), we show a repaired version that is automatically generated by our technique. The repaired version is similar to the one identified by authors in [9]; note however that [9] suggested an addition of a new state and two new transitions. Our repair mechanism achieves the same result by introducing one new transition between two existing states.

We have also analyzed the "Meta Conversation" protocol developed by IBM [12] and discussed in [7]. Two peers P_1 and P_2 race to decide the initiator of the interaction. The protocol is illustrated in Fig. 8(a). It is un-realizable because the peers can both send the start messages (aStartcp and bStartcp) which is not allowed in the protocol. The restriction based solution (Fig. 8(b)) only allows peer P_1 to start the interaction.

Note that the repair only considers the transitions and their labels, and not their semantics. For instance, in Fig. 6, the added bold blue edges (relaxation) do not follow the semantics of the messages being exchanged. Consider the new path in the interaction, where "cancel" from client to server can be followed by "succeed" from the server to client. This is present in the repair in order to allow any ordering between "succeed" and "cancel" messages (as "succeed" followed by "cancel" is allowed in the original contract), which may not make sense in the con-

(a)

(b)

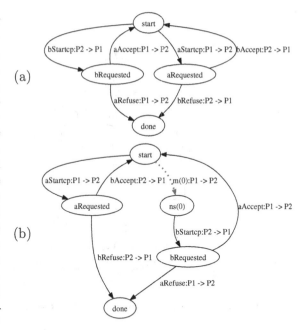

Fig. 8. (a) Meta conversation, (b) repaired.

text of the contract. Therefore, it is sometimes necessary to obtain certain application-domain specific information from the user such that relaxations can be guided appropriately. If the user had provided additional information that "cancel" can never be followed by "succeed", then relaxation would have been impossible and the only choice for removing difference between the un-realizable choreography and the corresponding 1-bounded system will be restriction. We allow users to provide such domain knowledge in our implementation. We have also allowed user-interaction to decide on whether relaxation or restriction is preferred for repair. The user-interaction essentially involves examination of the difference (as presented by our tool) and deciding on the choice between relaxation and restriction. Figure 9 presents an alternative solution for repairing the contract in Fig. 6 generated by our tool. Observe that in this solution, a combination of relaxation and restriction has been applied.

6 Related Work

Realizability of choreographies has been studied before. The authors in [7,9] use state machine based specifications while the authors in [6,10] use session types; both present sufficient conditions for realizability. In [4], we have proved the decidability of choreography realizability in terms of send sequences[1] by presenting a necessary and sufficient condition for realizability.

---

[1] Note that, the realizability problem for the MSC-graphs, which considers both send and receive actions for realizability, is undecidable [1].

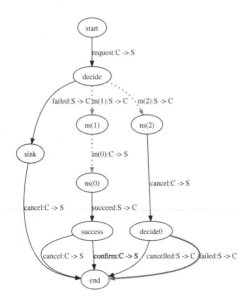

Fig. 9. Alternative repair strategy for ReservationSession (Fig. 2(b))

In [15], the realizability of choreography requires the developer to specify a "dominant" process for each branch and loop construct, which allows the projection mechanism to synthesize necessary synchronization messages between the dominant process and others. Similarly, techniques proposed in [3,8,14,19] rely on introducing new processes, monitors and central controllers to ensure realizability. These may not be viable options if one is using a distributed computing paradigm. Moreover these techniques can be conservative in the sense that unnecessary synchronization messages can be added to even realizable choreographies. Furthermore, the focus of these works is technically different from that of our–for instance, the technique in [3] coordinates the activities of the peers in a distributed fashion such that their coordinated behavior conforms to the given choreography. The repair technique developed by authors in [13] focuses on process algebraic description of choreographies and repair by restriction in the context of independent sequences (referred to as connected choreography by the authors); additionally, the description does not take into consideration iterations, which makes the technique inapplicable to choreographies with cycles.

In contrast, our work (which includes both relaxation and restriction mechanisms) does not require introduction of new processes, does not require a central controller, and does not require use of synchronous communication between any entities/peers. As our technique is based on finite state machines and their language equivalence, it is applicable to choreographies and interactions which are specified at different levels of abstractions, such as session-types [10] and collaboration diagrams [5], as long as these specifications are translated to state-machine based representation described in [4] and used in this paper.

7   Conclusion

We present techniques for automatically repairing un-realizable choreographies based on two strategies: (1) relaxation, where new behaviors are added to the choreography as part of the repair and (2) restriction, where un-desired (excluded by the choreography) behaviors in the system obtained by projecting the choreography are removed as part of the repair. We prove that our repair algorithm always terminates with a realizable choreography. To the best of our knowledge, our method is the first to consider automatically repairing choreographies and to provide formal guarantees of correctness.

References

1. Alur, R., Etessami, K., Yannakakis, M.: Realizability and verification of MSC graphs. In: Proceedings of 28th International Colloquium on Automata, Languages, and Programming, pp. 797–808 (2001)
2. Armstrong, J.: Getting Erlang to talk to the outside world. In: Proceedings of ACM SIGPLAN Workshop on Erlang, pp. 64–72 (2002)
3. Autili, M., Di Ruscio, D., Di Salle, A., Inverardi, P., Tivoli, M.: A model-based synthesis process for choreography realizability enforcement. In: Cortellessa, V., Varró, D. (eds.) FASE 2013 (ETAPS 2013). LNCS, vol. 7793, pp. 37–52. Springer, Heidelberg (2013)
4. Basu, S., Bultan, T., Ouederni, M.: Deciding choreography realizability. In: ACM SIGPLAN-SIGACT Symposium on Principles of Programming Languages (2012)
5. Bultan, T., Fu, X.: Specification of realizable service conversations using collaboration diagrams. Serv. Oriented Comput. Appl. **2**(1), 27–39 (2008)
6. Deniélou, P.-M., Yoshida, N.: Multiparty session types meet communicating automata. In: Seidl, H. (ed.) Programming Languages and Systems. LNCS, vol. 7211, pp. 194–213. Springer, Heidelberg (2012)
7. Fu, X., Bultan, T., Su, J.: Conversation protocols: a formalism for specification and verification of reactive electronic services. In: Ibarra, O.H., Dang, Z. (eds.) CIAA 2003. LNCS, vol. 2759, pp. 188–200. Springer, Heidelberg (2003)
8. Güdemann, M., Salaün, G., Ouederni, M.: Counterexample guided synthesis of monitors for realizability enforcement. In: Chakraborty, S., Mukund, M. (eds.) ATVA 2012. LNCS, vol. 7561, pp. 238–253. Springer, Heidelberg (2012)
9. Hallé, S., Bultan, T.: Realizability analysis for message-based interactions using shared-state projections. In: SIGSOFT Foundations of Software Engineering (2010)
10. Honda, K., Yoshida, N., Carbone, M.: Multiparty asynchronous session types. In: Proceedings of Symposium Principles of Programming Languages (2008)
11. Hunt, G.C., Larus, J.R.: Singularity: rethinking the software stack. Operating Syst. Rev. **41**(2), 37–49 (2007)
12. Kumaran, S., Nandi, P., Hanson, J., Heath, T., Patnaik, Y.: Conversational browser. IBM Techreport (2004)
13. Lanese, I., Montesi, F., Zavattaro, G.: Amending choreographies. In: Automated Specification and Verification of Web Systems (2013)
14. Lohmann, N., Wolf, K.: Realizability is controllability. In: Laneve, C., Su, J. (eds.) WS-FM 2009. LNCS, vol. 6194, pp. 110–127. Springer, Heidelberg (2010)
15. Qiu, Z., Zhao, X., Cai, C., Yang, H.: Towards the theoretical foundation of choreography. In: Proceedings of Conference on World Wide Web (2007)

16. Singularity design note 5: Channel contracts. singularity rdk documentation (v1.1) (2004). http://www.codeplex.com/singularity
17. Stengel, Z., Bultan, T.: Analyzing singularity channel contracts. In: Proceedings of 18th International Symposium on Software Testing and Analysis (ISSTA), pp. 13–24 (2009)
18. Web Service Choreography Description Language (WS-CDL) (2005). http://www.w3.org/TR/ws-cdl-10/
19. Yoon, Y., Ye, C., Jacobsen, H.-A.: A distributed framework for reliable and efficient service choreographies. In: Proceedings of the 20th International Conference on World wide web, WWW 2011, pp. 785–794. ACM (2011)

A Graph-Based Semantics Workbench
for Concurrent Asynchronous Programs

Claudio Corrodi[1,2]([⊠]), Alexander Heußner[3], and Christopher M. Poskitt[1,4]

[1] Department of Computer Science, ETH Zürich, Zürich, Switzerland
[2] Software Composition Group, University of Bern, Bern, Switzerland
corrodi@inf.unibe.ch
[3] Software Technologies Research Group, University of Bamberg, Bamberg, Germany
[4] Singapore University of Technology and Design, Singapore, Singapore

Abstract. A number of novel programming languages and libraries have been proposed that offer simpler-to-use models of concurrency than threads. It is challenging, however, to devise execution models that successfully realise their abstractions without forfeiting performance or introducing unintended behaviours. This is exemplified by SCOOP—a concurrent object-oriented message-passing language—which has seen multiple semantics proposed and implemented over its evolution. We propose a "semantics workbench" with fully and semi-automatic tools for SCOOP, that can be used to analyse and compare programs with respect to different execution models. We demonstrate its use in checking the consistency of semantics by applying it to a set of representative programs, and highlighting a deadlock-related discrepancy between the principal execution models of the language. Our workbench is based on a modular and parameterisable graph transformation semantics implemented in the GROOVE tool. We discuss how graph transformations are leveraged to atomically model intricate language abstractions, and how the visual yet algebraic nature of the model can be used to ascertain soundness.

1 Introduction

To harness the power of multi-core and distributed architectures, software engineers must program with concurrency, asynchronicity, and parallelism in mind. Classical thread-based approaches to concurrent programming, however, are difficult to master and error prone. To address this, a number of programming APIs, libraries, and languages have been proposed that provide safer and simpler-to-use models of concurrency, such as the block-dispatch model of Grand Central Dispatch [14], or the message-passing-based model of SCOOP [40]. The concurrent programming abstractions that these languages provide rely on the existence of effective execution models for realising them; *effective* in the sense that they do

C. Corrodi and C.M. Poskitt—Research done whilst employed by the Chair of Software Engineering, ETH Zürich.

P. Stevens and A. Wąsowski (Eds.): FASE 2016, LNCS 9633, pp. 31–48, 2016.
DOI: 10.1007/978-3-662-49665-7_3

so without forfeiting performance or introducing unintended behaviours. Devising execution models that successfully reconcile these requirements, however, is challenging: a model that is too restrictive can deny desirable concurrency and lead to unnecessary bottlenecks; a model that is too permissive can lead to surprising and unexpected executions.

This challenge is exemplified by SCOOP [40], a message-passing paradigm for concurrent object-oriented programming that aims to preserve the well-understood modes of reasoning enjoyed by sequential programs, such as pre- and postcondition reasoning over blocks of code. Although the high-level language mechanisms for achieving this were described informally as early as the '90s [24,25], it took several years to understand how to effectively implement them: execution models [6,26,40], prototypes [28,37], and contrasting versions of a production-level implementation [11] gradually appeared over the last decade, and can be seen as representing multiple, partially conflicting semantics for realising SCOOP. They are also unlikely to be the last, as new language features continue to be proposed, prototyped, and integrated, e.g. [27]. Despite the possible ramifications to behavioural and safety properties of existing programs, little work has been done to support formal and automatic *comparisons* of the program executions permitted by these different semantics. While general, tool-supported formalisations exist—in *Maude*'s conditional rewriting logic [26], for example, and in a custom-built CSP model checker [6]—these are tied to particular execution models, do not operate on program source code, and are geared towards "testing" the semantics rather than general verification tasks. Furthermore, owing to the need to handle waiting queues, locks, asynchronous remote calls, and several other intricate features of the SCOOP execution models, these formalisations quickly become complex, making it challenging to ascertain their soundness with language designers who lack a formal methods background.

The Challenge. There is a need for languages like SCOOP to have tools that not only support the prototyping of new semantics (and semantic extensions), but that also facilitate formal, automatic, and practical analyses for comparing the executions permitted by these semantics, and highlighting where behavioural and safety-related discrepancies arise. The underlying formalism for modelling the semantics should not be ad hoc; rather, it should support re-use, a modular design, and be easily extensible for language evolutions and changes. Furthermore, such tools should be usable in practice: the modelling formalism must be accessible to and understandable by software engineers, and the analyses must support several idiomatic uses of the language mechanisms.

Our Contributions. We propose a "semantics workbench" equipped with fully and semi-automatic tools for SCOOP, that can be used to analyse and compare programs with respect to different execution models for the purpose of checking their consistency. We demonstrate its use by formalising the two principal execution models of SCOOP, analysing a representative set of programs with respect to both, and highlighting some behavioural and deadlock-related discrepancies that the workbench uncovers automatically. Our workbench is based on a modular and parameterisable graph transformation system (GTS) semantics, built upon our preliminary modelling ideas in [18], and implemented in the general-purpose GTS analysis tool GROOVE [16]. We leverage this powerful formalism to atomically model complex programmer-level abstractions, and show how its inherently visual yet algebraic nature can be used to ascertain soundness. For language designers, this paper presents a transferable approach to checking the consistency of competing semantics for realising concurrency abstractions. For the graph transformation community, it presents our experiences of applying a state-of-the-art GTS tool to a non-trivial and practical problem in programming language design. For the broader verification community, it highlights a need for semantics-parameterised verification, and shows how GTS-based formalisms and tools can be used to derive an effective and modular solution. For software engineers, it provides a powerful workbench for crystallising their mental models of SCOOP, thus helping them to write better quality code and (where need be) port it across different SCOOP implementations.

Plan of the Paper. After introducing the SCOOP concurrency paradigm and its two most established execution models (Sect. 2), we introduce our formal modelling framework based on GTS, and show how to formalise different, parameterisable SCOOP semantics (Sect. 3). Implementing our ideas in a small toolchain (Sect. 4) allows us to check the consistency of semantics across a set of representative SCOOP programs (Sect. 5), and highlight both a behavioural and deadlock-related discrepancy. To conclude, we summarise some related work (Sect. 6), our contributions, and some future research directions (Sect. 7).

2 SCOOP and its Execution Models

SCOOP [40] is a message-passing paradigm for concurrent object-oriented programming that aims to preserve the well-understood modes of reasoning enjoyed by sequential programs; in particular, pre- and postcondition reasoning over blocks of code. This section introduces the programmer-level language mechanisms and reasoning guarantees of SCOOP, as well as its two most established execution models. These will be described in the context of SCOOP's production-level implementation for Eiffel [11], but the ideas generalise to any object-oriented language (as explored, e.g. for Java [37]).

Language Mechanisms. In SCOOP, every object is associated with a *handler* (also called a *processor*), a concurrent thread of execution with the exclusive right to call methods on the objects it handles. In this context, object references may point to objects with the same handler (*non-separate* objects) or to objects with distinct handlers (*separate* objects). Method calls on non-separate objects are executed immediately by the shared handler. To make a call on a separate object, however, a *request* must be sent to the handler of that object to process it: if the method is a *command* (i.e. it does not return a result) then it is executed asynchronously, leading to concurrency; if it is a *query* (i.e. a result is returned and must be waited for) then it is executed synchronously. Note that handlers cannot synchronise via shared memory: only by exchanging requests.

The possibility for objects to have different handlers is captured in the type system by the keyword separate. To request method calls on objects of separate type, programmers simply make the calls within *separate blocks*. These can be explicit (we will use the syntax separate x,y, ... do ... end); but they also exist implicitly for methods with separate objects as parameters.

Reasoning Guarantees. SCOOP provides certain guarantees about the order in which calls in separate blocks are executed to help programmers avoid concurrency errors. In particular, method calls on separate objects will be logged as requests by their handlers in the order that they are given in the program text; furthermore, there will be no intervening requests logged from other handlers. These guarantees exclude object-level data races by construction, and allow programmers to apply pre- and postcondition reasoning within separate blocks independently of the rest of the program. Consider the following example (adapted from [40]), in which two distinct handlers are respectively executing blocks that set the "colours" of two separate objects:

```
separate x,y
do
    x.set_colour (Green)
    y.set_colour (Green)
end
```

```
separate x,y
do
    x.set_colour (Indigo)
    a_colour = x.get_colour
    y.set_colour (a_colour)
end
```

The guarantees ensure that whilst a handler is inside its separate x,y block, the other handler cannot log intervening calls on x or y. Consequently, if the colours are later queried in another separate x,y block, both of them will be Green or both of them will be Indigo; interleavings permitting any other combination to be observed are entirely excluded. This additional control over the order in which requests are processed represents a twist on classical message-passing models, such as the actor model [1], and programming languages like Erlang [2] that implement them.

Execution Models. The abstractions of SCOOP require an execution model that can realise them without forfeiting performance or introducing unintended behaviours. Two contrasting models have been supported by different versions of the implementation: initially, a model we call Request Queues (RQ) [26], and a model that has now replaced it which we will call Queues of Queues (QoQ) [40].

The RQ execution model associates each handler with a single FIFO queue for storing incoming requests. To ensure the reasoning guarantees, each queue is protected by a lock, which another handler must acquire to be able to log a request on the queue. Realising a separate x,y,... block then boils down to acquiring locks on the request queues attached to the handlers of x,y,... and exclusively holding them for the duration of the block. This coarse-grained solution successfully prevents intervening requests from being logged, but leads to performance bottlenecks in several situations (e.g. multiple handlers vying for the lock of a highly contested request queue).

In contrast, the QoQ execution model associates each handler with a FIFO queue that itself contains (possibly several) FIFO subqueues for storing incoming requests. These subqueues represent "private areas" for handlers to log requests without interference from other handlers. Realising a `separate` x,y,... block no longer requires vying for locks; instead, the handlers of x,y,... simply generate private subqueues on which requests can be logged without interruption for the duration of the block. If another handler also wants to log requests, then a new private subqueue is generated for it and its requests can be logged at the same time. The QoQ model removes the performance bottlenecks caused by the locks of RQ, while still ensuring the SCOOP reasoning guarantees by completely processing subqueues in the order that they were generated.

Figure 1 visualises three handlers (h_1, h_2, h_3) logging requests (green blocks) on another handler (h_0) under the two execution models. Note that the RQ and QoQ implementations (i.e. compilers and runtimes) include additional optimisations, and strictly speaking, can themselves be viewed as competing semantics.

Fig. 1. Logging requests under the RQ (left) and QoQ (right) execution models

Semantic Discrepancies. Discrepancies between the execution models can arise in practice. In the mental model of programmers, with RQ, separate blocks had become synonymous with acquiring and holding locks—which are not implied by the basic reasoning guarantees or the QoQ model. This discrepancy comes to light with the classical dining philosophers program (as provided in the official SCOOP documentation [11]), which will form a running example for this paper. Under RQ, Listing 1 ("eager" philosophers) solves the problem by relying on the implicit parallel acquisition of locks on the forks' handlers; no two adjacent philosophers can be in their separate blocks (representing "eating") at the same time. Under RQ, Listing 2 ("lazy" philosophers) can lead to circular deadlocks, as philosophers acquire the locks in turn. With QoQ however—where there is no implicit locking—neither version represents a solution, and neither can cause a deadlock; yet the basic guarantees about the order of logged requests remain satisfied. We will return to this example in later sections, and show how such discrepancies can be detected by our workbench.

3 A Graph-Based Semantic Model for the SCOOP Family

There are several established and contrasting semantics of SCOOP [6,18,26,29, 40], including a comprehensive reference semantics for RQ in *Maude*'s conditional rewriting logic [26], and a semantics for the core of QoQ in the form of

```
separate left_fork, right_fork
do
   left_fork.use
   right_fork.use
end
```

```
separate left_fork
do
   separate right_fork
   do
      left_fork.use
      right_fork.use
   end
end
```

Listing 1. Eager philosophers   **Listing 2.** Lazy philosophers

simple structural operational rules [40]. These formalisations, however, cannot easily be used for semantic comparisons, due to their varying levels of detail, coverage, extensibility, and tool support. Hence we present in this section "yet another" semantic model, called SCOOP-GTS, based on our preliminary modelling ideas for RQ in [18], using the formalism of graph transformation systems (GTS).

Our reasons to introduce SCOOP-GTS are manifold: (a) we need a common modelling ground that can be parameterised by models of RQ and QoQ; (b) known models based on algebra, process calculi, automata, or Petri nets do not straightforwardly cover SCOOP's asynchronous concurrent nature, or would hide these features in intricate encodings; (c) existing approaches are often proposed from a theoretician's point of view and are not easily readable by software engineers, whereas graphs and diagrammatic notations (e.g. UML) might already be used in their everyday work. Choosing graph transformations as our base formalism is well-justified, as they satisfy the above requirements, and reconcile the goal to have a theoretically rigorous formalisation with the goal to be accessible to software engineers, e.g. for expert interviews with the language implementers (see [31] for a detailed discussion of the pros and cons of GTS in this setting). The "non-linear" context of graph rewriting rules proves to be a powerful mechanism for defining semantics and their interfaces for parameterisation.

We formalised SCOOP-GTS using the state-of-the-art GTS tool GROOVE [17]. Due to limited space, we provide all the files necessary to browse our GTS model as supplementary material [36], including input graphs generated from the example programs of Sect. 5 that can be simulated, analysed, and verified.

SCOOP-Graphs. Each global configuration of a SCOOP program, i.e. snapshot of the global state, is represented by a directed, typed attributed graph consisting of (i) *handler nodes* representing SCOOP's handlers, i.e. basic execution units; (ii) a representation of each handler's *local memory* (i.e. "heap" of non-separate objects) and its known neighbourhood, consisting of references to separate objects that can be addressed by queries and commands; (iii) a representation of each handler's *stack*, via stack frames that model recursive calls to non-separate objects; (iv) *requests* for modelling separate calls, which are stored in (v) subgraphs representing each handler's *input work queue*; (vi) a global *control flow graph* (CFG) presenting the program's execution blocks (consisting of states and actions/transitions in-between); (vii) relations to model inter-handler and handler-memory relations (e.g. locking, waiting, etc.) and to assign each

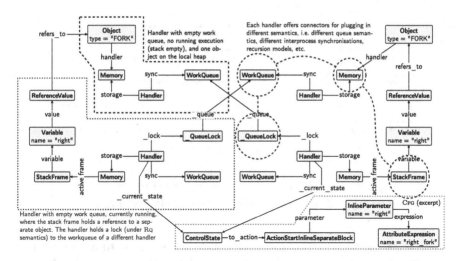

Fig. 2. Reachable deadlock under RQ for the lazy philosophers program (Listing 2) simplified from GROOVE output with additional highlighting and information in colour

handler to its current state in the CFG; and (viii) additional bookkeeping nodes, e.g. containing information on detected deadlocks, and nodes to model the interfaces/contexts for semantic parameterisation. An example SCOOP-Graph can be seen in Fig. 2, depicting a configuration with two concurrently running and two idle handlers.

GTS-Based Operational Semantics. The operational semantics of SCOOP-GTS is given by graph-rewriting rules that are regimented by *control programs*. An example rule, concisely written using nesting as supported by GROOVE, can be seen in Fig. 3. Note that nested rules (including ∀- and ∃-quantification) allow us to express complex, atomic rule matchings in a relatively straightforward and brief way (compared to rules in classical operational semantics, e.g. in [40] for multiple handler reservations). A simplified, example control program can be seen in Listing 3. Control programs allow us to make an execution model's scheduler explicit (and thus open to parameterisation) and help us to implement "garbage collection" for the model (e.g. removing bookkeeping edges no longer needed). Furthermore, they provide a fine-grained way to control the atomicity of SCOOP operations, by wrapping sequences of rule applications into so-called *recipes*.

Semantic Modularity of SCOOP-GTS. We support semantic parameterisation for SCOOP-GTS by providing fixed module interfaces in the graph via special "plug-in nodes/edges" (e.g. WorkQueue, Memory, StackFrame in Fig. 2), and changing only the set of GTS rules that operate on the subgraphs that they guard. We have modelled both RQ and QoQ with distinct sets of rules that operate on the subgraphs guarded by WorkQueue: we call the model parameterised by RQ and QoQ respectively SCOOP-GTS(RQ) and SCOOP-GTS(QoQ).

```
initialize_model;                                    // call gts rule for initialisation
while (progress & no_error) {
    for each handler p:                              // choose handlers under some scheduling strategy
        alap handler_local_execution_step(p)+;       // each handler executes local actions as long as possible
    try synchronisation_step;                        // then try (one) possible global synchronisation step
}
recipe handler_local_execution_step (p){
    try separate_object_creation(p)+;                // try local actions that are possibly applicable
    else try assignment_to_variable(p)+;
    else try ... ;                                   // sequentially try all other possible actions
    try clean_up_model+;                             // do some"garbage collection" to keep the model small
}
recipe synchronisation_step (){
    reserve_handlers | dequeue_task | ...;           // non-deterministically try to synchronise
}
...                                                  // remaining recipes (core functionality)
// ---------- plug in ------------------------------------------------------------------------------
recipe separate_object_creation(p){                  // provide different implementations for RQ and QoQ
    ...                                              // and parameterise the control program
}
...                                                  // remaining recipes that are plugged in
```

Listing 3. Simplified control program (in GROOVE syntax)

As well as parameterising the queue semantics, it is possible to model different recursion schemes, memory models, and global interprocess synchronisations.

This semantic modularity also permits us to directly apply abstractions to SCOOP-GTS, e.g. changing the queue's semantics to a bag's counting abstraction, or flattening recursion. This could prove useful for providing advanced verification approaches in the workbench.

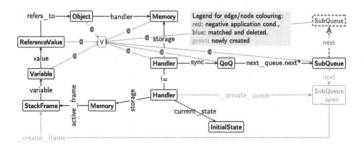

Fig. 3. Simplified QoQ rule for entering a `separate x,y,...` block, which uses ∀-quantification to atomically match arbitrarily many handlers. The rule assumes that the handlers' queues already contain some other private subqueues open

Soundness/Faithfulness. The relation of SCOOP-GTS to the most prominent execution models and runtimes is depicted in Fig. 4. Due to the varying levels of detail in the formalisations of the RQ and QoQ execution models (and lack of formalisations of their implementations/runtimes), there is no universal way to prove SCOOP-GTS's faithfulness to them. We also remark that SCOOP-GTS currently does not support some programming mechanisms of the Eiffel language (e.g. exceptions, agents), but could be straightforwardly extended to cover them.

We were able to conduct expert interviews with the researchers proposing the execution models and the programmers implementing the SCOOP compiler and runtimes, which helped to improve our confidence that SCOOP-GTS faithfully

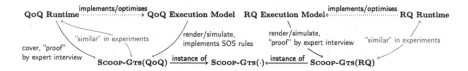

Fig. 4. Relation between Scoop-Gts, the execution models, and the runtimes

covers their behaviour. Here, Scoop-Gts's advantage of a visually accessible notation was extremely beneficial, as we were able to directly use simulations in Groove during the interviews, which were understood and accepted by the interviewees. In addition, we compared Groove simulations of the executions of Scoop programs (see the benchmarks of Sect. 5) against their actual execution behaviour in the official Scoop IDE and compiler (both the current release that implements QoQ, and an older one that implemented RQ). Again, this augmented our confidence. Furthermore, we were able to compare Scoop-Gts(QoQ) with the structural operational semantics for QoQ provided in [40]. Unfortunately, the provided semantic rules focus only on a much simplified core, preventing a rigorous bisimulation proof exploiting the algebraic characterisations of Gts. We can, however, straightforwardly implement and simulate them in our model.

To conclude, Scoop-Gts fits into the suite of existing Scoop formalisations, and is able to cover (avoiding the semantically overloaded word "simulate") both of the principal execution models.

Expressiveness. As previously discussed, Scoop-Gts is expressive enough to cover the existing RQ and QoQ semantic models of Scoop due to its modularity and the possibility to plug-in different queueing semantics. We currently plan to include other semantic formalisations of Scoop-like languages, e.g. the concurrent Eiffel proposed by [5] (similar to Scoop but differences regarding separate object calls), other actor-based object-oriented languages, and concurrency concepts like "co-boxes" [34]. Scoop-Gts is obviously Turing-complete (one can simulate a 2-counter Minsky machine by non-recursive models with one object per handler, similar to the construction in [15]). A proper formal investigation into its computational power (also that of subclasses of the model) is ongoing.

4   Toolchain for the Workbench

Our semantics workbench consists of a toolchain that bridges the gap between Scoop program code and the analysis of Scoop-Gts models in Groove. In particular, it translates source code into Scoop-Graphs, executes the appropriate analyses in Groove, and then collects and returns the results to the user.

Our toolchain is summarised in Fig. 5. Its principal component is a plug-in for the Eve IDE—a research version of the Scoop/Eiffel IDE (including the production compiler and runtime) which supports the integration of verification

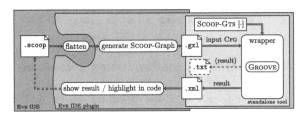

Fig. 5. Overview of our toolchain: a plugin integrated with the (research version of the) official Scoop IDE, which interfaces with a wrapper that utilises and controls Groove in the background. The wrapper can also be used as part of a standalone tool

tools [38]. For a given Scoop program, the plug-in uses the existing services of Eve to check that the code compiles, and then extracts a representation of it in which inheritance has been "flattened". From this flattened program, we generate a Scoop-Graph (encoded in the Graph eXchange Language) which corresponds very closely to the abstract syntax tree of the original program. See, for example, Fig. 6, which is generated from the code in Listing 2. Observe that between the `InitialState` and `FinalState`, the control-flow graph directly encodes the four actions of the original program: two declarations of `separate` blocks, and two commands within them. We provide a wrapper (written in Java) around the external Groove tool, which takes a generated Scoop-Graph as input, and launches a full state-space exploration in Groove with respect to Scoop-Gts(RQ) or Scoop-Gts(QoQ). The results—including statistics and detected error states—are then extracted from Groove and returned to the programmer for inspection. A standalone version of this wrapper without the Eve integration is also available and can be downloaded from [36].

Checking the Consistency of Semantics. The workbench can be used to check the consistency of program executions under RQ and QoQ with respect to various properties. These properties are encoded in Scoop-Gts as *error rules* that match on configurations if and only if they violate the properties. If they match, they generate a special `Error` node that encodes some contextual information for the toolchain to extract, and prevents the execution branch from being explored any further. Two types of error rules are supported: general, safety-related error rules for detecting problems like deadlock (whether caused by waiting for request queue locks in RQ, or waiting on cycles of queries in QoQ); but also user-specified error rules for program-specific properties (as we will use in Sect. 5). If any of these error rules are applied in a state-space exploration, this information is extracted and reported by the workbench toolchain; discrepancies between semantics exist when such rules match under only one. Figure 2 shows an actual deadlock between two handlers attempting to enter the nested separate block of Listing 2 under RQ. This configuration is matched by an error rule for deadlock (not shown), which catches the circular waiting dependencies exhibited by the edges.

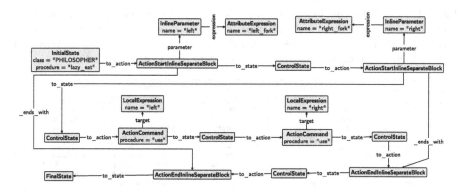

Fig. 6. Generated control-flow graph for Listing 2

5 Evaluation

To evaluate the use of our workbench for checking the consistency of semantics, we devised a representative set of benchmark programs, based on documented SCOOP examples [11] and classical synchronisation problems. We then deployed the toolchain to analyse their executions under RQ and QoQ with respect to behavioural and safety-related properties, and highlight the discrepancies uncovered by the workbench for our running example. Everything necessary to reproduce our evaluation is available at [36].

Benchmark Selection. Our aim was to devise a set of representative programs covering different, idiomatic usages of SCOOP's concurrency mechanisms. To achieve this, we based our programs on official, documented examples [11], as well as some classical synchronisation problems, in order to deploy the language mechanisms in a greater variety of usage contexts. Note that it is not (yet) our goal to analyse large software projects, but rather to compare executions of representative programs with manageable state spaces under different semantics.

We selected the following programs: dining philosophers—as presented in Sect. 2—with its two implementations for picking up forks (eagerly or lazily) which exploited the implicit locking of RQ; a third variant of dining philosophers without any commands in the separate blocks; single-element producer consumer, which uses a mixture of commands, queries, and condition synchronisation; and finally, barbershop and dining savages (based on [10]), both of which use a similar mix of features. These programs cover different usages of SCOOP's language mechanisms and are well-understood examples in concurrent programming. Note that while our compiler supports inheritance by flattening the used classes, these examples do not use inheritance; in particular, no methods from the implicitly inherited class ANY are used. By not translating these methods into the start graphs, we obtain considerably smaller graphs (which impacts the exploration speed, but not the sizes of the generated transition systems).

Benchmark Results. Table 1 contains metrics for the inspected examples, obtained using our GROOVE wrapper utility. The presented values correspond

Table 1. Results for the dining philosophers (DP, with the number of philosophers), producer-consumer (PC, with the number of elements), barbershop (with the number of customers), and dining savages (with the number of savages) programs; time and memory metrics are means over five runs (standard deviation in brackets)

Start graph	Semantics	Config-urations	Rule applications	Start graph size (nodes/edges)	Final graph size (nodes/edges)	Time [SD] (seconds)	Memory [SD] (GB)
DP 2 eager	RQ	4219	54441	226/343	261/396	19.34 [0.25]	1.60 [0.02]
	QoQ	5644	72762	226/343	284/462	25.61 [1.03]	1.63 [0.02]
DP 2 lazy	RQ	5679	72692	221/334	288/470	24.76 [0.34]	2.05 [0.10]
	QoQ	9609	123583	221/334	256/387	42.46 [0.65]	2.22 [0.06]
DP 2 eager	RQ	442	6010	254/395	300/473	6.08 [0.28]	0.57 [0.00]
(no commands)	QoQ	443	6135	254/395	300/473	5.84 [0.24]	0.57 [0.01]
DP 2 lazy	RQ	868	11211	250/387	325/541	9.53 [0.36]	0.66 [0.00]
(no commands)	QoQ	919	11935	250/387	296/465	10.66 [0.61]	0.66 [0.01]
DP 3 eager	RQ	99198	1270216	226/343	277/422	469.94 [11.93]	11.14 [0.17]
	QoQ	199144	2532882	226/343	304/498	1393.95 [31.06]	13.88 [0.08]
DP 3 lazy	RQ	170249	2166712	221/334	319/536	1149.07 [53.59]	13.33 [0.69]
	QoQ	444686	5683419	221/334	272/413	2564.45 [55.94]	11.99 [0.07]
DP 3 eager	RQ	3269	43967	254/395	316/499	37.31 [1.68]	1.70 [0.09]
(no commands)	QoQ	3286	45152	254/395	316/499	39.32 [0.65]	1.52 [0.00]
DP 3 lazy	RQ	10877	139216	250/387	355/604	114.26 [5.17]	3.39 [0.13]
(no commands)	QoQ	11774	151526	250/387	312/491	125.25 [4.19]	3.63 [0.07]
PC 5	RQ	4085	51283	307/476	353/548	45.87 [0.74]	2.07 [0.14]
	QoQ	12366	156210	307/476	353/548	140.86 [2.83]	3.14 [0.07]
PC 20	RQ	12890	159958	307/476	398/593	148.28 [2.85]	3.78 [0.25]
	QoQ	50286	632820	307/476	398/593	618.33 [15.42]	6.67 [0.20]
Barbershop 2	RQ	38509	494491	302/466	346/538	354.17 [16.58]	6.91 [0.19]
	QoQ	54325	702611	302/466	346/538	537.21 [8.19]	7.79 [0.16]
Savages 2	RQ	35361	448576	410/631	459/716	550.92 [14.99]	7.06 [0.07]
	QoQ	79398	1008596	410/631	459/716	1299.52 [54.96]	11.33 [0.11]

to full state-space exploration. Metrics for elapsed time (wall clock time) and memory usage (computed using Java's `MemoryPoolMXBean`) are the means of five runs, while the other values are the same for each run. The experiments were carried out on an off-the-shelf notebook with an Intel Core i7-4810MQ CPU and 16 GB of main memory. We used Oracle Java 1.8.0_25 with the `-Xmx 14g` option together with GROOVE 5.5.5.

Across all instances, the start and final graph sizes are comparable. This can be explained by the fact that our implementation contains a number of simple "garbage collection" rules that remove edges and nodes that are no longer needed (e.g. the results of intermediate computations). Final graphs simply contain the control-flow graph and heap structure after the executions. Note that we do not perform real garbage collection. For example, unreachable objects are not removed; the graph size increases linearly with the number of created objects.

The number of configurations denotes the number of recipe applications. This value is of interest because it allows one to directly compare explorations under different semantics (i.e. how much more concurrency is permitted). Recall that scheduler-specific rules are wrapped inside recipes. For example, enqueueing a work item may trigger more bookkeeping rules in QoQ than in RQ. Since the corresponding logic (see Listing 3) is implemented in a recipe, we end up with just one more configuration in both cases, independently of how many individual rule applications are triggered within the recipe. Differences in the number of configurations arise from different branching at synchronisation points. For example, we can see that in most instances, QoQ generates considerably more configurations than the RQ implementation, which suggests that SCOOP programs are "more concurrent" under QoQ.

The time and memory columns show the raw power requirements of our toolchain. Unfortunately, the state-space explosion problem is inevitable when exploring concurrent programs. The number of configurations is, unsurprisingly, particularly sensitive to programs with many handlers and only asynchronous commands (e.g. dining philosophers). Programs that also use synchronous queries (e.g. producer-consumer) scale better, since queries force synchronisation once they reach the front of the queue. We note again that our aim was to facilitate automatic analyses of representative SCOOP programs that covered the different usages of the language mechanisms, rather than optimised verification techniques for production-level software. The results suggest that for this objective, the toolchain scales well enough to be practical.

Error Rules/Discrepancies Detected. In our evaluation of the various dining philosophers implementations, we were able to detect that the lazy implementation (Listing 2) can result in deadlock under the RQ model, but not under QoQ. This was achieved by using error rules that match circular waiting dependencies. In case a deadlock occurs that is not matched by these rules, we can still detect that the execution is stuck and report a generic error, after which we manually inspect the resulting configuration. While such error rules are useful for analysing SCOOP-Graphs in general, it is also useful to define rules that match when certain program-specific properties hold. For example, if we take a look at the eager implementation of the dining philosophers (Listing 1) and its executions under RQ and QoQ, we find that the program cannot deadlock under either. This does not prove however that the implementation actually solves the dining philosophers problem under both semantics. To check this, we defined an error rule that matches if and only if two adjacent philosophers are in their separate blocks at the same time, which is impossible if forks are treated as locks (as they implicitly are under RQ). Consequently, this rule matches only under the QoQ semantics, highlighting that under the new semantics, the program is no longer a solution to the dining philosophers problem. (We remark that it can be "ported" to QoQ by replacing the commands on forks with queries, which force the waiting.) We implemented program-specific correctness rules for the other benchmark programs analogously, but did not detect any further discrepancies.

6   Related Work

We briefly describe some related work closest to the overarching themes of our paper: frameworks for semantic analyses, GTS models for concurrent asynchronous programs, and verification techniques for SCOOP.

Frameworks for Semantic Analysis. The closest approach in spirit to ours is the work on K [21,33]. It consists of the K concurrent rewrite abstract machine and the K technique. One can think of K as domain specific language for implementing programming languages with a special focus on semantics, which was recently successfully applied to give elaborate semantics to Java [4] and JavaScript [30]. Both $\mathbb{K}$ and our workbench have the same user group (programming language designers and researchers) and focus on formalising semantics and analysing programs based on this definition. We both have "modularity" as a principal goal in our agendas, but in a contrasting sense: our modularity targets a semantic plug-in mechanism for parameterising different model components, whereas $\mathbb{K}$ focuses on modularity with respect to language feature reuse. In contrast to our approach, $\mathbb{K}$ targets the whole language toolchain—including the possibility to define a language and automatically generate parsers and a runtime simulation for testing the formalisation. Based on *Maude*'s formal power of conditional rewriting logic, $\mathbb{K}$ also offers axiomatic models for formal reasoning on programs and the possibility to also define complex static semantic features, e.g. advanced typing and meta-programming. Despite having similar formal underlying theoretical power ($\mathbb{K}$'s rewriting is similar to "jungle rewriting" graph grammars [35]), SCOOP-GTS models make the graph-like interdependencies between concurrently running threads or handlers a first-class element of the model. This is an advantage for analyses of concurrent asynchronous programs, as many concurrency properties can be straightforwardly reduced to graph properties (e.g. deadlocks as wait-cycles). Our explicit GTS model also allows us to compare program executions under different semantics, which is not a targeted feature of $\mathbb{K}$. We also conjecture that our diagrammatic notations are easier for software engineers to grasp than purely algebraic and axiomatic formalisations.

GTS Models for Concurrent Asynchronous Programs. Formalising and analysing concurrent object-oriented programs with GTS-based models is an emerging trend in software specification and analysis, especially for approaches rooted in practice. See [31] for a good overview discussion—based on a lot of personal experience—on the general appropriateness of GTS for this task. In recent decades, conditional rewriting logic has become a reference formalism for concurrency models in general; we refer to [22] and its recent update [23] for details. Despite having a comparable expressive power, our approach's original decision for GTS and for GROOVE as our state-space exploration tool led us to an easily accessible, generic, and parameterisable semantic model and tools that work in acceptable time on our representative SCOOP examples. Closest to our SCOOP-GTS model is the QDAS model presented in [15], which represents an asynchronous, concurrent waiting queue based model with *global memory* as GTS, for verifying programs written in Grand Central Dispatch [14]. Despite the formal work, there is currently no direct compiler to GTS yet. The Creol model of [20] focuses on asynchronous concurrent models but without more advanced remote calls via queues as needed for SCOOP. Analysis of the model can be done via an implementation in *Maude* [19]. Existing GTS-based models for Java only translate the code to a typed graph similar to the control-flow sub-graph of SCOOP-GTS [8,32]. A different approach is taken by [12], which abstracts a GTS-based model for concurrent OO systems [13] to a finite state model that can be verified using the SPIN model checker. GROOVE itself was already used for verifying concurrent distributed algorithms on an abstract GTS level [16], but not on an execution model level as in our approach. However, despite the intention to apply generic frameworks for the specification, analysis, and verification of object-oriented concurrent programs, e.g. in [9,41], there are no publicly available tools implementing this long-term goal that are powerful enough for SCOOP.

SCOOP Analysis/Verification. Various analyses for SCOOP programs have been proposed, including: using a SCOOP virtual machine for checking temporal properties [29]; checking Coffman's deadlock conditions using an abstract semantics [7]; and statically checking code annotated with locking orders for the absence of deadlock [39]. In contrast to our work, these approaches are tied to particular (and now obsolete) execution models, and do not operate on (unannotated) source code.

The complexity of other semantic models of SCOOP led to scalability issues when attempting to leverage existing analysis and verification tools. In [6], SCOOP programs were hand-translated to models in the process algebra CSP to perform, e.g. deadlock analysis; but the leading CSP tools at the time could not cope with these models and a new tool was purpose-built (but no longer available/maintained today). In a recent deadlock detection benchmark on the RQ execution model formalised in *Maude* [26], the tool was not able to give verification results in reasonable time (i.e. less than one day) even for simple programs like dining philosophers[1]; our benchmarks compare quite favourably to this. Note that since our work focuses more on semantic modelling and comparisons than it does on the underlying model checking algorithms, we did not yet evaluate the generic bounded model checking algorithms for temporal logic properties implemented in GROOVE and accessible for SCOOP-GTS models.

7   Conclusion and Future Work

We proposed and constructed a semantic workbench for a concurrent asynchronous programming language via the following, general work flow: (i) derive a GTS-based semantic model from existing semi-formal documentation of execution models; (ii) continuously compare the model by simulation runs against the actual implementations; (iii) exploit semantic paramaterisation to derive a versatile model; (iv) if possible, conduct expert interviews to ascertain the model's faithfulness; (v) apply existing generic model checking techniques for GTS to implement analyses against the different execution models; (vi) implement different analyses on top of this model. This workflow resulted in the formalisation SCOOP-GTS, which covered the two principal execution models of SCOOP, and allowed us to formally, automatically, and practically compare the executions of programs with respect to both. With the conducted expert interviews, and the results of applying our model to check the consistency of the semantics across a small but representative collection of SCOOP programs in reasonable time, we were reassured of our choice of GTS as an underlying formalism: theoretically

---

[1] From personal communication with the researchers behind this benchmark.

sound, yet diagrammatically accessible for software engineers, and able to scale to the sizes of programs we need for semantic comparisons.

We are currently working on extending SCOOP-GTS to cover some more advanced and esoteric features of SCOOP (including distributed exception handling) and to enlarge the benchmark set, with the eventual aim of producing a conformance test suite for SCOOP-like languages. As noted in [42], the shape of the rules and the control programs have a big influence on the running times of GROOVE. We are currently working on refactoring SCOOP-GTS for better performance (relative to benchmarking on the conformance test suite).

A more general line of research focuses on the shape of the SCOOP-Graphs contained in the reachable state space of SCOOP-GTS. Insights here would help us to devise better abstraction techniques (along the lines of [3]) with which we could implement better verification algorithms, and visualise the influence of different semantic parameters on SCOOP-Graphs. Generalising SCOOP-GTS to cover other actor-based concurrency languages would also extend this result towards differences between the semantics of programming language families expressed as SCOOP-Graph properties.

Acknowledgements. We thank our interviewees from the SCOOP development and research team for the many helpful and insightful discussions. We are also deeply grateful for the work of the GROOVE developers that we leverage in this paper, and especially for their GROOVE-y feedback and support. The underlying research was partially funded by ERC Grant CME #291389.

References

1. Agha, G.: ACTORS: A Model of Concurrent Computation in Distributed Systems. MIT Press, Cambridge (1986)
2. Armstrong, J., Virding, R., Williams, M.: Concurrent Programming in ERLANG, 2nd edn. Prentice Hall, Englewood Cliffs (1996)
3. Backes, P., Reineke, J.: Analysis of infinite-state graph transformation systems by cluster abstraction. In: D'Souza, D., Lal, A., Larsen, K.G. (eds.) VMCAI 2015. LNCS, vol. 8931, pp. 135–152. Springer, Heidelberg (2015)
4. Bogdanas, D., Rosu, G.: K-Java: A complete semantics of Java. In: Proceedings of POPL 2015, pp. 445–456. ACM (2015)
5. Brooke, P.J., Paige, R.F.: Cameo: an alternative model of concurrency for Eiffel. Formal Aspects Comput. **21**(4), 363–391 (2009)
6. Brooke, P.J., Paige, R.F., Jacob, J.L.: A CSP model of Eiffel's SCOOP. Formal Aspects Comput. **19**(4), 487–512 (2007)
7. Caltais, G., Meyer, B.: Coffman deadlocks in SCOOP. In: Proceedings of NWPT 2014 (2014). http://arxiv.org/abs/1409.7514
8. Corradini, A., Dotti, F.L., Foss, L., Ribeiro, L.: Translating Java code to graph transformation systems. In: Ehrig, H., Engels, G., Parisi-Presicce, F., Rozenberg, G. (eds.) ICGT 2004. LNCS, vol. 3256, pp. 383–398. Springer, Heidelberg (2004)
9. Dotti, F.L., Duarte, L.M., Foss, L., Ribeiro, L., Russi, D., dos Santos, O.M.: An environment for the development of concurrent object-based applications. In: Proceedings of GraBaTs 2004. ENTCS, vol. 127, pp. 3–13. Elsevier (2005)

10. Downey, A.B.: The Little Book of Semaphores. http://greenteapress.com/semaphores/. Accessed Jan 2016
11. Eiffel Documentation: Concurrent Eiffel with SCOOP. https://docs.eiffel.com/book/solutions/concurrent-eiffel-scoop. Accessed Oct 2015
12. Ferreira, A.P.L., Foss, L., Ribeiro, L.: Formal verification of object-oriented graph grammars specifications. In: Proceedings of GT-VC 2006. ENTCS, vol. 175, pp. 101–114. Elsevier (2007)
13. Ferreira, A.P.L., Ribeiro, L.: A graph-based semantics for object-oriented programming constructs. In: Proceedings of CTCS 2004. ENTCS, vol. 122, pp. 89–104. Elsevier (2005)
14. Grand Central Dispatch (GCD) Reference. https://developer.apple.com/library/mac/documentation/Performance/Reference/GCD_libdispatch_Ref/index.html. Accessed Oct 2015
15. Geeraerts, G., Heußner, A., Raskin, J.: On the verification of concurrent, asynchronous programs with waiting queues. ACM Trans. Embed. Comput. Syst. **14**(3), 58 (2015)
16. Ghamarian, A.H., de Mol, M., Rensink, A., Zambon, E., Zimakova, M.: Modelling and analysis using GROOVE. Int. J. Softw. Tools Technol. Transf. **14**(1), 15–40 (2012)
17. Groove (project web page). http://groove.cs.utwente.nl/. Accessed October 2015
18. Heußner, A., Poskitt, C.M., Corrodi, C., Morandi, B.: Towards practical graph-based verification for an object-oriented concurrency model. In: Proceedings of GaM 2015. EPTCS, vol. 181, pp. 32–47 (2015)
19. Johnsen, E.B., Owe, O., Axelsen, E.W.: A run-time environment for concurrent objects with asynchronous method calls. In: Proceedings of WRLA 2004. ENTCS, vol. 117, pp. 375–392. Elsevier(2005)
20. Johnsen, E.B., Owe, O., Yu, I.C.: Creol: a type-safe object-oriented model for distributed concurrent systems. Theor. Comput. Sci. **365**(1–2), 23–66 (2006)
21. Lucanu, D., Şerbănuţă, T.F., Roşu, G.: K framework distilled. In: Durán, F. (ed.) WRLA 2012. LNCS, vol. 7571, pp. 31–53. Springer, Heidelberg (2012)
22. Meseguer, J.: Conditioned rewriting logic as a united model of concurrency. Theor. Comput. Sci. **96**(1), 73–155 (1992)
23. Meseguer, J.: Twenty years of rewriting logic. J. Logic Algebraic Program. **81**(7–8), 721–781 (2012)
24. Meyer, B.: Systematic concurrent object-oriented programming. Commun. ACM (CACM) **36**(9), 56–80 (1993)
25. Meyer, B.: Object-Oriented Software Construction, 2nd edn. Prentice Hall, Upper Saddle River (1997)
26. Morandi, B., Schill, M., Nanz, S., Meyer, B.: Prototyping a concurrency model. In: Proceedings of ACSD 2013, pp. 170–179. IEEE (2013)
27. Morandi, B., Nanz, S., Meyer, B.: Safe and efficient data sharing for message-passing concurrency. In: Kühn, E., Pugliese, R. (eds.) COORDINATION 2014. LNCS, vol. 8459, pp. 99–114. Springer, Heidelberg (2014)
28. Nienaltowski, P.: Practical framework for contract-based concurrent object-oriented programming. Doctoral dissertation, ETH Zürich (2007)
29. Ostroff, J.S., Torshizi, F.A., Huang, H.F., Schoeller, B.: Beyond contracts for concurrency. Formal Aspects Comput. **21**(4), 319–346 (2009)
30. Park, D., Ştefănescu, A., Roşu, G.: KJS: a complete formal semantics of JavaScript. In: Proceedings of PLDI 2015, pp. 346–356. ACM (2015)

31. Rensink, A.: The edge of graph transformation — graphs for behavioural specification. In: Engels, G., Lewerentz, C., Schäfer, W., Schürr, A., Westfechtel, B. (eds.) Nagl Festschrift. LNCS, vol. 5765, pp. 6–32. Springer, Heidelberg (2010)

32. Rensink, A., Zambon, E.: A type graph model for Java programs. In: Lee, D., Lopes, A., Poetzsch-Heffter, A. (eds.) FMOODS 2009. LNCS, vol. 5522, pp. 237–242. Springer, Heidelberg (2009)

33. Rosu, G., Serbanuta, T.: An overview of the K semantic framework. J. Logic Algebraic Program. **79**(6), 397–434 (2010)

34. Schäfer, J., Poetzsch-Heffter, A.: JCoBox: generalizing active objects to concurrent components. In: D'Hondt, T. (ed.) ECOOP 2010. LNCS, vol. 6183, pp. 275–299. Springer, Heidelberg (2010)

35. Şerbănuţă, T.F., Roşu, G.: A truly concurrent semantics for the $\mathbb{K}$ framework based on graph transformations. In: Ehrig, H., Engels, G., Kreowski, H.-J., Rozenberg, G. (eds.) ICGT 2012. LNCS, vol. 7562, pp. 294–310. Springer, Heidelberg (2012)

36. Supplementary material. http://www.swt-bamberg.de/fase2016_supp/

37. Torshizi, F.A., Ostroff, J.S., Paige, R.F., Chechik, M.: The SCOOP concurrency model in Java-like languages. In: Proceedings of CpPA 2009. Concurrent Systems Engineering Series, vol. 67, pp. 7–27. IOS Press (2009)

38. Tschannen, J., Furia, C.A., Nordio, M., Meyer, B.: Usable verification of object-oriented programs by combining static and dynamic techniques. In: Barthe, G., Pardo, A., Schneider, G. (eds.) SEFM 2011. LNCS, vol. 7041, pp. 382–398. Springer, Heidelberg (2011)

39. West, S., Nanz, S., Meyer, B.: A modular scheme for deadlock prevention in an object-oriented programming model. In: Dong, J.S., Zhu, H. (eds.) ICFEM 2010. LNCS, vol. 6447, pp. 597–612. Springer, Heidelberg (2010)

40. West, S., Nanz, S., Meyer, B.: Efficient and reasonable object-oriented concurrency. In: Proceedings of ESEC/FSE 2015, pp. 734–744. ACM (2015)

41. Zambon, E., Rensink, A.: Using graph transformations and graph abstractions for software verification. In: Proceedings of ICGT-DS 2010. ECEASST, vol. 38 (2011)

42. Zambon, E., Rensink, A.: Solving the N-Queens problem with GROOVE - towards a compendium of best practices. In: Proceedings of GT-VMT 2014. ECEASST, vol. 67 (2014)

ABS-YARN: A Formal Framework for Modeling Hadoop YARN Clusters

Jia-Chun Lin[✉], Ingrid Chieh Yu, Einar Broch Johnsen,
and Ming-Chang Lee

Department of Informatics, University of Oslo, Oslo, Norway
{kellylin,ingridcy,einarj,mclee}@ifi.uio.no

Abstract. In cloud computing, software which does not flexibly adapt to deployment decisions either wastes operational resources or requires reengineering, both of which may significantly increase costs. However, this could be avoided by analyzing deployment decisions already during the design phase of the software development. Real-Time ABS is a formal language for executable modeling of deployed virtualized software. Using Real-Time ABS, this paper develops a generic framework called ABS-YARN for YARN, which is the next generation of the Hadoop cloud computing platform with a state-of-the-art resource negotiator. We show how ABS-YARN can be used for prototyping YARN and for modeling job execution, allowing users to rapidly make deployment decisions at the modeling level and reduce unnecessary costs. To validate the modeling framework, we show strong correlations between our model-based analyses and a real YARN cluster in different scenarios with benchmarks.

1 Introduction

Cloud computing changes the traditional business model of IT enterprises by offering on-demand delivery of IT resources and applications over the Internet with pay-as-you-go pricing [6]. The cloud infrastructure on which software is deployed can be configured to the needs of that software. However, software which does not flexibly adapt to deployment decisions either require wasteful resource over-provisioning or time-consuming reengineering, which may substantially increase costs in both cases. Shifting deployment decisions from the deployment phase to the design phase of a software development process can significantly reduce such costs by performing model-based validation of the chosen decisions during the software design [14]. However, virtualized computing poses new and interesting challenges for formal methods because we need to express deployment decisions in formal models of distributed software and analyze the non-functional consequences of these deployment decisions at the modeling level.

A popular example of cloud infrastructure used in industry is Hadoop [5], an open-source software framework available in cloud environments from vendors

Supported by the EU projects H2020-644298 *HyVar: Scalable Hybrid Variability for Distributed Evolving Software Systems* (http://www.hyvar-project.eu) and FP7-610582 *Envisage: Engineering Virtualized Services* (http://www.envisage-project.eu).

P. Stevens and A. Wąsowski (Eds.): FASE 2016, LNCS 9633, pp. 49–65, 2016.
DOI: 10.1007/978-3-662-49665-7_4

such as Amazon, HP, IBM, Microsoft, and Rackspace. YARN [27] is the next generation of Hadoop with a state-of-the-art resource negotiator. This paper presents ABS-YARN, a generic framework for modeling YARN infrastructure and job execution. Using ABS-YARN, modelers can easily prototype a YARN cluster and evaluate deployment decisions at the modeling level, including the size of clusters and the resource requirements for containers depending on the jobs to be executed and their arrival patterns. Using ABS-YARN, designers can focus on developing better software to exploit YARN in a cost-efficient way.

ABS-YARN is defined using Real-Time ABS, a formal language for the executable modeling of deployed virtualized software [10]. The basic approach to modeling resource management for cloud computing in Real-Time ABS is a separation of concerns between the resource costs of the execution and the resource provisioning at (virtual) locations [18]. Real-Time ABS has previously been used to model and analyze the management of virtual resources in industry [3] and compared to (informal) simulation tools [17]. Although Real-Time ABS provides a range of formal analysis techniques (e.g., [2,30]), our focus here is on obtaining results based on easy-to-use rapid prototyping, using the executable semantics of Real-Time ABS, defined in Maude [12], as a simulation tool for ABS-YARN.

To evaluate the modeling framework, we comprehensively compare the results of model-based analyses using ABS-YARN with the performance of a real YARN cluster by using several Hadoop benchmarks to create a hybrid workload and designing two scenarios in which the job inter-arrival time of the workload follows a uniform distribution and an exponential distribution, respectively. The results demonstrate that ABS-YARN models the real YARN cluster accurately in the uniform scenario. In the exponential scenario, ABS-YARN performs less well but it still provides a good approximation of the real YARN cluster.

The main contributions of this paper can be summarized as follows:

1. We introduce ABS-YARN, a generic framework for modeling software targeting YARN. Using Real-Time ABS, designers can develop software for YARN on top of the ABS-YARN framework and evaluate the performance of the software model before the software is realized and deployed on a real YARN cluster.
2. ABS-YARN supports dynamic and realistic job modeling and simulation. Users can define the number of jobs, the number of the tasks per job, task cost, job inter-arrival patterns, cluster scale, cluster capacity, and the resource requirement for containers to rapidly evaluate deployment decisions with the minimum costs.
3. We comprehensively evaluate and validate ABS-YARN under several performance metrics. The results demonstrate that ABS-YARN provides a satisfiable modeling to reflect the behaviors of real YARN clusters.

Paper Organization. Section 2 provides a background introduction to Real-Time ABS and YARN. Section 3 presents the details of the ABS-YARN framework. In Sect. 4, we validate ABS-YARN and compare it with a real YARN cluster. Section 5 surveys related work and Sect. 6 concludes the paper.

Syntactic categories.   Definitions.
T in GroundType $P ::= \overline{IF}\ \overline{CL}\ \{[\overline{T}\ \overline{x};]\ s\}$
x in Variable $IF ::= \textbf{interface}\ I\ \{[\overline{Sg}]\}$
s in Stmt $CL ::= \textbf{class}\ C\ [(\overline{T}\ \overline{x})]\ [\textbf{implements}\ \overline{I}]\ \{[\overline{T}\ \overline{x};]\ \overline{M}\}$
a in Annotation $Sg ::= T\ m\ ([\overline{T}\ \overline{x}])$
g in Guard $M ::= Sg\ \{[\overline{T}\ \overline{x};]\ s\}$
e in Expression $a ::= \text{Deadline:}\ e\ |\ DC : e\ |\ Cost : e\ |\ a, a$
$g ::= b\ |\ x?\ |\ g \wedge g$
$s ::= s; s\ |\ \textbf{skip}\ |\ \textbf{if}\ b\ \{s\}\ \textbf{else}\ \{s\}\ |\ \textbf{while}\ b\ \{s\}\ |\ \textbf{return}\ e$
$|\ \textbf{duration}(e, e)\ |\ \textbf{suspend}\ |\ \textbf{await}\ g\ |\ [a]\ s\ |\ x = rhs$
$rhs ::= e\ |\ cm\ |\ \textbf{new}\ C\ (\overline{e})\ |\ \textbf{new}\ DeploymentComponent\ (e, e)$
$cm ::= [e]!m(\overline{e})\ |\ x.\textbf{get}$

Fig. 1. Syntax for the imperative layer of Real-Time ABS. Terms $\overline{e}$ and $\overline{x}$ denote possibly empty lists over the corresponding syntactic categories, and square brackets [] denote optional elements.

2 Background

2.1 Modeling Deployed Systems Using Real-Time ABS

Real-Time ABS [10] is a formal, executable, object-oriented language for modeling distributed systems by means of concurrent object groups [16], akin to concurrent objects [11], Actors [1], and Erlang processes [7]. Concurrent objects groups execute in parallel and communicate by asynchronous method calls and futures. In a group, at most one process is active at any time, and a queue of suspended processes wait to execute on an object of the group. Processes, which stem from methods calls, are cooperatively scheduled, so active and reactive behaviors can be easily combined in the concurrent object groups. Real-Time ABS combines functional and imperative programming styles with a Java-like syntax and a formal semantics. Internal computations in an object are captured in a simple functional language based on user-defined algebraic data types and functions. A modeler may abstract from many details of the low-level imperative implementations of data structures, but maintain an overall object-oriented design. The semantics of Real-Time ABS is specified in rewriting logic [12], and a model written in Real-Time ABS can be automatically translated into Maude code and executed by the Maude tool.

The imperative layer of Real-Time ABS addresses concurrency, communication, and synchronization based on objects. The syntax is shown in Fig. 1. A program P consists of interfaces IF, classes CL with method definitions M, and a main block $\{[\overline{T}\ \overline{x};]\ s\}$. Our discussion focuses on interesting imperative language features, so we omit the explanations of standard syntax and the functional layer (see [16]).

In Real-Time ABS, communication and synchronization are decoupled. Communication is based on asynchronous method calls $f = o!m(\overline{e})$ where f is a future variable, o an object expression, m a method name, and $\overline{e}$ the parameter values for the method invocation. After calling $f = o!m(\overline{e})$, the caller may proceed with its execution without blocking on the method reply. Synchronization is controlled by operations on futures. The statement **await** f? releases the processor while waiting for a reply, allowing other processes to execute. When the reply arrives, the suspended process becomes enabled and the execution may resume. The return value is retrieved by the expression $f.$**get**, which blocks all execution in the object until the return value is available. The syntactic sugar $x =$ **await** $o!m(\bar{e})$ encodes the standard pattern $f = o!m(\bar{e})$; **await** f?; $x = f.$**get**.

In Real-Time ABS, the timed behavior of concurrent objects is captured by a *maximal progress* semantics. The execution time can be specified directly with *duration* statements, or be implicit in terms of observations on the executing model. Method calls have associated deadlines, specified by deadline annotations. The statement **duration**(e_1, e_2) will cause time to advance between a best case e_1 and a worst case e_2 execution time. Whereas duration-statements advance time at any location, Real-Time ABS also allows a separation of concerns between the *resource cost* of executing a task and the *resource capacity* of the location where the task executes. Cost annotations [Cost: e] are used to associate resource consumption with statements in Real-Time ABS models.

Real-Time ABS uses *deployment components* to capture the execution capacity of a location in the deployment architecture, on which a number of concurrent objects can be deployed [18]. Each deployment component has its own execution capacity, which will determine the performance of objects executing on the deployment component. Deployment components are dynamically created by $x =$ **new** *DeploymentComponent* (*descriptor*, *capacity*), where x is typed by the DC interface, *descriptor* is a descriptor for the purpose of monitoring, and *capacity* specifies the initial CPU capacity of the deployment component. Objects are deployed on a deployment component using the DC annotation on the object creation statement.

2.2   YARN: Yet Another Resource Negotiator

YARN [27] is an open-source software framework supported by Apache for distributed processing and storage of high data volumes. It inherits the advantages of its well-known predecessor Hadoop [5], including resource allocation, code distribution, distributed data processing, data replication, and fault tolerance. YARN further improves Hadoop's limitations in terms of scalability, serviceability, multi-tenancy support, cluster utilization, and reliability.

YARN supports the execution of different types of jobs, including MapReduce, graph, and streaming. Each job is divided into tasks which are executed in parallel on a cluster of machines. The key components of YARN are as follows:

– *ResourceManager* (RM): RM allocates resources to various competing jobs and applications in a cluster, replacing Hadoop's JobTracker. Unlike Job-Tracker, the scheduling provided by RM is job level, rather than task level. Thus, RM does not monitor each task's progress or restart any failed task. Currently, the default job scheduling policy of RM is CapacityScheduler [23], which allows cluster administrators to create hierarchical queues for multiple tenants to share a large cluster while giving each tenant a capacity guarantee.

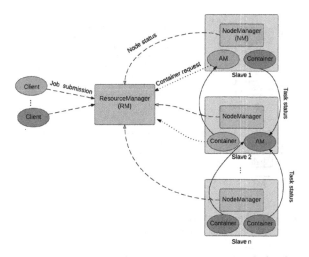

Fig. 2. The architecture of a YARN cluster.

The jobs in each queue are scheduled based on a First-in-First-out policy (FIFO), i.e., the first job to arrive is first allocated resources.

- *ApplicationMaster* (AM): This is an instance of a framework-specific library class for a particular job. It acts as the head of the job to manage the job's lifecycle, including requesting resources from RM, scheduling the execution of all tasks of the job, monitoring task execution, and re-executing failed tasks.
- *Containers*: Each container is a logical resource collection of a particular node (e.g., 1 CPU and 2GB of RAM). Clients can specify container resource requirements when they submit jobs to RM and run any kind of applications.

Figure 2 shows the architecture of a YARN cluster, which consists of RM and a set of slave nodes providing both computation resources and storage capacity to execute applications and store data, respectively. A slave node has an agent called NodeManager to periodically monitor its local resource usage and report its status to RM. The execution flow of a job on a YARN cluster is as follows:

1. Whenever receiving a job request from a client, RM follows a pre-defined job scheduling algorithm to find a container from an available slave and initiate the AM of the job on the container.
2. Once the AM is initiated, it starts requesting a set of containers from RM based on the client's container resource requirement and the number of tasks of the job. Basically, each task will be run on one container.
3. When RM receives a container request from the AM, it inserts the request into its queue and follows its job scheduling algorithm to allocate a desired container from an available slave node to the AM.
4. Upon receiving the container, the AM executes one task of the job on the container and monitors this task execution. If a task fails due to some errors such as an underlying container/slave node failure, the AM will re-request a container from RM to restart the task.
5. When all tasks of a job finish successfully, implying that the job is complete, the AM notifies the client about the completion.

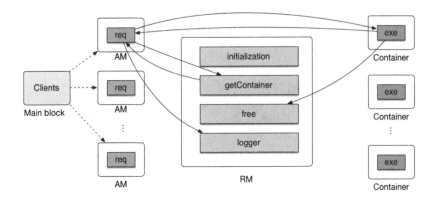

Fig. 3. The structure of the ABS-YARN framework.

3   Formal Model of the ABS-YARN Framework

Figure 3 shows the structure of ABS-YARN with classes RM, AM, and Container
reflecting the main components of a YARN cluster. In our framework, RM is
deployed as an independent deployment component with its own CPU capacity.
To model the most general case, we assume that RM has a single queue for all
job requests, implying that all jobs are served in a FIFO order. When a client
submits a job, an AM object is created for this job, and its **req** method starts
requesting containers from RM by invoking the **getContainer** method. If a
slave has sufficient resources, a container will be created and returned to the
AM. Then the AM submits one task of the job to the allocated container by
invoking the **exe** method. When the task terminates, the result is returned to
the associated AM, the **free** method is invoked to release the container, and the
logger method is used to record execution statistics.

ABS-YARN allows modelers to freely determine the scale and resource capacity of a YARN cluster, including (1) the number of slave nodes in the cluster,
(2) the CPU cores of each slave node, and (3) the memory capacity of each slave
node. To support dynamic and realistic modeling of job execution, ABS-YARN
also allows modelers to define the following parameters:

- Number of clients submitting jobs
- Number of jobs submitted by each client
- Number of tasks per job
- Cost annotation for each task
- CPU and memory requirements for each container
- Job inter-arrival pattern. Modelers can determine any kind of job inter-arrival
  distributions in ABS-YARN.

MapReduce jobs are the most common jobs in YARN, so we focus on modeling
their execution in this paper. Each MapReduce job has a map phase followed by
a reduce phase. In the map phase, all map tasks are executed in parallel. When

all the map tasks have completed, the reduce tasks are executed (normally, each jobs has only one reduce task). The job is completed when all the map and reduce tasks have finished.

The execution time of a task in a real YARN cluster might be influenced by many factors, e.g., the size of the processed data and the computational complexity of the task. To reduce the complexity of modeling the task execution time, ABS-YARN adopts the cost annotation functionality of Real-Time ABS to associate cost to the execution of a task. Hence, the task execution time will be the cost divided by the CPU capacity of the container that executes the task.

In the following, we limit our code presentation to the main building blocks and functionalities to simplify the description.

3.1   Modeling ResourceManager (RM)

The ResourceManager implements the RM interface:

```
1  interface RM {
2      Bool initialization(Int s, Int sc, Int sm);
3      Pair<Int, Container> getContainer(Int c, Int m);
4      Unit free(Int slaveID, Int c, Int m);
5      Unit logger(...);}
```

Method initialization initializes the entire cluster environment, including RM and s slaves. Each slave is modeled as a record in a database SlaveDB, with a unique SlaveID, sc CPU cores, and amount sm of memory capacity. After the initialization, the cluster can start serving client requests. Method getContainer allows an AM to obtain containers from RM. The size of the required container core and container memory are given by c and m, respectively. Method free is used to release container resources whenever a container finishes executing a task, and method logger is used to record job execution statistics, including job ID and job execution time.

The getContainer method, invoked by an AM, tries to allocate a container with c CPU cores and m amount of memory capacity from an available slave to the AM. Each container request is allowed at most thd attempts. Hence, as long as Find==False and attempt<=thd (line 3), the getContainer method will keep trying to obtain the database token to ensure a safe database access. The built-in function lookupDefault checks each slave in slaveDB to find a slave with sufficient resources. If such a slave exists (line 11), the corresponding container will be created as a deployment component with c cores, and the slave's resources will be reduced and updated accordingly (lines 12–14). The successfully generated container is returned to the AM.

However, if no slaves have enough resources, the process will suspend (line 21), allowing RM to process other method activations. The suspended process will periodically check whether any slaves can satisfy the request. If the desired container cannot be allocated within thd attempts, the method terminates and RM is unable to provide the desired container to the AM.

```
1  Pair <Int, Container> getContainer (Int c, Int m) {
2    Bool find=False; Int slaveID=1; Int attempt=1;
3    while (find==False && attempt<=thd){
4      await dbToken==True;
5      dbToken==False;
6      Int i=1;
7      while (find==False && i<=size(keys(slaveDB))){
8        Pair<Int,Int> slave= lookupDefault(slaveDB, i, Pair(1,1));
9        Int free_core= fst(slave);
10       Int free_mem= snd(slave);
11       if (free_core>=c && free_mem >= m){
12         slaveDB=put(slaveDB, i, Pair(free_core-c, free_mem-m));
13         DC s=new DeploymentComponent("slave", map[Pair(CPU,c)]);
14         [DC: s] Container container = new Container(this);
15         find=True;
16         slaveID=i;
17       }
18       i++;
19     }
20     ... // Release dbToken
21     await duration(1,1);
22     attempt++;
23   }
24   if (find==False){ container=null;}
25   return Pair(slaveID, container);
26 }
```

3.2 Modeling ApplicationMaster (AM)

An AM implements the AM interface with a req method to acquire a container
from RM and then execute a task on the container. For an AM, the total number
of times that req is called corresponds to the number of map tasks of a job (e.g.,
if a job is divided into 10 map tasks, this method will be called 10 times).

```
1  interface AM {
2    Unit req(Int mNum, Int c, Int m, Rat mCost, Rat rCost);}
```

The req method first invokes the getContainer method and sends a container-
resource request (i.e., the parameters c and m) to acquire a container from RM.
Since the call is asynchronous, the AM is able to request containers for other tasks
of jobID while waiting for the response.

```
1  Unit req(Int mNum, Int c, Int m, Rat mCost, Rat rCost) {
2    ...
3    Pair<Int, Container> p= await rm!getContainer(c, m);
4    Int slaveId=fst(p);
5    Container container=snd(p);
6    if (container!=null){
7      Fut<Bool> f = container!exe(slaveID, c, m, mCost);
8      await f?;
9      Bool map_result = f.get;
10     if (map_result==True){
11       returned_map++;
12       if (returned_map==mNum){
13         Bool red_result;
14         ...//Try to request a container and run the reduce task
15         if (red_result==True){
16           logging the job completion;
17         }
```

```
18              else{ logging the reducde-task failure;}
19           }
20         }
21      else{ logging the map-task failure;}
22    }
23    else{ logging unsuccessful container request;}
24  }
```

When a container is successfully obtained, a map task with cost mCost can be executed on the container (line 7). The process suspends while waiting for the result of the task execution. Each time when map_result==True, the req method increases the variable returned_map by one. When all map tasks of the job have successfully completed (line 12), the AM proceeds with a container request to run the reduce task of the job with cost rCost. Only when all map and reduce tasks are completed (line 15), the job is considered completed.

3.3 Modeling Containers

A container implements the Container interface:

```
1  interface Container{
2    Bool exe(Int slaveID, Int c, Int m, Rat tcost);}
```

Method exe is used to execute a task on a container. The formal parameters of exe consist of slaveID, CPU capacity c, memory capacity m, and the task cost tcost. Hence, the task execution time is tcost/c. When a task terminates, the free method of RM is invoked to release the container, implying that the corresponding CPU and memory resources will be returned back to the slave.

```
1  Bool exe(Int slaveID, Int c, Int m, Rat tcost){
2    [Cost: tcost] ... //executing a task;
3    rm!free(slaveID, c, m);
4    return true;}
```

4 Performance Evaluation and Validation

To compare the simulation results of ABS-YARN against YARN, we established a real YARN cluster using Hadoop 2.2.0 [5] with one virtual machine acting as RM and 30 virtual machines as slaves. Each virtual machine runs Ubuntu 12.04 with 2 virtual cores of Intel Xeon E5-2620 2 GHz CPU and 2 GB of memory. To achieve a fair validation, we also created an ABS-YARN cluster with 30 slaves; each with 2 CPU cores and 2 GB of memory. To realistically compare job execution performance between ABS-YARN and YARN clusters, we used the following five benchmarks from YARN [23]: **WordCount**, which counts the occurrence of each word in data files; **WordMean**, which calculates the average length of the words in data files; **WordStandardDeviation (WordSD)**, which counts the standard deviation of the length of the words in data files; **GrepSort**, which sorts data files; and **GrepSearch**, which searches for a pattern in data files.

We created a hybrid workload consisting of 22 WordCount jobs, 22 Word-Mean jobs, 20 WordSD jobs, 16 GrepSort jobs, and 20 GrepSearch jobs. The submission orders of all jobs were randomly determined. Each job processes 1 GB of enwiki data [13] with 128 MB block size (the default block size of YARN [23]). Hence, each job was divided into 8 (=1 GB/128 MB) map tasks and one reduce task, implying that 9 containers are required to execute each job. We assume that the resource requirement for each container is 1 CPU core and 1 GB RAM for both the ABS-YARN and YARN clusters.

We considered two job inter-arrival patterns in our experiments: Uniform and exponential distribution [20]. In the former, the inter-arrival time between two consecutive jobs submitted by clients are equal. In the latter, job inter-arrival time follows a Poisson process [20], i.e., job submissions occur continuously and independently at a constant average rate. Reiss et al. [25] show that job arrival patterns in a Google trace approximates an exponential distribution. This distribution has also been widely used as job arrival pattern in the literature (e.g., [22,24]). Based on these distributions, two scenarios were designed:

- *Uniform scenario:* The job inter-arrival time of the workload is 150 sec in the real YARN cluster. In ABS-YARN, this is normalized into 2 time units.
- *Exponential scenario:* The job inter-arrival time of the workload follows an exponential distribution with the average inter-arrival time of 158 sec and a standard deviation of 153 sec in the real YARN cluster. This is normalized into the average inter-arrival time of 158/75 time units and a standard deviation of 153/75 time units in the ABS-YARN cluster.

The following metrics were used to evaluate how well ABS-YARN can simulate job scheduling, job execution behavior, and job throughput of YARN:

- Starting time of all jobs of the workload
- Finish time of all jobs of the workload
- The number of cumulative completed jobs
- Total number of completed jobs

4.1 Validation Results in the Uniform Scenario

In order to achieve a fair comparison, we conducted the uniform scenario on the YARN cluster to obtain the average map-task execution time (AMT) and average reduce-task execution time (ART) for each job type. The results are listed in Table 1. After that, we respectively normalized each AMT and ART into a map-task cost and a reduce-task cost for ABS-YARN by dividing the AMT value by 75 and dividing the ART value by 75 (Note that 75 is half of the job inter-arrival time for the uniform scenario). With the corresponding map-task cost annotation (MCA) and reduce-task cost annotation (RCA), we simulated the uniform scenario on ABS-YARN.

Figure 4(a) shows the normalized starting time of all jobs in both clusters. We can see that the two curves are almost overlapping. The average time difference between ABS-YARN and YARN is 0.02 time units with a standard deviation of

Table 1. The average map-task execution time (AMT), average reduce-task execution time (ART), normalized map-task cost annotation (MCA), and normalized reduce-task cost annotation (RCA) in the uniform scenario.

Benchmark	AMT (sec)	ART (sec)	MCA	RCA
WordCount	162.64	251.01	2.17 (=162.64/75)	3.35 (251.01/75)
WordMean	107.10	139.94	1.43 (=107.10/75)	1.87 (=139.94/75)
WordSD	108.23	162.27	1.44 (=108.23/75)	2.16 (=162.27/75)
GrepSort	20.39	38.44	0.27 (=20.39/75)	0.51 (=38.44/75)
GrepSearch	31.22	55.97	0.42 (=31.22/75)	0.75 (=55.97/75)

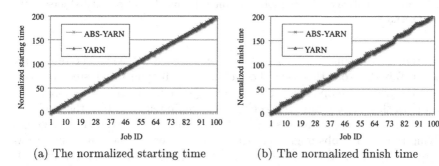

(a) The normalized starting time   (b) The normalized finish time

Fig. 4. The normalized time points of all jobs in the uniform scenario.

1.73 time units, showing that ABS-YARN is able to precisely capture the job scheduling of YARN in the uniform scenario. Figure 4(b) depicts all job finish time in both clusters. The average difference between ABS-YARN and YARN is 2.67 time units with a standard deviation of 1.81 time units, indicating that the framework can accurately model how containers execute jobs in a real YARN cluster. Based on the results shown in Fig. 4, we can derive that the cumulative numbers of completed jobs between the two clusters are close (see Fig. 5(a)). The average error is approximately 2.52 %, implying that ABS-YARN can precisely reflect the operation of YARN in the uniform scenario. Figure 5(b) shows that 100 jobs of the workload successfully finished in the ABS-YARN cluster, but 99 jobs of the workload completed in the YARN cluster since the remaining one job could not obtain sufficient containers to execute its tasks. The job completion error of ABS-YARN is only 1.01 %. Based on the above-mentioned results, it is evident that the ABS-YARN framework offers a superior modeling of YARN in the uniform scenario.

4.2 Validation Results in the Exponential Scenario

In this section, we compare ABS-YARN and YARN under the exponential scenario. Similar to the uniform scenario, we performed a normalization by executing the exponential scenario on the YARN cluster to derive a map-task cost

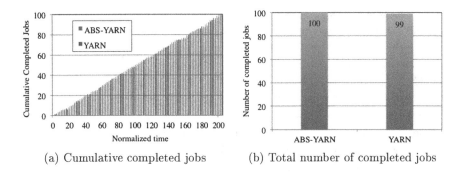

(a) Cumulative completed jobs   (b) Total number of completed jobs

Fig. 5. The cumulative completed jobs and the total number of completed jobs in the uniform scenario.

annotation and a reduce-task cost annotation for each job type. The results are listed in Table 2. Note that regardless of which job type was tested, the corresponding average map-task and reduce-task execution time were apparently higher than those in the uniform scenario. The main reason is that the job inter-arrival time in the exponential scenario had a much higher standard deviation, implying that many jobs might compete for containers at the same time. However, due to the limited container resources, these jobs had to wait for available containers and hence prolonged their execution time.

Table 2. The AMT, ART, MCA, and RCA in the exponential scenario.

Benchmark	AMT (sec)	ART (sec)	MCA	RCA
WordCount	295.47	430.24	3.94 (=295.27/75)	5.74 (430.24/75)
WordMean	139.98	201.11	1.87 (=139.98/75)	2.68 (=201.11/75)
WordSD	238.46	312.38	3.18 (=238.46/75)	4.17 (=312.38/75)
GrepSort	37.38	62.06	0.50 (=37.38/75)	0.83 (=62.06/75)
GrepSearch	173.92	205.94	2.32 (=173.92/75)	2.75 (205.94/75)

The normalized job starting time illustrated in Fig. 6(a) show that the ABS-YARN cluster follows the same trend as the YARN cluster. However, as more jobs were submitted, their starting time in ABS-YARN were later than those in the YARN cluster. The average time difference is around 19.48 with standard deviation of 12.92. The key reasons are two. First, the normalized map-task (reduce-task) cost annotations used by ABS-YARN were based on average map-task (reduce-task) execution time of the entire workload, which were longer than the actual map-task (reduce-task) execution time spent by the real YARN cluster in the early phase of the workload execution. Second, the number of available containers gradually decreased when more jobs were submitted to the ABS-YARN cluster. For these two reasons, the starting time of the subsequent jobs were delayed.

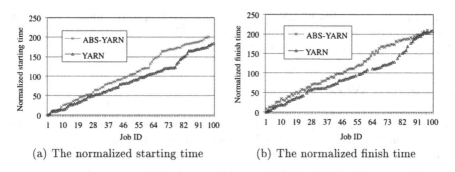

(a) The normalized starting time   (b) The normalized finish time

Fig. 6. The time points of all jobs in the exponential scenario.

Figure 6(b) depicts the normalized job finish time of the two clusters under the exponential scenario. We can see that during the workload execution, many jobs in the ABS-YARN cluster finished later than the corresponding jobs in the YARN cluster. The reasons are the same, i.e., the map-task (reduce-task) cost annotation values were derived from the corresponding average map-task (reduce-task) execution time, which were usually higher than the actual execution time in the YARN cluster during the early stage of the workload. Nevertheless, the results show that even under a heavy and dynamic workload, the ABS-YARN framework can still adequately model YARN.

The cumulative number of completed jobs illustrated in Fig. 7(a) shows that during most of the workload execution, the ABS-YARN cluster finished fewer jobs than the YARN cluster for the above mentioned reasons. However, in the late stage, the ABS-YARN cluster had more completed jobs than the YARN cluster. This phenomenon can also be deduced from Fig. 6 since seven jobs could not complete by the YARN cluster. The average difference of the cumulative workload completion between ABS-YARN and YARN is 14.49 %. Due to failing to get containers, 97 jobs and 93 jobs (as shown in Fig. 7(b)) were finished by the ABS-YARN cluster and the YARN cluster, respectively. Although the job

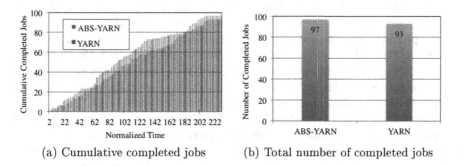

(a) Cumulative completed jobs   (b) Total number of completed jobs

Fig. 7. The cumulative completed jobs and the total number of completed jobs in the exponential scenario.

completion error of ABS-YARN is increased to 4.3 % from the uniform scenario to the exponential scenario, the above results still demonstrate that the ABS-YARN framework provides a satisfiable modeling for YARN.

5   Related Work

General-purpose modeling languages provide abstractions where the main focus has been on describing functional behavior and logical composition. However, this is inadequate for virtualized systems such as clouds when the software's deployment influences its behavior and when virtual processors are dynamically created. A large body of work on performance analysis using formal models can be found based on, e.g., process algebra [9], Petri Nets [26], and timed and probabilistic automata [4,8]. However, these works mainly focus on non-functional aspects of embedded systems without associating capacities with locations. A more closely related technique for modeling deployment can be found in an extension of VDM++ for embedded real-time systems [28], in which static architectures are explicitly modeled using buses and CPUs with fixed resources.

Compared to these languages, Real-time ABS [10,18] provides a formal basis for modeling not only timed behavior but also dynamically created resource-constrained deployment architectures, which enables users to model feature-rich object-oriented distributed systems with explicit resource management at an abstract yet precise level. Case studies validating the formalization proposed in Real-Time ABS include Montage [17] and the Fredhopper Replication Server [3]. Both case studies address resource management in clouds by combining simulation techniques and cost analysis. Different from these case studies, this paper uses Real-Time ABS to create a formal framework for YARN and comprehensively compare this framework with a real YARN cluster.

In recent years, many simulation tools have been introduced for Hadoop, including MRPerf, MRSim, and HSim. MRPerf [29] is a MapReduce simulator designed to understand the performance of MapReduce jobs on a specific Hadoop parameter setting, especially the impact of the underlying network topology, data locality, and various failures. MRSim [15] is a discrete event based MapReduce simulator for users to define the topology of a cluster, configure the specification of a MapReduce job, and simulate the execution of the job running on the cluster. HSim [21] models a large number of parameters of Hadoop, including nodes, cluster, and simulator parameters. HSim also allows users to describe their own job specification. All the above-mentioned simulators target Hadoop rather than YARN. Due to the fundamental difference between Hadoop and YARN, these simulators are unable to simulate YARN. Besides, these simulators concentrate on simulating the execution of a single MapReduce job and compare the corresponding simulation results with the actual results on real Hadoop systems. However, this is insufficient to confirm that they can faithfully simulate Hadoop when multiple jobs are running on Hadoop. Similar work can also be found in [19]. Different from all these simulators, the proposed ABS-YARN framework is designed to model a set of jobs running on YARN, rather than just one job. With ABS-YARN, users can comprehend the performance of YARN under a dynamic workload.

To our knowledge, the Yarn Scheduler Load Simulator (SLS) [31] is the only simulator currently designed for YARN, but it concentrates on simulating job scheduling in a YARN cluster. Besides, SLS does not provide any performance evaluation to validate its simulation accuracy. Compared with SLS, ABS-YARN provides a formal executable YARN environment. In this paper, we also present a comprehensive validation to demonstrate its applicability.

6   Conclusion and Future Work

This paper has presented the ABS-YARN framework based on the formal modeling language Real-Time ABS. ABS-YARN provides a generic model of YARN by capturing the key components of a YARN cluster in an abstract but precise way. With ABS-YARN, modelers can flexibly configure a YARN cluster, including cluster size and resource capacity, and determine job workload and job inter-arrival patterns to evaluate their deployment decisions.

To increase the applicability of formal methods in the design of virtualized systems, we believe that showing a strong correlation between model behaviors and real system results is of high importance. We validated ABS-YARN through a comprehensive comparison of the model-based analyses with the actual performance of a real YARN cluster. The results demonstrate that ABS-YARN is accurate enough to offer users a dependable framework for making deployment decisions about YARN at design time. In addition, the provided abstractions enable designers to naturally model and design virtual systems at this complexity, such as enhancing YARN with new algorithms.

In future work, we plan to further enhance ABS-YARN by incorporating multi-queue scheduler modeling, slave and container failure modeling, and distributed file-system modeling. Modeling different job types will also be considered. Whereas this paper has focussed on the accuracy of the ABS-YARN framework, our ongoing work on a more powerful simulation and visualization tool for Real-Time ABS will improve the applicability of ABS-YARN.

Acknowledgement. The authors thank NCLab at National Chiao Tung University, Taiwan for providing computation facilities for the YARN cluster used in our experiments.

References

1. Agha, G.A.: ACTORS: A Model of Concurrent Computations in Distributed Systems. The MIT Press, Cambridge (1986)
2. Albert, E., Arenas, P., Flores-Montoya, A., Genaim, S., Gómez-Zamalloa, M., Martin-Martin, E., Puebla, G., Román-Díez, G.: SACO: static analyzer for concurrent objects. In: Ábrahám, E., Havelund, K. (eds.) TACAS 2014 (ETAPS). LNCS, vol. 8413, pp. 562–567. Springer, Heidelberg (2014)

3. Albert, E., de Boer, F.S., Hähnle, R., Johnsen, E.B., Schlatte, R., Tapia Tarifa, S.L., Wong, P.Y.H.: Formal modeling and analysis of resource management for cloud architectures: An industrial case study using Real-Time ABS. J. Serv. Oriented Comput. Appl. **8**(4), 323–339 (2014)
4. Amnell, T., Fersman, E., Mokrushin, L., Pettersson, P., Yi, W.: TIMES: a tool for schedulability analysis and code generation of real-time systems. In: Larsen, K.G., Niebert, P. (eds.) FORMATS 2003. LNCS, vol. 2791, pp. 60–72. Springer, Heidelberg (2004)
5. Apache Hadoop. http://hadoop.apache.org/
6. Armbrust, M., Fox, A., Griffith, R., Joseph, A.D., Katz, R., Konwinski, A., Lee, G., Patterson, D., Rabkin, A., Stoica, I., Zaharia, M.: A view of cloud computing. Commun. ACM **53**(4), 50–58 (2010)
7. Armstrong, J.: Programming Erlang: Software for a Concurrent World. Pragmatic Bookshelf, Raleigh (2007)
8. Baier, C., Haverkort, B.R., Hermanns, H., Katoen, J.-P.: Performance evaluation and model checking join forces. Commun. ACM **53**(9), 76–85 (2010)
9. Barbanera, F., Bugliesi, M., Dezani-Ciancaglini, M., Sassone, V.: Space-aware ambients and processes. Theor. Comput. Sci. **373**(1–2), 41–69 (2007)
10. Bjørk, J., de Boer, F.S., Johnsen, E.B., Schlatte, R., Tapia, S.L.: Tarifa.: User-defined schedulers for real-time concurrent objects. Innov. Syst. Softw. Eng. **9**(1), 29–43 (2013)
11. Caromel, D., Henrio, L.: A Theory of Distributed Objects. Springer, New York (2005)
12. Clavel, M., Durán, F., Eker, S., Lincoln, P., Martí-Oliet, N., Meseguer, J., Talcott, C. (eds.): All About Maude - A High-Performance Logical Framework. LNCS, vol. 4350. Springer, Heidelberg (2007)
13. enwiki. http://dumps.wikimedia.org/enwiki/
14. Hähnle, R., Johnsen, E.B.: Designing resource-aware cloud applications. IEEE Comput. **48**(6), 72–75 (2015)
15. Hammoud, S., Li, M., Liu, Y., Alham, N.K., Liu, Z.: MRSim: A discrete event based MapReduce simulator. In: Seventh International Conference on Fuzzy Systems and Knowledge Discovery, FSKD 2010, pp. 2993–2997. IEEE (2010)
16. Johnsen, E.B., Hähnle, R., Schäfer, J., Schlatte, R., Steffen, M.: ABS: a core language for abstract behavioral specification. In: Aichernig, B.K., de Boer, F.S., Bonsangue, M.M. (eds.) Formal Methods for Components and Objects. LNCS, vol. 6957, pp. 142–164. Springer, Heidelberg (2011)
17. Johnsen, E.B., Schlatte, R., Tapia Tarifa, S.L.: Modeling resource-aware virtualized applications for the cloud in real-time ABS. In: Aoki, T., Taguchi, K. (eds.) ICFEM 2012. LNCS, vol. 7635, pp. 71–86. Springer, Heidelberg (2012)
18. Johnsen, E.B., Schlatte, R., Tapia Tarifa, S.L.: Integrating deployment architectures and resource consumption in timed object-oriented models. J. Log. Algebraic Methods Program. **84**(1), 67–91 (2015)
19. Kolberg, W., Marcos, P.D.B., Anjos, J.C., Miyazaki, A.K., Geyer, C.R., Arantes, L.B.: MRSG - a MapReduce simulator over SimGrid. Parallel Comput. **39**(4), 233–244 (2013)
20. Koralov, L.B., Sinai, Y.G.: Theory of Probability and Random Processes. Springer-Verlag, Berling (2007)
21. Liu, Y., Li, M., Alham, N.K., Hammoud, S.: HSim: a MapReduce simulator in enabling cloud computing. Future Gener. Comput. Syst. **29**(1), 300–308 (2013)

22. Luo, C., Zhan, J., Jia, Z., Wang, L., Lu, G., Zhang, L., Xu, C.-Z., Sun, N.: Cloudrank-d: benchmarking and ranking cloud computing systems for data processing applications. Front. Comput. Sci. **6**(4), 347–362 (2012)
23. Murthy, A., Vavilapalli, V., Eadline, D., Niemiec, J., Markham, J.: Apache Hadoop YARN: Moving Beyond MapReduce and Batch Processing with Apache Hadoop 2. Addison-Wesley Professional, San Francisco (2014)
24. Palanisamy, B., Singh, A., Liu, L., Bryan, L.: Cura: A cost-optimized model for MapReduce in a cloud. In: IEEE 27th International Symposium on Parallel and Distributed Processing, pp. 1275–1286. IEEE (2013)
25. Reiss, C., Tumanov, A., Ganger, G.R., Katz, R.H., Kozuch, M.A.: Towards understanding heterogeneous clouds at scale: Google traceanalysis.Technical Report ISTC-CC-TR-12-101, Intel Science and TechnologyCenter for Cloud Computing, Carnegie Mellon University, April 2012. http://www.pdl.cmu.edu/PDL-FTP/CloudComputing/ISTC-CC-TR-12-101.pdf
26. Sgroi, M., Lavagno, L., Watanabe, Y., Sangiovanni-Vincentelli, A.: Synthesis of embedded software using free-choice petri nets. In: Proceedings of the Design Automation Conference, DAC 1999, pp. 805–810. ACM (1999)
27. Vavilapalli, V.K., Murthy, A.C., Douglas, C., Agarwal, S., Konar, M., Evans, R., Graves, T., Lowe, J., Shah, H., Seth, S., Saha, B., Curino, C., O'Malley, O., Radia, S., Reed, B., Baldeschwieler, E.: Apache Hadoop YARN: yet another resource negotiator. In: Lohman, G.M. (ed.) ACM Symposium on Cloud Computing (SOCC 2013), pp. 5:1–5:16 (2013)
28. Verhoef, M., Larsen, P.G., Hooman, J.: Modeling and validating distributed embedded real-time systems with VDM++. In: Misra, J., Nipkow, T., Sekerinski, E. (eds.) FM 2006. LNCS, vol. 4085, pp. 147–162. Springer, Heidelberg (2006)
29. Wang, G., Butt, A.R., Pandey, P., Gupta, K.: A simulation approach to evaluating design decisions in MapReduce setups. In: IEEE International Symposium on Modeling, Analysis and Simulation of Computer and Telecommunication Systems, MASCOTS 2009, pp. 1–11. IEEE (2009)
30. Wong, P.Y.H., Albert, E., Muschevici, R., Proença, J., Schäfer, J., Schlatte, R.: The ABS tool suite: modelling, executing and analysing distributed adaptable object-oriented systems. J. Softw. Tools Technol. Transf. **14**(5), 567–588 (2012)
31. Yarn Scheduler Load Simulator (SLS). https://hadoop.apache.org/docs/r2.4.1/hadoop-sls/SchedulerLoadSimulator.html

Integrated Environment for Verifying and Running Distributed Components

Ludovic Henrio[1], Oleksandra Kulankhina[1,2], Siqi Li[3], and Eric Madelaine[1,2(✉)]

[1] University of Nice Sophia Antipolis, CNRS, Sophia Antipolis, France
Ludovic.Henrio@cnrs.fr
[2] INRIA Sophia Antipolis Méditérannée, Sophia Antipolis, France
{Oleksandra.Kulankhina,Eric.Madelaine}@inria.fr
[3] Shanghai Key Laboratory of Trustworthy Computing, ECNU, Shanghai, China
cathy.lsq09@gmail.com

Abstract. This paper targets the generation of distributed applications with safety guarantees. The proposed approach starts from graphical specification formalisms allowing the architectural and behavioral description of component systems. From this point, the user can automatically verify application properties using model-checking techniques. Finally, the specified and verified component model can be translated into executable Java code. We implement our approach in a tool suite distributed as an Eclipse plugin. This paper also illustrates our approach by modeling and verifying Peterson's leader election algorithm.

1 Introduction

Component-oriented programming has become a popular approach for distributed application development. Components enforce a clear design and specification stage of the applications, and provide a solid basis for safe and modular development of complex systems. This work aims at including systematic verification of behavioral properties in the development process of component-based applications. For this purpose we would like to provide the developers of distributed component-based systems with a set of tools supporting rigorous design and implementation of safe applications. Our tools should guide the user through all crucial phases of component software development: from application design specification to verification of the designed architecture and behavior properties as well as automated code generation.

Applying static analysis on hand-coded programs is complex and often imprecise, especially for distributed systems. Instead we chose a Model-Driven Engineering and a component-oriented approach in which the structure of the application is directly specified by the developer, and in which the final code is generated automaticaly, partialy or totaly.

VerCors[1] is a software platform which aims at supporting the creation of safe distributed component-based applications. VerCors[2] includes a set of graphical

---

[1] https://team.inria.fr/scale/software/vercors/vcev4-download/.

[2] Not to be confused with http://fmt.cs.utwente.nl/research/projects/VerCors/.

© Springer-Verlag Berlin Heidelberg 2016
P. Stevens and A. Wąsowski (Eds.): FASE 2016, LNCS 9633, pp. 66–83, 2016.
DOI: 10.1007/978-3-662-49665-7_5

designers based on UML where the user can specify the architecture and the business logic of his application, and check the static correctness of the component architecture [1]. The specification is then automatically transformed into a behavior graph that can be model-checked to prove its correctness. We rely on model-checking for verification, but we want to hide as much as possible the complexity of the underlying formal techniques to make our tools accessible to non-experts in model-checking. VerCors uses parametrized networks of asynchronous automata (pNets) as an intermediate format for behavior modeling and relies on CADP [2] model-checker to verify temporal properties. Last, Java code of the modeled application can be automatically generated and executed. We rely on ProActive[3] and the Grid Component Model (GCM) [3]. We chose GCM/ProActive because it targets distributed systems and features a well-defined semantics. Because of the chosen verification methodology, the current platform can only verify finite-state systems, but infinite-space systems can already be specified, modeled as pNets, and executed.

This paper shows that our approach is suitable for applications involving complex interactions between processes but without too much computational complexity. For the case studies involving such a computational complexity the model-checking approach might be limited. However in that case we advocate the use of the VerCors platform to specify and verify the core of the application, abstracting away computational details. The user can still generate the executable skeleton of the verified core application. He can then extend it with computational details. While the application logic is unchanged, the behavioral properties will still be valid.

The VerCors platform has already undergone several major generations, with significant evolutions for the underlying semantic model, as well as the modeling platform and the specification formalisms. The original version was using UML component structures for describing the application architecture, but this was too far from GCM needs, hence a new DSL and graphical formalism were defined. At the same time, aiming at better support for maintenance and usability, VerCors was moved to an Eclipse-based environment [4]. A series of publications described the support for several features of distributed component-based systems, including group communications, first-class futures, and reconfiguration. At that time, the platform was only able to generate part of the behavioral model and it relied on several manual steps only realizable by experts in formal methods. No code generation was supported. Starting from that preliminary work a new VerCors tool is presented in this paper. It includes the full set of modeling formalisms (architecture, types abstractions, and state-machines), the validation of static correctness, the full chain of tools for the generation of a pNet model for model-checking, as well as a new tool for automatic generation of executable GCM/ProActive code. More recently, theoretical papers defining the pNet model [5] and the behavioral semantics of GCM in terms of pNets [6] were published. They build a formal foundation for the VerCors tools.

---

[3] https://team.inria.fr/scale/software/proactive/.

First, Sect. 2 presents the background on GCM, the pNets formalism and our use-case (Peterson's leader election algorithm). In Sect. 3 we introduce a set of graphical formalisms to define abstractions of distributed component-based system architecture and behavior. In Sect. 4 we show how the specified models can be transformed into behavioral graphs accepted as input by a model-checker. We present in Sect. 5 the generation of executable code from the model specification. Finally, we discuss the related work in Sect. 6 and conclude in Sect. 7. We illustrate our contributions by modeling, verifying, and running Peterson's leader-election algorithm[4][7]. An extended version has been published as a research report [8]; it includes appendices with details on the usecase, the architecture of the tool, and the generation process.

2 Background

2.1 Grid Component Model and ProActive Platform

The Grid Component Model (GCM) [3] targets large-scale distributed component systems. Its reference implementation is GCM/ProActive.

Architecture. A GCM application consists of components, interfaces and bindings. Figure 2 illustrates an example of a GCM system. A component can be either *composite* (it consists of other subcomponents), e.g. `Application`, or *primitive* (a simple element encapsulating business code), e.g. `Comp1`. Components communicate through *interfaces* of two types: client and server (e.g. `C1` and `S1` correspondingly). A component sends requests and receives replies through *client* interfaces; a component receives requests and sends back results through *server* interfaces. The interfaces that communicate are connected with *bindings*.

ProActive is a Java library for distributed computing. Every component in GCM/ProActive is an active object made of a single applicative thread.

Informal semantics of ProActive components. Figure 1.a illustrates treatment of requests by primitive components. Every primitive component has a FIFO request queue, a body and an active object that serves requests. All requests to the server interfaces are first dropped to the queue. The body takes the first request from the queue and triggers the execution of the corresponding method of the active object. To process a request the component may need additional services provided by the other components, using operations calls on its client interfaces. Once a request is served, the component sends back a reply consisting of the value returned by the method. Then, the next can be served.

Figure 1.b illustrates the behavior of a GCM/ProActive composite. A composite has a FIFO request queue, a body, an associated active object, and some subcomponents. The body takes requests from the queue and forwards them to the subcomponents that serve them. In order to serve a request, a subcomponent may need to call methods of other subcomponents or outside of the composite, using client interfaces. Once a request has been served by the subcomponent, the

---

[4] Available at: https://github.com/Scale-VerCors/VCEv4/tree/master/Examples.

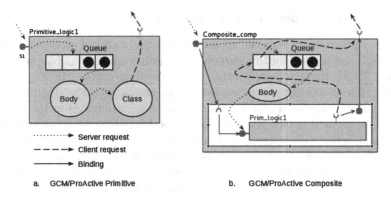

Fig. 1. GCM/ProActive component behavior

composite receives the reply and forwards it to the requester. Every request sent from a subcomponent towards the outside of a composite passes by the queue of the composite before being forwarded through the composite client interface.

GCM components communicate using futures. When a component sends a request to another component, the caller continues its execution as long as it does not need the result of the request. When the result is needed the caller blocks automatically. We call this behavior a "wait-by-necessity". In the meantime, an empty object called *future* represents the result of the request.

2.2   pNets

Parametrized networks of asynchronous automata (pNets) have been formalized in [5]. pNets are composition of labeled transition systems with parameters; they are used as an intermediate model for encoding behavior of GCM-based applications. The behavioural semantics of GCM has been formalized in [6,9]. A pNet is a hierarchical structure where leaves are pLTSs. A pLTS is a labelled transition system with variables, where labels are of the form $\langle \alpha, e_b, (x_j := e_j)^{j \in J} \rangle$, where e_b is a guard, the variables $x_j \in P$ are assigned when the transition is triggered, finally α is a parametrized action that has a label and a set of arguments, some of them are input variables, others are output expressions. By convention, we annotate actions with "!" and "?" depending on the information flow. We assume that the information goes from $!\alpha$ to $?\alpha$. A pNet is either a pLTS or the composition of several pNets; in the second case, the possible interaction between sub-entities are specified by *synchronisation vectors*: $pNet \triangleq pLTS \mid \langle\!\langle L, pNet_i^{i \in I}, SV_k^{k \in K} \rangle\!\rangle$ where L is the set of global actions, $pNet_i^{i \in I}$ is the family of sub-pNets. $SV_k^{k \in K}$ is a set of synchronization vectors. $SV_k = \alpha_j^{j \in J_k} \to \alpha'_k$ means that each of the sub-pNets in the set J_k can perform synchronously an internal action α_j; this results in a global action α'_k. Elements not taking part in the synchronization are denoted $-$ as in: $< -, -, \alpha, - > \to \alpha$.

2.3   Peterson's Leader Election Algorithm

Distributed processes often need to select a unique leader. Peterson's election algorithm [7] can be used for this purpose in a unidirectional ring of asynchronous processes. Every process participating in the elections has a FIFO queue and the order of sent messages is preserved by the communication channels. Each process can be either in active mode if the process participates in the election, or in passive mode if it only forwards messages. Initially, every process stores a unique number that will be modified during the election. The processes exchange two rounds of messages so that every active process learns the numbers stored by the two nearest active processes preceding it. If the maximum of the two previous values and the value held by the current process is the value received from the nearest predecessor of the process, then the active process takes this value as its own value; otherwise the process becomes passive. The rounds of messages and local decision steps are repeated until a process receives its own number, this process is the leader.

In details, every process P stores variables $max(P)$ and $left(P)$. $Max(P)$ is the number stored by P. $Left(P)$ is the number of the active process on the left of P. Processes exchange messages of the form $M(step, value)$ where $step$ is the phase of the algorithm. At the *preliminary phase*, each process P_i sends $M(1, max(P_i))$ to its neighbor. Then, if an active process P_i receives a message $M(1, x)$ and x is equal to its own number, the process is the leader, otherwise it assigns x to $left(P_i)$ and sends $M(2, x)$ to its neighbor. When an active process P_i receives $M(2, x)$ it compares $left(P_i)$ to x and $max(P_i)$. If $left(P_i)$ is greater than both values, P_i assigns $left(P_i)$ to $max(P_i)$ and sends $M(1, max(P_i))$; otherwise P_i becomes passive.

3   Graphical Designer

VerCors includes a graphical designer for modeling component-based system architecture and behavior. These models must be precise enough to be translated into both input for validation and for executable code. The graphical specification part of VerCors is based on Eclipse IDE; it was implemented using Sirius[5]. The VerCors platform includes graphical designers for four types of diagrams: Components, UML Class, UML State Machine, and Type diagrams. This section describes the four editors and the way they are integrated.

3.1   Architecture Specification

Component diagrams are used for the specification of a distributed application architecture. A component diagram includes primitives (grey boxes), and composites (white rectangles with grey border). Interfaces are attached to the borders of their containers. An interface has a set of characteristics, e.g. whether an

---

[5] Sirius is an open-source Eclipse project for development of graphical modeling environment based on EMF and GMF: http://www.eclipse.org/sirius/.

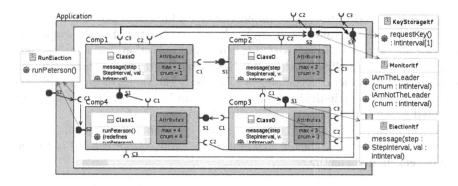

Fig. 2. Components diagram

interface is server or client. The icon representing an interface changes depending on the characteristics. Bindings are shown as arrows between interfaces.

UML Class diagrams are used to specify the list of attributes stored by components and the list of operations a component offers. The user can attach a UML class to a primitive component and a UML interface to client and server interfaces. If a class is attached to a component, it means that the attributes of the class are stored by the component and the operations of the class define the business logic of the component. A UML interface attached to a client or a server GCM interface stores the list of operations that can be called and served with this interface. Each operation defined in a class either has a reference to the operation of the interface it implements (or redefines in UML terms), or is a local method of the component.

The types of operations, attributes, and variables can be declared using Type diagrams. Enumerations, integer intervals, records (C-like structs) and infinite integers can be specified, while boolean and void types are created by default.

Use-case example. The Component diagram representing the architecture of our use-case model is shown on Fig. 2.

`Application` is a composite; it includes four primitives that participate in the leader election process. The primitives are connected in a ring topology and have similar structure. The entry point of the system is the *runPeterson()* operation of `Application` server interface S1. This request is forwarded to `Comp4` that triggers the election process. During the election, components invoke method *message* on their client interfaces C1. As defined in Sect. 2.3, each message transmits two parameters: *step* and *val*. The message is transmitted to the server interface S1 of the called component. The signature of *message* is specified in a UML interface `ElectionItf`. If a component decides to become a leader or a non-leader, it reports its decision to the environment by invoking an *IAmTheLeader(cnum)* or an *IAmNotTheLeader(cnum)* method on its client interface C2. These operations take the identifier of the component as a parameter.

All four components have the same set of attributes. They have the *message(...)* method implementing the leader election algorithm and a set of methods to access local attributes. `Comp4` implements an additional operation *runPeterson()*. `Comp1`, `Comp2`, and `Comp3` are implemented by `Class0` while `Comp4` uses `Class1` that extends `Class0` with *runPeterson()* operation. Initially, the components should have different default values of attribute `max` and `cnum`. `cnum` is a static unique identifier of a component. To specify the values of those attributes for every component individually, we define them in the **Attributes** field represented as a green box in every primitive definition.

In our model we define two integer interval types on Type diagram : *StepInterval = 0..2* for the parameter *step* of messages and *IntInterval = 1..4* for the component unique identifier.

3.2 Behavior Specification

UML State Machine diagrams are used for behavior specification in VerCors. Each State Machine defines the behavior of an operation of a UML Class.

A State Machine has a set of states connected by transitions. A state stores its name, while logic code is specified on transitions. To enable behavioral analysis we specify the syntax of UML transitions: a transition has a label of the form `[guard]/action1....actionN` where **Guard** is a boolean expression and an **action** is an assignment or a method call (to a local operation or a client interface). This set of actions is sufficient to encode any behaviour of distributed objects; control structures have to be encoded as guards on transitions.

The VerCors UML-based editors are based on Obeo UML Designer[6]. In particular, we integrated the State Machines graphical designer of Obeo UML Designer into VerCors, adding local variable declarations. A State Machine has access to its own local variables, to the client interfaces and to local methods of the component which behavior the State Machine describes. A State Machine can access the attributes of the component but only through getters and setters.

Figure 3 illustrates the State Machine of the *message* method of Peterson's leader election algorithm. It uses seven variables where *step* and *val* are input parameters of the method. The initial state is illustrated with a blue circle. First, `Choice6` checks the phase of the election algorithm. If the algorithm is in the preliminary (zero) phase either the component is active – it already participates in the election – or the component triggers the election process on its neighbor and performs the preliminary phase described in Sect. 2.3. If it is not the preliminary phase, either the component is passive and the message is forwarded to the neighbor `[isActive==false]/C1.message(step,val)`, or the actions of the State Machine correspond to the two cases $M(1,x)$ or $M(2,x)$ depending on the value of *step* (see Sect. 2.3).

To illustrate future-based communications in VerCors, we extend our use-case as follows. If a component decides to become the leader, it sends a *requestKey()* invocation on its client interface (see the transition from `State10` to `State12`). The request is forwarded to outside of `Application`. Then, the component claims itself as the leader by sending an *IamTheLeader(cnum)* request.

---

[6] http://www.umldesigner.org/.

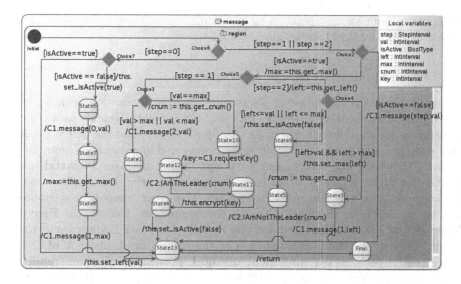

Fig. 3. Message state machine (Color figure online)

Finally, the component calls its local method *encrypt(key)* using the result of *requestKey()* as a parameter. The component should be able to claim itself as the leader before it receives the result of *requestKey()*. However, it cannot execute *encrypt(key)* if the *key* is not obtained. The VerCors user does not need to explicitly model future-based communications. Whenever a State Machine has a non-void client method invocation, it is interpreted as a future-based one.

To conclude, four integrated diagram editors are implemented in VerCors. Component diagrams correspond to architecture specification, Class diagrams represent attributes and method signatures of components, State Machine diagrams are used for behavior specification, and Type diagrams define type abstractions. They allow the user to easily describe his/her application and provide sufficient input both for model-checking and for code generation.

4 Behavior Verification

From user-defined architecture and behavior models VerCors produces input data for the CADP [2] model-checker following a chain of transformations presented in this section. First, we analyze input models and generate a corresponding pNet structure. Second, we generate a finite graph given as an input to CADP, together with auxiliary scripts for managing state-space explosion. Finally, the user can specify the properties that he wants to check on the generated graph and run CADP. While the specified system and the pNet model rely on parameterized state-machines potentially featuring infinite state-space, the model-checking phase can handle finite state-space only. As a consequence, the correctness of the finite abstraction should be checked by abstract interpretation techniques. From another point of view, the pNet model could also be checked by a different tool that handles infinite state-space.

4.1   From Application Design to pNets

We present here the generation of pNets specifying the application behavior [6].

A pNet of a **primitive** assembles pLTSs of two types: the generic ones whose structure is identical for all primitives (e.g. queue, body) and the pLTSs generated from the user-defined State Machines (server and local methods behavior). Figure 4 shows the pNet generated for Comp1 of our use-case. An **Attribute controller** pLTS is generated for each attribute of a primitive; it allows storing and modifying the value of this attribute. The list of component attributes can be derived from the UML Class of the component. **Proxy** and **Proxy-Manager** pLTSs are generated for every client operation having a non-void result. They model the implementation of the futures mechanism. A pLTS is generated for each **server and local method**. For this purpose we translate UML State Machines specifying methods behavior into pLTSs. To translate a State Machine into a pLTS we first map each state of a State Machine into a pLTS state and each transition to one or several pLTS transition (potentially adding intermediate states). For example, a State Machine transition [isActive==true]/max:=this.get_max() involves one guard condition and two actions: a call to a local function get_max and a return of its result. A pLTS transition can perform at most one action, hence, the result of the translation will consist in two sequential transitions.

The behavior of the components is modeled by synchronization vectors, expressing the synchronization and the data flow between pLTSs. As an example, the Body and the Queue pLTSs of a primitive are synchronized using:

$$< !Serve\_message(...), ?Serve\_message(...), -, -, -, -, - > \rightarrow Serve\_message(...)$$

in which, the subnets occur in the following order:

$$< Queue, Body, message, max\_ac, cnum\_ac, left\_as, isActive\_ac > .$$

Synchronization of the Queue with the environment under reception of a request is expressed by: $<?Q\_message(...), -, -, -, -, -, - > \rightarrow ?Q\_message(...)$ meaning that this action is exposed at the next level of pNet to synchronize with another pNet. The other vectors synchronize the following entities: the Body and a server method pLTS $(Call\_message(...))$; a server method pLTS and other local methods, or client method of the environment; the server method, the Body and the environment to return the result $(R\_message(...))$; the environment and the Queue when the Queue is saturated, raising an $Error\_queue$ event.

The pNet of a **composite** (Fig. 5) assembles pLTSs for queue, body and sub-entities enabling futures mechanism with pNets of the subcomponents. The request reception mechanism is similar to the one of a primitive. The only difference is that the body is synchronized with subcomponent pNets in order to forward them the requests. pNets of subcomponents are synchronized with each

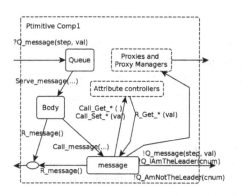

Fig. 4. pNet of Comp1   **Fig. 5.** pNet of application

other under internal method invocation (*e.g. Comp4_Comp1_message(...)*) and result reception. If a subcomponent invokes an operation outside of the composite, it synchronizes with the composite queue. Then, the queue synchronizes with the environment and forwards the request to outside of the composite.

Scenario. The user can specify a Scenario State Machine, encoding the legal sequences of actions performed by the environment, accessing only the server interfaces of the root component. The scenario of our use-case calls the *runPeterson* method on interface S1 of `Application` once. The scenario State Machine is translated into a pLTS and synchronized with the queue of the root component. This leads to a much smaller and meaningful behavior model.

4.2 From pNets to Model-Checking

Generation of verification input. As the next step, VerCors translates the pLTSs into the Fiacre format [10] and the synchronization vectors into EXP [11]. Then, the FLAC compiler translates the Fiacre specification into Lotos code. Finally the CADP front-end generates a labelled transition system in a format that can be used by the CADP model-checker. We generate a set of scripts for managing the execution of all steps: communication hiding, minimization, and hierarchical product using EXP files. In order to limit the state-space explosion phenomenon inherent to explicit-state model-checkers, the user should:

- use a scenario to limit acceptable inputs of the modeled system,
- specify the internal actions that he does not want to observe during model-checking (we generate a script transforming them into *internal* actions),
- limit the size of the data domains using the Types diagram.

All generated transition systems are minimized using branching bisimulation.
We have used the VerCors model-generation function to produce Fiacre, EXP and auxiliary scripts for our use-case. Table 1 presents size information for some

Table 1. Behavior graph files (all with Queue size of 3)

Graph	States	Transitions	Computation time
Behaviour of `Comp4`	3.217.983	45.055.266	2m48.520s
Comp4 (after hiding and minimization)	90.821	1.306.138	5m23.030s
full application	296	661	47m1.673s

of the intermediate behavior graphs. The last line is for the hierarchical construction of the full model of the application (including the Scenario), and the time includes the whole model-generation workflow. The time needed to generate Fiacre, EXP files and scripts from VerCors is neglectible.

Model-checking. We use the Model Checking Language (MCL [12]) to express the behavioral properties we want to prove on our system. MCL is a very expressive logic including first order predicates for the data part, and the alternation free μ-calculus for branching time logics. On top of MCL, we use *Specification Patterns* [13] for easier expression of some usual temporal logic properties, as in the examples below. We recall that in our example the properties are evaluated in the context of the scenario where the election algorithm is triggered.

First, we check that after a call to *runPeterson()*, it is inevitable (under fairness hypothesis) that either the leader is elected or one of the queues is saturated. The model-checker answers `true`: the election terminates. We also proved that with adequate queue size, they never saturate.

['Call_RunPeterson'] Inev ('Q_IamTheLeader.*' or'ErrorQueue.*')

Then, we prove that the event `Q_IamTheLeader` is emitted only once:

Absence_Before ('Q_IamTheLeader.*','Q_IamTheLeader.*')"

In order to check that the communications in the generated graph are indeed implementing futures properly, we verify the following formula which states that a key is always received before IamTheLeader() is invoked:

Existence_Between('R_RequestKey.*', 'Q_requestKey.*', 'Q_IamTheLeader.*')

The model-checker answers `false` and provides an example of system behavior where *IamTheLeader()* method is invoked before the key is received. This proves that a component is not blocked if the key is not needed.

To summarize, from the graphical models provided by the user we automatically generate a behavior description in the form of pNets, and translate these into an input for CADP verification tools. We tested our approach on our use-case and proved by model-checking the correctness of the application, including its safety, termination, and functional correctness.

5   Code Generation and Execution

5.1   Executable Code Generation

From the specified architecture and behavior we automatically generate executable code. We produce an ADL (XML) file defining architecture, and Java interfaces and classes files for the implementation of the methods specified by State Machines. This code can be run using the GCM/ProActive Java library.

Listing 1.1. Generated Java code of message

```
1   Boolean isActive = null;
2   Integer left = null, max = null, cnum = null;
3   State curState = State.Initial;
4   while(true) {
5    switch (curState) {
6     ...
7    case Choice2:
8           if(isActive == true) {
9              max=this.get_max();
10             curState = State.Choice5;
11             break; }
12          else if(isActive == false) {
13             C1.message(step, val);
14             curState = State.State13;
15             break; }... };}
```

We generate a Java interface for every UML interface and a Java class for every UML class. We translate each State Machine attached to a method into Java code. To do this we use a Java enumeration representing the state machine steps, a local variable **curState** holds the current state of the state machine and actions are taken depending on this state. Listing 1.1 shows a skeleton of the encoding of the *message* operation from Fig. 3. Note that if-else statements are used for states with more than one outgoing transition. For example in Choice 2, the guard label [**isActive==false**] is translated as an if-else statement in line 12; depending on the result, a *message* invocation is emitted (corresponding to **C1.message(...)**, line 13) and the value of **curState** is updated (line 14). A drawback of this approach is that such code may not be very convenient for the programmer since *do-while, for, while* constructs cannot be written as such in the state machine, but will rather be encoded within the state structure, separated by case instructions. We also generate skeleton code for getter and setter methods, which have no associated state machine.

The Java code generated by VerCors relies on futures. To implement their generation, we analyze the State Machines and mark the variables that store remote method invocation results. This information is used to generate the types of those variables and to access their values. For example, the **key** variable from our use-case State Machine will be generated with an *IntWrapper* type[7]. Then the statement **this.encrypt(key)** requires the value of **key** and it will be translated to the following Java code: **this.encrypt(key.intValue())**.

---

[7] Basic types need to be wrapped to enable future-based commnuications.

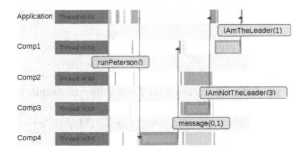

Fig. 6. Code execution (Color figure online)

5.2 Code Execution

We generated ProActive/Java code of our use-case example; the resulting execution is shown in Fig. 6[8]. Black arrows represent request emissions (the figure only shows some of them). Yellow and blue rectangles show request processing. For example, we can see how the call to *runPeterson* of Application is transmitted to Comp4 and at the end of the *runPeterson* request processing Comp4 triggers the elections on Comp1 by calling *message(0,1)*. At the end of the algorithm execution we can see how Comp3 reports to the Application that it is not the leader and Comp1 claims to be the leader.

To sum up, from the specification provided by the user VerCors automatically produces executable ProActive/Java code. We generated and executed code of our use-case model and we observed expected behavior of the produced system. The generated code is guaranteed to verify the temporal properties proven on the model. It can either be used as it is or serve as code skeleton if the programmer wants to add computational steps that he did not include in the model.

6   Related Work

There exist a number of languages, formalisms, and tools aiming at verification and safe code generation, we focus here on the ones that are dedicated to distributed systems and composition of distributed systems.

BIP (Behavior Interaction Priority) [14] allows rigorous design of complex component-based systems. BIP is supported by a toolset including translators of various source models to BIP, code generators, and verification mechanisms. BIP focuses on the design of systems based on the notion of interacting entities whereas our approach takes the point of view of the software developer, using classical UML-based descriptions augmented only by our graphical DSL for architecture, relying on notions the user knows well. Our approach is closely tied to the notion of distributed components interacting by requests and replies;

---

[8] We use a dedicated tool for the visualization of ProActive program execution: https://github.com/scale-proactive/A-viewer-tool-for-multiactive-objects.git.

while this reduces the field of applicability of our work, it allows us to generate the component interaction automatically, without additional input from the user.

Cadena [15] is a platform for the development of component-based applications, initially targeted for the Corba Component Model (CCM), and more recently extended to support Open-CCM, EJBs, and sensor networks specified with the nesC language. Cadena allows the user to specify component types, define and analyze inter-component dependencies, specify and model-check correctness properties, generate code in the various component formalisms, and even specify new user-defined component models. Unlike VerCors, it does not manage hierarchical components, so it could not be used for Fractal or GCM.

Palladio [16] is a tool for design, analysis and generation of hierarchical large-scale component-based systems. Palladio has less restrictions on types and allows more expressive modeling than VerCors. However, while Palladio has strong emphasis on simulation and system performance prediction, our approach benefits from the use of formal methods for validation.

Creol [17] is an object-oriented programming language based on concurrent objects that communicate asynchronously. Creol is supported by the Credo [18] toolset. In Credo the application description relies on Reo [19]. Credo provides an abstract but executable model of the application. Then, a test specification is derived to check compatibility between the two models. Creol is supported by a type-checker, a simulation and model-checking platform based on Maude. In VerCors we rely on UML-based formalisms, better known by the programmers than Reo. We also directly generate efficient code that can be executed on large-scale distributed infrastructures.

SOFA 2 [20] is a framework for distributed hierarchical component-based systems development. SOFA 2 is supported by a tool set comprising graphical designers and behavior validation instruments. SOFA 2 supports dynamic architectures, multiple communication styles and transparent distribution with the help of software connectors. Validation in SOFA 2 relies on behavioral protocols that are easy to understand for the programmer. This provides developers with validation capacities that require no expertise in any general logical formalism, though the expressivity may be lower than with temporal logic.

JHelena is a framework for modeling and generation of executable code of highly dynamic ensembles of autonomic distributed components that are modeled using Helena [21] technique. Our approach allows modeling systems with several levels of hierarchy while to our knowledge in Helena approach the composition only occurs at one level.

ABS [22] is a formal executable component modeling language supported by a deductive verification system Key-ABS. ABS is a powerful language for concurrent object-oriented programming, however it does not support any architectural description. The verification pattern is also quite different. Different tools for ABS either focus on specific properties (absence of deadlock for example) or use KeY to specify invariants of the program and verify them. Our approach allows us to target a wide range of properties while not asking the programmer to have the expertise necessary to write program invariants.

Concerning actor systems, the related work the closest to ours is Rebeca [23] that handles both functional and real-time verification. The first main difference between Rebeca and Vercors is the programming model: Rebeca has no *future* and no synchronisation operation, which makes the generation of behavioural model easier. The second one is that the Rebeca toolset does not provide a design tool or an execution platform as efficient as Vercors+ProActive. On the other side, Rebeca has strong results concerning the scalability of the approach, and the range of systems and of properties handled.

Several verification tools focus on "real-time aspects" allowing to reason on the time-sensitive properties [24]. In this section we have focused on the tools that explicitly handle asynchrony and we have not cited works on real-time systems in general.

7   Discussion and Perspectives

In this paper we presented our integrated environment for designing and implementing safe component-based systems. Our approach includes three main aspects. First, we provide graphical formalisms for the application architecture and the behavior specification, as well as type abstractions. The formalism extensively uses UML models that makes it easy to learn and use for the programmer. Second, we ensure behavioral correctness, by running a model-checker on the specified model. In practice, we transform graphical models into input for the CADP model-checker. As a result, the user can verify correctness properties of the modeled system even if he does not have a strong expertise in formal methods. Finally, we transform the models into executable application code. We implemented our approach in the VerCors platform and we tested it by modeling, verifying, and executing Peterson's leader election algorithm. Our approach was illustrated by generating GCM/ProActive code but it would be easy to generate code for any actor or active-object based language, or more generally any programming model made of components interacting by asynchronous requests and replies. Beyond the academic example of this paper, we have also published a study of a fault-tolerant protocol [25], showing how to handle scalability issues in the model-checking activities. In another paper, we showed an industrial-inspired study [26] in which we handle large state-spaces modeling an application with dynamic reconfiguration of components.

This paper raises the question of the relation between the semantics of the handled models: state-machines, pNets, finite-state models, and distributed Java programs. Previous usecases show that many applications and protocols can be encoded faithfully and executed correctly. It is not in the scope of this paper to study the semantic gap between these models or to formally prove that the behavioral model has the same semantics as the generated code. However, the formal semantics of ProActive [27], the semantics of pNets [5], and the formal definition of the translation from GCM to pNets [6] allowed us to check carefully that the semantics correspond faithfully. Considering the complexity of the system, an exhaustive formal proof of bisimulation between the semantics would require several years.

While creating the VerCors platform we tackled a number of challenges. First, the choice of the underlying technology was not trivial: we experimented with the Topcased platform, UML profiles, Eclipse Papyrus, before finding a usable environment with Sirius. Second, finding an expressive and easy to learn graphical formalism was a challenging task. We wanted to reuse UML notions as much as possible, but we realized that we needed our own graphical formalism, and had to find a way to map a large part of GCM specifications into UML models. Finally, the integration of all languages, models and formalisms involved in modeling, execution and verification was not trivial. For example, the syntax of State Machine had to be precisely specified to be able to translate them into Fiacre. Also, the translation between formalisms raised technical difficulties, some of them detailed in [6] and others related to the Fiacre language.

We are currently working on extensions of the VerCors platform that would address more features of distributed component-based applications. In particular, we want to address separation between functional code and application management and verify the correct interaction between those two aspects. Another challenge that we plan to address is the expression of the system properties using a higher level specification language. This should also include the translation from the model-checker diagnostics back to the user-level formalism, that is not implemented in the current version; it would make our approach even more attractive for users non-expert in model-checking.

References

1. Henrio, L., Kulankhina, O., Liu, D., Madelaine, E.: Verifying the correct composition of distributed components: formalisation and tool. In: FOCLASA, Rome, Italy, September 2014
2. Garavel, H., Lang, F., Mateescu, R., Serwe, W.: CADP 2010: a toolbox for the construction and analysis of distributed processes. In: Abdulla, P.A., Leino, K.R.M. (eds.) TACAS 2011. LNCS, vol. 6605, pp. 372–387. Springer, Heidelberg (2011)
3. Baude, F., Caromel, D., Dalmasso, C., Danelutto, M., Getov, V., Henrio, L., Pérez, C.: GCM: a grid extension to fractal for autonomous distributed components. Ann. Telecommun. **64**(1), 5–24 (2009)
4. Cansado, A., Madelaine, E.: Specification and verification for grid component-based applications: from models to tools. In: de Boer, F.S., Bonsangue, M.M., Madelaine, E. (eds.) FMCO 2008. LNCS, vol. 5751, pp. 180–203. Springer, Heidelberg (2009)
5. Henrio, L., Madelaine, E., Zhang, M.: pnets: an expressive model for parameterised networks of processes. In: 23rd Euromicro International Conference on Parallel, Distributed, and Network-Based Processing, PDP 2015, 4–6 March 2015, Turku, Finland, pp. 492–496 (2015)
6. Ameur-Boulifa, R., Henrio, L., Madelaine, E., Savu, A.: Behavioural semantics for asynchronous components. Rapport de recherche RR-8167, INRIA, December 2012
7. Dolev, D., Klawe, M.M., Rodeh, M.: An o(n log n) unidirectional distributed algorithm for extrema finding in a circle. J. Algorithms **3**(3), 245–260 (1982). http://dx.doi.org/10.1016/0196-6774(82)90023-2

8. Henrio, L., Kulankhina, O., Li, S., Madelaine, E.: Integrated environment for verifying and running distributed components - extended version. Research Report RR8841, INRIA Sophia-Antipolis, December 2015
9. Barros, T., Ameur-Boulifa, R., Cansado, A., Henrio, L., Madelaine, E.: Behavioural models for distributed fractal components. Ann. Telecommun. **64**(1–2), 25–43 (2009)
10. Berthomieu, B., Bodeveix, J., Filali, M., Garavel, H., Lang, F., Peres, F., Saad, R., Stoecker, J., Vernadat, F.: The syntax and semantics of Fiacre, March 2009
11. Lang, F.: Exp.Open 2.0: a flexible tool integrating partial order, compositional, and on-the-fly verification methods. In: Romijn, J.M.T., Smith, G.P., van de Pol, J. (eds.) IFM 2005. LNCS, vol. 3771, pp. 70–88. Springer, Heidelberg (2005)
12. Mateescu, R., Thivolle, D.: A model checking language for concurrent value-passing systems. In: Cuellar, J., Sere, K. (eds.) FM 2008. LNCS, vol. 5014, pp. 148–164. Springer, Heidelberg (2008)
13. Dwyer, M.B., Avrunin, G.S., Corbett, J.C.: Patterns in property specifications for finite-state verification. In: 21st International Conference on Software Engineering, May 1999
14. Basu, A., Bensalem, B., Bozga, M., Combaz, J., Jaber, M., Nguyen, T., Sifakis, J.: Rigorous component-based system design using the BIP framework. IEEE Softw. **28**(3), 41–48 (2011)
15. Childs, A., Greenwald, J., Jung, G., Hoosier, M., Hatcliff, J.: CALM and Cadena: metamodeling for component-based product-line development. IEEE Comput. **39**(2), 42–50 (2006)
16. Reussner, R., Becker, S., Burger, E., Happe, J., Hauck, M., Koziolek, A., Koziolek, H., Krogmann, K., Kuperberg, M.: The Palladio component model. Technical report, Karlsruhe Institute of Technology, March 2011
17. Leister, W., Bjork, J., Schlatte, R., Griesmayer, A.: Verifying distributed algorithms with executable Creol models, January 2011
18. Grabe, I., Jaghoori, M.M., Aichernig, B.K., Baier, C., Blechmann, T., de Boer, F.S., Griesmayer, A., Johnsen, E.B., Klein, J., Klüppelholz, S., Kyas, M., Leister, W., Schlatte, R., Stam, A., Steffen, M., Tschirner, S., Xuedong, L., Yi, W.: Credo methodology: modeling and analyzing A peer-to-peer system in Credo. Electron. Notes Theoret. Comput. Sci. **266**, 33–48 (2010)
19. Arbab, F.: A behavioral model for composition of software components. L'OBJET **12**(1), 33–76 (2006)
20. Hnětynka, P., Plášil, F.: Dynamic reconfiguration and access to services in hierarchical component models. In: Gorton, I., Heineman, G.T., Crnković, I., Schmidt, H.W., Stafford, J.A., Ren, X.-M., Wallnau, K. (eds.) CBSE 2006. LNCS, vol. 4063, pp. 352–359. Springer, Heidelberg (2006)
21. Klarl, A., Hennicker, R.: Design and implementation of dynamically evolving ensembles with the HELENA framework. In: Proceedings of the 23rd Australasian Software Engineering Conference, pp. 15–24. IEEE (2014)
22. Hähnle, R., Helvensteijn, M., Johnsen, E.B., Lienhardt, M., Sangiorgi, D., Schaefer, I., Wong, P.Y.H.: HATS abstract behavioral specification: the architectural view. In: Beckert, B., Damiani, F., de Boer, F.S., Bonsangue, M.M. (eds.) FMCO 2011. LNCS, vol. 7542, pp. 109–132. Springer, Heidelberg (2012)
23. Sirjani, M., Movaghar, A., Shali, A., de Boer, F.S.: Modeling and verification of reactive systems using Rebeca. Fundam. Inform. **63**(4), 385–410 (2004)
24. Burmester, S., Giese, H., Hirsch, M., Schilling, D.: Incremental design and formal verification with UML/RT in the FUJABA real-time tool suite. In: Proceedings of the International Workshop SVERTS (2004)

25. Ameur-Boulifa, R., Halalai, R., Henrio, L., Madelaine, E.: Verifying safety of fault-tolerant distributed components. In: Arbab, F., Ölveczky, P.C. (eds.) FACS 2011. LNCS, vol. 7253, pp. 278–295. Springer, Heidelberg (2012)
26. Gaspar, N., Henrio, L., Madelaine, E.: Formally reasoning on a reconfigurable component-based system – a case study for the industrial world. In: Fiadeiro, J.L., Liu, Z., Xue, J. (eds.) FACS 2013. LNCS, vol. 8348, pp. 137–156. Springer, Heidelberg (2014)
27. Caromel, D., Henrio, L.: A Theory of Distributed Objects. Springer, Berlin (2005). ISBN 3-540-20866-6

Model-Driven Development

Iterative and Incremental Model Generation by Logic Solvers

Oszkár Semeráth[✉], András Vörös, and Dániel Varró

Department of Measurement and Information Systems, Budapest University
of Technology and Economics, Budapest, Hungary
{semerath,vori,varro}@mit.bme.hu

Abstract. The generation of sample instance models of Domain-Specific Language (DSL) specifications has become an active research line due to its increasing industrial relevance for engineering complex modeling tools by using large metamodels and complex well-formedness constraints. However, the synthesis of large, well-formed *and* realistic models is still a major challenge. In this paper, we propose an iterative process for generating valid instance models by calling existing logic solvers as black-box components using various approximations of metamodels and constraints to improve overall scalability. (1) First, we apply enhanced metamodel pruning and partial instance models to reduce the complexity of model generation subtasks and the retrieved partial solutions initiated in each step. (2) Then we propose an (over-)approximation technique for well-formedness constraints in order to interpret and evaluate them on partial (pruned) metamodels. (3) Finally, we define a workflow that incrementally generates a sequence of instance models by refining and extending partial models in multiple steps, where each step is an independent call to the underlying solver (the Alloy Analyzer in our experiments).

Keywords: Domain-specific languages · Logic solvers · Model generation

1 Introduction

Motivation. The generation of sample instance models of Domain-Specific Language (DSL) specifications has become an active research line due to its increasing industrial relevance for engineering complex modeling tools by using large metamodels (MM) and complex well-formedness (WF) constraints [25]. Such instance models derived as representative examples [2] and counterexamples [18,32] may serve as test cases or performance benchmarks for DSL modeling tools, model transformations or code generators [4]. Existing approaches dominantly use either a logic solver or a rule-based instance generator in the background.

This paper is partially supported by the MTA-BME Lendület 2015 Research Group on Cyber-Physical Systems and by the ARTEMIS JU and the Hungarian National Research, Development and Innovation Fund in the frame of the R5-COP project.

P. Stevens and A. Wąsowski (Eds.): FASE 2016, LNCS 9633, pp. 87–103, 2016.
DOI: 10.1007/978-3-662-49665-7_6

Problem Statement. *Model finding using logic solvers* [16] (like SMT or SAT-solvers) is an effective technique (1) to identify inconsistencies of a DSL specification or (2) to generate well-formed sample instances of a DSL. This approach handles *complex global WF constraints* which necessitates to access and query several model elements during evaluation. Model generation for graph structures needs to satisfy complex structural global constraints (which is typical characteristic for DSLs), which restricts the direct use of logical numerical and constraint solvers despite the existence of various encodings of graph structures into logic formulae. As the metamodel of an industrial DSL may contain hundreds of model elements, any realistic instance model should be of similar size. Unfortunately, this cannot currently be achieved by a single direct call to the underlying solver [17,32], thus existing logic based model generators *fail to scale.* Furthermore, logic solvers tend to retrieve simple *unrealistic models* consisting of unconnected islands of model fragments and many isolated nodes, which is problematic in an industrial setting.

Rule-based instance generators [4,13,33] are effective in generating larger model instances by independent modifications to the model by randomly applying mutation rules. Such a rule-based approach offers *better scalability* for complex DSLs. These approaches may incorporate *local WF constraints* which can be evaluated in the context of a single model element (or within its 1-context). However, they *fail to handle global WF constraints* which require to access and navigate along a complex network of model elements. Since constraint evaluation is typically the final step of the generation process, the synthesized models may violate several WF constraints of the DSL in an industrial setting.

Contribution. The long term objective of our research is to synthesize large, well-formed *and* realistic models. In this paper, we propose an iterative process for incrementally generating valid instance models by calling existing logic solvers as black-box components using various abstractions and approximations to improve overall scalability. (1) First, we apply enhanced metamodel pruning [33] and partial instance models [32] to reduce the complexity of model generation subtasks and the retrieved partial solutions initiated in each step. (2) Then we propose an (over-)approximation technique for well-formedness constraints in order to interpret and evaluate them on partial (pruned) metamodels. (3) Finally, we define a workflow that incrementally generates a sequence of instance models by refining and extending partial models in multiple steps, where each step is an independent call to the underlying solver. We carried out experiments using the state-of-the-art Alloy Analyzer [16] to assess the scalability of our approach.

Added Value. Our approach increases the size of generated models by carefully controlling the information fed into and retrieved back from logic solvers in each step via abstractions. Each generated model (1) increases in size by only a handful number of elements, (2) satisfies all WF constraints (on a certain level of abstraction), and (3) it is realistic in the sense that each model is a single component (and not disconnected islands). The incremental derivation

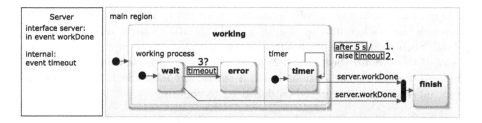

Fig. 1. Example Yakindu statechart with synchronisations.

of the result set provides graceful degradation, i.e. if the back-end solver fails to synthesize models of size N (due to timeout), all previous model instances are still available. From a practical viewpoint, the DSL engineer can influence or assist the instance generation process by selecting the important fragment of the analyzed metamodel (so called *effective metamodel* [4]). This is also common practice for testing model transformations or code generators.

Structure of the Report. Next, Sect. 2 introduces some preliminaries for formalizing metamodels, constraints and partial snaptshots. Our approach is presented in Sect. 3 followed by an initial experimental evaluation in Sect. 4. Related work is assessed in Sect. 5 while Sect. 6 concludes our paper.

2   Preliminaries

In this section we present an overview of model generation with logic solvers with a running case study of Yakindu statecharts. Yakindu Statecharts Tools [37] is an industrial integrated modeling environment developed by Itemis AG for the specification and development of reactive, event-driven systems based on the concept of statecharts captured in combined graphical and textual syntax. Yakindu simultaneously supports static validation of well-formedness constraints as well as simulation of (and code generation from) statechart models. A sample statechart is illustrated in Fig. 1. Yakindu provides two types of synchronization mechanisms: explicit synchronization nodes (marked as black rectangles) and event-based synchronization (i.e. raising and consuming events).

Validation is crucial for domain-specific modelling tools to detect conceptual design flaws early and ensure that malformed models does not processed by tooling. Therefore missing validation rules are considered as bugs of the editor. While Yakindu is a stable modeling tool, it is still surprisingly easy to develop model instances as corner cases which satisfy all (implemented) well-formedness constraints of the language but crashes the simulator or code generator due to synchronization issues. One of such problems is depicted in Fig. 1 where (1) after 5 s a (2) timeout event raised in region timer, but (3) it cannot be accepted in state wait in the simulator and in the generated code.

Our goal is to systematically synthesize such model instances by using logic solvers in the background by mapping DSL specifications to a logic problem [17,32]. Such model generation approach usually takes three inputs: (1) a *meta-model of the domain* (Sect. 2.1), (2) a set of *well-formedness constraints* of the language (Sect. 2.2), and optionally (3) a *partial snapshot* (Sect. 2.3) serving as an initial seed which generated models need to contain.

2.1   Domain Metamodel

Metamodels define the main concepts, relations and attributes of the target domain to specify the basic structure of the models. In this paper, the Eclipse Modeling Framework (EMF) is used for domain modeling, which is dominantly used in many industrial DSL tools and modeling environments. The main concepts are illustrated using Yakindu state graph metamodel [37] in Fig. 2.

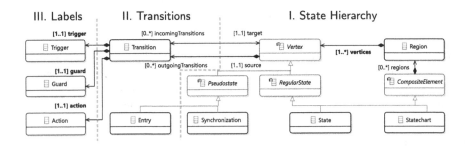

Fig. 2. Metamodel extract from Yakindu state machines

A state machine consists of **Regions**, which in turn contain states (called **Vertexes**) and **Transitions**. An abstract state **Vertex** is further refined into Regu-larStates (like **State**) and PseudoStates like **Entry** and **Synchronization** states. Note that we intentionally kept the generalization hierarchy unchanged and simplified the original metamodel only by removing some elements. Metamodel elements are mapped to a set of logic relations as defined in [17,32]:

- **Classes (CLS):** In EMF, *EClasses* can be instantiated to *EObjects*, where the set of objects of a model is denoted by *objects*. Additionally, the metamodel can specify finite types with predefined set of $enum = \{l_1, \ldots, l_n\}$ literals by *EEnums*. For both classes and enums, if an o is an instance of a type C it is denoted as $C(o)$.
- **References (REF):** *EReferences* between classes S and T capture a binary relation $R(S,T)$ of the metamodel. When two objects o and t are in a relation R, an *EReference* is instantiated leading from o to t denoted as $R(o,t)$.
- **Attributes (ATT):** *EAttributes* enrich a class C with values of predefined primitive types like integers, strings, etc. by binary relations $A(C,V)$. If an object o stores a value v as attribute A it is denoted as $A(o,v)$.

Further structural restrictions implied by a metamodel (and formalized in [32]) include (1) **Generalization (GEN)** which expresses that a more specific (child) class has every structural feature of the more general (parent) class, (2) **Type compliance (TC)** that requires that for any relation $R(o, t)$, its source and target objects o and t need to have compliant types, (3) **Abstract (ABS)**: If a class is defined as *abstract*, it is not allowed to have direct instances, (4) **Multiplicity (MUL)** of structural features can be limited with upper and lower bound in the form of "lower..upper" and (5) **Inverse (INV)**, which states that two parallel references of opposite direction always occur in pairs. EMF instance models are arranged into a strict *containment hierarchy*, which is a directed tree along relations marked in the metamodel as containment (e.g. regions or vertices).

An instance model M is an instance of a metamodel *Meta* (denoted with $M \models Meta$) if all the corresponding constraints above are satisfied, i.e. $Meta = CLS \wedge REF \wedge \cdots \wedge MUL \wedge INV$ [32]. Therefore a model generation task for a given size s and a metamodel *Meta* can be solved as logic problem, where the solver creates an interpretation for all class predicates, all reference and attribute relations over the set of $objects = \{o_1, \ldots, o_s\}$ and sets of enum literals, which satisfies all structural constraints.

2.2   Well-Formedness Constraints

Structural well-formedness (WF) constraints (aka design rules or consistency rules) complement metamodels with additional restrictions that have to be satisfied by a valid instance model (in our case, statechart model). Such constraints are frequently defined by graph patterns [36] or OCL invariants [27]. To abstract from the actual constraint language, we assume in the paper that WF constraints are defined in first order logic. Given a set *WF* of well-formedness constraints, a model M is called valid if $M \models Meta \wedge WF$.

Example. The Yakindu documentation states several constraints for statecharts including the following ones regulating the use of synchronization states. (Abbreviated names of classes and references are used as predicates).

Φ_1 Source states of a synchronization have to be contained in different regions!
$\forall syn, s_1, s_2, t_1, t_2, r_1, r_2 :$
(Synchron(syn) $\wedge$ outgoing(s_1, t_1) $\wedge$ outgoing(s_2, t_2) $\wedge$ target(t_1, syn)$\wedge$
target(t_2, syn) $\wedge$ vertices(r_1, s_1) $\wedge$ vertices(r_2, s_2) $\wedge s_1 \neq s_2$) $\Rightarrow r_1 \neq r_2$

Φ_2 Source states of a synchronization are contained in the same parent state!
$\forall syn, s_1, s_2, t_1, t_2, r_1, r_2 \exists p :$
(Synchron(syn) $\wedge$ outgoing(s_1, t_1) $\wedge$ outgoing(s_2, t_2) $\wedge$ target(t_1, syn)$\wedge$
target(t_2, syn) $\wedge$ vertices(r_1, s_1) $\wedge$ vertices(r_2, s_2) $\wedge s_1 \neq s_2$)
$\Rightarrow$ (regions(p, r_1) $\wedge$ regions(p, r_2))

Φ_3 Target states of a synchronization have to be contained in different regions!
$\forall syn, s_1, s_2, t_1, t_2, r_1, r_2 :$
(Synchron(syn) $\wedge$ incoming(s_1, t_1) $\wedge$ incoming(s_2, t_2) $\wedge$ source(t_1, syn)$\wedge$
source(t_2, syn) $\wedge$ vertices(r_1, s_1) $\wedge$ vertices(r_2, s_2) $\wedge s_1 \neq s_2$) $\Rightarrow r_1 \neq r_2$

Φ_4 Target states of a synchronization are contained in the same parent state!

$\forall syn, s_1, s_2, t_1, t_2, r_1, r_2 \exists p :$
(Synchron$(syn) \wedge$ incoming$(s_1, t_1) \wedge$ incoming$(s_2, t_2) \wedge$ source$(t_1, syn) \wedge$
source$(t_2, syn) \wedge$ vertices$(r_1, s_1) \wedge$ vertices$(r_2, s_2) \wedge s_1 \neq s_2)$
$\Rightarrow$ (regions$(p, r_1) \wedge$ regions$(p, r_2))$

Φ_5 A synchronization shall have at least two incoming or outgoing transitions!

$\forall syn :$ Synchron$(syn) \Rightarrow \exists t_1, t_2 : t_1 \neq t_2 \wedge ((\text{incoming}(t_1, syn) \wedge$
incoming$(t_2, syn)) \vee (\text{outgoing}(t_1, syn) \wedge \text{outgoing}(t_2, syn)))$

2.3   Partial Snapshots

Partial Snapshots (PS) specify required instance model fragments of a meta-model [32]. A partial snapshot is a model constructed from the same classes and relations as a valid instance model. Formally, a PS satisfies the constraints CLS, GEN, REF and TC, but it possibly violates ABS, ATT, MUL and INV, which means that even abstract classes can be instantiated, and multiplicity constraints, the inverse relation of references and containment hierarchy rules might be violated. If a PS is a partial snapshot of a metamodel it is denoted by $PS \models_P Meta$. A model M contains a partial snapshot PS (denoted with $M \models PS$) if there is a morphism $m : PS \rightarrow M$ (composed of a pair of morphisms $objects_{PS} \rightarrow objects_M$ and $references_{PS} \rightarrow references_M$ for mapping objects and references) which satisfies the following constraints for each $o_1, o_2 \in objects_{PS}$:

1. m is injective: $o_1 \neq o_2 \Rightarrow m(o_1) \neq m(o_2)$
2. For each class C the mapping preserves the type: $\mathsf{C}(o_1) \Rightarrow \mathsf{C}(m(o_1))$
3. For each reference R the mapping preserves the source and the target of the reference: $\mathsf{R}(o_1, o_2) \Rightarrow \mathsf{R}(m(o_1), m(o_2))$
4. For each attribute A the mapping preserves the attribute value v and the location: $\mathsf{A}(o_1, v) \Rightarrow \mathsf{A}(m(o_1), v)$

A partial snapshot can be generalized from a regular (fully specified) instance model by relaxing specific properties identified by the DSL developer [32] to guide testing in practical cases. In the current paper, we create partial snapshots by iteratively reusing the instance models generated in a previous run to achieve incremental model generation (see Sect. 3.3).

3   Incremental Model Generation by Approximations

Despite the precise definition of logic formulae for our statechart language using existing mappings [32], a major practical drawback is that a direct (single step) model generation using Z3 or Alloy as back-end solver only terminates for very small model sizes. If we aim to improve scalability by omitting certain constraints, the synthesized models are no longer well-formed thus they cannot be fed into Yakindu as sample models.

To increase the size of synthesized models while still keeping them well-formed, we propose an incremental model generation approach (Sect. 3.3) by iterative calls to backend solvers exploiting two enabling techniques of meta-model pruning (Sect. 3.1) and constraint approximation (Sect. 3.2).

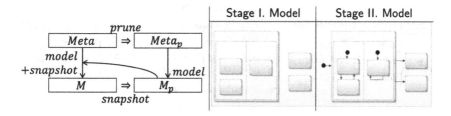

Fig. 3. Metamodel pruning with overapproximation

3.1 Metamodel Pruning

Metamodel pruning [13,33] takes a metamodel *Meta* as input and derives a simplified (pruned) metamodel *Meta$_P$* as output by removing some *EClasses*, *EReferences* and *EAttributes*. When removing a class from a metamodel, we need to remove all subclasses, all attributes and incoming or outgoing references to obtain a consistent pruned metamodel. Formally, we may iteratively remove certain predicates from *Meta* by pruning as follows:

- **EReference**: if $R(S,T) \in Meta$ then $R(S,T) \notin Meta_P$;
- **EAttributes**: if $A(C,V) \in Meta$ then $A(C,V) \notin Meta_P$;
- **EClasses**: if $C \in Meta$ and $sub(C,Sub) \notin Meta_P$ and $A(C,V) \notin Meta_P$ and $R(C,T) \notin Meta_P$ and $R(S,C) \notin Meta_P$ then $C \notin Meta_P$;

Example. We prune our statechart metamodel in two phases (see the slices in Fig. 2): classes Trigger, Guard and Action are omitted together with incoming references (Stage II), and then classes Transition, Pseudostate, Entry and Synchronization are removed (Stage I).

By using metamodel pruning, we first aim to generate valid instance models for the pruned metamodel and then extend them to valid instance models of the original larger metamodel. For that purpose, we exploit a property we call the *overapproximation property of metamodel pruning* (see Fig. 3), which ensures that if there exist a valid instance model M for a metamodel *Meta* (formally, $M \models Meta$) then there exists a valid instance model M_P for the pruned metamodel *Meta$_P$* (formally, $M_P \models Meta_P$) such that M_P is a partial snapshot of M ($M_P \subseteq M$). Consequently, if a model generation problem is unsatisfiable for the pruned metamodel, then it remains unsatisfiable for the larger metamodel. However, we may derive a pruned instance model M_P which cannot be completed in the full metamodel *Meta*, which is called a *false positive*.

Example. The statechart model in the middle of Fig. 3 corresponds to the pruned metamodel after Stage II. In our example, it can be extended by adding transitions and entry states to the model illustrated in the right side of Fig. 3, which now corresponds to the pruned metamodel of Stage I.

$$R(x)^O = \begin{cases} R(x) & \text{if } R \in Meta_P \\ true & \text{else} \end{cases}$$

$$R(x)^U = \begin{cases} R(x) & \text{if } R \in Meta_P \\ false & \text{else} \end{cases}$$

$$(\neg \Phi)^O = \neg(\Phi^U)$$
$$(\neg \Phi)^U = \neg(\Phi^O)$$
$$(\Phi_1 \wedge \Phi_2)^O = \Phi_1{}^O \wedge \Phi_2{}^O$$
$$(\Phi_1 \wedge \Phi_2)^U = \Phi_1{}^U \wedge \Phi_2{}^U$$
$$(\Phi_1 \vee \Phi_2)^O = \Phi_1{}^O \vee \Phi_2{}^O$$
$$(\Phi_1 \vee \Phi_2)^U = \Phi_1{}^U \vee \Phi_2{}^U$$

$$(\exists : \Phi(x))^O = \exists : \Phi(x)^O$$
$$(\exists : \Phi(x))^U = \exists : \Phi(x)^U$$
$$(\forall x : \Phi(x))^O = \forall x : \Phi(x)^O$$
$$(\forall x : \Phi(x))^U = \forall x : \Phi(x)^U$$

Fig. 4. Constraint pruning and approximation

3.2 Constraint Pruning and Approximation

When removing certain metamodel elements by pruning, related structural constraints (such as multiplicity, inverse, etc.) can be automatically removed, which trivially fulfills the overapproximation property. However, the treatment of additional well- formedness constraints needs special care since simple automated removal would significantly increase the rate of false positives in a later phase of model generation to such an extent that no intermediate models can be extended to a valid final model.

Based on some first-order logic representation of the constraints (derived e.g. in accordance with [32]), we propose to maintain approximated versions of constraint sets during metamodel pruning. In order to investigate the interrelations of constraints, we assume that logical consequences of a constraint set can be derived manually by experts or automatically by theorem provers [21]. The actual derivation approach falls outside the scope of the current paper. Given a DSL specification with a metamodel $Meta$ and a set of WF constraints $WF = \{\Phi_1, \ldots, \Phi_n\}$, let Φ be a formula derived as a theorem $WF \vdash \Phi$.

Now an *overapproximation* of formula Φ over metamodel $Meta$ for a pruned metamodel $Meta_P$ is a formula Φ_P such that (1) $\Phi \Rightarrow \Phi_P$, (2) Φ_P contains symbols only from $Meta_P$. The details of approximation are illustrated in Fig. 4 where R denotes a relation symbol derived for class or reference predicates in accordance with the metamodel. While more precise approximations can possibly be defined in the future, the current approximation is logically correct as if a model generation problem is unsatisfiable for an approximated set of constraints (over the pruned metamodel) then it remains unsatisfiable for the original set of constraints.

Example. Based on the set of WF constraints $\{\Phi_1, \Phi_2, \Phi_3, \Phi_4, \Phi_5\}$ defined in Sect. 2.2, a prover can derive the following formula as a theorem over the metamodel of Stage II: $\Phi_{syncout} \vee \Phi_{syncin}$, where $\Phi_1, \Phi_5 \models \Phi_{syncout} \vee \Phi_{syncin}$. The generated theorem $\Phi_{syncout}$ (and Φ_{syncin}) restricts the number of outgoing (ingoing) transitions from (to) a synchronization as follows:

$$\Phi_{syncout} = \forall syn \exists t_1, t_2, s_1, r_1, r_2, p : \mathsf{Synchron}(syn) \Rightarrow$$
$$(\mathsf{outgoing}(syn, t_1) \wedge \mathsf{target}(t_1, s_1) \wedge \mathsf{outgoing}(syn, t_2) \wedge \mathsf{target}(t_2, s_2) \wedge s_1 \neq s_2 \wedge$$
$$\mathsf{vertices}(r_1, s_1) \wedge \mathsf{vertices}(r2, s2) \wedge r_1 \neq r_2 \wedge \mathsf{regions}(p, r1) \wedge \mathsf{regions}(p, r2))$$

The variables and relations approximated in this phase are underlined: in Stage I the generation is restricted to the model by omitting transitions. The result of overapproximation states that if a model contains a synchronization, then needs to contain at least two regions:

$$\Phi^O_{syncout} \vee \Phi^O_{syncin} = \forall syn \exists s_1, r_1, r_2, p : \mathsf{Synchron}(syn) \Rightarrow$$
$$(s_1 \neq s_2 \wedge \mathsf{vertices}(r_1, s_1) \wedge \mathsf{vertices}(r2, s2) \wedge r_1 \neq r_2 \wedge \mathsf{regions}(p, r1) \wedge \mathsf{regions}(p, r2))$$

Applying the approximation rules of Fig. 4 directly on $\{\Phi_1, \Phi_5\}$ would lead to $\Phi^O_1 : true$ and $\Phi^O_5 : true$. These constraints are too coarse overapproximations providing no useful information to the model generator at this phase.

3.3   Incremental Model Generation by Iterative Solver Calls

By using metamodel pruning, we first aim to generate valid instance models for the pruned metamodel, which is a simplified problem for the underlying logic solver. Instance models of increasing size will be gradually generated by using valid models of the pruned metamodel as partial snapshots (i.e. initial seeds) for generating instances for a larger metamodel. Therefore, an incremental model generation task is also given with a target size s and a target metamodel $Meta$, but with an additional partial snapshot M_P. M_P is a valid instance of pruned metamodel $Meta_P$. M_P has s_P number of objects ($s_P \leq s$).

From a logic perspective, the partial snapshot defines a partial interpretation of relations for model generation, which may simplify the task of the solver compared to using fully uninterpreted relations. In order to exploit this additional information, the relations in the logic problem are partitioned into two sets of interpreted and uninterpreted symbols. $objects_P = \{o_1, \ldots, o_{s_P}\}$ are the objects in the partial snapshot. The extra objects to be generated in this step are denoted by $objects_N = \{o_{s_P+1}, \ldots, o_s\}$. The relations are partitioned according to the following rules:

- **Classes (CLS)**: Each class predicate $\mathsf{C}(o)$ in $Meta$ is separated into two: a fully interpreted $C_O(o)$ predicate for the objects in the partial snapshot $objects_P$, and an uninterpreted $C_N(o)$ for the newly generated objects $objects_N$. Therefore an object o is instance of a class C in the generated model if $C_O(o) \vee C_N(o)$ is satisfied. If the class is not in the pruned metamodel ($C \notin Meta_P$) then $C_O(o)$ is to be omitted, and if no new elements are created from a class then $C_N(o)$ can be omitted.
- **References (REF)**: Each reference predicate $\mathsf{R}(o, t)$ is separated into four categories: a fully interpreted $R_{OO}(o, t)$ between the objects of the partial snapshot ($objects_P$), an uninterpreted $R_{NN}(o, t)$ between the objects of the newly created objects ($objects_N$), and two additional uninterpreted relations $R_{ON}(o, t)$ and $R_{NO}(o, t)$ connecting the elements of the partial snapshot with the newly created elements (relations over $objects_O \times objects_N$ and $objects_N \times objects_O$ respectively). Therefore a reference $R(o, t)$ exists in the generated model if $R_{OO}(o, t) \vee R_{NN}(o, t) \vee R_{NO}(o, t) \vee R_{ON}(o, t)$. If the relation is not in the pruned metamodel ($R \notin Meta_P$) then $R_{OO}(o, t)$ can be omitted, and

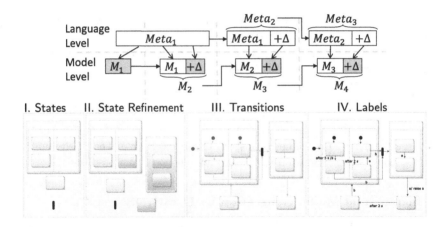

Fig. 5. Model generation iterations

if no new elements are created from a class then $R_{NN}(o,t)$, $R_{NO}(o,t)$ and $R_{ON}(o,t)$ can also be omitted.

– **Attributes (ATT)**: Attribute predicates are separated into a fully interpreted $A_O(o,v)$ for the objects in the partial snapshots $objects_P$, and an uninterpreted relation $A_N(o,v)$ for the newly created elements $objects_N$. An object o has an attribute value v $(A(o,v))$ if $A_O(o,v) \vee A_N(o,v)$. Attribute predicates are treated as reference predicates for omission.

The level of incrementality is still unfortunately limited from an important aspect. The background solvers typically provide no direct control over the simultaneous creation of new elements, i.e. we cannot provide domain- specific hints to the solver when the creation of an object always depends on the creation or existence of another object. This can still cause issues when a multitude of WF constraints are defined.

Example. In our running example, the instance models are generated in four steps, which is illustrated in Fig. 5. First, initial seeds are generated for the state hierarchy (M_1 over $Meta_1$), which are extended in the second step to model M_2 with the same metamodel elements. Then the metamodel is extended to $Meta_2$, and the transitions and the initial states are added to model M_3. Finally, triggers, guards and actions can be added to the model to obtain M_4.

4   Measurements

In order to assess the effectiveness of incremental model generation using constraint approximation for synthesizing well-formed instance models for domain-specific languages, we conducted some initial experiments using the Alloy Analyzer as background solver. We were interested in the following questions:

- Is incremental model generation with metamodel pruning and constraint approximation effective in increasing the size of models, the success rate or decreasing the runtime of the solver?
- Is incremental model generation still effective if metamodel pruning or constraint approximation is excluded?

Configurations. We conducted measurements on two versions of the Yakindu statechart metamodel: Phase 1 and Phase 2 (see Fig. 2). The pruned metamodel of Phase 1 (*MM1*) contains 8 classes and 2 references, and no well- formedness constraints by default. The metamodel of Phase 2 (*MM2*) contains 10 classes, 4 references and 8 constraints (including the 5 WF constraints listed in the paper and 3 more for restricting entry states).

- As a **base** configuration, the Alloy Analyzer is executed separately for the two problems with 1 min timeout. We record two cases: the largest model derived and a slightly larger model size where timeout was observed.
- Next, we run the solver incrementally with an initial model of size N and an increment of size K denoted as $N + K$ in Fig. 6 **without constraint approximation** but with metamodel pruning. Moreover, instance models derived for Phase 1 are used as partial snapshots for Phase 2.
- Then we run the solver incrementally with constraint approximation but **without metamodel pruning**. For that purpose, the constraint set for Phase 1 contains two approximated constraints: (1) Each region has a state where the entry state will point, and (2) There are orthogonal states in the model. Again, instance models derived for Phase 1 are used as partial snapshots for Phase 2, but the full metamodel is considered in Phase 2.
- Finally we configure the solver for **full** incrementally with constraint approximation and metamodel pruning by reusing instances of Phase 1 as partial snapshots in Phase 2.

Measurement Setup. Each model generation task was executed on the DSL presented in this paper 5 times using the Alloy Analyzer (with SAT4j- solver), then the median of the execution times was calculated. The measures are executed with one minute timeout on an average personal computer[1]. We measure the *runtime* of model generation, the *model size* denoting the maximal number of elements the derived model may contain, and the *success rate* denoting the percentage of cases when a well-formed model was derived, which satisfies all WF constraints within the given search scope.

Measurement Results. Results of our measurements are summarized in Fig. 6. We summarize our observations below.

---

[1] CPU: Intel Core-i5-m310M, MEM: 16GB but the back-end solver can use 4GB only, OS: Windows 10 Pro, Reasoner: Alloy Analyzer 4.2 with sat4j.

				MM1			MM2	
			#CLS:X	#REF:Y	#WF:Z	#CLS:X	#REF:Y	#WF:Z
			8	2	0 + 2	10	4	8
	Incre-mental	MM Pruning	Constraint Approx	Runtime (ms)	Model size (#)	Success rate (%)	Runtime (ms)	Model size (#)	Success rate (%)
Base	No	No	No	18349	60	100%	39040	12	0%
				Timeout	70	N/A	Timeout	16	N/A
W/o Prune	Yes	No	Yes	7327 + 11176	50+50	100%	Timeout	16	N/A
W/o Approx	Yes	Yes	No	12600+34804	50+50	100%	230 + 183465	20+30	0%
Full	Yes	Yes	Yes	7327 + 11176	50+50	100%	1644 + 44362	20+30	100%

Fig. 6. Measurement results

- **Base.** For *MM1*, Alloy was able to generate models with up to 60 objects. As there are no constraints at this level, many synchronizations are created (about half of the objects were synchronization and with only 5–10 states). Over 60 objects, the runtime grows rapidly as the SAT solver runs out of the maximal 4 GB memory. For *MM2*, Alloy was unable to create any models that satisfies all of the constraints as the search scope turned out to be too small to create valid models with synchronizations.

- **W/o Approx.** Alloy was able to generate models with 100 elements in two steps where each iterative step had comparable runtime. However, since no constraints are considered for *MM1*, Alloyed failed to extend partial snapshots of *MM1* to well-formed models for *MM2* (success rate: 0 %, although for this specific case, we executed over 100 runs of the solver due to the unexpectedly low success rate). Furthermore, we had to reduce the scope of search to 20 and 30 new elements with types taken from *MM2* \ *MM1* due to timeouts.

- **W/o Prune.** When metamodel pruning was excluded but approximated constraints were included for *MM1*, model generation succeeded for 100 elements, but extending them to models of *MM2* failed (as in this case, new elements could take any elements from *MM2*)

- **Full.** With incremental model generation by combining metamodel pruning and constraint approximation, we were able to generate well-formed models for both *MM1* and *MM2*, which was the only successful case for the latter.

Analysis of Results. While we used a reasonably sized statechart meta-model extracted from a real modeling tool (including everything to model state machines, but excluding imports and namespacing), we avoid drawing generic conclusions for the exact scalability of our results. Instead, we summarize some negative results which are hardly specific to the chosen example:

- Mapping a model generation problem to Alloy and running the Alloy Analyzer in itself will likely fail to derive useful results for practical metamodels, especially, in the presence of complex well-formedness constraints. Our observation is that many objects need to be created at the same time in consistent way, which cannot be efficiently handled by the underlying solver (either the scope is too small or out-of-memory). Altogether, the Alloy Analyzer was more effective in finding consistent model instance than proving that a problem is inconsistent, thus there are no solutions.

Table 1. Comparison of related approaches

		Logic Solvers	Uncertain Models	Rule-Based Generators	Iterative Solver Call
Inputs	Partial Snapshot	+	++	-	+
	Effective Metamodel	-	-	+	+
	Local Constraints	+	-	+	+
	Global Constraints	+	-	-	+
Outputs	Metamodel-compliant	+	+	+	+
	Well-formed	+	-	-	+
	Diverse	-	-	+	?
	Scalable	-	-	++	+/-
	Decidability	-	+	+	- (graceful degradation)

- An incremental approach with metamodel pruning but without constraint approximation will increase the overall size of the derived models, but the false positive rate would quickly increase.
- An incremental approach without metamodel pruning but with constraint approximation will likely have the same pitfalls as the original Alloy case: either the scope of search will become insufficient, or we run out of memory.
- Combining incremental model generation with metamodel pruning and constraint approximation is promising as a concept as it significantly improved wrt. the baseline case. But the underlying solver was still not sufficiently powerful to guarantee scalability for complex industrial cases.

5   Related Work

We compared our solution with existing model generation techniques with respect to the characteristics of *inputs* and *output results* in Table 1. As for *inputs*, the model generation can be (1) initiated from a *partial snapshot*, (2) focused on an *effective metamodel*. Additionally, an approach may support (3) *local* and (4) *global constraints* well-formedness constraints: a local constraint accesses only the attributes and the outgoing references of an object, while a global constraint specifies a complex structural pattern. Local constraints are frequently attached to objects (e.g. in UML class diagrams), while global constraints are widely used in domain-specific modeling languages. As *outputs*, the generated models may (i) be metamodel-compliant (ii) satisfy all *well-formedness* constraints of the language. When generated models are intended to be used as test cases, some approaches may guarantee a certain level of coverage or (iii) *diversity*. We consider a technique (iv) *scalable* if there is no hard limit on the model size (as demonstrated in the respective papers). Finally, a model generation approach may be (v) *decidable* which always terminates with a result. Our comparison excludes approaches like which do not guarantee metamodel-compliance of generated instance models.

Logic Solver Approaches. Several approaches map a model generation problem (captured by a metamodel, partial snapshots, and a set of WF constraints) into a logic problem, which are solved by underlying SAT/SMT-solvers. Complete frameworks with standalone specification languages include Formula [17] (which uses Z3 SMT- solver [26]), Alloy [16] (which relies on SAT solvers like Sat4j [23]) and Clafer [2] (using backend reasoners like Alloy).

There are several approaches aiming to validate standardized engineering models enriched with OCL constraints [14] by relying upon different back-end logic-based approaches such as constraint logic programming [6,8,9], SAT-based model finders (like Alloy) [1,7,22,34,35], first-order logic [3], constructive query containment [28], higher-order logic [5,15], or rewriting logics [10].

Partial snapshots and WF constraints can be uniformly represented as constraints [32], but metamodel pruning is not typical. Growing models are supported in [19] for a limited set of constraints. Scalability of all these approaches are limited to small models / counter-examples. Furthermore, these approaches are either a priori bounded (where the search space needs to be restricted explicitly) or they have decidability issues.

The main difference of our current approach is its *iterative derivation of models* and the *approximative handling of metamodels and constraints*. However, our approach is independent from the actual mapping of constraints to logic formulae, thus it could potentially be integrated with most of the above techniques.

Uncertain Models. Partial models are also similarity to uncertain models, which offer a rich specification language [12,29] amenable to analysis. Uncertain models provide a more expressive language compared to partial snapshots but without handling additional WF constraints. Such models document semantic variation points generically by annotations on a regular instance model, which are gradually resolved during the generation of concrete models. An uncertain model is more complex (or informative) than a concrete one, thus an a priori upper bound exists for the derivation, which is not an assumption in our case.

Potential concrete models compliant with an uncertain model can synthesized by the Alloy Analyzer [31], or refined by graph transformation rules [30]. Each concrete model is derived in a single step, thus their approach is not iterative like ours. Scalability analysis is omitted from the respective papers, but refinement of uncertain models is always decidable.

Rule-based Instance Generators. A different class of model generators relies on rule-based synthesis driven by randomized, statistical or metamodel coverage information for testing purposes [4,13]. Some approaches support the calculation of effective metamodels [33], but partial snapshots are excluded from input specifications. Moreover, WF constraints are restricted to local constraints evaluated on individual objects while global constraints of a DSL are not supported. On the positive side, these approaches guarantee the diversity of models and scale well in practice.

Iterative Approaches. An iterative approach is proposed *specifically for allocation problems* in [20] based on Formula. Models are generated in two steps to increase diversity of results. First, non-isomorphic submodels are created only from an effective metamodel fragment. Diversity between submodels is achieved by a problem-specific symmetry-breaking predicate [11] which ensures that no isomorphic model is generated twice. In the second step the algorithm completes the different submodels according to the full model, but constraints are only checked at the very final stage. This is a key difference in our approach where an approximation of constraints is checked at each step, which reduces the number of inconsistent intermediate models. An iterative, counter-example guided synthesis is proposed for higher-order logic formulae in [24], but the size of derived models is fixed.

6   Conclusion and Future Work

The validation of DSL tools frequently necessitates the synthesis of well-formed *and* realistic instance models, which satisfy the language specification. In the paper, we proposed an incremental model generation approach which (1) iteratively calls black- box logic solvers to guarantee well-formedness by (2) feeding instance models obtained in a previous step as partial snapshots (compulsory model fragments) to a subsequent phase to limit the number of new elements, and using (3) various approximations of metamodels and constraints. Our initial experiments show that significantly larger model instances can be generated with the same solvers using such an incremental approach especially in the presence of complex well-formedness constraints.

However, part of our experimental results are negative in the sense that the proposed iterative approach is still not scalable to derive large model instances of complex industrial languages due to restrictions of the underlying Alloy Analyzer and the SAT solver libraries. We believe that dedicated decision procedures and heuristics for graph models would be beneficial in the long run to improve the performance of model generation.

As future work, we aim to generate a structurally diverse set of test cases by enumerating different possible extensions of a partial snapshot in each iteration step. Additionally, we plan to check other underlying solvers and further approximations and strategies for deriving relevant formulae as logical consequences of constraints. And finally, we will investigate if the metamodel partitions and the iteration steps can be automatically created, thus creating a (semi-)automated process with improved DSL-specific heuristics.

References

1. Anastasakis, K., Bordbar, B., Georg, G., Ray, I.: On challenges of model transformation from UML to alloy. Soft. Syst. Model. 9(1), 69–86 (2010)
2. Bak, K., Diskin, Z., Antkiewicz, M., Czarnecki, K., Wasowski, A.: Clafer: unifying class and feature modeling. Softw. Syst. Model., pp. 1–35 (2013)

3. Beckert, B., Keller, U., Schmitt, P.H.: Translating the object constraint language into first-order predicate logic. In: Proceedings of the VERIFY, Workshop at Federated Logic Conferences (FLoC), Copenhagen, Denmark (2002)
4. Brottier, E., Fleurey, F., Steel, J., Baudry, B., Le Traon, Y.: Metamodel-based test generation for model transformations: an algorithm and a tool. In: 17th International Symposium on Software Reliability Engineering, ISSRE 2006, pp. 85–94, November 2006
5. Brucker, A.D., Wolff, B.: The HOL-OCL tool (2007). http://www.brucker.ch/
6. Büttner, F., Cabot, J.: Lightweight string reasoning for OCL. In: Vallecillo, A., Tolvanen, J.-P., Kindler, E., Störrle, H., Kolovos, D. (eds.) ECMFA 2012. LNCS, vol. 7349, pp. 244–258. Springer, Heidelberg (2012)
7. Büttner, F., Egea, M., Cabot, J., Gogolla, M.: Verification of ATL transformations using transformation models and model finders. In: Aoki, T., Taguchi, K. (eds.) ICFEM 2012. LNCS, vol. 7635, pp. 198–213. Springer, Heidelberg (2012)
8. Cabot, J., Clariso, R., Riera, D.: Verification of UML/OCL class diagrams using constraint programming. In: IEEE International Conference on Software Testing Verification and Validation Workshopp, ICSTW 2008, pp. 73–80, April 2008
9. Cabot, J., Clarisó, R., Riera, D.: UMLtoCSP: a tool for the formal verification of UML/OCL models using constraint programming. In: Proceedings of the 22nd IEEE/ACM International Conference on Automated Software Engineering (ASE 2007), pp. 547–548. NY, USA. ACM, New York (2007)
10. Clavel, M., Egea, M.: The ITP/OCL tool (2008). http://maude.sip.ucm.es/itp/ocl/
11. Crawford, J., Ginsberg, M., Luks, E., Roy, A.: Symmetry-breaking predicates for search problems. In: KR 1996, pp. 148–159 (1996)
12. Famelis, M., Salay, R., Chechik, M.: Partial models: Towards modeling and reasoning with uncertainty. In: Proceedings of the 34th International Conference on Software Engineering, pp. 573–583. IEEE Press, Piscataway, NJ, USA (2012)
13. Fleurey, F., Steel, J., Baudry, B.: Validation in model-driven engineering: Testing model transformations. In: International Workshop on Model, Design and Validation, pp. 29–40, November 2004
14. Gogolla, M., Bohling, J., Richters, M.: Validating UML and OCL models in USE by automatic snapshot generation. Softw. Syst. Model. **4**, 386–398 (2005)
15. Grönniger, H., Ringert, J.O., Rumpe, B.: System model-based definition of modeling language semantics. In: Lee, D., Lopes, A., Poetzsch-Heffter, A. (eds.) FMOODS 2009. LNCS, vol. 5522, pp. 152–166. Springer, Heidelberg (2009)
16. Jackson, D.: Alloy: a lightweight object modelling notation. ACM Trans. Softw. Eng. Methodol. **11**(2), 256–290 (2002)
17. Jackson, E.K., Levendovszky, T., Balasubramanian, D.: Reasoning about metamodeling with formal specifications and automatic proofs. In: Whittle, J., Clark, T., Kühne, T. (eds.) MODELS 2011. LNCS, vol. 6981, pp. 653–667. Springer, Heidelberg (2011)
18. Jackson, E.K., Sztipanovits, J.: Towards a formal foundation for domain specific modeling languages. In: Proceedings of the 6th ACM / IEEE International Conference on Embedded Software, EMSOFT 2006, pp. 53–62, NY, USA. ACM, New York (2006)
19. Jackson, E.K., Sztipanovits, J.: Constructive techniques for meta- and model-level reasoning. In: Engels, G., Opdyke, B., Schmidt, D.C., Weil, F. (eds.) MODELS 2007. LNCS, vol. 4735, pp. 405–419. Springer, Heidelberg (2007)

20. Kang, E., Jackson, E., Schulte, W.: An approach for effective design space exploration. In: Calinescu, R., Jackson, E. (eds.) Monterey Workshop 2010. LNCS, vol. 6662, pp. 33–54. Springer, Heidelberg (2011)
21. Kovács, L., Voronkov, A.: Interpolation and symbol elimination. In: Schmidt, R.A. (ed.) CADE-22. LNCS, vol. 5663, pp. 199–213. Springer, Heidelberg (2009)
22. Kuhlmann, M., Hamann, L., Gogolla, M.: Extensive validation of OCL models by integrating SAT solving into USE. In: Bishop, J., Vallecillo, A. (eds.) TOOLS 2011. LNCS, vol. 6705, pp. 290–306. Springer, Heidelberg (2011)
23. Le Berre, D., Parrain, A.: The sat4j library, release 2.2. J. Satisf. Boolean Model. Comput. **7**, 59–64 (2010)
24. Milicevic, A., Near, J.P., Kang, E., Jackson, D.: Alloy*: A general-purpose higher-order relational constraint solver. In: 37th IEEE/ACM International Conference on Software Engineering, ICSE, pp. 609–619 (2015)
25. Mougenot, A., Darrasse, A., Blanc, X., Soria, M.: Uniform random generation of huge metamodel instances. In: Paige, R.F., Hartman, A., Rensink, A. (eds.) ECMDA-FA 2009. LNCS, vol. 5562, pp. 130–145. Springer, Heidelberg (2009)
26. de Moura, L., Bjørner, N.S.: Z3: An efficient SMT solver. In: Ramakrishnan, C.R., Rehof, J. (eds.) TACAS 2008. LNCS, vol. 4963, pp. 337–340. Springer, Heidelberg (2008)
27. The Object Management Group: Object Constraint Language, v2.0., May 2006
28. Queralt, A., Artale, A., Calvanese, D., Teniente, E.: OCL-Lite: Finite reasoning on UML/OCL conceptual schemas. Data Knowl. Eng. **73**, 1–22 (2012)
29. Salay, R., Chechik, M.: A generalized formal framework for partial modeling. In: Egyed, A., Schaefer, I. (eds.) FASE 2015. LNCS, vol. 9033, pp. 133–148. Springer, Heidelberg (2015)
30. Salay, R., Chechik, M., Famelis, M., Gorzny, J.: A methodology for verifying refinements of partial models. J. Object Technol. **14**(3), 1–3–1–31 (2015)
31. Salay, R., Famelis, M., Chechik, M.: Language independent refinement using partial modeling. In: de Lara, J., Zisman, A. (eds.) Fundamental Approaches to Software Engineering. LNCS, vol. 7212, pp. 224–239. Springer, Heidelberg (2012)
32. Semeráth, O., Barta, A., Horváth, A., Szatmári, Z., Varró, D.: Formal validation of domain-specific languages with derived features and well-formedness constraints. Softw. Syst. Model., pp. 1–36 (2015)
33. Sen, S., Moha, N., Baudry, B., Jézéquel, J.-M.: Meta-model pruning. In: Schürr, A., Selic, B. (eds.) MODELS 2009. LNCS, vol. 5795, pp. 32–46. Springer, Heidelberg (2009)
34. Shah, S.M.A., Anastasakis, K., Bordbar, B.: From UML to Alloy and back again. In: MoDeVVa 2009: Proceedings of the 6th International Workshop on Model-Driven Engineering, Verification and Validation, pp. 1–10. ACM (2009)
35. Soeken, M., Wille, R., Kuhlmann, M., Gogolla, M., Drechsler, R.: Verifying UML/OCL models using boolean satisfiability. In: Design, Automation and Test in Europe, (DATE 2010), pp. 1341–1344. IEEE (2010)
36. Varró, D., Balogh, A.: The model transformation language of the VIATRA2 framework. Sci. Comput. Program. **68**(3), 214–234 (2007)
37. Yakindu Statechart Tools: Yakindu. http://statecharts.org/

Automated Model Merge by Design Space Exploration

Csaba Debreceni[1]([⊠]), István Ráth[1], Dániel Varró[1], Xabier De Carlos[2],
Xabier Mendialdua[2], and Salvador Trujillo[2]

[1] Department of Measurement and Information Systems,
Budapest University of Technology and Economics,
Magyar tudósok krt. 2, Budapest 1117, Hungary
{debreceni,rath,varro}@mit.bme.hu
[2] IK4-IKERLAN Research Center,
P.J.M. Arizmendiarrieta, 2, 20500 Arrasate, Spain
{xdecarlos,xmendialdua,strujillo}@ikerlan.es

Abstract. Industrial applications of model-driven engineering to develop large and complex systems resulted in an increasing demand for collaboration features. However, use cases such as model differencing and merging have turned out to be a difficult challenge, due to (i) the graph-like nature of models, and (ii) the complexity of certain operations (e.g. hierarchy refactoring) that are common today. In the paper, we present a novel search-based automated model merge approach where rule-based design space exploration is used to search the space of solution candidates that represent conflict-free merged models. Our method also allows engineers to easily incorporate domain-specific knowledge into the merge process to provide better solutions. The merge process automatically calculates multiple merge candidates to be presented to domain experts for final selection. Furthermore, we propose to adopt a generic synthetic benchmark to carry out an initial scalability assessment for model merge with large models and large change sets.

1 Introduction

Scalable collaborative model-driven engineering (MDE) for complex projects with multiple stakeholders and development groups working in a distributed way (both geographically and in time) is a major research challenge [21]. In traditional software engineering, version control systems (VCS) such as SVN or Git assist to work with textual documents in *off-line collaboration scenarios* having long transactions and complex modifications between commits. Since multiple collaborators may try to commit changes to the same document, a *comparison* or difference is calculated prior to local commit, which may cause *conflicts* between remote changes (already published to the server) and local changes (aimed to be

This paper is partially supported by the EU Commission with project MONDO (FP7-ICT-2013-10, #611125) and the MTA-BME Lendület 2015 Research Group on Cyber-Physical Systems.

© Springer-Verlag Berlin Heidelberg 2016
P. Stevens and A. Wąsowski (Eds.): FASE 2016, LNCS 9633, pp. 104–121, 2016.
DOI: 10.1007/978-3-662-49665-7_7

committed now). Such conflicts need to be resolved by *merging* the remote and local changes in a consistent way before a commit succeeds.

Unfortunately, the direct use of VCS in MDE is hindered by numerous factors implied by the differences between graph-based documents (e.g. models) and textual documents (e.g. source code). A major challenge is related to model comparison, which is also computationally more expensive over graphs, and it gave birth to advanced industrial strength frameworks like EMF Compare [1] or Diff/Merge [2] built into model-level version control systems (like in Papyrus UML or AMOR [5]). In order to achieve scalability for large models, these frameworks frequently assume that unique identifiers are available for model elements. That assumption results in more efficient model comparison algorithms.

While model comparison is computationally more challenging, resolving conflicting model changes is still a cumbersome task in practice, which is frequently performed manually by the engineers. EMF Compare and Diff/Merge enable automated conflict resolution in a programmatic way — but writing code for an automated merge is hardly a task for a domain expert. Furthermore, domain-specific conflict resolution strategies are rarely taken into consideration in industrial frameworks, hence the well-formedness of merge results is questionable.

In this paper, we propose a novel automated search-based model merge technique [20] which builds on off-the-shelf tools for the model comparison step, but uses guided rule-based design space exploration (DSE) [18] for merging models. In general, rule-based DSE aims to search and identify various design candidates to fulfill certain structural and numeric constraints. The exploration starts from an initial model and systematically traverses paths by applying operators. In our context, the results of model comparison will be the initial model, while target design candidates will represent the conflict-free merged models.

While many existing model merge approaches detect conflicts statically in a preprocessing phase, our DSE technique carries out *conflict detection dynamically* during exploration time as conflicting rule activations and constraint violations. Then *multiple consistent resolutions of conflicts* are presented to the domain experts. Our technique allows to incorporate domain-specific knowledge into the merge process by additional constraints, goals and operations to provide better solutions. Finally, we propose to adapt a generic scalability benchmark for assessing model merge performance for large models and large change sets, which is also an innovative aspect of the paper.

The rest of the paper is structured as follows: A motivating case study of modeling wind turbine control systems is presented in Sect. 2 together with the basics of model comparison and merge. A high-level overview of our approach is provided in Sect. 3. A detailed explanation of executing a merge process is discussed in Sect. 4. The case study will also serve as an initial assessment of the usefulness of a domain-specific merge technique while scalability evaluation will be carried out by adapting the Train Benchmark [29] in Sect. 5. Related work is summarized in Sect. 6 while Sect. 7 concludes our paper.

2   Preliminaries

2.1   From Model Comparison to Model Merge

Model comparison refers to identifying the differences between models. It requires reliability, precision and completeness as the merge process frequently relies on the output of this phase to detect conflicts and to resolve the detected conflicts. Altmanninger et al. [6] classifies model comparison methods based on the kind of information available. Only models are provided as input for *state-based* techniques, while *change-based* comparison relies on a list of the performed changes, e.g. $op_1, op_2, \ldots op_n$.

Based on the results of model comparison, *model merge* synthesizes a combined model which reconciles the identified differences. This is not always possible due to conflicts between model changes carried out by different collaborators. A merged model is called *syntactically correct* if it corresponds to its metamodel, and *consistent* when additional constraints of the domain are satisfied.

We use a simplified difference model derived from the EMF Compare tool [1] to store the changes in EMF models. This allows us to accept different types of comparison model (e.g. EMF Compare or Diff/Merge [2]) as an input of model merge. It contains the following default change types: (1) *create* or *delete* an object; (2) set, add or remove a value or an object to/from an *attribute* or a *reference*, respectively. Furthermore, we annotate the *priority* of changes as *may* or *must* which will be decided by users. Changes with *must* priority are mandatory to be involved in the solutions while the others with *may* priority can be omitted.

In the paper, we focus on *three-way merge*, which also uses the common ancestor O of local copy L and remote copy R to derive the merged model M. To determine the changes executed on O, a comparison is conducted between $O \leftrightarrow L$ and $O \leftrightarrow R$. The solution of merge M is obtained by applying a combination of changes performed either on L or R to the original model O.

2.2   A Motivating Model Merge Scenario

The domain of our motivating example describes *Wind Turbine Control Systems (WTCS)* developed by *IK4-Ikerlan* where different artefacts and algorithms for controlling a wind turbine are specified and connected to sensors and actuators. Models are specified by several collaborators, and consequently modifications could result in merge conflicts.

We introduce a simplified example of a wind turbine (WT1) in Fig. 1. Real models are obviously larger, sample models of this paper contain only artifacts related to the cooling of the Generator Subsystem:

- *Inputs*: Wind turbine WT1 gets data from a temperature sensor specified by the SystemInput identified as Temperature.
- *Outputs*: WT1 acts on two fans for cooling the wind turbine generator specified by the SystemOutputs: Fan1Activator and Fan2Activator.

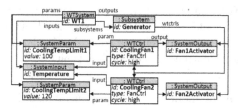

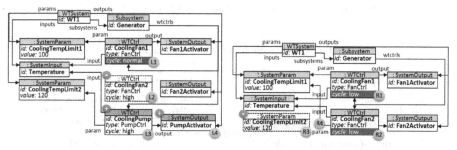

(a) Original model

(b) Local instance (modified by User1)   (c) Remote instance (modified by User2)

Fig. 1. Local and remote changes for 3-way merge

- *Params*: temperature limits for starting generator cooling can be specified by SystemParams: CoolingTempLimit1 and CoolingTempLimit2.

Subsystem Generator contains all the control units for cooling the Generator:

- CoolingFan1: this control unit (of type FanCtrl) specifies the control algorithm for fan #1 with High priority cycle with Temperature as SystemInput, Fan1Activator as SystemOutput, CoolingTempLimit1 as SystemParam.
- CoolingFan2: this control unit (of type FanCtrl) specifies the control algorithm for fan #2 with High priority cycle with Temperature as SystemInput, Fan2Activator as SystemOutput and CoolingTempLimit2 as SystemParam.

As a running example, we investigate the following scenario:

Local Changes. The first expert creates a Local version of the model with the following changes: (L1) the cycle attribute of CoolingFan1 is changed to Normal, (L2) CoolingFan2 instance is deleted. (L3) A new control unit (WTCtrl) is created with CoolingPump id. The new control unit is of type PumpCtrl with High cycle. Its input references the existing Temperature and its param references the existing CoolingTempLimit2. In contrast, (L4) its output references a new SystemOutput instance identified as PumpActivator.

Remote Changes. Another expert also remotely modified and already committed the model (before the first expert working on the local version managed to commit the model) to introduce the following remote changes: (R1) the cycle attribute of CoolingFan1 is changed to Low, (R2) the cycle attribute of CoolingFan2 is changed to Low, (R3) deletes SystemParam instance identified as CoolingTem-pLimit2 and (R4) changes param reference of control unit identified as CoolingFan2 to SystemParam instance identified as CoolingTempLimit1.

Model Comparison. Table 1 shows the result of model comparison between the different versions of the model calculated by using existing tools (using e.g. EMF Compare or Diff/Merge [2]). The differences between the local and the original model is denoted with $\Delta(L, O)$ (or shortly ΔL), while $\Delta(R, O)$ (or ΔR) represents the differences between the remote and the original model.

Table 1. Elements of $\Delta(L)$ and $\Delta(R)$

$\Delta(L,O)$comparison model	$\Delta(R,O)$comparison model
MAY attribute{CoolingFan1,cycle,Normal}	MAY attribute{CoolingFan1,cycle,Low}
MUST delete{CoolingFan2}	MUST attribute{CoolingFan2,cycle,Low}
MUST create{CoolingPump,WTCtrl,WT1,ctrls}	MAY delete{CoolingTempLimit2}
MAY attribute{CoolingPump,type,PumpCtrl}	MAY reference{CoolingFan2,param,
MAY attribute{CoolingPump,cycle,High}	CoolingTempLimit1}
MAY reference{CoolingPump,param,CoolingTempLimit2}	
MUST create{PumpActivator,SystemOutput,WT1,outputs}	
MAY reference{CoolingPump,output,PumpActivator}	

Change Annotation. After the comparison, the local collaborator annotates local changes $L2$, $L3$ and $L4$ and remote change $R2$ as *must* which prescribes that all such changes have to be present in the merged model unless some of them are in a conflict. In such a case, the merged model should contain as many (non-conflicting) *must* changes as possible, while some (conflicting) *must* changes might be omitted from the merged model. All other changes are marked as *may* to denote that the corresponding change may be included in the merged model.

Challenges. The following challenges need to be addressed for our example:

- Calculate *merged models* automatically as a maximal subset of non-conflicting changes from the local and remote change set. When there is a large number of possible combination of changes where some of them are selected from the local and the others from the remote branch, a merged model may be restricted to solutions compliant with *must* and *may* change annotations.
- Use *domain-specific goals and constraints* to restrict merged models to consistent ones (to ensure that all inputs and parameters are referenced by at least one control unit and each output is referenced by different control unit).
- Specify *domain-specific composite operations* to guide the merge process into a consistent solution (e.g. to remove inputs, parameters and outputs not referenced by any control unit).

3   Model Merge by Design Space Exploration: Concepts

3.1   Conceptual Overview

We propose to exploit guided rule-based *design space exploration (DSE)* [18] for automated model merge with an architecture depicted in Fig. 2. Rule-based DSE aims at finding optimal *solutions* from the several *design candidates* which satisfy several structural and numeric constraints, and they are reachable from an initial model along a trajectory by applying a sequence of exploration rules. The input of a rule-based DSE includes (1) the *initial model* used as the start of the exploration; (2) *goals* which need to be satisfied by solutions; (3) the set of *exploration rules*; (4) *constraints* that need to be respected in each exploration state and (5) further *guidance* for the exploration process.

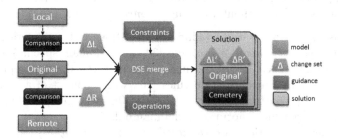

Fig. 2. Architecture of DSE Merge

We applied three-way model merge to a DSE problem as follows:

(1) the **initial model** contains the *original* model O and two *difference models* (ΔL and ΔR)
(2) the main **goal** is that there are no executable changes left in ΔL and ΔR along a specific exploration path.
(3) the **operations** are defined by change driven transformation rules to process generic change objects (*create, delete, set, add, remove*) of the difference models, and potentially composite (domain-specific) operators;
(4) **constraints** may identify inconsistencies and conflicts to eliminate certain trajectories;
(5) as main **exploration strategy**, any changes annotated as *must* are tried to be merged before resolving *may* changes.

Input. Our model merge approach takes three models as input: the original model O and the *difference models* between local and original models ΔL as well as the remote and original models ΔR. These together constitute the initial model for DSE. The calculation of the difference models ΔL and ΔR is carried out by an external comparison tool such as EMF Compare or Diff/Merge. Furthermore, in order to derive efficient state encoding for the exploration process, we assume that each element in the original model has some unique identifier.

Output. The output of the merge process automatically derived by DSE is a *set of solutions* where each solution consists of (i) the merged model M derived by applying a (non-extensible and non-conflicting) subset of local and remote changes on the original model O; (ii) the set of non-executed changes $\Delta L'$, $\Delta R'$; and (iii) the collection of the deleted objects stored in $Cemetery$.

3.2 Key Aspects of Exploration Process

Each solution is derived along a trajectory from the initial state to a solution state by *applying generic and domain-specific operations*. Along this trajectory, we transform the original model O into the merged model M, and the change models ΔL and ΔR are gradually reduced to $\Delta L'$ and $\Delta R'$. In each exploration step, *conflicts are detected and resolved* by incrementally tracking the matches (activations) of operations and constraints. Finally, a solution state is identified if all *goals* are satisfied without violating a *constraint* along the trajectory.

Operations. We incorporate two kinds of operations in the exploration based model merge: *generic merge operations* [30] and (domain-specific) *composite operations* [14,23] (such as refactorings, or repair rules). Each operation is captured by (graph) transformation rules [16], which consist of a *precondition* described as a graph pattern (using the EMF-IncQuery language [10] in our case) and an *action* part which captures model manipulations.

Generic merge operations are *change-driven transformations* [9], which consume or produce change models as additional input or output. The precondition selects an applicable change c from the deltas $\Delta L \cup \Delta R$ and may require the existence of certain model elements in the origin model O. The action part of a generic merge operation (1) modifies the original model O to apply a change, (2) moves the change c from the difference set $\Delta L \cup \Delta R$ into a completed set $Comp$ to prevent the application of the change multiple times. Thus such change-driven rules transform state-based merging into operation-based merging [12].

By default, domain-specific *composite operations* only manipulate the model O without consuming the deltas. Therefore, they need to be complemented with generic change-driven rules which identify the model-level changes carried out by them and record them as difference models in the completed set. In most cases, domain experts are responsible for capturing complex (domain-specific) operations only at the preparation of the merge tool for the specific domain. Collaborating engineers only use them as part of the merge process.

Conflict Detection and Resolution. A local change $l \in \Delta L$ and a remote change $r \in \Delta R$ may be conflicting, i.e. it is impossible to obtain a consistent merged model M by applying both l and r. Alternatively, in an operation-based interpretation, a conflict denotes a pair of operations o_1 and o_2, whereas one operation masks the effect of the other (i.e., they do not commute) or one operation disables the applicability of the other [23].

Instead of static (a priori) detection of conflicts as proposed in [17,24,27], we detect conflicts *on-the-fly* during the exploration process by relying upon the *incremental book-keeping of rule activations and constraints*. In each state of the

DSE, we investigate one by one all (enabled) activations of transformation rules, and try to find a solution by firing them. In case of a conflict, (1) firing one rule may prevent the application of another activation, or (2) both rules are fireable, but the result state violates a constraint. When two operations are confluent (i.e. they can be applied in arbitrary order), state encoding of DSE [19] helps identify that an already traversed state is reached. Hence applying operations in a different order has no impact on the results.

Activations of rules and constraints are continuously and efficiently maintained when firing an operation (either generic or composite), thus disabled rules and violated constraints are immediately identified. For that purpose, we rely upon the reactive VIATRA framework [8] and incremental model queries. The technicalities of conflict detection will be illustrated in Sect. 4.

Conflict Resolution by Exploration Strategy. In case of a conflict between two operations, DSE will investigate both trajectories as possible resolutions and derive two separate solutions correspondingly. Thus a merged model M derived automatically as a solution contains no conflicts by definition.

In case of many conflicts, the result set can too large to be presented to experts. Therefore, in order to reduce the number of solutions retrieved by DSE and guide the exploration in case of conflicts, model changes can be prioritized by the collaborators as *may* and *must* (see Table 1) prior to executing merge.

- If a change c_1 with *must* priority is in conflict with another change c_2 of *may* priority, then the merge will always select the former (c_1).
- If two conflicting changes c_1 and c_2 are both annotated with *may* than the merge will randomly select one.
- However, if two changes c_1 and c_2 of *must* priority are in conflict, then the merge process will enumerate both of them separately (in different solutions).

Goals. In generic, we aim to apply as many changes in ΔL and ΔR as possible to derive the merged model M. When extending a trajectory by any of the remaining changes in $\Delta L'$ or $\Delta R'$ would cause a conflict with some already applied change, a solution state of the DSE is reached. Technically, it is detected by the termination of the rule system, i.e. no operations are activated. Additionally, domain experts can provide domain-specific goals that act as heuristics for the exploration and provide consistent solutions.

Altogether, we define a *fully automated model merge approach* where all possible resolutions of conflicts are calculated, and all consistent merged models are prompted to experts, which was claimed to be beneficial in [31]. Representation of solutions contains several layouts (e.g. tree, graph) and metrics (e.g. number of executed changes) which help experts select the best solution for their purpose.

4   Elaboration of Model Merge on an Example

4.1   Operations and Goals

Change-Driven Rules for Generic Operations. We defined the following generic operations in the merge process for *creating/deleting object,* *setting/adding/removing attribute* and *setting/adding/removing reference*. For space considerations, we only discuss operations for setting an attribute (*setAttribute*) and deleting an object (*deleteObject*) in details (depicted in Fig. 3).

- *setAttribute(ac,o)*: The precondition prescribes that an attribute change *ac* is available in change set $\Delta L' \cup \Delta R'$ and its object *o* exists in the current model. Its action sets (i) attribute *ac.attribute* of object *o* to the given value *ac.value*, and (ii) moves the change *ac* to the completed set *Comp*.
- *deleteObject(dc,o)*: The precondition states that a delete change *dc* is available in the current change set $\Delta L' \cup \Delta R'$ and its referred object *o* exists in the current state of the model where *o* is a leaf in the containment hierarchy. The action part (i) deletes the object *o* from current state, (ii) puts it into *Cemetary* and (iii) moves the change *dc* to the completed set *Comp*.

Domain-Specific Goals and Operations. Our example introduced in Sect. 2 requires to extend model merge with domain-specific knowledge to guarantee the consistency of solutions. In the *Wind Turbine Control System (WTCS)* domain, it is mandatory that all SystemInput and SystemParam instances should be referenced by at least one control unit and each SystemOutput has to be referenced by a unique control unit. Model merge needs to respect such domain specific knowledge, which can be captured by additional goals specified as constraints and depicted in a graphical representation in Fig. 3c.

A domain-specific operation called *unreferencedPart* can be defined to eliminate unreferenced SystemInput, SystemOutput and SystemParam instances (see Fig. 3d). Here the precondition selects the unreferenced object *o* while the action part (i) initiates a new *delete change* independently from the current change set and (ii) executes the action part of the generic *delete* operation.

4.2   Conflict Detection in a Sample Exploration Step

Conflict detection and resolution is carried out during exploration by incrementally tracking rule activations and special constraints. We illustrate this step in the context of our running example (see Fig. 4, which is an extract of *iteration 3 and 9* of merge session from Sect. 4.3). It demonstrates a delete/use conflict: simultaneously setting the cycle attribute of CoolingFan2 and deleting CoolingFan2. Any solution of model merge may only contain one of the two changes.

1. In the beginning, both operations have an activation (left in Fig. 4) in the context of object CoolingFan2. Initially, all changes are located in ΔL or ΔR, cemetery and completed changes are empty. In this state, all constraints are satisfied, but goals are violated which means this state is not a solution.
2. Our merge process first selects and executes the deleteObject operation (top branch of Fig. 4) which removes CoolingFan2 from the model, moves CoolingFan2 to the *cemetery*, and the corresponding change is moved from ΔL to the completed set *Comp*. As a side effect, operation setAttribute loses its activation in the context of CoolingFan2 since its precondition is no longer be satisfied in

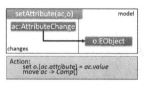

(a) Generic setAttribute

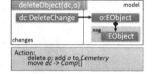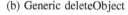

(b) Generic deleteObject

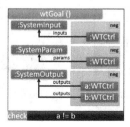

(c) Domain-specific goal

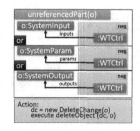

(d) Domain-specific operation

Fig. 3. Operations and goal

the new state. This fact is immediately identified by the underlying reactive transformation engine [8]. In the new state, the exploration incrementally checks that all constraints are satisfied and goals are violated, and then selects another enabled (activated) operation for execution.

3. Later, after backtracking to the first state, operation setAttribute is scheduled for execution on object CoolingFan2 (bottom branch of Fig. 4). As a result, *Cemetery* remains empty, the change is moved to the completed set, all goals are violated, and all constraints are satisfied. As a main conceptual difference, the activation of deleteObject is not disabled on CoolingFan2 as the corresponding object still exists, hence its precondition is satisfied.

4. Next, the process selects and executes deleteObject operation. As a result, CoolingFan2 is moved to the *cemetery* and the change is moved from ΔR to the completed set *Comp*. We detect this conflict by (incrementally) checking a generic merge constraint: there are two changes in the completed-set *Comp* which modifies the same object. In this case, exploration has to backtrack and finds another executable operation.

Obviously, the first type of constraint could also be detected by using similar constraints as for the second type. However, lost activations reduce the number of states to be traversed, thus they are preferred. Furthermore, note that when two operations are applicable in both order with a confluent result, the state encoding of DSE identifies that the same model is reached as a state.

4.3 A Merge Scenario on the Motivating Example

A possible execution of the DSE Merge is depicted in Fig. 5 which displays the completed changes for two solutions. In each iteration, one change is processed.

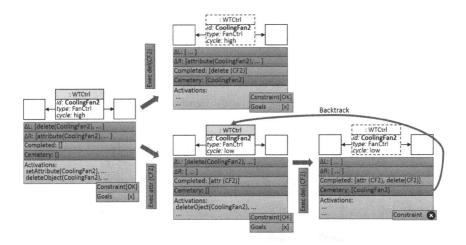

Fig. 4. Conflict resolution with incrementally tracking constraints and operations

- Itr. 1-2: all *must* changes are available and the algorithm randomly picked the createObject of CoolingPump and PumpActivator.
- Itr. 3: at this point only two conflicting transitions have activation; the algorithm picked deleteObject for CoolingFan2 non-deterministically. This leads to a state where the precondition of setAttribute operation cannot be satisfied any longer, thus it is disabled.
- Itr. 4-5: only *may* operations have activation where a setAttribute operation is selected that set the cycle attribute of CoolingFan1 to normal. Because of the generic constraint, the other setAttribute related to the same object (CoolingFan1) is disabled. The same happens when executing deleteObject for CoolingTempLimit2 that disables the setReference operation which should connect CoolingPump and CoolingTempLimit2.
- Itr. 6: this (aggregated) step is composed of all iterations that execution of operation setAttribute related to the newly created CoolingPump.
- Itr. 7: on this trajectory, deletion of CoolingFan2 leads the model into a state where the Fan2Activator output is not referenced by any control unit. Thus our domain-specific (composite) operation (unreferencedPart) has an activation that is executed on the model. After this iteration, there are no more activations and all goals are satisfied, so *Solution #1* is found.
- Itr. 8: after the solution, the strategy backtracks until it finds an activation for a *must* operation that should lead the model into a partially traversed state and forks the trajectory. Only the setAttribute operation related to *CoolingFan2* can be executed. After the execution, *deleteObject* of CoolingFan2 could have activation, but it is disabled by the generic constraint.
- Itr. 9-11: The same activations are available as for the 4th iteration except the domain-specific operation. The algorithm randomly executes these operations and finds *Solution #2*.

Resolved Conflicts. In iteration 3 and 8, two conflicting operations marked with *must* are executed which forks the exploration into two separate solutions to resolve the conflicts. At iterations of 4 and 9, two operations with *may* mark are in conflict. In each trajectory, only one of them is selected. Similar happens in iteration 5 and 10, but this time the same operation is selected in each branch.

Solution. There are two solutions in the output of the merge process. We discuss solution #1 in details where the merged model is depicted in Fig. 6. It also displays in dashed line the deleted objects stored in *Cemetery*, namely, CoolingTempLimit2, CoolingFan2 and Fan2Activator. There are four non-executed changes as shown in the bottom left corner of Fig. 6.

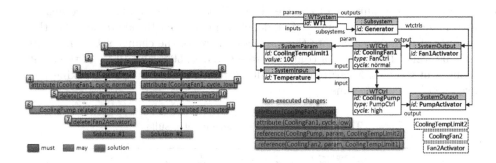

Fig. 5. Possible execution of the process

Fig. 6. Merged Model from Solution #1

5   Evaluation

As the state-of-the-art of model merge still lacks well-accepted benchmarks to measure *scalability* of model merging components (e.g. [22] measures precision and recall), we propose a new scalability benchmark for model merge by adapting of the Train Benchmark [29], which is an existing performance benchmark for model queries and well-formedness constraints (and also a case of the TTC 2015 contest [28]). The benchmark uses a domain-specific model of a railway system originating from the MOGENTES project [4]. From the existing benchmark, we reuse (1) the *model generator* to derive models of different size conforming to a railway metamodel, (2) the *fault injector* which changes the generated model (e.g. by changing structural features, and creating or deleting objects) to violate predefined well-formedness constraints, and (3) *repair actions* which pseudo-randomly resolve such violations in accordance with to a random seed value.

Based upon these components, we summarize how synthetic models are generated that contain conflicts serving as input for model comparison and model merge: (1) First, we generate a well-formed model. (2) Next, we inject several faults into the generated model. The result of this phase acts as *original (O)* model. (3) Then, local and remote changes are simulated by repairing these violations either in the local model *(L)* or remote model *(R)* or in both of them with different random seeds. In the latter case, the framework repairs the same problems in both cases by using different values, which leads to a conflict between two models. (4) We calculate the differences between the two with an existing comparison tool (EMF Compare). (5) Finally, these two model have to be merged with *may* annotations for changes using our merge tool.

We evaluate our DSE-based automated merge approach to assess its scalability using our benchmark where we investigate the scalability of the approach by measuring execution time for model comparison (carried out by EMF Compare) and model merge with respect to (i) the size of models, (ii) the size of change set, and (iii) the number of changes in conflict. For the evaluation, we generated models where the number of model elements is from 10,000 to 350,000, the number of faults injected into the models (i.e. size of the change set) is from 10 to 2000 while the number of conflicts are set to 0 %, 50 % and 100 % of the total number of changes. Measurement results are summarized in Table 2 taking the average of 5 separate runs.

Table 2. Scalability measurement results

Size	Δ	Diff (sec)	Merge (sec) 0% conflict	Merge (sec) 50% conflict	Merge (sec) 100% conflict	Size	Δ	Diff (sec)	Merge (sec) 0% conflict	Merge (sec) 50% conflict	Merge (sec) 100% conflict
	120	4.672	1.265	2.095	3.477		120	28.302	10.654	13.556	22.913
	240	7.329	2.241	3.345	4.109		240	30.711	20.285	24.377	37.501
11710	480	12.951	3.923	4.650	8.813	87396	480	36.378	38.154	48.655	76.703
	960	23.323	8.853	12.008	21.842		960	49.382	75.567	92.797	153.234
	1920	26.368	11.352	19.766	29.948		1920	80.934	162.845	205.423	367.357
	120	7.233	2.686	2.924	6.262		120	59.236	21.332	27.699	43.492
	240	7.569	4.355	5.106	8.596		240	79.068	42.308	50.843	79.492
23180	480	13.695	9.433	14.127	17.796	175754	480	93.395	80.130	95.332	162.106
	960	23.383	18.219	22.474	40.589		960	97.313	157.720	185.030	279.367
	1920	41.857	34.181	57.207	96.806		1920	118.439	311.525	362.841	626.946
	120	17.258	6.679	8.156	12.567		120	176.200	47.410	57.695	89.101
	240	18.592	10.625	12.623	20.047		240	177.280	84.678	104.739	166.990
46728	480	27.410	19.063	24.210	39.855	354762	480	188.028	156.568	198.307	317.629
	960	40.915	37.961	51.924	90.295		960	209.440	307.878	406.879	636.156
	1920	69.344	165.203	180.534	217.343		1920	257.355	1,342.081	1,401.882	1,535.091

Analysis of Results. As expected, merge time is linear in model and change size, and also proportional to comparison time. Furthermore, fewer conflicts imply faster merge time. Our results also show that runtime of merge is lower than compare time in case of smaller change sets (120, 240), and gradually outgrows it as the change set increases. However, change sets of an average commit in real projects are even smaller than our smallest case (see also the evaluation in [23]), which means that our scalability results represent a pessimistic setup.

6   Related Work

Several approaches address the model merge as depicted in Table 3. To position them against our approach, we use several characteristics proposed in a survey on model versioning [6], which also guides the structure of this section.

Table 3. Comparison of model merge approaches

	Basis	Conflict detection	Merge automation	Merge operations	Objectives	Guidance	Evaluation
EMF Compare [1]	state	static	semi	generic	-	-	scalability
EMF Diff/Merge [2]	state	static	semi	generic	-	-	scalability
Westfachtel [30]	state	runtime	semi	generic	goals	-	preliminary
N-way Merge [25]	state	static	semi	generic	-	-	preliminary
AMOR [13]	state	static	semi	generic, composite	goals	-	precision recall
Dam H.K. et al. [14]	state	static	auto	composite	goals, constraints	repair plan	scalability (closed)
MOMM [23]	operation	runtime	auto	composite	fixed goals	global search prioritized	real data
DSE Merge	state	runtime	auto	generic, composite	goals contraints	local search may/must	scalability (open)

Comparison Basis. Based on the model comparison technique, the approaches may be classified into *state-based* and *operation-based*. [1,2,13,14,25,30] and DSE Merge are *state-based* as they execute a comparison process between model states. However, [23] uses operations as input where even more complex operations as just the simple add, update, and delete operations are considered.

Conflict Detection. Finding the conflicting changes in the merge process is crucial task for a correct resolution. Most approaches use an initial phase to statically analyze the changes and look for conflicting pairs such as in [1,2,13,14,25]. Westfechtel [30] defines transformation rules for searching conflicts where the satisfied preconditions selects the conflicts in each iteration. Mansoor et al. [23] uses conflict detection algorithm between operations [12]. DSE Merge identifies conflicts incrementally as violations of constraints or as deactivations of merge operations, while dependencies between rules and constraints are handled automatically by the underlying DSE engine. This extends [14] where inconsistency constraints are handled incrementally while conflict detection happens as preprocessing.

Merge Automation. Most approaches [1,2,13,25,30] are semi-automated as they use a two-phase process: (i) they apply the non-conflicting operations and then (ii) let the user prioritize and select the operation to apply in case of two conflicting changes. This always results in a single solution due to the manual resolution by the user. In comparison, [14,23] and DSE Merge resolve the conflicts automatically in different ways and offer several solutions.

Merge Operations. In this context, merge operations are responsible for applying the changes in the merged model. [1,2,25,30] use generic operations for changes. The extension [11] of [30] adaptively learns resolution patterns from user that can be applied on the models which results in composite operations. [23] applies the input operations which are composite refactorings in their case. [14] uses basic generic operators for conflicts but generates composite operations as repair plans from the description of inconsistency constraints. Our DSE Merge approach allows to combine both generic and domain-specific composite operators in the form of change-driven transformation rules.

Objectives. Quality of the merge model can be improved by objectives that have to be satisfied during (*contraints*) or at the end (*goals*) of the merge process. This is an unsupported feature in [1,2,25]. [23] uses two fixed goals which are the base of the conflict resolution. [14] provides support for incrementally detecting violations of inconsistency constraints. [13] is connected to an additional model checker component [11] which allows to check OCL constraints as goals. [30] allows to define well-formedness constraints in OCL that act as goals. DSE Merge let the users to provide additional constraints and goals using graph patterns in addition to a built-in termination condition when no operations are activated.

Guidance. The execution of the merge process can use guidance to find the solution(s) faster. The tool [26] of [30] uses a dedicated fusing algorithm for the model merge phase using a fixed priority strategy of merge operations. [23] bases their tool to a global search genetic algorithm (NSGA-II [15]) where the operations are also prioritized related to their importance. DSE Merge is built on top of the ViatraDSE framework [19] using rule-based guided local search exploration. Furthermore, annotating changes with *may*/*must* can further reduce the result set retrieved to the user, which is another key difference wrt [14,23].

Evaluation. [23] provides an empirical evaluation of the tool based on real data, but its scalability is not discussed as their largest model was the same as our smallest. [14] represents an scalability evaluation of its tool with the largest size of 33.000 model element and 1,650 changes. [25] and [26] show a preliminary evaluation which show the relevance of the approach on very small models and change set. [13] evaluated by [22], but scalability is not discussed. For comparing models, [1] has a scalability test presented in [7]. Scalability of [2] is not well covered, however, we evaluated ourselves on the proposed benchmark [3]. DSE Merge is evaluated on an open scalability benchmark [29]. As future work, we plan to create an empirical user study from the usability aspect of our tool.

Summary. To summarize the key differences with [14] and [23], we rely on state-based comparison, apply a guided local-search strategy (vs. [23]), detect conflicts at runtime and allow complex generic merge operations (vs. [14]). Internally, we uniquely use incremental and change-driven transformations to derive the merged models. Finally, we report scalability of merge process for models which are at least one order of magnitude larger compared to [14] and [23].

7   Conclusion

The current paper presented an automated technique for three-way model merge exploiting design space exploration in the background. The original model and two difference models (original model↔remote version, and original model↔local version) calculated with existing model comparison tools (e.g. EMF Compare or Diff/Merge) serve as an input of our technique. Our technique automatically derives consistent and semantically correct merged models in all possible ways and also highlights the remaining (unresolved thus conflicting) model differences. Our approach incorporates the use of change-driven model transformations [9] to capture and execute merge operations, and relies on an incremental reactive model transformation engine [8] to detect and resolve merge conflicts. We proposed scalability benchmark for scalability aspect of merge components that demonstrates that DSE-based model merge can be executed for models around 350,000 elements and conflicting change sets with 1000 elements.

Our approach is fully implemented in a tool developed as part of a European project, which operates on well-known open source components of the Eclipse framework, such as EMF Compare [1] or Diff/Merge for [2] for model comparison and using the Viatra DSE [18,19] as underlying design space exploration framework built on reactive transformations [8].

As future work, we plan to improve our model merge technique by further search strategies to better exploit the dependencies between rules and constraints and compare it with other search-based merge techniques [23]. Currently, we are conducting an experimental user evaluation to compare the usability of the presented DSE Merge tool with EMF-Compare and Diff/Merge.

Acknowledgments. We thank to Gábor Szárnyas for improving the syntectic performance benchmark for the evaluation and András Szabolcs Nagy for his assistance on design space exploration.

References

1. EMF compare. https://www.eclipse.org/emf/compare/
2. EMF Diff/Merge. http://eclipse.org/diffmerge/
3. Evaluation of EMF Compare and Diff/Merge. https://github.com/FTSRG/publication-pages/wiki/Evaluation-of-EMF-Diff-Merge-and-EMF-Compare
4. Mogentes EU project. http://www.mogentes.eu/
5. Altmanninger, K., Kappel, G., Kusel, A., Retschitzegger, W., Seidl, M., Schwinger, W., Wimmer, M.: AMOR-towards adaptable model versioning. In: 1st International Workshop on Model Co-Evolution and Consistency Management, in conjunction with MODELS, vol. 8, pp. 4–50 (2008)
6. Altmanninger, K., Seidl, M., Wimmer, M.: A survey on model versioning approaches. IJWIS **5**(3), 271–304 (2009)
7. Barbero, M.: EMF compare 2.0: scaling to millions. In: EclipseCON 2013, Boston
8. Bergmann, G., Dávid, I., Hegedüs, Á., Horváth, Á., Ráth, I., Ujhelyi, Z., Varró, D.: Viatra 3: a reactive model transformation platform. In: Kolovos, D., Wimmer, M. (eds.) ICMT 2015. LNCS, vol. 9152, pp. 101–110. Springer, Heidelberg (2015)
9. Bergmann, G., Ráth, I., Varró, G., Varró, D.: Change-driven model transformations - change (in) the rule to rule the change. Softw. Syst. Model. **11**(3), 431–461 (2012)
10. Bergmann, G., Ujhelyi, Z., Ráth, I., Varró, D.: A graph query language for EMF models. In: Cabot, J., Visser, E. (eds.) ICMT 2011. LNCS, vol. 6707, pp. 167–182. Springer, Heidelberg (2011)
11. Brosch, P., Egly, U., Gabmeyer, S., Kappel, G., Seidl, M., Tompits, H., Widl, M., Wimmer, M.: Towards semantics-aware merge support in optimistic model versioning. In: Kienzle, J. (ed.) MODELS 2011 Workshops. LNCS, vol. 7167, pp. 246–256. Springer, Heidelberg (2012)

12. Brosch, P., Kappel, G., Langer, P., Seidl, M., Wieland, K., Wimmer, M.: An introduction to model versioning. In: Bernardo, M., Cortellessa, V., Pierantonio, A. (eds.) SFM 2012. LNCS, vol. 7320, pp. 336–398. Springer, Heidelberg (2012)

13. Brosch, P., Seidl, M., Wieland, K., Wimmer, M.: We can work it out: collaborative conflict resolution in model versioning. In: Wagner, I., Tellioğlu, H., Balka, E., Simone, C., Ciolfi, L. (eds.) ECSCW 2009, pp. 207–214. Springer, London (2009)

14. Dam, H.K., Reder, A., Egyed, A.: Inconsistency resolution in merging versions of architectural models. In: 2014 IEEE/IFIP Conference on Software Architecture, WICSA 2014, Sydney, Australia, pp. 153–162, 7–11 April 2014

15. Deb, K., Agrawal, S., Pratap, A., Meyarivan, T.: A fast and elitist multiobjective genetic algorithm: NSGA-II. IEEE Trans. Evol. Comput. **6**(2), 182–197 (2002)

16. Ehrig, H., Kreowski, H.J., Rozenberg, G.: Handbook of Graph Grammars and Computing by Graph Transformation, vol. 2. World Scientific, Singapore (1999)

17. Feather, M.S.: Detecting interference when merging specification evolutions. In: ACM SIGSOFT Software Engineering Notes. vol. 14, pp. 169–176. ACM (1989)

18. Hegedus, A., Horváth, A., Ráth, I., Varró, D.: A model-driven framework for guided design space exploration. In: Proceedings of the 2011 26th IEEE/ACM International Conference on Automated Software Engineering, pp. 173–182. IEEE Computer Society (2011)

19. Hegedüs, Á., Horváth, Á., Varró, D.: A model-driven framework for guided design space exploration. Autom. Softw. Eng. **22**(3), 399–436 (2015)

20. Kessentini, M., Werda, W., Langer, P., Wimmer, M.: Search-based model merging. In: Genetic and Evolutionary Computation Conference, GECCO 2013, Amsterdam, The Netherlands, pp. 1453–1460, 6–10 July 2013

21. Kolovos, D.S., Rose, L.M., Matragkas, N., Paige, R.F., Guerra, E., Cuadrado, J.S., De Lara, J., Ráth, I., Varró, D., Tisi, M., et al.: A research roadmap towards achieving scalability in model driven engineering. In: Proceedings of the Workshop on Scalability in Model Driven Engineering, p. 2. ACM (2013)

22. Langer, P., Wimmer, M.: A benchmark for conflict detection components of model versioning systems, vol. 33 (2013)

23. Mansoor, U., Kessentini, M., Langer, P., Wimmer, M., Bechikh, S., Deb, K.: MOMM: multi-objective model merging. J. Syst. Softw. **103**, 423–439 (2015)

24. Mens, T.: A state-of-the-art survey on software merging. IEEE Trans. Softw. Eng. **28**(5), 449–462 (2002)

25. Rubin, J., Chechik, M.: N-way model merging. In: Joint Meeting of the European Software Engineering Conference and the ACM SIGSOFT Symposium on the Foundations of Software Engineering, ESEC/FSE 2013, Saint Petersburg, Russian Federation, pp. 301–311, 18–26 August 2013

26. Schwägerl, F., Uhrig, S., Westfechtel, B.: Model-based tool support for consistent three-way merging of EMF models. In: Proceedings of the workshop on ACadeMics Tooling with Eclipse, p. 2. ACM (2013)

27. Steyaert, P., Lucas, C., Mens, K., D'Hondt, T.: Reuse contracts: managing the evolution of reusable assets. In: Proceedings of the 1996 ACM SIGPLAN Conference on Object-Oriented Programming Systems, Languages & Applications (OOPSLA 1996), San Jose, California, pp. 268–285, 6–10 October 1996

28. Szárnyas, G., Semeráth, O., Ráth, I., Varró, D.: The TTC 2015 train benchmark case for incremental model validation. In: Transformation Tool Contest, pp. 129–141 (2015)

29. Ujhelyi, Z., Bergmann, G., Hegedüs, Á., Horváth, Á., Izsó, B., Ráth, I., Szatmári, Z., Varró, D.: EMF-IncQuery: an integrated development environment for live model queries. Sci. Comput. Program. **98**, 80–99 (2015)

30. Westfechtel, B.: Merging of EMF models - formal foundations. Softw. Syst. Model. **13**(2), 757–788 (2014)

31. Wieland, K., Langer, P., Seidl, M., Wimmer, M., Kappel, G.: Turning conflicts into collaboration. Comput. Support. Coop. Work **22**(2-3), 181–240 (2013)

RuleMerger: Automatic Construction of Variability-Based Model Transformation Rules

Daniel Strüber[1]([✉]), Julia Rubin[2], Thorsten Arendt[1], Marsha Chechik[3], Gabriele Taentzer[1], and Jennifer Plöger[1]

[1] Philipps-Universität Marburg, Marburg, Germany
{strueber,arendt,taentzer,ploeger1}@informatik.uni-marburg.de
[2] Massachusetts Institute of Technology, Cambridge, USA
mjulia@csail.mit.edu
[3] University of Toronto, Toronto, Canada
chechik@cs.toronto.edu

Abstract. Unifying similar model transformation rules into variability-based ones can improve both the maintainability and the performance of a model transformation system. Yet, manual identification and unification of such similar rules is a tedious and error-prone task. In this paper, we propose a novel merge-refactoring approach for automating this task. The approach employs *clone detection* for identifying overlapping rule portions and *clustering* for selecting groups of rules to be unified. Our instantiation of the approach harnesses state-of-the-art clone detection and clustering techniques and includes a specialized *merge construction* algorithm. We formally prove correctness of the approach and demonstrate its ability to produce high-quality outcomes in two real-life case-studies.

1 Introduction

Model transformation is a key enabling technology for Model-Driven Engineering, pervasive in all of its activities, including the translation, optimization, and synchronization of models [1]. Algebraic graph transformation (AGT) is one of the main paradigms in model transformation, allowing rules to be specified in a high-level, declarative manner [2]. Recently, many complex transformations have been implemented using AGT [3–5]. AGT is gaining further importance due to its use as an analysis back-end for imperative transformation languages [6].

Transformation systems often contain rules that are substantially similar to each other. Yet, until recently, various model transformation languages lacked constructs suited to capture these similar *rule variants* in a compact manner [7]. The most frequently applied mechanism for creating variants was cloning: developers produced rules by copying and modifying existing ones. The drawbacks of cloning are well-known, e.g., the need to update all clones when a bug is found in one of the variants. Furthermore, creating a large set of mutually similar rules

P. Stevens and A. Wąsowski (Eds.): FASE 2016, LNCS 9633, pp. 122–140, 2016.
DOI: 10.1007/978-3-662-49665-7_8

also impairs the performance of transformation systems: each additional rule increases the computational effort, possibly rendering the entire transformation infeasible. Blouin et al. report that to be the case with as few as 250 rules [8].

Variability-based (VB) rules are an approach to address these issues [9]. Inspired by product line engineering (PLE) principles [10,11], a VB rule encodes a set of rule variants in a single-copy representation, explicating common and variable portions. In [9], we provide an algorithm for applying VB rules and show that it outperforms the application of classical rules in terms of execution time.

The VB rules in [9] were created manually, a tedious and error-prone task relying on the precise identification of (i) sets of rule variants, each to be unified into a single VB rule; (ii) rule portions that should be merged versus portions that should remain isolated. The choices made during these steps have a substantial impact on the quality of the produced rules.

In this work, we present *RuleMerger*, a novel approach for automating the merge-refactoring of model transformation rules. The approach includes a three-component framework (see Fig. 1). It applies *clone detection* [12] to identify overlapping portions between rules and *clustering* [13] to identify disjoint groups of similar rules. During *merge construction*, common portions are unified and variable ones are annotated to create VB rules. Each component can be instantiated and customized with respect to specific quality goals, e.g., to produce rules optimized for background execution or easy editing. Since the framework guarantees that all created rule sets are semantically equivalent, we envision a system that enables users to edit rules in a convenient representation and to automatically derive a highly efficient one.

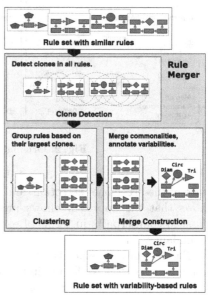

Fig. 1. Overview of *RuleMerger*

The distinguishing factors of this approach, compared to merge-refactoring approaches in the PLE domain [14–16], are its ability to detect overlapping *portions* rather than pairs of similar elements and to create *multiple* output VB rules rather than one single-copy representation of all rules. These factors allow us to address the performance and maintainability issues related to cloning.

Contributions. This paper makes the following contributions: (1) It presents a novel merge-refactoring approach for AGT-based model transformation rules. (2) It formally proves the correctness of the approach, showing the equivalence of the produced VB rules to their classical counterparts. (3) It instantiates the approach by providing a novel *merge construction* algorithm and harnessing

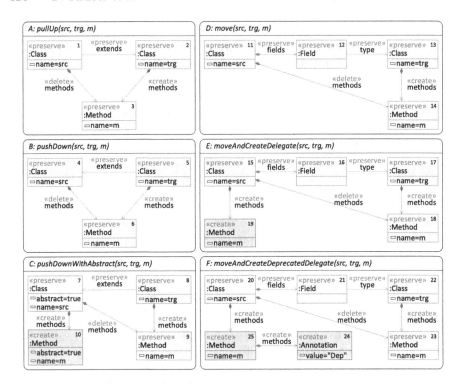

Fig. 2. Original transformation rules.

state-of-the-art clone detection and clustering techniques. (4) It empirically shows that the approach allows producing VB rules being superior to their classical counterparts in terms of execution time and the amount of contained redundancy.

The rest of this paper is structured as follows: Sect. 2 introduces a running example. In Sect. 3, we fix preliminaries. In Sect. 4, we outline the approach and argue for its correctness. Section 5 reports on our instantiation of *RuleMerger*. Section 6 presents our evaluation. In Sects. 7 and 8, we discuss related work and conclude.

2 Running Example

Consider a set of model transformation rules aimed at improving the structure of an existing code base by using *refactoring* [17]. Figure 2 shows six refactoring rules expressed in an abstract syntax notation [2]. The rules describe several simple ways of relocating a method between different classes. We present the rules in an integrated form, with the left- and right-hand sides of the transformation being represented in one graph. The left-hand side of a rule comprises all *delete* and *preserve* objects. The right-hand side contains all *preserve* and *create* objects.

Rule A takes as input two classes, one of them sub-classing the other, and a method. Each of these input objects is specified by its name. The rule moves the method from a sub-class to its super-class, by deleting it from the sub-class and adding it to the super-class. Similarly, rule B moves a method from the super-class to one of its sub-classes. Rule C also moves a method from the super- to a sub-class, but, in addition, creates an abstract method with the same name in the super-class. Rules D, E and F move a method across an association. The latter two rules also create a "wrapper" method of the same name in the source class. Rule F uses an annotation to mark this "wrapper" method as deprecated.

Such rule sets are often created by cloning, that is, copying a seed rule and modifying it to fit the new purpose. We consider the merge-refactoring of a rule set created using cloning. The result is a rule set with variability-based (VB) rules in which the common portions are unified and the differences are explicated, as shown in Fig. 3. Specifically, rules B and C are merged, producing a new VB rule $B + C$. Rules D, E, and F are merged into $D + E + F$. Rule A remains as is.

Each VB rule has a set of *variation points*, corresponding to the names of the original rules: Rule $B + C$ has the variation points B and C. In addition, each rule has a *variability model* specifying relations between variation points, such as their mutual exclusion: $B + C$ has the variability model $xor(B,C)$. VB rules are *configured* by binding each variation point to either *true* or *false*. Portions of VB rules are annotated with *presence conditions*. These portions are removed if the presence condition evaluates to *false* for the given configuration. Element #32 and its incoming edge, both annotated with C, are removed in the configuration $\{C{=}false, B{=}true\}$. These VB rules offer several benefits w.r.t. maintainability: The amount of redundancy is reduced, ensuring consistency between variants during changes; bugs are fixed in one place. The total number of rules is smaller.

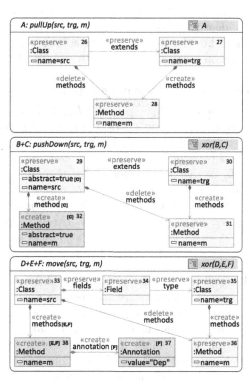

Fig. 3. Variability-based rules.

In this example, the user selects and configures one of theses rule at a time, to derive one specific rule variant – a process similar to that in PLE approaches [11]. In an alternative use-case, *all* rules of a rule set may be applied simultaneously. Configurations can then be determined automatically by the transformation engine [9], leading to considerable performance savings: The application sites or *matches* for the common portions are identified first and used as starting points for matching the variable portions. Such cases are demonstrated in Sect. 6.

3   Preliminaries: Variability-Based Model Transformation

We now give preliminaries, starting with simple transformation rules.

Definition 1 (Rule). *A rule* $r = L \xleftarrow{le} I \xrightarrow{ri} R$ *consists of graphs* L, I *and* R, *called* left-hand side, interface graph *and* right-hand side, *respectively, and two injective graph morphisms,* le *and* ri. *A rule is* connected *iff, treating all edges as undirected,* $\forall G \in \{L, R\}$ *there is a path between each pair of nodes in* G.

The rules in Fig. 2 follow this definition. Elements of I are annotated with the action *preserve*, elements of $L \setminus le(I)$ and $R \setminus ri(I)$ with *delete* and *create*.

Given a rule, a *subrule* encapsulates a subset of its actions on a substructure. To identify actions on substructures of *one* rule, we talk about subrule embeddings. For clone detection, the subrule relation must capture common actions on common patterns in *different* rules – we then talk about *subrule morphisms*.

Definition 2 (Subrule morphism). *Given a pair of rules* $r_0 = (L_0 \xleftarrow{le_0} I_0 \xrightarrow{ri_0} R_0)$ *and* $r_1 = (L_1 \xleftarrow{le_1} I_1 \xrightarrow{ri_1} R_1)$ *with injective mappings* le_i, ri_i *for* $i \in \{0, 1\}$, *a subrule mapping* $s : r_0 \to r_1$, $s = (s_L, s_I, s_R)$ *consists of injective mappings* $s_L : L_0 \to L_1$, $s_I : I_0 \to I_1$, *and* $s_R : R_0 \to R_1$ *such that in the diagram in Fig. 4 (1) and (2) commute. In addition, the intersection of* $s_L(L_0)$ *and* $le_1(I_1)$ *in* L_1 *as well as the intersection of* $s_R(R_0)$ *and* $ri_1(I_1)$ *in* R_1 *is isomorphic to* I_0. *Moreover,* $L_1 - (s_L(L_0) - s_L(le_0(I_0)))$ *is a valid graph.*

Subrule mapping s *is called a* subrule embedding *if all of its morphisms* s_L, s_I, *and* s_R *are inclusions. Given two subrule embeddings* $s : r_0 \to r_1$ *and* $s' : r_0' \to r_1'$, *we have that* $s \subseteq s'$ *if there are subrule embeddings* $t_0 : r_0 \to r_0'$ *and* $t_1 : r_1 \to r_1'$ *with* $s' \circ t_0 = t_1 \circ s$.

The conditions prefaced with "in addition" ensure that a subrule always performs the same actions on related elements as the original rule and that the larger pattern of the original rule does not prevent a subrule to be applied.

For example, in Fig. 2, B is a subrule of $B + C$ since B can be injectively mapped to $B + C$. The actions on the original and mapped elements are always the same.

We capture variability in rule sets by propositional expressions over a fixed set of independent *variation points*, calling these expressions *variability conditions*.

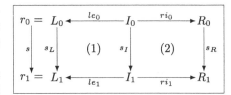

Fig. 4. Subrule morphism.

Definition 3 (Language of variability conditions). *Given a set of atomic terms V, called* variation points, *$\mathcal{L}_V$ is the set of all propositional expressions over V, called* variability conditions. *A* variability configuration *is a total function $cfg : V \rightarrow \{true, false\}$. cfg satisfies a variability condition vc if vc evaluates to* true *when each variation point vp in vc is substituted by $cfg(vp)$. A variability condition is* valid *if there is a variability configuration satisfying it. Given two variability conditions X and Y, X is* stronger *than Y iff $X \implies Y$.*

For example, in the rule $D + E + F$ in Fig. 2, $V = \{D, E, F\}$. True, E, and $E \vee F$ are valid variability conditions; $E \wedge \neg E$ is not valid. A possible configuration might bind the variation points D to *false*, E to *true* and F to *false*, which would satisfy the variability condition $E \vee F$.

In a VB rule, variability is formalized by means of subrule embeddings, each describing a single variant. The intersection of subrule embeddings is the part of the rule where all variants overlap, i.e., the *base rule*. Each subrule has a *variability condition* determining when this variant shall be active. Moreover, the entire rule has a *variability model*. The base rule does not have any annotations.

Definition 4 (Variability-based rule). *Given $\mathcal{L}_V$, a VB rule $\hat{r} = (r, S, v, pc)$ consists of a rule r, a set S of subrule embeddings to r, a variability condition v, called* variability model, *and a function $pc : S \cup \{id_r\} \rightarrow \mathcal{L}_V$. Function pc defines presence conditions for subrules s.t. $pc(id_r)$ is true and $\forall s \subseteq s' : pc(s') \implies pc(s)$. The* base rule *is determined by the intersection of all subrule embeddings.*

Rule $D + E + F$ in Fig. 3 is a compact representation of a VB rule over variation points D, E, and F with various subrule embeddings such as $\{s_E, s_{E \vee F}, s_{D \wedge E}, ...\}$. The base rule comprises all elements with the presence condition *true*: i.e., objects without annotations such as #33–36, and their relations. Elements #37 and #38 have non-*true* presence conditions and are therefore not present in all subrule embeddings. To ensure equivalence to the original three rules, the variability model v specifies mutual exclusion between variation points: $v = xor(v_D, v_E, v_F)$.

To show the correctness of our approach, we consider the *flattening* of a VB rule – an operation for generating the individual "flat" rules it represents.

Definition 5 (Flattening of a VB rule). *Let a VB rule $\hat{r} = (r, S, v, pc)$ over $\mathcal{L}_V$ be given. For each variability condition c in $\mathcal{L}_V$, the following holds: if $c \wedge v$ is valid, $S_c \subseteq S$ is a set of subrule embeddings iff $\forall s \in S : s \in S_c$ if $c \implies pc(s)$. Merging all subrule embeddings in S_c by first computing the intersections of all pairs of embeddings and merging them along these interfaces afterwards, yields a subrule embedding $r_c \rightarrow r$. r_c is the flat rule for condition c. $Flat(\hat{r})$ is the set of all flattened rules: $\{r_c \mid c \in \mathcal{L}_V \wedge (c \wedge v) \text{ is valid}\}$.*

For example, consider just the rule $D + E + F$ in Fig. 3. $c \wedge v$ becomes valid if $xor(cfg(v_D), cfg(v_E), cfg(v_F))$ is *true*. Hence, $Flat(D + E + F) = \{D, E, F\}$. In [9], it is shown that the application of a VB rule is equal to the application of flattened rules. This result is key to argue for the correctness of *RuleMerger*.

4   Framework

Given a rule set with similar rules, *RuleMerger*, outlined in Fig. 1, aims to find an efficient representation of these rules using a set of variability-based (VB) rules. At its core is a framework of three components called *clone detection, clustering* and *merge construction*. We specify the input and output of each component and show correctness of *RuleMerger* based on these specifications. Each component may be instantiated in various ways, as long as its specification is implemented.

4.1   Clone Detection

Clone detection allows identifying overlapping portions between the input rules. We use clone detection as a prerequisite for both clustering and merge construction: Rules with a large overlap are clustered together. Merging overlapping portions rather than individual elements allows us to preserve the essential structural information expressed in the rules. Moreover, the execution performance of the created VB rules can be considerably improved by restricting clone detection to *connected* portions: Connected patterns can be matched much more efficiently than multiple independent patterns [18].

Formally, given a set of rules, a *clone* is a largest subrule that can be embedded into a subset of this rule set. To account for the optional restriction of clone detection to connected portions, we analogously define *connected clones* based on largest connected subrules. To establish a well-defined merge construction, we define a *compatibility relation*, ensuring that two clones never assign the same object contained in one rule to diverging objects contained in another one.

Definition 6 (Clone group). *Given a set $\mathcal{R} = \{r_i | i \in I\}$ of rules, a (connected) clone group $CG_\mathcal{R} = (r_c, \mathcal{C})$ over $\mathcal{R}$ consists of a (connected) rule r_c, called* clone, *and set $\mathcal{C} = \{c_i | i \in I\}$ of subrule mappings $c_i : r_c \to r_i$ iff there is no set $\mathcal{C}' = \{c_i' | i \in I\}$ of subrule mappings $c_i' : r_c' \to r_i$ with a subrule mapping $i : r_c \to r_c'$ where r_c' is a (connected) rule.*

Given a clone group $CG_\mathcal{R}$ and a subset $\mathcal{R}' \subseteq \mathcal{R}$, $CG_\mathcal{R}$ is reduced to $\mathcal{R}'$, written $Red(CG_\mathcal{R}, \mathcal{R}') = (r_c, \mathcal{C}')$, by $\mathcal{C}' = \mathcal{C} \setminus \{c_j | r_j \notin \mathcal{R}'\}$. Clone groups $CG_\mathcal{R} = (r_c, \{c_k | k \in K\})$ and $CG_{\mathcal{R}'} = (r_c', \{c_l' | l \in L\})$ with $\mathcal{R} \subseteq \mathcal{R}$ and $K \subset L$ are compatible if there is a subrule mapping $in : r_c \to r_c'$ with $\forall k \in K : c_k = c_k' \circ in$.

Table 1 shows the result of applying clone detection to rules shown in Fig. 2. Each row denotes a clone group, comprising a set of rules and a clone present in each of these rules. Clones are indicated by their *size*, calculated as the total number of involved nodes and edges. The rows are ordered by the size of the clone. In particular, CG2 represents objects #15–18, #20–23 and their

Table 1. Clone groups, as reported by clone detection.

Name	Rules	Size
CG1	$\{E, F\}$	10
CG2	$\{D, E, F\}$	8
CG3	$\{C, E, F\}$	7
CG4	$\{B, C\}$	6
CG5	$\{A, B, C, D, E, F\}$	5

interrelations. CG1 incorporates objects #19 and #25 and their incoming relationships in addition. Clone groups CG1 and CG2 are compatible: The clone of CG2 extends the one of CG1. CG2 can be reduced to rule set $\{E, F\}$ by discarding the embedding into rule D. CG2 and CG3 are not compatible: their rule sets are not in subset relation. Each clone group in Table 1 is connected.

The output of clone detection is a set of clone groups – in the example, all rows of Table 1. These clone groups may be pair-wise incompatible.

4.2   Clustering

As a prerequisite for merge construction, we introduce *clustering*, an operation that splits a rule set into a cluster partition based on similarity between rules. Its input are a set of rules and a set of clone groups over these rules.

Definition 7 (Cluster). *Given a set $\mathcal{R}$ of rules and a set CG of clone groups over $\mathcal{R}$, a cluster Cl over $\mathcal{R}$ is a set of clone groups $CG_{\mathcal{R}'} \subset CG$ over each subset $\mathcal{R}' \subseteq \mathcal{R}$. Given a partition $\mathcal{P}$ of $\mathcal{R}$, a cluster partition is a set $Par(Cl)_{\mathcal{P}}$ of clusters over Cl where for each $P \in \mathcal{P}$ there is a cluster $Cl_P \in Par(Cl)_{\mathcal{P}}$ comprising clone groups $Red(CG_{\mathcal{R}'}, P)$ and $CG_{P'} \subseteq CG_P$ over subsets P' of P. Each cluster $Cl_P \in Par(Cl)_{\mathcal{P}}$ is called a sub-cluster of Cl.*

In the example, there is a cluster partition over the rule set with sub-clusters over $\{A\}$, $\{B, C\}$, and $\{D, E, F\}$. We consider the sub-cluster over $\{D, E, F\}$: The clone groups over this set are obtained by reducing the mappings of $\{CG2, CG5\}$ to rules D, E and F, i.e., discarding all mappings not referring to either rule. To obtain the clone groups over subset $\{E, F\}$, we include CG1 and CG3 as well and reduce the mappings of $\{CG1, CG2, CG3, CG5\}$ to E and F.

The output of clustering is one clustering partition over the rule set. Given multiple possible partitions, the instantiation of clustering has to choose one.

4.3   Merge Construction

Merge construction takes a cluster partition over the entire rule set as input. Each sub-cluster becomes a VB rule in the output. The available information on overlapping, given by clone groups, is considered to merge corresponding elements. Merging requires that the clone groups over each sub-cluster are compatible. Incompatible clone groups have to be discarded before merging, a nontrivial task requiring a strategy to determine what to discard. The instantiation in Sect. 5 provides such a strategy. To maintain traceability between original and new rules, we define a variation point for each original rule. The variability model is set over the variation points, specifying that exactly one of them is valid at a time.

Definition 8 (Cluster merge). *Given a cluster partition $Par(Cl)_{\mathcal{P}}$ over a cluster Cl over $\mathcal{R}$, each sub-cluster $Cl_P \in Par(Cl)_{\mathcal{P}}$ is merged to a variability-based rule $\hat{r} = (r, S, v, pc)$ by merging all rules in $P = \{r_j | j \in J\}$ over compatible* clone groups in Cl_P. The result is a rule r. $S = \{s_i : r_i \rightarrow r\}$ consists of all resulting subrule embeddings. Variation points V are determined by the rules in P: $V = \{v_j | j \in J\}$. Moreover, $v = \text{Xor}_{j \in J}(v_j)$ and $pc(s_j) = v_j$. We use the notation $Merge(Cl_P)$ to indicate $\hat{r}$ and $Merge(Cl) = \{Merge(Cl_P) | Cl_P \in Par(Cl)_P\}$.

Rules are merged over compatible clone groups by gluing those rule elements that are in relation via subrule mappings. This relation is extended to an equivalence relation, so in particular, the transitive closure is considered as well. All elements not in the relation are merged in disjointly.

In the example, considering all clone groups identified for the sub-cluster over $\{D, E, F\}$, CG1–2 are compatible; since we consider the reduction to $\{D, E, F\}$ they are incompatible to CG3 and CG5. Merging the sub-cluster based on clone groups CG1–2 yields a VB rule isomorphic to $D + E + F$ in Fig. 3. The variability model v is set to $xor(cfg(v_D), cfg(v_E), cfg(v_F))$. In the compact representation of VB rules shown in Fig. 3, the presence condition of an element is the disjunction of all variation points whose corresponding subrules contain the element.

As a key well-definedness result, we obtain that merging a rule set and then flattening it produces the original set. We provide a proof in [19].

Theorem 1 (Correctness of rule merger). *For any cluster Cl over a set $\mathcal{R}$ of flat rules, we have $Flat(Merge(Cl)) = \mathcal{R}$.*

Note that the opposite operation, first flattening a VB rule set and then merging the resulting flat rules, may not yield the same VB rule set: In general, there are several VB rules with the same flattening. In fact, Theorem 1 ensures that *all* VB rule sets created by instantiations of *RuleMerger* have the same flattening, i.e., they are semantically equivalent.

5   Instantiating RuleMerger

We now present our instantiation of the *RuleMerger* framework based on state-of-the-art *clone detection* and *clustering* algorithms and a new *merge construction* algorithm. We describe two input parameters enabling customizations with respect to specific quality goals. For implementation details, see [19].

Clone Detection. We considered the applicability of three techniques for clone detection, each of them allowing to identify *connected clones* as per Definition 6. First, we applied *gSpan*, a general-purpose graph pattern mining tool [20]. Using this tool, we experienced heap overflows even on small rule sets. Second, we reimplemented eScan [21], which terminated with *insufficient memory* errors for larger rule sets. While our implementation could be flawed, [22] reports on a similar experience with their re-implementation of eScan. Finally, we applied ConQAT [22], a heuristic technique which delivers fast performance at the expense of precision. It was able to analyze rule sets of 5000 elements in less than 10 seconds while reporting a large portion of relevant clones. We used ConQAT in our experiments on realistic rule sets.

We provide a customization to increase the speed-up produced by the constructed rules: The performance-critical task in rule application, *matching*, considers just the rule left-hand sides. Consequently, performance is optimized when rules are merged based on their overlap in left-hand sides. To this end, a Boolean parameter *restrictToLhs* allows to restrict the rule portions considered by clone detection. When set to *true*, it only finds and reports clones for left-hand sides.

Clustering. From a large variety of approaches to cluster a set of objects based on their similarity [13], we chose *AverageLinkage*, a hierarchical agglomerative method, due to its convenient application to our approach. It assumes a distance function – a measure of similarity between the clustered elements. We consider the similarity of rule pairs, defining it as the size of the rules' largest common clone divided by their average size. In the example, similarity of rules E and F is calculated based on CG1, evaluating to $\frac{10}{11} = 0.91$. It further assumes a customizable *cutting-level threshold* parameter that we describe in what follows.

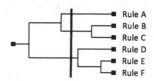

The method builds a cluster hierarchy, often visualized using a *dendrogram* – a tree diagram arranging the input elements, as shown in Fig. 5. Tree nodes describe proximity between rule sets. The "lower" in the tree two nodes are connected, the more similar are their corresponding rules. For example, rule D is similar to E and F, but the similarity is not as strong as that between just E and F. The clustering result is obtained by "cutting" using the cutting-level threshold, marked by a vertical bar in Fig. 5, and collecting the obtained subtrees.

Fig. 5. Cluster dendrogram, as reported by clustering.

Merge Construction. We propose a custom algorithm for merge construction. It proceeds in two steps: determining *what* is to be merged and *how* to do the merging. The first step, called *merge computation*, takes as input the cluster partition created by clustering (see Definition 7). To ensure a well-defined merge, merge computation refines the given cluster partition by discarding incompatible clone groups (Definition 6), retaining sub-clusters for which a set of compatible clone groups is available. To this end, we apply a greedy strategy that aims to capture a high degree of overlap. Each sub-cluster becomes a `MergeRule` in the output of merge computation, a `MergeSpecification`. The second step, *merge refactoring*, creates VB rules according to this `MergeSpecification` as per Definition 8.

Figure 6 specifies a metamodel for the interface between merge computation and merge refactoring. `Merge Specification`, corresponding to the

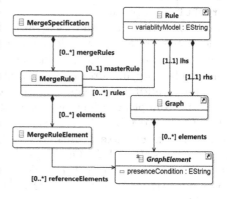

Fig. 6. MergeSpecification metamodel.

overall rule set, acts as an overarching container for a set of `MergeRule`s. One `MergeRule` identifies a sub-cluster that is to be merged into a VB rule. In order to preserve the graphical layout of the contained rules, one rule is stated as *masterRule*; this rule is used as a starting point in creating the VB rule. To retain as much layout information as possible, it is best to select the largest input rule as the *masterRule*. A `MergeRule` specifies all elements to be unified in the created VB rule. For each element in the resulting rule, a `MergeRuleElement` is defined, referring to the elements to be represented by it. In a consistent specification, each rule element is referred to by exactly one `MergeRuleElement`.

Figure 7 sketches the merge computation algorithm. The output `MergeSpecification` is created in line 2 and incrementally filled by considering each cluster. In each iteration of the loop starting in line 5, a new sub-cluster is constructed. We apply a greedy strategy to integrate as many compatible clone groups as possible, starting with the *top* – the largest available – clone group in lines 6–8 and incrementally adding the next largest compatible ones in 9–14. For each clone group, we temporarily create a new `MergeRule`, integrating

```
1: function COMPUTEMERGE(cl : Cluster[ ])
2:     var mergeSpecification = ∅
3:     for each c ← cl do
4:         var cg = c.cloneGroups
5:         while cg ≠ ∅ do        ▷ Create a new sub-cluster
6:             var top = FINDTOPCLONEGROUP(cg)
7:             var mergeRule = CREATEMERGERULE(top)
8:             var considered = {top}
9:             while HASCOMPATIBLE(considered, cg) do
10:                var comp = FINDTOPCOMPATIBLE(cg)
11:                var temp = CREATEMERGERULE(comp)
12:                INTEGRATE(mergeRule, temp)
13:                considered.ADD(comp)
14:            end while
15:            mergeSpecification.rules.ADD(mergeRule)
16:            cg.REMOVEMAPPINGS(mergeRule.rules)
17:            cg.REMOVEALLEMPTY
18:            cg.REMOVEALL(considered)
19:        end while        ▷ Done with current sub-cluster
20:    end for
21:    return mergeSpecification
22: end function
```

Fig. 7. Merge computation.

its contents with the result `MergeRule` in line 12. When no more compatible clone groups are found, we add the `MergeRule` to the result and discard mappings that concern its rules from the remaining clone groups, from which we remove all empty and already considered clone groups, in lines 15–18. We repeat this process until no clone groups are left to consider.

In the example, considering cluster $\{D, E, F\}$ containing clone groups CG1, CG2, CG3, and CG5, the largest one CG1 is chosen as top group in line 6. In line 7, a `MergeRule` is created based on CG1, specifying the merge of the involved rules E and F. One `MergeRuleElement` is created for each pair of clone elements and for each non-clone element, e.g., one for $\{\#15, \#20\}$ and one for $\{\#24\}$. In lines 9–14, CG2 is identified as the next largest compatible clone. Its temporary merge rule, specifying the merge of rules D, E and F, is created. The two merge rules are integrated by establishing that each rule element finally belongs to exactly one `MergeRuleElement`, which involves the deletion of redundant `MergeRuleElements`. Then, as no compatible clone groups can be found, the `MergeRule` comprising the information of CG1 and CG2 is added to the resulting `MergeSpecification`. In lines 17–18, the mappings of CG3 and CG5 for D, E and F are removed, leaving them empty and leading to their discarding.

Based on a given `MergeSpecification`, the merge refactoring procedure follows Definition 8 (see [19] for a detailed description): non-master-rule elements are moved to the master rule; non-master rules are deleted; a variability model is set for the master rule; and a presence condition is set for each contained element.

6 Evaluation

We focus on two research questions: **RQ1**: *How well does* RuleMerger *achieve its goal of creating high-quality rule sets?* **RQ2**: *What is the impact of design decisions made by* RuleMerger *on the quality of the created rules?*

To answer these questions, we applied our instantiation of *RuleMerger* on rule sets from two real-life model transformation scenarios, called OCL2NGC and FMRECOG, and one adapted from literature, called COMB. The main quality goal in these scenarios is performance: OCL2NGC and COMB were considered as benchmarks in [9] and [23]; FMRECOG is an automatically derived rule set used in the context of model differencing [24], a task that necessitates low latency. Thus, we optimized the two input parameters described in Sect. 5 for performance. We describe the rule sets and associated test input models in [19].

We assess the quality of the produced rules with respect to performance and reduction in redundancy. To quantify *performance*, we applied the rule sets on all input models and measured cumulative execution time on all input models. We repeated each experiment ten times to account for variance. To quantify *redundancy reduction*, we measured the relative decrease in the number of rule elements, based on the rationale that we produce semantically equivalent, yet syntactically compacted rules (Theorem 1). As discussed in Sect. 2, reducing redundancy in rules is related to benefits for their maintainability.

6.1 Methods and Set-Up

To address RQ1, we investigated three subquestions: **RQ1.1:** *How do VB rules created by* RuleMerger *compare to the equivalent classical rules?* **RQ1.2:** *How do VB rules created by* RuleMerger *compare to those created manually?* **RQ1.3:** *How do the VB rules created by* RuleMerger *scale to large input models?* For RQ1.1, we considered all three rule sets. For RQ1.2, we considered the scenario where a manually created rule set was available: OCL2NGC [9]. For RQ1.3, we considered the COMB scenario, as it features a procedure to increase the input model automatically (increasing the size of the input grid [23]); we measured the impact of model size on execution time until we ran out of memory.

To address RQ2, we investigated two questions: **RQ2.1** *What is the impact of clone detection?* **RQ2.2** *What is the impact of clustering?* For RQ2.1, we randomly discarded 25 %–100 % of the reported clone groups. For RQ2.2, we replaced the default clustering strategy by one that assigns rules to clusters randomly. We measured the execution time of the rules created using the modified input.

As clone detection techniques, we applied ConQat [22] on OCL2NGC and FMRECOG, as it was the only tool scaling to these scenarios. We applied gSpan [20] on the COMB rule set as it allowed us to consider all clones instead of an approximation. The input parameters were optimized independently for each scenario by applying the technique repeatedly until the execution time was minimized. Moreover, the Henshin transformation engine features an optimization concerning the order of nodes considered during matching. To avoid biasing the performance of the FMRECOG rule set by that optimization, we deactivated it. We ran all experiments on a Windows 7 workstation (3.40 GHz processor; 8 GB of RAM).

Table 2. Results for RQ1.1 and RQ1.2: Quality characteristics of the rule sets.

		Size		*Execution time (sec.)*			
Scenario	*Rule set*	#Rules	#Elements	Total	Sd	Median	Sd
OCL2NGC	Classic	36	3045	916.6	96.3	46.0	7.1
	Manual merge	10	1018	181.8	27.1	10.8	2.4
	RuleMerger	12	2147	5.8	0.4	0.4	0.1
FMRECOG	Classic	53	4626	799.9	41.4	63.2	3.5
	RuleMerger	12	2790	211.4	46.0	15.9	0.3
COMB NOMATCH	Classic	6	252	1.39	0.09	0.12	0.01
	RuleMerger	1	62	0.24	0.09	0.02	0.01
COMB SEVERALMATCHES	Classic	6	252	10.4	0.18	0.83	0.02
	RuleMerger	1	62	14.2	0.26	1.07	0.05

6.2   Results and Discussion

Table 2 shows the size and performance characteristics for all involved rule sets. Execution time is provided in terms of the total and median amount of time required to apply the whole rule set on each test model, each of them paired with the standard deviation *(SD)*. The number of elements refers to edges and nodes, including both left-hand and right-hand side of the involved rules.

RQ1.1. The execution time observed for OCL2NGC after the *RuleMerger* treatment showed a decrease by the factor of 158. This substantial speed-up can be partly explained by the merging component of *RuleMerger* that eliminates the anti-pattern *Left-hand side not connected (LhsNC)* [18]: In the automatically constructed VB rules, connected rules are used as base rules, while in the classic rules, we found multiple instances of *LhsNC*. In the FMRECOG and COMB rule sets, the speed-up was less drastic, amounting to the factors of 4.5 and 5.8, respectively. When applying the COMB rule set on the SEVERALMATCHES scenario, which involves an artificial input model with many possible matches [23], execution time increased by the factor 1.36, showing a limitation of VB rules: If the number of base matches is very high, the initialization overhead for extending the base matches outweighs the initial savings. This overhead may be reduced by extending the transformation engine implementation. The amount of redundancy was reduced by 29 % in OCL2NGC, 40 % in FMRECOG, and 75 % in COMB.

RQ1.2. In OCL2NGC, we found a speed-up by the factor of 36. To study this observation further, we inspected the manually created rules, again finding several instances of the *LhsNC* antipattern. This observation gives rise to an interesting interpretation of the manual merging process: While the designer's *explicit* goal was to optimize the rule set for performance, they implicitly performed the more intuitive task of optimizing for compactness. Indeed, the amount of reduced redundancy in the manually created rules (67 %) was significantly greater than in those created by *RuleMerger* (29 %), highlighting an inherent trade-off between performance- and compactness-oriented merging: Not including overlap elements into the base rule leads to duplications in the variable portions.

RQ1.3. As shown in Fig. 8, the last supported input model was a 480x480 grid for both rule sets. We observed that the ratio between the execution time of applying the classic (dark-gray bars) and the VB rules (light-gray bars) stayed the same in each iteration, independent of the size of the input grid: The VB rules were always faster by the factor of 6. In terms of the total execution time, the speed-up provided by the VB rules became more important as the size of input models increased.

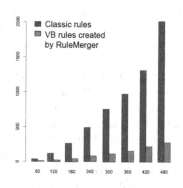

Fig. 8. Results for RQ1.3: Execution time in sec. (y) related to length of grid (x).

RQ2.1. As presented in Table 3, the execution time for the FMRECOG rule set increased monotonically when we increased the amount of discarded overlap, denoted as *d*. OCL2NGC behaved almost monotonically as well. The slightly decreased execution time reported for *d*=0.25 can be explained by the heuristic merge construction strategy. While the merge of rules based on their largest clones might be adequate in general, in some cases it may be preferable to discard a large clone in favor of a more homogeneous distribution of rules. The reported execution time for *d*=0.75 was higher than that for the set of classic rules. In this particular case, small clones were used during merging, leading to small base rules, which resulted in many detectable matches and thus in a high initialization overhead

Table 3. Results for RQ2.1: Impact of considered overlap on execution time (sec.).

	d: Discarded portion				
Scenario	0.0	0.25	0.5	0.75	1.0
Ocl2Ngc	5.8	5.6	251	981	917
FmRecog	211	252	604	690	800

Table 4. Results for RQ2.2: Impact of clustering strategy on execution time (sec.).

	Clustering strategy	
Scenario	AvLinkage	Random
Ocl2Ngc	5.8	80
FmRecog	211	788

for extending these matches. To mitigate this issue, one could define a lower threshold for clone size.

RQ2.2. As indicated in Table 4, the employed clustering strategy had a significant impact on performance, amounting to factors of 13.7 for the Ocl2Ngc and 3.7 for the FmRegoc rule set. Interestingly, in Ocl2Ngc, random clustering still yielded better execution times than manual clustering did (see Table 2) – this is related to the fact that *RuleMerger* removed the *LhsNC* antipattern. In FmRecog, randomly clustered rules were comparable to the classic ones.

6.3   Threats to Validity and Limitations

Factors affecting *external validity* include our choice of rule sets, test models and matching strategy, and the capability to optimize the two input parameters. While the considered rule sets represent three heterogeneous use cases, examples to show that our approach scales to more diverse and larger scenarios are required. To ensure that our test models were realistic, we employed the original test or benchmark models. The performance of rule application depends on the chosen matching strategy, in our case, mapping this task to a constraint satisfaction problem [25]. We aim to consider the effect of other strategies in the future. Parameter tuning requires the existence of realistic test models. If a rule set is designed for productive use, it is reasonable to assume such models to exist.

With regard to *construct validity*, we focus on one aspect of maintainability, the amount of redundancy. Giving a definitive answer on how to unify rules for their optimal maintainability is outside the scope of this work. Specifically, several unrelated rules may be unified, impairing understandability. To mitigate this issue, we recommend to inspect the clustering result before merging. Furthermore, our approach increases the size of individual rules, a potential impediment to readability [26]. We believe that this limitation can be mitigated by tool support. Inspired by related approaches to address the readability issues associated with *#ifdef* directives [27,28], we aim to provide *editable views*, representing portions of a VB rule that correspond to user-selected configurations.

7   Related Work

Our work is related to a number of approaches that create feature-annotated representations of products lines. In [29], an approach to merge statecharts based on structural and behavioral commonalities is applied to models of telecommunication features. In [16], an approach for merging and identifying variability in Matlab product variants is proposed. In [14,30], a formal merge framework is defined and instantiated for class models and state machines. It is studied how a number of desired qualities of the resulting model can be obtained. In [31,32], a technique for the reverse engineering of variability from block diagrams based on their data-flow structures is introduced. In [15], a language-independent approach for the reverse-engineering of product lines is proposed. These approaches operate on the basis of an element-wise comparison using names and as well as structural and behavioral similarities. In model transformation rules, the essential information lies in isomorphic structural patterns. To our knowledge, our approach is the first that utilizes clone detection to identify such patterns.

Our work can be considered a performance optimization for the NP-complete problem of transformation rule matching [33]. Earlier approaches in this area are mostly complementary to ours as they focus on the matching of single rules [34–37]. Mészáros et al. [38] first explored the idea of considering overlapping portions in multiple rules. Their custom technique for detecting these sub-patterns, however, did not scale up to complete rule sets. Instead, they considered just two rules at once, enabling a moderate performance improvement of 11 %. In our approach, applying clone detection and clustering techniques gives rise to an increased speed-up. In, [39] shared sub-patterns are considered dynamically during incremental pattern matching to mitigate the memory issue of Rete networks. Yet, the authors report on deteriorated execution times: The index tables mapping sub-patterns to partial matches grow so large that performance is impaired. Multi-query optimization has also been investigated for relational databases [40]. In graph databases, only single-query optimization has been considered [41].

The maintainability effects of cloning have been studied intensively [14,42]. In an empirical study, Kim et al. [43] identified three types of clones: *short-lived clones* vanishing over the course of few revisions, *"unfactorable" clones* related to language limitations, and *repeatedly changing clones* where a refactoring is recommended. We second the idea that an aggressive refactoring style directed at short-lived clones should be avoided. Instead, targeting clones of the two latter categories, we propose to apply our approach to stable revisions of the rule set. Specifically, clones that were previously "unfactorable" due to the lack of suitable reuse concepts may benefit from the introduction of VB rules. An approach complementary to clone refactoring is *clone management*, based on a tool that detects and updates clones automatically [44]. This approach has a low initial cost, but requires constant monitoring. Further works propose the refactoring of transformation rules towards pre-defined patterns [45], modular interfaces [46], and abstract metamodels [47]. None of these considers clones.

8   Conclusion and Future Outlook

In this work, we introduced an approach for constructing variability-based (VB) model transformation rules automatically. Our experiments showed that the approach is effective: The created rules always had preferable quality characteristics when compared to classical rules, unless the number of expected matches was very high. It is apparent that using the approach, the performance of model transformation systems as well as redundancy-related maintainability concerns can be considerably improved, making the benefits of VB rules available while imposing little manual effort.

In the future, we aim to provide tool support to address the readability issue brought by the increased amount of information in each rule. Moreover, we plan to increase the expressiveness of VB rules. Covering all important transformation features such as application conditions and amalgamation will make VB rules applicable to the existing variety of model transformation languages [48–50].

Acknowledgements. We thank Felix Rieger and the anonymous reviewers for their valuable comments on the present and earlier drafts of this manuscript.

References

1. Sendall, S., Kozaczynski, W.: Model transformation: the heart and soul of model-driven software development. IEEE Softw. **20**(5), 42–45 (2003)
2. Czarnecki, K., Helsen, S.: Feature-based survey of model transformation approaches. IBM Syst. J. **45**(3), 621–646 (2006)
3. Hermann, F., Gottmann, S., Nachtigall, N., Braatz, B., Morelli, G., Pierre, A., Engel, T.: On an automated translation of satellite procedures using triple graph grammars. In: Duddy, K., Kappel, G. (eds.) ICMB 2013. LNCS, vol. 7909, pp. 50–51. Springer, Heidelberg (2013)
4. Mann, M., Ekker, H., Flamm, C.: The graph grammar library - a generic framework for chemical graph rewrite systems. In: Duddy, K., Kappel, G. (eds.) ICMB 2013. LNCS, vol. 7909, pp. 52–53. Springer, Heidelberg (2013)
5. Famelis, M., et al.: Migrating automotive product lines: a case study. In: Kolovos, D., Wimmer, M. (eds.) ICMT 2015. LNCS, vol. 9152, pp. 82–97. Springer, Heidelberg (2015)
6. Richa, E., Borde, E., Pautet, L.: Translating ATL model transformations to algebraic graph transformations. In: Kolovos, D., Wimmer, M. (eds.) ICMT 2015. LNCS, vol. 9152, pp. 183–198. Springer, Heidelberg (2015)
7. Kusel, A., Schonbock, J., Kappel, G., Wimmer, M., Retschitzegger, W., Schwinger, W.: Reuse in model-to-model transformation languages: are we there yet? Softw. Syst. Model. **14**, 537–572 (2013)
8. Blouin, D., Plantec, A., Dissaux, P., Singhoff, F., Diguet, J.-P.: Synchronization of models of rich languages with triple graph grammars: an experience report. In: Di Ruscio, D., Varró, D. (eds.) ICMT 2014. LNCS, vol. 8568, pp. 106–121. Springer, Heidelberg (2014)
9. Strüber, D., Rubin, J., Chechik, M., Taentzer, G.: A variability-based approach to reusable and efficient model transformations. In: Egyed, A., Schaefer, I. (eds.) FASE 2015. LNCS, vol. 9033, pp. 283–298. Springer, Heidelberg (2015)
10. Clements, P., Northrop, L.: Software Product Lines: Practices and Patterns. Series in Software Engineering. Addison-Wesley, Boston (2001)
11. Czarnecki, K., Antkiewicz, M.: Mapping features to models: a template approach based on superimposed variants. In: Glück, R., Lowry, M. (eds.) GPCE 2005. LNCS, vol. 3676, pp. 422–437. Springer, Heidelberg (2005)

12. Roy, C.K., Cordy, J.R., Koschke, R.: Comparison and evaluation of code clone detection techniques and tools: a qualitative approach. Sci. Comput. Program. **74**(7), 470–495 (2009)
13. Xu, R., Wunsch, D., et al.: Survey of clustering algorithms. IEEE Trans. Neural Netw. **16**(3), 645–678 (2005)
14. Rubin, J., Chechik, M.: Combining related products into product lines. In: de Lara, J., Zisman, A. (eds.) Fundamental Approaches to Software Engineering. LNCS, vol. 7212, pp. 285–300. Springer, Heidelberg (2012)
15. Ziadi, T., Henard, C., Papadakis, M., Ziane, M., Le Traon, Y.: Towards a language-independent approach for reverse-engineering of software product lines. In: SAC 2014, pp. 1064–1071. ACM (2014)
16. Ryssel, U., Ploennigs, J., Kabitzsch, K.: Automatic variation-point identification in function-block-based models. In: GPCE 2010, pp. 23–32. ACM (2010)
17. Fowler, M.: Refactoring: Improving the Design of Existing Code. Pearson Education India, New Delhi (2002)
18. Tichy, M., Krause, C., Liebel, G.: Detecting performance bad smells for Henshin model transformations. In: AMT 2013, vol. 1077 (2013)
19. Strüber, D.: Model-driven engineering in the large: refactoring techniques for models and model transformation systems. Ph.D. thesis, Philipps University Marburg pending publication (2016)
20. Yan, X., Han, J.: gspan: graph-based substructure pattern mining. In: ICDM 2003, pp. 721–724. IEEE (2002)
21. Pham, N.H., Nguyen, H.A., Nguyen, T.T., Al-Kofahi, J.M., Nguyen, T.N.: Complete and accurate clone detection in graph-based models. In: ICSE 2009, pp. 276–286. IEEE (2009)
22. Deissenboeck, F., Hummel, B., Juergens, E., Pfaehler, M., Schaetz, B.: Model clone detection in practice. In: the 4th International Workshop on Software Clones, pp. 57–64. ACM (2010)
23. Varró, G., Schürr, A., Varró, D.: Benchmarking for graph transformation. In: ISVL-HCC 2005, pp. 79–88. IEEE (2005)
24. Bürdek, J., Kehrer, T., Lochau, M., Reuling, D., Kelter, U., Schürr, A.: Reasoning about product-line evolution using complex feature model differences. Autom. Softw. Eng. 1–47 (2015). Springer
25. Rudolf, M.: Utilizing constraint satisfaction techniques for efficient graph pattern matching. In: Workshop on Theory and Application of Graph Transformations, p. 238. Springer Science & Business Media (1998)
26. Störrle, H.: On the impact of layout quality to understanding UML diagrams: size matters. In: Dingel, J., Schulte, W., Ramos, I., Abrahão, S., Insfran, E. (eds.) MODELS 2014. LNCS, vol. 8767, pp. 518–534. Springer, Heidelberg (2014)
27. Kästner, C.: Virtual separation of concerns. Ph.D. thesis, University of Magdeburg (2010)
28. Walkingshaw, E., Ostermann, K.: Projectional editing of variational software. In: GPCE 2014, pp. 29–38. ACM (2014)
29. Nejati, S., Sabetzadeh, M., Chechik, M., Easterbrook, S., Zave, P.: Matching and merging of variant feature specifications. IEEE TSE **38**(6), 1355–1375 (2012)
30. Rubin, J., Chechik, M.: Quality of merge-refactorings for product lines. In: Cortellessa, V., Varró, D. (eds.) FASE 2013 (ETAPS 2013). LNCS, vol. 7793, pp. 83–98. Springer, Heidelberg (2013)
31. Wille, D.: Managing lots of models: the famine approach. In: FSE 2014, pp. 817–819. ACM (2014)

32. Holthusen, S., Wille, D., Legat, C., Beddig, S., Schaefer, I., Vogel-Heuser, B.: Family model mining for function block diagrams in automation software. In: SPLC 2014: Workshops, Demonstrations and Tools Companion, pp. 36–43. ACM (2014)

33. Atallah, M.: Algorithms and Theory of Computation Handbook. CRC, Boca Raton (2002)

34. Varró, G., Friedl, K., Varró, D.: Adaptive graph pattern matching for model transformations using model-sensitive search plans. ENTCS **152**, 191–205 (2006)

35. Horváth, Á., Varró, G., Varró, D.: Generic search plans for matching advanced graph patterns. Elec. Comm. of the EASST **6**, 58 (2007)

36. Krause, C., Tichy, M., Giese, H.: Implementing graph transformations in the bulk synchronous parallel model. In: Gnesi, S., Rensink, A. (eds.) FASE 2014 (ETAPS). LNCS, vol. 8411, pp. 325–339. Springer, Heidelberg (2014)

37. Acretoaie, V., Störrle, H.: Efficient model querying with VMQL. In: CMSEBA 2014, pp. 7–16. CEUR-WS.org (2015)

38. Mészáros, T., Mezei, G., Levendovszky, T., Asztalos, M.: Manual and automated performance optimization of model transformation systems. Int. J. Softw. Tools Technol. Transfer **12**(3–4), 231–243 (2010)

39. Varró, G., Deckwerth, F.: A rete network construction algorithm for incremental pattern matching. In: ICMT 2013, pp. 125–140 (2013)

40. Sellis, T.K.: Multiple-query optimization. ACM Trans. Database Syst. (TODS) **13**(1), 23–52 (1988)

41. Zhao, P., Han, J.: On graph query optimization in large networks. VLDB Endowment **3**(1–2), 340–351 (2010)

42. Kapser, C., Godfrey, M.W.: "cloning considered harmful" considered harmful. In: Working Conference on Reverse Engineering, pp. 19–28. IEEE (2006)

43. Kim, M., Sazawal, V., Notkin, D., Murphy, G.: An empirical study of code clone genealogies. In: ACM SIGSOFT Software Engineering Notes, vol. 30, pp. 187–196. ACM (2005)

44. Nguyen, H.A., Nguyen, T.T., Pham, N.H., Al-Kofahi, J., Nguyen, T.N.: Clone management for evolving software. IEEE Trans. Softw. Eng. **38**(5), 1008–1026 (2012)

45. Syriani, E., Gray, J.: Challenges for addressing quality factors in model transformation. In: ICST 2012, pp. 929–937. IEEE (2012)

46. Rentschler, A.: Model transformation languages with modular information hiding. Ph.D. thesis, Karlsruher Institut für Technologie (2015)

47. Sánchez Cuadrado, J., Guerra, E., de Lara, J.: Reverse engineering of model transformations for reusability. In: Di Ruscio, D., Varró, D. (eds.) ICMT 2014. LNCS, vol. 8568, pp. 186–201. Springer, Heidelberg (2014)

48. Balasubramanian, D., Narayanan, A., van Buskirk, C., Karsai, G.: The graph rewriting and transformation language: GReAT. ECEASST **1** (2007)

49. Geiß, R., Batz, G.V., Grund, D., Hack, S., Szalkowski, A.: GrGen: a fast SPO-based graph rewriting tool. In: Corradini, A., Ehrig, H., Montanari, U., Ribeiro, L., Rozenberg, G. (eds.) ICGT 2006. LNCS, vol. 4178, pp. 383–397. Springer, Heidelberg (2006)

50. Acretoaie, V., Störrle, H., Strüber, D.: Transparent model transformation: turning your favourite model editor into a transformation tool. In: Kolovos, D., Wimmer, M. (eds.) ICMT 2015. LNCS, vol. 9152, pp. 121–130. Springer, Heidelberg (2015)

Two-Step Transformation of Model Traversal EOL Queries for Large CDO Repositories

Xabier De Carlos[1]([⊠]), Goiuria Sagardui[2], and Salvador Trujillo[1]

[1] Ikerlan Research Center, P.J.M. Arizmendiarrieta 2, 20500 Arrasate, Spain
{xdecarlos,strujillo}@ikerlan.es
[2] Mondragon Unibertsitatea, Goiru 2, 20500 Arrasate, Spain
gsagardui@mondragon.edu

Abstract. Recent approaches persist models in databases to overcome performance and memory limitations of XMI. Among them, Connected Data Objects (CDO) is a database-based model repository widely used in Model Based Engineering by academia and industry. Model traversal queries are intensively used in modelling scenarios and their performance greatly impacts tools performance and user experience. In this paper, we introduce the CDO-QT framework to transform model traversal queries from Epsilon Object Language (EOL) into SQL queries and execute them at CDO repositories. This way, model engineers can define queries using domain concepts at performance similar to SQL. We have evaluated CDO-QT executing a set of queries over repositories from 15 MB to 5 GB size. CDO-QT results in better performance and memory consumption with respect to other approaches (Plain EMF, MDT OCL, CDO-OCL).

Keywords: Model driven development · Query · Model persistence · Eclipse modelling framework · Connected data objects · Large models

1 Introduction

Model Based Engineering (MBE) raises the abstraction level of software development promising productivity increases and greatly improved quality of the code and development process [11]. In this paradigm, models automate and guide the development processes and engineers focus on domain concepts rather than on implementation details.

Modelling scenarios in industry can be really complex [1], with large models of size of 100 MB and beyond, and with millions of model elements. Engineers use modelling tools for model transformation, validation or execution. Performance might have adverse effect on development, which makes MBE adoption difficult in industry. Among all the activities, model queries are intensively used. Therefore the impact of query performance on tool performance and user experience is significant [4]. In practise, model traversal queries are the most commonly used type of queries [9]. These queries obtain all the instances of a specific type and require traversing the entire model.

© Springer-Verlag Berlin Heidelberg 2016
P. Stevens and A. Wąsowski (Eds.): FASE 2016, LNCS 9633, pp. 141–157, 2016.
DOI: 10.1007/978-3-662-49665-7_9

The Eclipse Modelling Framework (EMF) is a mature framework widely used by the industry and academia. By default, EMF models are persisted using XML Metadata Interchange (XMI). XMI entails memory problems for models [9,15] and requires to completely load them in-memory for model traversal queries. EMF provides also a binary format which improves scalability of XMI, but it also requires loading entire models. Alternative proposals to XMI for large models choose databases for persistence, overcoming limitations by partial loading of models. Different back-end strategies have been proposed: noSQL databases (e.g. Morsa, MongoDB, NeoEMF/Map, NeoEMF/Graph or EMF Fragments); relational databases (e.g. Teneo); or several kinds of databases (e.g. CDO). Databases improve significantly performance in model operation for large models. For example, a database-based prototype introduced at [2] executes a model traversal query (GraBaTs query) 20 times faster than XMI and requires 57 % of the memory used by XMI.

Matureness and collaboration support makes Connected Data Objects (CDO) [17] the most widely used model repository in academia and industry [8]. CDO provides support for model operation from Plain EMF and EMF-based model query languages executed at *client-side* (e.g. MDT OCL or EMF query), model query languages executed at *server-side* (CDO OCL) and persistence-specific query languages (e.g. HQL and SQL). Persistence-specific languages improve significantly model operation performance. For example, GraBaTs query for CDO with H2 relational back-end for a model of almost 5 millon elements[1] requires 6 seconds and 289 MB of memory usage from SQL, while in the best case of model query languages, it requires 28 s using 525 MB. However, in model query languages model engineers use domain specific concepts, while in persistence-specific query languages engineers should be aware of the way information is persisted and learn database specific concepts and languages. This increases programming effort to get complex queries correct.

The main contribution of this paper is a framework (CDO-QT) that transforms queries from a model query language (Epsilon Object Language [12]) to a persistence specific query language (SQL) and executes them at a CDO repository. Generated queries are fully integrated with the versioning/branching of CDO. This way, model engineers can define queries using domain concepts at performance similar to SQL. CDO-QT is designed in a two-step transformation process to provide re-usability and extensibility. We evaluate performance and memory usage of different model traversal queries using Plain EMF, MDT OCL, CDO OCL, SQL and CDO-QT. We have executed the queries over ten CDO repositories from 15.3 MB to 5 GB. Results show that CDO-QT is able to execute all the queries faster and requiring less memory than the other solutions (Plain EMF, MDT OCL and CDO-OCL).

The rest of the paper is organized as follows: Sect. 2 introduces CDO and describes the motivation of this work. Section 3 describes the query transformation process performed by CDO-QT. In Sect. 4 we evaluate CDO-QT comparing performance and memory usage for executing different model traversal queries

---

[1] More details about the evaluation scenario and metrics in Sect. 4.

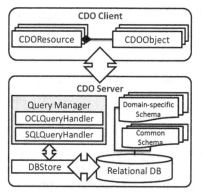

Fig. 1. Simplified CDO architecture for relational backends.

Table 1. Execution time (s) and memory usage (MB) for the GraBaTs query.

		Set0	Set1	Set2	Set3	Set4
Plain EMF	time	18	48	473	1069	1140
	mem	400	1028	3407	5672	6133
MDT OCL	time	18	46	453	1023	1101
	mem	322	934	3112	5731	6110
CDO OCL	time	1	2	11	26	28
	mem	67	67	337	525	590
SQL	time	0	1	2	5	6
	mem	65	126	154	289	289

and using different model query languages. This paper concludes with related work and conclusions in Sects. 5 and 6.

2   Operation with CDO Repositories

CDO provides transparent persistence of models in all kinds of back-end strategies, with load on demand mechanisms and caching policies to operate persisted models. CDO supports features such as: multi-user access, off-line collaboration, model-level locking, branching and versioning. Figure 1 illustrates the client/server architecture of CDO. **CDO Server** interacts with the database back-end through an IStore implementation. *DBStore* is the most mature and complete[2], and in practice mainly relational back-ends are used with CDO [3]. For relational back-ends, CDO provides a common data-schema with dedicated tables for change history, branches, commits or user access; additionally it generates automatically one data-schema for each different domain-metamodel.

EMF-based applications (editors, querying utilities, transformations, etc.) can operate with CDO repositories. For this purpose, **CDO Client** provides a custom extension of EMFs Resource (CDOResource) and EObjects (CDOObjects). Elements of the model are loaded in memory to operate them. CDO Client can also communicate with a server side query manager. CDO provides support for OCL queries (OCLQueryHandler) and SQL (SQLQueryHandler). Table 1 shows execution time and memory usage results for the GraBats case study [16] using Plain EMF, OCL, CDO-OCL and SQL on five CDO repositories with H2 relational database (Set0–4)[3]. Best results are obtained when operating from server-side query manager. In particular, CDOs' SQL query handler significantly improves performance of operation. However, the programming effort for model engineers to get complex queries right in SQL can be high, and they should be aware of database schema and persistence related issues.

---

[2] Comparison of CDO stores: http://goo.gl/cEemcL.

[3] For extended information about the evaluation, please refer to Sect. 4.

Fig. 2. EOL to SQL query transformation and execution process of CDO-QT.

3   CDO-QT

Some works have proposed query transformation from model query languages to SQL [5–7,10,13,14]. Inspired in these works, and with the aim of improving performance in CDO when operating with model query languages, we present Query Transformation Engine for CDO (CDO-QT).

CDO-QT inputs model traversal queries in a model query language (EOL [12]) and transforms automatically to SQL queries that are executed directly in CDO relational back-ends. Figure 2 illustrates the transformation process: (i) model engineers use EOL; (ii) CDO-QT transforms at runtime EOL statements into a language independent model; (iii) CDO-QT transforms the model into SQL statements; and (iv) SQL statements are executed directly over the database.

3.1   Query Language Independent Metamodel

CDO-QT uses a Query Language Independent Metamodel (QLI Metamodel) to specify queries in a language-independent way, separating the transformation to SQL from the model-query language. At this time, CDO-QT supports transformation of model traversal and self-contained EOL queries. A simplification of QLI Metamodel for model traversal EOL queries is illustrated in Fig. 3:

- `Query`: Root element of the model. Attribute `returnType` specifies the type of result returned by the query and `root` reference contains an `IModelTraversal` instance. `IModelTraversal` specifies statements that full-traverse models and is implemented by `AllInstancesOfKind` and `CollectionMethod`.
- `AllInstancesOfKind`. Abstraction for statements that traverse models searching instances of an specific kind (specified by `type`). Sample EOL statement is *MethodDeclaration.all*.
- `CollectionMethod`. Abstraction for query statements where all values of an input collection are evaluated (e.g. *.select(md:MethodDeclaration | ...)* EOL statement). `name` specifies type of the `CollectionMethod` (e.g. select, collect, etc.); `iterator` reference contains the input collection (`VariableIterator` instance); and `body` optional reference contains a `IQueryStatement` instance.
- `VariableIterator`. Specifies variables that iterate a collection values within a query. `type` contains `EClass` of the iterated values; `name` specifies the variable name; and `alias`, contains an unique name of the variable. `VariableIterator` contains an `ISource` instance (`source` reference). `ISource` is implemented by classes that specify collection of values iterated by a `VariableIterator` instance. Sample EOL statement is *md:MethodDeclaration*.

- IQueryStatement is an interface implemented by all classes that specify statements that could be contained by a CollectionMethod (LogicalOP, ComparisonOP and Value). getType() returns type of the value returned by the specified statement.
- LogicalOP. Abstraction for logical comparison of two statements[4] (contained by left and right) and returns a boolean value (getType()=Boolean). Operator specifies the logical operator type (AND, OR, NOT, etc.) Sample EOL statement is: mod.private and mod.static.
- ComparisonOP. Similar to LogicalOP but for comparison of values (e.g. EQUALS, LOWER, etc.). Sample EOL statement is mod.private=true.
- Value. Extended by PrimitiveValue, CollectionMethod, ValueMethod and VariableValue classes, and specifies statements returning a value.
- PrimitiveValue. Abstraction for primitive values (e.g. true boolean value).
- ValueMethod. For query statements that evaluate a single-value. name specifies method type; params contains parameters of the method; and variable reference contains a VariableValue instance which is evaluated. Sample EOL statement is md.isOfType(MethodDeclaration).
- VariableValue. Extended by LocalVariableValue and VariableIterator classes, is an abstraction for statements returning values derived from a variable specified within the query.
- LocalVariableValue. Abstraction for statements that specify value of a variable within the query. It contains parentVariable feature that references a VariableValue instance and sf attribute that specifies a EStructuralFeature. If sf is empty, this class specifies the value returned by the instance referenced at parentVariable. By contrast, if sf contains a feature, the class specifies the feature value in the parentVariable class values.

Figure 4 illustrates a sample QLI model that conforms to the QLI Metamodel. Section 3.3 describes this model and provides information about its generation.

3.2 CDO-QT Design

Figure 5 illustrates the class-diagram of CDO-QT:

- **Language independent** (CDO-QT.generic package). Classes and interfaces to be extended by EOL- and CDO-Specific packages. This design facilitates inclusion of new query languages. MLDriver transforms model queries into a language independent representation (QLI Model). PLDriver transforms into a database-specific language and executes the query.
- **EOL-Specific** (CDO-QT.eol-specific package). Deals with EOL and is responsible for parsing and transforming EOL queries into a QLI Model. EOLDriver extends MLDriver and implements IModel interface of the EMC API (provided by EOL) to interact with EOL queries. generateQLIM() method supports transformation of EOL queries into QLI model.

---

[4] With the exception of NOT operator that only has one statement contained by right reference.

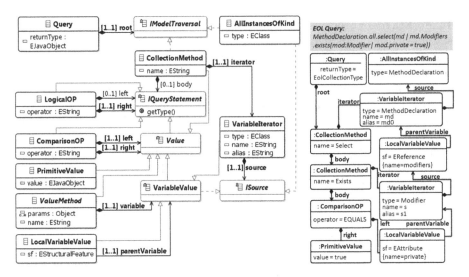

Fig. 3. Simplified QLI Metamodel

Fig. 4. QLI Model for a sample EOL query.

– **CDO-Specific** (CDO-QT.dbstore-specific package). Deals with CDO and is responsible for: (i) transforming QLI Model into a database specific language; and (ii) executing the query. We provide implementation for DBStore (SQL). CDODriver extends PLDriver. generateQuery() method that generates a SQL query from a language independent model. execQuery() method executes the generated SQL query through a CDOQuery instance (provided by CDO to execute SQL queries at server-side). CDODriver also implements getVersionBranchInfo() (which adds version and branch information to SQL queries) and postProcessResults() (for post-processing SQL results).

As shown in Fig. 6 user interacts with the EOLDriver (execQuery method). EOLDriver generates the QLI Model (generateQLIModel method) and calls getResult method of the CDODriver. CDODriver executes generateQuery method to obtain SQL query. Then, SQL query is completed with version/branch information (addVersionBranchInfo()). Next, query is executed, obtained results post-processed, and returned to EOLDriver and to the user.

3.3 From EOL to QLI Model

CDO-QT generates an intermediate and query language independent QLI Model from EOL queries: the EOLDriver receives from EOL an AST Tree that specifies the EOL Query, which is the input point of the transformation. Listing 1.1 illustrates a fragment of the transformation algorithm (genQLIElem(AST n)), where AST nodes are visited and artifacts of the QLI Model are instantiated. The algorithm is called recursively until all nodes are visited.

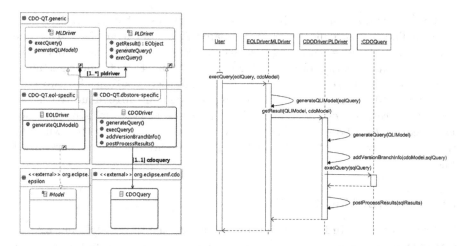

Fig. 5. CDO-QT class diagram   **Fig. 6.** CDO-QT sequence diagram

Following, QLI Model generation process for the EOL query illustrated on Fig. 4 is described: the transformation process starts with the AST node corresponding with the *MethodDeclaration.all* EOL statement. The transformation algorithm obtains the AST node and generates corresponding abstraction (`AllInstancesOfKind` instance). Next, AST node that specifies *.select(md — ...)* statement is processed by the algorithm and creates a `CollectionMethod` instance (with 'select' name value). This instance contains a `VariableIterator` instance that specifies the collection iterator (*md*). `VariableIterator` iterates values returned by *MethodDeclaration.all* statement and consequently it contains the previously instantiated `AllInstancesOfKind`.

```
1 Object genQLIElem(AST n){
2 if ...
3 else if(n.hasChildren() && isComparison(n.getText())){
4    ComparisonOP obj = createComparisonOP();
5    obj.setLeft(genQLIElem(n.getFirstChild()));
6    obj.setRight(genQLIElem(n.getSecondChild()));
7    obj.setOperator(n.getText());
8    return obj;
9 } ... }
```

Listing 1.1. Fragment of the QLI Model generation algorithm.

The condition of the `CollectionMethod` instance is specified by *md.modifiers.exists(mod:Modifier | ...)* EOL statement and a `CollectionMethod` (named '`exists`') instance is created under the body reference. It contains a `VariableIterator` instance that contains a `LocalVariableValue` that specifies iterated values (*md.modifiers*). `CollectionMethod` body reference is filled with a `ComparisonOP` (abstraction of condition *mod.private=true* condition). The fragment shown in Listing 1.1 contains code related to the generation of the `ComparisonOP` instances. In this case, it satisfies `n.hasChildren()` condition of line 3 (one child for each compared side) and `n.getText()` of line 3 returns the string = satisfying also second condition. Satisfying conditions involves the instantiation of a new `ComparisonOP`(line 4). Left and right references are obtained executing the algorithm `genQLIElem(AST n)` for two children (lines 5,6). In this case, `left` contains a `LocalVariableValue` that specifies *mod.private* statement, and `right` contains a `PrimitiveValue` instance that specifies *true* boolean value. Finally, operator feature is setted with the value returned by `n.getText()`(line 7) and the instantiated element is returned (line 8).

3.4   From QLI Model to SQL

`EOLDriver` calls `CDODriver` passing by arguments the `QLI Model` and a `CDO-Resource` instance (queried model). At this point, the prototype uses the default mapping strategy of the DBStore (horizontal mapping). We can distinguish two different types of tables within the domain-specific data-schema: (a) **Object-Tables**: contain information about all the instances of an specific type. The name of the each table corresponds with name of the type of the containing elements (e.g. *MethodDeclaration*); (b) **Many-Value-Ref-Tables**: contain information about a many-value reference of an specific type. The name of the table will follow this format: TypeName_FeatureName_List (e.g. *MethodDeclaration_BodyDeclarations_List*).

Table 2 describes a simplified version of SQL queries that are generated from each `QLI Model` element. Branching and versioning related statements are added in generated SQL queries:

- **WHERE** **statements that obtain information from an Object-Table.** Following, simplified version of the added SQL statement that is described: `CDO_VERSION>0 AND ((CDO_BRANCH =:branchID AND CDO_CREATED <= :commit AND (CDO_REVISED=0 OR CDO_REVISED>:commit)) OR (:hasBase AND CDO_BRANCH =:baseID AND CDO_CREATED<=:basetime AND (CDO_REVISED=0 OR CDO_REVISED>:basetime)))`. The statement contains the following parameters: (1) `commit`, specifies the timestamp of the commit corresponding with the model version; (2) `branchID`, specifies the identifier of the branch that is being queried; (3) `hasBase`, boolean value that specifies if the branch is based in another branch; (4) `baseID`, specifies the identifier of the base branch; and (5) `baseTime`, specifies the timestamp of the corresponding version of the base branch.
- **INNER JOIN statements that join an Object-Table with a Many-Value-Ref-Table.** This is a simplified version of the SQL statement that is added: `objectTable.CDO_VERSION = referenceTable.CDO_VERSION AND objectTable.CDO_BRANCH = referenceTable.CDO_BRANCH`.

Table 2. SQL queries generated for each QLI model element.

QLI Element	Generated SQL
AllKindInstances	types: `SELECT * FROM TypeTable WHERE ...` subtypes: `(SELECT * FROM SubType1Table)` `UNION (SELECT * FROM SubType2Table) ...`
LogicalOP	`(rightStatementSQL (AND │ OR │ ...) leftStatementSQL)`
ComparisonOP	`(rightStatementSQL ( = │ < │ ...)leftStatementSQL)`
PrimitiveValue	strings: `'value'`; other types: `value`

ValueMethod	method-specific SQL. Ex.: var.feature.isTypeOf(type):
	`EXISTS(SELECT * FROM TypeTable AS T`
	`WHERE var.feature=T.CDO_ID AND ...)`

CollectionMethod	method-specific SQL. Ex.: var.feature.exists(it — cond):
	`EXISTS (SELECT iteratorName.*`
	`FROM (VariableIteratorSQL) AS iteratorName`
	`WHERE condSQL)`

VariableIterator	`IteratorParentType_IteratorParentFeature_List` `INNER JOIN (iteratorType) AS iteratorName ON`

LocalVariableValue	multi-value refs: `SELECT featureName.CDO_VALUE`
	`FROM ParentType_Feature_List`
	`INNER JOIN FeatureType AS featureName ON`
	`WHERE ParentType_Feature_List.CDO_SOURCE =`
	`parent.CDO_ID AND ... )`
	attributes and single-value refs: `SELECT parent.feature`
	`FROM ParentTable WHERE 1`

3.5 Executing the Query

Version and branch parameters are set using the `CDOResource`. Listing 1.2 illustrates the parameter setting process: (1) parameter values are obtained from the `CDOResource` instance; (2) obtained values are set to the generated SQL through the `CDOQuery` instance (`cqo`); and (3) the SQL query is executed over the CDO repository using the `CDOQuery` class provided by CDO. Obtained results correspond to all the models (`CDOResource`) of the repository. To provide results for a specific model, CDO-QT filters and/or analyses the SQL results. For example, to obtain all *MethodDeclaration* instances, the post-process selects those that are part of the model (`object.cdoResource() == resource`). To check if a `MethodDeclaration` exists in a model, SQL results are analysed (e.g. `while(res.hasNext()){ if (res.getNext().cdoResource == resource)` `return true;} return false;`). We have decided to do this post-process as including it in the transformation would require complex SQL queries that could have impact in performance.

```
void setQueryParameters(CDOResource resource, CDOQuery cqo){
boolean hasParent = false;
long commit = getTimeStamp(resource.cdoView)
long branchID = resource.cdoView().getBranch().getID();
if(existsBase(resource)) hasParent = true;
long baseID = getBaseID(resource);
long baseTime = getBaseTime(resource);
cqo.setParameter("commit", Long.toString(commit));
cqo.setParameter("branchID", Long.toString(branchID));
cqo.setParameter("hasParent", hasParent);
cqo.setParameter("baseID",Long.toString(baseID));
cqo.setParameter("baseTime",Long.toString(baseTime));}
```

Listing 1.2. Setting paramater values of the generated SQL queries.

4 Evaluation

All the experiments have been executed as a standalone application over a Microsoft Azure[5] virtual machine configured with a 4 Core processor, 14 GB of RAM, 200 GB SSD, and running 64-Bit Windows Server 2012 and Java SE v1.8.0. We have used Eclipse Mars with CDO 4.4. CDO repositories have been executed in embedded mode[6] to measure total memory usage and avoid the uncertainty of connections in the execution time. Repositories run on top of H2 v1.3.168, using the DBStore with its default mapping, caching and pre-fetching values, and supporting audits and branches.

Correctness of query-results has been ensured by automatically comparing the results of each query using different languages. In order to get reliable numbers, each query was processed 5 times for each evaluation case and Java Virtual Machine has been restarted for each execution. Results have been evaluated against the following quantitative metrics: M1: Average Execution Time (in seconds) and M2: Maximum Memory Usage (in MB). M2 includes memory used by the CDO Client and Server. We have used three different queries in the evaluation: Q1: Number of classes (TypeDeclaration instances) existing within the model, Q2: Number of private methods (MethodDeclaration instances) existing within the model and Q3: Number of singletons (TypeDeclaration instances) existing within the model (GraBaTs case study query). All queries traverse model but with increasing complexity. We have expressed queries in Plain EMF, OCL (used by MDT OCL and CDO-OCL), SQL and EOL (used by CDO-QT). We have used metamodel and model instances from the GraBaTs 2009 case study [16]. Models specify source code of different Java packages and conform to the *JDTAST* metamodel which contains abstractions of the Java source code. Table 3 shows results of queries for each model.

In this evaluation we address: *Which is the performance of querying models within a CDO repository using EMF Plain, MDT OCL, CDO_OCL, SQL*

---

[5] Azure: https://azure.microsoft.com/en-us/services/virtual-machines/.

[6] CDO/Embedded: https://wiki.eclipse.org/CDO/Embedded.

Table 3. Properties of the GraBaTs models.

	XMI size	Repository size	Numb. of models	Model Elem	Q1 Results	Q2 Results	Q3 Results
Set0	8,8	15.3 MB	1	70447	14	4	1
Set1	27	43.8 MB	1	198466	40	38	2
Set2	271	307 MB	1	2082841	1605	1793	41
Set3	598	784 MB	1	4852855	5314	9275	155
Set4	646	1.17 GB	1	4961779	5984	10086	164
Set5	n/a	2.01 GB	2	9923558	5984	10086	164
Set6	n/a	2.88 GB	3	14885337	5984	10086	164
Set7	n/a	3.67 GB	4	19847116	5984	10086	164
Set8	n/a	4.45 GB	5	24808895	5984	10086	164
Set9	n/a	5 GB	6	29770674	5984	10086	164

and CDO-QT? We distinguish two different configuration factors (F) that may impact:

- **F1, Size of the model**: We measure how the increasing size of the model may influence on the performance (execution time and memory). We measure the size of a model in number of elements. For this factor, each model has been persisted in a different CDO Repository (from Set0 to Set4 of Table 3).
- **F2, Size of the repository**: As in CDO we can save many models in the repository, we have measured how the increasing size of the repository may influence on the performance. We measure the size of the repository in number of models and elements within the repository. For this factor, we have stored set4 model copies within the same CDO Repository (from Set4 to Set9 of Table 3).

Extended information in http://xdecarlos.bitbucket.org/fase_2016/.

4.1 Discussion

F1: Model-Size Influence (Set0-Set4). Size of the queried model has a great impact over the time and memory required in Plain EMF and MDT OCL, and three queries result in similar values (entire model is always loaded in memory). In Set4, these client-side solutions require more than 6000 % of time of Set0 and more than 1100 % of memory. *Plain EMF* requires 17-18 s and 396-513 MB for querying the smallest model (Set0) and 1140-1166 s and 6-6.1 GB for the largest (Set4). Model size impact is slightly lower for *MDT OCL* as it requires 17-18 s and 322-342 MB for Set0 and 1090-1101 s and 6-6.1 GB for Set4.

Figure 7 illustrates time and memory results and they show that, the impact of the model size is lower if queries are executed at server-side. In Set4, these

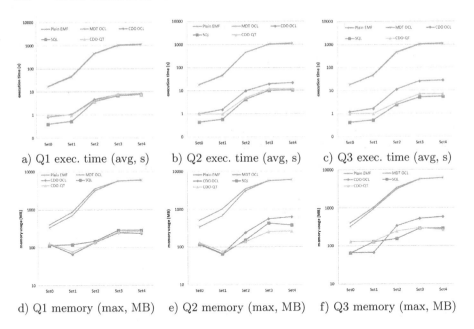

a) Q1 exec. time (avg, s)   b) Q2 exec. time (avg, s)   c) Q3 exec. time (avg, s)

d) Q1 memory (max, MB)   e) Q2 memory (max, MB)   f) Q3 memory (max, MB)

Fig. 7. Execution time and memory results of queries from Set0 to Set4.

solutions require up to 2400 % of time of Set0 and up to 800 % of memory. However, increase values are much lower than on client-side solutions.

CDO-OCL is more than 17 times faster than Plain EMF and MDT OCL, and it only requires 1 s for executing queries in Set0. Memory usage is also reduced to 123 MB (Q1-Q2) and 67 MB (Q3). In case of other sets, results vary depending on the query: Q1 requires less time than Q2 and Q3, and Q2 less than Q3. For example, in Set4 Q1 requires 8 s, Q2 22 s and Q3 28 s. However, Q3 is more than 38 times faster than any query in Plain EMF or MDT OCL. In terms of memory, Q1 requires less than Q2 and Q3: in Set4 Q1 needs 235 MB, Q2 636 MB and Q3 590 MB. Worst memory value (636 MB) is more than 9 times lower than the best memory usage result of the client-side solutions. *SQL* shows better results: queries require less than a second and 118 MB in Set0; and less than 12 s and 375 MB in Set4. Q1 requires less time and memory than Q2 and results are similar of CDO-OCL. In the case of Q2 it is 2 times faster than CDO-OCL and memory usage is reduced by 40 % for Set4. Q3 time and memory results are lower than Q1 and Q2, and it is more than 4 times faster than CDO-OCL requiring less than 50 % of memory.

Performance and memory results of *CDO-QT* for executing queries using EOL are similar to SQL. Execution time results show that CDO-QT requires between 1 and 2 s more than SQL to be executed. The generated SQL query is the same that is used in the SQL experiments, and it indicates that the extra-time corresponds with the EOL to SQL transformation. CDO-QT requires 1 s and less than 130 MB for executing queries in Set0, and less than 8 s and 315 MB

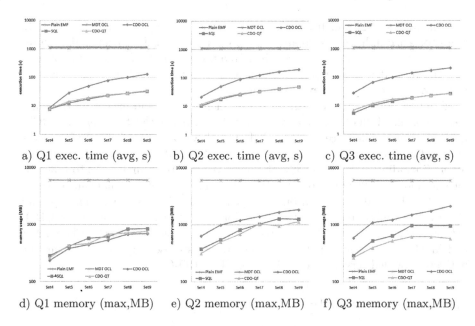

a) Q1 exec. time (avg, s)   b) Q2 exec. time (avg, s)   c) Q3 exec. time (avg, s)

d) Q1 memory (max,MB)   e) Q2 memory (max,MB)   f) Q3 memory (max,MB)

Fig. 8. Execution time and memory results of queries from Set4 to Set9.

in Set4. As occurs in SQL, Q3 requires less time and memory than Q1 and Q2, and Q1 less than Q2. For example in Set4: Q1 requires 8 s and 263 MB, Q2 12 s and 315 MB, and Q3 7 s and 263 MB. CDO-QT results are significantly better than using the other server-side solution (CDO-OCL), and much better than using a client-side solution (Plain EMF and MDT-OCL).

F2: Repository-Size Influence (Set4-Set9). Time and memory results obtained querying F2 models (set4-set9) indicate that the size of the repository has not influence in queries executed at the client-side: In the case of *Plain EMF* execution time value for executing queries is between 1140-1174 s and requires around 6 GB of memory; in the case of *MDT OCL* the execution time is slightly lower (between 1081-1113 s) and also requires around 6 GB of memory.

As Fig. 8 illustrates, this scenario changes in case of the server-side solutions, where the size of the repository has influence. *CDO-OCL* results show a constant increase of the query execution time from one repository to the subsequent one (e.g. from Set5 to Set6). The increase changes according to query: between 20-28 s for Q1, 31-41 s for Q2, and 35-42 s for Q3. Memory usage increases: from 235 MB to 695 MB in Q1; from 636 MB to 1860 MB in Q2; and from 590 MB to 2171 MB of Q3. The influence of the repository size is greater in Q3, which requires more time and memory. In Set4, CDO-OCL requires around 1100 % of time of Set0 and around 330 % of memory. The trend is similar in *SQL*, but the time increase between repositories is lower: 4-6 s for Q1, 7-8 s for Q2, and 4-5 s for Q3. Memory values increase from 285 MB to 849 MB for Q1; from 375 MB to 1249 MB for Q2; and from 289 MB to 968 MB for Q3. In the case of SQL, repository-size influence is greater in Q2. Q3 is resolved faster and Q1 requires less memory than others. In Set4, SQL requires around 430 % of time of Set0 and around 300 % of memory. While increase is similar to CDO-OCL in case of memory, increment of the execution time is lower.

CDO-QT results agree with those obtained in SQL and execution time and memory is also influenced by repository size, but it is lower than in CDO-OCL. Execution time difference between SQL and CDO-QT is only of 1-2 s (transformation time overhead). In terms of memory, CDO-QT uses less memory than others (including SQL): from 263 MB to 761 MB for Q1, from 315 MB to 1136 MB for Q2, and from 264 MB to 579 MB for Q3. The filtering mechanism provided by CDO-QT could be the reason of memory usage difference between SQL and CDO-QT. Results show that the execution time and memory usage of CDO-QT is much lower than the required by the client-side solutions (Plain EMF and MDT OCL). Additionally, CDO-QT resolves these queries faster than the natively provided server-side version of OCL (CDO-OCL).

4.2   Threats to Validity

All the queries full traverse the model, therefore they start the computation by obtaining all the instances of an specific type that exists within the queried model. This type of queries covers the majority of computational-demanding queries in real industrial domains such as reverse engineering domain [9]. However, there are other types of queries (e.g. non-traversal queries or queries that modify the model) that have not been tested. Moreover, models have been generated for test-case purpose. Using industrial models and real model operations would be more realistic. We plan to perform it in a future version of this work.

5   Related Work

Query Transformation. [10] describes a framework that supports mapping of UML models to arbitrary data-schemas and mapping of OCL invariants to a declarative query language. [14] transforms OCL constraints into SQL to check integrity of UML models persisted in relational repositories. [7] generates SQL queries from OCL constraints and executes over MySQL databases. [6] provides a tool based on OCL2SQL that generates views from OCL constraints. All these approaches provide generation at compilation-time from OCL (declarative language) to SQL (declarative language). By contrast, CDO-QT transforms at run-time EOL, an imperative model-level language, into a declarative persistence-specific query language (SQL).

CDO Evaluation. [15] includes evaluation of CDO by comparing results of performing different model operations (store, query and modify) with XMI and Morsa. [2] describes the performance and memory usage required by different persistence mechanisms (Teneo, CDO, Neo4J and OrientDB) for executing the GraBaTs case study query. These studies show CDO results for three models of

GraBaTs (Set0–2), by contrast, our evaluation includes results of all the Gra-BaTs models (Set0–4). [3,9,15] include an analysis of CDO and other persistence mechanisms through the execution of different types of queries. While they use one query language for executing queries in CDO, our study shows results for different query languages (Plain EMF, MDT OCL, CDO OCL, SQL and EOL with CDO-QT). [8] focuses the evaluation in the model query languages and describes the GraBaTs query results using different query languages and persistences (XMI, CDO and MORSA). While the GraBats query is included in this study, we have executed two additional queries using different query languages that are executed against CDO repositories.

Improve Query Performance. EMF-IncQuery provides support for executing model queries in an incremental way only over model parts that have changed [18]. [19] focuses on improving efficiency of model traversal EOL queries. While these approaches provide improvements on user-side query execution, CDO-QT provides support for generating SQL queries that are executed over persistence (relational back-end) and at server-side.

6   Conclusions and Future Work

In this paper, we have presented CDO-QT, an approach that: (i) provides a two-step transformation process that generates SQL queries from EOL queries; and (ii) executes generated SQL at server-side over CDO repositories. CDO-QT is able to execute model traversal queries in a model query language (EOL), but with a performance similar to SQL. We have compared the performance and memory usage results of executing different model query languages: Plain EMF, MDT OCL, CDO OCL, SQL and EOL using CDO-QT. GraBaTs 2009 Case Study models have been persisted in different CDO repositories with size from 15.3 MB to 5 GB. Execution time and memory results show that CDO-QT is a promising alternative for making queries from EOL to CDO repositories. Results indicate that CDO-QT is much faster and use less memory than model query languages executed at client-side of CDO (Plain EMF and MDT OCL). Moreover, obtained results are better than the natively supported CDO-OCL that executes OCL queries at server-side.

This prototype of CDO-QT provides support for executing self-contained and model traversal EOL queries. However, we plan to extend it to support more types of EOL queries (e.g. non-traversal queries, queries that modify models, query chains, etc.). For future work, we plan to provide CDO-QT implementations of additional model query languages, supporting transformation of other types of languages (e.g. IncQuery or OCL). We also plan to provide implementations for other stores of CDO and for other persistence mechanisms.

Acknowledgements. The authors wish to thank Xabier Mendialdua for his contributions. This work is partially supported by the EC, through the Scalable Modelling and Model Management on the Cloud (MONDO) FP7 STREP project (#611125).

References

1. Bagnato, A., Brosse, E., Sadovykh, A., Maló, P., Trujillo, S., Mendialdua, X., De Carlos, X.: Flexible and scalable modelling in the MONDO project: industrial case studies. In: Proceedings of the 3rd Workshop on Extreme Modeling Co-located with ACM/IEEE 17th International Conference on Model Driven Engineering Languages & Systems, XM@MoDELS 2014, 29 September 2014, Valencia, Spain, pp. 42–51 (2014)

2. Barmpis, K., Kolovos, D.S.: Evaluation of contemporary graph databases for efficient persistence of large-scale models. J. Object Technol. **13**(3), 3:1–3:26 (2014)

3. Benelallam, A., Gómez, A., Sunyé, G., Tisi, M., Launay, D.: Neo4EMF, a scalable persistence layer for EMF models. In: Cabot, J., Rubin, J. (eds.) ECMFA 2014. LNCS, vol. 8569, pp. 230–241. Springer, Heidelberg (2014)

4. Bergmann, G., Horváth, Á., Ráth, I., Varró, D., Balogh, A., Balogh, Z., Ökrös, A.: Incremental evaluation of model queries over EMF models. In: Petriu, D.C., Rouquette, N., Haugen, Ø. (eds.) MODELS 2010, Part I. LNCS, vol. 6394, pp. 76–90. Springer, Heidelberg (2010)

5. De Carlos, X., Sagardui, G., Murguzur, A., Trujillo, S., Mendialdua, X.: Model query translator - a model-level query approach for large-scale models. In: MODELSWARD 2015 - Proceedings of the 3rd International Conference on Model-Driven Engineering and Software Development, ESEO, 9–11 February 2015, Angers, Loire Valley, France, pp. 62–73 (2015)

6. Demuth, B., Hussmann, H., Loecher, S.: OCL as a specification language for business rules in database applications. In: Gogolla, M., Kobryn, C. (eds.) UML 2001. LNCS, vol. 2185, pp. 104–117. Springer, Heidelberg (2001)

7. Egea, M., Dania, C., Clavel, M.: MySQL4OCL: a stored procedure-based MySQL code generator for OCL. Electron. Commun. EASST **36**, 1–16 (2010)

8. Pagán, J.E., Molina, J.G.: Querying large models efficiently. Inf. Softw. Technol. **56**(6), 586–622 (2014)

9. Gómez, A., Tisi, M., Sunyé, G., Cabot, J.: Map-based transparent persistence for very large models. In: Egyed, A., Schaefer, I. (eds.) FASE 2015. LNCS, vol. 9033, pp. 19–34. Springer, Heidelberg (2015)

10. Heidenreich, F., Wende, C., Demuth, B.: A framework for generating query language code from OCL invariants. Electron. Commun. EASST **9**, 1–10 (2007)

11. Kärnä, J., Tolvanen, J.-P., Kelly, S.: Evaluating the use of domain-specific modeling in practice. In: Proceedings of the 9th OOPSLA Workshop on Domain-Specific Modeling (2009)

12. Kolovos, D.S., Rose, L., Garcia-Dominguez, A., Paige, R.: The Epsilon Book. Eclipse, Newyork (2010)

13. Kolovos, D.S., Wei, R., Barmpis, K.: An approach for efficient querying of large relational datasets with OCL based languages. In: Proceedings of the Workshop on Extreme Modeling co-located with ACM/IEEE 16th International Conference on Model Driven Engineering Languages & Systems (MoDELS 2013), 29 September 2013, Miami, Florida, USA, pp. 46–54 (2013)

14. Marder, U., Ritter, N., Steiert, H.P.: A DBMS-based approach for automatic checking of OCL constraints. Proc. OOPSLA **99**, 1–5 (1999)

15. Pagán, J.E., Cuadrado, J.S., Molina, J.G.: A repository for scalable model management. Softw. Syst. Model. **14**, 1–21 (2013)

16. Sottet, J.-S., Jouault, F., et al.: Program comprehension. In: Proceedings of the 5th International Workshop on Graph-Based Tools (2009)

17. Stepper, E.: CDO (2009). http://eclipse.org/cdo/. Accessed 30 January 2015
18. Ujhelyi, Z., Bergmann, G., Hegedüs, Á., Horváth, Á., Izsó, B., Ráth, I., Szatmári, Z., Varró, D.: EMF-IncQuery: an integrated development environment for live model queries. Sci. Comput. Program. **98**, 80–99 (2015)
19. Wei, R., Kolovos, D.S.: An efficient computation strategy for allInstances(). In: Proceedings of the 3rd Workshop on Scalable Model Driven Engineering Part of the Software Technologies: Applications and Foundations (STAF 2015) Federation of Conferences, 23 July 2015, L'Aquila, Italy, pp. 32–41 (2015)

Mind the Gap! Automated Anomaly Detection for Potentially Unbounded Cardinality-Based Feature Models

Markus Weckesser[1]([⊠]), Malte Lochau[1], Thomas Schnabel[1],
Björn Richerzhagen[2], and Andy Schürr[1]

[1] Real-Time Systems Lab, TU Darmstadt, Darmstadt, Germany
`markus.weckesser@es.tu-darmstadt.de`
[2] Multimedia Communications Lab, TU Darmstadt, Darmstadt, Germany

Abstract. Feature models are frequently used for specifying variability of user-configurable software systems, e.g., software product lines. Numerous approaches have been developed for automating feature model validation concerning constraint consistency and absence of anomalies. As a crucial extension to feature models, cardinality annotations and respective constraints allow for multiple, and even potentially unbounded occurrences of feature instances within configurations. This is of particular relevance for user-adjustable application resources as prevalent, e.g., in cloud computing. However, a precise semantic characterization and tool support for automated and scalable validation of cardinality-based feature models is still an open issue. In this paper, we present a comprehensive formalization of cardinality-based feature models with potentially unbounded feature multiplicities. We apply a combination of ILP and SMT solvers to automate consistency checking and anomaly detection, including novel anomalies, e.g., interval gaps. We present evaluation results gained from our tool implementation showing applicability and scalability to larger-scale models.

Keywords: Software product lines · Cloud-based systems · Cardinality-based feature models · Integer Linear Programming (ILP)

1 Introduction

Feature models become more and more established for specifying *variability* of highly-configurable software, e.g., software product lines [11]. Feature models are used during domain engineering to tailor configuration spaces of product lines in terms of available configuration parameters (*features*) and respective *constraints*, restricting their combinations within valid *configurations*. Each feature constitutes a user-visible (Boolean) configuration option from the problem domain, being mapped onto variable implementation artifacts within the solution space. This way, customer-tailored products are derivable from a common code base during application engineering. The FODA feature diagram notation

© Springer-Verlag Berlin Heidelberg 2016
P. Stevens and A. Wąsowski (Eds.): FASE 2016, LNCS 9633, pp. 158–175, 2016.
DOI: 10.1007/978-3-662-49665-7_10

is a frequently used graphical representation for feature models [6,22]. FODA feature diagrams organize features as nodes in a tree-like layout to denote a parent-child hierarchy. This feature tree is enriched with constructs to describe logical dependencies among features. Semantically, a feature model specifies a set of valid product configurations, i.e., those feature combinations satisfying all constraints. Recent approaches to formalizing feature model semantics either use algebraic representations [19,34], or transformations into equivalent constraint problems, e.g., propositional formulas (SAT) [5,25], and CSP [7]. The latter approach allows for applying off-the-shelf constraint-solvers for automatically validating desirable semantic properties of feature models such as constraint consistency and absence of anomalies, e.g., dead features [6].

However, FODA feature diagram notation is, in many cases, not expressive enough for capturing all user-configurable properties of real-world applications. In particular, two major extensions to feature models have been proposed, usually summarized under the term *extended feature models* (EFM), namely (1) non-Boolean feature attributes and respective constraints to denote *extra-functional properties of features*, and (2) UML-like feature multiplicities [32] in terms of cardinality annotations and respective constraints to allow selections of *multiple feature instances* (also referred to as *copies*), including (recursive) *clones* of their corresponding sub-trees [14]. Semantically, both concepts impose extensions to the notion of product configurations by means of (1) feature types beyond Boolean, and (2) multi-sets of selected feature instances. Both extensions complicate feature model semantics, thus automated consistency checking and anomaly detection becomes even more important for their applicability in practice. Concerning (1), various promising approaches have been proposed for analyzing non-Boolean configuration constraints [7,9,20,23]. In contrast, concerning (2), only preliminary attempts exist so far [12,14,26,29,30], although cardinality-based variability modeling is emerging in nowadays applications and, therefore, recently found its way into novel modeling approaches like CVL [16] and Clafer [3]. As a prominent example, for cloud-based systems, not only the *type*, but also the *amount* of available resources is explicitly configurable by the user [28], especially including (virtually) *unrestricted* resources [35]. The resulting *compound* cardinality intervals lead to novel kinds of anomalies by means of *dead cardinality, cardinality interval gaps* and *false unbounded cardinality*.

In this paper, we present a comprehensive formalization and automated validation technique for cardinality-based feature models (CFM). We support cardinality annotations including compound cardinality intervals and unbounded cardinality for singleton features, feature groups, as well as cross-tree constraints. Our approach is motivated by a real-world cloud-based application [31]. We further introduce a *normal form* for cardinality constraints and enhance established notions of feature model consistency and anomaly to explicitly take feature cardinality constraints into account. Our tool implementation, presented in full detail in an accompanying tool paper [33], combines ILP solvers for interval-bound analysis and SMT solvers for interval-gap analysis to automate validation of cardinality-based feature models. We provide evaluation results from experiments investigating applicability and scalability of our validation approach for input models of varying sizes and complexity.

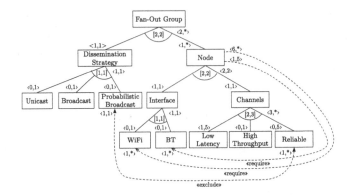

Fig. 1. CFM for fan-out group configuration of the event dissemination system

2   Cardinality-Based Feature Models

2.1   Background

Our running example is part of a cloud-based mobile augmented reality (AR) multi-player game scenario [31]. During a game, players (*nodes*) move and carry devices according to a predefined goal. Players communicate via cellular connections with a cloud-based service provider which delivers relevant game data and disseminating events. Players interact with the physical environment and other players located nearby. For this purpose, an Area of Interest (AoI) virtually surrounds each player's physical location, where overlapping AoI may form *Fan-Out Groups* to establish decentralized ad-hoc connections. This *bypassing* of the service provider may reduce latency of the cellular network.

All components of an AR game are highly configurable, including dynamic reconfigurations for run-time adaptation. Configuration decisions not only comprise *presence* or *absence* of functionality, but also the *available amount* of particular resources. Thus, CFM provide a suitable formalism to capture all relevant configuration choices and respective constraints of AR games. Figure 1 shows the CFM for configuring the *Dissemination Strategy*, the communication *Interface* and *Channel* properties of a (potentially unbounded) number of *Nodes* forming a *Fan-Out Group*. Similar to FODA notation [22], configuration parameters (*features*) reside in a tree-like diagram denoting a feature *decomposition* hierarchy. As a crucial extension, CFM differentiate between selectable/deselectable feature *types* as usual and, additionally, for each selected feature type, the *multiplicity* of occurrences of *feature instances* together with copies of their corresponding subtrees within configurations [14]. Restrictions on selections of both feature types and instances are specified by *cardinality intervals* (l, u), where l denotes the *lower* bound and u denotes the *upper* bound for the number of feature types or instances [32]. In particular, the CFM language considered in this paper provides the following constructs.

- *Feature instance cardinality*, annotated as $\langle l, u \rangle$ on the left-most position on top of each feature rectangle, restricts the minimum and maximum number of feature instances selectable from the sub-tree clone of respective parent feature instances. In our example, $\langle 1, 1 \rangle$ denotes that exactly one *Dissemination Strategy* is selectable, whereas $\langle 1, * \rangle$ denotes that arbitrary many, but at least one *Node* must be part of a *Fan-Out Group*.
- *Feature group type cardinality*, annotated as $[l, u]$, restricts the minimum and maximum number of types of feature instances selectable from the set of all immediate sub-features of a selected feature instance. In our example, $[1, 1]$ denotes that either instances of *WiFi*, or of *BT* must be selected for the *Interface*, whereas $[2, 3]$ denotes that at least two types of *Channels* from the given three options must be instantiated in a *Fan-Out Group*.
- *Feature group instance cardinality*, annotated as $\langle l, u \rangle$ at the right-hand side of each group arc, restricts the minimum and maximum number of feature instances of any type selectable from the set of all immediate sub-feature types. In our example, $\langle 3, * \rangle$ denotes that arbitrary many, but at least three *Channel* instances are required for each *Node*.
- *Cross-tree edges* by means of require- and exclude-edges annotated with $\langle l, u \rangle$ constraints at both the source and target feature rectangles [30], define constraints on the number of instances of arbitrary pairs of features. In our example, if at least one instance of *Reliable* is selected in a sub-tree clone, then no instance of *Probabilistic Broadcast* is allowed in the *Fan-Out Group* and vice versa. In addition, if between 1 and 5 *Nodes* are selected in a *Fan-Out Group*, then *BT* is used for all *Nodes* and *WiFi*, otherwise.

Combining different cardinality annotations in one CFM may lead to complicated dependencies among feature types and their possible number of instances. In order to provide a precise characterization of CFM configuration semantics, we provide a CFM formalization in the following. We first define the abstract syntax of CFM. Therefore, we introduce an *interval language* to express cardinality intervals (l, u) as pairs of *lower* and *upper* cardinality bounds, both given by natural numbers, or, in case of upper bounds, also by the special symbol $*$ denoting *unbounded* cardinality. By convention, $k < *$ holds for any $k \in \mathbb{N}_0$. *Compound cardinality intervals* are defined as the *union* of multiple (non-overlapping) intervals $(l_1, u_1), (l_2, u_2), \ldots, (l_n, u_n)$.

Definition 1 (Cardinality Interval). *The set of cardinality intervals is defined as* $\mathcal{I} \subset \mathbb{N}_0 \times (\mathbb{N}_0 \cup \{*\})$, *where* $(l, u) \in \mathcal{I}$ *iff* $l \leq u$ *holds. The set* $\mathcal{L} \subset_{fin} 2^{\mathcal{I}}$ *of compound cardinality intervals contains all finite subsets* $L \in \mathcal{L}$ *of* $\mathcal{I}$ *such that for all pairs* $(l_i, u_i) \in L$, $(l_j, u_j) \in L$, $i \neq j$, *either* $l_i > u_j$, *or* $u_i < l_j$ *holds.*

We further require compound intervals $L \in \mathcal{L}$ to be defined as concise as possible, e.g., $\{(1, 4)\}$ instead of $\{(1, 2), (3, 4)\}$. Intervals $L \in \mathcal{L}$ are used for all kinds of cardinality annotations in a CFM as described above. A CFM consists of a finite set F of features together with a hierarchy relation $\prec_F$ defining the tree hierarchy on F such that $f \prec_F f'$ denotes f to be the *parent feature* of f'.

In addition, a feature instance cardinality interval $\lambda_I^F(f) \in \mathcal{L}$ is assigned to every feature $f \in F$ by a function λ_I^F, as well as a group type cardinality interval $\lambda_T^G(f) \in \mathcal{L}$ by a function λ_T^G, and a group instance cardinality interval $\lambda_I^G(f) \in \mathcal{L}$ by a function λ_I^G. Both $\lambda_T^G(f)$ and $\lambda_I^G(f)$ define cardinality intervals on the set of *direct sub-features* of feature f with respect to $\prec_F$, hence we do not allow multiple direct sub-groups below one feature node. Furthermore, we require for every non-leaf feature $f \in F$ $\lambda_I^F(f)$, as well as $\lambda_T^G(f)$ and λ_I^G to be properly defined, even if f only contains a singleton sub-feature f', e.g., by assuming default group cardinality constraints $\lambda_T^G(f) = (0,1)$ and $\lambda_I^G(f) = (0,*)$. Cross-tree edges consist of four components, i.e., the source feature and the target feature and corresponding cardinality annotations restricting the number of feature instances. Due to the binary nature of cross-tree edges, cardinality intervals referring to feature types are meaningless and, therefore, not supported.

Definition 2 (CFM). *A cardinality-based feature model (CFM) defined over a non-empty, finite set F is a tuple $(\prec_F, \lambda_I^F, \lambda_T^G, \lambda_I^G, \Phi_R, \Phi_X)$, where*

- $\prec_F \subseteq F \times F$ *is a* feature decomposition *relation,*
- $\lambda_I^F : F \to \mathcal{L}$ *is a* feature instance cardinality *function,*
- $\lambda_T^G : F \to \mathcal{L}$ *is a* feature group type cardinality *function,*
- $\lambda_I^G : F \to \mathcal{L}$ *is a* feature group instance cardinality *function,*
- $\Phi_R \subseteq F \times \mathcal{L} \times \mathcal{L} \times F$ *is a* feature instance require-edge cardinality *relation,*
- $\Phi_X \subseteq F \times \mathcal{L} \times \mathcal{L} \times F$ *is a* feature instance exclude-edge cardinality *relation.*

For a CFM to be *syntactically well-formed*, it must satisfy further properties.

- $\prec_F$ forms a *finite rooted tree* on F, i.e., $\prec_F^+$ is a *strict partial order* on F with root feature $f_r \in F$ as unique minimal element, and for each $f \in F$, $f \neq f_r$, there is exactly one direct predecessor node $f' \in F$ with $f' \prec_F f$.
- Root feature f_r is a mandatory single-instance feature, i.e., $\lambda_I^F(f_r) = (1,1)$.
- Leaf nodes have empty group cardinality intervals, i.e., for each $f \in F$ with $\nexists f' \in F : f \prec_F f'$, $\lambda_G^I(f) = \lambda_G^T(f) = (0,0)$ holds.

Further well-formedness criteria may be imposed, e.g., forbidding $*$ as upper bound for feature group type cardinality. However, these and far more complicated cases are comprehensively treated by the normal form in Definition 6.

Obviously, CFM syntax constitutes a conservative extension to FODA feature diagrams [14,30]. However, concerning CFM semantics, the structure of valid CFM configurations essentially differs from FODA configurations. In particular, a CFM configuration not only contains information about the *presence*, or *absence* of features, but also the *number of instances* selected for each feature, as well as their memberships to the cloned sub-tree related to its parent feature instance. In this regard, one crucial semantic consideration for CFM concerns the interpretation of cardinality intervals restricting the number of feature instances. As already pointed out by Michel et al. in [26], one may either apply a *local*, or a *global* interpretation. For illustration purposes, we use the artificial CFM in Fig. 2 with sample configurations C_1, C_2, C_3, and C_4. Each feature instance constitutes the root of a (recursively) cloned sub-tree which can be configured

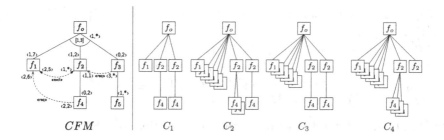

Fig. 2. CFM with sample configurations

individually for that instance. Considering, e.g., the require-edge from f_4 to f_1, a global interpretation would require this constraint to hold for the entire set of selected feature instances of f_4 and f_1, whereas in case of a local interpretation, the constraint must hold for every individual sub-tree clone. As a result, C_1 is invalid in case of a global interpretation, as the overall number of instances of f_4 is 2, but there is only one instance of f_1 in C_1. Hence, C_2 is valid as the overall number of instances of f_4 is 3 and, therefore, the precondition of the require-edge does not hold. C_3 is also valid as a sufficient number of instances of f_1 is selected. In contrast, in case of a local interpretation, C_1, C_2, and C_3 are all valid as either the precondition of the require-edge is not satisfied by any sub-tree clone of f_2 (C_1 and C_3), or the number of instances of f_1 is sufficient (C_2). Finally, although C_2 and C_4 have the same *number* of instances of each feature type, C_2 is valid for both interpretations, whereas C_4 is invalid in both cases as the feature instance cardinality of f_4 is violated. This example shows that the membership of feature instances to their corresponding parent feature instance sub-tree clones is a crucial part of CFM configuration semantics.

Here, we apply the global interpretation, constituting – in our opinion – the more intuitive and graspable CFM semantics. *CFM configuration semantics* characterizes those valid feature sub-tree copies with corresponding parent-child feature instance dependencies satisfying all cardinality constraints. Our CFM semantics is based on multi-sets M over set F to denote the number of feature instances selected in a configuration. A multi-set $M : F \rightarrow \mathbb{N}_0$ over set F defines a mapping from each element $f \in F$ onto a natural number $k = M(f)$, defining the *multiplicity* of f, where $k = 0$ denotes *absence* of f in M. We write $f_i^k \in M$, $1 \le k \le M(f_i)$ for short to refer to the kth instance of feature $f_i \in F$ within multi-set M with $M(f_i) > 0$. Furthermore, given a compound interval $L = \{(l_1, u_1), (l_2, u_2), \dots, (l_n, u_n)\} \in \mathcal{L}$ and $k \in \mathbb{N}_0$, we write $k \sqsubseteq L$ if $(l_i, u_i) \in L$ such that $l_i \le k \le u_i$ holds. We further denote a relation $\prec_F^M \subseteq M \times M$ on multi-set M, relating child feature instances to parent feature instances.

Definition 3 (CFM Configuration). *A configuration of a cardinality-based feature model* $(\prec_F, \lambda_I^F, \lambda_I^G, \lambda_T^G, \Phi_R, \Phi_X)$ *defined over a set F is a pair* $(M, \prec_F^M)$. *A configuration* $(M, \prec_F^M)$ *is valid iff*

- $M(f_r) = 1$,
- *if* $f_i^k \prec_F^M f_j^l$ *then* $f_i \prec_F f_j$ *and* $(\prec_F^M)^+$ *forms a rooted tree on M,*

- if $f_i^k \in M$, then for each $f_j \in F$ with $f_i \prec_F f_j$ it holds that $|\{f_j^l \in M | f_i^k \prec_F^M f_j^l\}| \sqsubseteq \lambda_F^I(f_j)$,
- if $f_i^k \in M$, then it holds that $|\{f_j^l \in M | f_i^k \prec_F^M f_j^l\}| \sqsubseteq \lambda_G^I(f_i)$,
- if $f_i^k \in M$, then it holds that $|\{f_j \in F | \exists f_j^l \in M : f_i^k \prec_F^M f_j^l\}| \sqsubseteq \lambda_G^F(f_i)$,
- if $(f_i, L_i, L_j, f_j) \in \Phi_R$ and $M(f_i) \sqsubseteq L_i$ then $M(f_j) \sqsubseteq L_j$, and
- if $(f_i, L_i, L_j, f_j) \in \Phi_X$ and $M(f_i) \sqsubseteq L_i$ then $M(f_j) \not\sqsubseteq L_j$ and vice versa.

By $[\![CFM]\!]$, we refer to the set of all valid configurations of CFM.

2.2   Analysis of Cardinality-Based Feature Models

We are now able to characterize fundamental validity properties of CFM. In particular, we define *consistency* of CFM in terms of the absence of inconsistent cardinality constraints. By including $*$ as cardinality bound, CFM allow to select an a-priori unbounded number of feature instances and, therefore, a potentially infinite number of configurations.

Definition 4 (Consistent and Bounded CFM). *A CFM is* consistent *iff it holds that $[\![CFM]\!] \neq \emptyset$. A CFM is* bounded *iff $*$ does not occur in a cardinality annotation. A CFM is* false *unbounded iff $*$ occurs in at least one cardinality annotation and $|[\![CFM]\!]| < \infty$ holds, and CFM is* unbounded, *else.*

False unboundedness is one example for an undesirable CFM property going beyond syntactic well-formedness criteria. To generalize, we recall the notion of *anomaly* to summarize undesirable semantic CFM properties. For FODA feature models, several types of anomalies and accompanying validation techniques have been proposed, e.g., dead features and false optional features [6]. First proposals exist to lift the anomaly notion also to CFM, e.g., *dead cardinality* anomaly [30].

Definition 5 (Dead Feature Instance Cardinality). *$k \sqsubseteq \lambda_F^I(f_i)$ is a* dead feature instance cardinality *of $f_i \in F$, if no $(M, \prec_F^M) \in [\![CFM]\!]$ with $f_j^k \in M$ and $f_j \prec_F f_i$ exists such that $|\{f_i^l \in M | f_j^k \prec_f^M f_i^l\}| = k$ holds.*

For other kinds of cardinality intervals of a CFM, the notion of dead cardinality can be defined, accordingly. Hence, for a feature f to be *dead* in a CFM, every cardinality $k \sqsubseteq \lambda_F^I(f_i)$ must be dead, thus the *actual* feature cardinality instance interval of f is $(0, 0)$, and a CFM is inconsistent if all features are dead.

The example in Fig. 2 exhibits several subtle cases of CFM anomalies. For example, the group instance cardinality $\langle 1, * \rangle$ of f_0 is *false unbounded* as the maximum number of possible child-feature instances is 11. The same holds for the interval $\langle 1, * \rangle$ on the right-hand side of the exclude-edge between f_1 and f_2 whose upper bound is actually limited to 2. In contrast, feature f_5 is *truly unbounded* thus making the entire CFM unbounded. Besides (false) unbounded intervals, this CFM contains further anomalies concerning bounded cardinality intervals. The lower bound 1 of the group instance cardinality interval $\langle 1, * \rangle$ of f_0 is a *dead cardinality*, as at least one instance of both f_1 and f_2 must be selected. Thus, lower bound 1 of group type cardinality $[1, 3]$ of f_0 is also *dead*. In addition, the lower bound of the target feature node cardinality interval $\langle 2, 6 \rangle$ of the require-edge from f_4 to f_1 is actually 6 instead of 2. Besides CFM anomalies affecting upper and/or lower bounds of cardinality intervals, a dead cardinality might be also located *within* intervals, thus imposing *interval gaps*. For example, the group instance cardinality of f_0 contains a gap at $(6, 6)$ as no valid combination of feature instances of f_1, f_2, and f_3 with an overall number of 6 is possible. As an even more subtle case, feature instance cardinality interval $\langle 1, 7 \rangle$ of f_1 contains the interval gap $(2, 5)$.

Due to the predominant role of cardinality constraints in CFM, any kind of potential semantic inconsistency can be explained through dead cardinality. To this end, we define a *normal form* for any given CFM by narrowing its declared cardinality intervals down to the *actual* ones, while preserving its feature-tree layout and configuration semantics. In case of gaps, closed interval declarations can be replaced by *compound* intervals, e.g., replacing group instance interval $(1, *)$ of f_0 in Fig. 2 by $\{(2, 5), (7, 11)\}$. In this way, a normal form $\overline{CFM}$ characterizes all dead cardinality anomalies compared to the original model CFM by means of those (sub-)ranges of feature cardinality intervals being removed from CFM to obtain $\overline{CFM}$. Hence, a CFM with $*$ occurring in some cardinality interval, but having no $*$ in its normal form is *false unbounded*. Furthermore, if a given CFM is *inconsistent*, all feature cardinality intervals of $\overline{CFM}$ are narrowed down to $(0, 0)$ (if we permit $\lambda_F^I(f_r) = (0, 0)$). Finally, to handle *redundant* cross-tree edges, we have to allow removals of edges from CFM to obtain a semantically equivalent normal form $\overline{CFM}$. For example, the precondition of the require-edge leading from f_3 to f_2 in Fig. 2 is not satisfiable thus making this edge redundant in $\overline{CFM}$. To formalize CFM normal form, we define an *inclusion hierarchy relation* $\precsim \subseteq \mathcal{L} \times \mathcal{L}$ as

$$L \precsim L' :\Leftrightarrow \forall k \in \mathbb{N}_0 : k \sqsubseteq L \Rightarrow k \sqsubseteq L'$$

thus requiring L to be a sub-range of L'.

Definition 6 (CFM Normal Form). $\overline{CFM}$ *is a normal form of CFM if*

- $[\![\overline{CFM}]\!] = [\![CFM]\!]$,
- $\overline{F} = F$, $\overline{\prec}_F = \prec_F$, $\overline{\Phi}_R \subseteq \Phi_R$, $\overline{\Phi}_X \subseteq \Phi_X$, *and*
- *for each* $f_i, f_j \in \overline{F}$, $\overline{\lambda}_I^F(f_i)$, $\overline{\lambda}_T^F(f_i)$, $\overline{\lambda}_I^G(f_i)$, *as well as* L_i *and* L_j *in each* $(f_i, L_i, L_j, f_j) \in \overline{\Phi}_R$ *and* $(f_i, L_i, L_i, f_j) \in \overline{\Phi}_X$ *are minimal with respect to* $\precsim$.

Applied to the CFM in Fig. 2, the resulting normal form is shown in Fig. 3(a). The following property is a direct consequence of Definitions 5 and 6.

Theorem 1. *For any CFM according to Definition 2, a normal form $\overline{CFM}$ exists and $\overline{CFM}$ contains no dead cardinality.*

In contrast, a normal form is, in general, not *unique* as removals of (mutually depending) redundant cross-tree edges may yield ambiguous results. A procedure for computing normal forms would allow for automatically consolidating

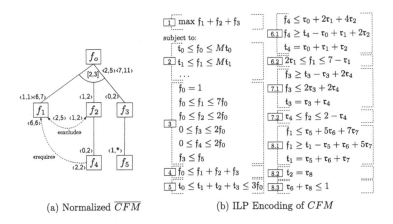

(a) Normalized $\overline{CFM}$ (b) ILP Encoding of CFM

Fig. 3. Sample CFM normal and ILP encoding of CFM semantics

and validating CFM, e.g., during domain analysis. However, constraint-solvers for SAT and CSP, usually used for validating FODA feature models, are not applicable for CFM validation due to the potentially unbounded search space.

3 Automated Anomaly Detection for CFM

We observe two potential causes for anomalies in CFM during normal form computation due to faulty declarations of cardinality intervals: (1) unsatisfiable lower/upper bounds (including false unbounded), and (2) unsatisfiable subranges (gaps). For (1), we encode CFM semantics in an ILP representation and use a respective ILP-solver for bound analysis, whereas for (2), we apply an SMT-solver to find interval gaps. To keep the presentation concise, we focus our considerations on input models CFM with non-compound cardinality intervals $L \in \mathcal{I}$.

Analysis of Interval Bounds. An ILP consists of a set of linear inequalities on a set of k integer-valued *decision variables*. The resulting convex hull forms the *feasible region* within a k-dimensional search space. An *objective function* states that either lower (minimum), or upper (maximum) boundary integer values for decision variables should be found by an ILP-solver. Encoding CFM semantics as ILP thus enables automated detection of dead cardinality potentially located at the *boundary* of cardinality intervals.

The ILP encoding of the CFM from Fig. 2 is given in Fig. 3(b). As decision variables, we introduce for each feature $f_i \in F$ a *feature multiplicity variable* $f_i \in \mathbb{N}_0$, denoting the *number* $M(f_i)$ of instances of type f_i being selected, and a *feature selection variable* $t_i \in \{0,1\}$, denoting whether at least one instance of f_i is selected in a CFM configuration. Consistency between variables f_i and corresponding variables t_i is enforced by constraints $M \cdot t_i \geq f_i$ and $t_i \leq f_i$ for all $f_i \in F$, (cf. $\boxed{2}$ in Fig. 3(b)). Here, we incorporate a coefficient M, frequently referred to as *big M* in the literature [37], by means of a sufficiently large number for coupling binary variables t_i to integer variables f_i. Coefficient M is conservatively approximated by multiplying the maximum upper bounds of cardinality intervals occurring in each branch of the feature tree and choosing the overall maximum value. The upper bound is derived from the syntactic context of the cardinality interval under consideration. Occurrences of $*$ are replaced in the same way. Due to monotonicity of aggregated cardinality interval bound values imposed by the CFM tree structure (cf. Definition 3), the restriction of the ILP search space to M, therefore, yields correct analysis results also for unbounded CFM.

To encode CFM semantics of feature instance cardinality intervals and subtree cloning, we introduce inequalities $l \cdot f_i \leq f_j \leq u \cdot f_i$ for all parent-child pairs $f_i \prec_F f_j$ and $(l, u) = \lambda_F^I(f_j)$ for child feature $f_j \in F$ (cf. $\boxed{3}$ in Fig. 3(b)). The inequality restricting the upper bound u is only introduced if u is bounded which does not hold, e.g., for feature f_5 in our example. For root feature f_r (denoted f_0), we have a special constraint $f_0 = 1$. For group instance cardinality intervals, we introduce inequalities

$$l \cdot f_i \leq \sum_{f_i \in F: f_i \prec_F f_j} f_j \leq u \cdot f_i$$

for all parent-child pairs $f_i \prec_F f_j$ and $(l, u) = \lambda_G^I(f_i)$ for parent feature $f_i \in F$. Again, in the unbounded case, we only restrict the lower bound. Semantics of group type cardinality intervals can be encoded, accordingly. The resulting group constraints for our example are depicted at $\boxed{4}$ and $\boxed{5}$ in Fig. 3(b), where the constraint at $\boxed{4}$ for f_0 only contains one inequality due to unboundedness.

Finally, cross-tree edges constitute the most complicated part potentially obstructing linearity of the ILP constraint set. To handle those cases, we use additional decision variables by means of fresh *interval selection variables* $\mathfrak{r}_k \in \{0, 1\}$ denoting a particular interval being selected or not. For each cross-tree edge $(f_i, L_i, L_j, f_j)_k \in \Phi_Y, Y \in \{R, X\}$, we define inequalities for source and target feature node intervals. For the source feature node f_i, we introduce three *interval selection variables* $\mathfrak{r}_{k-1}, \mathfrak{r}_k$, and $\mathfrak{r}_{k+1}$ to encode selection conditions for $L_i = (l_i, u_i)$. We encode the lower bounds of matching conditions of interval selection variables by

$$f_i \geq \mathfrak{r}_{k-1} + (l_i + 1) \cdot \mathfrak{r}_k + (u_i + 2) \cdot \mathfrak{r}_{k+1} - 1$$

and, for the upper bounds, by

$$f_i \leq (l_i - 1) \cdot \mathfrak{r}_{k-1} + u_i \cdot \mathfrak{r}_k + M \cdot \mathfrak{r}_{k+1},$$

respectively. To this end, $\mathfrak{r}_{k-1}$ indicates that the value of f_i is below l_i, $\mathfrak{r}_k$ indicates that the value of f_i is within interval L_i, and $\mathfrak{r}_{k+1}$ indicates that value of f_i is above u_i. If the source feature node cardinality interval is either unbounded, or its lower bound equals 1, the inequality is adapted, accordingly. In addition, the constraint $t_i = \mathfrak{r}_{k-1} + \mathfrak{r}_k + \mathfrak{r}_{k+1}$ ensures the interval not be selected and deselected at the same time if f_i is present. Applied to our example, the resulting encoding of source feature node cardinality intervals of the four cross-tree edges is shown in Fig. 3(b) at $\boxed{5.1}$, $\boxed{6.1}$, $\boxed{7.1}$, and $\boxed{8.1}$. Due to symmetry of exclude-edge semantics, target feature node cardinality intervals can be encoded in the same way as shown at $\boxed{8.2}$. To ensure mutual exclusion, an inequality such as at $\boxed{8.3}$ is added for each exclude-edge. For encoding target feature node cardinality intervals of require-edges $(f_i, L_i, L_j, f_j) \in \Phi_R$ with $(l_j, u_j) = L_j$, we introduce the constraint

$$l_j - M \cdot (1 - \mathfrak{r}_k) \leq \mathfrak{f}_j \leq u_j + M \cdot (1 - \mathfrak{r}_k)$$

to ensure that if the source node condition holds ($\mathfrak{r}_k = 1$), then f_j is within L_j (cf. $\boxed{5.2}$, $\boxed{6.2}$ and $\boxed{7.2}$ in Fig. 3(b)).

Based on this ILP encoding, CFM bound analysis can be performed for intervals $(l, u) \in \mathcal{I}$ by employing a corresponding ILP objective function, i.e., either minimization for lower bound analysis, or maximization for upper bound analysis. In Fig. 3(b), we analyze the upper bound of the group instance cardinality interval of f_0 by using the objective function $max\ f_1 + f_2 + f_3$ (cf. $\boxed{1}$), which returns 11. Considering unbounded cardinality intervals, we have two cases. In case of false unbounded intervals, e.g., the upper bound of the group instance cardinality of f_0, the solver run returns a *bounded* result with an objective value less than M. In case of a truly unbounded cardinality interval, e.g., the upper bound of feature instance cardinality of f_5, the solver either reports *unbounded but feasible*, or returns a value equal to M. To sum up, ILP-based interval bound analysis is *sound* in the sense that bounds of the search space reported feasible do not contain any dead cardinality. Similarly, the technique is *complete* in the sense that any dead cardinality at the bounds of the search space is detectable.

Detection of Interval Gaps. The ILP-based approach for interval-bound analysis is not directly applicable for interval-gap analysis as gaps are, by definition, not located at minima/maxima locations of the search space. For example, for detecting the group instance cardinality interval gap at $(6, 6)$ of f_0 in Fig. 2, we have to check whether $(6, 6)$ is a feasible value for the corresponding feature multiplicity variables. Hence, detecting interval gaps does not constitute an *optimization* problem, but rather a *constraint satisfaction* problem incorporating integer inequalities. To this end, an SMT-solver is applicable, being capable of interpreting first-order logics equipped with linear Integer arithmetics theory according to our ILP encoding of CFM semantics (cf. Fig. 3). For gap analysis, every sub-range of all cardinality intervals of a CFM has to investigated, where in case of unbounded intervals, analysis has to be performed up to M.

Normal Form Computation. We can now combine interval-bound analysis and interval-gap analysis to compute CFM normal forms. By ILP(CFM, interval) we denote ILP-solver calls to investigate a particular cardinality interval of CFM. The call returns the *actual* lower and upper bound of that interval to potentially replace the declared intervals within the normal form. For lower bounds of cardinality intervals defined by λ_I^F, λ_I^G and λ_T^G, the result is either greater than, or equal to the declared lower bound. For upper bounds, the result is either lower than, or equal to the declared upper bound. In case of unbounded intervals, the call either returns a concrete value in case of false unboundedness, or reports unboundedness. In case of infeasible intervals, the call returns $(0, 0)$. For interval-gap analysis, we denote SMT(CFM,interval,range) for respective SMT-solver calls, where range is a sub-range of interval to be investigated. For reducing the search space for gap detection, parameter range can be obtained from ILP-based bound analysis. The SMT call reports invalid sub-ranges within range leading to compound intervals within the normal form. Finally, for cardinality intervals L_i, L_j of cross-tree edges $(f_i, L_i, L_j, f_j) \in \Phi_Y$, $Y \in \{R, X\}$, bound and gap analysis is, in general, performed as described above. In contrast, infeasibility of source and/or target feature node intervals imposes incremental removals of the corresponding edges from Φ_Y during normal form computation.

4   Experimental Evaluation

We implemented CFM bound analysis and gap detection in a tool providing textual syntax for specifying input CFM models [33]. Here, we present evaluation results gained from several experiments performed with our tool. We address the following research questions.

(RQ1)   Is CFM normal form computation *applicable* to real-world input models?
(RQ2)   How does the size and complexity of CFM affect *scalability* of CFM analysis?
(RQ3)   How does the ILP-based feasibility check perform on FODA feature models compared to a SAT-based satisfiability check?

To address **(RQ1)**, we applied our tool to the real-world CFM in Fig. 1. To address **(RQ2)** and **(RQ3)**, we used synthetically generated CFM models by extending the *BeTTy* tool [36] with cardinality interval generation capabilities including adjustable *maximum feature instance cardinality* and *unbounded interval probability*. We generated CFM by randomly varying all CFM generation criteria using uniformly distributed random variables. Experiments were performed on a Unix machine with Intel Core i5 (2,3 GHz, 8 GB RAM). For bound analysis, we employed as ILP-solvers *CPLEX* [21], *Gurobi* [18], and *GLPK* [17]. For gap detection, we used SMT-solver *Z3* [27] and for **(RQ3)**, we utilized *Sat4j* [24].

For **(RQ1)**, we computed the normal form for the AR game CFM which includes bound analysis for 27 intervals, thus requiring 54 ILP-solver calls. The *CPLEX* ILP-solver took about 10 ms per call. Gap analysis included 27 intervals which took about 15.71 s per call. The resulting normal form exposed a false unbounded group instance interval anomaly for the *Channels* group, thus the unbounded interval symbol ∗ is replaced by 11.

Concerning **(RQ2)**, we performed regression analysis to estimate influences of model characteristics on CFM analysis performance metrics. To identify significant coefficients, we applied multiple linear regression analysis on input data sets by randomly varying all generation criteria. We applied *t-tests* to check

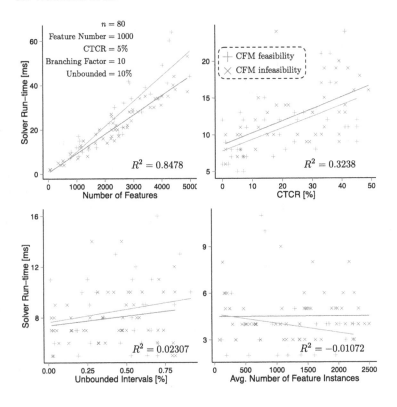

Fig. 4. Evaluation results for **(RQ2)**

significance of regression coefficients. With significance level $p < 0.05$, we identified (a) *number of features*, and (b) *cross-tree constraint ratio (CTCR)*, (c) *ratio of unbounded cardinality intervals*, as well as (d) *CFM feasibility* as coefficients with potentially high influences on run-time of ILP-based bound analysis. In contrast, the influence of *average number of feature instances* is not significant. Figure 4 contains the results of one bound analysis run for individual variation of coefficients (a)–(d). The plots show that run-time of ILP-based bound analysis is dominated by (a) and (b), as the size of the feature tree and the number of cross-tree edges directly affects the number of decision variables and constraints. The results show that ILP-based analysis of one particular bound for CFM with 5,000 features takes about 50 ms and thus about 21 min. for complete bound analysis. This can be considered industrial strength. In contrast, for SMT-based gap analysis, we were only able to obtain run-time analysis results for small-sized (and mostly bounded) CFM up to at most 200 features. As expected, run-time of SMT-based gap analysis tends to show exponential growth with increasing average size of cardinality intervals. For **(RQ3)** we conducted multiple linear regression to estimate influences of FODA feature model characteristics, i.e., with CFM restricted to cardinality intervals between 0 and 1, for comparing run-time of satisfiability checks using SAT and ILP-solvers. We identified coefficients

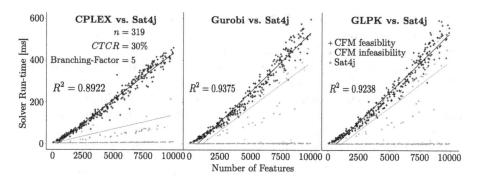

Fig. 5. Evaluation results for **(RQ3)**

number of features, *CTCR* and *CFM feasibility* as highly significant ($p < 0.01$). For *CPLEX*, the *maximum branching factor* has no significant influence. As shown in Fig. 4, the SAT-solver exhibits lower run-time metrics with increasing model size compared to ILP. Nevertheless, ILP-solvers perform remarkably well, with differences in run-time metrics by means of a constant factor only up to models with 5,000 features (Fig. 5).

Threats to Validity. Threats to validity may arise from our experimental input data selection. Concerning **(RQ1)**, the cloud-based AR game is part of a major research project and has already been used for experimental evaluation [31]. Similarly, our design choices for CFM syntax and semantics are derived from requirements of cloud-domain experts. Concerning synthetic data for **(RQ2)** and **(RQ3)**, we employed the well-established *BeTTy* tool for generating FODA-like feature trees, additionally augmented with cardinality intervals. The cardinality interval test data is dimensioned according to characteristics of our case study in order to obtain realistic models. To the best of our knowledge, there does neither exist a fully-fledged CFM generator, nor related approaches for comprehensive CFM analysis as in our approach. Hence, neither a qualitative, nor a quantitative comparison to existing other approaches has been possible so far.

5   Related Work

Formalization of Cardinality-Based Feature Models. Riebisch et al. first propose to extend FODA notation with UML-like multiplicities by means of feature group cardinality [32]. Czarnecki et al. extend feature models with group and feature cardinality, but forbid combinations of both [13]. Thereupon, Czarnecki et al. define CFM semantics based on sub-tree clones and propose their translation into a context-free grammar [14]. They also permit unbounded cardinality but do no investigate their semantic impact. Quinton et al. introduce source and target cardinality for require-edges [30]. However, their approach does neither consider exclude-edges, nor combinations of feature instance and group cardinality. Quinton et al. also mention unbounded cardinality, but neither address it in

CFM semantics, nor as part of CFM analysis. Michel et al. investigate semantic ambiguities due to combinations of feature and group cardinality and distinguish local clone-based from global feature-based interpretation of group type cardinality intervals, being similar to our notion of group instance and group type cardinality intervals [26]. However, they only consider global feature-based interpretation being similar to our notion of group type cardinality intervals. Cordy et al. allow combinations of feature and group cardinality, but for the latter only consider group type cardinality intervals [12]. Again, neither Michel et al., nor Cordy et al. handle unboundedness semantically and during CFM analysis.

Automated Analysis of Cardinality-Based Feature Models. Quinton et al. define inconsistent CFM similar to our notion of dead cardinality anomaly and perform inconsistency detection using CSP [28–30]. Cordy et al. in [12] and Zhang et al. in [38] present BDD-based CFM consistency analysis. However, neither of these approaches is able to handle unbounded configuration spaces and/or interval gaps, nor provide a normal form for CFM.

Analyzing Models with Unbounded Cardinality. Other modeling languages also employ the concept of cardinality to restrict instance multiplicities of model entities. CVL [16] provide *iterators* to mimic cardinality in feature diagrams including unbounded intervals, and the specification language CLAFER combines concepts from UML and feature modeling including group and feature instance cardinality [2]. However, no systematic analysis of unbounded cardinality is provided yet. In addition, several approaches have been proposed for analyzing multiplicities in UML class diagrams using Alloy [1], CSP [10], and ILP [15] but none of them explicitly handles unboundedness. Balaban et al. present a graph-based algorithm for tightening multiplicities in UML class diagrams [4]. However, the approach essentially differs from CFM normal form computation as no (recursively) cloned sub-tree hierarchy, cross-tree edges and multiple cardinality constraints per entities occur in class diagrams. Amongst others, Boufares et al. consider inconsistency in cardinality constraints of data-base schema definitions including unbounded cardinality, but do not take interval gaps into account [8].

6   Conclusion

We presented a comprehensive formalization of CFM configuration semantics including unbounded cardinality intervals. We further presented evaluation results gained from experiments conducted with our tool implementation for computing normal forms of CFM. The results show the general applicability and scalability of ILP-based bound analysis. For scalable gap analysis, we aim at replacing the SMT-solver also by an ILP-solver in our future work. We also plan to conduct further experiments including real-world case studies and alternative CFM semantics [26]. For integrating CFM into a fully-fledged engineering process with accompanying tool support, we plan to develop a methodology for mapping feature instances to solution space artifacts as, e.g., propagated by CVL [16].

Acknowledgment. This work was partially supported by the DFG (German Research Foundation) as part of projects B01 and C02 within CRC 1053 – MAKI and under SPP 1593: Design For Future – Managed Software Evolution.

References

1. Anastasakis, K., Bordbar, B., Georg, G., Ray, I.: On challenges of model transformation from UML to Alloy. Softw. Syst. Model. **9**(1), 69–86 (2010)
2. Bąk, K., Czarnecki, K., Wąsowski, A.: Feature and meta-models in Clafer: mixed, specialized, and coupled. In: Malloy, B., Staab, S., Brand, M. (eds.) SLE 2010. LNCS, vol. 6563, pp. 102–122. Springer, Heidelberg (2011)
3. Bak, K., Diskin, Z., Antkiewicz, M., Czarnecki, K., Wasowski, A.: Clafer: unifying class and feature modeling. Softw. Syst. Model. 1–35 (2014)
4. Balaban, M., Maraee, A.: Simplification and correctness of UML class diagrams – focusing on multiplicity and aggregation/composition constraints. In: Moreira, A., Schätz, B., Gray, J., Vallecillo, A., Clarke, P. (eds.) MODELS 2013. LNCS, vol. 8107, pp. 454–470. Springer, Heidelberg (2013)
5. Batory, D.: Feature models, grammars, and propositional formulas. In: Obbink, H., Pohl, K. (eds.) SPLC 2005. LNCS, vol. 3714, pp. 7–20. Springer, Heidelberg (2005)
6. Benavides, D., Segura, S., Ruiz-Cortés, A.: Automated analysis of feature models 20 years later: a literature review. Inf. Syst. **35**(6), 615–636 (2010)
7. Benavides, D., Trinidad, P., Ruiz-Cortés, A.: Automated reasoning on feature models. In: Pastor, Ó., Falcão e Cunha, J. (eds.) CAiSE 2005. LNCS, vol. 3520, pp. 491–503. Springer, Heidelberg (2005)
8. Boufares, F., Bennaceur, H.: Consistency problems in ER-schemas for database systems. Inf. Technol. **163**(4), 263–274 (2004)
9. Bürdek, J., Lity, S., Lochau, M., Berens, M., Goltz, U., Schürr, A.: Staged configuration of dynamic software product lines with complex binding time constraints. In: VaMoS 2014, pp. 16: 1–16: 8 (2014)
10. Cadoli, M., Calvanese, D., De Giacomo, G., Mancini, T.: Finite model reasoning on UML class diagrams via constraint programming. In: Basili, R., Pazienza, M.T. (eds.) AI*IA 2007. LNCS (LNAI), vol. 4733, pp. 36–47. Springer, Heidelberg (2007)
11. Clements, P., Northrop, L.: Software Product Lines: Practices and Patterns. Addison-Wesley Longman Publishing Co., Inc, Boston (2001)
12. Cordy, M., Schobbens, P.Y., Heymans, P., Legay, A.: Beyond boolean product-line model checking: dealing with feature attributes and multi-features. In: ICSE 2013, pp. 472–481 (2013)
13. Czarnecki, K., Helsen, S.: Staged configuration using feature models. In: Nord, R.L. (ed.) SPLC 2004. LNCS, vol. 3154, pp. 266–283. Springer, Heidelberg (2004)
14. Czarnecki, K., Helsen, S., Eisenecker, U.W.: Formalizing cardinality-based feature models and their specialization. Softw. Process Improv. Pract. **10**(1), 7–29 (2005)
15. Falkner, A., Feinerer, I., Salzer, G., Schenner, G.: Computing product configurations via UML and integer linear programming. Int. J. Mass Customisation **3**(4), 351–367 (2010)
16. Fleurey, F., Haugen, Ø., Møller-Pedersen, B., Svendsen, A., Zhang, X.: Standardizing variability – challenges and solutions. In: Ober, I., Ober, I. (eds.) SDL 2011. LNCS, vol. 7083, pp. 233–246. Springer, Heidelberg (2011)

17. GNU Linear Programming Kit, Version 4.55. http://www.gnu.org/software/glpk/glpk.html
18. Gurobi Optimization, I.: Gurobi Optimizer Reference Manual (2015). http://www.gurobi.com
19. Heymans, P., Schobbens, P.Y., Trigaux, J.C., Bontemps, Y., Matulevicius, R., Classen, A.: Evaluating formal properties of feature diagram languages. IET Softw. **2**(3), 281–302 (2008)
20. Hubaux, A., Heymans, P., Schobbens, P.-Y., Deridder, D.: Towards multi-view feature-based configuration. In: Wieringa, R., Persson, A. (eds.) REFSQ 2010. LNCS, vol. 6182, pp. 106–112. Springer, Heidelberg (2010)
21. IBM ILOG CPLEX V12.6 User's Manual for CPLEX. IBM Corp. (2015). http://www-01.ibm.com/software/commerce/optimization/cplex-optimizer/
22. Kang, K.C., Cohen, S.G., Hess, J.A., Novak, W.E., Peterson, S.A.: Feature oriented domain analysis (FODA). Technical report, CMU (1990)
23. Karataş, A.S., Oğuztüzün, H., Doğru, A.: Mapping extended feature models to constraint logic programming over finite domains. In: Bosch, J., Lee, J. (eds.) SPLC 2010. LNCS, vol. 6287, pp. 286–299. Springer, Heidelberg (2010)
24. Le Berre, D., Parrain, A.: The Sat4j Library, Release 2.2. J. Satisfiability Boolean Model. Comput. **7**, 59–64 (2010)
25. Mendonça, M., Wasowski, A., Czarnecki, K.: SAT-based analysis of feature models is easy. In: 13th SPLC, pp. 231–240 (2009)
26. Michel, R., Classen, A., Hubaux, A., Boucher, Q.: A formal semantics for feature cardinalities in feature diagrams. In: VaMoS 2011, pp. 82–89 (2011)
27. de Moura, L., Bjørner, N.S.: Z3: an efficient SMT solver. In: Ramakrishnan, C.R., Rehof, J. (eds.) TACAS 2008. LNCS, vol. 4963, pp. 337–340. Springer, Heidelberg (2008)
28. Quinton, C., Romero, D., Duchien, L.: Automated selection and configuration of cloud environments using software product lines principles. In: IEEE Cloud 2014, pp. 144–151 (2014)
29. Quinton, C., Pleuss, A., Berre, D.L., Duchien, L., Botterweck, G.: Consistency checking for the evolution of cardinality-based feature models. In: SPLC 2014, pp. 122–131 (2014)
30. Quinton, C., Romero, D., Duchien, L.: Cardinality-based feature models with constraints: a pragmatic approach. In: SPLC 2013, pp. 162–166 (2013)
31. Richerzhagen, B., Stingl, D., Hans, R., Groß, C., Steinmetz, R.: Bypassing the cloud: peer-assisted event dissemination for augmented reality games. In: P2P 2014, pp. 1–10 (2014)
32. Riebisch, M., Böllert, K., Streitferdt, D., Philippow, I.: Extending feature diagrams with UML multiplicities. In: 6th World Conference on Integrated Design & Process Technology (IDPT) (2002)
33. Schnabel, T., Weckesser, M., Kluge, R., Lochau, M., Schürr, A.: CardyGAn: tool support for cardinality-based feature models. In: VaMoS 2016 (2016) (to appear)
34. Schobbens, P.Y., Heymans, P., Trigaux, J.C.: Feature diagrams: a survey and a formal semantics. In: Proceedings of RE 2006, pp. 139–148 (2006)
35. Schroeter, J., Mucha, P., Muth, M., Jugel, K., Lochau, M.: Dynamic configuration management of cloud-based applications. In: SPLC 2012, pp. 171–178 (2012)
36. Segura, S., Galindo, J., Benavides, D., Parejo, J., Ruiz-Cortés, A.: BeTTy: benchmarking and testing on the automated analysis of feature models. In: VaMoS 2012, pp. 63–71 (2012)

37. Williams, H.P.: Model Building in Mathematical Programming. John Wiley & Sons, Hoboken (2013)
38. Zhang, W., Yan, H., Zhao, H., Jin, Z.: A BDD-based approach to verifying clone-enabled feature models' constraints and customization. In: Mei, H. (ed.) ICSR 2008. LNCS, vol. 5030, pp. 186–199. Springer, Heidelberg (2008)

Analysis and Bug Triaging

Cut Branches Before Looking for Bugs: Sound Verification on Relaxed Slices

Jean-Christophe Léchenet[1,2]([envelope]), Nikolai Kosmatov[1], and Pascale Le Gall[2]

[1] CEA, LIST, Software Reliability and Security Laboratory, P.C. 174,
91191 Gif-sur-Yvette, France
{`jean-christophe.lechenet,nikolai.kosmatov`}`@cea.fr`
[2] Laboratoire de Mathématiques et Informatique pour la Complexité et les Systèmes,
CentraleSupélec, Université Paris-Saclay, 92295 Châtenay-Malabry, France
`pascale.legall@centralesupelec.fr`

Abstract. Program slicing can be used to reduce a given initial program to a smaller one (a *slice*) which preserves the behavior of the initial program with respect to a chosen criterion. Verification and validation (V&V) of software can become easier on slices, but require particular care in presence of errors or non-termination in order to avoid unsound results or a poor level of reduction in slices.

This article proposes a theoretical foundation for conducting V&V activities on a slice instead of the initial program. We introduce the notion of *relaxed slicing* that remains efficient even in presence of errors or non-termination, and establish an appropriate soundness property. It allows us to give a precise interpretation of verification results (absence or presence of errors) obtained for a slice in terms of the initial program. Our results have been proved in Coq.

1 Introduction

Context. Program slicing was initially introduced by Weiser [32,33] as a technique allowing to decompose a given program into a simpler one, called a program slice, by analyzing its control and data flow. In the classic definition, a *(program) slice* is an executable program subset of the initial program whose behavior must be identical to a specified subset of the initial program's behavior. This specified behavior that should be preserved in the slice is called *slicing criterion*. A common slicing criterion is a program point l. For the purpose of this paper, we prefer this simple formulation to another criterion (l, V) where a set of variables V is also specified. Informally speaking, program slicing with respect to the criterion l should guarantee that any variable v at program point l takes the same value in the slice and in the original program.

Since Weiser's original work, many researchers have studied foundations of program slicing (e.g. [4–6,8,11,14,20,26–28]). Numerous applications of slicing have been proposed, in particular, to program understanding, software maintenance, debugging, program integration and software metrics. Comprehensive

© Springer-Verlag Berlin Heidelberg 2016
P. Stevens and A. Wąsowski (Eds.): FASE 2016, LNCS 9633, pp. 179–196, 2016.
DOI: 10.1007/978-3-662-49665-7_11

surveys on program slicing can be found e.g. in [9,29,30,35]. In recent classifi-cations of program slicing, Weiser's original approach is called *static backward slicing* since it simplifies the program statically, for all possible executions at the same time, and traverses it backwards from the slicing criterion in order to keep those statements that can influence this criterion. Static backward slicing based on control and data dependencies is also the purpose of this work.

Goals and Approach. Verification and Validation (V&V) can become easier on simpler programs after "cutting off irrelevant branches" [13,15,17,22]. Our main goal is to address the following research question:

> **(RQ)** Can we soundly conduct V&V activities on slices instead of the initial program? In particular, if there are no errors in a program slice, what can be said about the initial program? And if an error is found in a program slice, does it necessarily occur in the initial program?

We consider errors determined by the current program state such as runtime errors (that can either interrupt the program or lead to an undefined behavior). We also consider a realistic setting of programs with potentially non-terminating loops, even if this non-termination is unintended. So we assume neither that all loops terminate, nor that all loops do not terminate, nor that we have a preliminary knowledge of which loops terminate and which loops do not.

Dealing with potential runtime errors and non-terminating loops is very important for realistic programs since their presence cannot be a priori excluded, especially during V&V activities. Although quite different at first glance, both situations have a common point: they can in some sense interrupt normal exe-cution of the program preventing the following statements from being exe-cuted. Therefore, slicing away (that is, removing) potentially erroneous or non-terminating sub-programs from the slice can have an impact on soundness of program slicing.

While some aspects of **(RQ)** were discussed in previous papers, none of them provided a complete formal answer in the considered general setting (as we detail in Sects. 2 and 6 below). To satisfy the traditional soundness property, program slicing would require to consider additional dependencies of each statement on previous loops and error-prone statements. That would lead to inefficient (that is, too large) slices, where we would *systematically preserve all potentially erroneous or non-terminating statements* executed before the slicing criterion. Such slices would have very limited benefit for our purpose of performing V&V on slices instead of the initial program.

This work proposes *relaxed slicing,* where additional dependencies on previ-ous (potentially) erroneous or non-terminating statements are not required. This approach leads to smaller slices, but needs a new soundness property. We state and prove a suitable soundness property using a trajectory-based semantics, and show how this result can justify V&V on slices by characterizing possible ver-ification results on slices in terms of the initial program. The proof has been formalized in the Coq proof assistant [7] and is available in [1].

The Contributions of this work include:

- a comprehensive analysis of issues arising for V&V on classic slices;
- the notion of relaxed slicing (Definition 6) for structured programs with possible errors and non-termination, that keeps fewer statements than it would be necessary to satisfy the classic soundness property of slicing;
- a new soundness property for relaxed slicing (Theorem 1);
- a characterization of verification results, such as absence or presence of errors, obtained for a relaxed slice, in terms of the initial program, that constitutes a theoretical foundation for conducting V&V on slices (Theorems 2, 3);
- a formalization and proof of our results in Coq.

Paper Outline. Section 2 presents our motivation and illustrating examples. The considered language and its semantics are defined in Sect. 3. Section 4 defines the notion of relaxed slice and establishes its main soundness property. Next, Sect. 5 formalizes the relationship between the errors in the initial program and in a relaxed slice. Finally, Sects. 6 and 7 present the related work and the conclusion with some future work.

2   Motivation and Running Examples

Errors and Assertions. We consider errors that are determined by the current program state[1] including runtime errors (division by zero, out-of-bounds array access, arithmetic overflows, out-of-bounds bit shifting, etc.). Some of these errors do not always interrupt program execution and can sometimes lead to an (even more dangerous) undefined behavior, such as reading or writing an arbitrary memory location after an out-of-bounds array access in C. Since we cannot take the risk to overlook some of these "silent runtime errors", we assume that all threatening statements are annotated with explicit assertions `assert(C)` placed before them, that interrupt the execution whenever the condition C is false. This assumption will be convenient for the formalization in the next sections: possible runtime errors will always occur in assertions. Such assertions can be generated syntactically (for example, by the RTE plugin of the FRAMA-C toolset [21] for C programs). For instance, line 10 in Fig. 1a prevents division by zero at line 11, while line 13 makes explicit a potential runtime error at line 14 if the array a is known to be of size N. In addition, the `assert(C)` keyword can be also used to express any additional user-defined properties on the current state.

Most previous applications of slicing to debugging used slices in order to *better understand an already detected error,* by analyzing a simpler program rather than a more complex one [8,29,30]. Our goal is quite different: to perform V&V on slices in order to discover yet unknown errors, or show their absence (cf. **(RQ)**). The interpretation of absence or presence of errors in a slice in terms of the initial program requires solid theoretical foundations.

Classic Soundness Property. Let p be a program, and q a slice of p w.r.t. a slicing criterion l. The classic soundness property of slicing (cf. [6, Definition 2.5] or [28, Slicing Th.]) can be informally stated as follows.

---

[1] Temporal errors (e.g. use-after-free in C) cannot be directly represented in this way.

```
1   s1 = 0;
2   s2 = 0;
3   i = 0;
4   while (i < N){
5       assert (i < N);
6       s1 = s1 + a[i];
7       i = i + k;
8   }
9   j = 0;
10  assert (k != 0);
11  last = N/k;
12  while (j <= last){
13      assert (k*j < N);
14      s2 = s2 + a[k*j];
15      j = j + 1;
16  }
17  assert (N != 0);
18  avg1 = s1 / N;
19  assert (N != 0);
20  avg2 = s2 / N;
21  if(avg1 == avg2)
22      print("equal");
```

(a)

```
1   s1 = 0;
2
3   i = 0;
4   while (i < N){
5       assert (i < N);
6       s1 = s1 + a[i];
7       i = i + k;
8   }
9
10
11
12
13
14
15
16
17  assert (N != 0);
18  avg1 = s1 / N;
19
20
21
22
```

(b)

```
1
2   s2 = 0;
3
4
5
6
7
8
9   j = 0;
10  assert (k != 0);
11  last = N/k;
12  while (j <= last){
13      assert (k*j < N);
14      s2 = s2 + a[k*j];
15      j = j + 1;
16  }
17
18
19  assert (N != 0);
20  avg2 = s2 / N;
21
22
```

(c)

Fig. 1. (a) A program computing in two ways the average of elements of a given array a of size N whose only nonzero elements can be at indices $\{0, k, 2k, \ldots\}$, and its two slices: (b) w.r.t. line 18, and (c) w.r.t. line 20.

Property 1. Let σ be an input state of p. Suppose that p halts on σ. Then q halts on σ and the executions of p and q on σ agree after each statement preserved in the slice on the variables that appear in this statement.[2]

This property was originally established for classic dependence-based slicing for programs without runtime errors and only for executions with terminating loops: nothing is guaranteed if p does not terminate normally on σ. Let us show why this property does not hold in presence of potential runtime errors or non-terminating loops.

Illustrating Examples. Figure 1a presents a simple (buggy) C-like program that takes as inputs an array a of length N and an integer k (with $0 \leqslant k \leqslant 100$, $0 \leqslant N \leqslant 100$), and computes in two different ways the average of the elements of a. We suppose that all variables and array elements are unsigned integers, and all elements of a whose index is not a multiple of k are zero, so it suffices to sum array elements over the indices multiples of k and to divide the sum by N. The sum is computed twice (in s1 at lines 3–8 and in s2 at lines 9–16), and the averages avg1 and avg2 are computed (lines 17–20) and compared (lines 21–22). We assume that necessary assertions with explicit guards (at lines 5, 10, 13, 17, 19) are inserted to prevent runtime errors.

Figure 1b shows a (classic dependence-based) slice of this program with respect to the statement at line 18. Intuitively, it contains only statements

---

[2] Formally, using the notation introduced hereafter in the paper (cf. Definition 8), their *projections* are equal: $\mathrm{Proj}_L(\mathcal{T}[\![p]\!]\sigma) = \mathrm{Proj}_L(\mathcal{T}[\![q]\!]\sigma)$.

Initial state	Inputs	(a)	(b)	(c)
σ_1	$k = 2, N = 5$	—	—	—
σ_2	$k = 2, N = 4$	ϟ line 13	—	ϟ line 13
σ_3	$k = 0, N = 4$	↻ line 4	↻ line 4	ϟ line 10
σ_4	$k = 2, N = 0$	ϟ line 13	ϟ line 17	ϟ line 13
σ_5	$k = 0, N = 0$	ϟ line 10	ϟ line 17	ϟ line 10

Fig. 2. Errors (ϟ), non-termination (↻) and normal termination (—) of programs of Fig. 1 for some inputs.

(at lines $1, 3, 4, 6, 7, 18$) that can influence the slicing criterion, i.e. the values of variables that appear at line 18 after its execution.[3] In addition, we keep the assertions to prevent potential errors in preserved statements. Similarly, Fig. 1c shows a slice with respect to line 20, again with protecting assertions.

Figure 2 summarizes the behavior of the three programs of Fig. 1 on some test data. The elements of **a** do not matter here. Suppose we found an error at line 17 in slice (**b**) provoked by test datum σ_4. Program (**a**) does not contain the same error: it fails earlier, at line 13. We say that the error at line 17 in slice (**b**) is *hidden by the error* at line 13 of the initial program. Similarly, test datum σ_5 provokes an error at line 17 in slice (**b**) while this error is hidden by an error at line 10 in (**a**). In fact, the error at line 17 cannot be reproduced on the initial program, so we say that it is *totally hidden* by other errors.

For slice (**c**), detecting an error at line 10 on test datum σ_5 would allow us to observe the same error in (**a**). However, if this error in slice (**c**) is also provoked by test datum σ_3, this test datum does not provoke any error in (**a**) because the loop at line 4 does not terminate. We say that this error is *(partially) hidden by a non-termination* of the loop at line 4.

These examples clearly show that Property 1 is not true in presence of errors or non-terminating loops for classic slices. Indeed, the executions of p and q may disagree at least for two reasons:

(**i**) a previously executed non-terminating loop not preserved in the slice, or
(**ii**) a previously executed failing statement not preserved in the slice.

Let us consider another example related to error-free programs. If we suppose that $0 < k \leqslant 100$, $0 < N \leqslant 100$, and replace N/k by (N-1)/k at line 11 of Fig. 1, neither slice contains any error. If we manage to verify the absence of errors on both slices, can we be sure that the initial program is error-free as well?

Bigger Slices vs. Weaker Soundness Property. One solution (adopted by [18, 25, 26], cf. Sect. 6) proposes to ensure Property 1 even in presence of errors and potentially non-terminating loops by considering additional dependencies. This approach would basically lead to always preserving in the slice any

---

[3] By formal definitions of Sect. 4, one easily checks that line 18 is data-dependent on line 6, that is in turn data-dependent on lines 1,3,7 and control-dependent on line 4.

(potentially non-terminating) loop or error-prone statement that can be executed before the slicing criterion. The resulting slices would be much bigger, and the benefit of performing V&V on slices would be very limited.

For instance, to ensure that the executions of program **(a)** and slice **(b)** activated by test datum σ_4 agree on all statements of slice **(b)**, line 13 should be preserved in slice **(b)**. That would result (by transitivity of dependencies) in keeping e.g. the loop at line 12 and lines 9–11 in slice **(b)** as well. Similarly, the loop at line 4 should be kept in slice **(c)** to avoid disagreeing executions for test datum σ_3. The slices can become much bigger in this approach.

In this paper we propose *relaxed slicing*, an alternative approach that does not require to keep all loops or error-prone statements that can be executed before the slicing criterion, but ensures a weaker soundness property. We demonstrate that the new soundness property is sufficient to justify V&V on slices instead of the initial program. In particular, we show that reasons **(i)** and **(ii)** above are the only possible reasons of a hidden error, and investigate when the absence of errors in slices implies the absence of errors in the initial program.

3   The Considered Language and Its Semantics

Language. In this study, we consider a simple WHILE language (with integer variables, fixed-size arrays, pure expressions, conditionals, assertions and loops) that is representative for our formalization of slicing in presence of runtime errors and non-termination. The language is defined by the following grammar:

$$
\begin{aligned}
Prog \quad &::= \quad Stmt^* \\
Stmt \quad &::= \quad l : \texttt{skip} \mid \\
&\qquad l : x = e \mid \\
&\qquad \texttt{if } (l : b) \ Prog \ \texttt{else} \ Prog \mid \\
&\qquad \texttt{while } (l : b) \ Prog \mid \\
&\qquad l : \texttt{assert} \ (b, l')
\end{aligned}
$$

where l, l' denote labels, e an expression and b a boolean expression. A program ($Prog$) is a possibly empty list of statements ($Stmt$). The empty list is denoted λ, and the list separator is ";". We assume that the labels of any given program are distinct, so that a label uniquely identifies a statement. Assignments, conditions and loops have the usual semantics. As its name suggests, skip does nothing.

The assertion $\texttt{assert}(b, l')$ stops program execution in an error state (denoted ε) if b is false, otherwise execution continues normally. As said earlier, we assume that assertions are added to protect all threatening statements. The label l' allows us to associate the assertion with another statement that should be protected by the assertion (e.g. because it could provoke a runtime error). An assertion often protects the following line (like in Fig. 1, where the protected label is not indicated). Two simple cases however need more flexibility (cf. Fig. 3). Some assertions have to be themselves protected by assertions when they contain a threatening expression. Figure 3a gives such an example where, instead

```
 ┌ 13 : assert (z != 0, 11);                ┌ 11 : assert (k != 0, 1);
 │┌ 12 : assert (w != 0, 1);                │     while (1 : j <= N/k) {
 ││► 11 : assert ((y/z) + 1 != 0, 1);       ┤       ...
 └└─► 1  : z = x / ((y/z) + 1) + v/w;       └ 12 :   assert (k != 0, 1); }
```

(a) Chained assertions   (b) Loop condition

Fig. 3. Two special cases of assertions

of creating three assertions pointing to 1, assertions 11 and 12 point to 1, and assertion 13 points to another assertion 11. Figure 3b (inspired by the second loop of Fig. 1) shows how assertions with explicit labels can be used to protect a loop condition from a runtime error. The arrows in Fig. 3 indicate the protected statement.

Assertions can be also added by the user to check other properties than runtime errors. If the user does not need to indicate the protected statement, they can choose for l' either the label l of the assertion itself or any label not used elsewhere in the program. User-defined assertions should be also protected against errors by other assertions if necessary.

Semantics. Let p be a program. A program state is a mapping from variables to values. Let Σ denote the set of all valid states, and $\Sigma_\varepsilon = \Sigma \cup \{\varepsilon\}$, where ε is the error state. Let σ be an initial state of p. The *trajectory* of the execution of p on σ, denoted $T[\![p]\!]\sigma$, is the sequence of pairs $\langle (l_1, \sigma_1) \dots (l_k, \sigma_k) \dots \rangle$, where $l_1, \dots, l_k, \dots$ is the sequence of labels of the executed instructions, and σ_i is the state of the program *after* the execution of instruction l_i. T can be seen as a (partial) function

$$T : Prog \to \Sigma \to Seq(L \times \Sigma_\varepsilon)$$

where $Seq(L \times \Sigma_\varepsilon)$ is the set of sequences of pairs $(l, \sigma) \in L \times \Sigma_\varepsilon$. Trajectories can be finite or (countably) infinite. A finite subsequence at the beginning of a trajectory T is called a *prefix* of T. The empty sequence is denoted $\langle \rangle$.

Let $\oplus$ be the concatenation operator over sequences. For a finite trajectory T, we denote by $LS_\sigma(T)$ the last state of T (i.e. the state component of its last element) if $T \neq \langle \rangle$, and σ otherwise. The definition of $T_1 \oplus T_2$ is standard if T_1 is finite. If T_1 is infinite or ends with the error state ε, then we set $T_1 \oplus T_2 = T_1$ for any T_2 (and even if T_2 is not well-defined, in other words, $\oplus$ performs lazy evaluation of its arguments).

We denote by $\mathcal{E}$ an evaluation function for expressions, that is standard and not detailed here. For any (pure) expression e and state $\sigma \in \Sigma$, $\mathcal{E}[\![e]\!]\sigma$ is the evaluation of expression e using σ to evaluate the variables present in e. The error state is only reached through a failed `assert`. Thanks to the assumption that all potentially failing statements are protected by assertions, we do not need to model errors in expressions or other statements: errors always occur in assertions. We also suppose for simplicity that all variables appearing in p are initialized in any initial state of p, that ensures the absence of expressions that

$$\mathcal{T}[\![\lambda]\!]\sigma \;\;=\;\; \langle\rangle,$$

$$\mathcal{T}[\![s;\ p]\!]\sigma \;\;=\;\; \mathcal{T}[\![s]\!]\sigma \oplus \mathcal{T}[\![p]\!](LS_\sigma(\mathcal{T}[\![s]\!]\sigma)),$$

$$\mathcal{T}[\![l:\texttt{skip}]\!]\sigma \;\;=\;\; \langle(l,\sigma)\rangle,$$

$$\mathcal{T}[\![l:x=e]\!]\sigma \;\;=\;\; \langle(l,\sigma[x \leftarrow \mathcal{E}[\![e]\!]\sigma])\rangle,$$

$$\mathcal{T}[\![\texttt{if}\ (l:b)\ p\ \texttt{else}\ q]\!]\sigma \;\;=\;\; \langle(l,\sigma)\rangle \oplus (\mathcal{E}[\![b]\!]\sigma \rightarrow \mathcal{T}[\![p]\!]\sigma, \mathcal{T}[\![q]\!]\sigma),$$

$$\mathcal{T}[\![\texttt{while}\ (l:b)\ p]\!]\sigma \;\;=\;\; \langle(l,\sigma)\rangle \oplus (\mathcal{E}[\![b]\!]\sigma \rightarrow$$
$$\mathcal{T}[\![p]\!]\sigma \oplus \mathcal{T}[\![\texttt{while}\ (l:b)\ p]\!](LS_\sigma(\mathcal{T}[\![p]\!]\sigma)), \langle\rangle),$$

$$\mathcal{T}[\![l:\texttt{assert}(b,l')]\!]\sigma \;\;=\;\; (\mathcal{E}[\![b]\!]\sigma \rightarrow \langle(l,\sigma)\rangle, \langle(l,\varepsilon)\rangle),$$

where for any trajectories T, T' and boolean value v, we define

$$(v \rightarrow T, T') = \begin{cases} T \text{ if } v = True, \\ T' \text{ if } v = False. \end{cases}$$

Fig. 4. Trajectory-based semantics of the language (for a valid state $\sigma \in \Sigma$)

• cannot be evaluated due to an uninitialized variable. These assumptions slightly simplify the presentation without loss of generality for our purpose: loops and errors (in assertions) are present in the language.

Figure 4 gives the inductive definition of $\mathcal{T}$ for any valid state $\sigma \in \Sigma$. The definitions for a loop and a conditional rely on the notation $(v \rightarrow T_1, T_2)$ also defined in Fig. 4. For any state σ, variable x and value v, $\sigma[x \leftarrow v]$ denotes σ overridden by the association $x \mapsto v$. Notice that in the definitions for a sequence and a loop, it is important that $\oplus$ does not evaluate the second parameter when the first trajectory is infinite or ends with the error state since the execution of the remaining part is not defined in this case. Thus ε can appear only once at the very end of a trajectory.

We illustrate these definitions on slice **(b)** of Fig. 1, denoted p_b. For every initial state σ of p_b and unsigned integer i, we define $\sigma^i = \sigma[s_1 \leftarrow (i \cdot a[0] \mod M_u)]$, where M_u denotes the maximal representable value of an unsigned integer. Then the trajectory on σ_3 is infinite, while the trajectory on σ_5 leads to an error:

$$\mathcal{T}[\![p_b]\!]\sigma_3 = \langle(1,\sigma_3^0)(3,\sigma_3^0)(4,\sigma_3^0)(5,\sigma_3^0)(6,\sigma_3^1)(7,\sigma_3^1)(4,\sigma_3^1)(5,\sigma_3^1)(6,\sigma_3^2)(7,\sigma_3^2)\ldots\rangle,$$
$$\mathcal{T}[\![p_b]\!]\sigma_5 = \langle(1,\sigma_5^0)(3,\sigma_5^0)(4,\sigma_5^0)(17,\varepsilon)\rangle.$$

4   Relaxed Program Slicing

4.1   Control and Data Dependences

Let $L(p)$ denote the set of labels of program p. Let us consider here a more general slicing criterion defined as a subset of labels $L_0 \subseteq L(p)$, and construct a slice with respect to all statements whose labels are in L_0. In particular, this generalization can be very useful when one wants to perform V&V on a slice with respect to several threatening statements. In this work we focus on dependence-based slicing, where a dependence relation $\mathcal{D} \subseteq L(p) \times L(p)$ is used to construct a slice. We write $l \xrightarrow[p]{\mathcal{D}} l'$ to indicate that l' depends on l according to $\mathcal{D}$, i.e. $(l, l') \in \mathcal{D}$. The definitions of control and data dependencies, denoted respectively $\mathcal{D}_c$ and $\mathcal{D}_d$, are standard, and given following [6].

Definition 1 (Control Dependence $\mathcal{D}_c$). *The control dependencies in p are defined by* if *and* while *statements in p as follows:*

for any statement if $(l : b)$ q else r *and* $l' \in L(q) \cup L(r)$, *we define* $l \xrightarrow[p]{\mathcal{D}_c} l'$;

for any statement while $(l : b)$ q *and* $l' \in L(q)$, *we define* $l \xrightarrow[p]{\mathcal{D}_c} l'$.

For instance, in Fig. 1a, lines 5–7 are control-dependent on line 4, while lines 13–15 are control-dependent on line 12.

To define data dependence, we need the notion of (finite syntactic) paths. Let us denote again by $\oplus$ the concatenation of paths, extend $\oplus$ to sets of paths as the set of concatenations of their elements, and denote by "$*$" Kleene closure.

Definition 2 (Finite Syntactic Paths). *The set of finite syntactic paths $\mathcal{P}(p)$ of a program p is inductively defined as follows:*

$$\mathcal{P}(\llbracket \lambda \rrbracket) = \{\lambda\},$$
$$\mathcal{P}(\llbracket s;\ p \rrbracket) = \mathcal{P}(s) \oplus \mathcal{P}(p),$$
$$\mathcal{P}(\llbracket l : \mathtt{skip} \rrbracket) = \{l\},$$
$$\mathcal{P}(\llbracket l : x = e \rrbracket) = \{l\},$$

$$\mathcal{P}(\llbracket \mathtt{if}\ (l : b)\ p\ \mathtt{else}\ q \rrbracket) = \{l\} \oplus (\mathcal{P}(p) \cup \mathcal{P}(q)),$$
$$\mathcal{P}(\llbracket \mathtt{while}\ (l : b)\ p \rrbracket) = (\{l\} \oplus \mathcal{P}(p))^* \oplus \{l\},$$
$$\mathcal{P}(\llbracket l : \mathtt{assert}(b, l') \rrbracket) = \{l\}.$$

For a given label l, let def(l) denote the set of variables defined at l (that is, def$(l) = \{v\}$ if l is an assignment of variable v, and $\emptyset$ otherwise), and let ref(l) be the set of variables referenced at l. If l designates a conditional (or a loop) statement, ref(l) is the set of variables appearing in the condition; other variables appearing in its branches (or loop body) do not belong to ref(l). We denote by used(l) the set def$(l) \cup$ ref(l).

Definition 3 (Data Dependence $\mathcal{D}_d$). *Let l and l' be labels of a program p. We say that there is a data dependency $l \xrightarrow[p]{\mathcal{D}_d} l'$ if* def$(l) \neq \emptyset$ *and* def$(l) \subseteq$ ref(l') *and there exists a path $\pi = \pi_1 l \pi_2 l' \pi_3 \in \mathcal{P}(p)$ such that for all $l'' \in \pi_2$,* def$(l'') \neq$ def(l). *Each π_i may be empty.*

For instance, in Fig. 1b, line 18 is data-dependent on line 1 (with $\pi = 1, 3, 4, 17, 18$) and on line 6 (with $\pi = 1, 3, 4, 5, 6, 7, 4, 17, 18$, while line 6 is data-dependent on lines 1, 3, 6 and 7.

A slice of p is expected to be a *quotient* of p, that is, a well-formed program obtained from p by removing zero, one or more statements. A quotient can be identified by the set of labels of preserved statements. Notice that when a conditional (or a loop) statement is removed, it is removed with all statements of its both branches (or its loop body) to preserve the structure of the initial program in the quotient.

Given a dependence relation $\mathcal{D}$ and $L_0 \subseteq L(P)$, the slice based on $\mathcal{D}$ w.r.t. L_0 will be also identified by the set of labels of preserved statements. The following lemma justifies the correctness of the definitions of slices given hereafter. We denote by $\mathcal{D}^*$ the reflexive transitive closure of $\mathcal{D}$, and by $(\mathcal{D}^*)^{-1}(L_0)$ the set of all labels $l' \in L(p)$ such that there exists $l \in L_0$ with $l' \xrightarrow[p]{\mathcal{D}^*} l$.

Lemma 1. *Let $L_0 \subseteq L(P)$. If $\mathcal{D}$ is a dependence relation on p such that $\mathcal{D}_c \subseteq \mathcal{D}$, then $(\mathcal{D}^*)^{-1}(L_0)$ is the set of labels of a (uniquely defined) quotient of p.*

Lemma 1 can be easily proven by structural induction. It allows us to define a slice as the set of statements on which the statements in L_0 are (directly or indirectly) dependent.

Definition 4 (Dependence-based Slice). *Let $\mathcal{D}$ be a dependence relation on p such that $\mathcal{D}_c \subseteq \mathcal{D}$, and $L_0 \subseteq L(P)$. A dependence-based slice of p based on $\mathcal{D}$ with respect to L_0 is the quotient of p whose set of labels is $(\mathcal{D}^*)^{-1}(L_0)$. A classic dependence-based slice of p with respect to L_0 is based on $\mathcal{D} = \mathcal{D}_c \cup \mathcal{D}_d$.*

4.2   Assertion Dependence and Relaxed Slices

Soundness of classic slicing for programs without runtime errors or non-terminating loops can be expressed by Property 1 in Sect. 2. As we illustrated, to generalize this property in presence of runtime errors and for non-terminating executions one would need to add additional dependencies and systematically preserve in the slice all potentially erroneous or non-terminating statements executed before (a statement of) the slicing criterion. We propose here an alternative approach, called *relaxed slicing*, where only one additional dependency type is considered.

Definition 5 (Assertion Dependence $\mathcal{D}_a$). *For every assertion $l :$ assert (b, l') in p with $l, l' \in L(p)$, we define an assertion dependency $l \xrightarrow[p]{\mathcal{D}_a} l'$.*

Definition 6 (Relaxed Slice). *A relaxed slice of p with respect to L_0 is the quotient of p whose set of labels is $(\mathcal{D}^*)^{-1}(L_0)$, where $\mathcal{D} = \mathcal{D}_c \cup \mathcal{D}_d \cup \mathcal{D}_a$.*

For instance, in Fig. 1a, there would be an assertion dependence of each threatening statement on the corresponding protecting assertion (written on the previous line). Therefore both slices **(b)** and **(c)** of Fig. 1 (in which we artificially preserved assertions in Sect. 2) are in fact relaxed slices where assertions are naturally preserved thanks to the assertion dependence.

Assertion dependence brings two benefits. It ensures that a potentially threatening instruction is never kept without its protecting assertion. At the same time, an assertion can be preserved without its protected statement, that is quite useful for V&V that focus on assertions: slicing w.r.t. assertions may produce smaller slices if we do not need the whole threatening statement. For example, a relaxed slice w.r.t. the assertion at line 17 would contain only this unique line.

Notice that a relaxed slice does not require to include potentially erroneous or non-terminating statements that can prevent the slicing criterion from being executed (like in [18,25,26]). For example, slice (b) does not include the potential error at line 13, and slice (c) does not include the loop of line 4.

4.3   Soundness of Relaxed Slicing

We cannot directly compare the trajectory of the original program with a slice, since it may refer to statements and variables not preserved in the slice. We use projections of trajectories that reduce them to selected labels and variables.

Definition 7 (Projection of a State). *The projection of a state σ to a set of variables V, denoted $\sigma{\downarrow}V$, is the restriction of σ to V if $\sigma \neq \varepsilon$, and ε otherwise.*

Definition 8 (Projection of a Trajectory). *The projection of a one-element sequence $\langle (l,\sigma) \rangle$ to a set of labels L, denoted $\langle (l,\sigma) \rangle{\downarrow}L$, is defined as follows:*

$$\langle (l,\sigma) \rangle{\downarrow}L = \begin{cases} \langle (l, \sigma{\downarrow}\,\mathrm{used}(l)) \rangle & \text{if } l \in L, \\ \langle \rangle & \text{otherwise.} \end{cases}$$

The projection of a trajectory $T = \langle (l_1,\sigma_1) \ldots (l_k,\sigma_k) \ldots \rangle$ to L, denoted $\mathrm{Proj}_L(T)$, is defined element-wise: $\mathrm{Proj}_L(T) = \langle (l_1,\sigma_1) \rangle{\downarrow}L \oplus \ldots \oplus \langle (l_k,\sigma_k) \rangle{\downarrow}L \oplus \ldots$.

We can now state and prove the soundness property of relaxed slices.

Theorem 1 (Soundness of a Relaxed Slice). *Let $L_0 \subseteq L(p)$ be a slicing criterion of program p. Let q be the relaxed slice of p with respect to L_0, and $L = L(q)$ the set of labels preserved in q. Then for any initial state $\sigma \in \Sigma$ of p and finite prefix T of $\mathcal{T}[\![p]\!]\sigma$, there exists a prefix T' of $\mathcal{T}[\![q]\!]\sigma$, such that:*

$$\mathrm{Proj}_L(T) = \mathrm{Proj}_L(T')$$

Moreover, if p terminates without error on σ, $\mathcal{T}[\![p]\!]\sigma$ and $\mathcal{T}[\![q]\!]\sigma$ are finite, and

$$\mathrm{Proj}_L(\mathcal{T}[\![p]\!]\sigma) = \mathrm{Proj}_L(\mathcal{T}[\![q]\!]\sigma)$$

Proof. Let $\sigma \in \Sigma$, $\mathcal{T}[\![p]\!]\sigma = \langle (l_1,\sigma_1)(l_2,\sigma_2) \ldots \rangle$, and $\mathcal{T}[\![q]\!]\sigma = \langle (l'_1,\sigma'_1)(l'_2,\sigma'_2) \ldots \rangle$. Let $T = \langle (l_1,\sigma_1) \ldots (l_i,\sigma_i) \rangle$ be a finite prefix of $\mathcal{T}[\![p]\!]\sigma$. By Definition 8, the projections of $\mathcal{T}[\![q]\!]\sigma$ and T to $L = L(q)$ have the following form

$$\mathrm{Proj}_L(\mathcal{T}[\![q]\!]\sigma) = \langle (l'_1,\sigma'_1{\downarrow}\,\mathrm{used}(l'_1))(l'_2,\sigma'_2{\downarrow}\,\mathrm{used}(l'_2)) \ldots \rangle,$$
$$\mathrm{Proj}_L(T) = \langle (l_{f(1)},\sigma_{f(1)}{\downarrow}\,\mathrm{used}(l_{f(1)})) \ldots (l_{f(j)},\sigma_{f(j)}{\downarrow}\,\mathrm{used}(l_{f(j)})) \rangle,$$

where $j \leq i$ and f is a strictly increasing function.

Let us denote by k the greatest natural number such that $k \leq j$ and such that the prefix of $T[\![q]\!]\sigma$ of length k exists and satisfies $(\mathrm{Proj}_L(T))^k = \mathrm{Proj}_L((T[\![q]\!]\sigma)^k)$, where we denote by U^k the prefix of length k for any trajectory U. Let $T' = \langle (l'_1, \sigma'_1) \ldots (l'_k, \sigma'_k) \rangle$ be the prefix $(T[\![q]\!]\sigma)^k$. By Definition 8 we have

$$\mathrm{Proj}_L(T') = \langle \, (l'_1, \sigma'_1 {\downarrow} \, \mathrm{used}(l'_1)) \, \ldots \, (l'_k, \sigma'_k {\downarrow} \, \mathrm{used}(l'_k)) \, \rangle.$$

Since $(\mathrm{Proj}_L(T))^k = \mathrm{Proj}_L(T')$, for any $m = 1, 2, \ldots, k$ we have $l'_m = l_{f(m)}$ and $\sigma'_m {\downarrow} \, \mathrm{used}(l'_m) = \sigma_{f(m)} {\downarrow} \, \mathrm{used}(l_{f(m)})$. Set $\sigma_0 = \sigma'_0 = \sigma$.

Let us prove that $k = j$. We reason by contradiction and assume that $k < j$. By maximality of k, there can be three different cases:

1. $T[\![q]\!]\sigma$ is of size k, or
2. l'_{k+1} exists, but $l'_{k+1} \neq l_{f(k+1)}$, or
3. l'_{k+1} exists, $l'_{k+1} = l_{f(k+1)}$, but $\sigma'_{k+1} {\downarrow} \, \mathrm{used}(l'_{k+1}) \neq \sigma_{f(k+1)} {\downarrow} \, \mathrm{used}(l_{f(k+1)})$.

Since $l'_k = l_{f(k)}$, cases 1 and 2 can be only due to a diverging evaluation of a control flow statement (i.e. if, while or assert) situated in the execution of p between $l_{f(k)}$ and $l_{f(k+1)-1}$. If such a statement occurs at label $l'_k = l_{f(k)}$, its condition would be evaluated identically in both executions since $\sigma'_k {\downarrow} \, \mathrm{used}(l'_k) = \sigma_{f(k)} {\downarrow} \, \mathrm{used}(l_{f(k)})$. The first non-equal label $l_{f(k+1)}$ cannot be part of the body of some non-preserved if or while statement between $l_{f(k)} + 1$ and $l_{f(k+1)-1}$ in p by definition of control dependence (cf. Definition 1). Finally, the divergence cannot be due to an assert in p between $l_{f(k)+1}$ and $l_{f(k+1)-1}$ either, because a passed assert has no effect, while a failing assert would make it impossible to reach $l_{f(k+1)}$ in p. Thus a divergence leading to cases 1 and 2 is impossible.

In case 3, the key idea is to remark that $\sigma'_k {\downarrow} \, \mathrm{ref}(l'_{k+1}) = \sigma_{f(k+1)-1} {\downarrow} \, \mathrm{ref}(l_{f(k+1)})$. Indeed, assume that there is a variable $v \in \mathrm{ref}(l'_{k+1}) = \mathrm{ref}(l_{f(k+1)})$ such that $\sigma'_k(v) \neq \sigma_{f(k+1)-1}(v)$. The last assignment to v in the execution of p before its usage at $l_{f(k+1)}$ must be preserved in q because of data dependence (cf. Definition 3), so it has a label $l'_u = l_{f(u)}$ for some $1 \leqslant u \leqslant k$. By definition of k, the state projections after this statement were equal: $\sigma'_u {\downarrow} \, \mathrm{used}(l'_u) = \sigma_{f(u)} {\downarrow} \, \mathrm{used}(l_{f(u)})$, so the last values assigned to v before its usage at $l_{f(k+1)}$ were equal, that contradicts the assumption $\sigma'_k(v) \neq \sigma_{f(k+1)-1}(v)$. This shows that all variables referenced in $l_{f(k+1)}$ have the same values, so the resulting states cannot differ, and case 3 is not possible either. Therefore $k = j$, and T' satisfies $\mathrm{Proj}_L(T) = \mathrm{Proj}_L(T')$.

If p terminates without error on σ, by the first part of the theorem we have a prefix T' of $T[\![q]\!]\sigma$ such that $\mathrm{Proj}_L(T[\![p]\!]\sigma) = \mathrm{Proj}_L(T')$. If T' is a strict prefix of $T[\![q]\!]\sigma$, this means as before that a control flow statement executed in p causes the divergence of the two trajectories. By hypothesis, there are no failing assertions in the execution of p, therefore it is due to an if or a while. By the same reasoning as in cases 1, 2 above we show that its condition must be evaluated in the same way in both trajectories and cannot lead to a divergence. Therefore, $T' = T[\![q]\!]\sigma$. $\square$

5 Verification on Relaxed Slices

In this section, we show how the absence and the presence of errors in relaxed slices can be soundly interpreted in terms of the initial program.

Lemma 2. *Let q be a relaxed slice of p and $\sigma \in \Sigma$ an initial state of p. If the preserved assertions do not fail in the execution of q on σ, they do not fail in the execution of p on σ either.*

Proof. Let us show the contrapositive. Assume that $T[\![p]\!]\sigma$ ends with (l, ε) where $l \in L(q)$ is a preserved assertion. Let $L = L(q)$. From Theorem 1 applied to $T = T[\![p]\!]\sigma$, it follows that there exists a finite prefix T' of $T[\![q]\!]\sigma$ such that $\mathrm{Proj}_L(T) = \mathrm{Proj}_L(T')$. The last state of $\mathrm{Proj}_L(T')$ is ε, therefore the last state of T' is ε too. It means that ε appears in $T[\![q]\!]\sigma$, and by definition of semantics (cf. Sect. 3) this is possible only if ε is its last state. Therefore $T[\![q]\!]\sigma$ ends with (l, ε) as well. □

The following theorem and corollary immediately follow from Lemma 2.

Theorem 2. *Let q be a relaxed slice of p. If all assertions contained in q never fail, then the corresponding assertions in p never fail either.*

Corollary 1. *Let $q_1, \ldots, q_n$ be relaxed slices of p such that each assertion in p is preserved in at least one of the q_i. If no assertion in any q_i fails, then no assertion fails in p.*

The last result justifies the detection of errors in a relaxed slice.

Theorem 3. *Let q be a relaxed slice of p and $\sigma \in \Sigma$ an initial state of p. We assume that $T[\![q]\!]\sigma$ ends with an error state. Then one of the following cases holds for p:*

(†) $T[\![p]\!]\sigma$ *ends with an error at the same label, or*
(††) $T[\![p]\!]\sigma$ *ends with an error at a label not preserved in q, or*
(†††) $T[\![p]\!]\sigma$ *is infinite.*

Proof. Let $L = L(q)$ and assume that $T[\![q]\!]\sigma$ ends with (l, ε) for some preserved assertion at label $l \in L$. We reason by contradiction and assume that $T[\![p]\!]\sigma$ does not satisfy any of the three cases. Then two cases are possible.
    First, $T[\![p]\!]\sigma$ ends with (l', ε) for another preserved assertion at label $l' \in L$ (with $l' \neq l$). Then reasoning as in the proof of Lemma 2 we show that $T[\![q]\!]\sigma$ ends with (l', ε) as well, that contradicts $l' \neq l$.
    Second, $T[\![p]\!]\sigma$ is finite without error. Then the second part of Theorem 1 can be applied and thus $\mathrm{Proj}_L(T[\![p]\!]\sigma) = \mathrm{Proj}_L(T[\![q]\!]\sigma)$. This is contradictory since $T[\![q]\!]\sigma$ contains an error (at label $l \in L$) and $T[\![p]\!]\sigma$ does not. □

For instance, consider the example of Fig. 1 with $0 < \mathtt{k} \leqslant 100$, $0 < \mathtt{N} \leqslant 100$. In this case we can prove that slice (**b**) does not contain any error, thus we can deduce by Theorem 2 that the assertions at lines 5 and 17 (preserved in slice (**b**)) never fail in the initial program either. If in addition we replace N/k by (N-1)/k at line 11 of Fig. 1, we can show that neither of the two slices of Fig. 1 contains any error. Since these slices cover all assertions, we can deduce by Corollary 1 that the initial program is error-free.

Theorem 3 shows that despite the fact that an error detected in q does not necessary appear in p, the detection of errors on q has a precise interpretation. It can be particularly meaningful for programs supposed to terminate, for which a non-termination within some time τ is seen as an anomaly. In this case, detection of errors in a slice is sound in the sense that if an error is found in q for initial state σ, there is an anomaly (same or earlier error, or non-termination within time τ) in p whose type can be easily determined by running p on σ.

It can be noticed that a result similar to Theorem 3 can be established for non-termination: if $\mathcal{T}[\![q]\!]\sigma$ is infinite, then either (††) or († † †) holds for p.

6   Related Work

Weiser [34] introduced the basics of intraprocedural and interprocedural static slicing. A thorough survey provided in [30] explores both static and dynamic slicing and compares the different approaches. It also lists the application areas of program slicing. More recent surveys can be found at [9,29,35]. Foundations of program slicing have been studied e.g. in [4–6,8,11,14,20,26–28]. This section presents a selection of works that are most closely related to the present paper.

Debugging and Dynamic Slicing. Program debugging and testing are traditional application domains of slicing (e.g. [2,19,33]) where it can be used to better understand an already detected error, to prioritize test cases (e.g. in regression testing), simplify a program before testing, etc. In particular, dynamic slicing [8] is used to simplify the program for a given (e.g. erroneous) execution. However, theoretical foundations of applying V&V on slices instead of the initial program (like in [13,22]) in presence of errors and non-termination, that constitute the main purpose of this work, have been only partially studied.

Slicing and Non-terminating Programs. A few works tried to propose a semantics preserved by classic slicing even in presence of non-termination. Among them, we can cite the lazy semantics of [11], and the transfinite one of [16], improved by [24]. Another semantics proposed in [6] has several improvements compared to the previous ones: it is intuitive and substitutive. Despite the elegance of these proposals, they turn out to be unsuitable for our purpose because they consider non-existing trajectories, that are not adapted to V&V techniques, for example, based on path-oriented testing like in [13,15].

Ranganath, et al. [26] provides foundations for the slicing of modern programs, i.e. programs with exceptions and potentially infinite loops, represented by control flow graphs (CFG) and program dependence graphs (PDG). Their work gives two definitions of control dependence, non-termination sensitive and non-termination insensitive, corresponding respectively to the weak and strong control dependences of [25] and further generalized for any finite directed graph in [14]. [26] also establishes the soundness of classic slicing with non-termination sensitive control dependence in terms of weak bisimulation, more adapted to deal with infinite executions. Their approach requires to preserve all loops, that results in much bigger slices than in relaxed slicing.

Amtoft [4] establishes a soundness property for non-termination insensitive control dependence in terms of simulation. Ball and Horwitz [5] describes program slicing for arbitrary control flow. Amtoft and Ball [4,5] state that an execution in the initial program can be a prefix of that in a slice, without carefully formalizing runtime errors. Our work establishes a similar property, and in addition performs a complete formalization of slicing in presence of errors *and* non-termination, explicitly formalizes errors by assertions and deduces several results on performing V&V on slices.

Slicing in Presence of Errors. Harman, et al. [18] notes that classic algorithms only preserve a lazy semantics. To obtain correct slices with respect to a strict semantics, it proposes to preserve all potentially erroneous statements through adding pseudo-variables in the def(l) and ref(l) sets of all potentially erroneous statements l. Our approach is more fine-grained in the sense that we can independently select assertions to be preserved in the slice and to be considered by V&V on this slice. This benefit comes from our dedicated formalization of errors with assertions and a rigorous proof of soundness using a trajectory-based semantics. In addition, we make a formal link about the presence or the absence of errors in the program and its slices. Harman and Danicic [17] uses program slicing as well as meaning-preserving transformations to analyze a property of a program not captured by its own variables. For that, it adds variables and assignments in the same idea as our assertions. Allen and Horwitz [3] extends data and control dependences for Java program with exceptions. In both papers, no formal justification is given.

Certified Slicing. The ideas developed in [4,26] were applied in [10,31]. Wasserrab [31] builds a framework in Isabelle/HOL to formally prove a slicing defined in terms of graphs, therefore language-independent. Blazy, et al. [10] proposes an unproven but efficient slice calculator for an intermediate language of the CompCert C compiler [23], as well as a certified slice validator and a slice builder written in Coq [7]. The modeling of errors and the soundness of V&V on slices were not specifically addressed in these works.

To the best of our knowledge, the present work is the first complete formalization of program slicing for structured programs in presence of errors and non-termination. Moreover, it has been formalized in the Coq proof assistant on a representative structured language, that provides a certified program slicer and justifies conducting V&V on slices instead of the initial program.

7   Conclusion

In many domains, modern software has become very complex and increasingly critical. This explains both the growing efforts on verification and validation

(V&V) and, in many cases, the difficulties to analyze the whole program. We revisit the usage of program slicing to simplify the program before V&V, and study how it can be performed in a sound way in presence of possible runtime errors (that we model by assertions) and non-terminating loops. Rather than preserving more statements in a slice in order to satisfy the classic soundness property (stating an equality of whole trajectory projections), we define smaller, *relaxed slices* where only assertions are kept in addition to classic control and data dependences, and prove a weaker soundness property (relating prefixes of trajectory projections). It allows us to formally justify V&V on relaxed slices instead of the initial program, and to give a complete sound interpretation of presence or absence of errors in slices. First experiments with SANTE [12,13], where all-path testing is used on relaxed slices to confirm or invalidate alarms initially detected by value analysis, show that using relaxed slicing allowed to reduce the program in average by 51 % (going up to 97 % for some examples) and accelerated V&V in average by 43 %.

The present study has been formalized in Coq for a representative programming language with assertions and loops, and the results of this paper (as well as many helpful additional lemmas on dependencies and slices) were proved in Coq, providing a certified correct-by-construction slicer for the considered language [1]. This Coq formalization represents an effort of 8 person-months of intensive Coq development resulting in more than 10,000 lines of Coq code.

Future work includes a generalization to a wider class of errors, an extension to a realistic programming language and a certification of a complete verification technique relying on program slicing. Another research direction is to precisely measure the reduction rate and benefits for V&V of relaxed slicing compared to slicing approaches systematically introducing dependencies on previous loops and erroneous statements. In an ongoing work in DEWI project, we apply relaxed slicing for verification of protocols of wireless sensor networks.

Acknowledgments. Part of the research work leading to these results has received funding for DEWI project (www.dewi-project.eu) from the ARTEMIS Joint Undertaking under grant agreement No. 621353. The authors thank Omar Chebaro, Alain Giorgetti and Jacques Julliand for many fruitful discussions and earlier work that lead to the initial ideas of this paper. Many thanks to the anonymous reviewers for lots of very helpful suggestions.

References

1. Formalization of relaxed slicing (2016). http://perso.ecp.fr/~lechenetjc/slicing/
2. Agrawal, H., DeMillo, R.A., Spafford, E.H.: Debugging with dynamic slicing and backtracking. Softw. Pract. Exper. **23**(6), 589–616 (1993)
3. Allen, M., Horwitz, S.: Slicing java programs that throw and catch exceptions. In: PEPM 2003, pp. 44–54 (2003)
4. Amtoft, T.: Slicing for modern program structures: a theory for eliminating irrelevant loops. Inf. Process. Lett. **106**(2), 45–51 (2008)

5. Ball, T., Horwitz, S.: Slicing programs with arbitrary control-flow. In: Fritzson, P.A. (ed.) AADEBUG 1993. LNCS, vol. 749, pp. 206–222. Springer, Heidelberg (1993)
6. Barraclough, R.W., Binkley, D., Danicic, S., Harman, M., Hierons, R.M., Kiss, A., Laurence, M., Ouarbya, L.: A trajectory-based strict semantics for program slicing. Theor. Comp. Sci. **411**(11–13), 1372–1386 (2010)
7. Bertot, Y., Castéran, P.: Interactive Theorem Proving and Program Development. Springer, Heidelberg (2004)
8. Binkley, D., Danicic, S., Gyimóthy, T., Harman, M., Kiss, Á., Korel, B.: Theoretical foundations of dynamic program slicing. Theor. Comput. Sci. **360**(1–3), 23–41 (2006)
9. Binkley, D., Harman, M.: A survey of empirical results on program slicing. Adv. Comput. **62**, 105–178 (2004)
10. Blazy, S., Maroneze, A., Pichardie, D.: Verified validation of program slicing. CPP **2015**, 109–117 (2015)
11. Cartwright, R., Felleisen, M.: The semantics of program dependence. In: PLDI (1989)
12. Chebaro, O., Cuoq, P., Kosmatov, N., Marre, B., Pacalet, A., Williams, N., Yakobowski, B.: Behind the scenes in SANTE: a combination of static and dynamic analyses. Autom. Softw. Eng. **21**(1), 107–143 (2014)
13. Chebaro, O., Kosmatov, N., Giorgetti, A., Julliand, J.: Program slicing enhances a verification technique combining static and dynamic analysis. In: SAC (2012)
14. Danicic, S., Barraclough, R.W., Harman, M., Howroyd, J., Kiss, Á., Laurence, M.R.: A unifying theory of control dependence and its application to arbitrary program structures. Theor. Comput. Sci. **412**(49), 6809–6842 (2011)
15. Ge, X., Taneja, K., Xie, T., Tillmann, N.: DyTa: dynamic symbolic execution guided with static verification results. In: the 33rd International Conference on Software Engineering (ICSE 2011), pp. 992–994. ACM (2011)
16. Giacobazzi, R., Mastroeni, I.: Non-standard semantics for program slicing. High. Order Symbolic Comput. **16**(4), 297–339 (2003)
17. Harman, M., Danicic, S.: Using program slicing to simplify testing. Softw. Test. Verif. Reliab. **5**(3), 143–162 (1995)
18. Harman, M., Simpson, D., Danicic, S.: Slicing programs in the presence of errors. Formal Aspects Comput. **8**(4), 490–497 (1996)
19. Hierons, R.M., Harman, M., Danicic, S.: Using program slicing to assist in the detection of equivalent mutants. Softw. Test. Verif. Reliab. **9**(4), 233–262 (1999)
20. Horwitz, S., Reps, T., Binkley, D.: Interprocedural slicing using dependence graphs. In: PLDI (1988)
21. Kirchner, F., Kosmatov, N., Prevosto, V., Signoles, J., Yakobowski, B.: Frama-C: a software analysis perspective. Formal Asp. Comput. **27**(3), 573–609 (2015)
22. Kiss, B., Kosmatov, N., Pariente, D., Puccetti, A.: Combining static and dynamic analyses for vulnerability detection: illustration on heartbleed. In: Piterman, N., et al. (eds.) HVC 2015. LNCS, vol. 9434, pp. 39–50. Springer, Heidelberg (2015). doi:10.1007/978-3-319-26287-1_3
23. Leroy, X.: Formal verification of a realistic compiler. Commun. ACM **52**(7), 107–115 (2009)
24. Nestra, H.: Transfinite semantics in the form of greatest fixpoint. J. Log. Algebr. Program. **78**(7), 573–592 (2009)
25. Podgurski, A., Clarke, L.A.: A formal model of program dependences and its implications for software testing, debugging, and maintenance. IEEE Trans. Softw. Eng. **16**(9), 965–979 (1990)

26. Ranganath, V.P., Amtoft, T., Banerjee, A., Hatcliff, J., Dwyer, M.B.: A new foundation for control dependence and slicing for modern program structures. ACM Trans. Program. Lang. Syst. **29**(5) (2007). Article number (27)
27. Reps, T.W., Yang, W.: The semantics of program slicing and program integration. In: TAPSOFT (1989)
28. Reps, T.W., Yang, W.: The semantics of program slicing. Technical report, University of Wisconsin (1988)
29. Silva, J.: A vocabulary of program slicing-based techniques. ACM Comput. Surv. **44**(3), 12 (2012)
30. Tip, F.: A survey of program slicing techniques. J. Prog. Lang. **3**(3), 121–189 (1995)
31. Wasserrab, D.: From formal semantics to verified slicing: a modular framework with applications in language based security. Ph.D. thesis, Karlsruhe Inst. of Techn (2011)
32. Weiser, M.: Program slicing. In: ICSE (1981)
33. Weiser, M.: Programmers use slices when debugging. Commun. ACM **25**(7), 446–452 (1982)
34. Weiser, M.: Program slicing. IEEE Trans. Softw. Eng. **10**(4), 352–357 (1984)
35. Xu, B., Qian, J., Zhang, X., Wu, Z., Chen, L.: A brief survey of program slicing. ACM SIGSOFT Softw. Eng. Notes **30**(2), 1–36 (2005)

The Influences of Edge Instability on Change Propagation and Connectivity in Call Graphs

Lei Wang$^{(\boxtimes)}$, Han Li, and Xinchen Wang

School of Computer Science and Engineering, Beihang University, Beijing, China
{wanglei,sy1406228,wxc11061106}@buaa.edu.cn

Abstract. During the lifetime of any software there are numerous changes, which lead to a large number of versions over time. The amount of effort in programming and debugging for these updates and therefore the reliability of the software depends substantially on how far the change propagates. We introduced the concept of Propagation Scope (*PS*) to quantify change propagation and investigated several open-source software systems. We found that the propagation property varies even with systems of similar scales. According to the asymmetry between the in-degree and out-degree distributions in call graphs of software, we defined Edge Instability (*EI*) to measure the change propagation of a call graph. Analyzing newly added nodes in six software, we found that the new nodes exhibited preferential attachment behaviors and were more likely to call new nodes. We proposed a model based on these observations to adjust *EI* and Clustering Coefficient (*CC*). *CC* has been believed to be the major factor determining the propagation scope in a network. Our experiments showed, however, that *EI* had a larger impact on the propagation of call graphs. In both real software and our model, we measured the connectivity of call graphs with *EI* and evaluated connectivity under three edge-removal strategies. Our experiments showed that removing edges with high *EI*s hurt network connectivity the most.

Keywords: Complex networks · Software evolution · Change propagation · Network model · Call graph

1 Introduction

It has been observed that ideas, information, viruses, and diseases often propagate in the form of complex networks [30] and a network's topological structure has a significant impact on the dynamics of change propagation [28]. In the domain of computer science, it has been demonstrated that class diagrams [34,35], collaboration graphs [29], package dependency networks [23], the object graphs [31], software component graphs [20], and call graphs in large-scale software systems [37] are all complex networks. In this paper, we studied change propagation in call graphs, a critical aspect in software evolution. As developers code to introduce new features or fix bugs for one part of a software system, other parts need to be updated accordingly to stay consistent with the changes.

© Springer-Verlag Berlin Heidelberg 2016
P. Stevens and A. Wąsowski (Eds.): FASE 2016, LNCS 9633, pp. 197–213, 2016.
DOI: 10.1007/978-3-662-49665-7_12

For example, when a function's prototype changes, its callers have to be modified to call through the new interface. To understand the evolution of software systems, we collected call graphs of a large number of software systems of multiple versions. A call graph describes the calling relationship between functions in a program. Specifically, functions in the program are represented as nodes in a call graph. If one function calls another, an edge from the node representing the caller to the node of the callee function is added to the graph. We generated a call graph for each version of a selected software system and, by comparing the graphs of different versions, investigated change propagation as software evolves.

We selected 35 stable Linux kernels from version 1.0 to version 2.2.26 (available at http://ftp.kernel.org) and generated their call graphs using a modified version of GCC 3.4.6 [2]. To compare update propagation characteristics among different software, we collected call graphs for five additional open-source projects, including 80 versions of Samba, 25 versions of BIND, 55 versions of Sendmail, 76 versions of OpenSSH, and 59 versions of vsftpd obtained from the code repository [7]. To identify updates between two adjacent versions of a software system, we use *ctags* [1] to get the start and end points of a function in one version. We then compared the functions of the same name in the two versions to decide if the function is updated. We also identified functions removed from the older version or added in the newer version. All these changes, including updates, additions, and removals of functions, can be identified in the call graphs when they are propagated to other functions in the software. In this paper, we name the versions with ordered sequence numbers starting from 0 following their chronological order.

We quantified network propagation with Propagation Scope (PS). The scope that a change propagation can reach is mostly determined by the topological structure of the corresponding call graph, which can be characterized by many factors, including the graph's node count, edge count, average node degree, etc. Among the factors, the clustering coefficient (CC) measures how tightly nodes in a network are clustered and is believed to be the most powerful factor determining the propagation of networks [38,41]. We found, however, that propagation in a call graph was not sensitive to CC changes. In fact, for the studied software, the asymmetry between the in-degree and out-degree distributions were manifest [36] and have a significant influence on the change propagation of software [8]. Given the asymmetry, we introduce Edge Instability (EI) to measure the propagation. We found that the new nodes exhibit preferential attachment behaviors and are more likely to call new nodes. With these observations, we propose a model to adjust CC and EI based on Barabási and Albert (BA) model and it's extension [6,18]. Experiments showed that EI has a larger impact than CC on the propagation of call graph.

Inspired by the influences of EI on change propagation, we use EI to measure the connectivity of call graphs. In complex networks, researchers often study robustness by measuring connectivity after removing nodes or edges [10,32]. We adopted the same methodology to evaluate the connectivity of call graphs and compare three strategies to attack generated graphs by our model: 1. Removing edges randomly. 2. Removing edges with higher EIs. 3. Removing edges with higher "edge degrees" [19]. Our experiments showed that removing edges with high EIs hurt network robustness more than removing edges with high "edge degrees" or randomly.

The rest of this paper is organized as follows. Section 2 introduces the concept of propagation scope, edge instability and statistics with various software systems. Connectivity of call graphs under three edge-removal strategies are discussed in Sect. 3. Section 4 describes behaviors of new nodes and an innovative model of software evolution. The correlation among parameters of the proposed model, change propagation and connectivity are also discussed in Sect. 4. Section 5 introduces the related work briefly. The paper closes with our conclusions in Sect. 6.

2   Change Propagation

To quantify the change propagation in a network, we introduce the concept of propagation scope (PS), derived from the concepts of *Change Cost* [26] and *Average Propagation Ratio* [25], and edge instability. To reveal impact of the structure of a call graph on PS, we will measure the number of nodes and edges, the average node degree, the diameter, the clustering coefficient and the edge instability of the call graphs under investigation.

2.1   Propagation Scope

The concept of propagation scope is motivated by the observation that in a call graph a change propagates in one direction. For example, if Function A calls Function B and B's interface is changed, Function A has to change accordingly, or the change of B propagates to A. Changes do not propagate in the opposite direction. For example, the change of Function A does not affect function B. Formally, we state that Node n_i can reach Node n_j within a distance of 1 if there is a directed edge $< n_i, n_j >$ in a network G. We use R_j^d to denote the set of nodes that can reach n_j within distance d. Formally, we use Eq. (1) to define the propagation scope of Network G within distance d, or PS_G^d.

$$PS_G^d = \frac{\sum\limits_{j=1}^{|N|} |R_j^d|}{|N|^2} \tag{1}$$

where $|N|$ is the number of nodes in Network G.

According to Eq. (1) and the definition of R_j^d, if $d_1 > d_2$, then $PS_G^{d1} \geqslant PS_G^{d2}$, because R_j^d monotonically increases with d. Using D to denote network diameter, we have $PS_G^d = PS_G^D$ for any d larger than D. Finally, the propagation scope of Network G, PS_G, can be defined using Eq. (2).

$$PS_G = PS_G^D = \frac{\sum\limits_{j=1}^{|N|} |R_j^D|}{|N|^2} \tag{2}$$

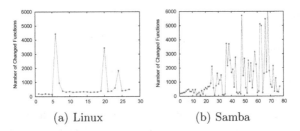

(a) Linux   (b) Samba

Fig. 1. Number of changed functions in Linux and Samba.

The propagation scope can be used to differentiate networks of different topologies in terms of impact of a node's change on other nodes. The larger the propagation scope, the greater the number of nodes affected by changes taking place at a node.

By definition, *PS* is obviously related to the number of nodes, the number of edges and the average node degree. We compare some versions of Linux with versions of Samba of similar scale. The results are shown in Table 1. In the table, "Linux1" stands for set of the Linux versions from 1.2.0 to 1.2.10, "Linux2" stands for set of the Linux versions from 2.0.0 to 2.0.40. "Samba1" stands for set of Samba versions from 2.2.8 to 2.2.12, and "Samba2" stands for set of Samba versions from 3.0.25 to 3.0.34. As shown in Table 1, Linux1 and Samba1 have similar node count and edge count. This is also the case for Linux2 and Samba2. However, we can see that the PS_G values of different Linux versions is always smaller than those of Sambas in Table 1.

Table 1. Statistics with Linux and Samba of similar scale.

software	Linux1	Samba1	Linux2	Samba2
Avg. node	3993	3803	8099	7373
Avg. edge	14996	13849	31400	30513
Ave. degree	7.51	7.28	7.75	8.27
PS_G	0.0135	0.0297	0.0112	0.0295

We also investigate changes between two adjacent versions of Linux and Samba, respectively. Figures 1 and 2 showed the number of changed functions and the size of the maximal connected subgraphs. To compare Linux with Samba using their call graphs of similar scales, we chose Linux 2.0.40 and Samba 3.0.34 as the last tested version shown in Figs. 1 and 2. For most versions, the number of changed functions in Linux was fewer than that of Samba. For the maximal connected subgraphs, the sizes in the two versions of Linux were larger than 200, and those in other versions were less than 90. On the other hand, in over one third of the versions of Samba, the sizes of the maximal connected subgraphs were larger than 200, with the largest of 1501. The change propagation in Samba seemed substantially larger than that in Linux. This observation is consistent with Table 1. Therefore, *PS* could be used to measure the change propagation in call graphs of software.

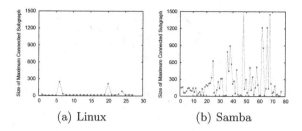

(a) Linux   (b) Samba

Fig. 2. Size of maximal connected subgraphs in Linux and Samba.

2.2   Edge Instability

The asymmetry between the in-degree and out-degree distributions of software appears obviously [9,29,34,36]. The in-degree distribution of software systems obviously obeys the power-law while the out-degree distribution are similar to the power-law distribution with a cutoff. Inspired by the asymmetry of degree distribution and direction of change propagation in software, we propose the Edge Instability of a call graph.

Firstly, we define the node stability S_i for Node n_i in Eq. (3).

$$S_i = \frac{k_{in}^i}{k_{in}^i + k_{out}^i} \tag{3}$$

where k_{in}^i and k_{out}^i are the in- and out-degree of node n_i, respectively. A greater value of S_i means that n_i has a smaller out-degree and therefore the changes of other nodes are less likely to propagate to n_i. Thus we say a node with a greater S_i is more stable. The value of S_i is always in the range of [0, 1].

The instability I_{ij} of the edge $< n_i, n_j >$ is derived from node stability and defined by Eq. (4).

$$I_{ij} = S_i - S_j \tag{4}$$

where S_i and S_j are the node stability of nodes n_i and n_j, respectively. With this definition, an edge with a greater I_{ij} propagates changes to more nodes. Thus we call I_{ij} as edge instability. The edge instability, EI, of a graph is the average I_{ij} of the edges in the graph.

Figure 3 includes two examples to explain this observation.

1. In Fig. 3(a), S_i is 3/4 and S_j is 1/4. Accordingly, I_{ij} of Edge $< i, j >$ is 1/2. A change at Nodes j, a, b or c will propagate to Nodes i, d, e, and f across Edge $< i, j >$, as indicated by the dotted lines.
2. In Fig. 3(b), S_i is 0 and S_j is 1/4. Accordingly, I_{ij} of Edge $< i, j >$ is -1/4. Changes at Nodes j, a, b, and c only spread to Node i but do not reach nodes d, e, and f.

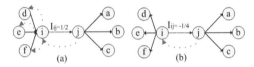

Fig. 3. Comparison between the effects of two edges with the higher and lower I_{ij} for the neighboring nodes

Apparently, Edge $< i, j >$ with higher EI in the first example has a higher impact on the propagation scope.

2.3 Statistics with Six Open Source Software

For a node in a call graph, the out-degree is the number of other functions that the function represented by this node calls, and the in-degree is the number of other functions that call the function of this node. The sum of the in-degree and out-degree is the degree of the node. We calculated average degree of the nodes in the call graphs of the selected systems. We found that the average degrees stayed stable as the software systems evolve over many versions. For each call graph, we measure the diameter, denoted as D.

Clustering, the tendency that a node's neighbors are likely to be neighbors themselves, has been commonly considered as one of the most important factors in the study of propagation [38]. We calculated the clustering coefficient (CC) in C_i of Node i using Eq. (5):

$$C_i = \frac{2E_i}{k_i(k_i - 1)} \tag{5}$$

where E_i is the number of edges connecting neighbors of Node i, and k_i is the degree of Node i. The clustering coefficient C of a graph is the average clustering coefficient of the nodes in the graph.

The number of nodes, the number of edges, the average node degree, the diameter (D), the clustering coefficient (CC), the edge instability (EI) and the propagation scope (PS_G) of six selected systems are showed in Fig. 4. Figure 4 shows that for all the systems both the number of nodes and the number of edges grow over time. A number of observations can be made as below.

1. Table 2 summarizes the correlation coefficient results between PS_G and other features of six software. Compared with the number of nodes, the number of edges, the average node degree, the diameter (D) and the clustering coefficient, the edge instability is the only one that had a positive correlation with PS_G in all six software.
2. As the increase of node number, the corresponding PS_G decreases except for BIND. In fact, PS_G is the ratio of the number of nodes a propagation reaches to the number of all nodes. The propagation of changes in a system is hard to maintain the same rate as a software system becomes larger.

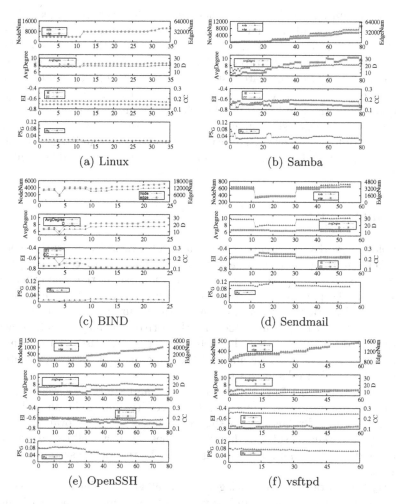

Fig. 4. The number of nodes, the number of edges, the average degree, *CC*, *EI* and *PS_G* of six software. X axis indicates the sequence numbers of versions.

Table 2. The correlation coefficient results between *PS_G* and other features.

Software	Node	Edge	Ave. deg	D	CC	EI
Linux	−0.99	−0.99	−0.96	−0.96	0.42	**0.41**
Samba	−0.11	−0.11	0.086	0.05	0.03	**0.29**
BIND	0.29	0.58	0.94	0.85	−0.75	**0.48**
Sendmail	−0.80	−0.80	−0.79	−0.37	0.76	**0.68**
OpenSSH	−0.96	−0.96	−0.85	−0.94	0.97	**0.94**
vsftpd	−0.93	−0.92	−0.91	−0.26	−0.21	**0.90**

3. Per the definition of *PS*, as the increases of the average degree, *PS* of a software system would also increase. This phenomenon can be observed clearly in BIND system (Fig. 4(c)). It is easy to understand that the more edges a system has, the faster the propagation would be. The tendency, however, is not apparent in other software systems. It is difficult to tell the impact of the average degree on PS_G in two cases: 1. The average degree is very stable. 2. The average degree and node number change at the same time.

4. Previous works suggest that as *CC* increases the propagation scope in a network would decrease [38]. This can be clearly observed in BIND and vsftpd. It is not apparent, however in other systems as *CC* is very stable in different versions.

3   Connectivity

In complex networks, researchers often study robustness by measuring connectivity after removing nodes or edges [10,32]. As many error conditions do not cause the crash of the whole software system, we assume that the other parts of the software keep working. For example, when the kernel panics in a loadable module of an Ethernet driver it can contain the failure and give out messages. The other parts of the system cannot use this driver but may be able to access the Ethernet device from other channels and certainly a user can continue to work in a text editor. Thus, we adopted the same methodology to evaluate the connectivity of call graphs in this paper.

We remove the edge to simulate the failure, and study how well the other nodes in the call graph stay connected. Connectivity among the nodes left represents a measure of robustness of the graph under edge removal. It is not a measure of how well the software handles crashes but how well its functions are designed and coded to minimize the impact on the rest of the system when one or more parts fail.

We try three strategies to attack generated call graphs. The first strategy, the "RA removal", removes edges randomly. The second removes edges with higher *EI*s and is called the "HL removal". The third strategy is proposed by Ref. [19] where the edge degree is defined by Eq. (6):

$$k_e = k_v * k_w \tag{6}$$

where the edge e connects two nodes v and w with node degrees k_v and k_w, respectively. The attack strategy selects the edges in descending degrees. We name this strategy as "ED removal".

We select Linux 2.0.1, Samba 3.0.10, BIND 9.2.4rc5, Sendmail 8.11.3, OpenSSH 2.5.2p1 and vsftpd 1.1.2 to compare the three strategies. Each time, 5 percent of edges are removed. We measure the change of the size of the maximal connected subgraph, S, with Eq. (7):

$$S = \frac{N_a}{N_i} \tag{7}$$

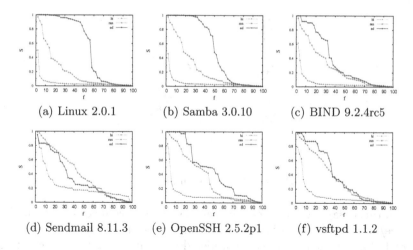

(a) Linux 2.0.1   (b) Samba 3.0.10   (c) BIND 9.2.4rc5

(d) Sendmail 8.11.3   (e) OpenSSH 2.5.2p1   (f) vsftpd 1.1.2

Fig. 5. Six software under three attack strategies.

where N_i and N_a are the numbers of nodes in the maximal connected subgraph before and after the attack, respectively.

The results are shown in Fig. 5 when a fraction f of the edges is removed in six software. In Fig. 5, it is difficult to distinguish the impact of the connectivity between the RA and ED removal. When the call graphs undergo the HL removal attacks, however, the sizes of maximal connected subgraph decreases rapidly. We observed the top 20 edges with high EI in Linux and found the similar structure as Fig. 6 when we extract all edges that directly connect to the edge with high EI from call graph. The edges with high EI behave like some kind of "weak ties" [15] between two parts of software modules. Removing these edges results in quick disintegration of the call graphs.

4   Features of Call Graphs and Evolution Model

To understand how software systems evolve into particular structures, we studied the ways new nodes were added into call graphs.

4.1   Preferential Attachment

Call graphs show that their in-degree distribution largely obeys the power-law while the out-degree exhibits the power-law distribution with a cutoff [36]. Thus, we investigated whether new nodes would contribute to the distributions of in-degree and out-degree. Specifically, for in-degree distribution we would like to know whether new nodes are more likely to be connected to existing nodes of higher in-degrees (in terms of function calls, the functions corresponding to the new nodes are the callers in this case). For out-degree distribution, we would like to know whether existing nodes of higher out-degree are more likely to be connected to the new nodes (the functions corresponding to the new nodes are the

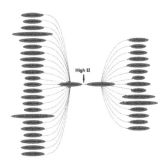

Fig. 6. The edge with high *EI*.

callees in this case). The tendency for new nodes to be connected to either high in-degree/out-degree nodes is commonly known as "preferential attachment". Preferential attachment has been considered as an important factor contributing to the scale-free feature of complex networks [5]. We would like to know whether in-degree and out-degree preferential attachments exist when the new nodes are added.

We studied how the newly added nodes are connected to the top 5 % nodes with the highest in-degrees and the top 5 % nodes with the highest out-degrees in each software version. To quantify the preferential attachment tendency, we define the concept of connecting probability (*CP*) as the probability that a new node is connected to the top 5 % nodes with the highest in-degree/out-degrees. Formally, *CP* can be calculated using Eq. (8):

$$CP = \frac{N_c}{N_t} \tag{8}$$

where N_c is the number of new nodes that call the top 5 % nodes with the highest in-degrees when we consider in-degree preferential attachment (the resulting *CP* is called in-degree *CP*) and N_t is the total number of new nodes in the corresponding version. When we consider out-degree preferential attachment, N_c is the number of new nodes that are called by the top 5 % nodes with the highest out-degrees and N_t stays the same (the resulting *CP* is called out-degree *CP*). The average in-degree and out-degree *CP* are summarized in Table 3. Table 3 indicates that the in-degree *CP* is consistently large for each system, which suggests high in-degree preferential attachment behaviors in all systems. Table 3 also shows that the out-degree *CP* is consistently lower than the corresponding in-degree *CP* for each version. The out-degree preferential attachment tendency, if any, seems much weaker than that of the in-degree preferential attachment.

4.2   Callers of New Nodes

In Sect. 4.1, the out-degree *CP* results indicate that the top 5 % nodes with the highest out-degrees do not call the new nodes extensively. It is interesting to

Table 3. Average connecting probability.

Software	Linux	Samba	BIND	Sendmail	OpenSSH	vsftpd
Avg. In-degree	73.06 %	60.28 %	60.36 %	60.66 %	62.46 %	64.65 %
Avg. Out-degree	4.43 %	12.35 %	5.79 %	6.99 %	10.91 %	34.32 %

know which nodes call the new nodes the most. We used N_{new} and N_{old} to denote the number of the new nodes that call the new nodes and the number of the old nodes that call the new nodes in each version, respectively. We use R_{new} to quantify the ratio of N_{new} to $(N_{new}+N_{old})$. It can be calculated using the Eq. (9):

$$R_{new} = \frac{N_{new}}{N_{new} + N_{old}} \tag{9}$$

Thus, we can obtain R_{new} for each software version. The average R_{new} of the Linux, Samba, BIND, Sendmail, OpenSSH, and vsftpd are 47.3 %, 38.6 %, 37.6 %, 23.4 %, 41.0 %, and 29.1 %, respectively. Note that the average ratio of the number of new nodes to that of old nodes for all Linux versions is only 1.8 %. These results indicate that compared with old nodes, new nodes are more likely to call new nodes. In other words, the "age" of a node is one factor to determine whether the node calls another node in real-life software, which ultimately will have an impact on the degree distribution.

4.3   Evolution Model for Software

The "age" of a node seemed to be critical to determine the likelihood for connecting new nodes. With these observations and analysis, we propose a novel model to compare the impact of CC and EI on propagation, in which the two properties can be tuned by changing some parameters. We build our model based on Barabási and Albert (BA) model [6,18] and extend it to adjust clustering coefficient and edge instability as follows:

1. In the beginning, a network consists of m_0 nodes and no edges. m_0 is a small integer. In our experiments it is set to 3.
2. Add Node v ($v = m_0 + 1$ intially).
3. Repeat the following two steps for Node v until m edges are added.
   (a) Preferential attachment (PA): Each edge of Node v is then attached to an existing node with the probability proportional to its degree and age, i.e., the probability for Node w ($w = 1, 2, ..., m_0 + v$ - 1) to be attached to v is

$$P_w = \frac{k_w}{\sum_{i=1}^{m_0+v-1} k_i} \tag{10}$$

where $k_i = (age_i)^{-\beta} * k_i'$. age_i, with the initial value of 1, represents the age of Node i. When a new node is added to the network, the age of each existing node is incremented by 1. k_i' is the degree of Node i. β controls the influence of a node's age.

(b) Triad formation (TF): If an edge between Nodes v and w was added in the previous PA step, then add one more edge from Node v to a randomly chosen neighbor of Node w. If all neighbors of Node w have been connected to Node v, go back to Step 3(a).

4. If $v < |N| - m_0 + 1$, increment v by 1 and go back to step 2. Otherwise, the network is generated.

In generating the network, the total number of the PA and TF steps that produces edges for each new node is m. After one PA, we perform a TF step with a probability of P_t. P_t is a parameter that adjusts the CC of the generated network.

Equation (2) shows that the diameter of a graph has a major impact on PS_G. When a new edge does not cause the current diameter to exceed a threshold, LD, the edge is added. Otherwise, the new edge is dropped and a new possible edge is selected to repeat the above step.

Following [34], we first generate undirected graphs and then transform them into directed graphs by making edges to start from the newly added nodes and end at the existing nodes.

There are five parameters in our model (N, m, P_t, β, and LD). In the experiments, we used $N = 10000$ and $m = 3$. To understand the effect of the P_t and β, we select P_t and β in the ranges of 0 to 0.8 and 0 to 1.0, respectively. Figure 7 showed the relationship among PS_G, CC and EI with the different P_t and β parameters of the generated graphs by our model. We have some observations:

- P_t correlated positively with CC as shown in Fig. 7 (a) and (d).
- β correlated positively with EI as shown in Fig. 7 (b) and (e).
- β, which determines PS_G of a network, has a larger impact on the propagation than P_t, as shown in Fig. 7 (c) and (f). Thus, in our model, the propagation scope was highly correlated with β and therefore EI but less affected by the changes in CC.

To study the impact of EI on connectivity, we use the three strategies to attack graphs generated by different βs. Figure 8 summarized the results. Figure 8(a) showed that, under different βs (between 0 and 1), the effect of node age on network structure changed significantly. The effect of the node ages limited the preferential attachment and prevented a scale-free distribution of connectivities [4]. It seemed to be a critical point in a network and the network became scale-free when β was below a certain value. With large βs, the network showed no power law characteristics and the degree became exponentially distributed. As shown in Fig. 8(a), overall and for different βs, the networks had a good connectivity. This result was consistent with the experiments on network connectivity [3]. This suggested that the network was connected under the random attack due to the scale-free feature. When β fell between 0.4 and 0.8, however, the degree distribution of network transited from scale-free to exponential and the network more vulnerable to random attacks.

Figure 8(b) showed a fast decay for different values of β and f between 0.2 and 0.3. The network was less connected and therefore it became "harder" for

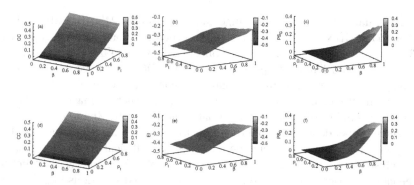

Fig. 7. Summary of PS_G, clustering coefficient and edge instability under different parameters. (a) CC with P_t and β, LD is 20. (b) EI with P_t and β, LD is 20. (c) PS_G with P_t and β, LD is 20. (d) CC with P_t and β, LD is 25. (e) EI with P_t and β, LD is 25. (f) PS_G with P_t and β, LD is 25.

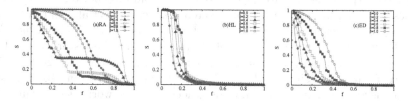

Fig. 8. Three attack strategies applied to the graphs generated with P_t 0.30, LD 20 and β from 0 to 1. (a) The RA attack strategies. (b) The HL attack strategies. (c) The ED attack strategies.

the remaining nodes to communicate with each other when the unstable edges (the edges with the EI values close to 1) were removed.

Figure 8(b) with 8(c) showed that when β is small the HL and ED removals had a similar effect for network connectivity. When β is large, however, the HL removal hurt the connectivity more than ED. As β increased the distribution of degree morphs from scale-free to exponential. Under exponential degree distribution, each node in the network has approximately the same degree, and therefore the damage to network connectivity by ED removal was less obvious. In HL removal, however, the EI highly affected the propagation of networks when β increased (see Fig. 7) and the edges with high EI had a structure of "weak ties" (see Fig. 6). Thus, removing the edges with high EIs in HL removal broke the network into small pieces fast for all β values. HL instead of ED removal became a good indicator for attacks when the degree distribution of networks shifts from scale-free to exponential.

5   Related Work

Two main approaches to study change propagation in software are Impact Analysis (IA) and Mining Software Repositories (MSR). IA uses dependency or traceability information and MSR uses historical information [21]. An in-depth review of impact analysis for software change can be found in [24]. Mirarab et al. [27] propose to use BBNs for impact analysis, and their approach achieves a precision of 63 % with a recall of 26 %. Formal Concept Analysis (FCA) [14], probabilistic approach [33], and Family Dependence Graph (FDG) [39] have been employed for change impact analysis. In the context of complex technical systems, Giffin et al. [13] analyze change propagation with design structure matrix (DSM) and categorize a number of typical change patterns. Recently, Zhang et al. [40] use requirement dependency as a tool to conduct change propagation analysis. They investigate whether existing dependency types are sufficient for change propagation analysis. In our work, we analyze the impact of software network structures on the change propagation without tracing the affected functions in software.

Hassan and Holt propose to determine how changes propagate with developer information, historical co-change information of entity, code structure, and code layout heuristic [16]. Hassan and Malik further improve the approach with an adaptive heuristic method [17]. Zimmermann et al. [42] apply data mining techniques to analyze version histories, and to uncover couplings between fine-grained entities to guide programmers among related changes. Gall et al. [12] propose an approach to extract software evolution patterns and dependencies from the CVS data. Their proposed methodology, QCR, is to examine the historical development of classes by analyzing changes of classes and common change behavior obtained from CVS. They further [11] classify changes according to their significance levels (low, medium, high, or crucial). In our work, we explain why asymmetric structures inside the software are formed after analyzing call graphs of many software system versions, and propose an evolution model capturing the way new nodes are added during the process of software evolution. By varying the parameters of the proposed model, we study the relationship between the change propagation and software structure.

Asymmetric structures can increase the fragility of software [8]. Studies on the mechanism of asymmetric software structures can help optimization of software. Myers points out that the asymmetry typically is due to the common practice of software reuse [29]. Others [34] argue that the asymmetry is rooted right in the economization of development effort and related costs. Additionally [9] notes that the out-degree of the class in the object oriented software systems is limited by the size of the class. They have found that the limitation leads to the asymmetry of degree distributions. We found, however, that the manner in which new nodes are added into the call graphs during software evolution contributes to the asymmetric feature of software, and that the asymmetric structures have a significant impact on the change propagation of software.

Many network models have been proposed in the past decade. In BA model [5], each newly added node is connected to nodes selected with a probability proportional to their respective degrees. Although the degree distribution of the BA model follows the power-law distribution, the resulting clustering coefficient is much lower than those measured in software systems. In the Copying model [22], each newly added node randomly selects a target node and connects to it, as well as to all neighbor nodes of the target node. The Copying model has a large clustering coefficient. In the process of selecting the target node in the Copying model, however, older nodes have greater priority to be connected to the newly added nodes. This feature is different from actual new node behavior demonstrated in real software systems, in which new nodes are more likely to be connected among themselves.

6   Conclusions

Using propagation scope, we quantified change propagation in different versions of six open-source software systems. Inspired by the asymmetry of degree distribution and direction of change propagation in software, we proposed the edge instability to measure the change propagation of a call graph. We calculated the number of nodes, the number of edges, the average node degree, the diameter, *CC*, *EI* in the call graphs of the selected systems, and found that *EI* is the only one that had a positive correlation with propagation scope in all six studied software. To compare the impact of *CC* and *EI* on change propagation, we have proposed a novel model allowing us to adjust these properties. Although *CC* is traditionally considered one of the most important factors in the study of propagation, our experimental results indicated that *EI* had a much bigger impact in call graphs. Furthermore, we showed the correlation between the connectivity of call graphs and *EI*, i.e., eliminating the edges with high *EI* breaks a network into small pieces faster in real software and networks generated by our model. In summary, we demonstrated that *EI* could be a good indicator of the change propagation and connectivity of software networks.

Acknowledgments. This work was supported by National Natural Science Foundation of China (No. 61272167).

References

1. ctags 5.8 release. http://ctags.sourceforge.net
2. Gcc 3.4 release series. http://gcc.gnu.org/gcc-3.4/
3. Albert, R., Jeong, H., Barabósi, A.: Error and attack tolerance of complex networks. Nature **406**(6794), 378–382 (2000)
4. Amaral, L., Scala, A., Barthélémy, M.: Classes of small-world networks. Proc. Nat. Acad. Sci. **97**, 11149–11152 (2000)
5. Barabási, A.L., Albert, R.: Emergence of scaling in random networks. Science **286**, 509–512 (1999)
6. Barabási, A.L., Albert, R.: Emergence of scaling in random networksscience. Science **286**(5439), 509–512 (1999)
7. Bhattacharya, P., Iliofotou, M., Neamtiu, I., Faloutsos, M.: Graph-based analysis and prediction for software evolution. In: ICSM, pp. 419–429 (2012)
8. Challet, D., Lombardoni, A.: Bug propagation and debugging in asymmetric software structures. Phys. Rev. E **70**, 046109 (2004)
9. Concas, G., Marchesi, S.P.M., Serra, N.: Powerlaws in a large object-oriented software system. IEEE Trans. Softw. Eng. **33**(10), 687–708 (2007)

10. Crucittia, P., Latorab, V., Marchiori, M., Rapisarda, A.: Error and attacktolerance of complex networks. Phys. A **340**, 388–394 (2004)
11. Fluri, B., Gall, H.C.: Classifying change types for qualifying change couplings. In: ICPC, pp. 35–45 (2006)
12. Gall, H., Jazayeri, M., Krajewski, J.: Cvs release history data for detecting logical couplings. In: IWPSE (2003)
13. Giffin, M., de Weck, O., Bounova, G., Keller, R., Eckert, C., Clakson, J.: Change propagation analysis in complex technical systems. J. Mech. Des. **131**(8), 081001-1–081001-14 (2009)
14. Girba, T., Ducasse, S., Kuhn, A.: Using concept analysis to detect co-change patterns. In: Ninth International Workshop on Principles of Software Evolution: In conjunction with the 6th ESEC/FSE, pp. 83–89 (2007)
15. Granovetter, M.: The strength of weak ties. Am. J. Socio. **78**(6), 1360–1380 (1973)
16. Hassan, A.E., Holt, R.C.: Predicting change propagation in software systems. In: International Conference on Software Maintenance, pp. 284–293 (2004)
17. Hassan, A.E., Malik, H.: Supporting software evolution using adaptive change propagation heuristics. In: ICSM, pp. 177–186 (2008)
18. Holme, P., Kim, B.: Growing scale-free networks with tunable clustering. Phys. Rev. E **65**(2), 026107 (2000)
19. Holme, P., Kim, B., Yoon, C.: Attack vulnerability of complex networks. Phys. Rev. E **65**(2), 056109 (2002)
20. Ichii, M., Matsushita, M., Inoue, K.: An exploration of power-law in use-relation of java software systems. In: 19th Australian Software Engineering Conference, pp. 422–4311 (2008)
21. Kagdi, H., Maletic, J.: Software-change prediction: estimated+actual. In: Software Evolvability, pp. 38–43 (2006)
22. Krapivsky, P.L., Redner, S.: Network growth by copying. Phys. Rev. E **71**(3), 036118 (2005)
23. LaBelle, N., Wallingford, E.: Inter-package dependency networks in open-source software. CoRR, cs.SE/0411096 (2004)
24. Lehnert, S.: A review of software change impact analysis. Technical University Ilmenau, pages Report ilm1-200618 (2011)
25. Liu, J., Lu, K.H.J., Li, B., Tse, C.: Characterizing the structural quality of general complex software networks. Int. J. Bifurcat. Chaos **18**(02), 605–613 (2008)
26. MacCormack, A., Rusnak, J., Baldwin, C.: Exploring the structure of complex software designs: an empirical study of open source and proprietary code. Manag. Sci. **52**(7), 1015–1030 (2006)
27. Mirarab, S., Hassouna, A., Tahvildari, L.: Using bayesian belief networks to predict change propagation in software systems. In: ICPC, pp. 177–188 (2007)
28. Moore, C., Newman, M.E.J.: Epidemics and percolation in small-world networks. Phys. Rev. E **61**(5), 5678 (2000)
29. Myers, C.R.: Software systems as complex networks: structure, function, and evolvability of software collaboration graphs. Phys. Rev. E **68**, 046116.1–046116.15 (2003)
30. Newman, M.E.J.: The structure and function of complex networks. SIAM Rev. **45**, 167–256 (2003)
31. Potanin, A., Noble, J., Frean, M., Biddle, R.: Scale-free geometry in oo programs. Commun. ACM **48**(5), 99–103 (2005)
32. Albert, A.B.R., Jeong, H.: Error and attack tolerance of complex networks. Nature **406**, 378–382 (2000)

33. Sharafat, A.R., Tahvildari, L.: Change prediction in object-oriented software systems: a probabilistic approac. J. Softw. **3**(5), 26–39 (2008). (1796217X)
34. Valverde, S., Cancho, R.F., Solé, R.V.: Scale-free networks from optimal design. Europhys. Lett. **60**, 512–517 (2002)
35. Valverde, S., Solé, R.V.: Hierarchical small worlds in software architecture. cond-mat/0307278 (2003)
36. Wang, L., Wang, Y., Zhao, Y.: Mechanism of asymmetric software structures: a complex network perspective from behaviors of new nodes. Phys. A Stat. Mech. Appl. **413**, 162–172 (2014)
37. Wang, L., Wang, Z., Yang, C., Zhang, L., Ye, Q.: Linux kernels as complex networks: a novel method to study evolution. In: ICSM, pp. 41–50 (2009)
38. Wu, X., Liu, Z.: How community structure influences epidemic spread in social networks. Phys. A **387**, 623–630 (2008)
39. Yazdanshenas, A.R., Moonen, L.: Fine-grained change impact analysis for component-based product families. In: ICSM, pp. 119–128 (2012)
40. Zhang, H., Li, J., Zhu, L., Zhu, L., Jeffery, R., Liu, Y., Wang, Q., Li, M.: Investigating dependencies in software requirements for change propagation analysis. Inf. Softw. Technol. **56**(1), 40–53 (2014)
41. Zhou, T., Yan, G., Wang, B.: Maximal planar networks with large clustering coefficient and power-law degree distribution. Phys. Rev. E **71**(4), 046141 (2005)
42. Zimmermann, T., Zeller, A., Weissgerber, P., Diehl, S., Zeller, A.: Mining version histories to guide software changes. IEEE Trans. Softw. Eng. **31**(6), 429–445 (2005)

Modeling and Abstraction of Memory Management in a Hypervisor

Pauline Bolignano[1,2($\boxtimes$)], Thomas Jensen[1], and Vincent Siles[2]

[1] Inria, Rennes, France
{pauline.bolignano,thomas.jensen}@inria.fr
[2] Prove & Run, 77 Avenue Niel, 75017 Paris, France
{pauline.bolignano,vincent.siles}@provenrun.com

Abstract. Hypervisors must isolate memories of guest operating systems. This paper is concerned with proving memory isolation properties about the virtualization of the memory management unit provided by a hypervisor through shadow page tables. We conduct the proofs using abstraction techniques between high-level and low-level descriptions of the system, based on techniques from previous work on formally proving memory isolation in micro-kernels. The present paper shows how a hypervisor developed by Technische Universität Berlin has been formalized and presents the isolation properties we have proved on the targeted abstract model. In particular, we provide details about how the management of page tables has been formally modeled.

1 Introduction

A hypervisor is a software that makes it possible to run several guest operating systems (OS) on the same hardware. It is responsible for enforcing isolation between guests, for supervising their communication, *etc.* Hypervisors usually run at a privileged level, where all instructions are executable, whereas only some instructions are available to the guests. Their key role in managing the resources of the hardware make them highly security-critical components.

An OS running on bare metal manages the piece of hardware responsible for the memory management, called the Memory Management Unit (MMU). On every memory access, the MMU translates the virtual addresses manipulated by the software into physical addresses. The mappings from virtual to physical addresses are kept in page tables (PT) and managed by the OS. However when an OS runs on top of a hypervisor, the latter is the one managing the MMU and the translations. The hypervisor emulates the MMU for the guest OS and supervises the translations by maintaining PTs that *shadow* the PTs of the guest OS, called the Shadow Page Tables (SPTs). The SPT algorithms control the access of the guests to memory resources, and are thus central when proving security properties of guest OSes. Yet, they are definitely non-trivial, and considered an important challenge in formal OS development [1,6,7].

The motivation for our approach is obtaining the certification of isolation properties between guest OSes according to criteria such as Common Criteria [8].

© Springer-Verlag Berlin Heidelberg 2016
P. Stevens and A. Wąsowski (Eds.): FASE 2016, LNCS 9633, pp. 214–230, 2016.
DOI: 10.1007/978-3-662-49665-7_13

One key element of this methodology is designing an abstract model of the concrete target of certification, and proving properties on this abstraction. We first build a low-level model of the hypervisor in the form of a transition system which represents its behavior precisely. This model is abstracted into a simpler transition system, in which properties are simpler to express and prove. We have written our model and conducted our proof with the language and tools developed at Prove & Run. These tools have already shown to be efficient in proving this kind of systems [12]. It should be stressed though, that the work presented here is independent of the particular tool used for its mechanized formalization.

The central part of our approach is that we abstract the *paged* address space (the memory and a pointer to the SPT) into a *linear* memory address space. To do this, we first provide a low-level model of the hypervisor and prove a set of key invariants of this model that are needed to prove isolation. This low-level model is then abstracted into a high-level model with separated memory segments. We have designed the abstract model to be as small as possible while keeping enough expressiveness to state our isolation property. This property guarantees that some resources of the guests are isolated from other guests. It can be divided in two sub-properties, concerning integrity and confidentiality, respectively. The *integrity* property for one guest ensures that its resources are not modified by other guests, unless it has given the authorization to do so. The *confidentiality* for one guest ensures that executions of other guests do not depend on its resources, unless it has given the authorization to do so. By its structure, the abstract model has inherent properties that ensure isolation, e.g. each guest has its own memory segments, whereas in the concrete model the memory is an array of bytes possibly shared with all the guests. To link the two models, we prove invariants on the concrete model which show that the whole system can be divided into well-separated subsystems.

Section 2 introduces the concept of page tables and shadow data structures. In Sect. 3, we outline the concrete model of a paravirtualized ARM version of a hypervisor developed by the SecT team at TU Berlin [17]. We give a classification of the transitions regarding the effects they have on the global state. We present the proof of an invariant which is essential for isolation. In Sect. 4 we present our abstract model, which is novel and interesting because it allows to precisely observe the memory while avoiding the notion of PTs. We show how we abstract the concrete memory. We then present the properties of integrity and confidentiality that we proved, and which taken together guarantee the isolation of guest memories. Finally, in Sect. 5 we discuss related work.

2   Memory Management in Hypervisors

When memory is virtualized, each entity runs as if it had the whole memory for itself, while the underlying platform shares the memory between several entities. In a classic OS with MMU, the OS keeps and manages the translations from virtual pages to physical pages in PTs. In the case of hypervision, a level of translation is added. The hypervisor may either use a hardware virtualization extension (if available) or implement a virtualization mechanism in software. We cover the latter scenario.

The hypervisor on which we work uses the most common software solution, based on SPT. SPTs are maintained by the hypervisor and translate guest virtual addresses (GVA) to physical addresses (PA), as illustrated in Fig. 1. The hypervisor creates and manages them by combining the Guest Page Tables (GPT), which translate GVA into guest physical addresses (GPA), and the Host Page Tables (HPT), which translate host virtual addresses HVA to PA. To simplify the presentation, we here consider that GPA and HVA are equal. The algorithm of managing SPTs we are working on is similar to those governing the Translation Lookaside Buffer (TLB) [5, Chapter 19]. For example when a page fault occurs at GVA gva, the hypervisor is notified. It goes through the GPTs to find out if any HVA hva was mapped to gva in the GPTs. If there is one, it computes the physical address pa corresponding to hva and, provided the guest is allowed to access this part of the memory, it adds the mapping from gva to pa in the SPTs. If the gva was not present in the GPTs, the hypervisor injects the page fault into the guest, so that the guest can add the mapping to the GPTs. Then the execution faults again on gva, because it is not yet in the SPTs, and it brings us back to the first case. Similarly when the guest switches PTs, when there is a TLB invalidation, the hypervisor handles the trap and updates the SPTs. In the hypervisor on which we work, the HPTs are allocated during system initialization, and a contiguous segment of PA corresponds to a contiguous segment of HVA.

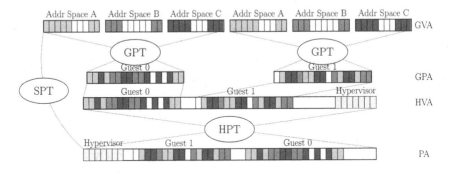

Fig. 1. Page tables of the hypervisor

3   The Concrete Hypervisor Model

The concrete model is the lowest level of our modeling effort; we kept it close to the implementation. However, unlike the C implementation, the effects of hypervisor and guest commands on memory are made explicit. We use untyped memory at this level to remain close to the C code. The closer the concrete model is to the C code, the smaller the gap is between what is proved and what is executed. Using untyped memory permits us to reason about type misinterpretation, and allows casts that are legitimate. We represent the memory as an array of bytes on which we use arithmetic computations to prove that there are no aliasing problems or overlapping data structures.

The memory that we model does not take the hypervisor memory space into account, except for the PTs about which we want to reason. Indeed, each time the hypervisor performs an action, it has an impact on its memory (e.g.pushing/popping something on its stack), and reasoning about these side-effects while reasoning about the effects of the action is not realistic. Moreover, we do not handle DMA and we do not model the devices' memory (cf Sect. 6).

3.1   Global State

We decompose a transition in three sub-transitions, the flow of execution is shown in Fig. 2. The hypervisor first restores the execution of the guest $(0 \rightarrow 1)$, in particular, it sets the processor to *user mode*, which is an unprivileged mode, i.e.in the Privilege Level of execution 0 (PL0). Then the guest executes until it raises an exception or makes a hypercall, making the hardware switch to a privileged mode of execution $(1 \rightarrow 2)$. A privileged mode is in the Privilege Level 1 (PL1). Depending on the level of privilege, some registers may or may not be visible, and accesses to registers may raise an exception. Finally the hypervisor saves the registers of the guest, then handles the call or the fault, while fixing the saved registers as necessary (step $2 \rightarrow 0$).

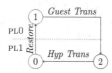

Fig. 2. Execution flow

The state $\sigma = \langle \sigma_{\mathrm{HW}}, \sigma_{\mathrm{HYP}}, exception \rangle$ of the system is made of three components: the hardware state, the hypervisor state (which itself contains the states of the n guests) and an exception. The state of the hardware σ_{HW} is a tuple: $\langle mem, base, level, regs_{gp}, regs_{mmu}, regs_{gic} \rangle$.

Let $Addr$ be the set of all the 32 bit addresses, $Byte$ the set of all the bytes. The physical memory is a function from addresses to bytes: $mem \in Mem = Addr \rightarrow Byte$. In the hardware state σ_{HW}, the tuple $regs_{gp}$ represents the values of the thirteen general purpose registers, the stack pointer, the link register and the program counter currently in the hardware, $regs_{gp} = \langle r0, ..., r12, sp, lr, pc \rangle$. The $base$ is the pointer to the root of the PT used by the processor for address translations. The tuple $regs_{mmu}$ represents the fault status registers related to the MMU, which are needed to solve a page fault. The hardware state also provides the privilege level $level \in \{pl0, pl1\}$, and the registers of the Generic Interrupt Controller ($regs_{\text{gic}}$), which concern the management of the interrupts.

In a configuration with n guests, a guest is identified by an index in $\{1, ..., n\}$. The hypervisor state σ_{HYP} keeps the index of the current guest, its internal state, and the states of all the guests.

$$\sigma_{\text{HYP}} = \langle curr, \sigma_{\text{int}}, \langle \sigma_{G1}, ..., \sigma_{Gn} \rangle \rangle$$
$$\text{where}, \forall i, \sigma_{Gi} = \langle vbase, vmode, vbnk, vregs_{\text{gp}}, vregs_{\text{mmu}}, vregs_{\text{gic}} \rangle$$

The emulated PT base pointer ($vbase$) of the guest contains a pointer to the GPT, i.e. from GVA to GPA. When a page fault occurs, the hypervisor uses the $vbase$ to walk the GPT. However the hardware $base$ pointer never contains the $vbase$ pointer but rather the pointer to the SPT or the HPT.

3.2   Page Tables

A PT maps virtual addresses to physical addresses and provides the access rights to the address. The set of rights is denoted by $Rights$ and contains two elements: $\{rw, ro\}$. We define the total order relation $\geq$ over $Rights$ by $rw \geq ro$. The set of page tables PT is defined by $PT = Addr \rightarrow Addr \times Rights$, these functions are not total, a virtual address $va \in Addr$ not in the domain corresponds to an address for which there is no translation, i.e. the access to va would raise a fault. The function pt takes a memory and a pointer and returns the PT located there: $pt(mem, base)$ is read as "the page table at address $base$ in memory mem", $pt \in Mem \rightarrow Addr \rightarrow PT$. We denote by Γ_f the graph of function f, in particular $\Gamma_{pt(mem,base)}$ is the set of mappings present in the PT at address $base$ in memory mem. In practice, when looking for the physical address corresponding to the virtual address va, va is split in three parts: the first part is an index i_1 in the first level of PT, the second is an index i_2 in a second level of PT, and the last is an offset in a page. The $base$ address in $pt(mem, base)$ is the base address of the first level of PT, each entry of the first level of PT either holds a fault or the address to a second level of PTs. Similarly to pt, we note pt_2 the function that takes a memory and a base address and returns a second level of PT.

An address which is not in the image of a PT is *not mapped*, whereas an address in the image is *mapped* with some rights. For a page table $table \in PT$, we denote the first projection of $Im(table)$ by $Map(table)$. Similarly, we use $Map_{\text{RW}}(table)$ to denote the set of all the physical addresses mapped with RW rights by $table$: $Map_{\text{RW}}(table) = \{pa | (pa, rw) \in Im(table)\}$. The hypervisor associates a SPT to each GPT, we note $\mathcal{B}_{\text{SPT}}(\sigma_{\text{int}}, i)$ the set of base addresses of the SPTs of guest i.

We define m non-overlapping intervals $I_1, ..., I_m$ of physical addresses, such that $\bigcup_{k=1}^{m} I_k \subset Dom(mem)$. We let I represent the set $\{I_1, ..., I_m\}$. During the execution, the hypervisor ensures that the addresses of each interval are only mapped in the SPT of the allowed guests. The permissions for each interval are provided by the initial configuration through the *region* function. The function *region* takes an interval and a guest index and returns the maximum rights that the guest can have on this interval: $region \in (I \times \{1,..,n\}) \rightarrow Rights$. The function is partial, $(I_j, i) \notin Dom(region)$ means that the guest i has no rights on the interval I_j. The hypervisor ensures that an address in an interval is always mapped in the SPT of a guest with rights inferior or equal to the rights defined by the $region$ function (see Invariant 1 in Sect. 3.4). The relation $allowed(a, i, r)$ is true if the address a is in a region of guest i with rights r: $\exists k, a \in I_k \wedge region(I_k, i) = r$. An interval might be private or shared between two guests. If shared, one guest has RO access and the other RW access to it, i.e. it is a one way buffer. Let j be in $\{1, ..., m\}$. Let i and k be in $\{1, ..., n\}$. The following predicates formalize the two possible configurations of an interval:

- $private(I_j, i) \Leftrightarrow \forall a \in I_j, \forall l \neq i, allowed(a, i, rw) \wedge \neg allowed(a, l, \_)$
- $shared(I_j, i, k) \Leftrightarrow \forall a \in I_j, (allowed(a, i, rw) \wedge allowed(a, k, ro) \wedge \forall l \notin \{i, k\}, \neg allowed(a, l, \_))$

3.3 Concrete Transitions

A transition of the system is decomposed into three transitions, as defined in Fig. 2. The *restore transition* models the change from privileged mode to user mode. The hypervisor injects an interrupt to the guest beforehand if any is pending. We define the two other types of sub-transitions below.

Guest transitions occur in user mode. We confine the possible effects they can have on the system by making two hypotheses on the processor. First, the guest may only change the non-privileged registers $regs_{gp}, regs_{mmu}$ and $regs_{gic}$. In particular, it *cannot* change the PT base register. Secondly, it may only change the memory mapped in RW by the PT currently used by the hardware ($pt(mem, base)$). This second hypothesis only makes sense if the so-called current PT is constant during a guest transition. This is ensured by an invariant stating that the memory space where SPT are stored is not mapped in RW by any guest. We denote by $wf(mem, base)$ the property stating that the PT at address $base$ does not map itself in the memory mem. The guest transition is depicted in Fig. 3, where the notation $mem' \cong mem[map_{RW}(pt(mem, base))]$ means that mem and mem' are equal except at the physical addresses mapped in RW by the PT at address $base$ in mem. For readability, fields modified by the transition are represented bolded.

As previously explained, the guest execution gives back the control to the hypervisor when it raises an exception. That is why when the guest ends, the field exception e is always updated. In the case of an abort, information about the fault is stored in the $regs_{mmu}$. As stated, the guest transition does not capture a third hypothesis on the processor, which is fundamental to prove confidentiality. Thus, in Axiom 1 we state that a guest transition only depends on the part of the memory mapped by the current PTs. Here, $\sigma \stackrel{A}{=} \sigma'$ means that the restriction to A of the memories of two states σ and σ' are equal and that all their other fields are equal.

Axiom 1. Let σ_1 and σ_2 be two states such that $\sigma_1 \stackrel{A}{=} \sigma_2$, where $A = map(pt(\sigma_1.base, \sigma_1.mem))$. If $\sigma_1 \xrightarrow{GuestTrans} \sigma_1'$ then $\sigma_2 \xrightarrow{GuestTrans} \sigma_2'$ and $\sigma_1' \stackrel{A}{=} \sigma_2'$.

GUEST TRANS:

$$\frac{wf(mem, base) \qquad mem' \cong mem[map_{RW}(pt(mem, base))]}{\left\langle \begin{matrix} \langle mem, base, \mathbf{pl0}, \mathbf{regs_{gp}}, \mathbf{regs_{mmu}}, \mathbf{regs_{gic}} \rangle \\ \sigma_{\text{HYP}} \\ e \end{matrix} \right\rangle \rightarrow \left\langle \begin{matrix} \langle mem', base, \mathbf{pl1}, \mathbf{regs'_{gp}}, \mathbf{regs'_{mmu}}, \mathbf{regs'_{gic}} \rangle \\ \sigma_{\text{HYP}} \\ e' \end{matrix} \right\rangle}$$

PG FAULT:

$$\frac{\begin{matrix} decode(abt, \sigma_{\text{HW}}) = pf(gva) \\ \sigma_{Gi}.vregs_{mmu}.pg = enabled \qquad hpt(\sigma_{Gi}.vbase) = (pbase, \_) \\ \{(gva, (gpa, r_0))\} \in \Gamma_{pt(mem, pbase)} \qquad hpt(gpa) = (pa, \_) \\ \exists r_1 \geq r_0, allowed(pa, i, r_1) \qquad \Gamma_{pt(mem', base)} = \Gamma_{pt(mem, base)} \cup \{(gva, (pa, r_0))\} \\ \sigma'_{\text{HYP}} = \sigma_{\text{HYP}}[\sigma_{\text{int}} \leftarrow alloc(\sigma_{\text{int}}, mem, gva)] \end{matrix}}{\left\langle \begin{matrix} \langle mem, base, regs_{mmu}, regs_{gp}, pl1, regs_{gic} \rangle \\ \sigma_{\text{HYP}} \\ abt \end{matrix} \right\rangle \rightarrow \left\langle \begin{matrix} \langle mem', base, regs_{mmu}, regs_{gp}, pl1, regs_{gic} \rangle \\ \sigma'_{\text{HYP}} \\ abt \end{matrix} \right\rangle}$$

Fig. 3. Concrete guest transition and page fault transition

Hypervisor transitions happen in a privileged mode. There are fourteen hypervisor transitions, that can be grouped as follows. The first group contains the six transitions related to the memory management: they either modify the current SPTs or the base pointer. The second group only contains the scheduling transition. It corresponds to the guest context switch, that loads the registers of the new guest. In particular, it changes the PT base pointer. The third group contains three transitions that inject a fault to the guest. These transitions only have an impact on general purpose registers. The fourth group contains the emulation of the access to privileged registers. The hypervisor writes to the corresponding emulated privileged register, or reads its value and put it in one of the general purpose registers. This transition may have an impact on the general purpose register or on the guest's GIC. Finally, the transitions of the fifth group concern the IRQs, they have an impact on the GIC registers of the hypervisor or of the guests.

As an example, a transition corresponding to a page fault is presented in Fig. 3. A page fault occurs when the guest tries to access an address gva which is not mapped in the current SPT, the first premise illustrates the decoding of the fault by the hypervisor. The second premise indicates that the MMU of the guest is activated. The GPA $vbase$ is the base of the GPT that the guest is currently using, $pbase$ is the corresponding physical address. The faulting address gva is in the domain of the GPT, and is bound to pa with the rights r_0. The physical address pa corresponds to gpa in the HPT, guest i is allowed to map it with r_0 rights. The memory mem' of the resulting state is such that the graph of the current SPT in mem' contains the new mapping $(gva, (pa, r_0))$. The internal state σ_{int} of the hypervisor might be modified if the addition of a new mapping necessitates the allocation of a new PT (it changes the state of the allocator), we do not detail the behavior of the $alloc$ function here.

3.4 SPT Invariants

The main invariant needed in the concrete model is that if a physical address pa is mapped by one of the SPTs of a guest i with some rights r_0, then pa is in one of the intervals to which this guest has access, with compatible rights. We express this invariant formally, using the notations introduced in Sect. 3.2:

Invariant 1. $(base \in \mathcal{B}_{\mathrm{SPT}}(\sigma_{\mathrm{int}}, i) \wedge (pa, r_0) \in Im(pt(mem, base))) \Rightarrow \exists r_1 \geq r_0 \wedge allowed(pa, i, r_1)$

We have seen in Sect. 3.3 that the page fault handling may lead to the addition of a new mapping in the SPT of the guest. The addition and removal of mappings in a SPT are the crucial parts of the algorithm when it comes to isolation. We have proved the preservation of Invariant 1 during this sensitive operation. We present below the main invariants needed for the proof.

We denote by $Pool(i)$ the set of physical addresses where the SPT of the guest i might be located. The static configuration ensures that the physical addresses of the pools are not in a part of memory attributed to a guest: $\forall i, \forall pa \in Pool(i) \Rightarrow \forall j, r, \neg allowed(pa, j, r)$. We say that $part\_of(mem, b, a)$ is true if the byte at address a holds any value of the PT at base address b.

Invariant 2 ensures that the SPTs of a guest are located within its pool. For each guest, the hypervisor references the free slots available to allocate a new SPT, we write $free\_pt_2(\sigma_{\mathrm{int}}, j, b)$ if b is the address of a free slot for guest j. Invariant 3 states that the free slots for a guest are in its pool, it allows to prove that the former invariant holds after the allocation of a new level of SPT.

Invariant 2 (SPTs disjoint Pools). $b \in \mathcal{B}_{\mathrm{SPT}}(\sigma_{\mathrm{int}}, i) \wedge part\_of(mem, b, pa) \Rightarrow pa \in Pool(i)$.

Invariant 3 (Free PTs disjoint Pools). $free\_pt_2(\sigma_{\mathrm{int}}, j, b_2) \Rightarrow b_2 \in Pool(j)$.

In order to maintain Invariant 1 during the allocation of a new PT in the SPT of guest i, we need to know that the new PT does not map any physical address outside the range allowed to guest i. This property can be stated more easily if a new PT is flushed before being attributed, yet Invariant 4 is sufficient in order to ensure isolation.

Invariant 4 (Free PT allowed). $free\_pt_2(\sigma_{\mathrm{int}}, j, b_2) \wedge (pa, r_a) \in Im(pt_2(mem, b_2)) \Rightarrow (\exists r_b \geq r_a \wedge allowed(pa, j, r_b))$.

Last but not least, SPTs must not overlap, i.e. addresses where a part of a SPT is kept must not correspond to addresses where another part of any SPT is kept. We write $overlap(mem, b, b')$ if the SPT at base b in memory mem overlaps with the SPT at base b'. In particular $overlap(mem, b, b)$ means that the different branches of the same PT overlap. In order to prove that this invariant holds after the allocation of a new second level PT, we must also ensure that a free PT was not allocated in another SPT of that guest beforehand. Note that Invariant 2 already ensures that the PT was not allocated to another guest.

Invariant 5 (No overlap). $b, b' \in \mathcal{B}_{\mathrm{SPT}}(\sigma_{\mathrm{int}}, j) \Rightarrow \neg overlap(mem, b, b')$.

Invariant 6 (Free PT not allocated). $free\_pt_2(\sigma_{\mathrm{int}}, j, b_2) \Rightarrow \forall b \in \mathcal{B}_{\mathrm{SPT}}(\sigma_{\mathrm{int}}, j), \neg part\_of(mem, b, b_2)$.

Preservation of Invariant 1: Consider the case where the hypervisor adds a new mapping m_{new} from the GVA va to the physical address pa in a SPT of guest j, with rights r such that $allowed(pa, j, r)$. We write $base$ for the physical base address of the SPT, and let i_1 and i_2 be the indexes in the first and second level PTs for va. The hypervisor evaluates the i_1^{th} descriptor of the first level of PT. Suppose that this descriptor is a fault. The hypervisor performs three steps: (1) it searches for a free second level PT in the pool of guest j, marks it as used and returns its base address $base_2$, (2) it modifies the first level descriptor at the i_1^{th} entry in the first level PT at base $base$ so that it points to $base_2$, (3) it modifies the second level descriptor at the i_2^{th} entry in the second level of PT freshly allocated so that it leads to pa with the rights r.

We sketch the proof of preservation of Invariant 1. Let mem (resp. mem') be the memory before (resp. after) the transition. We assume that Invariant 1 holds for mem (H_{inv}). Assume that there exists a mapping $m_{bad} = (va', (pa', r'))$ which contradicts Invariant 1 in mem' (H_{break}). Let $base_k$ be the base of a SPT of a guest k in which the mapping m_{bad} is: $m_{bad} \in \Gamma_{pt(mem', basek)}$. We write i_1' and i_2' for the decomposition of the virtual address va' into indexes in the first and second level PT. We proceed by analyzing all the possible branches in all the SPTs where m_{bad} can be, and for each case we refute the existence of such a mapping. The following lines summarize the hypotheses:

- $m_{new} = (va, (pa, r))$ is the new mapping added in the SPT of guest j, located at base $base_j$.
- $base_2$ is the base of the second level of PT freshly allocated.
- H_{pa}: The mapping to be inserted is allowed $(allowed(pa, j, r))$.
- H_{inv}: Invariant 1 holds for mem.
- $m_{bad} = (va', (pa', r'))$.
- H_{break}: Invariant 1 does not holds for mem ($m_{bad} \in \Gamma_{pt(mem', basek)} \wedge \nexists r_0 \geq r', allowed(pa', j, r_0)$).
- va can be decomposed in i_1 and i_2.
- va' can be decomposed in i_1' and i_2'.

Proof. Case $k = j$, $base_k = base_j$ and $i_1' = i_1$: this case means that m_{bad} is one of the mapping that we have just added, i.e. that the address pa' is mapped by the second level of PT we have just allocated.

$\diamond$ *Case $i_2' = i_2$:* it means that m is the very mapping we have added, $m = (va, (pa, r))$[1]. Yet we know that this mapping is allowed for guest j $(allowed(pa, j, r))$, which contradicts H_{break}.

$\diamond$ *Case $i_2' \neq i_2$:* it means that the address pa' is mapped by the second level PT we have just added but does not correspond to the page at index i_2. From Invariant 4 we know that all the indexes of the new PT are in an allowed range for the guest, so it contradicts H_{break}.

---

[1] In reality we just know that m is in the page that we have just mapped, other invariants and conditions on the arguments must be verified (e.g. that the addresses va and pa are aligned to the size of a page) but we do not introduce all the details here.

Case $k \neq j$, or $base_k \neq base_j$ or $i'_1 \neq i_1$: these are the cases where m is in another branch than the modified one, we show that it was necessarily present before, thus contradicting H_{inv}.

◇ Case $k \neq j$: From Invariants 2 and 3, we know that $pt(mem, base_k) = pt(mem', base_k)$. Thus H_{break} yields that m_{bad} was already present in mem ($m_{bad} \in \Gamma_{pt(mem, base_k)}$), which contradicts H_{inv}.

◇ Case $k = j \land base_k \neq base_j$: Invariants 6 and 5 lead to the same conclusion as the precedent case.

◇ Case $k = j \land base_k = base_j \land i'_1 \neq i_1$: From Invariants 6 and 5 we know that the change we made in one branch i_1 of the SPT does not affects other branches, in particular the one in i'_1. Thus m_{bad} was necessarily in the SPT before the addition of the mapping, contradicting H_{inv}.

Note that the hypervisor itself is virtualized by the HPT (i.e. it manipulates virtual addresses which are translated by the processor with the HPT). The addition of a new mapping in the SPT that we have described hides that when the hypervisor accesses the ith entry of a PT located at some physical address, it refers to the entry by its virtual address. Hence one must ensure that the traversal of the SPTs made by the hypervisor with *virtual* addresses is equivalent as the one that would be made with *physical* addresses. We do not present the invariants here, yet it must be underlined that these invariants are used in each case of the proof to specify the effects of the actions of the hypervisor.

The invariants presented are not tight to implementation, they concern SPT algorithms in general. We do have some properties for free due to our particular static configuration, e.g. we know that the pools and the guest regions are disjoint. In a dynamic configuration, this kind of properties would have to be proved, but the reasoning stays unchanged.

The preservation of Invariant 1 under the addition of a mapping is the major requirement to formally link the page fault transition that we have presented in Fig. 3 to the abstract transition mm that we present later in Sect. 4.2.

4 The Abstract Hypervisor Model

This section presents the abstract model used to prove that SPTs provide memory isolation between guests. Some data structures and algorithms of the concrete model have no impact on the isolation property. Thus, provided the right invariants are proved on the concrete model, there is no need to project them on the abstract state. For example, in our case the generic interruption controller has no effect on the memory management; therefore we can remove it from the abstract model and remove all the derived operations. That is why the abstract state is much smaller.

The abstract state contains the index of the current guest and the states of all the guests:

$$\sigma_\alpha = \langle curr, \sigma_1, ...\sigma_n \rangle, \text{ where } \sigma_i = \langle abs\_regs, priv, \langle s_1, ..., s_n \rangle, \langle r_1, ..., r_n \rangle \rangle$$

The guest state is composed of some abstract registers and an address space. We model the address space as a set of segments. Each guest has: (1) a private segment, (2) n shared segments to which it has *write* access, called the *send* segments, (3) n shared segments to which it has *read* access, called the *receive* segments. A segment has the type $Addr \rightarrow Cell$, where $Cell$ represents a byte either mapped or not: $Cell = Byte \times Bool^2$. We say that two cells have the same value if they have the same byte value. We say that two cells have the same tag if they have the same boolean value. The segment function is not total. The segment s_j of σ_i represents the segment in which i can write and j can read. The segment r_j of σ_i represents the segment in which i can read and j can write. The segments are duplicated, such that the jth send segment of guest i is synchronized with the ith receive segment of guest j. Two segments are said to be synchronized if they have the same values but possibly different tags. The notion of synchronization instead of a mere equality allows to reason about sharing, by capturing the fact that a byte value at some address in some segment of a guest can change even if the guest does not map the address. Such an abstraction allows to have a precise view of the memory while discarding the PTs.

4.1   Link Between the Concrete and the Abstract Model

In this section we show how the concrete and the abstract models can be linked.

For a guest i, the abstract cell corresponding to the byte b at address pa in memory mem is such that (1) the value of the cell is b (2) the tag of the cell is mapped if pa is mapped by the current SPT of guest i, unmapped otherwise.

However not all the memory addresses of the concrete model are to be abstracted in the segments of a guest i, we define below which addresses are abstracted for each guest, and in which segment they are located. Recall from the concrete guest transition that when a guest runs, it only has access to the addresses mapped by the PT currently in the base register of the processor. We assume in the sequel that when a guest runs, only one of its own SPT can be used by the processor (the preservation of this invariant is obvious).

All the addresses which are in the domain of a segment of the abstract guest i correspond to all the physical addresses that the concrete guest i can possibly access. Thus it corresponds to all the addresses that the guest i might map in its SPTs, formally it corresponds to the set:

$$\{pa \in Addr | \exists r_0, \exists base \in \mathcal{B}_{\mathrm{SPT}}(\sigma_{\mathrm{int}}, i) \wedge (pa, r_0) \in Im(pt(mem, base))\}$$

When Invariant 1 is verified, we can characterize this set by the addresses located in the intervals on which guest i has some rights, that is the set:

$$\{pa \in Addr | \exists r_1, allowed(pa, i, r_1)\}$$

Thus, we can bound the domains of the segments to the intervals defined in Sect. 3.2. The fact that this part of the abstraction does not depend on the SPTs

---

[2] In fact we differentiate a byte mapped in RW and a byte mapped in RO, but we omit the details here for clarity's sake.

but rather on the definition of intervals is convenient. Indeed it simplifies the proof of correspondence between an abstract and a concrete action, particularly if the action has an impact on the SPTs.

Now that we have a characterization of all the addresses that are in the segments of a guest, we dispatch them in the segments with the right properties. For example if an address is in an interval over which guest i has RW access and guest k has RO access, it appears in the kth send segment of guest i and in the ith receive segment of guest k. Recall from Sect. 3.2 that an interval can be in two configurations, shared or private. The correspondence between the concrete intervals and the segments is defined as follow:

- $pa \in I_j \wedge private(I_j, i) \Leftrightarrow pa \in Dom(\sigma_i.priv)$
- $pa \in I_j \wedge shared(I_j, i, k) \Leftrightarrow pa \in Dom(\sigma_i.s_k) \wedge pa \in Dom(\sigma_k.r_i)$

4.2 Abstract Transitions

We present here the abstractions of the transitions presented in Sect. 3.3, i.e. the *restore*, *guest*, and *hypervisor transitions*.

The view of the concrete **restore transition** does either nothing (in case just the PL is changed) or injects an IRQ into the guest, which only impacts the registers.

The whole **guest transition** is represented in Fig. 4, but in practice, we split the guest transition in two steps. The first part, called the *abstract run*, is the view of the concrete guest transition seen from the current guest. Invariants on the concrete level allow to state that only the writable segments of the abstract guest (private and send segments) are modified during the run, formally: $\sigma' = run(\sigma) \Rightarrow \sigma' \cong \sigma[r_1...r_n]$. Secondly, changes in the send segments of the current guest are mirrored in the corresponding receive segments of the other guests. In other terms, the receive segments of the other guests are synchronized with the send segment of the current guest. The synchronization seg'_1 of segment seg_1 with seg_2, i.e. updating all the values of seg_1 with those of seg_2 without changing its tags, is denoted by $seg'_1 = seg_1 \xleftarrow{VAL} seg_2$.

We distinguish four types of **hypervisor transitions**, depending on their impact on the guest states. Each transition corresponds to one or several groups of the hypervisor concrete transitions presented in Sect. 3.3. The *change register* (*chreg*) transition is the abstraction of the concrete injection transitions and of the access to privileged register transition. The particularity of these transitions is that their only observable impact is on registers. The *memory management* (*mm*) transition captures the effects of the concrete transitions concerning the memory management virtualization. These concrete transitions have an impact on the registers and on memory. In particular, they do not change the value of memory cells but only the active SPT. It means that the impact of the *mm* transition on the segments is only on their tag (i.e. mapped or not). The *nop* transition is the abstraction of all the concrete transitions which do not have any observable impact on the abstract state. It abstracts all the IRQ transitions, indeed, all these transitions only impact the GIC which we do not represent in the abstract model. The *scheduling* (*sched*) transition corresponds to the concrete scheduling transition.

$$\frac{\sigma'_i = run(\sigma_i) \qquad \forall k \neq i, \sigma'_k = \sigma_k[r_i \xleftarrow{VAL} \sigma'_i.s_k]}{\langle i, \sigma_1, ...\sigma_n \rangle \to \langle i, \sigma'_1, ...\sigma'_n \rangle} \text{ GUEST TRANS}$$

$$\frac{decode(\sigma_i.abs\_regs) = inject(r') \qquad \sigma'_i = \sigma_i[abs\_regs \leftarrow r']}{\langle i, \sigma_1, ..., \sigma_i, ...\sigma_n \rangle \to \langle i, \sigma_1, ..., \sigma'_i, ...\sigma_n \rangle} \text{ CHREG}$$

$$\frac{decode(\sigma_i.abs\_regs) = sched(nxt)}{\langle i, \sigma_1, ...\sigma_n \rangle \to \langle nxt, \sigma_1, ...\sigma_n \rangle} \text{ SCHED}$$

$$\frac{decode(regs) = nop}{\langle i, \sigma_1, ...\sigma_n \rangle. \to \langle i, \sigma_1, ...\sigma_n \rangle} \text{ NOP}$$

$$\frac{decode(\sigma_i.abs\_regs) = mm(\sigma'_i)}{\langle i, \sigma_1, ...\sigma_i, ...\sigma_n \rangle \to \langle i, \sigma_1, ...\sigma'_i, ...\sigma_n \rangle} \text{ MM}$$

$$\frac{\sigma_i \cong \sigma'_i[abs\_regs]}{\langle i, \sigma_1, ...\sigma_i, ...\sigma_n \rangle \to \langle i, \sigma_1, ...\sigma'_i, ...\sigma_n \rangle} \text{ RESTORE}$$

Fig. 4. Abstract sub-transitions

In order to establish a formal link between the two models, we need to prove the correspondence between all the transitions of the models. More specifically, we need to prove that if a concrete and an abstract state are related by the abstract relation defined in Sect. 4.1, the two states resulting from two corresponding transitions are also related. The correspondence proofs rely on the proof of preservation of invariants presented in Sect. 3.4. The preservation of the low-level invariants is the most difficult part of the proof. Therefore the correspondence of the transitions related to memory management are the most subtle to prove, because they may modify the SPT, making the preservation of the invariant more difficult to ensure. We have already proved the preservation of our invariants under the map operation which is used in the page fault transition, in order to prove its correspondence with the abstract *mm* transition. We have completed the proof of correspondence between the abstract and the concrete guest transitions. We have thus partially validated our abstraction.

4.3 Properties

Guests may interfere with each other (e.g.through shared memory), so we cannot prove non-interference. Instead we prove an *isolation* property on some resources of the guests, i.e. we prove their integrity and their confidentiality. The resources on which we prove isolation are the registers and the memory segments. Below, we detail the properties on segments, as our main focus is the memory isolation. We express the properties on one transition step. More exactly, to state a property for one guest, we confine the effects that the execution of another guest can have on the former. Thus, as our system is sequential, we consider a transition where the former guest does not run. We prove the extension of these properties to any sequence of transitions where a guest does not run. The proof sketch of integrity shows the simplicity with which we can bound the effects of a transition in our model. The proof of confidentiality is done in a similar way.

Integrity for a guest i means that if another guest j runs, then the private segment and the send segments of i are not modified, and only its jth receive segment might have change.

Theorem 1 (Integrity). *Let i and j be two guest indexes such that $i \neq j$. Consider a transition where j is the running guest. If*

$$\langle j, \sigma_1, ..., \sigma_i, ..., \sigma_n \rangle \rightarrow \langle j', \sigma'_1, ..., \sigma'_i, ..., \sigma'_n \rangle$$

then $\sigma'_i.priv = \sigma_i.priv$ and $\forall k, \sigma'_i.s_k = \sigma_i.s_k$ and $\forall k \neq j, \sigma'_i.r_k = \sigma_i.r_k$.

Proof. Let i and j be two guest indexes such that $i \neq j$. We consider a transition from the state $\langle j, \sigma_0, ..., \sigma_n \rangle$. The first part of the transition is the restore transition, which does not change the running guest nor the state of guest i. The second part of the transition is the guest transition. From the definition of the guest transition (Fig. 4) we know that the running guest is not changed, and that the state σ'_i of guest i after the transition is such that: $\sigma'_i = \sigma_i[r_j \xleftarrow{VAL} \sigma'_j.s_i]$. Hence the three following facts are verified: $\sigma'_i.priv = \sigma_i.priv$ and $\forall k, \sigma'_i.s_{ik} = \sigma_i.s_k$ and $\forall k \neq j, \sigma'_i.r_k = \sigma_i.r_k$. The third part of the transition is the hypervisor transition. None of the four hypervisor transitions changes the state of guest i. Therefore integrity is verified for any transition.

To express confidentiality properties, we compare one step of execution from two states which differ only on some resources of guest i. If the guest j which runs in this step has no authorization to access these resources, then the two states resulting from the transition are equal except on guest i. Notice that we cannot prove our property on a non-deterministic system because we reason on the very fact that two executions end in similar states. Yet the scheduling and restore sub-transitions are non-deterministic, indeed we have not included in our model sufficient information to decide whether an interrupt is to be injected or which guest is to be run on a scheduling. We address this issue by making two assumptions that allow us to add some extra information which make these sub-transitions deterministic. We suppose that when a guest does not run, its memory does not interfere with the scheduler nor with the interrupt management of other guests. There is no major difficulty in proving these properties but we set them aside in the first instance in order to focus on memory isolation. Therefore, we reason with two extra arguments which make the system deterministic: a guest to be run next (nxt) and the optional registers corresponding to the IRQ injection ($oirq$). We write $\xrightarrow{nxt,oirq}$ for such an enhanced transition.

Theorem 2 (Confidentiality). *Let i, k and j be three guest indexes such that $i \neq j$ and $k \neq j$. Let $\hat{\sigma}_i$ be a guest state such that $\hat{\sigma}_i \cong \sigma_i[priv, s_k, r_k]$. If*

$$\langle j, \sigma_1, ...\sigma_i, ..., \sigma_n \rangle \xrightarrow{nxt,oirq} \langle j', \sigma'_1, ..., \sigma'_i, ..., \sigma'_n \rangle$$

then

$$\langle j, \sigma_1, ...\hat{\sigma}_i, ..., \sigma_n \rangle \xrightarrow{nxt,oirq} \langle j', \sigma'_1, ...\hat{\sigma}_i{}', ..., \sigma'_n \rangle.$$

5   Related Work

Daum et al. [10] strengthened the refinement between the abstraction layers of the micro-kernel seL4 to reason about virtual memory management. It allows them to reason at a finer granularity and to have an abstract model upon which they can extend their previous proofs [14] to prove isolation between processes. Although OSes and hypervisors have much in common, the memory management part is quite different, since the SPTs are not present in OSes.

Barthe et al. formalized in Coq an idealized model of a paravirtualized hypervisor [6]. They included the caches in their model and considered cache-based side-channel attacks, which is out of our scope. They do not refine their model to an implementation level, and they make several simplifications, such as considering only one level of page tables. In addition they do not consider any sharing between guests.

Blanchard et al. present a case study on the creation of a new mapping in a page table [7]. Their method is quite different from ours. They work on a part (i.e. one function) independently of the rest of the system whereas we model the interactions between the several parts of the system, to prove high-level properties on the whole system. In contrast to us, they consider parallelism and show that their model is valid for weak memory models.

In [1,11], Kovalev et al. present the proof of a correctness property of the TLB virtualization code, using the verifier VCC [9]. They prove that if a translation is present in the virtual TLB (i.e. the TLB that the guest would have if it were running directly on the hardware), it is also present, modulo some translation stages, in the hardware TLB (i.e. the cache of the SPT). Their property does not provide isolation, it is complementary to ours. Their hardware model is very complete and detailed, but their SPT algorithm is rather simplified. For example, they suppose that there is always a free SPT slot available when allocating a new one, whereas we go in deeper details in the model of the SPT allocator, as we consider that the proof of its well-formedness is a key aspect of the isolation proof.

Nemati et al. [15] prove isolation properties on a hypervisor which uses direct paging. Direct paging does not use shadow data structures. Though still supervised by the hypervisor, the guest OS directly manages mappings from GVA to PA. This solution requires additional modifications of the guest.

On a hypervisor supporting one guest, Vasudevan et al. [16] proved that the guest cannot write in hypervisor memory, i.e. they proved the integrity of the hypervisor memory. They verified automatically some modules of the hypervisor, using the CBMC model checker, and other manually, due to the limitation of the tool. Andrabi extended the automatic verification by proving the well-formedness of the PT setup in [3]. They do not virtualize the memory with SPTs, but rather use the hardware virtualization solution.

6   Conclusion

The management of page tables (PT) is a core task for a hypervisor and involves non-trivial algorithms which make it difficult to prove -and even to state- that the hypervisor enforces isolation between its guest OSes. In this paper we have argued that it is possible to construct an abstract model of a hypervisor, on which it is considerably simpler to conduct such proof. To this end, we have presented a concrete model of a hypervisor (in which six out of the fourteen hypervisor transitions concern the PTs), and established a number of invariants on this model. Based on these invariants, it is possible to construct an abstract model in which the management of PTs has been abstracted away. We have proved isolation on the resulting abstract model.

Handling page faults that lead to the addition of a mapping in the SPTs, is the most complex and security-critical operation of the SPT algorithm. Complex, because it modifies the structure of the SPT, requiring a substantial number of well-formedness invariants to capture the effects of the modifications. Security-critical, because it gives guests access to new parts of the memory. A central part of the work reported here has been to state and prove the low-level invariants needed to prove the correspondence of the concrete page fault operation with its abstract counterpart. The major part of the other operations of the SPT algorithm do not threaten our current invariants, and are therefore less complex to integrate.

Reaching a level of abstraction where the PTs are no longer present simplifies the whole model and alleviates the proof effort for the other dependent subsystems. Our abstract model can be extended to integrate additional features such as management of devices, that we have not taken into account in this paper, since the focus is on the SPT algorithm. More specifically, if we virtualize devices, the hypervisor controls the guest accesses to memory of the devices, so, in this case, we can ensure isolation. If we do not virtualize devices, every guest who has access rights to a device memory region can access it, in this case there might be channels between the guests accessing this part of memory. Another feature not currently accommodated by the hypervisor model is direct memory access (DMA) from devices. DMA hardware extensions (I/O MMU [2], SMMU [4,13]) allow the hypervisor to control the access to memory by a PT mechanism similar to the MMU, and can be proved secure. Without such extensions, DMA-aware devices can access any part of the memory and make it impossible to establish isolation within any model. Further work will investigate how to integrate device management and DMA into our models.

References

1. Alkassar, E., Cohen, E., Kovalev, M., Paul, W.J.: Verification of TLB virtualization implemented in C. In: Joshi, R., Müller, P., Podelski, A. (eds.) VSTTE 2012. LNCS, vol. 7152, pp. 209–224. Springer, Heidelberg (2012). http://www-wjp.cs.uni-saarland.de/publikationen/ACKP12.pdf
2. AMD I/O virtualization technology (IOMMU) specification (2015). http://support.amd.com/TechDocs/48882_IOMMU.pdf
3. Andrabi, S.J.: Verification of XMHF HPT protection setup. Technical report, University of North Carolina (2013). http://cs.unc.edu/~sandrabi/Project_work/VerificationofXMHFHPTProtectionSetup.pdf
4. ARM system memory management unit (2012). http://infocenter.arm.com/help/index.jsp?topic=/com.arm.doc.ihi0062b/index.html

5. Arpaci-Dusseau, R.H., Arpaci-Dusseau, A.C.: Operating Systems: Three Easy Pieces, 0.80th edn. Arpaci-Dusseau Books, Wisconsin (2014)
6. Barthe, G., Betarte, G., Campo, J., Luna, C.: Cache-leakage resilient OS isolation in an idealized model of virtualization. In: 2012 IEEE 25th Computer Security Foundations Symposium (CSF), pp. 186–197, June 2012
7. Blanchard, A., Kosmatov, N., Lemerre, M., Loulergue, F.: A case study on formal verification of the anaxagoros hypervisor paging system with frama-C. In: Núñez, M., Güdemann, M. (eds.) Formal Methods for Industrial Critical Systems. LNCS, vol. 9128, pp. 15–30. Springer, Heidelberg (2015). http://dx.doi.org/10.1007/978-3-319-19458-5_2
8. Common criteria portal. http://www.commoncriteriaportal.org/
9. Cohen, E., Dahlweid, M., Hillebrand, M., Leinenbach, D., Moskal, M., Santen, T., Schulte, W., Tobies, S.: VCC: a practical system for verifying concurrent C. In: Berghofer, S., Nipkow, T., Urban, C., Wenzel, M. (eds.) TPHOLs 2009. LNCS, vol. 5674, pp. 23–42. Springer, Heidelberg (2009). http://research.microsoft.com/apps/pubs/default.aspx?id=117859
10. Daum, M., Billing, N., Klein, G.: Concerned with the unprivileged: user programs in kernel refinement. Formal Asp. Comput. **26**(6), 1205–1229 (2014). http://dx.doi.org/10.1007/s00165-014-0296-9
11. Kovalev, M.: TLB virtualization in the context of hypervisor verification. Ph.D. thesis, Universität des Saarlandes, Postfach 151141, 66041 Saarbrücken (2013). http://scidok.sulb.unisaarland.de/volltexte/2013/5215
12. Lescuyer, S.: ProvenCore: towards a verified isolation micro-kernel. In: International Workshop on MILS: Architecture and Assurance for Secure Systems (2015). http://milsworkshop2015.euromils.eu/downloads/hipeac_literature/04-mils15_submission_6.pdf
13. Mijat, R., Nightingale, A.: Virtualization is coming to a platform near you (2011). https://www.arm.com/files/pdf/System-MMU-Whitepaper-v8.0.pdf
14. Murray, T.C., Matichuk, D., Brassil, M., Gammie, P., Bourke, T., Seefried, S., Lewis, C., Gao, X., Klein, G.: sel4: from general purpose to a proof of information flow enforcement. In: 2013 IEEE Symposium on Security and Privacy, SP 2013, Berkeley, CA, USA, 19–22 May 2013. pp. 415–429 (2013). http://dx.doi.org/10.1109/SP.2013.35
15. Nemati, H., Guanciale, R., Dam, M.: Trustworthy virtualization of the ARMv7 memory subsystem. In: Italiano, G.F., Margaria-Steffen, T., Pokorný, J., Quisquater, J.-J., Wattenhofer, R. (eds.) SOFSEM 2015-Testing. LNCS, vol. 8939, pp. 578–589. Springer, Heidelberg (2015). http://dx.doi.org/10.1007/978-3-662-46078-8_48
16. Vasudevan, A., Chaki, S., Jia, L., McCune, J., Newsome, J., Datta, A.: Design, implementation and verification of an extensible and modular hypervisor framework. In: Proceedings of the 2013 IEEE Symposium on Security and Privacy, SP 2013, pp. 430–444. IEEE Computer Society, Washington (2013). http://dx.doi.org/10.1109/SP.2013.36
17. Vetter, J., Petschik-Junker, M., Nordholz, J., Peter, M., Danisevskis, J.: Uncloaking rootkits on mobile devices with a hypervisor-based detector. In: ICISC (International Conference on Information Security and Cryptology), Seoul, Republic of Korea (2015)

Crowdsourced Bug Triaging: Leveraging Q&A Platforms for Bug Assignment

Ali Sajedi Badashian[(✉)], Abram Hindle, and Eleni Stroulia

University of Alberta, Edmonton, Canada
{alisajedi,abram.hindle,stroulia}@ualberta.ca

Abstract. Bug triaging, *i.e.*, assigning a bug report to the "best" person to address it, involves identifying a list of developers that are qualified to understand and address the bug report, and then ranking them according to their expertise. Most research in this area examines the description of the bug report and the developers' prior development and bug-fixing activities. In this paper, we propose a novel method that exploits a new source of evidence for the developers' expertise, namely their contributions in *Stack Overflow*, the popular software Question and Answer (Q&A) platform. The key intuition of our method is that the questions a developer asks and answers in *Stack Overflow*, or more generally in software Q&A platforms, can potentially be an excellent indicator of his/her expertise. Motivated by this idea, our method uses the bug-report description as a guide for selecting relevant *Stack Overflow* contributions on the basis of which to identify developers with the necessary expertise to close the bug under examination. We evaluated this method in the context of the 20 largest *GitHub* projects, considering 7144 bug reports. Our results demonstrate that our method exhibits superior accuracy to other state-of-the-art methods.

1 Introduction

Software development, today more than ever, is a community-of-practice activity. Developers often work on multiple projects, hosted on large-scale software repository platforms, such as *GitHub* and *BitBucket*. They access and contribute information to open question-answering web sites, such as *Java Forum, Yahoo! Answers* and *Stack Overflow*[1]. Through the developers' participation on these code-sharing and question-answering platforms, rich evidence of their software development expertise is collected. Understanding the developers' expertise is relevant to many software-engineering activities, including "onboarding" of new project members so that their expertise is best utilized in the new context, forming new teams that have the necessary expertise to take on new projects, and bug triaging and assignment to the person that is best skilled to fix it.

In this paper we focus on the bug-triaging-and-assignment task, which has already received substantial attention by the software-engineering community

---

[1] http://www.coderanch.com/forums, http://answers.yahoo.com, and http://stackoverflow.com/.

© Springer-Verlag Berlin Heidelberg 2016
P. Stevens and A. Wąsowski (Eds.): FASE 2016, LNCS 9633, pp. 231–248, 2016.
DOI: 10.1007/978-3-662-49665-7_14

[2,8,10,15,16,19]. The typical formulation of **bug triaging** problem aims at ranking a number of developers that could potentially fix a given bug report. Most solutions to date have considered developers' expertise, using their past development and bug-resolving contribution as evidence. In contrast, we describe and report on the effectiveness of a bug-assignment method that uses expertise networks extracted from social software-development platforms.

At a high level, based on our initial study on the crowdsourced approach [26], our work makes two novel contributions to the bug-triaging research. First, we demonstrate that as a software focused Q&A web site, *Stack Overflow* contains valuable information about the expertise of the participating developers, which may be exploited to support bug triaging. Second, we comparatively investigate a family of methods for analyzing *Stack Overflow* posts to precisely understand how to improve state-of-the-art bug-triaging methods.

The rest of the paper is as follows. Section 2 sets the background context for our work. Section 3 describes in detail our new bug-assignment method, ranking the expertise of developers based on a new metric relying on *Stack Overflow*. Section 4 reports on the evaluation of our method. Finally, Sect. 6 concludes with a summary of the take-home lessons of this work.

2   Literature Review

There are two categories of previous research relevant to this body of work: (a) expertise identification and recommendation; and (b) bug triaging.

Expertise Identification and Recommendation: Venkaratamani *et al.* [32] described a system for recommending specific questions to *Stack Overflow* members qualified to answer them. The system infers the developers' expertise based on the names of the classes and methods to which the developers have contributed. Similarly, Fritz *et al.* [9] developed the "Degree of Knowledge" (DOK) metric to determine the level of a developer's knowledge regarding a code element (class, method or field), based on the developer's contribution to the development of this element. Mockus and Herbsleb [17] developed the Expertise Browser (EB), a tool that identifies the developers' expertise from their code and documentation, considering system commits and changes to classes, sub-systems, packages, etc.

Zhang *et al.* [33] described a method for constructing a "Community Expertise Network" (CEN) from the post-reply relations of Java Forum users. They then ranked the users' expertise using the PageRank [6] and HITS (Hyperlink-Induced Topic Search) [11] algorithms on this network.

Bug Triaging: Previous research in bug-triaging has produced a number of different techniques for selecting the (list of k) most capable developer(s) to resolve a given bug report. Typically the first developer in the list is selected as the bug assignee but, if this developer is unavailable or somehow unsuitable to work on the bug report, the other developers in the recommendations list may be tasked with the bug. Given this problem formulation, most researchers evaluate their methods by reporting *top-k* "accuracy" [1,5,8,10,13,14,28–30] (hit ratio in the *top-k* recommended list) or precision-and-recall [1–3,7,16,27] (precision is the percentage of the suggested developers who were actual bug fixers and recall is the percentage of bug fixers who were actually suggested).

Machine Learning (ML) Approaches: Čubranić and Murphy [8] used a Naive Bayes classifier to assign each bug report (a "text document" consisting of the bug summary and description) to a developer (seen as the "class"). Their classifier was able to predict the bug assignee with a *top-1* accuracy of up to 30 %.

Next, Anvik *et al.* [2] proposed a Support Vector Machine (SVM) method as a more effective text classifier for this problem, reporting up to 57 %, 64 % and 18 % *top-3* accuracy. Additionally considering the bug-report severity and priority [3] resulted in 75 %, 70 %, 84 %, 98 % and 98 % *top-5* accuracy. Note that the last two high-accuracy results are were obtained in very small projects, with 6 and 11 developers respectively. A subsequent method, taking also into account information about the components linked to bugs and the list of active developers resulted in 64 % and 86 % accuracies in two projects [1].

Lin *et al.* [14] used SVM and C4.5 classifiers, considering the bug-report textual data (title and description) as well as the bug type, class, priority, submitter and the module IDs, and obtained up to 77 % accuracy.

Considering severity and component of the bug reports in addition to the textual descriptions, Lamkanfi *et al.* [13] compared the effectiveness of four ML approaches, Naive Bayes, Multinomial Naive Bayes, 1NN and SVM in predicting the real assignee. They reported Multinomial Naive Bayes as the most accurate method with 79 % accuracy.

Naguib *et al.* [18] used LDA to assign the bug reports to topics. Then, mining the activity profiles of the developers in a bug-tracking repository, they associate topics to developers. Finally, they suggest the developers with the most topics matching with the bug-report topics. They obtained up to 75 % *top-5* accuracy.

Information Retrieval (IR) Approaches: Canfora and Cerulo [7] consider each developer as a document by aggregating the textual descriptions of the change requests that the developer has addressed. Given a new bug report, the textual description of the new request is used as a query to the document repository to retrieve the candidate developer. This method achieved 62 % and 85 % accuracy in two projects.

Develect, by Matter *et al.* [16], employs the Vector Space Model (VSM) and relies on a vocabulary of "technical terms" collected from the developers' source-code commits and the bug-report keywords. The developer's expertise is modeled as a term vector, based on that developer's commit history. Given a new bug report, the closest –according to the cosine distance– developer is identified. This method achieved up to 34 % and 71 % *top-1* and *top-10* accuracies.

Linares-Vásquez *et al.* [15] applied IR-based concept-location techniques [20] to locate the source code files relevant to the text-change request. Source-code authorship information of these files was used to recommend expert developers and they obtained up to 65 % precision.

Shokripour *et al.* [28] proposed an assignee recommender for the bug reports based on information extracted from the developers' source code, comments, previously fixed bugs, and source code change locations. A subsequent study [27] improved these results using additional data, such as the source-code files, commits and comments of the developers, names of classes, methods, fields and parameters in the source code. The maximum *top-5* accuracy of their approach on three different projects was 62 %. They obtained 48 % and 48 % *top-1* and 60 % and 89 % *top-5* accuracies on two projects (between 57 and 9 developers respectively).

Other Approaches: Tamrawi *et al.* [29] introduced a fuzzy approach that computes a score for each "developer - technical term" based on the technical terms available in previous bug reports and their fixing history by the developers. Considering the new bug report, they calculate a score for each developer as a candidate assignee by combining his/her scores for all the technical terms associated with the bug report in question. This method was shown to achieve between b40 % and 75 % for *top-1* and *top-5* accuracy over 7 projects.

A number of studies have examined bug reassignments, the reasons that cause them, and ways to reduce them [4,34]. To reduce bug reassignments, Jeong *et al.* [10] introduced "tossing graphs" of developers (as nodes) and edges between them, weighed by the number of times the destination developer was assigned a bug originally assigned to the source developer. Then, beginning with the first prediction (developer candidate) in hand, they used this graph to predict the next developer by consulting this graph, obtaining up to 77 % *top-5* accuracy.

All the above studies use some combination of the bug textual and categorical attributes, the bug code components, and the developers' coding and bug-fixing contributions. Our method is unique in that it uses the developers' *Stack Overflow* questions and answers, the semantic tags of these artifacts, as well as the developers' previous bug assignments to determine the relevance of a developer to a particular bug report.

3   A Social Bug-Triaging Model

Software developers today contribute to a variety of social platforms, including social software-development platforms, question-and-answering communities, technical blogs, and presentation-sharing web sites. The key intuition of our work is that these contributions constitute evidence of expertise that can be exploited in the context of bug triaging. More specifically, in this paper, we analyze the developers' contributions in *Stack Overflow* for assigning them to *GitHub* bug reports. Focusing on the overlap of the two social platforms [25], our approach examines the questions and answers in *Stack Overflow* that pertain to the terms mentioned in a bug report's title and description. It uses *Stack Overflow* tags for cross-referencing *GitHub* bug reports with *Stack Overflow* questions and answers. Tags categorize the questions and their corresponding answers in terms of a few well-known technical terms. The community curates these tags to improve their quality: the person asking a question selects the initial tags for the question

Bug report title: TooManyOpenFiles might cause data-loss in *ElasticSearch Lucene*
Bug report body: Under certain circumstances a TooManyOpenFiles exception in *Java* thrown as FileNotFoundException might cause *data* loss where entire shards *lucene* indices are deleted. This is mainly caused by Lucene-4870 *https* issues.apache.org *jira* browse LUCENE-4870 - currently all *Elasticsearch* releases are affected by this.
Project title: *elasticSearch*
Project description: *Open Source* Distributed RESTful *Search* Engine
Project language: *Java*

Fig. 1. An example bug report (selected fields)

Table 1. The activity of some developers in *Stack Overflow*, and their various expertise scores.

Question/Answerer	upVotes	Bob	Ali	Joe	Mike	Jane	Tom	Ben
Q1/Mike; version control, **open source**	3	46	5	53		28		
Q2/Jane; ajax, **data**, **search**, jquery, php	1	20	16	22	6			
Q3/Mike; **elasticsearch**, php, **java**, **lucene**	21	11	14	29		10		
Q4/Ali; **https**, css, **java**, **jira**, **data**	0	27			0		86	
Q5/Ben; search,java,lucene, elasticsearch,https	70	1	18	42	-4	14	98	
AnswerNum		5	4	4	3	3	2	0
Z_score		2.24	1.34	2	0.45	1	1.41	-1
A_score		$\frac{(46+1).1+(20+1).2+(11+1).3+(27+1).4+(1+1).5}{247}$	$\frac{(5+1).1+(16+1).2+(14+1).3+(18+1).5}{180}$	$\frac{(53+1).1+(22+1).2+(29+1).3+(42+1).5}{405}$	$\frac{(6+1).2+(0+1).4+(-4+1).5}{3}$	$\frac{(28+1).1+(10+1).3+(14+1).5}{137}$	$\frac{(86+1).4+(98+1).5}{843}$	0
Q_score $(\mu=20)$		0	$20.(\frac{4}{0+1})$ $=80$	0	$20.(\frac{1}{3+1}+\frac{3}{21+1})$ $=7.7$	$20.(\frac{2}{1+1})$ $=20$	0	$20.(\frac{5}{70+1})$ $=1.41$
SSA_Z_score		15.72	6.20	20.12	-1.44	9.34	29.03	-1.19

(out of around 40,000 available but evolving tags) and expert community members, who enjoy a reputation above some threshold, can edit them. Tags are also used as indication of expertise; for example, the person answering a question tagged with *Android* and *Java* is assumed to be knowledgeable in these two domains. Furthermore, the more upVotes this answers collects, the more knowledgeable this answerer is assumed to be.

Figure 1 summarizes the elements of interest in a real bug report[2]. Some of the words in the bug-report's title and description are shown as *italic* because they also appear as tags in the *Stack Overflow* questions reported in Table 1,

---

[2] https://github.com/elasticsearch/elasticsearch/issues/2812 2014-08-20.

where they are shown in bold. Note that the only characters allowed in *Stack Overflow* tags are alphanumeric and the four characters '+', '-', '.' and '#'. So all other caracters in the bug report were converted to white space.

Table 1 reports partial information about five questions in *Stack Overflow* and the answers provided by 7 developers. Each question is associated with the developer who asked it, the number of upVotes it received, and its thematic tags. The questions are sorted based on the number of their tags that match with the bug-report textual information (in Fig. 1) and are shown in bold under each question. The more tags the question shares with the bug-report terms, the more relevant it is to the bug report. We will use these tags to characterize the *expertise areas* required to address the bug report in question.

3.1   Social Metrics of Expertise

Zhang *et al.* [33] introduced a family of metrics for measuring expertise in social networks. The simplest one is *AnswerNum*, the number of answers contributed by a user. However, while answering a question is an indication of expertise, asking a question is an indication of lack of expertise. Z_score is a more sophisticated metric that considers both questions and answers: $Z = (a - q)/\sqrt{(a+q)}$. In this formula, q and a are the numbers of the questions and answers correspondingly posted by user u. If a user asks as many questions as he answers, his Z_score will be close to 0. Developers who answer more questions than they ask have positive Z_scores, and vice versa. The *Z_score* is undefined for users who have not asked nor answered a question. The developers in Table 1 are ordered (left to right) in descending *AnswerNum* order.

3.2   A Bug-Specific Social Metric of Expertise

The *Z_score* would likely identify the most active question answerers as the preferred bug assignees every time, consistently ignoring all other developers. To prevent this phenomenon, we have chosen to refine the *Z_score* with bug-specific information, making a social and subject-aware version called *SSA_Z_score*. As discussed before, we use *Stack Overflow* tags as a cross-referencing mechanism between *GitHub* bug reports and *Stack Overflow* questions and answers. Developers facing problems with their tasks, use these tags, which are indexed by search engines [23], to search for earlier questions and their answers that could be helpful to them. Tags are generic enough to convey semantic topics and, yet, specific enough to relate to programming concepts and expertise needed to fix *GitHub* bugs. As a sanity check against the possibility that tags may drastically limit the relevant information between *GitHub* and *Stack Overflow*, we examined the bug reports in three selected *GitHub* projects (out of the 20 projects considered in this study) and found that in the textual information of each bug report, there were between 2 to 89 *Stack Overflow* tags mentioned (avg = 14.9, var = 132 and $\sigma = 11.5$). In effect, the *Stack Overflow* tags define a common vocabulary for developers to exchange information. This vocabulary has a fundamental advantage over natural languages; all tags are useful and there is no need for stop-word and noise-word removal from the bug-report texts.

Our approach limits the search for potential bug assignees to the *Stack Overflow* members that have asked questions or provided answers with at least one tag in common with the text of the bug report under examination, b. To that end, we define the followings:

- **match_tags$_{SO,b}$**: all the *Stack Overflow* tags that appear in the title and description of the bug report; these are, in effect, the *Stack Overflow* topics that are important for the bug report in hand.
- **match_tags$_{q,b}$**: the shared tags between a question (q) and b.
- **match_tags$_{a,b}$**: the tags that annotate the question of an answer (a) that also appear in b.

$$A\_score_{u,b} = \sum_{a \in uanswers} (upVotes_a + 1) \cdot (match\_tags_{a,b}) \quad (1)$$

$$Q\_score_{u,b} = \mu \cdot \sum_{q \in uquestions} \frac{(match\_tags_{q,b})}{(upVptes_q + 1)} \quad (2)$$

$$Z\_score_u = \frac{(a - q)}{\sqrt{(a + q)}} \quad (3)$$

$$SSA\_Z\_score_{u,b} = \frac{(A\_score_{u,b} - Q\_score_{u,b})}{\sqrt{(A\_score_{u,b} + Q\_score_{u,b})}} \quad (4)$$

For user u and bug report b, we define the $A\_score_{u,b}$ (Eq. 1) and $Q\_score_{u,b}$ (Eq. 2) to replace a and q respectively in the original definition of the Z_score. At any point in time, for every answer the user has contributed in the past that is relevant to the bug in question (*i.e.*, is associated with a tag that appears in the bug report), the number of $match\_tags_{a,b}$ is multiplied with the number of the answer's upVotes (plus one, for the answer itself). In effect, each answer contributes to the calculation of the user's expertise, taking into account the number of upVotes that the answer has received, which reflects the community's judgement on the answer's quality and usefulness. The sum of these terms make up $A\_score_{u,b}$. Each question is considered as evidence of lack of relevant expertise but this weakness is compensated by promotion of the question by other users (upVotes). To reflect the intuition that the "asker of a naive question is less knowledgeable than asker of a good one", we divide $match\_tags_{a,b}$ by the number of upVotes (plus one for the question itself). This tends to make the value of $Q\_score_{u,b}$ very small relative to $A\_score_{u,b}$, which is why we use the μ *normalization factor* to adjust it. The *social subject-aware Z_score* (*SSA_Z_score*) can then be defined as shown in Eq. 4. This formula involves the terms relevant to the user's expertise (as $match\_tags_{q,b}$ and $match\_tags_{a,b}$ used in $A\_score_{u,b}$ and $Q\_score_{u,b}$ for different questions and answers). Furthermore, it takes into account the votes of the users to the answers and questions to advance good ones. The $SSA\_Z\_score_{u,b}$ as a measure of expertise of u regarding b focuses on answers and questions related to the bug under examination.

Table 1 shows different scores for the users. Each cell at the intersection of a question and a developer contains the number of upVotes for the answer posted by that developer to the question. *Tom* has the best $SSA\_Z\_score_{u,b}$: he provided two answers to questions relevant to the bug, which received many upVotes.

Note that our implementation of the above score is aware of the temporal aspect of a developer's expertise. The activity of a developer in *Stack Overflow* accumulates over time but the estimation of the developer's expertise for a given bug report, reported in time t, is based only on his contributions up to date: the $SSA\_Z\_score_{u,b}$ considers questions and answers of the user u posted in time $t1 < t$.

3.3 A Recency-Aware, Social and Subject-Aware Expertise Metric

The expertise of the developers shifts over time as they work on different projects with potentially different technologies [16]. Developers actively working in a particular domain are more appropriate to be assigned to a bug in this domain. This is why Matter *et al.* consider a decay factor in their model of developers' expertise. Shokripour *et al.* [28] also consider this idea in their bug-assignment method: the older the evidence for a particular expertise is, the less relevant it is for current expertise needs. Anvik *et al.* [2] used filtering approaches to capture the recency of work.

Motivated by the intuition that "more recent evidence of expertise is more relevant", we define the *recency-aware, social, subject-aware* $RA\_SSA\_Z\_score_{u,b}$ as follows.

$$RA\_SSA\_Z\_score\_u, b = \alpha \cdot (SSA\_Z\_score_{u,b})$$
$$+ \beta \cdot (\sum_{\substack{i \in previous\ bugs \\ assigned\ to\ u}} \frac{1}{1 + number\ of\ bugs\ occurred\ between\ i\ and\ b})$$

$$(5)$$

In this formula, α and β are tuning parameters and we explain how we tuned them in Sect. 4.4. Having the $RA\_SSA\_Z\_score_{u,b}$ for all users in the community over a bug report, our algorithm sorts the users and reports the top k as the most capable developers to fix the bug.

4   Evaluation

We obtained two *Stack Overflow* data sets [21,22] (approximately 65 GB and 90 GB). They consist of several XML files including information of 2,332,403 and 3,080,577 users, their posts, tags, votes, etc. In order to link these users to *GitHub*, their emails are normalized by a hash algorithm and they are joined via their emailHash [25,31], which is provided by the older data set. We merged these two data sets to get a large data set including the newer posts with old users.

We used a MySQL database dump [24] (with a size of about 21 GB) containing information of 4,212,377 *GitHub* users and their project memberships. However, this data set did not include the textual information of the bug reports. We obtained this information from a set of MongoDB dumps provided by the same web site [24] (with a size of about 210 GB) including information of 2,908,292 users. Again, we also merged the two data sets and obtained a large data set including information about *GitHub* users, projects and bug reports.

As our method assigns bugs to developers with a presence in both *GitHub* and *Stack Overflow*, we used identity merging [25, 31] to identity the common users in *GitHub* and *Stack Overflow*. The *GitHub* data set contains the e-mails of the users, but *Stack Overflow* data set includes e-mail hash. So for each *GitHub* user, using MD5 function, we obtained the e-mail hash and compared it with e-mail hashes in *Stack Overflow*. With this approach, we found 358,472 common users.

4.1   Experiment Setup

For each *GitHub* project, we first calculated the union of the sets of project members, committers, bug reporters and bug assignees, and we removed from this set all developers without any *Stack Overflow* activity, to calculate the project's community-members set. Next, we sorted the projects based on the cardinality of their community-member sets and we identified the top 20 projects[3] with the highest number of community members and the highest number of bug assignees.

For the selected 20 projects, the number of community members vary from 28 to 822 (average=127, median=87). Out of 14,172 bug reports in all the selected projects, we examined 7144 bug reports that have been assigned to one of the project's community members. Note that we could not use the rest of bug reports since they were assigned to developers with no *Stack Overflow* activity. For each bug report in each of the 20 chosen projects, we ran our algorithm to recognize the $RA\_SSA\_Z\_score_{u,b}$ for all project-community members. Then, we ranked the users from the highest score to the lowest and compared the top ones against the real assignee. We used bug reports from three of these projects for training and tuning purposes (*e.g.*, the parameters of $RA\_SSA\_Z\_score_{u,b}$ or investigating the inclusion of *Stack Overflow* tags) and 17 for final evaluation.

We report the average *top-k* recommendation accuracies. We compare our results for k=1 and k=5 with several implemented methods, as well as previously published results. We also report our results based on MAP (Mean Average Precision) as a precise, synthesized, rank-based evaluation measure.

---

[3] rails/rails, scala/scala, adobe/brackets, JuliaLang/julia, mozilla/rust, mozilla-b2g/gaia, angular/angular.js, bundler/bundler, lift/framework, dotcloud/docker, edx/edx-platform, elasticsearch/elasticsearch, fog/fog, html5rocks/www.html5rocks.com, Khan/khan-exercises, saltstack/salt, travis-ci/travis-ci, NServiceBus/NServiceBus, TryGhost/Ghost and yui/yui3.

4.2   Comparison to State of the Art

Direct comparison with earlier methods is not possible since none of the previous studies we reviewed above have made available their bug-assignment algorithm implementation and data sets. To approximate this comparison, we experimented with the scikit-learn[4] implementations of a number of algorithms classifying bugs to developers, which we applied to our own data set. Considering the previous bug reports and the real assignee for each one, these algorithms use word-based features of the bug reports to predict the most probable developer who would fix the bug.

1NN, 3NN and 5NN. In this family of classifier methods, each bug report is considered a point in a multi-dimensional space, each dimension defined by a distinct word. Each developer (class) corresponds to a hyper-plane in this space, consisting of all the bugs closed by the developer. Then, given a new bug report and a corresponding new point in the space, the closest existing point is selected. The class of the selected point (bug report) is the recommendation for the new bug report. This process is called Nearest Neighbor (1NN). In 3NN and 5NN, we look for 3 or 5 nearest points (bug reports) to that point and simply get their average to determine a hyper-plane and its class (developer) as the recommendation. Lamkanfi, et al. [13] and Anvik [3] used this method for their predictions about bug reports.

Naive Bayes (NB) and Multinomial Naive Bayes (MNB). In this family of algorithms, the developers' features are the words included in the textual elements of the bug reports they have handled before. These features are considered by the learner as a bag of words. Given a new bug report, the classifier returns the classes (developers) with the highest number features in common with the bug. Bhatacharya et al. [5], Čubranić and Murphy [8] and Anvik [2] are from those researchers who used this method for bug triaging. Building on the above method, a group of Naive Bayes classifiers, one per developer, may be constructed to decide the developer to which a given bug report belongs, and to calculate the probability of that being the case. Then, this probability is compared over all the developers to infer the most probable bug fixers. Lamkanfi et al. [13] and Anvik [3] used this method for bug triaging.

SVM. This approach represents bug reports as vectors in a multi-dimensional space –similar to 1NN, 3NN and 5NN. With each word being a dimension, this classifier considers each bug report a point in this multidimensional space. Then, considering all the bug reports that are already assigned to each developer as a *category*, the optimal hyper-planes between these points to separate different categories is inferred. This method also assigns a label (name of a developer) to each category. Then, given a new bug report, it reports the label of its category. Lin et al. [14], Anvik et al. [2] and Bhattacharya et al. [5] used this method for bug triaging.

---

[4] http://scikit-learn.org/stable/.

4.3   Implementation

The Java implementation of our approach as well as our data sets (3 training and tuning and 17 final evaluation projects and their bug reports) and output results are available online at http://github.com/alisajedi/BugTriaging for consideration or future comparisons.

Regarding the implemented Machine-Learning approaches, given that no open implementations were available for the previous bug-assignment methods reported in the literature, we made fair effort toward the best implementation of the competitor algorithms. We processed bug reports' title and body words with TF-IDF, producing TF-IDF word vectors. In order to make the process competitive enough to our approach, we made the process online; train them on first n-1 bug reports and then test on the nth. Then train on first n bug reports and test on $n+1^{th}$ and so on.

We used the followings parameters for `scikit-learn` machine learners. For KNN, we chose k as the parameter (1, 3 or 5), weights='uniform', algorithm= 'auto', leaf_size=30, p=2, metric='minkowski' and metric_params=None. For Multinomial Naive Bayes, we used Laplace smoothing priors ($\alpha = 1.0$) fit to prior distribution using OneVsRestClassifier classifier strategy. Similarly for Naive Bayes, but it uses multiclass classification. For SVM, we used Support Vector Classification (SVC) class. We chose RBF kernel type, used shrinking heuristic, with gamma kernel coefficient $1/n$ for n features, error penalty=1 and probability=true. More details as well as the Python implementation of the mentioned approaches are available online at: http://github.com/abramhindle/ bug-triager-scikit/blob/ali/dumpbayes.py.

4.4   Performance of Variant Social Metrics of Expertise

In Sect. 3 we incrementally developed our *Triage_score* starting with the simple social measures of expertise a and q. To gain an insight on how each aspect of this measure contributes to the bug-assignment effectiveness, we applied several intermediate variants of the metric, representing different intuitions in its evolutionary construction process, to three test projects with 490 bug reports in total, randomly selected from the 20 projects of our study.

The performance of the simplest measure, *i.e.*, the number of answers, *AnswerNum* [33], tagged with at least one of those $match\_tags_{SO,b}$ is shown in Table 2. The triaging accuracy is poor and does not recommend this naive measure for the bug-assignment task.

The original Z_score [33], which considers answers as indication of expertise and questions as indication of lack of expertise, does not perform much better. The problem was that the Z_score metric measures general expertise rather than expertise specific to the bug under examination, and, as a result, it is inadequate to compete with the approaches reported in the literature.

Next we evaluated the subject-aware Z_score, *SA_Z_score*, which measures expertise of the developers in $match\_tags_{SO,b}$, without considering upVotes.

Table 2. Accuracy results for preliminary approaches and tuning

Method		Top-1	Top-5	MAP
AnswerNum		3.40	21.00	0.1384
Z_score		3.49	21.05	0.1453
SA_Z_score (μ=1, upVotes=0)		9.12	23.59	0.1801
SSA_Z_score	μ=1	**12.33**	56.97	0.3216
	μ=10	12.06	52.68	0.3153
	μ=20	11.79	50.67	0.3128
	μ=1+avg(upVotes)	12.06	53.61	0.3166
	μ=1+avg(upVotes)^2	11.66	53.73	0.3130
	μ=1+HM(upVotes)	**12.33**	**58.45**	**0.3223**
recency-aware SSA_Z_score	α=0.001	42.65	88.37	0.618
	α=0.01	**43.06**	**88.57**	**0.621**
	α=0.1	41.84	86.33	0.609
	α=1	39.59	77.96	0.565
	α=10	38.98	77.14	0.559

This score is in effect equivalent to *SSA_Z_score*, but with μ=1 and without considering upVotes. μ was the *normalization factor* which we used to balance the values of $Q\_score_{u,b}$ with $A\_score_{u,b}$ when it was divided by "1+number of upVotes of the question". In other words, we set $\mu = 1$ for *SA_Z_score* because it does not consider upVotes. Again, a small improvement was observed in the performance, evidence that, not surprisingly, awareness of the bug under examination is useful in selecting the right bug assignee. Still this score is not competitive with the literature results.

Our next step was to consider the community's curation of the questions and answers. Instead of uniformly considering all *Stack Overflow* answers of a developer as evidence of expertise and all questions as evidence of lack of expertise, we evaluated whether weighing "good" answers and questions more than "bad" ones would make a difference. The *Stack Overflow* users' upVotes are evidence for the quality of the questions and answers and the *social subject-aware Z_score* (*SSA_Z_score*) was designed to take them into account, as well as being aware of the bug context. This metric involves the μ *normalization factor* that determines the importance of considering "asking" as "lack of expertise" with respect to answers. It can be assigned a static value, or, it may be tuned for different projects. In our main experiments, we set it to "*1+Harmonic Mean of upVotes of all related questions*" (all questions containing at least one $match\_tags_{SO,b}$) which has slightly better performance. The tuning results are shown in Table 2. Note that for the example of Table 1, we have μ=20, obtained simply based on the average of upVotes of the questions mentioned in the first column.

The final improvement leading to our triage score was to make it sensitive to the recency of the relevant *Stack Overflow* activity. The key intuition here is that "the fixing activity has locality" meaning that "the recent fixing developers are likely to fix bug reports in the near future" [29]. Inspired by this idea, we considered the recency of the developers" activities, highlighting recent ones more than past ones. As we anticipated, the results improved further.

Finally, we examined the impact of the various parameters of our metrics to the bug-triaging performance. For the purpose of tuning and calibrating our method, we needed to determine the values for α and β in the $RA\_SSA\_Z\_score_{u,b}$ (Eq. 5). We set the value of β to 1 in order to reduce the variables to one. Then, changed α and measured the accuracy and MAP on three test projects. The best results obtained with α=0.01. This is because of very large numbers attained for $Social\_Z\_score$ (i.e., number of upVotes multiplied by number of tags, summed over all answers of each user). Later in this section, we apply the parameter values (μ, α and β) obtained from the three projects into the remaining 17 projects in our final evaluation.

4.5   Performance of the $RA\_SSA\_Z\_score_{u,b}$

As the final evaluation, we ran our algorithm over 17 projects (holding out the three projects used for tuning) including 6654 bug reports and sorted the recommended developers for each bug report. We measured the average *top-k* accuracies as well as MAP. The average *top-k* accuracies of our approach for k from 1 to 5 are 45.17 %, 66.41 %, 77.50 %, 84.79 % and 89.43 % respectively. We also obtained the MAP as 0.633, which is very strong and shows that the harmonic mean of the real assignee is 1.58 over all the bug reports.

We also implemented the other approaches discussed in Sect. 4.2. We ran those experiments to compare the results of our method with other approaches on the same data set. The results for average *top-1* and *top-5* accuracies as well as MAP are shown in Table 3.

Note that all the values reported in Table 3 are averages over all the 17 projects examined; due to paper-length limitations, the per-project values are not shown here. However, we examined the detailed results for each project and found them close to the mean (var=60.97 and σ=7.81 for *top-5* accuracies). Our results demonstrate that our $RA\_SSA\_Z\_score_{u,b}$, relying on evidence of developers' expertise from their *Stack Overflow* activities, is very effective in selecting the right assignee for the right bug, much more so than all competing machine-learning algorithms relying exclusively on *GitHub* data. In the next section, we analyze these results and compare the details with the other methods.

Table 3. Accuracy results for different simulated approaches compared with ours

	1NN	3NN	5NN	Naive Bayes	Multinomial Naive Bayes	SVM	Our Approach
Top1 Accuracy (%)	43.09	**46.48**	45.60	43.77	42.75	45.46	45.17
Top5 Accuracy (%)	70.46	75.63	75.00	78.98	75.97	81.82	**89.43**
MAP	0.575	0.610	0.596	0.609	0.606	0.617	**0.633**

5 Analysis

First, we compare our approach against implemented machine-learning methods. The results in Table 3 show that our method outperforms all of the other machine learning methods in terms of *top-5* accuracy and MAP. 3NN, 5NN and SVM do well for top-1 accuracy, slightly better than our approach. Our average *top-5* accuracy is between 8 to 19 percent better than other approaches. The MAP value of our approach, 0.633, corresponds to the harmonic mean 1.58 for the rank of the real assignee (implying that the real assignee frequently appeared in the rank-1 and rank-2 positions in the results). MAP varies from 0.575 (for 1NN) to 0.617 (for SVM as the best approach after ours). Comparing the different algorithms on the same data set demonstrates the usefulness of our method. The improved MAP and accuracy of our approach over these other methods shows that our approach is trustworthy and capable of precise assignee recommendation.

Let us now compare the accuracy of our approach against the accuracy reported in previous published contributions. Due to differences in the experimental design and collected metrics of the various studies, it is impossible to have an exact and fair comparison. Some of these earlier methods reported the maximum accuracy over different projects instead of the average accuracy. Also they differ in reported values for k in *top-k* accuracies, with *top-1* and especially *top-5* being the most frequently used. As one of the best obtained accuracies in the previous studies, Shokripour *et al.* obtained 48 % *top-1* and 60 % and 89 % *top-5* accuracies on two projects (between 57 and 9 developers respectively). Our *top-5* accuracy outperforms theirs, but their approach performs 3 % better on *top-1*. Note that their best results were obtained in a project with only 9 candidate developers (our projects included between 28 and 822 developers). Also note that their approach was tested only on 80 and 85 bug reports, as opposed to our 7144 bug reports. In fact, some of the features and meta-data that are required for their method (*e.g.,* product and component of the bug reports) are quite difficult to obtain [13], which makes this study quite challenging to replicate.

To summarize our comparison findings, it is important to mention the following. Our evaluation of our metric is the most thorough reported in the literature (with 20 projects and 7144 bug reports). Our metric highly outperforms all previously reported methods in terms of average *top-5* accuracy, and most of them in terms of average *top-1* accuracy. More importantly, our metric exhibits the highest MAP.

Limitations and Threats to Validity. The most important concern with respect to the validity of our method is that the common users (between *Stack Overflow* and *GitHub*) who constitute the project community are a small part of the complete set of developers associated with each project. The common users between *Stack Overflow* and *GitHub* represent up to 20 % of the total number of users, in each of these networks. There are many users about whom we do not have information, because we could not match their profile in the two networks.

However, to mitigate this limitation, unlike most previous studies, we examined our approach on a large number (*i.e.*, 20) of big projects with thousands of users and bug reports which is quite substantial, limiting threats to external validity. We can even argue that this phenomenon may be an advantage of our approach that focuses on high-quality evidence of developers' expertise established in the actively curated *Stack Overflow* community and ignores developers who do not have such credentials. If our method performs well by accessing parts of the developers' contributions, it should improve when accessing the complete information. Looking from another point of view, regarding commercial and non-open source software, while the users may or may not participate in Q&A networks, there are tracks of developers' activities in their private networks and documents. These information supplement the sources of expertise that are introduced in this study, compensating the limitation.

Currently, for privacy reasons, much of the Q&A content at the software social networks is provided anonymously. One could envision however that project managers could request their developers to provide their *Stack Overflow* IDs. Thus, the step of identifying users common across the two networks through their e-mails should become unnecessary and a larger community of developers, with far more extensive Q&A contributions, will become available to the bug-assignment process.

One concern, is the practice of some developers answering their own questions on *Stack Overflow* for announcing a commonly encountered issue with some API, library, etc. However, we investigated the questions and answers of members of three (out of the 20) chosen projects and found that only 3 % of their answers are answers to one's own questions, and only in around half of these cases the question is up-voted, meaning that the case did not indicate expertise, but lack of expertise (as we assumed).

6 Conclusions and Future Work

The fundamental novelty of our work lies in that it is the first bug-assignment method to consider evidence of developers' expertise beyond their contributions to software development, examining instead their contributions to a Q& A platform. Our method takes advantage of the fact that many developers participate in both platforms. Relying on the expertise of the community to recognize good (and bad) questions and answers, our method taps into a rich, and as yet unexploited, social source of expertise information. To consider this information in the context of the software-development task at hand, our method relies on the intersection between *GitHub* bug-report text and tags of the *Stack Overflow* questions and answers. We believe *Stack Overflow* is a rich source of expertise for software engineering purposes since the privilege of important *Stack Overflow* contributions like up/downVoting is only available to community members who have established a minimum reputation.

We have thoroughly evaluated our method with 20 popular *GitHub* projects, comparing its performance (a) against six traditional machine-learning approaches that have been widely used for bug assignment before, and

(b) against the reported accuracies of previous bug-triaging publications. Our approach exploits expertise information found in *Stack Overflow* and readily outperforms the competition. We believe that in order to achieve even better performance, a project manager may ask the ID of his developers in the software social networks and identify their full Q&A contributions.

Generalizing beyond *Stack Overflow*, how helpful it is for bug assignment, and what limitations it suffers, we envision a new research agenda studying the application of third-party expertise networks to bug triaging. The biggest open question is how to generalize this approach to multiple expertise networks. As well as various Q&A networks and code forums, perhaps there are wikis, project documentation, or developer performance histories that could be mined for expertise networks to exploit for bug triage.

In addition to considering multiple social platforms, we also plan to consider tag synonyms: *Stack Overflow* introduces lists of tag synonyms and suggests the users to use the primary definitions (e.g., "servlets" instead of "webservlet", "authentication" instead of "login"), but does not enforce the practice. In the future, we plan to consider integration of the synonyms in their primary definitions in code and data sets.

As a useful application, the methods mentioned in this paper can be exploited in the onboarding programs [12] to guide the newcomers in the process of fixing bugs. Since these users have no previous background in the current project, the utilization of expertise scores proposed in this paper, based on the users' Q&A contributions will be very useful.

Acknowledgments. This work has been partially funded by IBM, the Natural Sciences and Engineering Research Council of Canada (NSERC) and the GRAND NCE.

References

1. Anvik, J.: Automating bug report assignment. In: Proceedings of the 28th International Conference on Software Engineering (Doctoral Symposium), ICSE 2006, pp. 937–940. ACM (2006)
2. Anvik, J., Hiew, L., Murphy, G.C.: Who should fix this bug? In: Proceedings of the 28th International Conference on Software Engineering, ICSE 2006, pp. 361–370. ACM (2006)
3. Anvik, J.K.: Assisting Bug Report Triage through Recommendation. Ph.D. thesis, University of British Columbia, November 2007
4. Baysal, O., Holmes, R., Godfrey, M.W.: Revisiting bug triage and resolution practices. In: Proceedings of the User evaluation for Software Engineering Researchers (USER) Workshop at the International Conference on Software Engineering (ICSE), 2012, pp. 29–30. IEEE (2012)
5. Bhattacharya, P., Neamtiu, I., Shelton, C.R.: Automated, highly-accurate, bug assignment using machine learning and tossing graphs. J. Syst. Softw. **85**(10), 2275–2292 (2012)
6. Brin, S., Page, L.: The anatomy of a large-scale hypertextual web search engine. Computer networks and ISDN systems **30**(1), 107–117 (1998)

7. Canfora, G., Cerulo, L.: Supporting change request assignment in open source development. In: Proceedings of the 2006 ACM Symposium on Applied Computing, SAC 2006, pp. 1767–1772. ACM (2006)

8. Čubranić, D., Murphy, G.C.: Automatic bug triage using text categorization. In: SEKE 2004: Proceedings of the Sixteenth International Conference on Software Engineering & Knowledge Engineering. Citeseer (2004)

9. Fritz, T., Ou, J., Murphy, G.C., Murphy-Hill, E.: A degree-of-knowledge model to capture source code familiarity. In: Proceedings of the 32Nd ACM/IEEE International Conference on Software Engineering, ICSE 2010, vol. 1, pp. 385–394. ACM (2010)

10. Jeong, G., Kim, S., Zimmermann, T.: Improving bug triage with bug tossing graphs. In: Proceedings of the 7th Joint Meeting of the European Software Engineering Conference and the ACM SIGSOFT Symposium on The Foundations of Software Engineering, ESEC/FSE 2009, pp. 111–120. ACM (2009)

11. Kleinberg, J.M.: Hubs, authorities, and communities. ACM Comput. Surv. (CSUR) **31**(4es), 5 (1999)

12. Labuschagne, A., Holmes, R.: Do onboarding programs work? In: Proceedings of the 12th Working Conference on Mining Software Repositories, MSR 2015 (2015)

13. Lamkanfi, A., Demeyer, S., Soetens, Q.D., Verdonck, T.: Comparing mining algorithms for predicting the severity of a reported bug. In: 2011 15th European Conference on Software Maintenance and Reengineering (CSMR), pp. 249–258. IEEE (2011)

14. Lin, Z., Shu, F., Yang, Y., Hu, C., Wang, Q.: An empirical study on bug assignment automation using chinese bug data. In: Proceedings of the 2009 3rd International Symposium on Empirical Software Engineering and Measurement, ESEM 2009, pp. 451–455. IEEE Computer Society (2009)

15. Linares-Vásquez, M., Hossen, K., Dang, H., Kagdi, H., Gethers, M., Poshyvanyk, D.: Triaging incoming change requests: Bug or commit history, or code authorship? In: 2012 28th IEEE International Conference on Software Maintenance (ICSM), pp. 451–460. IEEE (2012)

16. Matter, D., Kuhn, A., Nierstrasz, O.: Assigning bug reports using a vocabulary-based expertise model of developers. In: 6th IEEE International Working Conference on Mining Software Repositories, MSR 2009, pp. 131–140, May 2009

17. Mockus, A., Herbsleb, J.D.: Expertise browser: A quantitative approach to identifying expertise. In: Proceedings of the 24th International Conference on Software Engineering, ICSE 2002, pp. 503–512. ACM (2002)

18. Naguib, H., Narayan, N., Brugge, B., Helal, D.: Bug report assignee recommendation using activity profiles. In: 2013 10th IEEE Working Conference on Mining Software Repositories (MSR). IEEE(2013)

19. Nguyen, T.T., Nguyen, A.T., Nguyen, T.N.: Topic-based, time-aware bug assignment. SIGSOFT Softw. Eng. Notes **39**(1), 1–4 (2014)

20. Poshyvanyk, D., Marcus, A.: Combining formal concept analysis with information retrieval for concept location in source code. In: 15th IEEE International Conference on Program Comprehension, ICPC 2007, pp. 37–48. IEEE (2007)

21. Stack Exchange Community: Is there a direct download link with a raw data dump of stack overflow? http://meta.stackexchange.com/questions/198915/is-there-a-direct-download-link-with-a-raw-data-dump-of-stack-overflow-not-a-t. Accessed on 20 Auguest 2014

22. Stack Exchange Inc: Stack exchange data dump. https://archive.org/details/stackexchange. Accessed 20 Auguest 2014

23. Stack Exchange Team: What are tags, and how should i use them? http:// stackoverflow.com/help/tagging. Accessed on 17 March 2015

24. The GHTorrent Project: Mysql database dumps. http://GHTorrent.org/ downloads/mysql-2014-08-18.sql.gz. Accessed on 20 Auguest 2014

25. Sajedi Badashian, A., Esteki, A., GholiPour, A., Hindle, A., Stroulia, E.: Involvement, contribution and influence in github and stack overflow. In: Proceedings of the 2014 Conference of the Center for Advanced Studies on Collaborative Research, CASCON 2014. ACM, Markham (2014)

26. Sajedi Badashian, A., Hindle, A., Stroulia, E.: Crowdsourced bug triaging. In: 2015 IEEE International Conference on Software Maintenance and Evolution (ICSME), pp. 506–510. IEEE (2015)

27. Shokripour, R., Kasirun, Z., Zamani, S., Anvik, J.: Automatic bug assignment using information extraction methods. In: 2012 International Conference on Advanced Computer Science Applications and Technologies (ACSAT), pp. 144–149, November 2012

28. Shokripour, R., Anvik, J., Kasirun, Z.M., Zamani, S.: Why so complicated? simple term filtering and weighting for location-based bug report assignment recommendation. In: Proceedings of the 10th Working Conference on Mining Software Repositories, MSR 2013, pp. 2–11. IEEE Press (2013)

29. Tamrawi, A., Nguyen, T.T., Al-Kofahi, J., Nguyen, T.N.: Fuzzy set-based automatic bug triaging (nier track). In: Proceedings of the 33rd International Conference on Software Engineering, ICSE 2011, pp. 884–887. ACM (2011)

30. Tamrawi, A., Nguyen, T.T., Al-Kofahi, J.M., Nguyen, T.N.: Fuzzy set and cache-based approach for bug triaging. In: Proceedings of the 19th ACM SIGSOFT Symposium and the 13th European Conference on Foundations of Software Engineering, ESEC/FSE 2011, pp. 365–375. ACM (2011)

31. Vasilescu, B., Filkov, V., Serebrenik, A.: Stackoverflow and github: associations between software development and crowdsourced knowledge. In: 2013 International Conference on Social Computing (SocialCom), pp. 188–195. IEEE (2013)

32. Venkataramani, R., Gupta, A., Asadullah, A., Muddu, B., Bhat, V.: Discovery of technical expertise from open source code repositories. In: Proceedings of the 22nd International Conference on World Wide Web Companion, WWW 2013 Companion, International World Wide Web Conferences Steering Committee, pp. 97–98 (2013)

33. Zhang, J., Ackerman, M.S., Adamic, L.: Expertise networks in online communities: Structure and algorithms. In: Proceedings of the 16th International Conference on World Wide Web, WWW 2007, pp. 221–230. ACM (2007)

34. Zimmermann, T., Nagappan, N., Guo, P.J., Murphy, B.: Characterizing and predicting which bugs get reopened. In: 34th International Conference on Software Engineering (ICSE), 2012, pp. 1074–1083. IEEE (2012)

Probabilistic and Stochastic Systems

Model-Based Testing of Probabilistic Systems

Marcus Gerhold and Mariëlle Stoelinga(✉)

University of Twente, Enschede, The Netherlands
m.gerhold@utwente.nl, marielle@cs.utwente.nl

Abstract. This paper presents a model-based testing framework for probabilistic systems. We provide algorithms to generate, execute and evaluate test cases from a probabilistic requirements model. In doing so, we connect *ioco*-theory for model-based testing and statistical hypothesis testing: our *ioco*-style algorithms handle the functional aspects, while statistical methods, using χ^2 tests and fitting functions, assess if the frequencies observed during test execution correspond to the probabilities specified in the requirements.

Key results of our paper are the classical soundness and completeness properties, establishing the mathematical correctness of our framework; Soundness states that each test case is assigned the right verdict. Completeness states that the framework is powerful enough to discover each probabilistic deviation from the specification, with arbitrary precision.

We illustrate the use of our framework via two case studies.

1 Introduction

Probability. Probability plays an important role in many computer applications. A vast number of randomized algorithms, protocols and computation methods use randomization to achieve their goals. Routing in sensor networks, for instance, can be done via random walks [1]; speech recognition is based on hidden Markov models [32]; population genetics use Bayesian computation [2], security protocols use random bits in their encryption methods [10], control policies in robotics, leading to the emerging field of probabilistic robotics, concerned with perception and control in the face of uncertainty networking algorithms assign bandwidth in a random fashion. Such applications can be implemented in one of the many probabilistic programming languages, such as Probabilistic-C [26] or Figaro [28]. At a higher level, service level agreements are formulated in a stochastic fashion, stating that the average uptime should be at least 99 %, or that the punctuality of train services should be 95 %.

Key question is whether such probabilistic systems are correct: is bandwidth distributed fairly among all parties? Is the up-time, packet delay and jitter according to specification? Do the trains on a certain day run punctual

This work has been supported by the NWO project BEAT (612.001.303), the STW project SUMBAT (13859), the EU FP7 project SENSATION (318490) and by the STW and ProRail project ArRangeer (12238).

P. Stevens and A. Wąsowski (Eds.): FASE 2016, LNCS 9633, pp. 251–268, 2016.
DOI: 10.1007/978-3-662-49665-7_15

enough? To investigate such questions, probabilistic verification has become a mature research field, putting forward models like probabilistic automata (PAs) [33,38], Markov decision processes [30], (generalized) stochastic Petri nets [23], with verification techniques like stochastic model checking [31], and tools like Prism [20].

Testing. In practice, the most common validation technique is testing, where we subject the system under test to many well-designed test cases, and compare the outcome to the specification. Surprisingly, only few papers are concerned with the testing of probabilistic systems[1], with notable exceptions being [16,18].

This paper presents a model-based testing framework for probabilistic systems. Model-based testing (MBT) is an innovative method to automatically generate, execute and evaluate test cases from a requirements model. By providing faster and more thorough testing at lower cost, MBT has gained rapid popularity in industry. A wide variety of MBT frameworks exist, capable of handling different system aspects, such as functional properties [40], real-time [5,8,22], quantitative aspects [7], and continuous behaviour [27]. As stated, MBT approaches dealing with probability are underdeveloped.

Our Approach. Our specification is given as *probabilistic input/output transition system pIOTS*, a mild generalization of the PA model. As usual, pIOTSs contain two type of choices, *non-deterministic choices* model choices that are not under the control of the system. As argued in [33], these are needed to model phenomena like implementation freedom, scheduler choices, intervals of probability and interleaving. *Probabilistic choices* model random choices made by the system (e.g., coin tosses) or nature (e.g., failure probabilities, degradation rates).

Important contribution are our algorithms to automatically generate, execute and evaluate test cases from a specification pIOTS. These test cases are probabilistic and check if both the functional and the probabilistic behaviour conform to the specification. Probability is observed through frequencies, hence we execute each test multiple times. We use statistical hypothesis testing, in particular the χ^2 test, to assess whether a test case should pass or fail. Technical complication here is the non-determinism in pIOTSs, which prevents us from directly using the χ^2 test. Rather, we first need to find the best resolution of the non-determinism that could have led to these observations. To do so, we set up a non-linear optimization problem that finds the best fit for the χ^2 test.

Key result of our paper is the soundness and completeness of our framework. *Soundness* states that each test case we derive contains the correct verdict: a pass if the behaviour observed during testing conforms to the requirements; a fail if it does not. *Completeness* states that the framework is powerful enough to discover each deviation of non-conforming implementations. Formulating the soundness and completeness results requires a formal notion of conformance. Here, we propose the *pioco*-relation, which pins down when an implementation

---

[1] Note that the popular topic of statistical testing is concerned with choosing the test inputs probabilistically; it does not check for the correctness of the random choices made by a system itself.

modelled as pIOTS conforms to a specification pIOTs. We prove several properties of the *pioco*-relation, in particular it being a conservative extension of *ioco*. Lastly, we illustrate our approach with two case studies: the exponential binary back off protocol, and the IEEE 1394 root contention protocol.

While test efficiency is important, this paper focusses on the methodological set up and correctness. Important future work is to optimize the statistical verdicts we derive and to provide a fully fledged implementation of our methods.

Related Work. Probabilistic testing preorders and equivalences are well studied [11,13,34], defining when two probabilistic transition systems are equivalent, or one subsumes the other. In particular, early and influential work by [21] introduces the fundamental concept of probabilistic bisimulation via hypothesis testing. Also, [9] shows how to observe trace probabilities via hypothesis testing. Executable test frameworks for probabilistic systems have been defined for probabilistic finite state machines [17,24], dealing with mutations and stochastic timing, Petri nets [6], and CSL [35,36]. The important research line of statistical testing [4,42,43] is concerned with choosing the inputs for the SUT in a probabilistic way in order to optimize a certain test metric, such as (weighted) coverage. The question on when to stop statistical testing is tackled in [29].

An approach similar in the spirit of ours is by Hierons et al. [16]. However, our model can be considered as an extension of [16] reconciling probabilistic and non-deterministic choices in a fully fledged way. Being more restrictive enables [16] to focus on individual traces, whereas we use trace distributions.

Furthermore, the current paper extends a workshop paper by [14] that introduced the *pioco*-relation and roughly sketched the test case process. Novel contributions of our current paper are 1. a more generic model pIOTS model that includes internal transitions, 2. the soundness and completeness results, 3. solid definitions of test cases, test execution, and verdicts, 4. the treatment of quiescence, i.e., absence of outputs, 5. the handling of probabilistic test cases.

Overview of the Paper. Section 2 sets the mathematical framework and introduces pIOTSs, adversaries and trace distributions. Section 3 shows how we generate and execute probabilistic tests and evaluate them functionally and statistically. Section 4 introduces the *pioco* relation and shows the soundness and completeness of our testing method. Two case studies can be found in Sect. 5. Lastly Sect. 6 ends the paper with future work and conclusions.

2 Preliminaries

2.1 Probabilistic Input/Output Systems

We start by introducing some standard notions from probability theory. A *discrete probability distribution* over a set X is a function $\mu : X \longrightarrow [0,1]$ such that $\sum_{x \in X} \mu(x) = 1$. The set of all distributions over X is denoted by $Distr(X)$. The probability distribution that assigns 1 to a certain element $x \in X$ is called the *Dirac* distribution over x and is denoted $Dirac(x)$.

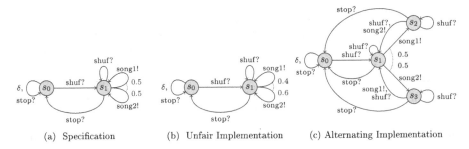

(a) Specification   (b) Unfair Implementation   (c) Alternating Implementation

Fig. 1. Specification and two implementations of a shuffle music player. Actions separated by commas indicate that two transitions are enabled from the state.

A *probability space* is a triple $(\Omega, \mathcal{F}, \mathbb{P})$, such that Ω is a set, $\mathcal{F}$ is a σ-field of Ω, and $\mathbb{P} : \mathcal{F} \to [0,1]$ a probability measure such that $\mathbb{P}(\Omega) = 1$ and $\mathbb{P}(\bigcup_{i=0}^{\infty} A_i) = \sum_{i=0}^{\infty} \mathbb{P}(A_i)$ for $A_i \in \mathcal{F}$, $i = 1, 2, \ldots$ pairwise disjoint.

Definition 1. *A* probabilistic input/output transition system *is a sixtuple* $\mathcal{A} = (S, s, L_I, L_O, L_H, \Delta)$, *where*

- S *is a finite set of states,*
- s_0 *is the unique starting state,*
- L_I, L_O *and* L_H *are disjoint sets of input, output and internal labels respectively, containing a special quiescence label* $\delta \in L_O$. *We write* $L = L_I \cup L_O^{\delta} \cup L_H$ *for the set of all labels.*
- $\Delta \subseteq S \times Distr(L \times S)$ *a finite transition relation such that for all input actions* $a?$, $\mu(a?, s') > 0$ *implies* $\mu(b, s'') = 0$ *for all* $b \neq a?$.

We use "?" to suffix input and "!" to suffix output. We write $s \xrightarrow{\mu,a} s'$ *if* $(s, \mu) \in \Delta$ *and* $\mu(a, s') > 0$; *and* $s \to a$ *if there are* $\mu \in Distr(L \times S)$ *and* $s' \in S$ *such that* $s \xrightarrow{\mu,a} s'$ ($s \not\to a$ *if not*). *We write* $s \xrightarrow{\mu,a}_{\mathcal{A}} s'$, *etc. to clarify ambiguities if needed. Lastly,* $\mathcal{A}$ *is* input-enabled *if for all* $s \in S$ *we have* $s \to a?$ *for all* $a \in L_I$.

Following [15], pIOTSs are *input-reactive* and *output-generative*. Upon receiving an input, the pIOTS decides probabilistically which next state to move to. On producing an output, the pIOTS chooses both the output action and the state probabilistically. As required in clause 4 of Definition 1, this means that each transition can either involve a single input action, or several outputs, quiescence or internal actions. Note that a state can enable input and output transitions albeit not in the same distribution. Furthermore, in testing, a verdict must also be given if the system-under-test is quiescent, i.e., produces no output at all. Hence, the requirements model must explicitly indicate when quiescence is allowed, which is expressed by a special output label δ, for details see [39,41].

Example 2. Figure 1 shows three models of a simple shuffle mp3 player with two songs. The pIOTS in (Fig. 1a) models the requirements: pressing the shuffle button enables the two songs with probability 0.5 each, repeatedly until stop is pressed.

Implementation (Fig. 1b) is subject to a small probabilistic deviation. In implementation (Fig. 1c) the same song cannot be played twice in a row without intervention of the shuffle button. States without enabled output transition allow quiescence, denoted by δ transitions. The model-based testing framework established in the paper is capable of detecting all of the above flaws.

Parallel composition is defined in a standard fashion. Two pIOTSs in composition synchronize on shared actions, and evolve independently on others. Since the transitions in the component pIOTSs are stochastically independent, we multiply the probabilities when taking shared actions, denoted by $\mu \times \nu$. To avoid name clashes, we only compose compatible pIOTSs. Note that parallel composition of two input-enabled pIOTSs yields a pIOTS.

Definition 3. *Two pIOTSs* $\mathcal{A} = (S, s_0, L_I, L_O, L_H, \Delta)$ *and* $\mathcal{A}' = (S', s_0', L_I', L_O', L_H', \Delta')$, *are compatible if* $L_O \cap L_O' = \{\delta\}$, $L_H \cap L' = \emptyset$ *and* $L \cap L_H' = \emptyset$. *Their* parallel composition *is the tuple*

$$\mathcal{A} \parallel \mathcal{A}' = (S'', (s_0, s_0'), L_I'', L_O'', L_H'', \Delta''), \text{ where}$$

$S'' = S \times S'$, $L_I'' = (L_I \cup L_I') \setminus (L_O \cup L_O')$, $L_O'' = L_O \cup L_O'$, $L_H'' = L_H \cup L_H'$, *and finally* $\Delta'' = \{((s, t), \mu) \in S'' \times Distr(L'' \times S'') \mid$

$$\mu \equiv \begin{cases} \nu_1 \times \nu_2 & \text{if } \exists a \in L \cap L' \text{ such that } s \xrightarrow{\nu_1, a} \wedge t \xrightarrow{\nu_2, a} \\ \nu_1 \times \mathbb{1} & \text{if } \forall a \in L \text{ with } s \xrightarrow{\nu_1, a} \text{ we have } t \not\xrightarrow{a} \\ \mathbb{1} \times \nu_2 & \text{if } \forall a \in L' \text{ with } t \xrightarrow{\nu_2, a} \text{ we have } s \not\xrightarrow{a} \end{cases} \},$$

where $(s, \nu_1) \in \Delta, (t, \nu_2) \in \Delta'$ *respectively, and* $\nu_1 \times \mathbb{1}((s, t), a) = \nu_1(s, a) \cdot 1$ *and* $\mathbb{1} \times \nu_2((s, t), a) = 1 \cdot \nu_2(t, a)$.

2.2   Paths and Traces

We define the usual language concepts for LTSs. Let $\mathcal{A} = (S, s_0, L_I, L_O, L_H, \Delta)$ be a pIOTS. A *path* π of $\mathcal{A}$ is a (possibly) infinite sequence of the following form

$$\pi = s_1 \mu_1 a_1 s_2 \mu_2 a_2 s_3 \mu_3 a_3 s_4 \ldots,$$

where $s_i \in S$, $a_i \in L$ and $\mu_i \in Distr(L \times S)$, such that each finite path ends in a state and $s_i \xrightarrow{\mu_{i+1}, a_{i+1}} s_{i+1}$ for each non-final i. We use $last(\pi)$ to denote the last state of a finite path ($last(\pi) = \infty$ for infinite paths). The set of all finite paths of $\mathcal{A}$ is denoted by $Path^*(\mathcal{A})$ and all infinite paths by $Path(\mathcal{A})$.

The associated *trace* of a path π is obtained by omitting states, distributions and internal actions, i.e. $trace(\pi) = a_1 a_2 a_3 \ldots$. Conversely, $trace^{-1}(\sigma)$ gives the set of all paths, which have trace σ. The *length* of a path is the number of occurring actions on its associated trace. All finite traces of $\mathcal{A}$ are summarized in $traces(\mathcal{A})$. The set of *complete traces*, $ctraces(\mathcal{A})$, contains every trace based on paths ending in states that do not enable any more actions. We write $out_\mathcal{A}(\sigma)$ for the set of all output actions enabled with positive probability after trace σ.

2.3   Adversaries and Trace Distributions

Very much like traces of LTSs are obtained by first selecting a path and by then removing all states and internal actions, we do the same in the probabilistic case. First, we resolve all non-deterministic choices in the pIOTS via an adversary and then we remove all states to get the trace distribution.

The resolution of the non-determinism via an adversary leads to a purely probabilistic system, in which we can assign a probability to each finite path. A classical result in measure theory [12] shows that it is impossible to assign a probability to all sets of traces, hence we use σ-fields $\mathcal{F}$ consisting of cones.

Adversaries. Following the standard theory for probabilistic automata [38], we define the behaviour of a pIOTS via adversaries (a.k.a. policies or schedulers) to resolve the non-deterministic choices in pIOTSs; in each state of the pIOTS, the adversary may choose which transition to take or it may also halt the execution.

Given any finite history leading to a state, an adversary returns a discrete probability distribution over the set of next transitions. In order to model termination, we define schedulers such that they can continue paths with a halting extension, after which only quiescence is observed.

Definition 4. *An* adversary E *of a pIOTS* $\mathcal{A} = (S, s_0, L_I, L_O, L_H, \Delta)$ *is a function*

$$E : Path^* (\mathcal{A}) \longrightarrow Distr\,(Distr\,(L \times S) \cup \{\bot\}),$$

such that for each finite path π, *if* $E\,(\pi)\,(\mu) > 0$, *then* $(last\,(\pi), \mu) \in \Delta$ *or* $\mu \equiv \bot$. *We say that* E *is deterministic, if* $E\,(\pi)$ *assigns the Dirac distribution to every distribution after all* $\pi \in Path^* (\mathcal{A})$. *The value* $E\,(\pi)\,(\bot)$ *is considered as interruption/halting. An adversary* E *halts on a path* π, *if* $E\,(\pi)\,(\bot) = 1$. *We say that an adversary halts after* $k \in \mathbb{N}$ *steps, if it halts for every path of length greater or equal to* k. *We denote all such finite adversaries by* $adv\,(\mathcal{A}, k)$.

Intuitively an adversary tosses a multi-faced and biased die at every step of the computation, thus resulting in a purely probabilistic computation tree. The probability assigned to a path π is obtained by the probability of its cone $C_\pi = \{\pi' \in Path\,(\mathcal{A}) \mid \pi \sqsubseteq \pi'\}$. We use the inductively defined path probability function Q^E, i.e. $Q^E\,(s_0) = 1$ and $Q^E\,(\pi\mu as) = Q^E\,(\pi)\,E\,(\pi)\,(\mu)\,\mu\,(a, s)$. This function enables us to assign a unique probability space $(\Omega_E, \mathcal{F}_E, P_E)$ associated to an adversary E. Thus, the probability of π is $P_E\,(\pi) = P_E\,(C_\pi) = Q^E\,(\pi)$.

Trace Distributions. A trace distribution is obtained from (the probability space of) an adversary by removing all states. Thus, the probability assigned to a set of traces X is the probability of all paths whose trace is an element of X.

Definition 5. *The* trace distribution H *of an adversary* E, *denoted* $H = trd\,(E)$ *is the probability space* $(\Omega_H, \mathcal{F}_H, P_H)$ *given by*

1. $\Omega_H = L^\omega$,
2. $\mathcal{F}_H$ *is the smallest* σ-field containing the set $\{C_\beta \subseteq \Omega_H \mid \beta \in L^\omega\}$,
3. P_H *is the unique prob. measure on* $\mathcal{F}_H$ *such that* $P_H\,(X) = P_E\,(trace^{-1}\,(X))$ *for* $X \in \mathcal{F}_H$.

We write $trd(\mathcal{A})$ for the set of all trace distributions of $\mathcal{A}$ and $trd(\mathcal{A}, k)$ for those halting after $k \in \mathbb{N}$. Lastly we write $\mathcal{A} =_{TD} \mathcal{B}$ if $trd(\mathcal{A}) = trd(\mathcal{B})$, $\mathcal{A} \sqsubseteq_{TD} \mathcal{B}$ if $trd(\mathcal{A}) \subseteq trd(\mathcal{B})$ and $\mathcal{A} \sqsubseteq_{TD}^{k} \mathcal{B}$ if $trd(\mathcal{A}, k) \subseteq trd(\mathcal{B}, k)$ for $k \in \mathbb{N}$.

The fact that $(\Omega_E, \mathcal{F}_E, P_E)$ and $(\Omega_H, \mathcal{F}_H, P_H)$ define probability spaces, follows from standard measure theory arguments (see for example [12]).

Example 6. Consider (c) in Fig. 1 and an adversary E starting from the beginning state s_0 scheduling probability 1 to shuf?, 1 to the distribution consisting of song1! and song2! and $\frac{1}{2}$ to both shuffle? transitions in s_2. Then choose the paths $\pi = s_0\mu_1$shuf?$s_1\mu_2$song1!$s_2\mu_3$shuf?s_2 and $\pi' = s_0\mu_1$shuf?$s_1\mu_2$song1!$s_2\mu_4$shuf?s_1.

We see that $\sigma = trace(\pi) = trace(\pi')$ and $P_E(\pi) = Q^E(\pi) = \frac{1}{4}$ and $P_E(\pi') = Q^E(\pi') = \frac{1}{4}$, but $P_{trd(E)}(\sigma) = P_E(trace^{-1}(\sigma)) = P_E(\{\pi, \pi'\}) = \frac{1}{2}$.

3 Testing with pIOTS

3.1 Test Generation

Model-based testing entails the automatic test case generation, execution and evaluation based on a requirements model. We provide two algorithms for test case generation: an *offline* or *batch* algorithm that generates test cases before their execution; and an *online* or *on-the-fly* algorithm generating test cases during execution.

First, we formalize the notion of a (offline) test case over an action signature (L_I, L_O). In each state of a test, the tester can either provide some stimulus $a? \in L_I$, or wait for a response of the system or stop the testing process.[2] Each of these possibilities can be chosen with a certain probability, leading to probabilistic test cases. We model this as a probabilistic choice between the internal actions τ_{obs}, τ_{stop} and τ_{stim}. Note that, even in the non-probabilistic case, the test cases are often generated probabilistically in practice, but this is not supported in theory. Thus, our definition fills a small gap here.

Furthermore, note that, when waiting for a system response, we have to take into account all potential outputs in L_O, including the situation that the system provides no response at all, modelled by δ. Since the continuation of a test depends on the history, offline test cases are formalized as trees.

Definition 7. *A test or test case over an action signature (L_I, L_O) is a pIOTS of the form $t = (S, s_0, L_O \setminus \{\delta\}, L_I \cup \{\delta\}, \{\tau_{obs}, \tau_{stim}, \tau_{stop}\}, \Delta)$ such that*

- *t is internally deterministic and does not contain an infinite path;*
- *t is acyclic and connected;*
- *For every state $s \in S$, we either have*
  - *after $(s) = \emptyset$, or*
  - *after $(s) = \{\tau_{obs}, \tau_{stim}, \tau_{stop}\}$, or*
  - *after $(s) = L_I \cup \{\delta\}$, or*
  - *after $(s) = L_{out}$, such that $L_{out} \subseteq L_O \setminus \{\delta\}$,*

---

[2] Note that in more recent version of *ioco* theory [41], test cases are input-enabled. This can easily be incorporated into our framework.

where after (*s*) *is the set of actions in state s. A* test suite *T is a set of test cases. A* test case (suite) *for a pIOTS* $\mathcal{A}_S = (S, s_0, L_I, L_O, L_H, \Delta)$, *is a test case (suite) over* (L_I, L_O).

Note that the action signature of tests has switched input and output label sets.

Definition 8. *For a given test t a* test annotation *is a function*

$$a : ctraces\,(t) \longrightarrow \{pass, fail\}.$$

A pair $\hat{t} = (t, a)$ *consisting of a test and a test annotation is called an* annotated test. *The set of all such* $\hat{t}$, *denoted by* $\widehat{T} = \{(t_i, a_i)_{i \in \mathcal{I}}\}$ *for some index set* $\mathcal{I}$, *is called an* annotated test suite. *If t is a test case for a specification* $\mathcal{A}_S$ *we define the test annotation* $a_{\mathcal{A}_S, t} : ctraces\,(t) \longrightarrow \{pass, fail\}$ *by*

$$a_{\mathcal{A}_S, t}(\sigma) = \begin{cases} fail & if\ \exists \varrho \in traces\,(\mathcal{A}_S)\,, a! \in L_O^\delta : \varrho a! \sqsubseteq \sigma \wedge \varrho a! \notin traces\,(\mathcal{A}_S)\,; \\ pass & otherwise. \end{cases}$$

Example 9. Figure 2 shows two derived tests for the specification in Fig. 1. Note that the action signature is mirrored. Therefore if $s \xrightarrow{\mu, a}_{\hat{t}} s'$ with a an output action of the specification, then we have $\mu = Dirac$. Test $\hat{t}_2$ shows how we apply stimuli, observe or stop with probabilities $\frac{1}{3}$ each. If we stimulate, we apply stop! and shuf! with probability $\frac{1}{2}$ each.

Algorithms. The procedure *batch* in Algorithm 1 generates test cases from a specification, given a specification pIOTSs $\mathcal{A}_S$ and a history σ, which is initially ϵ. Each step a probabilistic choice is made to return an empty test, to observe or to stimulate, denoted with probabilities $p_{\sigma,1}, p_{\sigma,2}$ or $p_{\sigma,3}$ respectively. The latter two call the procedure *batch* again. If erroneous output is detected, we stop immediately. We require that $p_{\sigma,1} + p_{\sigma,2} + p_{\sigma,3} = 1$.

Algorithm 2 shows a sound way to derive tests on-the-fly. The inputs are a specification $\mathcal{A}_S$, a concrete implementation $\mathcal{A}_\mathcal{I}$ and a test length $n \in \mathbb{N}$. The algorithm returns a verdict of whether or not the implementation is *ioco* correct in the first n steps. If erroneous output was detected, the verdict will be *fail* and *pass* otherwise. With probability $p_{\sigma,1}$ we observe and with probability $p_{\sigma,2}$ we stimulate. The algorithm stops after n steps. Thus, $p_{\sigma,1} + p_{\sigma,2} = 1$.

Theorem 10. *All test cases generated by Algorithm 1 are test cases according to Definition 7. All test cases generated by Algorithm 2 assign the correct verdict according to Definition 8.*

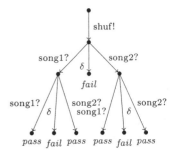

(a) Annotated test $\hat{t}_1$

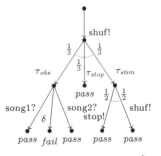

(b) Prob. annotated test $\hat{t}_2$

Fig. 2. Two tests derived from the specification in Fig. 1

ALGORITHM 1: Batch test generation for *pioco*.	**ALGORITHM 2:** On-the-fly test case derivation for *pioco*.

ALGORITHM 1: Batch test generation for *pioco*.

Input: Specification pIOTS $\mathcal{A}_S$ and history $\sigma \in traces(\mathcal{A}_S)$.
Output: A test case t for $\mathcal{A}_S$.
1 **Procedure** batch($\mathcal{A}_S, \sigma$)
2    $p_{\sigma,1}\cdot[\text{true}] \rightarrow$
3   **return** $\{\tau_{stop}\}$
4    $p_{\sigma,2}\cdot[\text{true}] \rightarrow$
5   result := $\{\tau_{obs}\}$
6   **forall** $b! \in L_O$ **do:**
7   **if** $\sigma b! \in traces(\mathcal{A}_S)$:
8   result := result $\cup \{b!\sigma' \mid \sigma' \in$ batch$(\mathcal{A}_S, \sigma b!)\}$
9   **else:**
10   result := result $\cup \{b!\}$
11   **end**
12   **end**
13   **return** result
14    $p_{\sigma,3}\cdot[\sigma a? \in traces(\mathcal{A}_S)] \rightarrow$
15   result := $\{\tau_{stim}\} \cup \{a?\sigma' \mid \sigma' \in$ batch$(\mathcal{A}_S, \sigma a?)\}$
16   **forall** $b! \in L_O$ **do:**
17   **if** $\sigma b! \in traces(\mathcal{A}_S)$:
18   result := result $\cup \{b!\sigma' \mid \sigma' \in$ batch$(\mathcal{A}_S, \sigma b!)\}$
19   **else:**
20   result := result $\cup \{b!\}$
21   **end**
22   **end**
23   **return** result

ALGORITHM 2: On-the-fly test case derivation for *pioco*.

Input: Specification pIOTS $\mathcal{A}_S$, an implementation $\mathcal{A}_I$ and an upper bound for the test length $n \in \mathbb{N}$.
Output: Verdict *pass* if Impl. was ioco conform in the first n steps and *fail* if not.
1 $\sigma := \epsilon$
2 **while** $|\sigma| < n$ **do:**
3    $p_{\sigma,1}\cdot[\text{true}] \rightarrow$
4   *observe next output b! (possibly δ) of* $\mathcal{A}_I$
5      $\sigma := \sigma b!$
6   **if** $\sigma \notin traces(\mathcal{A}_S)$:
7   **return** *fail*
8    $p_{\sigma,2} \cdot [\sigma a? \in traces(\mathcal{A}_S)] \rightarrow$
9   **try:**
10   **atomic**
11   *stimulate I with a?*
12          $\sigma := \sigma a?$
13   **end**
14   **catch** *an output b! occurs before a? could be applied*
15        $\sigma := \sigma b!$
16   **if** $\sigma \notin traces(\mathcal{A}_S)$:
17   **return** *fail*
18
19   **end**
20 **end**
21 **return** *pass*

3.2 Test Evaluation

In our framework, we assess functional behaviour by the test verdict $a_{\mathcal{A}_S,t}$ and probabilistic behaviour via statistics, as elaborated below.

Statistical Verdict. Given a (black box) implementation, the idea is to run an offline or online test case multiple times, in order to collect a sample. Then, we check if the frequencies of the traces contained in this sample match the probabilities in the specification via statistical hypothesis testing. However, since the specification contains non-determism, we cannot apply statistical means directly. Rather, we check if the observed trace frequencies can be explained, if we resolve occurring non-determinism in the specification according to some scheduler.

We formulate a hypothesised scheduler that makes the occurrence of the sample most likely. This gives rise to a purely probabilistic computation tree and probabilities and expected values for each trace can be calculated. Based on a predefined level of significance $\alpha \in (0, 1)$ we use null hypothesis testing to determine whether to accept or reject the hypothesised scheduler. If it is accepted, we have no reason to assume that the implementation differs probabilistically from the specification and give the *pass* label. If it is rejected, we assign the *fail* verdict, because there is no scheduler to explain the observed frequencies.

Sampling. To collect a sample, we define the length $k \in \mathbb{N}$ and width $m \in \mathbb{N}$ of an experiment first, i.e. how long shall we observe the machine and how many times do we want to run it before stopping. Thus, we collect $\sigma_1, \ldots, \sigma_m \in traces\,(\mathcal{A}_\mathcal{I})$ with $|\sigma_i| = k$ for $i = 1, \ldots, m$. We call $O = (\sigma_1, \ldots, \sigma_m) \in (L^k)^m$ a *sample*. We assume the system is governed by a trace distribution D_i in every run, thus running the machine m times, means that a sample is generated by a sequence of m (possibly) different trace distributions $\boldsymbol{D} = (D_1, D_2, \ldots, D_m) \in trd\,(\mathcal{A}_\mathcal{I}, k)^m$.

Each run the implementation makes two choices. (1) It chooses a trace distribution D_i and (2) D_i chooses a trace σ_i. Once a trace distribution D_i is chosen, it is solely responsible for the trace σ_i, meaning that for $i \neq j$ the choice of σ_i by D_i is independent of the choice σ_j by D_j.

Frequencies. The frequency function is defined as $freq : (L^k)^m \rightarrow Distr\,(L^k)$, such that $freq\,(O)\,(\sigma) = \frac{|\{i=1,\ldots,m \wedge \sigma=\sigma_i\}|}{m}$. Assume that $k, m \in \mathbb{N}$, $\boldsymbol{D}$ and $\sigma \in L^k$ are fixed. Then a sample O can be treated as a Bernoulli experiment of length m, where success occurs in position $i \in \{1, \ldots, m\}$ if $\sigma = \sigma_i$. Thus, the success probability in the i-th step is given by $P_{D_i}\,(\sigma)$. So assume X_i are Bernoulli distributed random variables for $i = 1, \ldots, m$. We define a new random variable as $Z = \frac{1}{m} \sum_{i=1}^{m} X_i$, which represents the frequency of success in m steps governed by $\boldsymbol{D}$. Thus the expected frequency is given as

$$\mathbb{E}_\sigma^{\boldsymbol{D}} := \mathbb{E}\,(Z) = \frac{1}{m} \sum_{i=1}^{m} \mathbb{E}\,(X_i) = \frac{1}{m} \sum_{i=1}^{m} P_{D_i}\,(\sigma).$$

It is $\sum_\sigma \mathbb{E}_\sigma^{\boldsymbol{D}} = 1$, which means $\mathbb{E}^{\boldsymbol{D}}$ is the distribution expected under $\boldsymbol{D}$.

Acceptable Outcomes. We will accept a sample O if $freq\,(O)$ lies within some distance r of the expected distribution $\mathbb{E}^{\boldsymbol{D}}$. Recall the definition of a ball centred at $x \in X$ with radius r as $B_r\,(x) = \{y \in X \mid dist\,(x, y) \leq r\}$. All distributions deviating at most by r from the expected distribution are contained within the ball $B_r\,(\mathbb{E}^{\boldsymbol{D}})$, where $dist\,(u, v) := \sup_{\sigma \in L^k} |\,u\,(\sigma) - v\,(\sigma)\,|$ and u and v are distributions. In order to minimize the error of falsely accepting a sample, we choose the smallest radius, such that the error of falsely rejecting a sample is not greater than a predefined level of significance $\alpha \in (0, 1)$ by $\bar{r} := \inf \{r \mid P_{\boldsymbol{D}}\,(freq^{-1}\,(B_r\,(\mathbb{E}^{\boldsymbol{D}}))) > 1 - \alpha\}$.

Definition 11. *For $k, m \in \mathbb{N}$ and a pIOTS $\mathcal{A}$ the acceptable outcomes under $\boldsymbol{D} \in trd\,(\mathcal{A}, k)^m$ of significance level $\alpha \in (0, 1)$ are given by the set of observations $Obs\,(\boldsymbol{D}, \alpha, k, m) = \{O \in (L^k)^m \mid dist\,(freq\,(O), \mathbb{E}^{\boldsymbol{D}}) \leq \bar{r}\}$. The set of observations of $\mathcal{A}$ of significance level $\alpha \in (0, 1)$ is given by*

$$Obs\,(\mathcal{A}, \alpha, k, m) = \bigcup_{\boldsymbol{D} \in trd(\mathcal{A},k)^m} Obs\,(\boldsymbol{D}, \alpha, k, m).$$

The defined set of observations of a pIOTS $\mathcal{A}$ therefore has two properties, reflecting the error of false rejection and false acceptance respectively.

1. For $D \in trd(\mathcal{A})$ of length k, we have $P_D(Obs(\mathcal{A}, \alpha, k, m)) \geq 1 - \alpha$,
2. For $D' \notin trd(\mathcal{A})$ of length k, we have $P_{D'}(Obs(\mathcal{A}, \alpha, k, m)) \leq \beta_m$,

where α is the predefined level of significance and β_m is unknown but minimal by construction. Note that $\beta_m \to 0$ as $m \to \infty$, thus the error of falsely accepting an observation decreases with increasing sample width.

Application. This framework has two problems for practical applications: (1) the parameter $\bar{r}$ may be hard to find and (2) for a given sample, it is no trivial task to find the trace distribution, that gives it maximal likelihood, i.e.

$$\mathbb{P}_{\mathcal{A}}^{k,m}(O) := \max_{D \in (trd(\mathcal{A},k) \setminus trd(\mathcal{A},k-1))^m} P_D(O).$$

The parameter $\bar{r}$ gives the best fit, but finding it is no trivial task. It is of interest for the soundness and completeness proofs, but in practice we will use χ^2 hypothesis testing. The empirical value $\chi^2 = \sum_{i=1}^{m}(n(\sigma_i) - mE_{\sigma_i}^D)^2/mE_{\sigma_i}^D$, where $n(\sigma)$ is the amount σ occurred in the sample, is compared to critical values of given degrees of freedom and levels of significance. These values can be calculated or looked up in a χ^2 table.

Since expectations in our construction depend on a scheduler/trace distribution to explain a possible sample, it is of interest to find the best fit. Hence, we are trying to solve the minimisation

$$\min_{D} \sum_{i=1}^{m} \frac{(n(\sigma_i) - mE_{\sigma_i}^D)^2}{mE_{\sigma_i}^D}. \tag{1}$$

By construction, we want to optimize the probabilities p_i used by a scheduler to resolve non-determinism. This turns (1) into a minimisation of a rational function $f(p)/g(p)$ with inequality constraints on the vector p. As shown in [25], minimizing rational functions is **NP**-hard. This approach optimizes one possible trace distribution to fit the sample data instead of finding m different ones. This topic could be handled in future research, with the assumption of one distribution which lets the implementation choose different trace distributions.

Verdict Function. With this framework, the following decision process summarizes if an implementation fails for functional and/or statistical behaviour.

Definition 12. *Given a specification* $\mathcal{A}_\mathcal{S}$, *an annotated test* $\hat{t}$ *for* $\mathcal{A}_\mathcal{S}$, $k, m \in \mathbb{N}$ *where* k *given by the trace length of* $\hat{t}$ *and a level of significance* $\alpha \in (0, 1)$, *we define the* functional verdict *as the function* $v_{\hat{t}} : pIOTS \longrightarrow \{pass, fail\}$, *with*

$$v_{\hat{t}}(\mathcal{A}_\mathcal{I}) = \begin{cases} pass & if \; \forall \sigma \in ctraces(\mathcal{A}_\mathcal{I} \,\|\, t) \cap ctraces(t) : a(\sigma) = pass \\ fail & otherwise, \end{cases}$$

the statistical verdict *as the function* $v_t^{\alpha, m} : pIOTS \longrightarrow \{pass, fail\}$, *with*

$$v_t^{\alpha, m}(\mathcal{A}_\mathcal{I}) = \begin{cases} pass & if \; \mathbb{P}_{\mathcal{A}_\mathcal{S}}^{k,m}(Obs(\mathcal{A}_\mathcal{I} \,\|\, t, \alpha, k, m)) \geq 1 - \alpha \\ fail & otherwise, \end{cases}$$

and finally the overall verdict as the function $V_{\hat{t}}^{\alpha,m} : pIOTS \rightarrow \{pass, fail\}$, with $V_{\hat{t}}^{\alpha,m}(A_{\mathcal{I}}) = pass$ if $v_{\hat{t}}(A_{\mathcal{I}}) = v_t^{\alpha,m}(A_{\mathcal{I}}) = pass$ and $V_{\hat{t}}^{\alpha,m}(A_{\mathcal{I}}) = fail$ otherwise. For an annotated test suite $\hat{T}$ for $A_{\mathcal{S}}$ we lift this to $V_{\hat{T}}^{\alpha,m}(A_{\mathcal{I}}) = pass$ if $V_{\hat{t}}^{\alpha,m}(A_{\mathcal{I}}) = pass$ for each $\hat{t} \in \hat{T}$ and $V_{\hat{T}}^{\alpha,m}(A_{\mathcal{I}}) = fail$ otherwise.

4   Conformance, Soundness and Completeness

A key result of our paper is the correctness of our framework, formalized as soundness and completeness. *Soundness* states that each test case is assigned the correct verdict. *Completeness* states that the framework is powerful enough to discover each deviation from the specification. Formulating these properties requires a formal notion of conformance that we formalize as the *pioco*-relation.

4.1   Probabilistic Input/Output Conformance $\sqsubseteq_{pioco}$

The classical *ioco* relation [40] states that an implementation conforms to a specification, if it never provides any unspecified output or quiescence, i.e. for two IOTSs $A_{\mathcal{I}}$ and $A_{\mathcal{S}}$, with $A_{\mathcal{I}}$ input-enabled, we say $A_{\mathcal{I}} \sqsubseteq_{ioco} A_{\mathcal{S}}$, iff

$$\forall \sigma \in traces(A_{\mathcal{S}}) : out_{A_{\mathcal{I}}}(\sigma) \subseteq out_{A_{\mathcal{S}}}(\sigma).$$

To generalize *ioco* to pIOTSs, we introduce two auxiliary concepts:

1. the prefix relation for trace distributions $H \sqsubseteq_k H'$ is the analogue of trace prefixes, i.e. $H \sqsubseteq_k H'$ iff $\forall \sigma \in L^k : P_H(\sigma) = P_{H'}(\sigma)$
2. for a pIOTSs A and a trace distribution H of length k, the *output continuation* of H in A contains all trace distributions, which are equal up to length k and assign every trace of length $k+1$ ending in input probability 0. We set

$$outcont(H, A) := \{H' \in trd(A, k+1) \mid H \sqsubseteq_k H' \wedge \forall \sigma \in L^k L_I : P_{H'}(\sigma) = 0\}.$$

Intuitively an implementation should conform to a specification, if the probability of every trace in $A_{\mathcal{I}}$ specified in $A_{\mathcal{S}}$, can be matched. Just like in *ioco*, we neglect unspecified traces ending in input actions. However, if there is unspecified output in the implementation, there is at least one adversary that schedules positive probability to this continuation.

Definition 13. *Let $A_{\mathcal{I}}$ and $A_{\mathcal{S}}$ be two pIOTSs. Furthermore let $A_{\mathcal{I}}$ be input-enabled, then we say $A_{\mathcal{I}} \sqsubseteq_{pioco} A_{\mathcal{S}}$ iff*

$$\forall k \in \mathbb{N} \forall H \in trd(A_{\mathcal{S}}, k) : outcont(H, A_{\mathcal{I}}) \subseteq outcont(H, A_{\mathcal{S}}).$$

The *pioco* relation conservatively extends the *ioco* relation, i.e. both relations coincide for IOTSs.

Theorem 14. *Let A and B be two IOTSs and A be input-enabled, then*

$$A \sqsubseteq_{ioco} B \Longleftrightarrow A \sqsubseteq_{pioco} B.$$

The implementation is always assumed to be input-enabled. If the specification is input-enabled too, then *pioco* coincides with trace distribution inclusion. Moreover, our results show that *pioco* is transitive, just like *ioco*.

Theorem 15. *Let $\mathcal{A}$, $\mathcal{B}$ and $\mathcal{C}$ be pIOTSs and let $\mathcal{A}$ and $\mathcal{B}$ be input-enabled, then*

- *$\mathcal{A} \sqsubseteq_{pioco} \mathcal{B}$ if and only if $\mathcal{A} \sqsubseteq_{TD} \mathcal{B}$.*
- *$\mathcal{A} \sqsubseteq_{pioco} \mathcal{B}$ and $\mathcal{B} \sqsubseteq_{pioco} \mathcal{C}$ then $\mathcal{A} \sqsubseteq_{pioco} \mathcal{C}$.*

4.2 Soundness and Completeness

Talking about soundness and completeness when referring to probabilistic systems is not a trivial topic, since one of the main inherent difficulties of statistical analysis is the possibility of false rejection or false acceptance.

The former is of interest when we refer to soundness (i.e. what is the probability that we erroneously assign *fail* to a correct implementation), and the latter is important when we talk about completeness (i.e. what is the probability that we assign *pass* to an erroneous implementation). Thus, a test suite can only fulfil these properties with a guaranteed (high) probability (c.f. Definition 12).

Definition 16. *Let $\mathcal{A}_S$ be a specification over an action signature (L_I, L_O), $\alpha \in (0, 1)$ the level of significance and $\widehat{T}$ an annotated test suite for $\mathcal{A}_S$. Then*

- *$\widehat{T}$ is sound for $\mathcal{A}_S$ with respect to $\sqsubseteq_{pioco}$, if for all input-enabled implementations $\mathcal{A}_i \in pIOTS$ and sufficiently large $m \in \mathbb{N}$ it holds that*

$$\mathcal{A}_{\mathcal{I}} \sqsubseteq_{pioco} \mathcal{A}_S \Longrightarrow V_{\widehat{T}}^{\alpha, m} (\mathcal{A}_{\mathcal{I}}) = pass.$$

- *$\widehat{T}$ is complete for $\mathcal{A}_S$ with respect to $\sqsubseteq_{pioco}$, if for all input-enabled implementations $\mathcal{A}_{\mathcal{I}} \in pIOTS$ and sufficiently large $m \in \mathbb{N}$ it holds that*

$$\mathcal{A}_{\mathcal{I}} \not\sqsubseteq_{pioco} \mathcal{A}_S \Longrightarrow V_{\widehat{T}}^{\alpha, m} (\mathcal{A}_{\mathcal{I}}) = fail.$$

Soundness for a given $\alpha \in (0, 1)$ expresses that we have a $1 - \alpha$ chance that a correct system will pass the annotated suite for sufficiently large sample width m. This relates to false rejection of a correct hypothesis or correct implementation respectively.

Theorem 17 *(Soundness). Each annotated test for a pIOTS $\mathcal{A}_S$ is sound for every level of significance $\alpha \in (0, 1)$ wrt pioco.*

Completeness of a test suite is inherently a theoretic result. Since we allow loops, we require a test suite of infinite size. Moreover, there is still the chance of falsely accepting an erroneous implementation. However, this is bound from above by construction, and will decrease for bigger sample sizes (c.f. Definition 11).

Theorem 18 *(Completeness). The set of all annotated test cases for a specification $\mathcal{A}_S$ is complete for every level of significance $\alpha \in (0, 1)$ wrt pioco.*

5   Experimental Validation

To apply our framework, we implemented two well-known randomized communication protocols in Java, and tested these with the MBT tool JTorX [3]. The statistical verdicts were calculated in MatLab with a level of significance $\alpha = 0.1$.

5.1   Binary Exponential Backoff

The Binary Exponential Backoff protocol is a data transmission protocol between N hosts, trying to send information via one bus [19]. If two hosts send simultaneously, then their messages collide and they pick a new waiting time before trying again: after i collisions, they randomly choose a slot in $\{0, \dots 2^i - 1\}$ until the message gets through.

A sample of the protocol is shown in Table 1. Note that our specification of this protocol contains no non-determinism. Thus, calculations in this example are not subject to optimization to find the best trace distribution.

Table 1. A sample O of trace length $k = 5$ and depth (number of test runs) $m = 10^5$. Calculations yield $\chi^2 = 14.84 < 17.28 = \chi^2_{0.1}$, hence we accept the implementation.

#	Trace σ	n	$\approx mE_\sigma$	$[l_{0.1}, u_{0.1}]$	$\approx \frac{(n-mE_\sigma)^2}{mE_\sigma}$
1	collide! send! collide! send! send!	18656	18750	[18592, 18907]	0.47
2	collide! send! collide! send! collide!	18608	18750	[18592, 18907]	1.08
3	collide! collide! send! collide! send!	16473	16408	[16258, 16557]	0.26
4	collide! collide! send! send! collide!	12665	12500	[12366, 12633]	2.18
5	collide! send! collide! collide! send!	11096	10938	[10811, 11064]	2.28
6	collide! collide! collide! send! send!	8231	8203	[8091, 8314]	0.10
7	collide! collide! send! send! send!	6108	6250	[6152, 6347]	3.23
8	collide! collide! collide! send! collide!	2813	2734	[2667, 2800]	2.28
9	collide! collide! send! collide! collide!	2291	2344	[2282, 2405]	1.20
10	collide! send! collide! collide! collide!	1538	1563	[1512, 1613]	0.40
11	collide! collide! collide! collide! send!	1421	1465	[1416, 1513]	1.32
12	collide! collide! collide! collide! collide!	100	98	[85, 110]	0.04
				$\chi^2 =$	14.84
				Verdict:	*Accept*

n in Table 1 shows how many times each trace occurred and E_σ gives the expected value. The interval $[l_{0.1}, r_{0.1}]$ represents the 90 % confidence interval under the assumption of a normal distribution. It gives a rough idea how much values will deviate for the given level of confidence. However, we are interested in the multinomial deviation (i.e. less deviation of one trace allows higher deviation for another trace). For that purpose we use the χ^2 score, given by the sum of the entries of the last column. Calculation shows $\chi^2 = 14.84 < 17.28 = \chi^2_{0.1}$, which is the critical value for 11 degrees of freedom and $\alpha = 0.1$. Consequently, we accept the hypothesis of the probabilities being implemented correctly.

5.2 IEEE 1394 FireWire Root Contention Protocol

The IEEE 1394 FireWire Root Contention Protocol [37] elects a leader between two nodes via coin flips: If *head* comes up, node i picks a waiting time $fast_i \in [0.24\,\mu s, 0.26\,\mu s]$, if *tail* comes up, it waits $slow_i \in [0.57\,\mu s, 0.60\,\mu s]$. After the waiting time has elapsed, the node checks whether a message has arrived: if so, the node declares itself leader. If not, the node will send out a message itself, asking the other node to be the leader. Thus, the four outcomes of the coin flips are: $\{fast_1, fast_2\}$, $\{slow_1, slow_2\}$, $\{fast_1, slow_2\}$ and $\{slow_1, fast_2\}$. The protocol contains inherent non-determinism [37]; If different times were picked, the protocol always terminates. However, if equal times were picked, it may either elect a leader, or retry depending on the resolution of the non-determinism.

Table 2. A sample O of length $k = 5$ and depth $m = 10^5$ of the FireWire root contention protocol. Calculations of χ^2 are done after optimization in p.

#	Trace σ	$\approx m E_\sigma^D (p)$	Correct n_c	M_1 n_{M_1}	M_2 n_{M_2}	M_3 n_{M_3}	M_4 n_{M_4}
1	c1? slow$_1$! c2? slow$_2$! retry!	$6250 \cdot p$	3148	1113	3091	3055	3161
2	c1? slow$_1$! c2? slow$_2$! done!	$18750 \cdot p$	9393	3361	9047	9242	9329
3	c1? slow$_1$! c2! fast$_2$! done!	$25000 \cdot p$	12531	40507	18163	15129	12982
4	c1? fast$_1$! c2! fast$_2$! retry!	$8333 \cdot p$	4254	1467	4037	4066	4179
5	c1? fast$_1$! c2! fast$_2$! done!	$16667 \cdot p$	8227	3048	7858	8474	8444
6	c1? fast$_1$! c2? slow$_2$! done!	$25000 \cdot p$	12438	504	7918	10128	11867
7	c2? slow$_2$! c1? slow$_1$! retry!	$6250 \cdot (1-p)$	3073	1137	2961	3256	3135
8	c2? slow$_2$! c1? slow$_1$! done!	$18750 \cdot (1-p)$	9231	3427	9069	9456	9368
9	c2? slow$_2$! c1? fast$_1$! done!	$25000 \cdot (1-p)$	12657	447	8055	9685	11975
10	c2? fast$_2$! c1? fast$_1$! retry!	$8333 \cdot (1-p)$	4211	1466	4008	4131	4199
11	c2? fast$_2$! c1? fast$_1$! done!	$16667 \cdot (1-p)$	8335	2977	7969	8295	8312
12	c2? fast$_2$! c1? slow$_1$! done!	$25000 \cdot (1-p)$	12502	40546	17824	15083	13049
		$p_{opt} \approx$	0.499	0.498	0.502	0.500	0.499
		$\chi^2 \approx$	9.34	169300	8175	2185	99.22
		Verdict	*Accept*	*Reject*	*Reject*	*Reject*	*Reject*

Table 2 shows the recorded traces, where c1? and c2? denote coin1 and coin2 respectively. We have tested five implementations: Implementation *Correct* implements fair coins, while the mutants M_1, M_2, M_3 and M_4 were subjects to probabilistic deviations giving advantage to the second node, i.e. $P(fast_1) = P(slow_2) = 0.1$, $P(fast_1) = P(slow_2) = 0.4$, $P(fast_1) = P(slow_2) = 0.45$ and $P(fast_1) = P(slow_2) = 0.49$ for mutants 1, 2, 3 and 4 respectively. The expected value E_σ^D depends on resolving one non-determinism by varying p (which coin was flipped first). Note that other non-determinism was not subject to optimization, but immediately clear by trace frequencies. The calculated χ^2 scores are based on an optimized value for p for each sample and compared to the critical value $\chi_{0.1}^2 = 17.28$ resulting in the verdicts shown.

6 Conclusions and Future Work

We defined a sound and complete framework to test probabilistic systems, defined a conformance relation in the *ioco* tradition called *pioco* and showed how to derive probabilistic tests of a requirements model. Verdicts that handle the functional and statistical behaviour are assigned after a test is applied. We showed that the correct verdict can be assigned up to arbitrary precision by setting a level of significance and sufficiently large sample size.

Future work should focus on the practical aspects of our theory: tool support, larger case studies and more powerful statistical methods to increase efficiency.

References

1. Al-Karaki, J.N., Kamal, A.E.: Routing techniques in wireless sensor networks: a survey. IEEE Wireless Commun. **11**(6), 6–28 (2004)
2. Beaumont, M.A., Zhang, W., Balding, D.J.: Approximate bayesian computation in population genetics. Genetics **162**(4), 2025–2035 (2002)
3. Belinfante, A.: JTorX: a tool for on-line model-driven test derivation and execution. In: Esparza, J., Majumdar, R. (eds.) TACAS 2010. LNCS, vol. 6015, pp. 266–270. Springer, Heidelberg (2010)
4. Beyer, M., Dulz, W.: Scenario-based statistical testing of quality of service requirements. In: Leue, S., Systä, T.J. (eds.) Scenarios: Models, Transformations and Tools. LNCS, vol. 3466, pp. 152–173. Springer, Heidelberg (2005)
5. Bohnenkamp, H.C., Belinfante, A.: Timed testing with TorX. In: Fitzgerald, J.S., Hayes, I.J., Tarlecki, A. (eds.) FM 2005. LNCS, vol. 3582, pp. 173–188. Springer, Heidelberg (2005)
6. Böhr, F.: Model based statistical testing of embedded systems. In: IEEE 4th International Conference on Software Testing, Verification and Validation Workshops (ICSTW), pp. 18–25 (2011)
7. Bozga, M., David, A., Hartmanns, A., Hermanns, H., Larsen, K.G., Legay, A., Tretmans, J.: State-of-the-art tools and techniques for quantitative modeling and analysis of embedded systems. In: DATE, pp. 370–375 (2012)
8. Briones, Laura Brandán, Brinksma, Ed: A test generation framework for *quiescent* real-time systems. In: Grabowski, Jens, Nielsen, Brian (eds.) FATES 2004. LNCS, vol. 3395, pp. 64–78. Springer, Heidelberg (2005)
9. Cheung, L., Stoelinga, M., Vaandrager, F.: A testing scenario for probabilistic automata. J. ACM **54**(6), 45 (2007). Article No. 29
10. Choi, S.G., Dachman-Soled, D., Malkin, T., Wee, H.: Improved non-committing encryption with applications to adaptively secure protocols. In: Matsui, M. (ed.) ASIACRYPT 2009. LNCS, vol. 5912, pp. 287–302. Springer, Heidelberg (2009)
11. Cleaveland, R., Dayar, Z., Smolka, S.A., Yuen, S.: Testing preorders for probabilistic processes. Inform. Comput. **154**(2), 93–148 (1999)
12. Cohn, D.L.: Measure Theory. Birkhäuser, Boston (1980)
13. Deng, Y., Hennessy, M., van Glabbeek, R.J., Morgan, C.: Characterising Testing Preorders for Finite Probabilistic Processes. CoRR (2008)
14. Gerhold, M., Stoelinga, M.: Ioco Theory for Probabilistic Automata. In: Proceedings of the Tenth Workshop on MBT, pp. 23–40 (2015)

15. van Glabbeek, R.J., Smolka, S.A., Steffen, B., Tofts, C.: Reactive, Generative, and Stratified Models of Probabilistic Processes, pp. 130–141. IEEE Computer Society Press (1990)
16. Hierons, R.M., Núñez, M.: Testing probabilistic distributed systems. In: Hatcliff, J., Zucca, E. (eds.) FMOODS 2010, Part II. LNCS, vol. 6117, pp. 63–77. Springer, Heidelberg (2010)
17. Hierons, R.M., Merayo, M.G.: Mutation testing from probabilistic and stochastic finite state machines. J. Syst. Softw. **82**, 1804–1818 (2009)
18. Hwang, I., Cavalli, A.R.: Testing a probabilistic FSM using interval estimation. Comput. Netw. **54**, 1108–1125 (2010)
19. Jeannet, B., D'Argenio, P.R., Larsen, K.G.: Rapture: a tool for verifying markov decision processes. In: Tools Day (2002)
20. Kwiatkowska, M., Norman, G., Parker, D.: PRISM: probabilistic symbolic model checker. In: Field, T., Harrison, P.G., Bradley, J., Harder, U. (eds.) TOOLS 2002. LNCS, vol. 2324, pp. 200–204. Springer, Heidelberg (2002)
21. Larsen, K.G., Skou, A.: Bisimulation Through Probabilistic Testing, pp. 344–352. ACM Press (1989)
22. Larsen, K.G., Mikucionis, M., Nielsen, B.: Online testing of real-time systems using UPPAAL. In: Grabowski, J., Nielsen, B. (eds.) FATES 2004. LNCS, vol. 3395, pp. 79–94. Springer, Heidelberg (2005)
23. Marsan, M.A., Balbo, G., Conte, G., Donatelli, S., Franceschinis, G.: Modelling with Generalized Stochastic Petri Nets. Wiley, New York (1994)
24. Merayo, M.G., Hwang, I., Núñez, M., Cavalli, A.: A statistical approach to test stochastic and probabilistic systems. In: Breitman, K., Cavalcanti, A. (eds.) ICFEM 2009. LNCS, vol. 5885, pp. 186–205. Springer, Heidelberg (2009)
25. Nie, J., Demmel, J., Gu, M.: Global minimization of rational functions and the nearest GCDs. J. Global Optim. **40**(4), 697–718 (2008)
26. Paige, B., Wood, F.: A Compilation Target for Probabilistic Programming Languages. CoRR arXiv:1403.0504 (2014)
27. Peters, H., Knieke, C., Brox, O., Jauns-Seyfried, S., Krämer, M., Schulze, A.: A test-driven approach for model-based development of powertrain functions. In: Cantone, G., Marchesi, M. (eds.) XP 2014. LNBIP, vol. 179, pp. 294–301. Springer, Heidelberg (2014)
28. Pfeffer, A.: Practical probabilistic programming. In: Frasconi, P., Lisi, F.A. (eds.) ILP 2010. LNCS, vol. 6489, pp. 2–3. Springer, Heidelberg (2011)
29. Prowell, S.J.: Computations for Markov Chain Usage Models. Technical Report (2003)
30. Puterman, M.L.: Markov Decision Processes: Discrete Stochastic Dynamic Programming. Wiley, New York (2014)
31. Remke, A., Stoelinga, M. (eds.): Stochastic Model Checking. LNCS, vol. 8453. Springer, Heidelberg (2014)
32. Russell, N., Moore, R.: Explicit modelling of state occupancy in hidden markov models for automatic speech recognition. In: Acoustics, Speech, and Signal Processing, IEEE International Conference on ICASSP 1985, vol. 10, pp. 5–8 (1985)
33. Segala, R.: Modeling and verification of randomized distributed real-time systems. Ph.D. thesis, Cambridge, MA, USA (1995)
34. Segala, R.: Testing Probabilistic Automata. In: Sassone, V., Montanari, U. (eds.) CONCUR 1996. LNCS, vol. 1119, pp. 299–314. Springer, Heidelberg (1996)
35. Sen, K., Viswanathan, M., Agha, G.: Statistical model checking of black-box probabilistic systems. In: Alur, R., Peled, D.A. (eds.) CAV 2004. LNCS, vol. 3114, pp. 202–215. Springer, Heidelberg (2004)

36. Sen, K., Viswanathan, M., Agha, G.: On statistical model checking of stochastic systems. In: Etessami, K., Rajamani, S.K. (eds.) CAV 2005. LNCS, vol. 3576, pp. 266–280. Springer, Heidelberg (2005)

37. Stoelinga, M., Vaandrager, F.W.: Root contention in IEEE 1394. In: Katoen, J.-P. (ed.) AMAST-ARTS 1999, ARTS 1999, and AMAST-WS 1999. LNCS, vol. 1601, pp. 53–74. Springer, Heidelberg (1999)

38. Stoelinga, M.: Alea jacta est: verification of probabilistic, real-time and parametric systems. Ph.D. thesis, Radboud University of Nijmegen (2002)

39. Stokkink, W.G.J., Timmer, M., Stoelinga, M.I.A.: Divergent quiescent transition systems. In: Veanes, M., Viganò, L. (eds.) TAP 2013. LNCS, vol. 7942, pp. 214–231. Springer, Heidelberg (2013)

40. Tretmans, J.: Test generation with inputs, outputs and repetitive quiescence. Softw. Concepts Tools **17**(3), 103–120 (1996)

41. Tretmans, J.: Model based testing with labelled transition systems. In: Hierons, R.M., Bowen, J.P., Harman, M. (eds.) FORTEST. LNCS, vol. 4949, pp. 1–38. Springer, Heidelberg (2008)

42. Walton, G.H., Poore, J.H., Trammell, C.J.: Statistical Testing of Software Based on a Usage Model. Softw. Pract. Exper. **25**(1), 97–108 (1995)

43. Whittaker, J.A., Thomason, M.G.: A markov chain model for statistical software testing. IEEE Trans. Softw. Eng. **20**(10), 812–824 (1994)

An Iterative Decision-Making Scheme for Markov Decision Processes and Its Application to Self-adaptive Systems

Guoxin Su[1(✉)], Taolue Chen[2], Yuan Feng[3], David S. Rosenblum[1], and P.S. Thiagarajan[4]

[1] School of Computing, National University of Singapore, Singapore, Singapore
guoxinsu@gmail.com
[2] Department of Computer Science, Middlesex University London, London, UK
[3] Centre for Quantum Computation and Intelligent Systems,
University of Technology Sydney, Sydney, Australia
[4] Laboratory of Systems Pharmacology, Harvard Medical School, Boston, USA

Abstract. Software is often governed by and thus adapts to phenomena that occur at runtime. Unlike traditional decision problems, where a decision-making model is determined for reasoning, the adaptation logic of such software is concerned with empirical data and is subject to practical constraints. We present an *Iterative Decision-Making Scheme* (IDMS) that infers both point and interval estimates for the undetermined transition probabilities in a Markov Decision Process (MDP) based on sampled data, and iteratively computes a confidently optimal scheduler from a given finite subset of schedulers. The most important feature of IDMS is the flexibility for adjusting the criterion of confident optimality and the sample size within the iteration, leading to a tradeoff between accuracy, data usage and computational overhead. We apply IDMS to an existing self-adaptation framework Rainbow and conduct a case study using a Rainbow system to demonstrate the flexibility of IDMS.

1 Introduction

Software is often governed by and thus adapts to phenomena that occur at runtime [22]. One typical example is the control software of autonomous systems, such as driverless vehicles. Because the occurrence of runtime phenomena is asynchronous with respect to the flow of the application logic, because not all information about the phenomena is available at the design time, and because the specification of the adaptive behavior may evolve over time, it is advantageous to gather the complex adaptation logic into a component separated from

This work was partially supported by the Singapore Ministry of Education (Grant Nos. R-252-000-458-133 and MOE2015-T2-1-137), the Australian Research Council (Grant Nos. DP130102764 and DP160101652), the National Natural Science Foundation of China (Grant Nos. 61428208 and 61502260), the CAS/SAFEA International Partnership Program for Creative Research Team, and an overseas grant from the State Key Laboratory of Novel Software Technology at Nanjing University.

© Springer-Verlag Berlin Heidelberg 2016
P. Stevens and A. Wąsowski (Eds.): FASE 2016, LNCS 9633, pp. 269–286, 2016.
DOI: 10.1007/978-3-662-49665-7_16

the application logic. In contrast to traditional decision problems where a decision model, such as a Markov Decision Process (MDP) [27], is determined for reasoning, the adaptation logic of autonomous systems is governed by empirical data and is subject to practical constraints. In many situations, one has to sacrifice the optimality of an adaptive solution to a certain extent in order to satisfy various Quality-of-Service (QoS) constraints.

Consider a Web system that provides news content services. At some moment, the system may detect high latency of content delivery. Suppose that the system can lower the content fidelity (such as delivering multimedia contents in the text mode) and/or increase the server pool size, and that the benefits or costs of these operations are measured quantitatively. Further, to achieve more sophisticated effects, operations can be combined to form a strategy. For example, one simple strategy could be the following: Once "high latency" is detected, increase the number of Virtual Machine (VM) instances by one; if "high latency" persists, switch from the multimedia mode to the text mode. Because multiple strategies built into the adaptation logic may be triggered by the same condition, an additional mechanism is required to select one of them.

A key challenge of the strategy selection for the Web system is that some probability parameters, such as successful chances of operations, are not fixed. For example, if the VM number is increased by one, the probability that latency will drop below the threshold may increase, but it still has to be estimated based on runtime data. While the idealized goal is to select an optimal strategy, it is important to take into account the practical constraints. For example, obsolete data no longer reflects the current environmental situation; the time frame of data sampling may be constrained by the tolerance of adaptation delay; the sampling frequency may be restricted because of its performance overhead on the network; and last but not the least, the adaptation should not downgrade the functional performance of the system by consuming too much computational capacity (e.g., CPU and RAM). In short, besides decision accuracy, runtime decision-making has to address the limitation of data and computation resource.

The above adaptation model for the Web system can be formalized as an MDP in which actions represent operations and schedulers represent strategies. The runtime data are stored in a data structure (i.e., a set of integer matrices) for estimating the transition probabilities of the MDP. Therefore, the problem of strategy selection is an instance of the general problem of minimizing the (expected) cumulative cost for an MDP with empirically determined transition probabilities and a given subset of schedulers. Despite this problem is well understood in the theory of MDPs [27], our first contribution is an *Iterative Decision-Making Scheme* (IDMS) that supports a trade-off between three important metrics, namely, accuracy, data usage and computational overhead. The basic idea of IDMS is as follows:

1. We infer both point and interval estimates of transition probabilities for the MDP decision model based on the data structure for runtime data.
2. Next, we compute a scheduler that minimizes the cumulative cost for a given reachability problem.

3. We then determine whether this scheduler meets a criterion called *confident optimality*. If yes, or if the maximal number of iterative steps is reached, the iteration terminates; otherwise, the iteration returns to data sampling.

We formalize three metrics for IDMS: (i) the probability that a confidently optimal scheduler is truly optimal, namely accuracy; (ii) the average sample size of the iteration, which is a direct metric of data usage; and (iii) the average time of iteration, which measures computational overhead conveniently. The trade-off among these three metrics is realized by adjusting the criterion of confident optimality and the sample size during the iteration. The core method of IDMS is a value-iteration algorithm developed from probabilistic model checking [19].

The second contribution of this paper is an application of IDMS to self-adaptive systems. Several high-level frameworks and approaches based on probabilistic model checking have been proposed to aid the design of self-adaptive systems, but with emphasis on different aspects of the adaptation [3,4,18,20,23]. However none of these works address the problem of making the aforementioned tradeoff in the adaptation. We demonstrate that IDMS can be naturally embedded into the Rainbow framework [11] which employs a standard, point-valued MDP as its decision model, and thus extends the adaptation function of the latter. We present a case study on a Rainbow system and the empirical evidence that demonstrates the flexibility of IDMS.

The remainder of the paper is organized as follows. Section 2 presents the formal models and core method. Section 3 presents the IDMS scheme. Section 4 describes the application to self-adaptive systems. Section 5 presents the case study. Section 6 reports the related work. Section 7 concludes the paper.

2 Formal Model and Value-Iteration Method

In this section, we present our formal models and value-iteration method. The position of our method in the state of the art is discussed in Sect. 6.

Definition 1 (MDP). *An MDP is a tuple $\mathcal{M} = (S, Act, \mathcal{P}, \alpha, C)$ where*

- *S is a finite, non-empty state space,*
- *Act is a finite non-empty set of actions,*
- *α is the initial distribution over S,*
- *$\mathcal{P} = \{\mathcal{P}_a\}_{a \in Act}$ is a family of transition probability matrices indexed by $a \in Act$, and*
- *$C : S \to \mathbf{R}_{\geq 0}$ is a cost function.*

We require that, for each $a \in Act$ and $s \in S$, $\mathcal{P}_a[s,t] \geq 0$ for all $t \in S$ and $\sum_{t \in S} \mathcal{P}_a[s,t] \in \{0,1\}$. We say action a is enabled at s if $\sum_{t \in S} \mathcal{P}_a[s,t] = 1$.

Schedulers play a crucial role in the analysis of MDPs. For our purposes, it suffices to consider *simple* schedulers, in which for each state s, the scheduler fixes one of the enabled actions at s and selects the same action every time when the system resides in s. Formally, a simple scheduler is a function $\sigma : S \to Act$

such that $\sigma(s)$ is one of the actions enabled at state s. In our setting, instead of considering the whole set of schedulers, we work only with a (finite) subset of simple schedulers Σ specified by the user. A *path* in $\mathcal{M}$ under σ is an infinite sequence of states $\rho = s_0 s_1 \cdots$ such that, for all $i \geq 0$, $\mathcal{P}_a[s_i, s_{i+1}] > 0$ for $a = \sigma(s_i)$. Let $Path_{\mathcal{M},\sigma}$ be the set of paths in $\mathcal{M}$ under σ. Let $Path_{\mathcal{M},\sigma}(s)$ be the subset of paths that start from s. Let $Pr_{\mathcal{M},\sigma}$ be the standard *probability distribution* over $Path_{\mathcal{M},\sigma}$ as defined in the literature [1, Chap. 10].

The *expected cumulative cost*, or simply *cumulative cost*, of reaching a set $G \subseteq S$ of *goal* states (called G-states hereafter) in $\mathcal{M}$ under σ, denoted $C_{\mathcal{M},\sigma}(G)$, is defined as follows: First, let $C_{\mathcal{M},\sigma}(s, G)$ be the expected value of random variable $X : Path_{\mathcal{M},\sigma}(s) \to \mathbf{R}_{\geq 0}$ such that (i) if $s \in G$ then $X(\rho) = 0$, (ii) if $\rho[i] \notin G$ for all $i \geq 0$ then $X(\rho) = \infty$, and (iii) otherwise $X(\rho) = \sum_{i=0}^{n-1} C(s_i)$ where $s_n \in G$ and $s_j \notin G$ for all $j < n$. Then, let $C_{\mathcal{M},\sigma}(G) = \sum_{s \in S} \alpha(s) \cdot C_{\mathcal{M},\sigma}(s, G)$.

By the above definitions, for those states which do *not* reach the goal states almost surely (viz. with probability less than 1), the cumulative cost is ∞. We remark that other definitions on the costs of paths not reaching the goal states do exist and can be found in [8]. However, they are more involved and are not needed in the current setting. In order to compute the cumulative cost, we first have to identify the set of states $S_{=1}$ from which the probability to reach the goal states in G is 1. This can be done by a standard graph analysis [1, Chap. 10]. Next, we solve the following system of linear equations with variables $(x_s)_{s \in S_{=1}}$:

$$
\begin{aligned}
x_s &= 0 && \text{if } s \in G \\
x_s &= C(s) + \sum_{t \in S_{=1}} \mathcal{P}_a[s, t] \cdot x_t && \text{if } s \notin G
\end{aligned}
\tag{1}
$$

where $a = \sigma(s)$. When the scheduler is fixed, the MDP is reduced to a discrete-time Markov chain (DTMC) and hence solving (1) is straightforward. One can employ standard Jacobi or Gauss-Seidel itertaion methods to compute the least fixpoint [31]. In detail, one starts from $\boldsymbol{x}^{(0)}$ where $x_s^{(0)} = 0$ for all $s \in S_{=1}$, and computes $x_s^{(n+1)} = C(s) + \sum_{t \in S_{=1}} \mathcal{P}_a[s, t] \cdot x_t^{(n)}$ if $s \notin G$ and 0 otherwise, until $\max_{s \in S} |x_s^{(n+1)} - x_s^{(n)}| < \epsilon$ for some predetermined $\epsilon > 0$. In practice, and especially in probabilistic verification, this is usually more efficient than the Gaussian elimination [19].

Interval-valued MDPs (IMDP) are MDPs where some of the transition probabilities are specified as real intervals.

Definition 2 (IMDP). *An IMDP is a tuple* $\mathcal{M}^I = (S, Act, \mathcal{P}^+, \mathcal{P}^-, \alpha, C)$ *where*

- *S, Act, α and C are defined the same as in Definition 1,*
- *$\mathcal{P}^+ = \{\mathcal{P}_a^+\}_{a \in Act}$, $\mathcal{P}^- = \{\mathcal{P}_a^-\}_{a \in Act}$ are two families of nonnegative matrices indexed by $a \in Act$, giving the upper and lower bounds of transition probabilities respectively. Further, for each $a \in Act$, $\mathcal{P}_a^+$ and $\mathcal{P}_a^-$ have the same corresponding 0- and 1-entries.*

With $\mathcal{M}^I = (S, Act, \mathcal{P}^+, \mathcal{P}^-, \alpha, C)$ we associate a set of MDPs $[\![\mathcal{M}^I]\!]$ such that $\mathcal{M} = (S, Act, \mathcal{P}, \alpha, C) \in [\![\mathcal{M}^I]\!]$ if and only if for each $a \in Act$, $\mathcal{P}_a^- \leq \mathcal{P}_a \leq \mathcal{P}_a^+$. where $\leq$ is interpreted entry-wise. We call an $\mathcal{M} \in [\![\mathcal{M}^I]\!]$ an *instance* of $\mathcal{M}^I$.

Given an IMDP $\mathcal{M}^I$ and a simple scheduler σ, since the possible cumulative cost of reaching G-states is in the form of an interval, we are interested in the *bounds* of such an interval. The *minimum* cumulative cost of reaching G-states in $\mathcal{M}^I$ under σ is

$$C_{\mathcal{M}^I,\sigma}^{\min}(G) = \inf_{M \in [\![\mathcal{M}^I]\!]} C_{\mathcal{M},\sigma}(G).$$

Because the *maximum* cumulative cost $C_{\mathcal{M}^I,\sigma}^{\max}(G)$ is symmetrical to the minimum case, in the remainder of this section, we mainly deal with the latter.

To this end, as before we first identify states that reach the goal states G almost surely (under σ) and are denoted by $S_{=1}$. Owing to the assumption made on IMDPs in Definition 2, this can be done by graph-analysis as on MDPs $\mathcal{M}^I$. For those states not in $S_{=1}$, the minimal cost is ∞ according to our convention. We then consider the following Bellman equation over the variables $(x_s)_{s \in S_{=1}}$:

$$
\begin{aligned}
x_s &= 0 && \text{if } s \in G \\
x_s &= \min_{\mathcal{P}_a^- \le \mathcal{P}_a \le \mathcal{P}_a^+} \{C(s) + \sum_{t \in S_{=1}} \mathcal{P}_a[s,t] \cdot x_t\} && \text{if } s \notin G
\end{aligned}
\tag{2}
$$

where $a = \sigma(s)$. Note that $\mathcal{P}_a$ is required to be a transition probability matrix. Let $\boldsymbol{x} = (x_s)_{s \in S_{=1}}$ be the *least* fixpoint of (2). We easily obtain:

Proposition 1. $C_{\mathcal{M}^I,\sigma}^{\min}(G) = \sum_{s \in S} \alpha(s)x_s.$

To solve (2), there are essentially two approaches. The first one is to reduce it to linear programming (LP). However, despite theoretically elegant, this is not practical for real-life cases. Instead, we apply the second approach, i.e., the value-iteration method. For each iteration, the crucial part is to compute

$$\min_{\mathcal{P}_a^- \le \mathcal{P}_a \le \mathcal{P}_a^+} \left\{C(s) + \sum_{t \in S_{=1}} \mathcal{P}_a[s,t] \cdot x_t\right\}$$

for a given $\boldsymbol{x}$. This problem can be reduced to a standard linear program. Indeed, for each s, introduce variables $(y_t)_{t \in S}$ and consider the problem:

minimize $C(s) + \sum_{t \in S_{=1}} y_t x_t$

subject to $\sum_{t \in S_{=1}} y_t = 1$ and $\mathcal{P}_a^-[s,t'] \le y_{t'} \le \mathcal{P}_a^+[s,t']$ for all $t' \in S_{=1}$.

This can be solved efficiently via off-shelf LP solvers (note that here x_t's and a are given). Hence each iteration takes polynomial time. We also remark that the LP here admits a very simple structure and only contains at most $|S|$ variables (and usually much less for practical examples), while the direct approach (based on LP as well) requires at least $|S|^2 + |S|$ variables and is considerably more involved. Although it might take exponentially many iterations to reach the least fixpoint, in practice one usually sets a stopping criteria such as $\max_{s \in S} |x_s^{(n+1)} - x_s^{(n)}| < \epsilon$ for a fixed error bound $\epsilon > 0$.

Let $C^{\text{dif}}_{\mathcal{M}^I,\sigma}(G) = C^{\text{max}}_{\mathcal{M}^I,\sigma}(G) - C^{\text{min}}_{\mathcal{M}^I,\sigma}(G)$. Because $\mathcal{M}$, $\mathcal{M}^I$ and G are clear in the context, to simplify notations we make the following abbreviations:

FULLY-SPELLED	$C_{\mathcal{M},\sigma}(G)$	$C^{\text{min}}_{\mathcal{M}^I,\sigma}(G)$	$C^{\text{max}}_{\mathcal{M}^I,\sigma}(G)$	$C^{\text{dif}}_{\mathcal{M}^I,\sigma}(G)$
ABBREVIATED	C_σ	C^{min}_σ	C^{max}_σ	C^{dif}_σ

3   Iterative Decision-Making Scheme

In this section, we present main stages and techniques of IDMS and describe the realization of trade-offs between the three metrics.

3.1   IDMS Preview and Example

IDMS is an iterative process that contains one pre-stage and five runtime stages (i.e., Stage 1 to 5), as depicted in Fig. 1. The pre-stage builds up a parametric MDP with transition probability parameters in the design time. At runtime Stage 1 collects data samples and Stage 2 infers point and interval estimates based on the samples. By instantiating the parameters with the point and interval estimates, Stage 3 builds up a (concrete) MDP and an IMDP. Stage 4 attempts to compute a confidently optimal scheduler. Then the process either moves to Stage 5 where a decision is made or goes back to Stage 1. The process terminates when either a confidently optimal scheduler is returned, or the maximal time of iteration (namely the maximal number of steps within the iteration) is reached. Note as the decision making may need to be repeated periodically at runtime, Stage 5 may be followed by Stage 1.

A parametric MDP example $\mathcal{M}_{eg}(\boldsymbol{\theta})$ is described in Fig. 2. The state space of $\mathcal{M}_{eg}(\boldsymbol{\theta})$ is $\{s_0, \ldots, s_7, s_G\}$ with s_0 being the only initial state (i.e., the initial distribution assigns 1 to s_0 and 0 to other states) and s_G being the only goal state. The dashed arrows are probabilistic transitions, labeled by parameters $\boldsymbol{\theta} = (\theta_1, \ldots, \theta_5)$. The solid arrows are non-probabilistic transitions (or, equivalently, transitions with the fixed probability 1). The wavy arrows represent non-deterministic transitions, with a and b being two actions. For $\mathcal{M}_{eg}(\boldsymbol{\theta})$, the two actions induce two schedulers, denoted σ_a and σ_b, respectively. States of $\mathcal{M}_{eg}(\boldsymbol{\theta})$ are associated with costs ranging from 0 to 2.

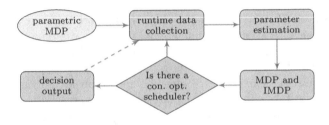

Fig. 1. Pre-stage and runtime stages of IDMS

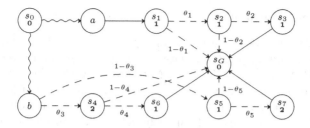

Fig. 2. A parametric MDP example $\mathcal{M}_{eg}(\boldsymbol{\theta})$

3.2 Data Structure and Parameter Estimation

IDMS does not presume a particular method for collecting runtime data but it stores them in a specific data structure, namely a set of non-negative integer matrices that are related to schedulers of the parametric MDP. The integer in each entry represents the number of times that the corresponding transition is recorded in the sampling time frame. For example, the two integer matrices related to σ_a and σ_b of $\mathcal{M}_{eg}(\boldsymbol{\theta})$ are as follows:

$$M_a : \begin{array}{c} \\ s_1 \\ s_2 \end{array} \begin{array}{cccc} s_1 & s_2 & s_3 & s_G \\ \begin{bmatrix} 0 & N_{1,2} & 0 & N_{1,G} \\ 0 & 0 & N_{2,3} & N_{2,G} \end{bmatrix} \end{array} \qquad M_b : \begin{array}{c} \\ s_0 \\ s_4 \\ s_5 \end{array} \begin{array}{ccccc} s_4 & s_5 & s_6 & s_7 & s_G \\ \begin{bmatrix} N_{0,4} & N_{0,5} & 0 & 0 & \\ 0 & 0 & N_{4,5} & 0 & N_{4,G} \\ 0 & 0 & 0 & N_{5,7} & N_{5,G} \end{bmatrix} \end{array}$$

where $N_{\sharp,\natural} > 0$, with $\sharp$ and $\natural$ denoting (some) elements in $\{0,\ldots,7,G\}$, are integer variables. $N_{\sharp,\natural}$ is increased by 1 (i.e., $N_{\sharp,\natural} \leftarrow N_{\sharp,\natural}+1$) if a transition from $s_\sharp$ to $s_\natural$ is newly observed. Note that zero entries in M_a and M_b remain unchanged for all time, because according to the structural specification of $\mathcal{M}_{eg}(\boldsymbol{\theta})$, the correspondent transitions are impossible to occur.

The data structure is used to estimate parameters in the parametric MDP. IDMS adopts two forms of estimation, namely point estimation and interval estimation, which we illustrate using M_a. Note that M_a is used to estimate parameters θ_1 and θ_2. For point estimation, θ_1 is estimated as the numerical value $N_{1,2}/(N_{1,2}+N_{1,G})$ and θ_2 is estimated as $N_{2,3}/(N_{2,3}+N_{2,G})$. For interval estimation, IDMS assumes that θ_1 (resp., θ_2) is the mean of a Bernoulli distribution and $(N_{1,2}, N_{1,G})$ (resp., $(N_{2,3}, N_{2,G})$) forms a random sample of the distribution. In other words, $(N_{1,2}, N_{1,G})$ denote a random sample containing $N_{1,2}$ copies of 1 and $N_{1,G}$ copies of 0, and $(N_{2,3}, N_{2,G})$ has a similar meaning. Therefore, one can employ the standard statistical inference method to derive a confidence interval for θ_1 and one for θ_2. By the laws of large numbers, if $N_{1,2} + N_{1,G}$ (resp., $N_{2,3} + N_{2,G}$) increases then the width of the resulted confidence interval for θ_1 (resp., θ_2) likely decreases (when the confidence level is fixed).

3.3   Confident Optimality

By instantiating the transition probability parameters in the parametric MDP with the corresponding point estimates and interval estimates, one obtains a concrete MDP $\mathcal{M}$ and an IMDP $\mathcal{M}^I$. Note that if $[p, q] \subset [0, 1]$ instantiates a parameter θ then, equivalently, $[1 - q, 1 - p]$ instantiates $1 - \theta$. Clearly, $\mathcal{M}$ and $\mathcal{M}^I$ share the same state space S, initial distribution α and cost function C. Moreover, $\mathcal{M}$ is an instance of $\mathcal{M}^I$, namely, $\mathcal{M} \in [\![\mathcal{M}^I]\!]$. From now on, for given $\mathcal{M}$ and $\mathcal{M}^I$, we always assume $\mathcal{M} \in [\![\mathcal{M}^I]\!]$. A key decision-making criterion in IDMS is formalized as follows:

Definition 3 (Confident Optimality). *Given* $\mathcal{M}$, $\mathcal{M}^I$, $G \subseteq S$ *of goal states and a finite nonempty subset* Σ *of schedulers,* $\sigma^* \in \Sigma$ *is* confidently optimal *if, for all* $\sigma \in \Sigma \backslash \sigma^*$, *the following two conditions hold:*

$$C_{\sigma^*} \leq C_\sigma \text{ and}$$
$$C_{\sigma^*}^{\max} \leq C_\sigma^{\min} + \gamma \cdot C_{\sigma^*}^{\mathrm{dif}} \quad \text{where } \gamma \geq 0. \tag{3}$$

In words, a scheduler σ^* in the given scheduler subset Σ of $\mathcal{M}$ (or, equivalently, $\mathcal{M}^I$) is confidently optimal if for *all other* schedulers σ in Σ (i.e., $\sigma \neq \sigma^*$):

- The cumulative cost (of reaching G-states) in $\mathcal{M}$ under σ^* is not larger than the cumulative cost in $\mathcal{M}$ under σ;
- The $(1/\gamma)$-portion of the difference between the maximum cumulative cost in $\mathcal{M}^I$ under σ^* and the minimum cumulative cost in $\mathcal{M}^I$ under σ is not larger than the maximum-minimum difference of cumulative cost in $\mathcal{M}^I$ under σ^*.

A correct illustrative example is presented in the latter text. It is noteworthy that, different from an standard MDP problem, a subset of schedulers is explicitly given in our definition.

The parameter γ, which is specified by the user, has the function of adjusting the criterion of confident optimality. A confidently optimal scheduler may not exist for the given MDP and IMDP; in some rare case, there may be more than one confidently optimal schedulers. Note that if a sufficiently large value for γ is selected, then the second condition in Eq. (3) is guaranteed to be true. If so, the definition is degenerated to the standard definition of optimal cumulative costs for MDPs with point-valued transition probabilities.

Given $\mathcal{M}, \mathcal{M}^I, G, \Sigma, \gamma$, the following procedure decides whether a confidently optimal scheduler σ^* exists and returns σ^* if it exists:

1. Compute C_σ for all $\sigma \in \Sigma$, and compute $\Sigma_1 \subseteq \Sigma$ such that $C_{\sigma_1} = \min_{\sigma \in \Sigma} C_\sigma$ if and only if $\sigma_1 \in \Sigma_1$.
2. Compute $C_{\sigma_1}^{\max}$ for all $\sigma_1 \in \Sigma_1$, and compute $C_\sigma^{\min}$ for all $\sigma \in \Sigma$.
3. If there is $\sigma^* \in \Sigma_1$ such that $C_{\sigma^*}^{\max} \leq C_\sigma^{\min} + \gamma \cdot C_{\sigma^*}^{\mathrm{dif}}$ where $\sigma \neq \sigma^*$, then return σ^*; otherwise, return "no confidently optimal scheduler".

The procedure relies on the core method of value-iteration presented in Sect. 2. The computational complexity of is dependent on the core value-iteration method and the size of Σ. Note that although the number of *all* schedulers in an MDP increases exponentially as the size of the MDP increases, in our case a *specific* subset of schedulers Σ is predefined by the model builder. If we suppose the value-iteration takes constant time (e.g., the model is fixed), then the time complexity of the procedure is linear in the size of Σ.

We present an example to explain how IDMS is affected by γ and the sample size. Suppose after instantiating $\boldsymbol{\theta}$ of $\mathcal{M}_{eg}(\boldsymbol{\theta})$ with point estimates and interval estimates, the cumulative cost intervals for schedulers σ_a and σ_b are $[l_1, u_1]$ and $[l_2, u_2]$, respectively. The positions of l_1, u_1, l_2 and u_2 are illustrated on the left side of the following drawing (where $0 \le p < q$).

If $u_1 \le l_2 + \gamma(u_1 - l_1)$, the above procedure returns σ_a. But if $u_1 > l_2 + \gamma(u_1 - l_1)$, neither σ_a nor σ_b is confidently optimal and so the procedure returns "no confidently optimal scheduler". If one lowers the value γ and/or increases the sample size, the computed cost intervals usually shrink, as depicted on the right side of the above drawing. Then there is a higher probability that a confidently optimal scheduler (namely σ_a) is returned from the procedure and the iteration of IDMS terminates.

3.4 Metrics and Tradeoff

One main advantage of IDMS is the flexibility that enables a tradeoff between the three important metrics for practical, especially runtime, decision-making. The three metrics are accuracy of the decision, data usage for making the decision and computational overhead on the runtime system. Because random sampling is involved in IDMS, under a specific scheduler of an MDP and an IMDP, the cumulative cost and the minimum/maximum cumulative costs (of reaching the goal states) are uncertain. Therefore, a confidently optimal scheduler may be decided at each iterative step with a certain probability. Further, a confidently optimal scheduler may not be the truly optimal one, which is defined based on the unknown real values of the transition probability parameters in the abstract MDP. In view of this, we define the three metrics as follows:

- Accuracy is the probability that a confidently optimal scheduler is optimal.
- Data usage is the average size of sampled data used in the iteration.
- Computational overhead is measured by the average iteration time (namely, the average number of iterative steps).

Ideally, one wants to maximize the first one while minimize the latter two. However, according to laws of statistics this is impossible. To obtain high accuracy in a statistical process (including IDMS), a large-sized sample has to be used; although it is possible to set a high accuracy threshold and then try to infer the result using a sample whose size is as small as possible, this usually leads to a costly iterative process. Therefore, a practical solution is to achieve a suitable tradeoff between the three metrics. In IDMS, to realize this tradeoff, one can adjust the constant γ and the sample size within the iteration.

4   Application to Self-adaptive System

In this section, we describe an application of IDMS to self-adaptive systems. A variety of frameworks are proposed to aid the design of self-adaptive systems [12,13,25] and we focus on the Rainbow framework.

4.1   Rainbow Framework

We illustrate Rainbow with the example Z.com [11] which is a fictional news website providing multi-media and textual news service while keeping the cost of maintaining its server pool within its operational budget. Z.com has a client-server architecture with three additional adaptation-relevant components, as shown in Fig. 3: The Sensor collects runtime data; the Manager controls the adaptation, such as switching the news content mode from multi-media to text and *vice versa*; and the Effector executes the adaptation to affect the system.

In Rainbow, the adaptation is specified as *strategies* in its customized language Stitch [9]. A strategy is a tree structure consisting of *tactics*, which in turn contain operations. Figure 4 specifies two strategies a and b, guarded by a common condition cond where SNo and MaxSNo refer to the current server number and the maximal server number, respectively.[1] If strategy a is selected, operation enlistSever[1] in tactic s1 is first executed. Next, if the variable hiLatency is true then enlistSever[1] in tactic s2 is executed; otherwise strategy a terminates. Last,

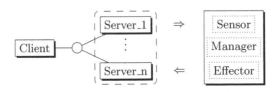

Fig. 3. Software architecture of Z.com

```
define  cond := hiLatency &! TextMode &(SNo<=MaxSNo−2);
strategy  a[cond]{
  tactic  s1: enlistServer[1]{
    tactic  s2: hiLatency −>enlistServer[1]{
      tactic  s3: hiLatency −>switchToTextMode;}}}
strategy  b[cond]{
  tactic  s4: hiLoad−>enlistServer[2]{
    tactic  s6: hiLatency −>switchToTextMode;}
  tactic  s5:! hiLoad−>switchToTextMode{
    tactic  s7: hiLatency −>enlistServer[2];}}
  ... % other strategy specification
```

Fig. 4. Strategy specification for Z.com in Stitch

---

[1] For simplicity, the specification does not strictly follow the syntax of Stitch.

Table 1. Costs of operations in strategies a and b

Utility Dimension	Operation						
	op(s1)	op(s2)	op(s3)	op(s4)	op(s5)	op(s6)	op(s7)
Content	0	0	1	0	1	1	0
Budget	1	1	0	2	0	0	2

if hiLatency persists to be true then switchToTextMode in tactic s3 is executed; otherwise strategy a terminates. Strategy b is specified in a similar style.

To evaluate strategies, Rainbow uses *utilities* to describe the costs and benefits of operations. The quantities of utilities are provided by human experts or stakeholders. Table 1 describes two utilities called *content* and *budget* and the costs of the operations in terms of the two. Note that because there is only one operation in each tactic of the adaptation specification in Fig. 4, we use tactic names to label operations—the correspondent operation to an tactic s is denoted op(s). For example, if switchToTextMode is executed, then the content cost is, say, 1; if enlistServer[i] with $i \in \{1, 2\}$ is executed, then the budget cost is, say, i. Then, the overall cost of an operation is the weighted sum of utilities. For simplicity, we let the weights of all utilities equal to 1.

Rainbow characterizes uncertainty in the detection of guarding conditions (such as hiLantency in tactic s2) as probabilities called *likelihoods*. The likelihoods in strategies a and b are specified in Table 2. Note that because there is one likelihood parameter in each tactic (except s1) of in Fig. 4, like for operations, we also use tactic names to label likelihoods—the correspondent operation to an tactic s is denoted lk(s). We explain how these likelihoods are elicited in Rainbow later; for now, they are viewed as undetermined parameters.

It is not hard to observe a correspondence between the adaptation specification of Z.com and an MPD model, where operations are represented by actions and strategies are represented by schedulers. Indeed, the Stitch specification under consideration can be translated into $\mathcal{M}_{eg}(\boldsymbol{\theta})$. Therefore, the adaptation problem in Rainbow is an instance of the problem of selecting a strategy that minimizes the cumulative cost (of reaching the goal states in the MDP).

4.2 Embedding IDMS into Rainbow

At least two methods to elicit likelihoods are supported in Rainbow. First, like utilities and their weights, concrete values of likelihoods can be explicitly given by human experts or stakeholders [9]. Second, sampling methods for estimating likelihoods are also implemented in Rainbow [7,10]. For example, the Manager can check the values of Boolean variables hiLatency and hiLoad as the system operates and record the result. Then, with respect to the condition probabilities described in Table 2, one easily obtains a sample for each parameter θ_i. Therefore, we can embed IDMS into Rainbow economically, just by enhancing the reasoning mechanism of strategy selection in the Manager with IDMS, but with little change made to the Sensor and the Effector

Table 2. Likelihood parameters in strategies a and b

Likelihood	Interpretation as a conditional probability
lk(s2)	Pr(hiLatency=true | SNo=MaxSNo - 1 & textMode=true)
lk(s3)	Pr(hiLatency=true | SNo=MaxSNo & textMode=true)
lk(s4)	Pr(hiLoad=true | hiLatency=true & SNo=MaxSNo - 2 & textMode=true)
lk(s4)	Pr(hiLoad=false | hiLatency=true & SNo=MaxSNo - 2 & textMode=true)
lk(s6)	Pr(hiLatency=true | hiLoad=true & SNo=MaxSNo & textMode=true)
lk(s7)	Pr(hiLatency=true | hiLoad=true & SNo=MaxSNo - 2 & textMode=false)

Rainbow exploits point estimates for likelihoods, as its decision model is a standard MDP. Because the runtime data set cannot be arbitrarily large, point estimates may be error-prone. Poor strategy selection often causes some extra cost and reduced benefit. Even worse, the extra cost and reduced benefit may accumulate if the non-optimal strategy is selected repeatedly. In view of this, the interval estimation method in IDMS can complement to the point estimation method in Rainbow, and leads to more stable decision-making outputs. By applying IDMS to Rainbow, another and more important benefit is the possibility of making a tradeoff between accuracy, data usage and computational overhead, thus improving the adaptation function of Rainbow.

5   Simulation-Based Experiment

5.1   Methodology and Setting

The general experimental methodology we adopt is simulation. Recall that IDMS assumes that likelihood parameters in Z.com are means of Bernoulli distributions. We use Matlab to simulate the generation and collection of runtime data. To this end, we need to fix the expected values of the Bernoulli random variables, namely the true values of $\boldsymbol{\theta}$ of $\mathcal{M}_{eg}(\boldsymbol{\theta})$. We let $\theta_1 = \frac{2}{3}$, $\theta_2 = \frac{4}{7}$, $\theta_3 = \frac{1}{3}$, $\theta_4 = \frac{4}{9}$ and $\theta_5 = \frac{4}{9}$. As the true values of $\boldsymbol{\theta}$ are given, we also know which scheduler is optimal. Indeed, by computation, the overall cost of strategy a is 2.0476 and that of strategy b is 2.0741. Thus, strategy a is optimal. It is noteworthy that the difference between the above two overall costs may seem small, but it is non-negligible because they are proportional to the weights of utility dimensions, which may be large in some case, and also because the extra cost may accumulate if the adaptation is triggered repeatedly.

To evaluate the flexibility of IDMS for making the intended tradeoff, we implement the computing procedure presented in Sect. 3.3 in Matlab. Given a sample of specific size for estimating each parameter θ_i of $\boldsymbol{\theta}$, and given a specific value of γ, IDMS terminates with a certain probability, called *termination probability* in the experiment. Based on the termination probability, we can immediately calculate the data usage and the computational overhead. Upon termination, with a certain probability, the selected scheduler is strategy a. This probability, called *correctness rate* in the experiment, is equal to the metric of accuracy. Since we can simulate IDMS (applied to $\mathcal{M}_{eg}(\boldsymbol{\theta})$), we can estimate the correctness rate and termination probability using the standard Monte Carlo estimation. In this experiment, we estimate the two for *different* sample sizes and values of γ. Note that the confidence level of interval estimation is fixed in IDMS and we set it to be 95 % in the experiment. The Matlab source code and data are available on http://www.comp.nus.edu.sg/~sugx/fase16/.

5.2   Experimental Data and Concrete Tradeoffs

The experimental data, summarized in Fig. 5, is generated from samples of n-size with n ranging from 200 to 5,000 in an increment of 200, and with a selection of values for γ as specified in the legends of the figures (where "large" refers to a sufficiently large value of γ such that the computing procedure is degenerated to a point estimation). For each n, the number of generalized samples is 10,000, based on which we calculate the correctness rate and termination probability.

Figure 5 demonstrates the dependence of the correctness rate and termination probability on γ and the sample size. Figure 5(a) shows that as γ decreases or as the sample size increases, the correctness rate increases. In particular, except for samples of small size (less than 1,000), IDMS provides a higher correctness rate than the point estimation method. Figure 5(b) shows that as γ increases or as the sample size increases, the termination probability increases. Note that if a sufficiently large value for γ is selected, the termination probability is 1 for samples of all selected sizes (and thus L8 is not depicted in Fig. 5(b).)

An important implication of Fig. 5 is that, by adjusting the value of γ and the sample size in different ways, one is able to achieve different tradeoffs between accuracy, data usage and computational overhead. To illustrate this flexibility, Table 3 describes three cases where the three metrics have different priorities. Based on Fig. 5, by selecting different pairs of γ and sample size, we obtain three

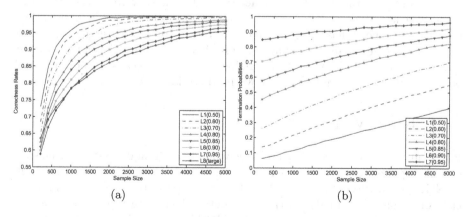

(a)   (b)

Fig. 5. (a) Correctness rates and (b) termination probabilities with different sample sizes and γ values

Table 3. Priorities of metrics in three different cases

Metric	Priority		
	A	B	C
Accuracy	high	medium	low
Data usage	low	medium	high
Computational overhead	low	high	high

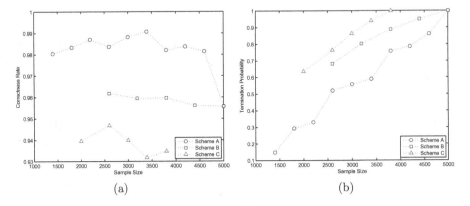

(a)   (b)

Fig. 6. Three iteration schemes in items of (a) correctness rates and (b) termination probabilities

examples of iteration schemes depicted in Fig. 6. Each marker in Fig. 6 refers to an iterative step with a specific value of γ and a specific sample size. For example, setting $\gamma = 0.5$ and the sample size as 1,400, according to Fig. 5, we obtain the leftmost marker of Scheme A in Fig. 6. The other markers in Fig. 6 are identified in the same way. All three schemes terminate with probability 1 before or when the sample size reaches 5,000. It is easy to observe that the schemes reflect the metric priorities in the corresponding cases in Table 3. For example, Scheme A has a high correctness rate compared with the other two schemes, because the priority of accuracy is high in Case A; it has a low average termination probability and a high number of markers, because the priorities of both data usage and computational overhead are low in Case A.

6   Related Work

Probabilistic model checking is a relatively mature technique that has been successfully applied to a wide range of domains, and we refer the readers to Forejt *et al.* [19] for a survey. The IMDP model considered in this paper falls into the class of probabilistic models with uncertainty, which have received substantial attention. For instance, in AI research, IMDPs were considered with different objectives such as discounted sum and limiting average [21,30]. The motivation of those works is to come up with an abstract framework, which is different from our motivation of runtime decision-making. In robust control theory, IMDPs or MDPs with more general forms of uncertainty are advocated to address the robustness of the controller under potential perturbation of the system [24,32]. In this paper, we consider expected cumulative costs of reachability properties. On the computational aspect, some of the mentioned approaches [21,24,30] also employed a value-iteration method. However, they mostly rely on ordering between intervals which is not needed in our case. Furthermore, Puggelli *et al.* [26] proposed polynomial algorithms for Markov chains with uncertainty based on optimization techniques, but only for reachability and PCTL properties.

Several high-level frameworks and approaches based on probabilistic model checking have been proposed for self-adaptive systems recently, but with emphasis on different aspects of the adaptation, such as QoS management and optimization [4], adaptation decisions [20], verification with information of confidence intervals [3], runtime verification efficiency and sensitivity analysis [18], and proactive verification and adaptation latency [23]. None of those works addressed the problem of making a practical tradeoff similar to the one supported by IDMS. Rainbow [9] supports the computation of cumulative costs and/or rewards when the likelihood parameters in the adaptation strategies are explicitly specified. Subsequent work [5,6] employs a combination of a simulation method and probabilistic model checking to evaluate properties such as resilience and adaptation latency. As mentioned, our IDMS can be economically embedded into Rainbow and extend the adaptation function of the latter.

We mention some other existing approaches to the design of self-adaptive systems, which rely on mathematical methods related to probability theory and statistics. Esfahani *et al.* [15,16] presented a general definition of adaptation optimality using fuzzy mathematics, which accounts for not only the current utility but also the optimal consequence of future operations. But IDMS estimates the probability parameters based on runtime data. Epifani *et al.* [14] presented the KAMI framework to deal with the inaccuracy of parameters related to the non-functional aspect of the system (such as reliability and performance), and Bencomo *et al.* [2] presented a Bayesian network for modeling self-adaptive systems. These two approaches rely on the Bayesian (point) estimation method while IDMS exploits both point and interval estimates from the frequentist statistics theory. Finally, Filieri *et al.* [17] constructed approximate dynamic models of a self-adaptive system and for synthesizing, from those models, a suitable controller that guarantees prescribed multiple non-functional system requirements. The method they used is from control theory, which is quite different from the theory of MDPs.

7   Conclusions

We have presented IDMS, an iterative framework that supports a tradeoff among three important metrics in practical runtime decision-making problems: accuracy, data usage and computational overhead. We have also instantiated IDMS on the Rainbow framework and presented a simulation-based evaluation.

For future work, we plan to enhance IDMS with a mechanism for automatically adjusting the confident optimality and the sample size based on the given priorities of the three metrics. Another interesting topic is a generalization of the value-iteration method in IMDP to synthesize a scheduler that minimizes the cumulative cost, without prescribing a subset of schedulers.

References

1. Baier, C., Katoen, J.-P.: Principles of Model Checking. The MIT Press, Cambridge (2008)
2. Bencomo, N., Belaggoun, A., Issarny, V.: Dynamic decision networks for decision-making in self-adaptive systems: A case study. In: Proceedings of the 8th International Symposium on Software Engineering for Adaptive and Self-Managing Systems, SEAMS 2013, pp. 113–122. IEEE Press, Piscataway, NJ, USA (2013)
3. Calinescu, R., Ghezzi, C., Johnson, K., Pezzé, M., Rafiq, Y., Tamburrelli, G.: Formal verification with confidence intervals: A new approach to establishing the quality-of-service properties of software systems. IEEE Trans. Reliab. **99**, 1–19 (2015)
4. Calinescu, R., Grunske, L., Kwiatkowska, M., Mirandola, R., Tamburrelli, G.: Dynamic QoS management and optimization in service-based systems. IEEE Trans. Softw. Eng. **37**(3), 387–409 (2011)
5. Camára, J., de Lemos, R.: Evaluation of resilience in self-adaptive systems using probabilistic model-checking. In: 2012 ICSE Workshop on Software Engineering for Adaptive and Self-Managing Systems (SEAMS), pp. 53–62, June 2012
6. Cámara, J., Moreno, G.A., Garlan, D.: Stochastic game analysis and latency awareness for proactive self-adaptation. In: Proceedings of the 9th International Symposium on Software Engineering for Adaptive and Self-Managing Systems, SEAMS, pp. 155–164. ACM, New York, NY, USA (2014)
7. Celiku, O., Garlan, D., Schmerl, B.: Augmenting architectural modeling to cope with uncertainty. In: Proceedings of the International Workshop on Living with Uncertainty (IWLU 2007), Atlanta, Georgia, USA (2007)
8. Chen, T., Forejt, V., Kwiatkowska, M.Z., Parker, D., Simaitis, A.: Automatic verification of competitive stochastic systems. Formal Method Syst. Des. **43**(1), 61–92 (2013)
9. Cheng, S.-W.: Rainbow: Cost-Effective Software Architecture-based Self Adaptation. Ph.D. thesis, Carnegie Mellon University (2008)
10. Cheng, S.-W., Garlan, D.: Handling uncertainty in autonomic systems. In: Proceedings of the International Workshop on Living with Uncertainty (IWLU 2007), Atlanta, Georgia, USA (2007)
11. Cheng, S.-W., Garlan, D., Schmerl, B.: Architecture-based self-adaptation in the presence of multiple objectives. In: ICSE Workshop on Software Engineering for Adaptive and Self-Managing Systems (SEAMS 2006), Shanghai, China (2006)
12. Cooray, D., Malek, S., Roshandel, R., Kilgore, D.: RESISTing reliability degradation through proactive reconfiguration. In: Proceedings of the IEEE/ACM International Conference on Automated Software Engineering, ASE 2010, pp. 83–92. ACM, New York, NY, USA (2010)
13. Elkhodary, A., Esfahani, N., Malek, S.: FUSION: A framework for engineering self-tuning self-adaptive software systems. In: Proceedings of the Eighteenth ACM SIGSOFT International Symposium on Foundations of Software Engineering, FSE 2010, pp. 7–16. ACM, New York, NY, USA (2010)

14. Epifani, I., Ghezzi, C., Mirandola, R., Tamburrelli, G.: Model evolution by runtime parameter adaptation. In: Proceedings of the 31st International Conference on Software Engineering, ICSE 2009, pp. 111–121. IEEE Computer Society, Washington, DC, USA (2009)

15. Esfahani, N., Kouroshfar, E., Malek, S.: Taming uncertainty in self-adaptive software. In: Proceedings of the 19th ACM SIGSOFT Symposium and the 13th European Conference on Foundations of Software Engineering, ESEC/FSE 2011, pp. 234–244. ACM, New York, NY, USA (2011)

16. Esfahani, N., Malek, S.: Uncertainty in self-adaptive software systems. In: de Lemos, R., Giese, H., Müller, H.A., Shaw, M. (eds.) Software Engineering for Self-Adaptive Systems. LNCS, vol. 7475, pp. 214–238. Springer, Heidelberg (2013)

17. Filieri, A., Hoffmann, H., Maggio, M.: Automated multi-objective control for self-adaptive software design. In: Proceedings of the 10th Joint Meeting on Foundations of Software Engineering, ESEC/FSE 2015, pp. 13–24 (2015)

18. Filieri, A., Tamburrelli, G., Ghezzi, C.: Supporting self-adaptation via quantitative verification and sensitivity analysis at run time. IEEE Trans. Softw. Eng. **42**, 75–99 (2015)

19. Forejt, V., Kwiatkowska, M., Norman, G., Parker, D.: Automated verification techniques for probabilistic systems. In: Bernardo, M., Issarny, V. (eds.) SFM 2011. LNCS, vol. 6659, pp. 53–113. Springer, Heidelberg (2011)

20. Ghezzi, C., Pinto, L.S., Spoletini, P., Tamburrelli, G.: Managing non-functional uncertainty via model-driven adaptivity. In: Proceedings of the International Conference on Software Engineering, ICSE 2013, pp. 33–42. IEEE Press (2013)

21. Givan, R., Leach, S.M., Dean, T.L.: Bounded-parameter Markov Decision Processes. J. Artif. Intell. **122**(1–2), 71–109 (2000)

22. Huebscher, M.C., McCann, J.A.: A survey of autonomic computing-degrees, models, and applications. ACM Comput. Surv. **40**(3), 7: 1–7: 28 (2008)

23. Moreno, G.A., Cámara, J., Garlan, D., Schmerl, B.: Proactive self-adaptation under uncertainty: A probabilistic model checking approach. In: Proceedings of the 10th Joint Meeting on Foundations of Software Engineering, ESEC/FSE 2015, pp. 1–12. ACM, New York, NY, USA (2015)

24. Nilim, A., Ghaoui, L.E.: Robust control of Markov Decision Processes with uncertain transition matrices. Oper. Res. **53**(5), 780–798 (2005)

25. Poladian, V., Garlan, D., Shaw, M., Satyanarayanan, M., Schmerl, B., Sousat, J.: Leveraging resource prediction for anticipatory dynamic configuration. In: First International Conference on Self-Adaptive and Self-Organizing Systems, SASO 2007, pp. 214–223 (2007)

26. Puggelli, A., Li, W., Sangiovanni-Vincentelli, A.L., Seshia, S.A.: Polynomial-time verification of PCTL properties of MDPs with convex uncertainties. In: Sharygina, N., Veith, H. (eds.) CAV 2013. LNCS, vol. 8044, pp. 527–542. Springer, Heidelberg (2013)

27. Puterman, M.L.: Markov decision processes. Handb. Oper. Res. Manage. Sci. **2**, 331–434 (1990)

28. Su, G., Feng, Y., Chen, T., Rosenblum, D.S.: Asymptotic perturbation bounds for probabilistic model checking with empirically determined probability parameters. IEEE Trans. Softw. Eng. **99**, 1–19 (2015)

29. Su, G., Rosenblum, D.S., Tamburrelli, G.: Reliability of run-time quality-of-service evaluation using parametirc model checking. In: Proceedings of the 38th International Conference on Software Engineering, ICSE 2016. ACM, New York, NY, USA (2016)

30. Tewari, A., Bartlett, P.L.: Bounded parameter markov decision processes with average reward criterion. In: Bshouty, N.H., Gentile, C. (eds.) COLT. LNCS (LNAI), vol. 4539, pp. 263–277. Springer, Heidelberg (2007)
31. Varga, R.S.: Matrix Iterative Analysis, Springer Series in Computational Mathematics. Springer, Heidelberg (2009)
32. Wiesemann, W., Kuhn, D., Rustem, B.: Robust markov decision processes. Math. Oper. Res. **38**(1), 153–183 (2013)

Family-Based Modeling and Analysis
for Probabilistic Systems – Featuring PROFEAT

Philipp Chrszon$^{(\boxtimes)}$, Clemens Dubslaff, Sascha Klüppelholz,
and Christel Baier

Faculty of Computer Science, Technische Universität Dresden, Dresden, Germany
{chrszon,dubslaff,klueppel,baier}@tcs.inf.tu-dresden.de

Abstract. Feature-based formalisms provide an elegant way to specify families of systems that share a base functionality and differ in certain features. They can also facilitate an all-in-one analysis, where all
systems of the family are analyzed at once on a single family model
instead of one-by-one. This paper presents the basic concepts of the tool
PROFEAT, which provides a guarded-command language for modeling
families of probabilistic systems and an automatic translation of family
models to the input language of the probabilistic model checker PRISM.
This translational approach enables a family-based quantitative analysis
with PRISM. Besides modeling families of systems that differ in system
parameters such as the number of identical processes or channel sizes,
PROFEAT also provides special support for the modeling and analysis
of (probabilistic) product lines with dynamic feature switches, multi-
features and feature attributes. By means of several case studies we show
how PROFEAT eases family-based modeling and compare the one-by-one
and all-in-one analysis approach.

1 Introduction

Feature orientation is a popular paradigm for the development of customizable
software systems (see, e.g., [3,7,29]). Formalisms with feature-oriented concepts
provide an elegant way to specify families of systems that can be seen as variants,
sharing some base functionality but differing in the combinations of features. The
most prominent application of feature-oriented formalisms are software product
lines [12]. Several techniques for the analysis of feature-oriented models and software product lines using testing, type checking, static analysis, theorem proving
or model checking have been proposed and implemented in tools (see, e.g., [35]
for an overview). The focus of the paper is on a feature-oriented formalism for the
quantitative analysis of families of probabilistic systems modeled by discrete- or
continuous-time Markov chains or Markov decision processes (MDPs). For this

The authors are supported by the DFG through the collaborative research centre HAEC (SFB 912), the Excellence Initiative by the German Federal and State
Governments (cluster of excellence cfAED and Institutional Strategy), the Research
Training Groups QuantLA (GRK 1763) and RoSI (GRK 1907), and the DFG/NWO-
project ROCKS, and Deutsche Telekom Stiftung.

© Springer-Verlag Berlin Heidelberg 2016
P. Stevens and A. Wąsowski (Eds.): FASE 2016, LNCS 9633, pp. 287–304, 2016.
DOI: 10.1007/978-3-662-49665-7_17

purpose, we introduce PROFEAT, a feature-oriented extension of the input language of the probabilistic model checker PRISM [28] together with an automatic translation of PROFEAT models to pure (feature-less) PRISM models. To specify valid feature combinations, we rely on a feature-model formalism similar to the Textual Variability Language (TVL) [8]. PROFEAT also allows for (numerical) feature attributes and multi-features [8,15,16].

PROFEAT follows the approach of [21] for modeling product lines using the parallel composition of (possibly interacting) feature modules and a feature controller that synchronizes with the feature modules when dynamic switches of the feature combinations occur. The dynamics of the feature controller and its interactions with the feature modules are crucial to model dynamic product lines [13,17,20,24]. Probabilistic dynamic product lines as presented in [21] allow, e.g., to model the frequencies of uncontrollable feature switches by stochastic distributions. The potential adaptations are then modeled by non-deterministic feature switches. In PROFEAT the operational behavior of the feature modules and the feature controller are represented by an extension of PRISM's guarded command language, supporting constraints for the feature combinations and synchronization actions for the activation and deactivation of features. Thus, whereas [21] uses MDP-like models for both the feature modules and the feature controller and handcrafted translations of the feature-oriented concepts into PRISM language, the PROFEAT framework provides an elegant way to specify the feature modules and feature controller and automatically generates corresponding PRISM code.

The quantitative analysis of PROFEAT models in terms of the (maximal or minimal) probabilities of path properties or expected costs can be carried out using PRISM or other probabilistic model checkers that support PRISM's input language. Besides the translation of PROFEAT models into PRISM models, our implementation also supports the analysis of product lines by providing commands to trigger the PRISM model-checking engines either for the family model ("all-in-one") or for each family member separately ("one-by-one"). The one-by-one analysis can be carried out sequentially or in parallel.

Besides static or dynamic product lines, PROFEAT can also be used to specify families of probabilistic systems with the same functionality, but different system parameters. Examples for such system parameters that may constitute a family of systems are initial values of discrete variables (and hence the set of starting states), threshold values triggering a certain behavior or reset values, the sizes of a buffer, a data package, an encryption key, the number of redundant components, or of retries and the energy consumption for some send operation.[1] In these cases, PROFEAT's family-based modeling approach and support for the one-by-one analysis offers a convenient way to perform analysis benchmarks which till now are usually done using handcrafted templates. To illustrate the capabilities of PROFEAT, we considered a series of examples and compared the performance of all-in-one and one-by-one analyses using the three PRISM engines MTBDD, HYBRID and SPARSE. While the MTBDD engine is fully symbolic and carries

---

[1] To ensure the finiteness of the family model (which is necessary to employ standard model-checking techniques) the range of the parameters is required to be finite.

out all computations using multi-terminal binary decision diagrams (MTBDD), the numerical computations of the SPARSE engine are carried out using sparse matrices, and the HYBRID engine relies on an MTBDD-representation of the model and a sparse representation of probability or expectation vectors. Our experimental results indicate that there is no clear superiority of the all-in-one analysis approach, no matter which of the three PRISM engines is used. However, for well-known product line models, where the base functionality contains most of the behaviors and features have comparably less behaviors, all-in-one approaches are feasible (especially within the MTBDD engine).

Related Work. Various authors have presented model-checking techniques for families of non-probabilistic systems. For the automatic detection of feature interactions, Plath and Ryan [36] introduced a feature-oriented extension of the input language of the model checker SMV and Apel et al. [5] presented the tool SPLVerifier. FeatureIDE [40] is a tool set supporting all phases of the software-product-line development with connections to the theorem prover KeY and the model checker JPF-BDD. Gruler et al. [25] introduced a feature-based extension of the process algebra CCS and presented model-checking algorithms to verify requirements expressed in the μ-calculus. We are not aware of any implementation of this approach. Lauenroth et al. [34] deal with family models based on I/O automata with may ("variable") and must ("common") transitions and a model checker for a CTL-like temporal logic that has been adapted for reasoning about the variability of product lines. Featured transition systems (FTS) are labeled transition systems with annotations for the feature combinations of static product lines [11] or a variant of dynamic product lines [13]. The SNIP tool [9,11,15] relies on FTS specified using a feature-based extension of the modeling language Promela and allows for checking FTS against LTL properties one-by-one or using a symbolic all-in-one verification algorithm. Its re-engineered version ProVeLines [14] provides several extensions, including verification techniques for reachability properties with real-time constraints. For branching-time temporal-logic specifications, [10,13] proposed a symbolic model-checking approach for (adaptive) FTS. We are not aware of an implementation of the approach of [13]. In [10], an all-in-one analysis based on the feature-oriented extension of the SMV input language by [36] has been proposed, which allows verifying static product lines using the (non-probabilistic) symbolic model checker NuSMV. This extension of SMV follows the compositional feature-oriented software design paradigm (as we do) but puts the emphasis on superimposition [1,2,30], rather than parallel composition of feature behaviors [21].

None of the approaches mentioned above deals with probabilistic behaviors. To the best of our knowledge, there is no other tool that provides support for family-based probabilistic model checking of dynamic product lines. The benefits of probabilistic model checking for the analysis of adaptive software has been already drawn by Filieri et al. [22]. The work on model-checking algorithms for parametric Markov chains [18,27] and tool support in the model checkers PARAM [26] (which has been reimplemented and integrated in PRISM) and PROPhESY [19] is orthogonal. By computing rational functions for the probabilities of reachability conditions or expected accumulated costs, these techniques can be seen as an all-in-one analysis of families of probabilistic systems with the same state space, but different transition probabilities. Ghezzi and Sharifloo [23] and the recent work by Rodrigues et al. [37] illustrate the potential of parametric probabilistic model-checking techniques for the analysis of product lines. The PROFEAT language can handle probability parameters as well and translate them to PRISM code. However, there is no direct connection between PROFEAT and the parametric probabilistic model checkers as they do not support multiple initial states. The recent work by Beek et al. [39] presents a framework for the analysis of software product lines using statistical model checking. An approach towards a family-based performance analysis of dynamic probabilistic product lines arising from UML activity diagrams has been presented by [32].

Outline. Section 2 presents the main principles of the PROFEAT language. Details on the automatic generation of PRISM code from PROFEAT models as well as explanations on PROFEAT's support for the all-in-one and one-by-one analysis will be given in Sect. 3. Section 4 reports on experimental studies. A brief conclusion is provided in Sect. 5. The source code of PROFEAT can be obtained at https://wwwtcs.inf.tu-dresden.de/ALGI/PUB/FASE16.

2   Modeling Families of Systems: The PROFEAT Language

A PROFEAT model might represent a family of randomized protocols or other probabilistic systems that can be modeled by finite-state Markovian models, such as discrete- or continuous-time Markov chains (DTMCs, or CTMCs, respectively) or Markov decision processes (MDPs). Therefore, the model consists of two parts: the declaration of the family, and a compact feature-oriented representation of the operational behavior of all family members. Inspired by the application of feature-oriented formalisms for software product lines, a family member is specified by some combination of features, each either *active* or *inactive*. The language constructs for the declaration of feature models, i.e., the valid feature combinations, are inspired by the *Textual Variability Language* (TVL) [8]. For the definition of the operational behaviors, we adopt the guarded-command input language of the model checker PRISM [28] and extend it by feature-specific concepts presented in [21]. Guards in commands of a PRISM module can contain constraints for feature combinations. To model dynamic product lines, dynamic feature switches may occur by interactions with a feature controller, which is represented by a separate PRISM module with synchronization actions for activating and deactivating features. Apart from feature models, other families of probabilistic systems that differ, e.g., in the number of processes, the queue size or other system parameters can easily be modeled. For instance, existing parametrized PRISM models are usually checked within PRISM's experiment environment in a one-by-one fashion. Within PROFEAT only minor modifications are necessary to represent the whole family of systems that differ in the system parameters.

We illustrate the modeling approach of PROFEAT using a simple producer-consumer model. The system consists of a single producer that enqueues jobs with probabilistic workload sizes into a FIFO buffer handed to one or more workers. One worker can only process one package at a time and the duration of the processing is determined by the work-package size. Varying the buffer size, the number of workers, the processing speed of individual workers or the load caused by the producer yields different variants, i.e., families of systems.

2.1 Feature Modeling

A product line comprises a set of feature combinations, which are defined through a *feature model*. For the producer-consumer product line, the following figure

```
1  root feature
2    all of Producer, Buffer, Workers, optional Fast;
3    constraint active(Fast)=>active(Worker[0])&active(Worker[1]);
4    constraint Worker[0].speed + Worker[1].speed < 7;
5  endfeature
6
7  feature Workers
8    some of Worker[3];
9  endfeature
10
11 feature Worker
12   speed:[1..5];
13 endfeature
```

depicts a feature diagram, the standard formalism to define feature models in the software-engineering domain, and a part of its declaration in PROFEAT. Similar to feature diagrams, where each feature is represented by a rectangular node, PROFEAT uses textual feature-blocks to declare features and also has a tree-like structure. The **root feature** (denoted by System in the diagram) is a special feature, representing the base functionality on which the product line is built upon. Each feature can be decomposed into one or more sub-features. Here, the System is decomposed into four sub-features. An **all of** decomposition indicates that all sub-features are required in every feature combination whenever their parent feature is active. As used by the Workers feature, the **some of** operator implies that at least one of the sub-features has to be active if the parent is active. In addition to the **one of** operator (which requires exactly one sub-feature), the decomposition can also be given by a cardinality. Optional features are preceded by the **optional** keyword, indicating that the feature may or may not be part of a valid feature combination, regardless of the decomposition operator. PROFEAT has built-in support for *multi-features* [15], i.e., features that can appear more than once in a feature combination. The number of instances is given in brackets behind the feature name. In the producer-consumer example, the Workers feature is decomposed into three distinct copies of the Worker feature. It is important to note that the decomposition operator ranges over the feature instances. Thus, the **some** operator could be replaced by cardinality

[1..3] in the above listing. Multi-features can be marked optional as well. Then, each individual copy of the multi-feature is an optional feature. Besides multi-features, the PROFEAT language supports non-Boolean features in the form of numeric *feature attributes* [8]. In the example shown above, the Worker has the attribute speed which can take any integer value from 1 to 5. Access to feature attributes is possible regardless of whether the corresponding feature is active or not. The combination of multi-features and feature attributes enables a compact representation of complex product lines.

The introduction of multi-features necessitates the distinction between features and feature instances. In PROFEAT, each feature instance is uniquely identified by its *fully qualified name*. Sub-feature instances as well as feature attributes are addressed using the familiar dot-notation. Instances of multi-features are referred to by an array-like syntax. For example, the fully qualified name of the second worker's speed attribute is root.Workers.Worker[1].speed. As long as the qualified name is unambiguous, the prefix can be omitted. For instance, the name Worker[1].speed is valid as well.

A feature block may also contain cross-tree constraints over feature instances and feature attributes. In our example, the first constraint given in the root feature expresses that the first two Worker instances must be active whenever the Fast feature is active. The second constraint limits the accumulated speed of the first two workers. A constraint can be preceded by the initial keyword, which only affects the initial set of valid feature combinations. Obviously, this distinction is only relevant for dynamic product lines.

Behavior of Features. In a PROFEAT model, the declarative feature model is strictly separated from the operational behavior of features. A feature may be "implemented" by one or more *feature modules*, which are listed after the modules keyword inside the feature block. In our running example, the Worker feature is implemented by the Worker_impl module. The listing on the left shows the feature module and the extended feature declaration of the Worker feature. For the definition of feature modules, we use an extension of PRISM's guarded command language. Besides Boolean or integer variables defined in feature modules as in PRISM, PROFEAT supports (one dimensional) arrays. A set of *commands* defines the behavior of the feature module, having the form *guard → stochastic-update*. If the guard evaluates to *true*, the module can transition (with some probability) into a successor state defined through the updates of the variables. Consider the following command of the producer feature module.

```
1  feature Worker
2    speed :[1..5];
3    block dequeue[id];
4    modules Worker_impl;
5  endfeature
6
7  module Worker_impl
8    t :[0..max_work_size] init 0;
9    [working[id]] t>0 ->
10        (t'=max(0, t-speed));
11    [dequeue[id]] t=0 ->
12        (t'=Buffer.cell[0]);
13  endmodule
```

[enqueue] !buffer_full -> 0.1:(size'=2) + 0.9:(size'=1);

Here, the producer enqueues a work package of size 2 with a probability 0.1 if the buffer is not full. The guard expression may reference the local variables of other feature modules. Furthermore, the built-in `active` function can be used in guards, evaluating to *true* if applied to a feature which is currently active.

Another means for communication besides shared variables is *synchronization* between feature modules. A command can be labeled with an *action* that is placed between the square brackets preceding the guard. If two or more modules share an action, they are forced to take the labeled transitions simultaneously. However, if any of those modules cannot take the transition (because its guard is not fulfilled), then the action is *blocked*, so that none of the modules can take the transition. In our running example, a worker synchronizes with the feature module implementing the FIFO buffer over the `dequeue` action to obtain a new work package (line 11). In PROFEAT, action labels can be indexed using an array-like syntax. In case of multi-features, the implicit `id` parameter evaluates to the index of the feature instance. Thus, there exist three distinct `dequeue` actions in our model. By default, feature modules of inactive features do not block actions. Thus, with regard to synchronization, deactivating a feature has the same effect as removing it entirely from the model. This is useful if the model is fully synchronous, i.e., if there is a global action that synchronizes over all transitions. However, in some cases it is crucial that an inactive feature hinders active features to synchronize with its actions. In the producer-consumer example, an inactive worker should not take a work package out of the queue (line 11). Therefore, its `dequeue` action is modeled as blocking using the `block` keyword inside the `feature` module (line 3).

Specification of Costs and Rewards. As in PRISM, states and transitions in PROFEAT can be augmented with costs and rewards. This allows reasoning

```
1  feature Worker
2     speed :[1..5];
3     rewards "energy"
4        [working[id]]
5           true : pow(2,speed);
6     endrewards
7  endfeature
```

about quantitative measures, such as energy consumption, performance and throughput. Costs and rewards are defined as a part of feature declarations using the keyword `rewards`. In the listing on the left, the energy consumption of a worker is specified depending on its processing speed.

Feature Controller. In a PROFEAT model, the feature combination is not necessarily static, but may also change over time. The *feature controller* is a special module that defines the rules for the dynamic activation and deactivation of features, whose declaration we exemplify within our producer-consumer model:

```
controller
    [] buffer_full & !active(Worker[2]) -> activate(Worker[2]);
    [] buffer_low & active(Worker[2]) -> deactivate(Worker[2]);
endcontroller
```

Essentially, a `controller` is a module, which can modify feature combinations using the `activate` and `deactivate` updates. In the controller shown above, the third worker is activated to speed up processing whenever the buffer is full. Once the buffer is nearly empty, the worker is deactivated. The definition of a feature controller is optional. If no controller is given, the defined product line is assumed to be static. Feature modules can synchronize with the controller over the `activate` and `deactivate` actions, which enables them to react or even block the activation or deactivation of their corresponding feature. For instance, by adding the following line to the `Worker_impl` module, the deactivation of the worker is blocked as long as it is still processing a work package:

```
[deactivate] t=0 -> true;
```

Templates and Metaprogramming. PROFEAT also provides constructs commonly found in template engines but not included in PRISM's input language. Commands can be generated at translation time by using `for` loops. Furthermore, `feature` blocks as well as feature modules can be parametrized, which, in turn, allows for parametrization of guards, probabilities and costs/rewards. These feature and module templates are instantiated by referencing them in a decomposition or using the `modules` keyword, respectively. Consider the following excerpt of the feature module implementing the FIFO buffer:

```
1 module fifo(capacity)
2    cell : array [0..capacity-1] of [-1..max_work_size] init -1;
3    for w in [0..2]
4      [dequeue[w]] cell[0] != -1 ->
5        (cell[capacity-1]'=-1) &
6        for i in [0..capacity-2] (cell[i]'=cell[i+1]) endfor;
7    endfor
8    ...
9 endmodule
```

The module is parametrized over the capacity of the buffer (line 1). The `for` loop stretching from line 3 to 7 generates a `dequeue` labeled command for each worker. The inner loop (lines 6) shifts the buffer entries to remove the first element from the buffer.

2.2 Parametrization

While PROFEAT provides special support for feature-oriented modeling, families can also be formed by ranging over system parameters. In our running example, such a parameter might be the FIFO buffer size. Parameters are declared in a `family` block, as shown on the left. Similar to feature attributes, system parameters can be constrained as well. Furthermore, a family declaration can be combined with a feature

```
1 family
2    buffer_size:[1..8];
3    initial constraint
4        buffer_size != 5;
5 endfamily
```

model, resulting in a family that is both defined by system parameters and all valid initial feature combinations. To declare subsets of valid feature combinations as initial ones, PROFEAT provides the `initial constraint` keyword (see line 3 of the listing). Valid feature combinations not fulfilling the listed constraints are still possible during runtime by dynamic feature switches.

System parameters can be used anywhere in the model description, including guards, probabilities and costs/rewards. In contrast to feature attributes, system parameters are constant for each instance of a family. This has an important consequence: parameters can be used to specify the range of variables, the size of arrays, the range of `for` loops and even the number of multi-feature instances. Thus, system parameters can directly influence the structure of the system.

3 Implementation

We have implemented a software tool[2] that translates a PROFEAT model into the input language of the model checker PRISM. This translation-based approach enables the use of existing machinery for the verification and quantitative analysis of PROFEAT models. The PROFEAT tool furthermore supports the translation of queries into PRISM's properties file format. Thus, queries can be formulated in the extended syntax of PROFEAT and allow reasoning about feature-specific properties. In this section, we provide a semantics for the PRO-FEAT language and highlight notable steps of the translation process. The compositional modeling framework for probabilistic dynamic product lines by [21] provides a translation of feature modules under a feature controller into the input language of PRISM, naturally mapping feature composition to the parallel composition of PRISM. Thus, the semantics of the behavioral model of PROFEAT is defined in terms of the PRISM language semantics. The semantics of PROFEAT's feature modeling formalism is given by the semantics of TVL [8] extended with multi-features as described in [15].

3.1 Translation of Feature-Specific Constructs

In PROFEAT, the access to the feature combination is provided through the use of the `active` function and the `activate` and `deactivate` updates of the feature controller. We encode feature combinations by a set of integer variables with range `[0..1]`, which simplifies the handling of feature cardinalities (compared to a Boolean encoding). Instead of creating one variable per feature instance, the tool generates one variable per *atomic set* to reduce the number of variables: An atomic set is a set of features that can be treated as a unit as they never appear separately in a feature combination [38]. Given this representation, the translation of the `active` function is simple: The call to `active` is replaced by a check testing whether the atomic-set variable evaluates to 1. Analogously, the `activate` and `deactivate` updates assign a 0 or a 1 to the corresponding variable, respectively. However, the feature controller cannot change the feature combination arbitrarily: As an update has to yield a valid feature combination,

---

[2] For the Haskell source code of the tool, we refer to https://wwwtcs.inf.tu-dresden. de/ALGI/PUB/FASE16.

the translation has to add a guard to commands containing atomic-set variable updates. This guard is synthesized from the feature model and evaluates to *false* if the transition described by the command would result in an invalid feature combination.

Another aspect of the translation concerns the synchronization between the feature controller and the feature modules in case of feature activation and deactivation. Implicitly, an *activate$_f$* action and a *deactivate$_f$* action is created for each feature instance f. In PRISM, commands can only be labeled with a single action. However, an update may activate or deactivate multiple feature instances at once, thus requiring multiple action labels per command for synchronization. To circumvent this restriction of the PRISM language, the set of action labels is merged into a single action label. This solution requires special care in the translation of feature modules. Let us assume a command C labeled with the action *activate$_f$*. Then, we collect the action labels of all feature-controller commands that activate the feature instance f. Finally, we create a copy of the command C for each collected action label. This translation realizes the intended synchronization between the feature controller and the feature modules, even in the case of multiple simultaneous feature activations and deactivations.

Lastly, the translation must ensure that feature modules of inactive features do not block actions, i.e., deactivating a feature should have the same effect as removing the corresponding feature modules from the model. To achieve this behavior, we take the following approach. Suppose the feature module M implements the feature instance f. Then, for each command in M that has the form $[\alpha]$ *guard* $\rightarrow$ *update*, a command $[\alpha]$ $\neg\texttt{active}(f) \rightarrow$ *true* is generated. Thus, if the feature instance f is not active, the translated module does not block the action α. However, this command is not generated if the user explicitly requests the blocking of action α by using the $\texttt{block}$ keyword in the feature declaration.

3.2 All-in-One and One-by-One Translation

Essentially, there are two different approaches for the analysis of a family of systems described by some PROFEAT model: The *one-by-one* and the *all-in-one* approach. Within a one-by-one approach, each member of the family is analyzed separately. Differently, within an all-in-one approach, the whole family is encoded into a single PRISM model and analyzed in a single run. The result of the all-in-one analysis is then interpreted for each member of the family, providing results as the members would have been analyzed separately. An all-in-one approach can potentially exploit the similarities between the family instances and speed up the analysis, but may require additional memory. However, a big advantage of the one-by-one approach is that it can be easily parallelized. As we illustrate in our case studies (see Sect. 4), it depends on the model as well as the time and memory constraints which approach is appropriate. For this reason, PROFEAT supports both, an all-in-one and a one-by-one translation of the family model. Switching from one analysis approach to the other requires no adjustments to the model.

In case of one-by-one translation, PROFEAT generates a PRISM model for every instance of the family. That is, for each valid valuation of the system parameters and for each initial feature combination, the system parameters are replaced by constants. If no `family` block is given, then one model for each valid initial feature combination is generated. The all-in-one translation generates a single PRISM model with multiple initial states, one for each instance of the family. However, there is a technical difficulty in the translation into an all-in-one model: Array sizes, numbers of multi-features and variable bounds can be defined in terms of system parameters. Hence, these parameters might depend on the initial state and thus are not known at translation time. Therefore, PROFEAT instantiates these parametrized structures with their maximal size.

4 Experimental Studies

As PROFEAT follows a translational approach, all-in-one and one-in-one analyses can be carried out using the same model-checking tool PRISM, allowing for a conceptual comparison of both approaches. Besides a sequential one-by-one analysis as usually performed within product-line verification (see, e.g., [4]), we also provide results for analyzing the models generated by the one-by-one translation in parallel. Clearly, under the quite unrealistic assumption that lots of CPU cores (which allow for parallelization) and enough memory is provided, a parallel execution is likely to outperform an all-in-one approach. For our experiments we used a Linux machine with two 8-core Intel Xeon E5-2680 CPUs running at 2.7 GHz and equipped with 384 GBytes of RAM, hyper-threading enabled. Thus, we restricted ourselves to an execution of 32 analyses in parallel.

4.1 The Producer-Consumer Example

In the base model of the producer-consumer example, as considered already in previous sections, the controller can activate or deactivate workers in the workers pool, increase or decrease the size of the buffer, and increase or decrease the processing speed of individual workers. For realizing fairness among regular actions and controller actions, we introduced an additional progress module. When considering expected costs, the goal will be to finish a certain number of jobs. For this we enriched the model with a counter. In this section, we consider three variants of the base model and corresponding analysis queries:

Best Buffer. A static product line which parametrizes over the buffer size. Here, we ask for the buffer size for which minimal expected storage costs arise until a certain number of jobs are processed.

Best Worker. This family parametrizes over all possible combinations of workers. Within this family model, we ask for the combination of workers where the minimal expected energy is required to finish a given number of jobs.

Distributions. Here, we consider different workload distributions as parameter space of the model. The goal is to compute the distribution where the expected energy required to finish a certain number of jobs is minimal.

Figure 1a shows the number of MTBDD nodes for representing the three model variants depending on the family parameter. Within all variants, the number of nodes in the all-in-one model is significantly smaller that the sum of the MTBDD nodes for the separate models, indicating shared behaviors between the family members. We evaluated the quantitative queries stated above using both, the MTBDD and the SPARSE engine of PRISM. In general, the SPARSE engine turned out to perform slightly better than the MTBDD engine, especially within expectation queries. The results are illustrated in Fig. 1b–d.

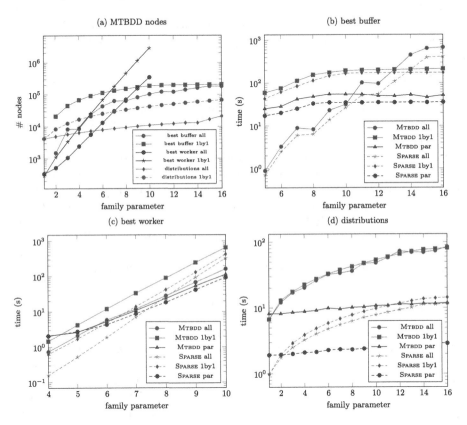

Fig. 1. Number of MTBDD nodes for the producer-consumer models (a), Analysis times of the variants best buffer (b), best worker (c) and distributions (d)

In some cases, where the number of instances is exponential in the family parameter (cf. Fig. 1c – Best Worker), the all-in-one analysis approach outperforms the one-by-one approach and can even keep up with the parallel computation. In other cases (cf. Fig. 1b – Best Buffer), the all-in-one approach was only superior up to a system size of 14. For the third model variant (cf. Fig. 1d – Distributions), the all-in-one and one-by-one approaches asymptotically displayed similar performance. Overall, there is a no clear trend on which approach is favorable, the one-by-one or the all-in-one analysis.

4.2 Feature-Aware Case Studies

The development of PROFEAT has been first and foremost motivated by several studies from the domain of feature-oriented systems such as product lines, where all-in-one analysis approaches turned out to outperform the traditional one-by-one analysis approach. In this section, we demonstrate how (probabilistic) versions of classical product lines can be modeled and analyzed with PROFEAT.

Body Sensor Network Product Line. A Body Sensor Network (BSN) system is a network of connected sensors sending measurements to a central entity which evaluates the data and identifies health critical situations. In [37], a BSN product line with features for several sensors has been introduced. The approach presented in [37] follows the ideas by [23] towards parameterized DTMC models: For each feature, a Boolean parameter f is 1 if the feature is active and 0 otherwise. A factor p is multiplied to the probability of every transition, where $p=f$ in case the feature enables the transition and $p = 1-f$ otherwise. Parametric model checkers are then used to compute a single formula which for each feature combination evaluates to the probability of reaching a successful configuration, i.e., the reliability of the BSN. The authors of [37] report that the parametric approach using PARAM can be seven times faster, a novel symbolic bounded-search approach can be eleven times faster, and a handcrafted (model dependent) compositional parametric approach can even be 100 times faster than a PRISM-based one-by-one analysis. For obtaining the results, three different model-checking tools have been used. Furthermore, special tailored scripts were required to perform the one-by-one analysis and to evaluate the formulas returned by the parametric model checkers. With PROFEAT the feature model of the BSN product line can be directly incorporated into the parametric model specified by [37], as PROFEAT's representation of features as Boolean parameters is compatible with the approach by [23]. Thus, PROFEAT allows for an all-in-one approach on the same model as of [37] and simplifies the comparison to one-by-one analysis also concerning different model-checking engines such as the explicit or symbolic engines of PRISM.

In the first line of Table 1, we show the results of our experiments for computing the same reliability probability as in [37]. The all-in-one approach turns out to be ≈100 times faster than the one-by-one approach, independent of the chosen engine. Hence, PROFEAT directly enables a speed up of the analysis time in the same magnitude as handcrafted decomposition optimizations by [37].

Elevator Product Line. A classical (non-probabilistic) product line considers an elevator system, introduced by [36] for checking feature interactions. It has been then considered in several case studies issuing family-based product-line verification (see, e.g., [4,15]). An elevator system is modeled by a cabin which can transport persons to floors of a building. The persons first have to push a button at the floor and then in the cabin for calling the elevator and defining a direction where to ride, respectively. In its basic version [36], the product line comprises 32 products built by five features, not changeable after deployment. We extend this product line in various aspects. First, we resolve some non-deterministic choices by probabilities when appropriate, e.g., modeling the request rate of a person and introducing a probability of failure. Second, we add a service feature, which enables to call technical staff repairing the elevator or change feature combinations. As a consequence, our elevator system is a dynamic product line where features can be changed during runtime. Third, we modeled dynamic feature changes as non-deterministic choices in the feature controller. This yields an MDP model for which a strategy-synthesis problem can be considered: Compute best- and worst-case strategies on how to activate or deactivate features to reach certain goals [21]. We deal with a simple instance of the elevator which can transport one person and where at most two persons act in the system. Our product lines have 64 feature combinations each, parametrized over the number of floors (2-4) in the building. We finally consider the family of the three product lines, containing 192 single instances of the elevator system. We asked for the minimal probability that if the cabin is on the ground floor and the top floor is requested, the probability to serve the top floor within the next three steps is greater than 0.99. Our analysis results are depicted in Table 1, where especially for larger instances the MTBDD all-in-one analysis outperforms other approaches and engines. Notice that the number of MTBDD nodes of the family model containing all three elevator product lines (cf. the row above the double rule) is greater than the sum of nodes of the family models for each product line. Possibly, other MTBDD variable orderings, e.g., provided by methods presented in [31], could yield smaller model representations and faster all-in-one analyses.

4.3 Benchmark Suite Examples

We used PROFEAT also to model and analyze some examples taken from the PRISM benchmark suite [33] and the probabilistic locking protocol PWCS [6] to investigate whether also standard parametrized models can profit from an all-in-one analysis. In the PWCS model, we consider two family parameters: The number of writers that intend to access a shared object (1) and the number of replicas for a given object (2). When providing PROFEAT code for the examples based on the existing models, the scripting and parameterization of PROFEAT yield a more compact model representation and required only mild modifications. Each row in the lower part of Table 1 stands for the evaluation of a query, which cover minimal and maximal expected values as well as probabilities for bounded and unbounded reachability. The HYBRID engine of PRISM does not yet support the computation of expectations. A reduction of the MTBDD size was only achieved for the self-stabilization protocol. In all other cases, the size of the family model was in the order of the sum of the separate models. The one-by-one approaches outperform the all-in-one approaches in almost all cases, even for the self-stabilization protocol.

Table 1. Analysis times (in seconds) of feature and benchmark suite models

Model	MTBDD nodes		MTBDD			HYBRID			SPARSE		
	family	separate	all	1by1	par	all	1by1	par	all	1by1	par
BSN	5651	111507	1	129	25	1	128	25	1	128	25
Elevator (2 floors)	42254	1329204	1	65	7	2	49	7	1	45	7
Elevator (3 floors)	151274	4924349	4	223	11	98	2531	96	7	286	18
Elevator (4 floors)	420448	13519274	15	910	32	2601	54262	1952	56	2008	83
Elevator (2-4 floors)	779569	19772827	29	1199	49	5089	56843	2052	74	2339	106
CSMA (2–4 processes)	633997	634076	timeout			not supported			1236	1251	1220
	"	"	timeout			3660	3577	3384	1078	1013	954
Stabilization (3–21 processes)	4340	10662	2036	1643	932	251	37	22	129	33	20
	"	"	≪1	1	2	not supported			122	24	15
	"	"	timeout			not supported			2629	476	269
	"	"	13	10	7	12	10	6	12	10	7
	"	"	13	10	7	13	10	7	13	10	6
Philosophers (3–12)	82995	82689	9056	6212	3945	9722	5949	4009	out of memory		
PWCS (3 replicas, 1–9 writers)	134236	134190	49	26	15	232	165	130	314	271	220
	"	"	6564	2247	960	not supported			5473	1544	1230
PWCS (3 writers, 1–7 replicas)	955505	958033	752	2279	1628	968	348	306	738	2209	1265
	"	"	timeout			not supported			1221	3857	2735

5 Conclusions

We presented the language PROFEAT for family-based modeling and analysis of probabilistic systems. To the best of our knowledge, PROFEAT is the first modeling language for probabilistic dynamic product lines with tool support for an all-in-one and one-by-one analysis without employing templates, scripting or different model descriptions. Whereas for experiments on product-line inspired case studies an all-in-one approach turns out to be usually faster than a one-by-one approach, this cannot be generalized to arbitrary families, e.g., when only a few common behaviors exist within the family members. There are various directions for further work, e.g., establishing an all-in-many approach clustering families and thus mixing both approaches. Symmetry reductions on the model could also speed up an all-in-one analysis, especially within multi-features.

References

1. Apel, S., Hutchins, D.: A calculus for uniform feature composition. ACM Trans. Program. Lang. Syst. **32**(5), 19:1–19:33 (2010)
2. Apel, S., Janda, F., Trujillo, S., Kästner, C.: Model superimposition in software product lines. In: Paige, R.F. (ed.) ICMT 2009. LNCS, vol. 5563, pp. 4–19. Springer, Heidelberg (2009)

3. Apel, S., Kästner, C.: An overview of feature-oriented software development. J. Object Technol. **8**(5), 49–84 (2009)

4. Apel, S., von Rhein, A., Wendler, P., Groesslinger, A., Beyer, D.: Strategies for product-line verification: Case studies and experiments. In: Proceedings of the International Conference on Software Engineering, ICSE 2013, pp. 482–491. IEEE (2013)

5. Apel, S., Speidel, H., Wendler, P., von Rhein, A., Beyer, D.: Detection of feature interactions using feature-aware verification. In: International Conference on Automated Software Engineering (ASE), pp. 372–375. IEEE (2011)

6. Baier, C., Engel, B., Klüppelholz, S., Märcker, S., Tews, H., Völp, M.: A probabilistic quantitative analysis of probabilistic-Write/Copy-select. In: Brat, G., Rungta, N., Venet, A. (eds.) NFM 2013. LNCS, vol. 7871, pp. 307–321. Springer, Heidelberg (2013)

7. Benavides, D., Segura, S., Ruiz-Cortés, A.: Automated analysis of feature models 20 years later: A literature review. Inf. Syst. **35**(6), 615–636 (2010)

8. Classen, A., Boucher, Q., Heymans, P.: A text-based approach to feature modelling: Syntax and semantics of TVL. Sci. Comput. Program. **76**(12), 1130–1143 (2011)

9. Classen, A., Cordy, M., Heymans, P., Legay, A., Schobbens, P.-Y.: Model checking software product lines with SNIP. STTT **14**(5), 589–612 (2012)

10. Classen, A., Cordy, M., Heymans, P., Legay, A., Schobbens, P.-Y.: Formal semantics, modular specification, and symbolic verification of product-line behaviour. Sci. Comput. Program. **80**, 416–439 (2014)

11. Classen, A., Cordy, M., Schobbens, P.-Y., Heymans, P., Legay, A., Raskin, J.-F.: Featured transition systems: Foundations for verifying variability-intensive systems and their application to LTL model checking. IEEE Trans. Softw. Eng. **39**(8), 1069–1089 (2013)

12. Clements, P., Northrop, L.: Software Product Lines: Practices and Patterns. Addison-Wesley Professional, Reading (2001)

13. Cordy, M., Classen, A., Heymans, P., Legay, A., Schobbens, P.-Y.: Model checking adaptive software with featured transition systems. In: Cámara, J., Lemos, R., Ghezzi, C., Lopes, A. (eds.) Assurances for Self-Adaptive Systems. LNCS, vol. 7740, pp. 1–29. Springer, Heidelberg (2013)

14. Cordy, M., Classen, A., Heymans, P., Schobbens, P.-Y., Legay, A.: ProVeLines: a product line of verifiers for software product lines. In: 17th International Software Product Line Conference (SPLC), pp. 141–146. ACM (2013)

15. Cordy, M., Schobbens, P.-Y., Heymans, P., Legay, A.: Beyond boolean product-line model checking: Dealing with feature attributes and multi-features. In: Proceedings of the International Conference on Software Engineering, ICSE 2013, pp. 472–481. IEEE Press (2013)

16. Czarnecki, K., Helsen, S., Eisenecker, U.W.: Formalizing cardinality-based feature models and their specialization. Softw. Process: Improv. Pract. **10**(1), 7–29 (2005)

17. Damiani, F., Schaefer, I.: Dynamic delta-oriented programming. In: Proceedings of the 15th International Software Product Line Conference, SPLC 2011. ACM (2011)

18. Daws, C.: Symbolic and parametric model checking of discrete-time markov chains. In: Liu, Z., Araki, K. (eds.) ICTAC 2004. LNCS, vol. 3407, pp. 280–294. Springer, Heidelberg (2005)

19. Dehnert, C., Junges, S., Jansen, N., Corzilius, F., Volk, M., Bruintjes, H., Katoen, J.-P., Ábrahám, E.: PROPhESY: A PRObabilistic parameter synthesis tool. In: Kroening, D., Păsăreanu, C.S. (eds.) CAV 2015. LNCS, vol. 9206, pp. 214–231. Springer, Heidelberg (2015)

20. Dinkelaker, T., Mitschke, R., Fetzer, K., Mezini, M.: A dynamic software product line approach using aspect models at runtime. In: Proceedings of the 1st Workshop on Composition and Variability (2010)
21. Dubslaff, C., Baier, C., Klüppelholz, S.: Probabilistic model checking for feature-oriented systems. In: Chiba, S., Tanter, É., Ernst, E., Hirschfeld, R. (eds.) Transactions on AOSD XII. LNCS, vol. 8989, pp. 180–220. Springer, Heidelberg (2015)
22. Filieri, A., Ghezzi, C., Tamburrelli, G.: A formal approach to adaptive software: Continuous assurance of non-functional requirements. Formal Aspects Comput. 24(2), 163–186 (2012)
23. Ghezzi, C., Sharifloo, A.M.: Model-based verification of quantitative non-functional properties for software product lines. Inf. Softw. Technol. 55(3), 508–524 (2013)
24. Gomaa, H., Hussein, M.: Dynamic software reconfiguration in software product families. In: van der Linden, F.J. (ed.) PFE 2003. LNCS, vol. 3014, pp. 435–444. Springer, Heidelberg (2004)
25. Gruler, A., Leucker, M., Scheidemann, K.: Modeling and model checking software product lines. In: Barthe, G., de Boer, F.S. (eds.) FMOODS 2008. LNCS, vol. 5051, pp. 113–131. Springer, Heidelberg (2008)
26. Hahn, E.M., Hermanns, H., Wachter, B., Zhang, L.: PARAM: A model checker for parametric markov models. In: Touili, T., Cook, B., Jackson, P. (eds.) CAV 2010. LNCS, vol. 6174, pp. 660–664. Springer, Heidelberg (2010)
27. Hahn, E.M., Hermanns, H., Zhang, L.: Probabilistic reachability for parametric Markov models. Softw. Tools Technol. Transf. 13(1), 3–19 (2011)
28. Hinton, A., Kwiatkowska, M., Norman, G., Parker, D.: PRISM: A tool for automatic verification of probabilistic systems. In: Palsberg, J., Hermanns, H. (eds.) TACAS 2006. LNCS, vol. 3920, pp. 441–444. Springer, Heidelberg (2006)
29. Kang, K.C., Cohen, S.G., Hess, J.A., Novak, W.E., Peterson, A.S.: Feature-oriented domain analysis (FODA) feasibility study. Technical Report CMU/SEI-90-TR-21, Carnegie-Mellon University (1990)
30. Katz, S.: A superimposition control construct for distributed systems. ACM Trans. Program. Lang. Syst. 15(2), 337–356 (1993)
31. Klein, J., Baier, C., Chrszon, P., Daum, M., Dubslaff, C., Klüppelholz, S., Märcker, S., Müller, D.: Advances in symbolic probabilistic model checking with PRISM. In: Proceedings of the 22th International Conference on Tools and Algorithms for the Construction and Analysis of Systems (TACAS), LNCS. Springer, to appear (2016)
32. Kowal, M., Schaefer, I., Tribastone, M.: Family-based performance analysis of variant-rich software systems. In: Gnesi, S., Rensink, A. (eds.) FASE 2014 (ETAPS). LNCS, vol. 8411, pp. 94–108. Springer, Heidelberg (2014)
33. Kwiatkowska, M.Z., Norman, G., Parker, D.: The PRISM benchmark suite. In: Proceedings of the Quantitative Evaluation of Systems (QEST 2012), pp. 203–204. IEEE, 2012. https://github.com/prismmodelchecker/prism-benchmarks/
34. Lauenroth, K., Pohl, K., Toehning, S.: Model checking of domain artifacts in product line engineering. In: 24th IEEE/ACM International Conference on Automated Software Engineering (ASE), pp. 269–280. IEEE (2009)
35. Meinicke, J., Thüm, T., Schröter, R., Benduhn, F., Saake, G.: An overview on analysis tools for software product lines. In: 18th International Software Product Lines Conference (SPLC), pp. 94–101. ACM (2014)
36. Plath, M., Ryan, M.: Feature integration using a feature construct. Sci. Comput. Program. 41(1), 53–84 (2001)

37. Rodrigues, G.N., Alves, V., Nunes, V., Lanna, A., Cordy, M., Schobbens, P.-Y., Sharifloo, A.M., Legay, A.: Modeling and verification for probabilistic properties in software product lines. In: High Assurance Systems Engineering (HASE), pp. 173–180. IEEE (2015)

38. Segura, S.: Automated analysis of feature models using atomic sets. In: SPLC (2), pp. 201–207 (2008)

39. ter Beek, M.H., Legay, A., Lluch-Lafuente, A., Vandin, A.: Statistical analysis of probabilistic models of software product lines with quantitative constraints. In: 19th International Conference on Software Product Line (SPLC), pp. 11–15. ACM (2015)

40. Thüm, T., Kästner, C., Benduhn, F., Meinicke, J., Saake, G., Leich, T.: FeatureIDE: An extensible framework for feature-oriented software development. Sci. Comput. Program. **79**, 70–85 (2014)

Statistical Model Checking of e-Motions Domain-Specific Modeling Languages

Francisco Durán[✉], Antonio Moreno-Delgado, and José M. Álvarez-Palomo

E.T.S.I. Informática, University of Málaga, Málaga, Spain
{duran,amoreno,alvarezp}@lcc.uma.es

Abstract. Domain experts may use novel tools that allow them to design and model their systems in a notation very close to the domain problem. However, the use of tools for the statistical analysis of stochastic systems requires software engineers to carefully specify such systems in low level and specific languages. In this work we line up both scenarios, specific domain modeling and statistical analysis. Specifically, we have extended the e-Motions system, a framework to develop real-time domain-specific languages where the behavior is specified in a natural way by in-place transformation rules, to support the statistical analysis of systems defined using it. We discuss how restricted e-Motions systems are used to produce Maude corresponding specifications, using a model transformation from e-Motions to Maude, which comply with the restrictions of the VeStA tool, and which can therefore be used to perform statistical analysis on the stochastic systems thus generated. We illustrate our approach with a very simple messaging distributed system.

1   Introduction

Model Driven Engineering advocates the use of models as the key artifacts in all phases of development, artifacts from which whole systems can be derived, analysed and implemented [21]. To be able to define such models in terms as close to the problem domain as possible, different technologies for the definition of *Domain Specific Modeling Languages* (DSMLs) have been proposed (see, e.g., [20]). The main goal of these DSMLs is to follow the domain abstractions and semantics, allowing modelers to perceive themselves as working directly with domain concepts. Model transformations may then be used to analyze certain aspects of models and then automatically synthesize various types of artifacts, such as source code, simulation inputs, or alternative model representations.

DSMLs are typically defined by means of its structural aspects (with its corresponding abstract and, in some cases, concrete syntaxes). These definitions allow the rapid development of languages and some of their associated tools, such as editors or browsers. Typically, to perform some type of analysis or to generate code, such models need to be transformed into formalisms or programming languages with the appropriate tool support. There are many success stories using this approach. However, the semantics of such DSMLs is embedded in the model

P. Stevens and A. Wąsowski (Eds.): FASE 2016, LNCS 9633, pp. 305–322, 2016.
DOI: 10.1007/978-3-662-49665-7_18

transformations, and provided by the target formalism, what constrains the rapid definition of such languages. To overcome this situation different authors have proposed different ways of providing an operational semantics as part of the definition of DSMLs, possibly being the most successful one the one using graph transformation systems (GTS) [33], with systems such as AToM3 [13], AGG [37] or e-Motions [29] implementing it.

The specification of the explicit behavioral semantics of DSMLs helps in MDE activities such as quick prototyping, simulation, or analysis. Ensuring semantic properties of models is important because any error in a model can easily become a systemic error in the system under development. E.g., AGG and e-Motions provide support for the simulation of models defined conforming to user-defined DSMLs. These and other languages provide support for different kinds of analysis as well, like termination checks, critical pair analysis, or reachability analysis (see, e.g., [31,37]). CheckVML [34], GROOVE [28] and e-Motions [29] support the model checking of systems whose behavior is specified by graph transformation systems.

This is, however, not enough, since applications become more and more complex, and model checking is a very expensive procedure, both in time and space, being infeasible in many cases. A very important class of systems that falls out of the scope of classical model checkers are real-time stochastic systems. The methods used to verify quantitative properties of stochastic systems are typically based on numerical methods [19], that iteratively compute the exact (or approximate) measure of paths satisfying relevant logical formulas. Although tools like PRISM [22] and UPPAAL [4] have shown very successful in the analysis of this kind of systems, explicitly constructing the corresponding probabilistic model is infeasible in many cases. An alternative method that solves this problem is based on statistical methods, similar to Monte Carlo simulations. By testing our hypothesis on many executions of a system, we may infer statistical evidence on the satisfaction or violation of the specification. Thus, properties like "the probability of completing task X with Y units of energy is greater than 0.3" or "the average amount of energy required to complete task X with confidence interval α and error bound β" are evaluable. YMER [39] and VeStA [36] were pioneering tools implementing these techniques. Latest releases of the well-established tools PRISM and UPPAAL have more recently also included capabilities for statistical model checking (see [9,23]).

Statistical methods has another advantage in the context of DSMLs: are "easy" to use and "cheap". As other model-checking methods, statistical model checking is completely automatic, and can be used where other methods fail. But can also be used for "normal" systems with a shorter computation time. Since statistical model checking assumes the existence of inaccuracy in its results, answers are calculated provided a confidence interval and an error bound. As may be expected, these requirements have an impact on the number of samples to be processed, and therefore on the evaluation time.

In this paper we describe how the e-Motions tool has been extended so the models built conforming to user-defined DSMLs are suitable for statistical model checking. e-Motions models are transformed into Maude specifications satisfying the requirements of the PVeStA tool [3] (an extension and parallelization of VeStA [36]). Such Maude specifications are therefore suitable to be stochastically analyzed using PVeStA. We illustrate the use of e-Motions to model systems and its statistical model checker with a very simple messaging system.

The remaining of the paper is structured as follows. Section 2 presents e-Motions and VeStA/PVeStA, and their underlying Maude system. Section 3 explains how e-Motions specifications are statistically analysed using PVeStA and how the connection between these two systems is established. The way systems are defined in e-Motions and how they can be statistically analysed is illustrated with a case study in Sect. 4. Section 5 discusses some related work and Sect. 6 wraps up presenting some conclusions and future work.

2   Preliminaries

In this section, we introduce the e-Motions language and tool, the Maude system and the Maude implementation of e-Motions, and the VeStA/PVeStA tool.

2.1   The e-Motions System

e-Motions [29] is a graphical language and framework that supports the specification, simulation, and formal analysis of real-time systems. It supports the graphical specification of the dynamic behavior of DSMLs using their concrete syntax, making this task very intuitive.[1] The abstract syntax of a DSML is specified as an Ecore metamodel, which defines all relevant concepts—and their relations—in the language. Its concrete syntax is given by a GCS (Graphical Concrete Syntax) model, which attaches an image to each language concept. Then, its behavior is specified with (graphical) in-place model transformations. e-Motions provides a model of time, supporting features like duration, periodicity, etc., and mechanisms to state action properties [29,30].

In-place transformations are defined by rules, each of which represents a possible *action* of the system. These rules are of the form [NAC]* × LHS → RHS, where LHS (left-hand side), RHS (right-hand side) and NAC (negative application conditions) are model patterns that represent certain (sub-)states of the system. The LHS and NAC patterns express the conditions for the rule to be applied, whereas the RHS represents the effect of the corresponding action. A LHS may also have positive conditions, which are expressed, as any expression in the RHS, using OCL. Thus, a rule can be applied, i.e., triggered, if a match of the LHS is found in the model, its conditions are satisfied, and none of its NAC patterns occur. If several matches are found, one of them is non-deterministically chosen and applied, giving place to a new model where the matching objects are substituted by the appropriate instantiation of its RHS pattern. The transformation of the model proceeds by applying the rules on sub-models of it in a non-deterministic order, until no further transformation rule is applicable.

---

[1] e-Motions got an "ease of use" award at the 7th Transformation Tool Contest [26].

In e-Motions, there are two types of rules to specify time-dependent behavior, namely, *atomic* and *on-going* rules. Atomic rules represent atomic actions with a duration, which is specified by an interval of time. Atomic rules with duration zero are called *instantaneous* rules. On the other hand, on-going rules represent continuous actions that may be interrupted at any time.

A special kind of object, named *Clock*, represents the current global time elapse. Designers can use it in their rules (using its attribute *time*) to know the amount of time that the system has been working.

Figure 1 shows the metamodel and concrete syntax for a very simple messaging system, where there are nodes interconnected via channels. Each node has an agenda (a set with the identifiers of the other nodes in the net), and may deliver messages to any other node in it. There are two types of messages in the system, namely Token and Message. Figure 2 shows a sample initial configuration conforming to the metamodel in Fig. 1a and using the concrete syntax in Fig. 1b. Figure 3 shows the atomic rules defining the possible actions that may happen in such systems. The NewMessage rule states that every time a node receives a token message with time zero, a new message is created addressed to another node chosen from the agenda following a uniform distribution, and will be sent through an outgoing channel also chosen probabilistically—WITH blocks state positive conditions that have to be hold on a given match of the LHS for the rule to be triggered. Mail objects will be moved from nodes to channels and from channels to nodes by rules Node2Channel and Channel2Node, respectively, both with a duration that follows a normal distribution (see the definition of variable STime at the bottom of the rule and its use in the header to establish the duration). The MessageArrival and DecreaseToken rules model, respectively, the arrival of a message to its destination node, where the observer gathers information about the time taken, and the pass of time for the token messages. NewMessage and MessageArrival are modelled as instantaneous actions (duration [0,0]). Node2Channel, Channel2Node and DecreaseToken have probabilistic durations, whilst the duration of the first two are calculated in the rule itself, for the third one the duration is given by the attribute t of the token, whose value was assigned in a previous NewMessage rule.

2.2   Maude

Maude [10,11] is an executable formal specification language based on rewriting logic [24], a logic of change that can naturally deal with states and non-deterministic concurrent computations. A rewrite logic theory is a tuple (Σ, E, R), where (Σ, E) is an *equational theory* that specifies the system states as elements of the initial algebra $\mathcal{T}_{(\Sigma,E)}$, and R is a set of rewrite rules that describe the one-step possible concurrent transitions in the system.

Rewriting will operate on congruence classes of terms modulo E. This of course does not mean that an implementation of rewriting logic must have an E-matching algorithm for each equational theory E that a user might specify. The equations are divided into a set A of structural axioms for which matching algorithms are available and a set E of equations. Then, for having a complete

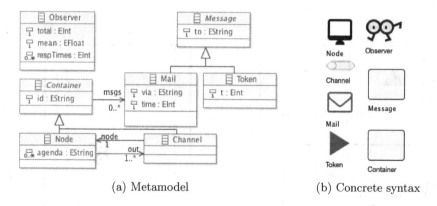

(a) Metamodel   (b) Concrete syntax

Fig. 1. Metamodel and concrete syntax for the messaging system

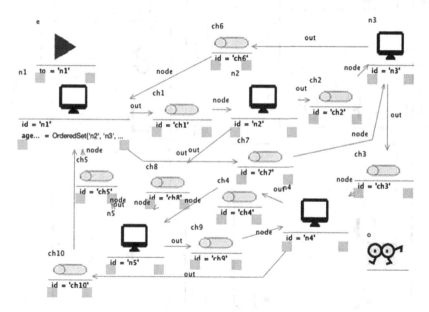

Fig. 2. Messaging system's initial configuration

agreement between the specification's initial algebra and its operational semantics by rewriting, a rewrite theory $(\Sigma, E \cup A, R)$ is assumed to be such that the set E of equations is (ground) Church-Rosser and terminating modulo A, and the rules R are (ground) coherent with the equations E modulo A (see [14,15]).

In the case of Maude, the equational logic is membership equational logic (MEL) [7], which can be seen as an extension of order-sorted logic with sorts, subsorts, and partial functions, and where atomic sentences include both equations $t = t'$ and memberships $t : s$, stating that term t has sort s. Maude provides support for rewriting modulo associativity, commutativity and identity, which perfectly captures the evolution of models made up of objects linked by references as in graph grammar.

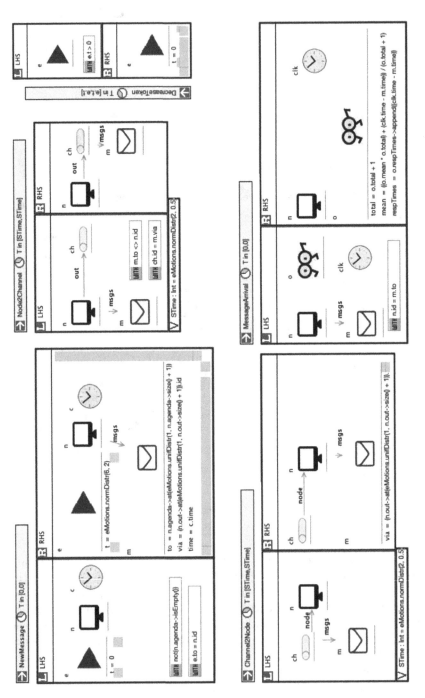

Fig. 3. Messaging system's rules

Maude counts with a rich set of validation and verification tools, increasingly used as support to the development of UML, MDA, and OCL tools (see, e.g., [32] for an overview). Furthermore, Maude has demonstrated to be a good environment for rapid prototyping, and also for application development (see [11]).

Among other applications, Maude may be seen as a general framework where to develop model transformations [6]. Maude is used as a formal notation to provide the precise semantics of the corresponding e-Motions specifications (as described in [30]), while at the same time the model transformations between e-Motions and Maude allow the Maude tools to become available in the e-Motions environment. More precisely, the generated Maude specification is a Real-Time Maude specification. Real-Time Maude [27] is a rewriting-logic-based specification language and formal analysis tool that extends the Maude system [11] to support the formal specification and analysis of *real-time systems*. Real-Time Maude provides a sort Time to model the time domain, which can be either discrete or dense. Then, pass of time is modelled with *tick rules* like

$$\texttt{crl } [l] \ : \ \{ \ t, \ T \ \} \ \Rightarrow \ \{ \ t', \ T + \tau \ \} \ \texttt{if } C.$$

where t and t' are system states (an evolving model in our case), T is the global time, and τ is a term of sort Time that denotes the *duration* of the rewrite, and that affects the *global time elapse*. Since tick rules affect the global time, in Real-Time Maude time elapse is usually modeled by one single tick rule, and the system dynamic behavior by instantaneous transitions [27]. Although there are other sampling strategies, in the most convenient one this single tick rule models time elapse by using two functions: the delta function, that defines the effect of time elapse over every model element, and the mte (maximal time elapse) function, that defines the maximum amount of time that can elapse before any action is performed. Then, time advances non-deterministically by any amount τ, which must be less or equal than the maximum time elapse of the system.

$$\texttt{crl } [\texttt{tick}] \ : \ \{ \ t, \ T \ \} \ \Rightarrow \ \{ \ \texttt{delta}(t, \ \tau), \ T + \tau \ \} \ \texttt{if } \tau \leq \texttt{mte}(t) \land C.$$

2.3 Maude Representation of e-Motions Models and Metamodels

As in [5,32], the algebraic semantics of an Ecore[2] metamodel MM is provided by a MEL theory $Spec_{MM}$ so that a model M conformant with MM is an element of the initial algebra $\mathcal{T}_{Spec_{MM}}$. The e-Motions definition of a domain specific language provided by a metamodel MM plus a set of transformation rules defining its dynamic semantics, is then represented as a rewrite theory extending $Spec_{MM}$ with some additional definitions and rules specifying such a behavior.

An ATL transformation transforms e-Motions models into Maude executable specifications, which can be used for simulation and analysis. Although a detailed presentation of this transformation can be found in [30], we give here a general account of it to understand the rest of the paper.

---

[2] Ecore is equivalent to the EMOF (Essential MOF) portion of MOF defined in the MOF 2 specification [25].

e-Motions' models are represented in Maude as structures of sort @Model of the form $mm\{obj_1 \ obj_2 \ ... \ obj_N\}$, where mm is the name of its metamodel and obj_i are the objects that constitute the model. An object is a record-like structure of the form $< o : c \mid a_1 : v_1\#...\#a_n : v_n >$ (of sort @Object), where o is the object identifier (of sort Oid), c is the class the object belongs to (of sort @Class), and $a_i : v_i$ are attribute-value pairs (of sort @StructuralFeature-Instance). Given appropriate definitions for all classes, attributes and references in its corresponding metamodel, a possible valid state could be as follows:

```
@smp-mm@ {
    < n1 : Node | id :"n1" # out : Set{"ch1", "ch2"} # agenda : ... >
    < ch1 : Channel | id : "ch1" # node : "n2" >
    ...
}
```

This code snippet shows part of a model in which there is a node object "n1" of class Node which is connected to channels "ch1" and "ch2", which in turn are connected to nodes "n2" and "n3".[3]

Although in e-Motions there are two kinds of rules, namely, atomic and on-going rules, for the purpose of the work at hand only atomic rules are used. So in what follows, we sketch the Maude specification of the atomic e-Motions rules.

Atomic rules are represented as two Real-Time Maude instantaneous rules, one modeling its *triggering* and another one modeling its actual *realization*. *Triggering rules* represent the action's preconditions. When a rule precondition is satisfied, the triggering Maude rule is applied and an atomic action execution (*AAE*) object is created. *AAE* objects represent atomic rules' executions, each one acting as a countdown to the finalization of the action. *AAE* objects gather the information needed for its instantiation: the rule's name (l), the identifiers of the elements involved in the action (ρ), and the variables used in it (ν). Initially, the timer (τ) is set to the given duration of the rule.

$$\text{crl } [l] \ : \ \{t, T\} \ => \ \{t, AAE(l, \rho, \nu, \tau), T\} \text{ if } C \, .$$

The *realization rule* represents the postcondition of the rule, which can be performed once the action's timer is consumed, and only if none of the action's participants have been deleted by other actions. Then, the subterm matching the LHS is substituted by the corresponding instantiation of the RHS and the attribute values are computed.

$$\text{crl } [l] \ : \ \{t, AAE(l, \rho, \nu, 0), T\} \ => \ \{t', T\} \text{ if } C \, .$$

As above explained, time elapse is modeled by using the delta and mte functions. Both functions need to be defined only over time-dependent elements, namely the Clock instance and *AAE* objects. The delta function decreases *AAE* timers and increases the clock value. The rest of objects remain unchanged.

---

[3] In e-Motions, all structural features are qualified with the name of the class they belong to, and all elements are qualified with the name of the metamodel they are defined in. All these qualifications have been removed to improve readability.

Action execution objects AAE gather additional information for dealing with scheduling, periodicity, etc. The interested reader is referred to [30] for a complete account on them and on the representation of on-going rules. From the point of view of executability by rewriting and, in particular, for the discussion on un-quantified non-determinism in the following sections the key idea is that AAE objects are required for the realization of actions.

2.4   The VeStA/PVeStA Tool

There are two main approaches for statistical model checking: sequential testing [40], implemented, e.g., in Ymer [39], and black-box testing [35], implemented, e.g., in VeStA [36]. In sequential testing, sample execution paths are generated until its answer can be guaranteed to be correct within the required error bounds. In black-box testing, the system is not controlled to generate specific execution traces. Instead, a quantitative measure of *confidence* is computed for given samples.

VeStA [36] performs discrete-event simulation from a Maude specification by invoking the Maude interpreter. Given a Maude model, an initial state (or configuration) and a temporal logical formula expressed in QuaTeX [2], VeStA is used to perform stochastic analysis. QuaTeX uses real-valued states and path functions to quantitatively specify properties about probabilistic models. Specifically, QuaTeX provides an expressive language for real-valued temporal properties through the combination of recursive function declarations, an if-then-else construct, and a next operator. The reader is referred to [2] for a detailed account on QuaTeX. For the soundness of the analysis carried out in VeStA, the specification to be analyzed has to have absence of *un-quantified non-determinism* [35].

AlTurki et al. have extended the VeStA tool with a parallel implementation, PVeStA [3], which makes the analysis substantially more efficiently. VeStA and PVeStA have been used for the analysis of systems and algorithms by different authors (see, e.g., [1, 8, 16]).

3   PVeStA-Compliant Representation of e-Motions Models

When rewriting a system, there might be different sources of non-determinism. Some of them are part of our specification, due to probabilistic choices and stochastic real-time. However, rewrite engines need to take their own choices. When there are several matches, for a given rule or for several rules, rewrite engines will choose an alternative following some internal criteria. For the statistical analysis used in VeStA/PVeStA to be sound the rewriting logic specification cannot contain un-quantified non-determinism [2].

The thus obtained specification may be used for rewriting in Maude, but other tools in the Maude formal environment, as its model checker or its reachability analysis tool, can also be used on it [31]. In Sect. 3.2 we show how, by meeting its requirements, we can also use the PVeStA tool for carrying on statistical model checking.

3.1   Un-quantified-non-determinism-free e-Motions Systems

Writing an arbitrary rewrite specification that meets the *un-quantified-non-determinism* free requirement is non-trivial. We could check whether a specification meets the requirement by performing a critical pair analysis and checking that there are no rules that can be applied simultaneously.[4] However, the checking would not be easy either. And although it may give us some hints on the sources of un-quantified non-determinism, we would still have to change the specification.

To avoid this problem, and to make easier to write a specification free from *un-quantified non-determinism*, Agha et al. propose in [2] the use of the *actor* model. To guarantee that only one rule can be fired at any time, messages are scheduled following a continuous probability distribution. To improve its executability, a centralized scheduler is used in [3], so that only one scheduled message or object is available for execution at any time. With this scheduler-based scheme, having a single message in the initial configuration, rules with one object and a message in its left-hand sides, and no two rules for the same message, are a sufficient condition to meet the requirement. Eckhardt et al. relaxed the requirements on systems in [16] by allowing nested configurations of objects. The basic idea is however the same one, if every rule is going to be fired by a message, this message determines the rule match, and there is only one message out of the scheduler at a time, there is only one rule that may be fired and in one possible way.

Given the direct transformation of e-Motions configurations of objects with references into Maude configurations of objects, we may use the same scheduler scheme with the following changes on the requirements:

- There is a distinguish class **Message** whose objects represent messages.
- Objects communicate through asynchronous message passing, avoiding direct synchronization among them. We allow several objects in the left-hand sides of rules, but only when they are related by a containment relation, and not to model communication between them.
- Message and action execution objects are scheduled so that there is only one of these objects out of the scheduler.
- In the initial configuration there is only one message object, and no action execution object. If there are more than one message objects, they have to be scheduled.
- Rules may be fired either by messages or by action execution objects AAE. Each rule has in its left-hand side either a message or an action execution object. There is no rule without one of these objects in its left-hand side.
- As in [3], there might be in the right-hand side of a rule any number of message and action execution objects, but only one may be non-scheduled. The rest must be scheduled so that only one remains in the under-execution configuration. When there are several messages in the left-hand side of a rule, the order of the messages is specified in the transformation.

---

[4] Critical pair analysis is available in Maude, and has been used for tools like its confluence and coherence checkers (see [15]).

- If there are two rules with the same message or action execution object in its LHS, they cannot be simultaneously applicable. This is a requirement often used in critical pair analysis (cf. [15]): if there is a critical pair between two rules, their conditions should not be simultaneously satisfiable.
- The duration intervals of all atomic rules must be of the form [n,n]. Intervals of the form [n,m] are a source of un-quantified no-determinism, since the actual duration of the corresponding action might be any value in that interval.

These requirements are a sufficient condition for the specification to meet the un-quantified-non-determinism-free condition. Given the direct transformation between e-Motions rules and Maude rules, these requirements can indeed be checked on the e-Motions model itself.

Our scheduler contains both messages and action execution objects, which are released one by one in every rewriting tick step. As in [3], the elements in the scheduler are ordered according to their scheduled time. Messages are always ahead of actions, as they are ready to be consumed as soon as they are generated by a realization rule. Those objects scheduled for the same time are served in accordance with the time they were inserted in the scheduler (FIFO). The order of AAE objects is determined by their timers, being the first action execution object the one with the smallest timer. If several action execution objects have the same countdown, they follow a FIFO order.

Thus, a Maude rule mapped from an e-Motions rule can be triggered by two reasons:

1. there is a message which matches the message of the left-hand side of an instantaneous rule or a triggering rule of a non-instantaneous rule, or
2. there is an AAE object whose countdown has reached zero.

Let us check these requirements on the example given in Sect. 2. The first observation is that there is a single message (Mail or Token) in the lefthand side of each rule. If we assume that the initial configuration has a single message (a Token object in our case), the scheduler will make sure that there is only one message at a time in the running configuration. Notice that NewMessage is the only rule that have two messages in its righthand side. In this case, the transformation generating the Maude specification will decide which one goes first in the scheduler. The other important observation is that there will never be two nodes referencing to the same Mail object. In those other cases in which there are possible overlaps, indicating that there may be more than one applicable rule, or multiple matches for the same rule, we can check that their conditions are not simultaneously satisfiable. See for example that with a Token object in the running configuration, there might be matches for rules NewMessage and DecreaseToken at the same time. Notice however that NewMessage requires e.t = 0 and DecreaseToken requires e.t > 0. There is a similar situation for rules Node2Channel and MessageArrival, in this case m.to <> n.id and m.to = n.id cannot be satisfied simultaneously.

3.2 Modifications of Maude Rules

The Maude modules supporting the e-Motions infrastructure and the Maude rules mapped from the e-Motions rules have been modified to make use of the scheduler. Regarding the infrastructure modules, a new module defines the scheduler, operations to insert and remove objects from the scheduler, and extensions to the operations `delta` and `mte`. This module is independent from the systems and is added to the resulting Maude specification.

Every Maude rule mapped from an e-Motions atomic instantaneous rule must be modified by wrapping all the messages in its right-hand side with the operator `schedule`, which takes a list of one or more elements and insert them in the scheduler, following equations defined in the infrastructure module. For the Maude rules mapped from e-Motions non-instantaneous rules, there are more modifications. Messages present in the left-hand side of the triggering rule cannot be removed when the rule is executed, they must be available in the system because they are required for the corresponding realization action. However, they cannot stay free in the configuration because they could be chosen again. Therefore, they must be wrapped with the operator `blocked`, allowing to free another scheduled message from the scheduler. AAE objects created on the RHSs of rules have to be included within `schedule` operators to be handled by the scheduler. For the realization rules, messages that appear on its LHS must be wrapped with `blocked` operators, since the have to match with those wrapped in the triggering rule. Finally, those messages created in such rules have to be enclosed within `schedule` operators. The e-Motions scheduler releases a new message or AAE object if the current state of the system has no free message or AAE after a rewriting step.

In e-Motions systems time advances by means of the `tick` rule which, given the current state, computes the minimum among the maximum time elapses (MTEs) of the actions that may be performed on the current state. If that value is greater than zero, it means that there is no action that can be triggered or realized at that time. In that case, the global time is advanced until that value and the countdown values of all the AAE objects are updated according to that value. The operation `delta` makes that update. The operations `delta` and `mte` have been modified to take into account the elements contained in the scheduler.

3.3 e-SMC: e-Motions & PVeStA Integration

A new extension for the e-Motions framework has been developed to allow automatic modifications of e-Motions specifications for them to hold the restrictions mentioned in Sect. 3.2. This extension is named e-SMC and it has been implemented as an Eclipse plugin, integrated with the e-Motions tool. e-SMC encapsulates all the process from the mapping from the e-Motions system to the Maude specification to the execution of PVeStA as statistical analyzer, and the presentation of the analysis results. e-SMC also allows the user to specify the QuaTeX query that describes the property to be analyzed. The e-SMC tool, its documentation and some examples are available at http://maude.lcc.uma.es/esmc.

In the e-Motions framework, the model described with the DSML passes through a series of transformations to finally generate a Maude specification. The first one is an ATL model-to-model transformation, which generates Maude models conforming the Maude metamodel. The second one is a *Xtend* transformation which generates the final Maude code. e-SMC includes a new model-to-model transformation from the generated Maude models by the ATL transformation to Maude models compliant with the PVeStA restrictions. This new Maude models are, in turn, passed as input to the *Xtend* transformation.

4   Case Study: A Simple Messaging System

We illustrate the kind of statistical model checking we may perform with the very simple messaging system introduced in Sect. 2. To better illustrate the possible kinds of analysis, we compare the first simple messaging protocol results with a second version of the system in which each node has a routing table to decide which channel the message will be sent through in rules NewMessage and Channel2Node. In this second version, instead of probabilistically choosing an output channel, the value of the via attribute is retrieved from a table storing the best channel for a given destination.

The most interesting property to be analyzed in these simple message passing systems is *how well connected is each node?* Or *how long does it take a message to reach its target?* However, this property has to be statistically analyzed, since it depends on the value of three stochastic parameters: (i) when is the next message going to be sent, (ii) which is the target node, and (iii) which channel chooses a node to send the message through. In terms of statistical model-checking, the property at hand could be expressed as "with a confidence of 99 %, which is the mean time a message takes to commute between the source and target nodes?".

We proceed by defining a state expression which retrieves the mean response time collected by the Observer object at that time. Our executions have been performed using 8 threads (servers in the PVeStA terminology) and a master (client in PVeStA terms) running batches of 30 samples on each thread. After several iterations PVeStA returns the mean time elapsed between the start node n_i sending the message and the target node receiving it.

For the case of simple message passing with routing tables the time elapsed for messages sent from each node has been drastically reduced. Note that in the first case there may be even messages looping without finding their target. In this case we run batches of 10 samples on each thread, since it takes a smaller amount of values to converge.

Table 1 shows the execution times for each node, the number of samples needed to reach the confidence interval, and finally value of the property under study. Of course, the case study with routing converges with less samples since we are fixing which is the route the message will follow. Graphs in Fig. 4 show the evolution of the mean of the arrival times for each of the nodes in the system. Notice how they converge after some number of samples to their respective final mean values, once the confidence interval is reached.

Table 1. Execution times and mean time for messages being sent

	Simple message passing			Simple message passing routing		
n_i	Ex. time	# samples	mean. time	Ex. time	# samples	mean. time
n_1	93 s	600	8.7795	23 s	240	2.9484
n_2	111 s	660	7.2204	18 s	160	2.9639
n_3	96 s	870	7.6253	16 s	160	2.9984
n_4	92 s	510	8.3019	18 s	160	3.0141
n_5	87 s	1080	7.7106	25 s	240	3.0233

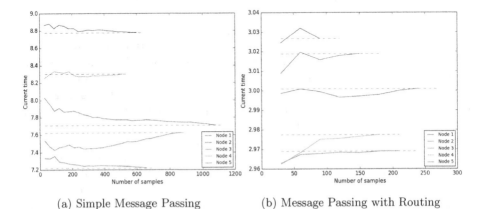

(a) Simple Message Passing   (b) Message Passing with Routing

Fig. 4. Mean message delivery time

5   Related Work

Heckel et al. propose in [17] the modeling and analysis of stochastic graphs transformation systems by defining Continuous Time Markov chains from GTSs with transition matrices representing the probabilities of the application of each rule. They provide some support using GROOVE [28] and PRISM. In later works [38], they handle distributions depending on pairs rule-match and may perform stocastic simulation. They develop GRaSS, with VIATRA as back-end, which can run multiples simulations limited by a time amount or number of steps. GRaSS may then calculate some statistical values with given confidence intervals.

GROOVE [28] supports the modeling of object-oriented systems, with graph transformations as a basis for model transformation and operational semantics. Systems thus defined may then be verified using model checking. CheckVML does something similar, although in this case system specifications into a tool-independent abstract representation of transition systems, from which Promela specifications are generated to model check using Spin.

Several attempts to reduce the complexity of model checking have also been proposed. Isenberg et al. propose in [18] the use of bounded model checking via SMT solving. Yousefian et al. use genetic algorithms in [41] to search specific states in large state spaces.

Based on ideas from Event Scheduling, de Lara et al. propose in [12] an interesting way of adding explicit time to graph transformation rules by scheduling rules in the future. Basically, they schedule all possible matches of rules (what they call *events*) and proceed by handling each of these events. To avoid the explosion in the number of matches, they use a control graph which establishes the possible sequences in which the rules may be applied. This idea could be an alternative way of guaranteeing the absence of un-quantified non-determinism, although at the cost of providing the control graph.

6 Conclusions

We have presented how the e-Motions tool has been extended so that the models built conforming to user-defined DSMLs are suitable for statistical model checking. e-Motions models are transformed into Maude specifications satisfying the requirements of the PVeStA tool [3], making them suitable to be stochastically analyzed. We have illustrated the use of e-Motions to model systems and its statistical model check with a very simple application for message delivery.

With our approach we provide statistical model checking capabilities to user-defined DSMLs in a user-friendly graphical environment. Statistical model checking offers a completely automatic procedure, with the possibility of adjusting the desired confidence interval and error bound.

Although the basic functionality and tooling is already available, much work remains ahead. For example, we would like to automate the check of the satisfaction of the non-quantified-non-determinism requirements. e-Motions features like periodicity, scheduling, or non-degenerate intervals are not yet supported. Moreover, although the response times obtained with PVeStA are acceptable, we would like to explore the possibility of using more powerful model checkers as back-end tools. Finally, we will complete the graphical representations of the obtained distributions of results inside our Eclipse plugin.

Acknowledgements. This work was partially supported by Research Project TIN2014-52034-R and by Universidad de Málaga (Campus de Excelencia Internacional Andalucía Tech).

References

1. Agha, G., Greenwald, M., Gunter, C.A., Khanna, S., Meseguer, J., Sen, K., Thati, P.: Formal modeling and analysis of DOS using probabilistic rewrite theories. In: Proceedings of FCS (2005)
2. Agha, G., Meseguer, J., Sen, K.: PMaude: rewrite-based specification language for probabilistic object systems. In: Proceedings of the QAPL, ENTCS, vol. 153, pp. 213–239 (2006)

3. AlTurki, M., Meseguer, J.: PVESTA: a parallel statistical model checking and quantitative analysis tool. In: Corradini, A., Klin, B., Cîrstea, C. (eds.) CALCO 2011. LNCS, vol. 6859, pp. 386–392. Springer, Heidelberg (2011)
4. Bengtsson, J., Larsen, K.G., Larsson, F., Pettersson, P., Yi, W.: UPPAAL - a tool suite for automatic verification of real-time systems. In: Alur, R., Sontag, E.D., Henzinger, T.A. (eds.) HS 1995. LNCS, vol. 1066, pp. 232–243. Springer, Heidelberg (1996)
5. Boronat, A., Meseguer, J.: An algebraic semantics for MOF. In: Fiadeiro, J.L., Inverardi, P. (eds.) FASE 2008. LNCS, vol. 4961, pp. 377–391. Springer, Heidelberg (2008)
6. Boronat, A., Meseguer, J.: MOMENT2: EMF model transformations in Maude. In: Proceedings of JISBD, pp. 178–179 (2009)
7. Bouhoula, A., Jouannaud, J.-P., Meseguer, J.: Specification and proof in membership equational logic. Theoret. Comput. Sci. **236**(1–2), 35–132 (2000)
8. Bruni, R., Corradini, A., Gadducci, F., Lluch Lafuente, A., Vandin, A.: Modelling and analyzing adaptive self-assembly strategies with Maude. In: Durán, F. (ed.) WRLA 2012. LNCS, vol. 7571, pp. 118–138. Springer, Heidelberg (2012)
9. Bulychev, P.E., David, A., Larsen, K.G., Mikucionis, M., Poulsen, D.B., Legay, A., Wang, Z.: UPPAAL-SMC: statistical model checking for priced timed automata. EPTCS **85**, 1–16 (2012). Proceedings of QAPL
10. Clavel, M., Durán, F., Eker, S., Lincoln, P., Martí-Oliet, N., Meseguer, J., Quesada, J.F.: Maude: specification and programming in rewriting logic. Theoret. Comput. Sci. **285**(2), 187–243 (2001)
11. Clavel, M., Durán, F., Eker, S., Lincoln, P., Martí-Oliet, N., Meseguer, J., Talcott, C.: All About Maude. LNCS, vol. 4350. Springer, Heidelberg (2007)
12. de Lara, J., Guerra, E., Boronat, A., Heckel, R., Torrini, P.: Domain-specific discrete event modelling and simulation using graph transformation. Softw. Syst. Model. **13**(1), 209–238 (2014)
13. de Lara, J., Vangheluwe, H.: AToM: a tool for multi-formalism and meta-modelling. In: Kutsche, R.-D., Weber, H. (eds.) FASE 2002. LNCS, vol. 2306, pp. 174–188. Springer, Heidelberg (2002)
14. Durán, F., Lucas, S., Marché, C., Meseguer, J., Urbain, X.: Proving operational termination of membership equational programs. Higher-Order Symbol. Comput. **21**(1–2), 59–88 (2008)
15. Durán, F., Meseguer, J.: On the Church-Rosser and coherence properties of conditional order-sorted rewrite theories. J. Log. Algebr. Program. **81**(7–8), 816–850 (2012)
16. Eckhardt, J., Mühlbauer, T., AlTurki, M., Meseguer, J., Wirsing, M.: Stable availability under denial of service attacks through formal patterns. In: de Lara, J., Zisman, A. (eds.) Fundamental Approaches to Software Engineering. LNCS, vol. 7212, pp. 78–93. Springer, Heidelberg (2012)
17. Heckel, R., Lajios, G., Menge, S.: Stochastic graph transformation systems. In: Ehrig, H., Engels, G., Parisi-Presicce, F., Rozenberg, G. (eds.) ICGT 2004. LNCS, vol. 3256, pp. 210–225. Springer, Heidelberg (2004)
18. Isenberg, T., Steenken, D., Wehrheim, H.: Bounded model checking of graph transformation systems via SMT solving. In: Beyer, D., Boreale, M. (eds.) FORTE 2013 and FMOODS 2013. LNCS, vol. 7892, pp. 178–192. Springer, Heidelberg (2013)
19. Jansen, D.N., Katoen, J.-P., Oldenkamp, M., Stoelinga, M., Zapreev, I.: How fast and fat is your probabilistic model checker? An experimental performance comparison. In: Yorav, K. (ed.) HVC 2007. LNCS, vol. 4899, pp. 69–85. Springer, Heidelberg (2008)

20. Kelly, S., Tolvanen, J.-P.: Domain-Specific Modeling: Enabling Full Code Generation. Wiley, New York (2008)
21. Caskurlu, B.: Model driven engineering. In: Butler, M., Petre, L., Sere, K. (eds.) IFM 2002. LNCS, vol. 2335, pp. 286–298. Springer, Heidelberg (2002)
22. Kwiatkowska, M., Norman, G., Parker, D.: Probabilistic symbolic model checking with PRISM: a hybrid approach. In: Katoen, J.-P., Stevens, P. (eds.) TACAS 2002. LNCS, vol. 2280, pp. 52–66. Springer, Heidelberg (2002)
23. Kwiatkowska, M., Norman, G., Parker, D.: PRISM 4.0: verification of probabilistic real-time systems. In: Gopalakrishnan, G., Qadeer, S. (eds.) CAV 2011. LNCS, vol. 6806, pp. 585–591. Springer, Heidelberg (2011)
24. Meseguer, J.: Conditional rewriting logic as a unified model of concurrency. Theoret. Comput. Sci. 96(1), 73–155 (1992)
25. Meta object facility (MOF) core specification, Version 2.4.1 (2013)
26. Moreno-Delgado, A., Durán, F.: The movie database case: a solution using the Maude-based e-Motions tool. In: 7th Transformation Tool Contest (TTC), vol. 1305, pp. 116–124. CEUR Workshop Proceedings (2014)
27. Ölveczky, P.C., Meseguer, J.: Semantics and pragmatics of Real-Time Maude. Higher-Order Symbol. Comput. 20(1–2), 161–196 (2007)
28. Rensink, A.: The GROOVE simulator: a tool for state space generation. In: Pfaltz, J.L., Nagl, M., Böhlen, B. (eds.) AGTIVE 2003. LNCS, vol. 3062, pp. 479–485. Springer, Heidelberg (2004)
29. Rivera, J.E., Durán, F., Vallecillo, A.: A graphical approach for modeling time-dependent behavior of DSLs. In: Proceedings of VL/HCC, pp. 51–55. IEEE (2009)
30. Rivera, J.E., Durán, F., Vallecillo, A.: On the behavioral semantics of real-time domain specific visual languages. In: Ölveczky, P.C. (ed.) WRLA 2010. LNCS, vol. 6381, pp. 174–190. Springer, Heidelberg (2010)
31. Rivera, J.E., Vallecillo, A., Durán, F.: Formal specification and analysis of domain specific languages using Maude. Simulation 85(11/12), 778–792 (2009)
32. Romero, J.R., Rivera, J.E., Durán, F., Vallecillo, A.: Formal and tool support for model driven engineering with Maude. J. Object Technol. 6(9), 187–207 (2007)
33. Rozenberg, G. (ed.): Handbook of Graph Grammars and Computing by Graph Transformations: Volume 1 Foundations. World Scientific, River Edge (1997)
34. Schmidt, Á., Varró, D.: CheckVML: a tool for model checking visual modeling languages. In: Stevens, P., Whittle, J., Booch, G. (eds.) UML 2003. LNCS, vol. 2863, pp. 92–95. Springer, Heidelberg (2003)
35. Sen, K., Viswanathan, M., Agha, G.: Statistical model checking of black-box probabilistic systems. In: Alur, R., Peled, D.A. (eds.) CAV 2004. LNCS, vol. 3114, pp. 202–215. Springer, Heidelberg (2004)
36. Sen, K., Viswanathan, M., Agha, G.A.: VeStA: a statistical model-checker and analyzer for probabilistic systems. In: Proceedings of QEST, pp. 251–252. IEEE (2005)
37. Taentzer, G.: AGG: a graph transformation environment for modeling and validation of software. In: Pfaltz, J.L., Nagl, M., Böhlen, B. (eds.) AGTIVE 2003. LNCS, vol. 3062, pp. 446–453. Springer, Heidelberg (2004)
38. Torrini, P., Heckel, R., Ráth, I.: Stochastic simulation of graph transformation systems. In: Rosenblum, D.S., Taentzer, G. (eds.) FASE 2010. LNCS, vol. 6013, pp. 154–157. Springer, Heidelberg (2010)
39. Younes, H.L.S.: Ymer: a statistical model checker. In: Etessami, K., Rajamani, S.K. (eds.) CAV 2005. LNCS, vol. 3576, pp. 429–433. Springer, Heidelberg (2005)

40. Younes, H.L.S., Simmons, R.G.: Probabilistic verification of discrete event systems using acceptance sampling. In: Brinksma, E., Larsen, K.G. (eds.) CAV 2002. LNCS, vol. 2404, pp. 223–235. Springer, Heidelberg (2002)
41. Yousefian, R., Rafe, V., Rahmani, M.: A heuristic solution for model checking graph transformation systems. Appl. Soft Comput. **24**, 169–180 (2014)

Proof and Theorem Proving

Towards Formal Proof Metrics

David Aspinall[1](✉) and Cezary Kaliszyk[2]

[1] LFCS, School of Informatics, University of Edinburgh,
Edinburgh EH8 9AB, Scotland, UK
David.Aspinall@ed.ac.uk
[2] University of Innsbruck, Technikerstr. 21a/2 6020, Innsbruck, Austria

Abstract. Recent years have seen increasing success in building large formal proof developments using interactive theorem provers (ITPs). Some proofs have involved many authors, years of effort, and resulted in large, complex interdependent sets of proof "source code" files. Developing these in the first place, and maintaining and extending them afterwards, is a considerable challenge. It has prompted the idea of *Proof Engineering* as a new sub-field, to find methods and tools to help. It is natural to try to borrow ideas from Software Engineering for this.

In this paper we investigate the idea of defining *proof metrics* by analogy with software metrics. We seek metrics that may help to monitor and compare formal proof developments, which might be used to guide good practice, locate likely problem areas, or suggest refactorings. Starting from metrics that have been proposed for object-oriented design, we define analogues for formal proofs. We show that our metrics enjoy reasonable properties, and we demonstrate their behaviour with some practical experiments, showing changes over time as proof developments evolve, and making comparisons across between different ITPs.

1 Introduction

Interactive formal proof has advanced to make some impressive achievements, demonstrating that large software and hardware systems can be verified and that large mathematical proofs can be completely captured on machine, giving very high degrees of confidence each case. Some examples are:

- Hales's *FlySpeck* formalisation of his proof of the Kepler Conjecture [13], which includes about 510,000 lines of code proving 27,451 lemmas in the HOL Light interactive theorem prover. This involved a team of 22 people, and an estimated total of 20 person-years of work [14].
- Klein's verification of the seL4 microkernel [20], the core of which consists of almost 400,000 lines of code with 59,000 lemmas, which verifies around 9,000 lines of C and assembler code in the Isabelle ITP. This project involved a team of 13 people, and an estimated total of 20 person-years of work.
- The Compendium of Complex Lattices book formalized in Mizar, performed by a team of 15 people led by Bancerek [3]: it consists of 57 articles with 2,566 theorems and 124,628 lines of proof; it took over 5 person-years.

© Springer-Verlag Berlin Heidelberg 2016
P. Stevens and A. Wąsowski (Eds.): FASE 2016, LNCS 9633, pp. 325–341, 2016.
DOI: 10.1007/978-3-662-49665-7_19

In each case, the result consists of instructions written in a dedicated *formal proof language* which direct the proof engine to check a formal proof of some logical statement; these instructions are sometimes called a (formal) *proof script*.

To give further background for those unfamiliar: a *proof script* is somewhat like a program written in an ordinary programming language; like a program it is usually stored in a plain text file. In *interactive* theorem proving, one works intensively with the machine's help to build the proof script; the system checks progress at intermediate points. There are several currently successful ITP systems in which large proofs have been constructed, including the three mentioned above, and others such as HOL4, Coq, ACL2 and PVS. Some ITPs are conceptually similar and use related logics, but each implementation has its own formal proof language so proofs scripts from one cannot be used in another; there are few, if any, useful tools that work for more than one system. This is like the situation with different programming languages, but the user community for each ITP is small. Learning an ITP requires expertise and typically takes months.

Despite the fragmentation, ITPs have continually advanced so that multi-person developments are more common. Leaders of large proof projects have become concerned about the engineering aspects of building and then maintaining large proof scripts, motivating a new sub-field of study: *Proof Engineering* [6,10,19]. There are many questions which we do not yet know how to answer. For example: How should a large proof be broken into separate modules? Given a large proof, how can we tell if it is well-structured or in need of improvement, perhaps to improve understanding or maintainability? If a basic definition needs to be changed, how much of the rest of the development will break? These are similar to the concerns of software engineering, so it is natural to ask if software engineering research and practice can provide ideas that transfer.

1.1   From Software Metrics to Proof Metrics

In this paper we make some first steps to investigate *proof metrics*, deliberately making a connection to software metrics that have been studied extensively and found utility in practice. Certainly it would be useful to get a handle on the size and complexity of a formal proof and its change over time. It would also be useful to understand how well-structured a formal proof is; one of the most painful proof engineering activities is refactoring existing proofs to change structure [11]; so much so that it is often avoided [12]. So the classic software design goals for modularity of high *coherence* (a module should contain related things) and low *coupling* (connected modules should only have a few connections) are equally applicable to formal proof development.

As our starting point, we take inspiration from the landmark metrics for object-oriented design that were introduced by Chidamber and Kemerer [7] ("C&K"). Although the C&K metrics have since been criticised and modified in a myriad of ways, they still stand as a plausible starting point for a new application area. In particular, they are appropriate because they have simple definitions and motivations and also because there is a rough analogy between the static structure of an object-oriented design and the structure of proof scripts.

OOP	Formal proof
class	proof module
class inheritance	proof module import
instance variable	declaration of a type or constant
method	theorem
method type	theorem statement
method body	theorem proof

Fig. 1. A loose analogy between object-oriented programming and formal proof

Just as with programs, large formal proofs are broken up into *modules*. Various sorts of module have been studied and are adopted in different systems, supporting both in-the-small structuring (e.g., capturing the notion of an algebraic structure with its operations and axioms: *locales* in Isabelle) and in-the-large (e.g., capturing a whole collection of definitions and properties about groups). Here we are concerned with in-the-large modules which form the basic top-level decomposition of a formal proof. In Isabelle modules are called *theories*, in Mizar they are called *articles*; in HOL Light, modules are identified with files.

Top-level modules contain statements to be proved and their proofs, which we (and most ITPs) call *theorems*. A formal proof also needs to define the subject of its concern: whether some mathematics or a proof of software correctness, *declarations* and *definitions* are needed to introduce types and constants of discourse. Although specific mechanisms differ, top-level modules have some *import* mechanism to allow access to other modules. Scoping mechanisms for restricting visibility are currently either primitive or little used; hence visibility of imported theorems usually extends transitively through imported modules, just as class inheritance extends member visibility transitively through the class hierarchy. (Section 2 shows some small example proofs and import graphs, along with the abstraction that we use to define metrics.)

This leads us to the loose analogy shown in Fig. 1. Classes in OO design or programming are like proof modules. Theorems are somewhat like methods: both have complex bodies that describe their implementation. In OO, instance variables capture the nature of what a class models; methods inspect and manipulate the variables. In ITP land, theorem statements describe properties of (immutable) types and constants. Proofs may refer to further types and constants and to other theorems: usually ones proved earlier in some well-founded ordering. This is analogous to methods that invoke other methods in their implementation. (As an aside: ITPs grudgingly admit theorems without proof: *assumptions* or *axioms* taken as given; this allows a form of top-down development, but does not really make up for the lack of any modeling language or technology.)

The plan is now clear. Using the analogy, size metrics that consider the number of methods in a class can be recast as metrics counting the number of theorems in a theory. Metrics based on the class hierarchy relationships can be recast to examine dependencies among proof modules. And so on; how we recast the C&K metrics is defined precisely and discussed in Sect. 3. We can also show that our metrics satisfy some analytical properties which have been studied in software metrics; this is covered in Sect. 4.

There is a risk that the investigation may be futile. Despite good properties, naive translations of software metrics using Fig. 1 could result in functions that are uninteresting or meaningless in the setting of formal proof. Our analogy is rough: the structuring mechanisms differ, and programs have dynamics which is the whole purpose of their construction. But the dynamics of a completed formal proof is a one-shot check and annotation: a black-box operation in which the ITP emits compilation errors if the developer made a mistake or a "QED" acknowledgement in the case of success.

To demonstrate that our metrics may be actually interesting in practice, we examine several large repositories of formal developments, taken from three different ITPs. Our metrics confirm some expected "folklore" aspects of the system differences. Looking at some version control history, we are able to correlate certain changes in formal proof files with changes in the expected metrics, and vice-versa. Our practical experiments are described in Sect. 5.

Contributions. We believe this is the first attempt to adapt ideas from software metrics to formal proof that goes beyond size-based metrics. We contribute:

1. a simple abstract model definition for formal proofs;
2. a precise definition of a set of *proof metrics* using this model;
3. (informal) proofs that our metrics satisfy some reasonable properties;
4. an implementation of the metrics for three different ITPs;
5. demonstration of metrics for various large proof corpora;
6. demonstration of the historical change of the metrics on 38 versions taken from the version control history of HOL Light.

As well as size measurements, our metrics include *complexity* against relationships and positions within a proof development and estimates of *interdependence* between parts of a formal proof.

Related Work. There is a large literature on software metrics concerning their definition and empirical study as well as (often) debating their utility. Despite any debate, metrics continue to be studied and used in practice. For example, metrics are used in cost estimations models (e.g., COCOMO and variants; see Trendowicz and Jeffrey for a recent overview [29]). They can also be used to implement heuristics to detect "bad smells" in code that may suggest when refactorings may be desirable [27] or where they have occured in the past [9].

On the side of formal proof, the topic is quite new. Researchers in the seL4 project have set out an agenda similar to ours [17] and empirically demonstrated a relationship between theorem statement size and proof size [23] in seL4 and, to a restricted extent, other Isabelle proofs (see Sects. 5 and 6 for more remarks). Also for Isabelle, Blanchette et al. [5] studied the dependencies and size of whole formalization libraries in the AFP contributed library. They found little entry reuse based on the import graph and showed that the size distribution of the entries follows the power law. Working with Mizar proofs, Pak investigated ways of improving proof readability using notions of legibility based on locality of reference, taking inspiration from models of cognitive perception [24]; this is similar to the software engineering idea of cohesion, which is a metric we define. We mention some other related work in the body of the paper.

2   Programming Formal Proofs

Languages of different ITPs vary considerably, but all provide the user with a way to express theorem statements and give proofs, which the system verifies. There are two predominant styles of proof script: *procedural*, where user instructions (*tactics*) are transformations that successively refine a state backwards from the goal; and *declarative*, where instructions drive the ITP forwards to its target, providing *justifications* "by" that gives the ITP hints. Some systems support both styles. Often, procedural proofs are easier to write and declarative proofs are easier to read. To give a flavour, Fig. 2 shows two formal proof excerpts.

In both styles, instructions used in a theorem's proof take arguments that are theorems themselves, creating dependencies between theorems. Circular dependencies are not allowed: to prove a theorem P using another theorem Q, Q must be provable itself without P. As proof libraries grow larger, theorems are collected together into modules; a well organised library collects related theorems together. Modules also have a cycle-free dependency ordering, as new modules are built from older ones. Figure 3 shows the dependencies between modules and theorems in the first part of the HOL Light library.

```
let REAL_INV_SGN = prove
  ('∀x. real_inv(real_sgn x)
    = real_sgn x',
  GEN_TAC THEN
  REWRITE_TAC[real_sgn] THEN
  REPEAT COND_CASES_TAC THEN
  REWRITE_TAC[REAL_INV_0;
    REAL_INV_1;
    REAL_INV_NEG]
  );;
```

```
lemma abs_triangle_ineq2:
  "|a| - |b| ≤ |a - b|"
proof -
  have "|a| = |b + (a - b)|"
    by (simp add: algebra_simps)
  then have "|a| ≤ |b| + |a - b|"
    by (simp add: abs_triangle_ineq)
  then show ?thesis
    by (simp add: algebra_simps)
qed
```

Fig. 2. A HOL Light procedural proof (left) and an Isabelle declarative proof (right).

2.1   Formal Proof Developments, Abstractly

We now model this situation. Suppose two sets of identifiers: the *module names* $\mathcal{M}$ and the *theorem names* $\mathcal{T}$. For simplicity (to avoid considering notions of scope) but without loss of generality, we assume that theorem names are globally unique. So each theorem belongs to a module: the mapping mn : $\mathcal{T} \to \mathcal{M}$ returns the module name of a given theorem. We use "theorem" in a general sense,

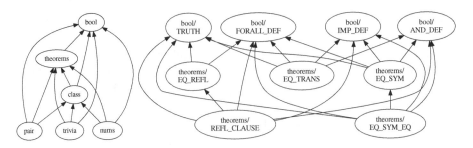

Fig. 3. Module dependencies and theorem dependencies in HOL Light.

in reality ITP modules can contain declarations or definitions of various other things (axioms, constants, types, syntax, etc.); we are agnostic whether these are included in the abstract notion of "theorem" or not.

Definition 1 (Proof Module and Proof Development)

- A proof module *is a pair* (M, T) *of a module name* $M \in \mathcal{M}$ *and a finite set of theorem names* $T \subset \mathcal{T}$ *such that* $\mathsf{mn}(t) = M$ *for all* $t \in T$.
- A proof development $P = \{(M, T_M)\}$ *is given by a finite set of proof modules having distinct module names* M.

Formal mathematics is a well-founded endeavour: later definitions or theorems may only depend on ones that have been given earlier. Theorem dependency relations have been investigated in practice before for real systems (e.g., [1,26]) but the next definition has not been spelled out before.

Definition 2 (Proof Development Dependency)

- A module dependency (uses) relation $\rightarrow^{\mathrm{M}}$ *is a well-founded relation on a subset of* $\mathcal{M}$. *We write* $\leq_{\mathrm{M}}$ *for the reflexive, transitive closure of* $\rightarrow^{\mathrm{M}}$.
- A theorem dependency (uses) relation $\rightarrow^{\mathrm{T}}$ *is a well-founded relation on a subset of* $\mathcal{T}$. *We write* $\leq_{\mathrm{T}}$ *for the reflexive, transitive closure of* $\rightarrow^{\mathrm{M}}$.
- A dependency for a proof development P *is given by a module dependency relation* $\rightarrow^{\mathrm{M}}$ *on the module names of* P, *together with a theorem dependency relation* $\rightarrow^{\mathrm{T}}$ *on all of the theorem names in* P, *which respects* $\rightarrow^{\mathrm{M}}$ *in the sense that* $t_1 \rightarrow^{\mathrm{T}} t_2 \implies \mathsf{mn}(t_1) \leq_{\mathrm{M}} \mathsf{mn}(t_2)$.

Thus, a proof development forms a DAG of modules which overlays a set of DAGs of theorems. Note that we distinguish direct or "immediate" dependencies from indirect ones: a theorem t_3 may use a theorem t_2, in its proof which in turn uses t_1 ($t_3 \rightarrow^{\mathrm{T}} t_2$ and $t_2 \rightarrow^{\mathrm{T}} t_1$); but t_3 may have a different proof that uses both t_2 and t_1 directly ($t_3 \rightarrow^{\mathrm{T}} t_1$ and $t_3 \rightarrow^{\mathrm{T}} t_2$). In both cases t_3 ultimately depends on t_1, so $t_3 \leq_{\mathrm{T}} t_1$.

Module dependencies suggest the proof checking (or compilation) order: we suppose that proofs of theorems in each module are checked together, and modules are checked in some defined or inferred order. Then $M_2 \leq_{\mathrm{M}} M_1$ says that

M_2 is the later module that may build on concepts and lemmas, etc., given in M_1. So whenever $t_2 \to^T t_1$, we require that t_1 has been checked in the same or an earlier module (perhaps transitively earlier) than t_1.

The converse implication need not hold; module dependencies can be "loose" in that they may not reflect any (direct or transitive) theorem dependencies; a bit like "redundant imports" in programming languages. We call a module dependency $M_1 \to^M M_2$ between different modules *strict* only when there is indeed some $t_1 \leq_T t_2$ for which $mn(t_1) = M_1$ and $mn(t_2) = M_2$. In our implementation of the metrics to follow, we take the theorem dependency relation to be primary, and derive $\to^M$ as the minimal strict relation between modules which respects $\to^T$. This is an implementation choice that conveniently unifies the treatment between different systems.

The theorem dependency relationship is all that we use to model the bodies of theorems (an axiom has no dependencies). But we need more to capture theorem statements. To avoid any detail of the logical language for statements we suppose that there is an abstract set of *features* $\mathcal{F}$ which capture the constants, types, etc. that a theorem statement may refer to. We suppose, for simplicity again, that every theorem name is associated globally with a statement, so there is a mapping $fea : \mathcal{T} \to Fin(\mathcal{F})$. Given a theorem t, $fea(t) \subset \mathcal{F}$ is the finite set of features used in its statement. For example, the Kepler conjecture, which gives an upper bound on ball packings in $\mathbb{R}^3$ with the formal HOL Light statement:

```
∀V. packing V ⟹ (∃c. ∀r. &1 ≤ r
              ⟹ &(CARD(V INTER ball(vec 0,r))) ≤
                pi * r pow 3 / sqrt(&18) + c * r pow 2)
```

can be characterized by the following features based on the constants and types appearing in its formal statement:

$$fea(\text{kepler\_conjecture}) = \{ \text{packing}, \text{sqrt}, \text{ball}, \text{pi}, \text{BIT0}, \text{BIT1}, \text{NUMERAL}, 0,$$
$$\text{real\_add}, \text{real\_div}, \text{real\_le}, \text{real\_mul}, \text{real\_of\_num}$$
$$\text{real\_pow}, \text{CARD}, \text{INTER}, 3, \text{cart}, \text{num}, \text{prod}, \text{real} \}.$$

3   Six Simple Proof Metrics

In their landmark paper [7], now over 20 years old, Chidamber and Kamerer proposed metrics for object-oriented design which are also applicable to implementations in object-oriented programs. They consolidated earlier work and aimed to set their metrics on a rigorous footing. They designed six metrics for OOD: each metric is a function on a class. The metrics were evaluated by checking analytically that they possess reasonable properties and by examining the result of their application in two real software projects.

Here we revisit C&K's metrics and recast them for formal proof developments. There have been many criticisms, variants and improvements on C&K's work, and empirical studies providing varying degrees of external validation. In this first study, we cannot expect to find perfect metrics for formal proof so we start off with a "straw-man" proposal inspired by this indisputably key work.

3.1   WTM: Weighted Theorems per Module

WTM is our analogue of C&K's WMC, *Weighted Methods per Class*, which is a basic size assessment of a module. Let the theorems of a proof module M be $T_M = \{t_1, \ldots, t_n\}$. Then WTM is defined by:

$$\text{WTM}(M) = \sum_{i=1}^{n} c(t_i)$$

where c is some complexity function applied to theorems t_i in the theory T.

The idea of the complexity function is that it allows more complex theorems to be given a higher weighting. For example, we could measure the size of the theorem statement (perhaps counting distinct constants unwinding definitions recursively [6,23]), or, we could instead measure proof size by counting the number of lines-of-code in the proof script for the theorem's proof. The simplest choice (and common in OOP studies) is to take c to be the identity, so WTM=n, the number of theorems in the theory.

3.2   DIT: Depth in Tree

The metric DIT calculates the maximum depth of the proof module in the module dependency graph; it corresponds to the DIT metric for a class in OOP which measures the depth of a class in the inheritance tree. Intuitively, higher DIT values in a proof development suggest modules that are potentially more complex since they rely on more levels of previously constructed proofs. We define:

$$\text{DIT}(M) = depth_P(M)$$

where $depth_P(M_n)$ is the length n of the longest path $M_n \to^M M_{n-1} \cdots \to^M M_0$.

3.3   NOC: Number of Children

The Number of Children, NOC, for a proof module is the number of immediate descendent modules that depend upon it. This is defined as:

$$\text{NOC}(M) = |\{ M' \mid M \to^M M' \}|$$

In OOP, this is a measure of scope of a class: how many other classes immediately depend on this one. Intuitively, modules with higher NOC values may incur greater cost to change, since a local change will have a broader effect. But at the same time, a higher NOC shows a greater reuse, indicating that the module is actually used in many places, demonstrating that it is good or important.

C&K suggest that too many children may indicate "improper" abstraction: superclasses should not be overly general. They found a case of this in a project they examined. In proof developments, we expect the core library modules to have many children. OOP languages often have a separate import mechanism for library functions, independently of subclassing. This is a tension in our analogy: class inheritance is arguably more akin to theories in-the-small, but in-the-small proof modules are less widely used and harder to compare across systems.

3.4   CBM: Coupling Between Modules

C&K define a metric called Coupling Between Object classes (CBO) which is a complexity measure on the class hierarchy. Two classes are coupled if one uses member functions or instance variables of the other. Our analogous metric is:

$$\text{CBM}(M) = |\, \{\, M' \mid M \to^{\text{M}} M' \lor M' \to^{\text{M}} M \,\}\,|$$

Intuitively, coupling refers to the degree of interdependence between parts of a design: it means dependency as ancestor or child. Modules with higher coupling values are more closely bound into the proof development hierarchy, meaning that they may be difficult to understand in isolation. The simple definition above doesn't account for a multiplicity of couplings between modules. Later work on OOP coupling metrics addressed this; we might similarly consider a metric which counts the number of strict theorem dependencies that cross module boundaries.

3.5   TDM: Total Dependencies for Module

C&K's next metric is RFC, Response For a Class, which counts the number of methods that could be executed in response to a message received by an object of that class. Intuitively this may estimate the potential (dynamic) complexity of behaviours of objects in the class; high RFC values might suggest classes that are harder to test. We re-interpret this using theorem dependency:

$$\text{TDM}(M) = |\, \{\, t' \mid t \to^{\text{T}} t' \land t \in T_M \,\}\,|$$

There is no analogue of "response" for a theorem, but just as invoking a method $m()$ leads to invoking other methods mentioned in the body of m, our metric counts the number of theorems depended on in the definition of a given theorem. Notice that this includes internal dependencies which do not cross the module boundary, as well as external ones.

In the proof setting, we hypothesise that this metric may suggest the overall brittleness of a theory: if (too) many other theorems are used in the construction of a module, it may break easily if the statements of those other theorems change.

3.6   LCOM: Lack of Cohesion in Module

The final metric given by C&K is LCOM, originally Lack of Cohesion of Methods in a class. Cohesion refers to internal consistency within a module; a high LCOM value suggests a module that gathers together many unrelated things. C&K's metric is defined as the difference between the number of pairs of methods which that entirely different instance variables (p), and the number of pairs of methods that access some of the same attributes (q); LCOM was taken to be $p - q$ or zero if $q > p$. Early on, LCOM was criticised for failing to fit empirical data [4], spawning a slew of alternatives (for partial surveys, see e.g. [2,22]).

As a first proposal for the formal proof setting, we suggest a metric based on theorem statement dissimilarity counted using features: two theorems are similar if they concern the same concepts, and so mention the same constant names, types, etc.[1] An overall measure of similarity for the module is given by summing up the Jaccard index for each pair of theorem statements:

$$\text{sim}(M) = \sum_{i=1}^{n} \sum_{j=i+1}^{n} \frac{|\text{ fea}(t_i) \cap \text{fea}(t_j)\,|}{|\text{ fea}(t_i) \cup \text{fea}(t_j)\,|}$$

Then we compute LCOM as the average dissimilarity:

$$\text{LCOM}(M) = 1 - \frac{\text{sim}(M)}{\frac{1}{2}(n^2 - n)}.$$

(this is similar to CC, among others [2]). Unlike the preceding metrics which are on an interval scale with no maximum, LCOM is a ratio in the range 0 to 1.

4   Properties of Proof Metrics

Weyuker [31] proposed desirable analytical properties for structured program metrics, six of which were adapted by C&K to OOD, again, generating much subsequent discussion and criticism. Here we briefly revisit the properties and their connection to our metrics.

Several properties relate to combinations of programs; for structured programming this meant, essentially simple juxtaposition of source code $P; Q$. Composition in OOP is more complicated. But for our simple model of formal proof languages, we suppose that the operation $M + M'$ stands for (disjoint) combination of modules.

Proposition 1. *Properties of formal proof metrics.*

W1 **Non-coarseness.** *Given a module M and a metric μ, one can always find a module M' st $\mu(M) \neq \mu(M')$.* This is satisfied by all of our metrics.

W2 **Non-uniqueness.** *There can be distinct modules M and M' with $\mu(M) = \mu(M')$.* This is satisfied by all of our metrics.

W3 **Design is important.** *Two modules M and M' may have the same meaning without $\mu(M) = \mu(M')$ holding.* If we take the semantics of an abstract module to be the set of (named) theorems it proves, then this property is not satisfied by the basic size metric WTM metric or the cohesion metric LCOM, which only consider the (number of) theorem statements and don't relate to design-in-the-large. Of course the property holds if we consider the full proof language, which has a complex concrete syntax, so many ways to describe the same module.

W4 **Monotonicity.** *For all M and M', $\mu(M) \leq \mu(M + M')$ and $\mu(M') \leq \mu(M + M')$.* This is true for all of our metrics except LCOM, since it is normalised for comparison between modules; LCOM can be reduced by adding theorems to a module that have an average greater similarity to those already there.

---

[1] A similar idea was in fact suggested by Matichuk et al. [23] as future work.

W5 **Combination can cause interaction.** $\exists M_1, M_2, M_3$ such that $\mu(M_1) = \mu(M_2)$ does not imply $\mu(M_1 + M_3) \neq \mu(M_1 + M_3)$. This property can be satisfied for all the dependency related metrics, but not the size measure WTM. It can be satisfied by LCOM since this is non-compositional.

W6 **Interaction can increase complexity.** $\exists M_1, M_2$ such that $\mu(M_1) + \mu(M_2) < \mu(M_1 + M_2)$. This opposite of the triangle inequality fails for all of our metrics except LCOM. C&K argued against it; all of their metrics failed it and it prevents μ being a distance metric in the mathematical sense.

5   Experimental Study

To test our metrics, we implemented a tool to make calculations using feature and dependency data exported from (suitably modified) ITPs during proof checking. Then we investigated the metrics on a range of existing formal proof developments and their version histories.

5.1   Large Proof Development Examples

We investigated large developments in three systems:

1. The Kepler formal proof, FlySpeck: we focused on the final version of the text formalization [13] together with the underlying core library of HOL Light and the formalization of Multivariate Analysis [15] (SVN revision 245).
2. The Isabelle HOL Main (core library) theory together with three formalizations: cryptographic protocols, Auth [25]; Java bytecode, Bali; and Probability theory [16] (Isabelle 2015 release version).
3. The Mizar Mathematical Library. We focused on the basic libraries of formalized topology and theory of lattices [3] (Mizar version 7.11.07, MML version 4.156.1112).

In each case, information was exported in a uniform format, containing theorem dependencies and statement features. To be as similar as possible across provers, we used symbol features (i.e., names of constants and types present in the theorem statement, as shown in Sect. 2.1), rather than more complex notions.

For HOL Light, we used the HOLyHammer proof advice tool [18] by Kaliszyk and Urban. For the Isabelle formalizations we used the Blanchette's TPTP/-Mash_Export [21], which can compute dependencies and MaSh features for a given set of Isabelle/HOL theories. For Mizar, used the data available in the MPTP2078 challenge by Urban [30]. The challenge includes the proof dependencies and statements for the selected Mizar articles. We extracted symbol features using standard TPTP tools [28].

Space precludes a complete breakdown of metric values, but the summary in Fig. 4 shows the averages for each development. From theorem count totals we can see, for example, how large Flyspeck is; but metrics give an idea of the form of its structure: it has a large number of modules with comparatively fewer theorems, compared to library code. This likely contributes to the better cohesion score. For module hierarchy, the development is, on average, almost twice as deep as the next deepest, Isabelle's highly structured Main HOL library.

		#mods	#thms	TDM	WTM	NOC	CBM	DIT	LCOM%
HOL Light	Core	21	2618	391	125	7.4	14.8	6.8	75.2
	Multivariate	19	11093	3091	584	7.0	34.9	7.6	75.6
	Flyspeck	237	12999	1582	55	12.6	44.1	27.6	62.0
Isabelle	Main	73	12731	357	174	8.9	17.9	17.6	72.2
	Auth	38	4282	202	209	2.9	12.7	3.9	57.1
	Bali	25	6946	261	502	4.7	16.8	4.2	66.8
	Multivariate	50	7821	245	287	2.1	16.5	3.9	61.0
	Probability	45	5928	460	246	4.7	26.5	7.7	62.7
Mizar	MPTP2078	33	3646	270	110	9.3	26.3	10.2	73.8

Fig. 4. The overall statistics for the considered proof libraries together with the mean values of the proposed proof metrics computed on these libraries.

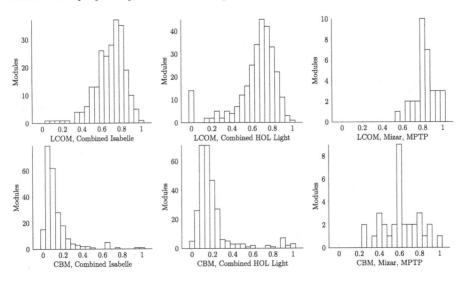

Fig. 5. Cohesion (top) and coupling (bottom) distributions across modules in the three ITPs. Coupling is normalized to $[0; 1]$ for comparison.

5.2 Distribution of Cohesion and Coupling

In general, the metrics differ widely across modules in the same formal library, so it is interesting to examine their distributions. Figure 5 shows the distributions of cohesion and coupling across the three considered ITPs. Cohesion shows a similar distribution across the systems, with slightly higher values for Mizar. For Mizar we focused on a more advanced part of the library without including all the foundational modules; perhaps suprisingly we see high dissimilarity scores within those modules. In HOL Light we see a peak on the histogram for the zero bracket. This is because of a few Flyspeck modules that export precisely one theorem with a large complicated proof. When it comes to coupling, we see that coupling is generally low, but higher for the Mizar case: this is to be expected because we considered a self-contained development in isolation.

5.3 LCOM, TDM, and WTM over Time

We compared metrics for the HOL Light core library over the last five years of HOL Light development, by exporting the data from 38 selected SVN revisions. The values of selected metrics for these revisions are depicted in Fig. 6. In general, the library has grown to prove more theorems over time without changing its modular structure. The average WTM and TDM both increase, showing the growing average number of theorems per module and complexity of the dependency relationship. The jump in LCOM and TDM between revisions 200 and 205 can be traced back to the removal of a module called ind_defs, the only change in modular structure that we see. As the library becomes more dense, similar theorems added to the same modules may decrease LCOM, which is seen around version 145. LCOM can also change because of library restructuring; we show an example of this next.

5.4 Case Study: HOL Light Refactoring

On Dec 1, 2011 John Harrison slightly reorganised the HOL Light library. He moved definitions of supremum and infimum of a set along with all the properties of these concepts from Multivariate/misc to sets. Three basic Archimedian properties moved from Multivariate/misc to real. Finding this history in the version control logs, we examined the impact on our metrics.

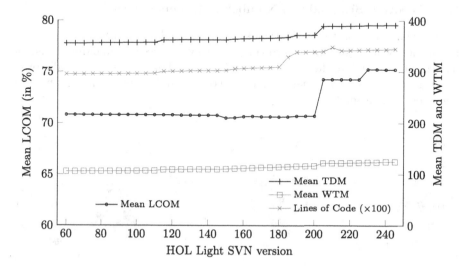

Fig. 6. The values of the metrics for the HOL Light core library compared to the number of lines of code over five years of HOL Light development.

		real	sets	infsup	misc	Ave.
LCOM (%)	before	68.8	90.5	-	84.7	81.3
	after	68.7	90.3	-	87.4	82.1
	separate	68.7	90.5	49.6	87.4	74.0
TDM	before	286	501	-	503	430.0
	after	292	542	-	482	438.7
	separate	292	501	237	482	376.5
WTM	before	286	468	-	155	303.0
	after	289	517	-	103	303.0
	separate	289	468	49	103	227.3

Fig. 7. The impact of a library reorganization on the proof metrics.

Figure 7 shows the results for LCOM, TDM and WTM. The latter metrics reflect moves but averages do not change, since the theorems proved and their proofs stay the same. For LCOM, there is small reduction for `real` and `sets` by the moves, reflecting that relocated theorems enjoyed similarity and/or were similar to those of their destination modules. But the `misc` module was left with a poorer score; less similarity remained among what was left. As an experiment we tested what would happen if a separate module `infsup` was added to hold the relocated theorems about infimum and supremum; the new module introduces few cross-module dependencies decreasing TDM and has a much better cohesion score which brings down the average LCOM value for the whole development.

5.5 Theorem Size and the Number of Dependencies

In a striking recent result, Matichuk et al. showed that proof size increases quadratically with statement size (measured by recursively unfolding constant names) in the seL4 verification [23]. This is potentially useful as a predictor of effort, in connection to earlier work that shows a relation between human effort and proof size in seL4.

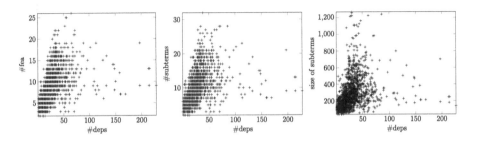

Fig. 8. The number of dependencies compared to three notions of theorem statement size on the Mizar/MPTP2078 proof library.

As a related comparison with a different ITP, and to investigate potential ways of measuring statement size, we compared the number of dependencies with the number of theorem features, the number of subterms in a statement and the size of the theorem statement in MPTP2078. The scatter plots in Fig. 8 show our results. Although increasing numbers of dependencies tend to correspond with larger statement sizes, there are no clear relationships, and plenty of outliers. This is not surprising: we are in a very different setting, with mathematical proofs constructed using an automation strategy, which is rather powerful for the considered domain.

6 Conclusions

This is the first (to our knowledge) investigation of formal proof metrics which considers both the *modular structure* of a proof development and its size profile. We also gave the first implementation and experimental data for metrics applied to proofs in more than one theorem proving system, raising intriguing questions of whether such measures can be used to compare developments across systems.

There are many caveats for this initial study. It is easy to imagine improvements to our definitions, or to spot potential flaws (e.g., one issue: we count dependencies manifested in final proofs, rather than ones the user mentioned).

Nevertheless, we are believe that our results give evidence of potential value for proof metrics. A central question around metrics — can we show that they actually measure something? — is perhaps even more thorny than for software. Notions of formal proof quality are not yet developed and there are questions over what to assess empirically. Defect prediction is not an obvious aim; bugs as such do not exist in formal proof. If a proof is found by the system, it must be correct! (Saying this, definitions and theorem statements *can* be wrong, even inconsistent, which is serious; dependency metrics might provide hints on that.) Effort prediction in general cannot be feasible: ITPs work in undecidable proof systems, which means that there are profound theorems that have short statements but will need immensely long proofs. The Kepler statement shown in Sect. 2.1 is (almost certainly) just such an example. So it is hard to imagine a mathematical analogue of "function points". Software or hardware verification is a more hopeful domain: where a body of proofs exists about some complex system, we may hope to see correlated scaling effects in proof size or effort as the system evolves, or as more properties are proven; Matichuk et al. [23] have demonstrated a case of this, as mentioned above. And a different, perhaps more transferable, use of proof metrics may be for *stability* tracking, to see where a development seems to be proceeding to an optimal design. This was found to be effective in a study of a particular object-oriented framework [8].

Even without general predictive models, we suspect that proof metrics will find a valuable use inside a range of future tools that provide monitoring of proof development progress, and perhaps hints of "bad smells" in a development. We look forward to their further investigation and application.

Acknowledgements. We're grateful to colleagues Iain Whiteside, Ajitha Rajan and the DReaM group at Edinburgh for discussions. The referees provided useful remarks. We acknowledge financial support from grants from UK EPSRC (EP/J001058/1) and the Austrian Science Fund (P26201). For tools and data, please visit http://homepages.inf.ed.ac.uk/da/proofmetrics/.

References

1. Alama, J., Mamane, L., Urban, J.: Dependencies in formal mathematics: applications and extraction for coq and mizar. In: Jeuring, J., Campbell, J.A., Carette, J., Dos Reis, G., Sojka, P., Wenzel, M., Sorge, V. (eds.) CICM 2012. LNCS, vol. 7362, pp. 1–16. Springer, Heidelberg (2012)
2. Al-Dallal, J., Briand, L.C.: A precise method-method interaction-based cohesion metric for object-oriented classes. ACM Trans. Softw. Eng. Methodol. **21**(2), 8:1–8:34 (2012)
3. Bancerek, G., Rudnicki, P.: A compendium of continuous lattices in MIZAR. J. Autom. Reasoning **29**(3–4), 189–224 (2002)
4. Basili, V.R., Briand, L.C., Melo, W.L.: A validation of object-oriented design metrics as quality indicators. IEEE Trans. Softw. Eng. **22**(10), 751–761 (1996)
5. Blanchette, J.C., Haslbeck, M., Matichuk, D., Nipkow, T.: Mining the archive of formal proofs. In: Kerber, M., Carette, J., Kaliszyk, C., Rabe, F., Sorge, V. (eds.) CICM 2015. LNCS, vol. 9150, pp. 3–17. Springer, Heidelberg (2015)
6. Bourke, T., Daum, M., Klein, G., Kolanski, R.: Challenges and experiences in managing large-scale proofs. In: Jeuring, J., Campbell, J.A., Carette, J., Dos Reis, G., Sojka, P., Wenzel, M., Sorge, V. (eds.) CICM 2012. LNCS, vol. 7362, pp. 32–48. Springer, Heidelberg (2012)
7. Chidamber, S.R., Kemerer, C.F.: A metrics suite for object oriented design. IEEE Trans. Softw. Eng. **20**(6), 476–493 (1994)
8. Demeyer, S., Ducasse, S.: Metrics, do they really help? In: Malenfant, J. (ed.) Proceedings LMO 1999 (Languages et Models a Objets), pp. 69–82 (1999)
9. Demeyer, S., Ducasse, S., Nierstrasz, O.: Finding refactorings via change metrics. In: Object-Oriented Programming Systems, Languages & Applications, OOPSLA 2000, pp. 166–177 (2000)
10. Gonthier, G., Mathematics, E.: The odd order theorem proof. In: Principles of Programming Languages, POPL 2013, pp. 1–2. ACM (2013)
11. Gonthier, G., Asperti, A., Avigad, J., Bertot, Y., Cohen, C., Garillot, F., Le Roux, S., Mahboubi, A., O'Connor, R., Ould Biha, S., Pasca, I., Rideau, L., Solovyev, A., Tassi, E., Théry, L.: A machine-checked proof of the odd order theorem. In: Blazy, S., Paulin-Mohring, C., Pichardie, D. (eds.) ITP 2013. LNCS, vol. 7998, pp. 163–179. Springer, Heidelberg (2013)
12. Hales, T.C.: The jordan curve theorem, formally and informally. Am. Math. Mon. **114**(10), 882–894 (2007)
13. Hales, T.C., et al.: A formal proof of the Kepler conjecture. In: CoRR abs/1501.02155 (2015)
14. Hales, T.C., et al.: A revision of the proof of the kepler conjecture. Discrete Comput. Geom. **44**(1), 1–34 (2010)
15. Harrison, J.: The HOL light theory of euclidean space. J. Autom. Reasoning **50**(2), 173–190 (2013)

16. Hölzl, J., Heller, A.: Three chapters of measure theory in Isabelle/HOL. In: van Eekelen, M., Geuvers, H., Schmaltz, J., Wiedijk, F. (eds.) ITP 2011. LNCS, vol. 6898, pp. 135–151. Springer, Heidelberg (2011)
17. Jeffery, R.D., et al.: An empirical research agenda for understanding formal methods productivity. Inf. Softw. Technol. 60, 102–112 (2015)
18. Kaliszyk, C., Urban, J.: Learning-assisted automated reasoning with flyspeck. J. Autom. Reasoning 53(2), 173–213 (2014)
19. Klein, G.: Proof engineering considered essential. In: Jones, C., Pihlajasaari, P., Sun, J. (eds.) FM 2014. LNCS, vol. 8442, pp. 16–21. Springer, Heidelberg (2014)
20. Klein, G., et al.: seL4: Formal verification of an OS kernel. In: Symposium on Operating Systems Principles SOSP, pp. 207–220. ACM (2009)
21. Kühlwein, D., Blanchette, J.C., Kaliszyk, C., Urban, J.: MaSh: Machine learning for sledgehammer. In: Blazy, S., Paulin-Mohring, C., Pichardie, D. (eds.) ITP 2013. LNCS, vol. 7998, pp. 35–50. Springer, Heidelberg (2013)
22. Marcus, A., Poshyvanyk, D.: The conceptual cohesion of classes. In: IEEE International Conference on Software Maintenance, ICSM 2005, pp. 133–142 (2005)
23. Matichuk, D., et al.: Empirical study towards a leading indicator for cost of formal software verification. In: International Conference on Software Engineering, ICSE 2015, pp. 722–732 (2015)
24. Pąk, K.: Automated improving of proof legibility in the mizar system. In: Watt, S.M., Davenport, J.H., Sexton, A.P., Sojka, P., Urban, J. (eds.) CICM 2014. LNCS, vol. 8543, pp. 373–387. Springer, Heidelberg (2014)
25. Paulson, L.C.: The inductive approach to verifying cryptographic protocols. J. Comput. Secur. 6(1–2), 85–128 (1998)
26. Pons, O., Bertot, Y., Rideau, L.: Notions of dependency in proof assistants. In: User Interfaces for Theorem Provers (UITP) (1998)
27. Simon, F., Steinbruckner, F., Lewerentz, C.: Metrics based refactoring. In: Software Maintenance and Reengineering, CSMR. 2001, pp. 30–38 (2001)
28. Sutcliffe, G.: The TPTP world – Infrastructure for automated reasoning. In: Clarke, E.M., Voronkov, A. (eds.) LPAR-16 2010. LNCS, vol. 6355, pp. 1–12. Springer, Heidelberg (2010)
29. Pąk, K.: Automated improving of proof legibility in the mizar system. In: Watt, S.M., Davenport, J.H., Sexton, A.P., Sojka, P., Urban, J. (eds.) CICM 2014. LNCS, vol. 8543, pp. 373–387. Springer, Heidelberg (2014)
30. Urban, J., Sutcliffe, G.: ATP cross-verification of the mizar MPTP challenge problems. In: Dershowitz, N., Voronkov, A. (eds.) LPAR 2007. LNCS (LNAI), vol. 4790, pp. 546–560. Springer, Heidelberg (2007)
31. Weyuker, E.J.: Evaluating software complexity measures. IEEE Trans. Software Eng. 14(9), 1357–1365 (1988)

Reduction Rules for Colored Workflow Nets

Javier Esparza[✉] and Philipp Hoffmann[✉]

Technische Universität München, Munich, Germany
esparza@in.tum.de, ph.hoffmann@tum.de

Abstract. We study Colored Workflow nets [8], a model based on Workflow nets [14] enriched with data. Based on earlier work by Esparza and Desel on the negotiation model of concurrency [3,4], we present reduction rules for our model. Contrary to previous work, our rules preserve not only soundness, but also the data flow semantics. For free choice nets, the rules reduce all sound nets (and only them) to a net with one single transition and the same data flow semantics. We give an explicit algorithm that requires only a polynomial number of rule applications.

1 Introduction

Workflow Petri nets [13,14] are a very successful formalism for modeling and analyzing business processes. They have become the most popular formal backend for graphical notations like BPMN (Business Process Modeling Notation), EPC (Event-driven Process Chain), or UML Activity Diagrams, which typically do not have a formal semantics. By translating the basic constructs of such languages into Petri nets one gets access to a large variety of analysis techniques and tools.

One of these analysis techniques is *reduction*. Reduction algorithms are a very efficient analysis technique for workflows, EPCs, AND-XOR graphs and other models (see for instance [11,15,18,21]). They consist of a set of *reduction rules*, whose application allows one to simplify the workflow while preserving important properties. Reduction aims to elude the state-explosion problem, and, when the property does not hold, provides error diagnostics in the form of an irreducible graph [15]. Moreover, for certain classes of nets the rules can be *complete*, meaning that they reduce all workflows satisfying the property to some unique canonical workflow (and only them); in this case, reduction provides a decision algorithm for the property that avoids any kind of state-space exploration. Reduction algorithms are an important part of the well-known Woflan tool [9,20].

Free choice workflow nets (also called workflow graphs) are a class of workflow nets that captures many control-flow constructs of BPMN, EPC, or Activity Diagrams (see [14], or [6] for a very recent study). In [15] it is shown that a certain set of reduction rules for free choice workflow models, originally presented in [2], preserves the *soundness* property, and is complete. Soundness is a fundamental analysis problem for workflows [14,16]. Loosely speaking, a workflow net is sound if a distinguished marking signaling successful termination is reachable from any reachable marking. The reduction algorithm provides a polynomial-time decision

---

This work was partially funded by the DFG Graduiertenkolleg 1480 (PUMA).

P. Stevens and A. Wąsowski (Eds.): FASE 2016, LNCS 9633, pp. 342–358, 2016.
DOI: 10.1007/978-3-662-49665-7_20

procedure for soundness, in sharp contrast with the fact that deciding soundness is at least PSPACE-hard for general workflow nets[1].

However, the rules of [2] have two important shortcomings. First, while they preserve soundness, they do not preserve any property concerning *data*. Workflows manipulating data can be modeled as *colored* workflow nets [8], where tokens carry data values, and transitions transform a tuple of values for its input places into a tuple of values for its output places. The *linearly dependent place rule* (Rule 2 in Chap. 7 of [2]) allows one to *remove* place p from a net, if it is redundant in the sense that there are other places which together have the same incoming and outgoing transitions as p. However, this reduction does not make sense for the colored workflow net: the tokens on p might hold a value needed by an outgoing transition t to compute the value of the produced tokens! Loosely speaking, the application of the rule destroys the dataflow semantics of the net.

The second shortcoming is that the linearly dependent place rule is not correct for arbitrary workflow nets, only for free choice ones ([2], p. 145[2]). Since not all industrial business processes are free choice (30 % of our benchmarks in Sect. 5 are non-free choice), this considerably reduces the applicability of the rules.

The most satisfactory solution to these two problems would be to replace the linearly dependent place rule by rules extensible to colored nets, while keeping completeness. However, this problem has remained open for over 15 years.

In this paper we solve this problem and present a set of surprisingly simple rules that overcomes the shortcomings. First, the rules can be applied to arbitrary colored workflow nets. Second, they preserve not only the sound/unsound character of the net, but also the *input/output relation* of the workflow; more precisely, the original workflow net has a firing sequence that transforms an entry token with value v_{in} into an exit token with value v_{out} iff the net after the reduction also has such a sequence. Therefore, the rules can be applied to decide any property of the input/output relation. Finally, the new rules are complete for free choice workflow nets.

Our results rely on previous work on *negotiations*, a model of concurrency introduced in [3,4]. Negotiations share many features with Petri nets, but, unlike Petri nets, are a structured model of communicating sequential agents. In [4] a complete set of reduction rules for the class of *deterministic negotiations* is presented. We generalize the results of [4] to show that a similar set of rules is correct for arbitrary workflow nets, and complete for free choice workflow nets. Since the proofs of [4] make strong use of the agent structure, we must substantially modify them, and in fact write many of them from scratch. Moreover, because of the agent structure of negotiations, workflow nets obtained as translations of negotiations are automatically 1-safe. Therefore, the results cannot be used to deal with variants of the soundness notion, like k-soundness or generalized

---

[1] The exact complexity depends on the specifics of the workflow model, for instance whether the workflow Petri net is assumed to be 1-safe or not.

[2] The example of page 145 is not a workflow net, but can be easily transformed into one.

soundness [16]. Making use of the theory of free choice nets we can however show that our rules are still correct and complete for these variants.

Finally, and as a third contribution of the paper, we report on some experimental results. In [4] only the rules and the completeness result are presented, but neither a specific algorithm prescribing a concrete strategy to decide which rule to apply at which point, nor an implementation and experimental validation. In this paper we report on a prototype implementation, and on experimental results on a benchmark suite of nearly 2000 workflows derived from industrial business processes.

Other Related Work. The soundness problem has been extensively studied, both from a theoretical and a practical point of view, and very efficient verification algorithms have been developed (see e.g. [16] for a comprehensive survey). Our approach is not more efficient for checking soundness than the ones of e.g. [5], but can also be applied to checking arbitrary properties of the input/output relation, while retaining completeness. In [10,12] state-space exploration of workflows is performed to identify data flow anti-patterns (like a variable being assigned a value during an execution, but never being read afterwards). Our technique aims at avoiding state-space exploration and considers properties of the input/output relation.

The paper is organized as follows. Section 2 defines workflow nets, free choice nets, and soundness. Section 3 presents our reduction rules and proves them correct. In Sect. 4 we first show completeness for acyclic nets and then extend the result to cyclic nets. Section 5 presents experimental results on the benchmarks of [5,17]. Finally, Sect. 6 contains some conclusions and open questions. The proofs of all results can be found in the arXiv version.

2   Workflow Nets and Colored Workflow Nets

We recall the definitions of workflow nets and the soundness property.

Definition 1 (Workflow Net [14]). *A Workflow net (WF net) is a quintuple* (P, T, F, i, o) *where*

– *P is a finite set of places.*
– *T is a finite set of transitions $(P \cap T = \emptyset)$.*
– *$F \subseteq (P \times T) \cup (T \times P)$ is a set of arcs.*
– *$i, o \in P$ are places such that i has no incoming arcs, o has no outgoing arcs.*
– *The graph $(P \cup T, F \cup (o, i))$ is strongly connected.*

We write $^\bullet p$ and $p^\bullet$ to denote the input and output transitions of a place p, respectively, and similarly $^\bullet t$ and $t^\bullet$ for the input and output places of a transition t. A marking M is a function from P to the natural numbers that assigns a number of tokens to each place. A transition t is enabled at M if all places of $^\bullet t$ contain at least one token in M. An enabled transition may fire, removing a token from each place of $^\bullet t$ and adding one token to each place of $t^\bullet$.

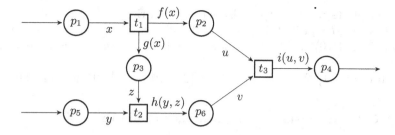

Fig. 1. A partial workflow net with data

The *initial marking* (*final marking*) of a workflow net puts one token on place i (on place o), and no tokens elsewhere. A marking is *reachable* if some sequence of transition firings leads from the initial marking to it. We call elements in $P \cup T$ the nodes of the workflow net.

Definition 2 (Soundness [14]). *A WF net* $\mathcal{W} = (P, T, F, i, o)$ *is sound if*

- *the final marking is reachable from any reachable marking, and*
- *every transition occurs in some firing sequence starting from the initial marking.*

When modeling a workflow, it is useful to model not only control flow but also data flow. We do so by means of Colored Workflow nets.

Definition 3 (Colored WF Net [8]). *A* colored WF net *(CWF net) is a tuple* $\mathcal{W} = (P, T, F, i, o, V, \lambda)$ *where* (P, T, F, i, o) *is a WF net,* V *is a function that assigns to every place* $p \in P$ *a color set* C_p *and* λ *is a function that assigns to each transition* $t \in T$ *a left-total relation* $\lambda(t) \subseteq \prod_{p \in \bullet t} C_p \times \prod_{p \in t \bullet} C_p$ *between the values of the input places and those of the output places of* t.

A colored marking *M of $\mathcal{W}$ is a function that assigns to each place p a multiset $M(p)$ over C_p, interpreted as a multiset of colored tokens currently on p. A colored marking is* initial *(*final*) if it puts one token on place i (on place o), of any color in C_i (C_o), and no tokens elsewhere.*

Observe that there are as many initial markings as elements in C_i. To distinguish between input and output values of a transformer λ, we separate them by a $\rightarrow$.

Consider the partial workflow net in Fig. 1 and take $C_p = \mathbb{N}$ for every place p of the net. An example of a colored marking could be the marking $(\{3\}, \emptyset, \emptyset, \emptyset, \{2, 4\}, \emptyset)$ which puts a token of color 3 on p_1 and two tokens, one of color 2 and one of color 4, on p_5. If $f(x) = x + 1$ and $g(x) = x + 2$, then we have $\lambda(t_1) = \{(n \rightarrow n + 1, n + 2) \mid n \geq 0\}$.

We call $\lambda(t)$ the transformer associated with t. When a transition t fires, the colored marking changes in the expected way [8]: (a) remove a token from each input place of t; (b) choose an element of $\lambda(t)$ whose projection onto the input places matches the tuple of removed tokens; (c) add the projection of $\lambda(t)$ onto the output places to the output places of t. We write $M \xrightarrow{t} M'$ to denote that t is enabled at M and its firing leads to M'. For example, the colored marking $(\{3\}, \emptyset, \emptyset, \emptyset, \{2, 4\}, \emptyset)$ enables transition t_1, and taking $h(y, z) = y \cdot z$ we have

$$(\{3\}, \emptyset, \emptyset, \emptyset, \{2, 4\}, \emptyset) \xrightarrow{t_1} (\emptyset, \{4\}, \{5\}, \emptyset, \{2, 4\}, \emptyset) \xrightarrow{t_2} (\emptyset, \{4\}, \emptyset, \emptyset, \{4\}, \{10\}).$$

2.1 A Colored Version of the Insurance Claim Example

We extend the well known insurance complaint process of [14] with data. The workflow is shown in Fig. 2. After initial registration of the complaint, a questionnaire is sent to the complainant. In parallel, the complaint is evaluated. The evaluation decides whether processing is required. In that case, the processing takes place (e.g. by some employee) and is checked for correctness (e.g. by a senior employee) which may either lead to another round of processing if an error is found, or the processing ends. Finally, the complaint is archived.

We add colors to keep track of the status of the complaint and its estimated cost for the company, modeled by a number in the interval [1..10] (see Table 1). Furthermore each claimant belongs to a customer group, either A or B. A's and B's insurance policies entitle them, respectively, to the full cost or to half the cost of the damage. The color sets of places i, o, c_2, c_6 are the pairs $\{A, B\} \times [1..10]$, modeling the customer group and the cost of the claim as estimated by the customer. The colors of place c_4 additionally contain the result of the evaluation: PR (process) or NPR (do not process). Colors of c_5 store the result of the questionnaire: the answer to the question "was it your fault?" (YES/NO), or a time out (TO). In place c_7, the information from c_4 and c_5 is put together, and in c_8 the result of the first processing is added. Finally, tokens in c_9 can have the same values as those in c_8, plus an additional value ERR if the check at transition check_processing reveals a miscalculation. Tokens in c_6 and o store

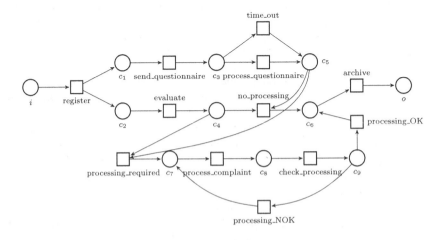

Fig. 2. Insurance claim process

Table 1. Color sets and transformers for the insurance claim workflow

$$C_i = C_o = C_{c_2} = C_{c_6} = \{A, B\} \times [1..10] \qquad C_{c_7} = C_i \times C_{c_5}$$
$$C_{c_1} = C_{c_3} = \{\bullet\} \qquad\qquad\qquad\qquad C_{c_8} = C_{c_7} \times [1..10]$$
$$C_{c_4} = C_i \times \{PR, NPR\} \qquad\qquad\quad C_{c_9} = C_{c_7} \times ([1..10] \cup \{ERR\})$$
$$C_{c_5} = \{YES, NO, TO\}$$

$$\lambda(\texttt{register}) = \{(x, k \to \{\bullet\} \times \{x, k\}) \mid 1 \le k \le 10\}$$
$$\lambda(\texttt{send\_questionnaire}) = \{(\bullet \to \bullet)\}$$
$$\lambda(\texttt{time\_out}) = \{(\bullet \to TO)\}$$
$$\lambda(\texttt{process\_questionnaire}) = \{(\bullet \to YES), (\bullet \to NO)\}$$
$$\lambda(\texttt{evaluate}) = \{(x, k \to x, k, NPR) \mid 1 \le k \le 3\}$$
$$\cup \{(x, k \to x, k, PR) \mid 4 \le k \le 10\}$$
$$\lambda(\texttt{no\_processing}) = \{(x, k, NPR, q \to x, k) \mid 1 \le k \le 3\}$$
$$\lambda(\texttt{processing\_required}) = \{(x, k, PR, q \to x, k, q) \mid 4 \le k \le 10\}$$
$$\lambda(\texttt{process\_complaint}) = \{(x, k, q \to x, k, q, v) \mid 4 \le k \le 10, 1 \le v \le k\}$$
$$\lambda(\texttt{check\_processing}) = \{(x, k, v, q \to x, k, q, v) \mid x = A, 4 \le k \le 10, v = k\}$$
$$\cup \{(x, k, v, q \to x, k, q, v) \mid x = B, 4 \le k \le 10, v = k/2\}$$
$$\cup \{(x, k, v, q \to x, k, q, ERR) \mid \text{otherwise}\}$$
$$\lambda(\texttt{processing\_NOK}) = \{(x, k, q, ERR \to x, k, q) \mid 4 \le k \le 10\}$$
$$\lambda(\texttt{processing\_OK}) = \{(x, k, q, v \to x, v) \mid 4 \le k \le 10, 1 \le v \le 10\}$$
$$\lambda(\texttt{archive}) = \{(x, v \to x, v) \mid (x, v) \in C_{c_6}\}$$

the amount that was actually paid by the company after the processing was successful (or without processing).

Assume that the company's policy is to accept all claims which are evaluated to a value of 3 or less without any further processing, and process all other claims. The transformers modeling this policy are given in Table 1, where $x \in \{A, B\}$ and $q \in \{YES, NO, TO\}$ unless otherwise stated. Division by 2 is assumed to be integer division.

All transformers are self-explanatory except perhaps process_complaint and check_processing. In process_complaint, an employee may lower the customer's estimate k to a new value v. In check_processing, a senior employee checks that the employee made no mistake (modeled by the fact that v must be $k/2$ or k depending on the customer group). If the check fails, an error flag is set and the processing is repeated.

Apart from the soundness of the workflow, we wish to check the following property: if two customers in the same group register insurance complaints, then the one claiming a higher also receives a higher amount (notice that our ideal insurance company does not reject any complaint). We shall use our reduction algorithm to check that the property holds for customers of group A, but not for customers of group B.

The attentive reader may have noticed that the semantics of colored nets allows, e.g., to take the transition no_processing even when the evaluation indicates that processing is necessary. This can easily be dealt with by introducing additional error values that are then propagated until the end. We omit them to ease the reading and assume that no_processing and processing are taken according to the result of evaluate, and similarly in other cases.

2.2 Summaries and Equivalence

Since a workflow net describes a process starting at i and ending at o, it is interesting to study the input/output relation or *summary* of the whole process.

Definition 4 (Summary and Equivalence). *Let $\mathcal{W}$ be a colored WF net. Let $\mathcal{M}_i$ and $\mathcal{M}_o$ be the sets of initial and final colored markings of $\mathcal{W}$. The summary of $\mathcal{W}$ is the relation $S \subseteq \mathcal{M}_i \times \mathcal{M}_o$ given by: $(M_i, M_o) \in S$ iff M_o is reachable from M_i. Two colored WF nets are equivalent iff they are both sound or both unsound, and have the same summary.*

Our rules aim to reduce CWF nets while preserving equivalence. If we are able to reduce a CWF to another one with one single transition t, then the summary is given by $\lambda(t)$, and we say that the CWF has been *completely reduced* and we have *computed the summary*. Since this CWF net is obviously sound and rules preserve equivalence, if a CWF net can be completely reduced, then it is sound. We prove that our rules preserve equivalence for all CWF nets, and give an algorithm that completely reduces all sound *free choice CWF nets*, defined below, by means of a polynomial number of rule applications.

In Sect. 4 we compute the summary of the free choice CWF net of Fig. 2 using our reduction procedure. The result (where we write $M_i \Rightarrow M_o$ instead of $(M_i, M_o) \in S$, and omit the error values) is:

$$\{(A, k \Rightarrow A, k) \mid 1 \le k \le 10\} \cup \{(B, k \Rightarrow B, k) \mid 1 \le k \le 3\}$$
$$\cup \{(B, k \Rightarrow B, k/2) \mid 4 \le k \le 10\}$$

Since the summary contains $(B, 3 \Rightarrow B, 3)$ and $(B, 4 \Rightarrow B, 2)$, the company policy does not satisfy the desired property for customers of group B.

2.3 Free Choice Workflow Nets

We recall the definition of free choice workflow nets [2,14].

Definition 5 (Free Choice Workflow Nets). *A workflow net $\mathcal{W} = (P, T, F, i, o)$ is free choice (FC) if for every two places $p_1, p_2 \in P$ either $p_1^\bullet \cap p_2^\bullet = \emptyset$ or $p_1^\bullet = p_2^\bullet$.*

The net of Fig. 2 is free choice. We also need to introduce clusters, and the new notion of free choice cluster and free choice node.

Definition 6 (Clusters, Free Choice Nodes [2]). *Let $\mathcal{W} = (P, T, F, i, o)$ be a workflow net. The cluster of $x \in P \cup T$ is the unique smallest set $[x] \subseteq P \cup T$ satisfying: $x \in [x]$, if $p \in P \cap [x]$ then $p^\bullet \subseteq [x]$, and if $t \in T \cap [x]$, then $^\bullet t \subseteq [x]$. A set $X \subseteq P \cup T$ is a cluster if $X = [x]$ for some x. A cluster c is free choice if $(p, t) \in F$ for every $p \in P \cap c$ and $t \in T \cap c$. A node x is free choice if $[x]$ is a free choice cluster.*

The sets $\{c_3\} \cup c_3^{\bullet}$ and $\{c_4, c_5\} \cup c_4^{\bullet} \cup c_5^{\bullet}$ are free choice clusters of the net of Fig. 2. It is easy to see that clusters are equal or disjoint, and therefore the clusters of $\mathcal{W}$ are a partition of $P \cup T$. Further, we have $[i] \cap P = \{i\}$ and $[o] = \{o\}$. Finally, we have that $\mathcal{W}$ is free choice iff all its nodes are free choice.

We say that a marking M marks a cluster c if it marks *all* places in c. Observe that if a cluster is marked, then all its transitions are enabled. We say that a cluster fires if one of its transitions fires.

3   Reduction Rules

We present a set of three *reduction rules* for CWF nets similar to those used for transforming finite automata into regular expressions [7].

A reduction rule, or just rule, is a binary relation on the set of CWF nets. For a rule R, we write $W_1 \xrightarrow{R} W_2$ for $(W_1, W_2) \in R$. A rule R is *correct* if it preserves equivalence, i.e., if $W_1 \xrightarrow{R} W_2$ implies that W_1 and W_2 are equivalent.

Given a set of rules $\mathcal{R} = \{R_1, \ldots, R_k\}$, we denote by $\mathcal{R}^*$ the transitive closure of $R_1 \cup \ldots \cup R_k$. We say that $\mathcal{R}$ is *complete* for a class of CWF nets if for every sound CWF net $\mathcal{W}$ in that class there is a CFW net $\mathcal{W}'$ consisting of a single transition between the two only places i and o such that $\mathcal{W} \xrightarrow{\mathcal{R}^*} \mathcal{W}'$.

We describe rules as pairs of a *guard* and an *action*. $W_1 \xrightarrow{R} W_2$ holds if W_1 satisfies the guard, and W_2 is a possible result of applying the action to W_1.

Merge rule. Intuitively, the *merge rule* merges two transitions with the same input and output places into one single transition.

Definition 7. *Merge rule*

Guard: $\mathcal{W}$ *contains two distinct transitions* $t_1, t_2 \in T$ *such that* ${}^{\bullet}t_1 = {}^{\bullet}t_2$ *and* $t_1^{\bullet} = t_2^{\bullet}$.

Action: *(1)* $T := (T \setminus \{t_1, t_2\}) \cup \{t_m\}$, *where* t_m *is a fresh name.*
        (2) $t_m^{\bullet} := t_1^{\bullet}$ *and* ${}^{\bullet}t_m := {}^{\bullet}t_1$.
        (3) $\lambda(t_m) := \lambda(t_1) \cup \lambda(t_2)$.

Iteration rule. Loosely speaking, the iteration rule replaces arbitrary iterations of a transition by a single transition with the same effect.

Definition 8. *Iteration rule*

Guard: $\mathcal{W}$ *contains a free choice cluster* c *with a transition* $t \in c$ *such that* $t^{\bullet} = {}^{\bullet}t$.

Action:
        (1) $T := (T \setminus \{t\})$.
        (2) For all $t' \in c \setminus \{t\}$: $\lambda(t') := \lambda(t)^* \cdot \lambda(t')$ *where* $\lambda(t)^* = \sum_{i \geq 0} \lambda(t)^i$,
        and $\lambda(t)^0$ *is the identity relation.*

Observe that $\lambda(t)^*$ captures the fact that t can be executed arbitrarily often.

Shortcut Rule. The shortcut rule merges transitions of two clusters, one of which will occur as a consequence of the other, into one single transition with the same effect.

Definition 9. *A transition t unconditionally enables a cluster c if $c \cap P \subseteq t^\bullet$.*

Observe that if t unconditionally enables c and a marking M enables t, then the marking M' given by $M \xrightarrow{t} M'$ enables every transition in c.

Definition 10. *Shortcut rule*

Guard: *$\mathcal{W}$ contains a transition t and a free choice cluster $c \notin \{[o], [t]\}$ such that t unconditionally enables c.*

Action:

  (1) $T := (T \setminus \{t\}) \cup \{t'_s \mid t' \in c\}$, where t'_s are fresh names.
  (2) For all $t' \in c$: ${}^\bullet t'_s := {}^\bullet t$ and $t'_s{}^\bullet := (t^\bullet \setminus {}^\bullet t') \cup t'^\bullet$.
  (3) For all $t' \in c$: $\lambda(t'_s) := \lambda(t) \cdot \lambda(t')$.
  (4) If ${}^\bullet p = \emptyset$ for all $p \in c$, then remove c from $\mathcal{W}$.

We also use a restricted version of this rule, called the *d-shortcut rule*. This rule is obtained by adding an additional guard to the shortcut rule: $|c \cap T| = 1$. This guard guarantees that the number of edges does not increase when the d-shortcut rule is applied.

Figure 3 shows a sequence of reductions illustrating the definitions of the rules. Notice that the graphical description does not contain the transformer information. A second example of reduction in which the workflow net also exhibits concurrency is shown in Sect. 4.1.

Theorem 1. *The merge, shortcut and iteration rules are correct for CWF nets.*

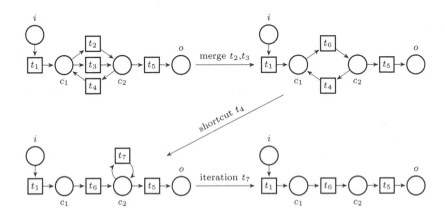

Fig. 3. Example of rule applications

4 Reduction Procedure

We show that the rules presented in the previous section summarize all sound FC-CWF nets in polynomial time. The proof is very involved, and we can only sketch it.

We first show that acyclic FC-CWF nets can be completely reduced.

Definition 11 (Graph). *The graph of a CWF net is the graph $(P \cup T, F)$. A CWF net is acyclic if its graph is acyclic.*

Theorem 2. *The merge and d-shortcut rule are complete for acyclic FC-CWF nets.*

In the cyclic case we need the notion of *synchronizer of a loop*. Although a similar concept was already used in [4], the definition there exploits the fact that negotiations are a structured model of communicating sequential agents. Since workflow nets do not have such a structure, we need a different definition.

Definition 12 (Loop). *Let $\mathcal{W}$ be a CWF net. A non-empty transition sequence σ is a loop of $\mathcal{W}$ if $M \xrightarrow{\sigma} M$ for some reachable marking M.*

Definition 13 (Synchronizer). *Let $\mathcal{W}$ be a WF net. A free choice transition t synchronizes a loop σ if t appears in σ and for every reachable marking M: if M enables t, then $M(p) = 0$ for every $p \in (\bigcup_{t' \in \sigma, t' \neq t} {}^\bullet t')$. A free choice transition is a synchronizer if it synchronizes some loop.*

Consider the insurance claim net, replacing the part between the places c_7 and c_9 by Fig. 4. The sequence process check1 check2 combine processing_NOK is a loop. Transitions process, combine, and processing_NOK are synchronizers, but check1 and check2 are not. We use synchronizers to define fragments of $\mathcal{W}$ on which to apply our rules.

Definition 14 (Fragment). *Let $\mathcal{W}$ be a CWF net and let t be a synchronizer of $\mathcal{W}$. The fragment $\mathcal{W}_t$ contains all transitions appearing in all loops synchronized by t, together with their input and output places, and the arcs connecting them.*

In our example, the fragment $\mathcal{W}_{process}$ is exactly the net of Fig. 4. Our procedure selects a synchronizer t and applies the rules to $\mathcal{W}_t$ until, loosely speaking, all loops synchronized by t are removed from the net, and t is no longer a synchronizer. The next lemma shows that when no synchronizers can be found anymore, the workflow net is acyclic, and so can be completely reduced by Theorem 2.

Lemma 1. *Every sound cyclic FC-CWF net has at least one synchronizer.*

Proof Sketch. We first show that in every sound cyclic FC-CWF net there exists a loop. We then inspect minimal loops and show that they must include a synchronizer. The proof constructs a transition sequence that pushes one token towards the final marking while all other tokens stay inside the loop. Should no synchronizer be present in the loop, this sequence ends in a dead lock contradicting soundness.

Given two synchronizers t and t', we say $\mathcal{W}_t \preceq \mathcal{W}_{t'}$ if every node of $\mathcal{W}_t$ is also a node of $\mathcal{W}_{t'}$. The relation $\preceq$ is a partial order on fragments. We have:

Lemma 2. *Let t be a synchronizer of a sound FC-CWF net. If $\mathcal{W}_t$ is minimal with respect to the partial order on fragments, then all non-synchronizers of $\mathcal{W}_t$ can be removed by means of applications of the d-shortcut and merge rules.*

Proof Sketch. Intuitively, synchronizers are points where loops begin and end. For two distinct synchronizers of a *minimal* fragment, any occurrence sequence starting from the marking enabling one of them, ending in the marking enabling the other, and in which no other synchronizers occur, is acyclic. Thus we can reduce the possible paths from one synchronizer to another to a single transition using our rules. We do so by constructing auxiliary acyclic workflow nets and reducing those, applying the same reduction rules to our original net.

In our example, the fragment of Fig. 4 on the left is reduced to the synchronizer-only fragment shown in Fig. 4 on the right. In such a fragment, a marking always marks exactly the places of one of the clusters, and nothing else. Intuitively, the synchronizer-only fragment is an *S-net*, i.e., a net where every transition has exactly one input and one output place, but in which some places are *duplicated*. Figure 3 shows an example of an S-net, while the net on the right of Fig. 4 is an S-net in which place c_{10} is duplicated in place c_{11}.

When reducing S-nets we must be careful that the shortcut rule does not "run into cycles". Consider for instance the second net in Fig. 3. If instead of shortcutting t_4 we shortcut t_1, we obtain a new transition t_7 with i and c_2 as input and output place. If we now shortcut t_7, we return to the original net with an additional transition connecting i and o. This problem is solved by imposing an (arbitrary) total order on the clusters. Using this order we classify transitions as "forward" (leading to a greater cluster) and "backward" (leading to a smaller cluster). Running into cycles is avoided by only applying the shortcut rule to the backward transition leading to a minimal cluster. Ultimately, this procedure reduces the fragment to an acyclic net. The total number of synchronizers is thus reduced, until none are left. At this point, by Lemma 1 the net is acyclic, and Theorem 2 can be applied. The complete reduction algorithm is listed as Algorithm 1. The algorithm contains several points where the computation might end if some condition is fulfilled. If the net was free choice, we can then conclude that it is unsound.

We have not yet discussed why a fragment could be malformed as mentioned in Line 3 of the algorithm. The proof that every minimal loop has a synchronizer also shows something more: tokens can only exit a loop at a cluster that contains a synchronizer, and all tokens exit the loop at the same time. Thus when we compute a fragment and find transitions that lead out of the fragment and whose cluster does not contain a synchronizer, or transitions that partially end outside and partially inside the fragment, we can already conclude that the net is unsound. For more information on how to compute fragments, see the next section.

Algorithm 1. Reduction procedure for cyclic workflow nets $\mathcal{W}$

1:	**while** $\mathcal{W}$ is cyclic **do**
2:	$c \leftarrow$ a minimal synchronizer of $\mathcal{W}$ ▷ If there is none, return
3:	$F \leftarrow$ the fragment of c ▷ If fragment is malformed, return
4:	**while** F contains non-synchronizers **do**
5:	apply the merge rule exhaustively
6:	apply the iteration rule exhaustively
7:	apply the d-shortcut rule to F ▷ If not possible, return
8:	**end while**
9:	fix a total order on F
10:	**while** F is cyclic **do**
11:	apply the merge rule exhaustively
12:	apply the iteration rule exhaustively
13:	apply the shortcut rule to the backward transition which ends at a minimal cluster
14:	**end while**
15:	**end while**
16:	**while** $\mathcal{W}$ is not reduced completely **do**
17:	apply the merge rule exhaustively
18:	apply the d-shortcut rule to F ▷ If neither was possible, return
19:	**end while**

With some analysis on the number of rule application in the acyclic case as well as the S-net case, we can bound the number of rule application to be polynomial:

Theorem 3. *Every sound FC-CWF net can be summarized in at most $\mathcal{O}(|C|^4 \cdot |T|)$ shortcut rule applications and $\mathcal{O}(|C|^4 + |C|^2 \cdot |T|)$ merge rule applications where C is the set of clusters of the net. Any unsound FC-CWF net can be recognized as unsound in the same time.*

4.1 Summarizing the Example

We illustrate our algorithm on the example of the insurance claim of Fig. 2. To better illustrate our approach, we replace the part between the places c_7 and c_9 by Fig. 4.

Our algorithm begins by checking whether $\mathcal{W}$ is cyclic and finds a minimal synchronizer. This could in our example be c_7, its fragment is exactly the part of the net depicted in Fig. 4 on the left. Since the fragment contains non-synchronizers c_{10}, c_{11}, the while loop of Line 4 is entered. The d-shortcut rule is applied to check1 and check2. The resulting fragment is depicted in Fig. 4 on the right. This fragment consists only of synchronizers and thus the while loop ends. We fix as total order $[c_7] \prec [c_{10}] \prec [c_9]$.

Transition processing_NOK is a backward transition as its post-set $[c_7]$ is smaller than its pre-set $[c_9]$ according to the total order. It is shortcut resulting in another backward transition ending in the cluster containing c_{10}, c_{11}, which is

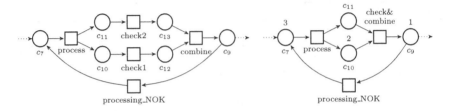

Fig. 4. Extension of the insurance claim net and the synchronizer-only fragment

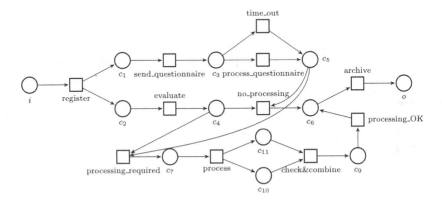

Fig. 5. After shortcutting backward transitions

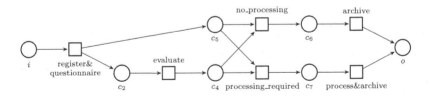

Fig. 6. After some rule applications

then shortcut again to a self-loop on c_9. The self-loop is removed via the iteration rule.

The resulting net is depicted in Fig. 5. This net is acyclic, thus now the d-shortcut and merge rule are applied exhaustively. An intermediate step is depicted in Fig. 6. First process_questionnaire and time_out are merged and the path from i to c_5 is shortcut. Then the linear path from c_7 to o is shortcut into a single transition. Next the path from i to c_4 is shortcut, resulting in the transition register to unconditionally enable no_processing and processing_required. Finally, with three more shortcuts and a merge, the net is completely reduced, and we obtain the transformer shown in Sect. 2.2.

4.2   Extension to Generalized Soundness

In [1, 19] (see also [16]), two alternative notions of soundness are introduced: k-soundness and generalized soundness. We show that for free choice workflow nets they coincide with the standard notion. Therefore, our rules are also complete with respect to these alternative notions.

Definition 15. *Let* $W = (P, T, F, i, o)$ *be a workflow net. For every* $k \geq 1$, *let* i^k *(o^k) denote the marking that puts k tokens on i (on o), and no tokens elsewhere.* W *is k-sound if o^k is reachable from every marking reachable from i^k. W is generalized sound if it is k-sound for every $k \geq 1$.*

Theorem 4. *Let* W *be a free choice workflow net. The following statements are equivalent: (1) W is sound; (2) W is k-sound for some $k \geq 1$; (3) W is generalized sound.*

5   Experimental Evaluation

We have implemented our reduction algorithm and applied it to a benchmark suite of models previously studied in [5, 17].[3]

The most complex part of the implementation[4] is the computation of synchronizers and their fragments. A crucial point is that we are only interested in fragments that consist of free choice places as those are the fragments we might be able to completely reduce. The computation of the synchronizers starts with an overapproximation: starting from a cluster c, we begin by marking for all transitions $t \in c_T$, the places in $t^\bullet$ that are free choice as visited. Whenever we have marked all places in a cluster as visited, we repeat the same for this cluster. In that way we overapproximate the set of clusters that can occur in an occurrence sequence as in the definition of synchronizer. Should all places in c be marked as visited at some point, we consider c a potential synchronizer.

We now compute the fragment of c in a backwards fashion. Starting with only c, we check for every transition whose out-places are contained in the currently identified fragment, whether its in-places were completely marked in the first step. If so, add its in-places and the transition to the fragment. We also check simple soundness properties, e.g. that no transition exists which starts in the fragment and ends partially inside and partially outside the fragment.

We have conducted some experiments to obtain answers to the following two questions: (1) Since our rules must preserve not only soundness, but also the input/output relation, they cannot be as "aggressive" as previous ones. So it could be the case that they only lead to a small reduction factor in the non-free choice case. To explore this question, we experimentally compute the reduction factor for non-free choice benchmarks. (2) While Theorem 3 is a strong theoretical result (compared to PSPACE-hardness of soundness for arbitrary workflow

---

[3] Nets can be obtained under http://svn.gna.org/viewcvs/service-tech/trunk/_meta/ nets/challenge/ in folders `sap-reference` and `ibm-soundness`.

[4] Can be obtained under https://www7.in.tum.de/tools/workflow/index.php.

Table 2. Analyzed workflow nets

	#	|P|			|T|			red	# rule
	nets	avg	med	max	avg	med	max	by	appl
Acyclic FC sound	446	20.7	13	154	13.1	9	95	—	12.8
Acyclic FC uns	761	60.4	49	264	41.1	33	285	73.6 %	38.0
Cyclic FC sound	24	46.1	43	118	34.3	26	93	—	43.2
Cyclic FC uns	155	73.2	61	274	51.1	44	243	78.1 %	53.2
Acyclic not FC	542	47.0	38	262	46.8	37	267	68.4 %	38.4
Cyclic not FC	30	85.6	72	193	88.1	72	185	66.4 %	82.7

nets), the $\mathcal{O}(|C|^4 \cdot |T|)$ bound has rather high exponents, and could potentially lead to an impractical reduction algorithm. To explore if the worst case appears in practice, we compute the number of rule applications for free choice benchmarks.

We have used the benchmark suites of [5,17], both consisting of industrial examples. We analyzed a total of 1958 nets, of which 1386 were free choice. Running the reduction procedure for all benchmarks took 6 seconds. The results are shown in Table 2. The number of places and transitions are always given as average/median/max. In the free choice case, our algorithm found that 470 nets were sound (i.e. those nets were reduced completely), and on average the nets were reduced to about 23 % of their original size. In the non-free choice case no net could be reduced completely (which does not necessarily mean they are all unsound). However, the size of the nets was still reduced to about 35 % of their original size. While we have omitted some more data on the number of rule applications due to lack of space, our experiments indicate that the number of rule applications is close to linear in the size of the net.

6 Conclusion

We have presented the first set of reduction rules for colored workflow nets that preserves not only soundness, but also the input/output relation, and is complete for free choice nets. We have also designed a specific reduction algorithm. Experimental results for 1958 workflow nets derived from industrial business processes show that the nets are reduced to about 30 % of their original size.

Our rules can be used to prove properties of the input/output relation by computing it. To reduce the complexity of the computation, we observe that our reduction rules are easily compatible with abstract interpretation techniques: given an abstract domain of data values, the rules can be adapted so that, instead of computing the transformers of the new transitions using the union, join, and Kleene-star operators, they compute their abstract versions. We plan to study this combination in future research.

Acknowledgements. Thank you very much to Karsten Wolf for pointing us to the benchmarks. Many thanks to the anonymous reviewers for the helpful comments.

References

1. Cortadella, J., Reisig, W. (eds.): ICATpPN 2004. LNCS, vol. 3099. Springer, Heidelberg (2004)
2. Desel, J., Esparza, J.: Free Choice Petri Nets, vol. 40. Cambridge University Press, Cambridge (2005)
3. Esparza, J., Desel, J.: On negotiation as concurrency primitive. In: D'Argenio, P.R., Melgratti, H. (eds.) CONCUR 2013 – Concurrency Theory. LNCS, vol. 8052, pp. 440–454. Springer, Heidelberg (2013)
4. Esparza, J., Desel, J.: On negotiation as concurrency primitive ii: deterministic cyclic negotiations. In: Muscholl, A. (ed.) FOSSACS 2014 (ETAPS). LNCS, vol. 8412, pp. 258–273. Springer, Heidelberg (2014)
5. Fahland, D., Favre, C., Jobstmann, B., Koehler, J., Lohmann, N., Völzer, H., Wolf, K.: Instantaneous soundness checking of industrial business process models. In: Dayal, U., Eder, J., Koehler, J., Reijers, H.A. (eds.) BPM 2009. LNCS, vol. 5701, pp. 278–293. Springer, Heidelberg (2009)
6. Favre, C., Fahland, D., Völzer, H.: The relationship between workflow graphs and free-choice workflow nets. Inf. Syst. **47**, 197–219 (2015)
7. Hopcroft, J.E., Motwani, R., Ullman, J.D.: Introduction to Automata Theory, Languages, and Computation, 3rd edn. Addison-Wesley Longman Publishing Co., Boston (2006)
8. Jensen, K., Kristensen, L.M.: Coloured Petri Nets: Modelling and Validation of Concurrent Systems. Springer Science & Business Media, New York (2009)
9. Ouyang, C., Verbeek, E., van der Aalst, W.M.P., Breutel, S., Dumas, M., ter Hofstede, A.H.M.: WofBPEL: A tool for automated analysis of BPEL processes. In: Benatallah, B., Casati, F., Traverso, P. (eds.) ICSOC 2005. LNCS, vol. 3826, pp. 484–489. Springer, Heidelberg (2005)
10. Sadiq, S., Orlowska, M., Sadiq, W., Foulger, C.: Data flow and validation in workflow modelling. In: Proceedings of the 15th Australasian Database Conference, vol. 27, pp. 207–214. Australian Computer Society Inc. (2004)
11. Sadiq, W., Orlowska, M.E.: Analyzing process models using graph reduction techniques. Inf. Syst. **25**(2), 117–134 (2000)
12. Trčka, N., van der Aalst, W.M.P., Sidorova, N.: Data-flow anti-patterns: discovering data-flow errors in workflows. In: van Eck, P., Gordijn, J., Wieringa, R. (eds.) CAiSE 2009. LNCS, vol. 5565, pp. 425–439. Springer, Heidelberg (2009)
13. Van Der Aalst, W., Van Hee, K.M.: Workflow Management: Models, Methods, and Systems. MIT press, Cambridge (2004)
14. van der Wil, M.P.: Aalst.: The application of petri nets to workflow management. J. Circ. Syst. Comput. **8**(1), 21–66 (1998)
15. van der Aalst, W.M.P., Hirnschall, A., Verbeek, H.M.W.E.: An alternative way to analyze workflow graphs. In: Pidduck, A.B., Mylopoulos, J., Woo, C.C., Ozsu, M.T. (eds.) CAiSE 2002. LNCS, vol. 2348, pp. 535–552. Springer, Heidelberg (2002)
16. van der Aalst, W.M.P., van Hee, K.M., ter Hofstede, A.H.M., Sidorova, N., Verbeek, H.M.W., Voorhoeve, M., Wynn, M.T.: Soundness of workflow nets: classification, decidability, and analysis. Formal Aspects Comput. **23**(3), 333–363 (2011)

17. van Dongen, B.F., Jansen-Vullers, M.H., Verbeek, H.M.W., van der Aalst, W.M.P.: Verification of the sap reference models using epc reduction, state-space analysis, and invariants. Comput. Ind. **58**(6), 578–601 (2007)

18. van Dongen, B.F., van der Aalst, W.M.P., Verbeek, H.M.W.E.: Verification of EPCs: Using reduction rules and petri nets. In: Pastor, Ó., Falcão e Cunha, J. (eds.) CAiSE 2005. LNCS, vol. 3520, pp. 372–386. Springer, Heidelberg (2005)

19. van Hee, K.M., Sidorova, N., Voorhoeve, M.: Generalised soundness of workflow nets is decidable. In: Cortadella, J., Reisig, W. (eds.) ICATPN 2004. LNCS, vol. 3099, pp. 197–215. Springer, Heidelberg (2004)

20. (Eric) Verbeek, M.H.W., Basten, T., van der Aalst, W.M.P.: Diagnosing workflow processes using woflan. Comput. J. **44**(4), 246–279 (2001)

21. Verbeek, H.M.W., Wynn, M.T., van der Aalst, W.M.P., ter Hofstede, A.H.M.: Reduction rules for reset/inhibitor nets. J. Comput. Syst. Sci. **76**(2), 125–143 (2010)

Many-Valued Institutions
for Constraint Specification

Claudia Elena Chiriță[1]([✉]), José Luiz Fiadeiro[1], and Fernando Orejas[2]

[1] Department of Computer Science,
Royal Holloway University of London, Egham, UK
`claudia.elena.chirita@gmail.com`, `jose.fiadeiro@rhul.ac.uk`
[2] Dep. de Llenguatges i Sistemes Informàtics,
Uni. Politècnica de Catalunya, Barcelona, Spain
`orejas@lsi.upc.edu`

Abstract. We advance a general technique for enriching logical systems with soft constraints, making them suitable for specifying complex software systems where parts are put together not just based on how they meet certain functional requirements but also on how they optimise certain constraints. This added expressive power is required, for example, for capturing quality attributes that need to be optimised or, more generally, for formalising what are usually called service-level agreements. More specifically, we show how institutions endowed with a graded semantic consequence can accommodate soft-constraint satisfaction problems. We illustrate our approach by showing how, in the context of service discovery, one can quantify the compatibility of two specifications and thus formalise the selection of the most promising provider of a required resource.

1 Introduction

The problem of supporting the process of building complex systems from simpler parts has deserved a lot of attention since the birth of software engineering, and has been addressed by formal methods of different kinds (e.g. [12]). One such family of formal methods is known under the general heading of 'algebraic specification' (e.g. [23]). In a nutshell, the method is based on the simple principle that parts of software applications (components, modules, and so on) should expose interfaces where they specify required and provided properties. Those parts can then be connected if their interfaces match (in the sense that required properties are met by those provided).

A well-known theory of algebraic specifications is based on the theory of 'institutions' [17]. Essentially, institutions provide logical languages for formulating the properties that will go on the interfaces of parts and an algebra of

Work partially supported by funds from the Spanish Ministry for Economy and Competitiveness (MINECO) and the European Union (FEDER funds) under grant COMMAS (ref. TIN2013-46181-C2-1-R).

P. Stevens and A. Wąsowski (Eds.): FASE 2016, LNCS 9633, pp. 359–376, 2016.
DOI: 10.1007/978-3-662-49665-7_21

models that provide mathematical abstractions of the parts; properties and models are related in a way that supports compositionality, i.e. that the properties of a complex whole can be derived from those of its parts.

That theory is based on exact matches between interfaces, i.e. either the provided properties satisfy the required ones or they do not. Whereas this has served well the specification of functional requirements, software development has evolved in ways that require the specification of properties that can be met in more than one way, i.e. that express 'soft' constraints. A typical example is service-oriented software development where software applications (requesters) can choose among several application suppliers (providers) every time a need for a service arises; the requester first needs to discover a provider that can guarantee, through an interface, the fulfilment of certain requirements, and then to bind to a provider that optimises the satisfaction of certain constraints (e.g. shipment costs in relation to delivery time) establishing a 'service-level agreement'. Another example arises in the context of software product lines, where the selection of features may require the optimisation of given quality attributes of the resulting software variant [18].

In this context, soft-constraint systems have been successfully employed for capturing such non-functional requirements in service-oriented architectures [20, 27], including the negotiation of service-level agreements [6], as well as in the context of software product lines (e.g. [2]). The two main approaches to soft constraint satisfaction problems, SCSP [4] and VCSP [9,24], generalise the classical crisp variant of constraint satisfaction problems (CSP) by evaluating constraints over c-semirings and valuation structures, respectively.

Our aim in this paper is to extend the institution-based theory of algebraic specifications to address soft constraints. Although the idea of extending abstract data types with soft constraints was already outlined, essentially through examples, in [15], it lacks a rigorous formalisation within the setting of institutions. Such an extension is essential to provide a logic-independent foundation that, on the one hand, can be used to support different specification languages and, on the other hand, can be integrated in development environments that, like HETS [21], offer automated support for the specification and analysis of systems.

To this end, in Sect. 2, we first extend the traditional notion of institution along the lines of [10] by replacing the boolean space of truth values with residuated lattices [16], which offer a unifying truth structure for both idempotent c-semirings and valuation structures [3]. Using a simple example, we explain how first-order logic specifications can be extended with soft constraints, and then show how this extension can be generalised to define a logical system of soft constraints as a many-valued institution parameterised by a stratified logic [1]. Based on this construction, in Sect. 3, we formalise the mechanism of selecting a most promising provider of a needed resource in the context of service discovery and binding on the quantification of the compatibility of two constraint specifications as a value of a residuated lattice; we achieve this by defining a compatibility score using the concept of graded semantic consequence [10]. Lastly, in Sect. 4 we study the evolutionary behaviour of service applications. We show how our framework captures situations where different service components (constraint specifications) are based on different truth spaces, which arise in heterogeneous complex systems. We also take into account the dynamicity of preferences during the development of a system (the change of the truth structures, or of the preferences expressed as sentences of the specifications), and underline the uncertainties of predicting the evolutionary behaviour of service applications. The paper relies on basic knowledge of category theory, for example at the level of [11,22].

2   Soft-Constraint Specification in Institutions

In this section, after briefly recalling the notion of institution, we focus on the construction of a particular type of institution that is suitable for defining soft CSP specifications. As an example, we describe in more detail how constraint specifications can be written over the institution of first-order logic. This allows us to identify the properties and the additional structure that an institution $\mathcal{I}$ should have in order to deal with soft constraints, and to further define a many-valued institution CSP($\mathcal{I}$).

2.1   Institutions

The notion of *institution* was introduced by Goguen and Burstall [17] at the beginning of the 80's to allow for studying concepts for structuring and modularising specifications, independently of the actual formalism to be used for writing the specifications. Intuitively, the notion of institution is an abstract view of the main ingredients of a logical or specification formalism. In particular, an institution consists of:

– A category of signatures, where signatures are the basic elements that we use for building formulas. For instance, in first-order logic, signatures are sets of sorts and function and predicate symbols together with their arity.
– A functor Sen that associates, to each signature Σ, the set of all the formulas that can be written using Σ. In the case of first-order logic, this would mean all the formulas that can be written using the predicate and function symbols in the signature, and including the standard logical connectives and quantifiers. Sen is a functor and not just a mapping, because we want to explicitly associate to each signature morphism $\varphi\colon \Sigma \to \Sigma'$ that translates symbols in Σ into symbols in Σ', the mapping Sen(φ) that translates formulas over Σ into formulas over Σ'.
– A functor Mod that associates, to each signature Σ, the category of all its models. In the case of first-order logic, Mod(Σ) is the category of all Σ-algebras. Again, Mod is a functor and not just a mapping, because we want to explicitly associate to each signature morphism $\varphi\colon \Sigma \to \Sigma'$ that translates symbols in Σ into symbols in Σ', the *reduct* associated to that morphism. In particular, if A' is a Σ'-algebra, its reduct along $\varphi\colon \Sigma \to \Sigma'$ would be a Σ-algebra A, where each symbol s in Σ is interpreted like the symbol $\varphi(s)$ in A'.

– A satisfaction relation that, given a Σ-formula ρ and a Σ-model M, tells us if M satisfies ρ. Moreover, it is required that institutions (i.e. the formalisms that we consider valid) satisfy the *satisfaction condition* that states that satisfaction does not depend on the choice of signature, i.e. satisfaction is invariant under language translation.

Definition 1 (Institution). *An* institution $\mathcal{I}$ *consists of*

– *a category* $\mathbb{Sig}^{\mathcal{I}}$ *whose objects are called* signatures,
– *a sentence functor* $\mathrm{Sen}^{\mathcal{I}} \colon \mathbb{Sig}^{\mathcal{I}} \to \mathbb{Set}$ *giving for every signature* Σ *the set* $\mathrm{Sen}^{\mathcal{I}}(\Sigma)$ *of* Σ-sentences *and for every signature morphism* φ *the* sentence translation map $\mathrm{Sen}^{\mathcal{I}}(\varphi)$,
– *a model functor* $\mathrm{Mod}^{\mathcal{I}} \colon (\mathbb{Sig}^{\mathcal{I}})^{\mathrm{op}} \to \mathbb{Cat}$ *defining for every signature* Σ *the category* $\mathrm{Mod}^{\mathcal{I}}(\Sigma)$ *of* Σ-models *and* Σ-model homomorphisms, *and for every signature morphism* φ *the* reduct functor $\mathrm{Mod}^{\mathcal{I}}(\varphi)$,
– *a satisfaction relation* $\models^{\mathcal{I}}_{\Sigma} \subseteq |\mathrm{Mod}^{\mathcal{I}}(\Sigma)| \times \mathrm{Sen}^{\mathcal{I}}(\Sigma)$ *for every signature* Σ,

such that the satisfaction condition $\mathrm{Mod}^{\mathcal{I}}(\varphi)(M') \models^{\mathcal{I}}_{\Sigma} \rho$ *iff* $M' \models^{\mathcal{I}}_{\Sigma'}$ $\mathrm{Sen}^{\mathcal{I}}(\varphi)(\rho)$ *holds for any signature morphism* $\varphi \colon \Sigma \to \Sigma'$, Σ'-model M' *and* Σ-sentence ρ.

We may omit sub- or super-scripts when there is no risk of confusion. The sentence translation $\mathrm{Sen}^{\mathcal{I}}(\varphi)$ and the reduct functor $\mathrm{Mod}^{\mathcal{I}}(\varphi)$ may also be denoted by $\varphi(\_)$ and $\_\!\restriction_{\varphi}$. When $M = M' \!\restriction_{\varphi}$ we say that M is a φ-*reduct* of M' and that M' is a φ-*expansion* of M.

A specification in an institution $\mathcal{I}$ is a pair (Σ, E) consisting of a signature and a collection of sentences (axioms) in the language of that signature, i.e. $E \subseteq \mathrm{Sen}^{\mathcal{I}}(\Sigma)$ – what is usually called a (theory) presentation. A morphism of specifications $\phi \colon (\Sigma, E) \to (\Sigma', E')$ is a signature morphism $\phi \colon \Sigma \to \Sigma'$ such that $E' \models \phi(E)$, i.e. the axioms of (Σ, E) are semantic consequences of (Σ', E') – such a morphism formalises the way (Σ, E) is a part of (Σ', E'). Presentations and their morphisms constitute a category, which we denote by $\mathbb{Pres}^{\mathcal{I}}$.

An example of a specification in first-order logic is given in Fig. 1 (written in a CASL-like syntax [8]) – the specification of residuated lattices, i.e. the first-order structures that satisfy the axioms of the specification are the residuated lattices, which play an essential role in this paper.[1]

2.2 Generalising the Truth Space

As said above, institutions are an abstraction of logical formalisms, where you describe its main ingredients, in particular, when a given formula is satisfied (or is not satisfied) by a given model. However, when dealing with soft constraints, we need to allow for different degrees of satisfaction. This means, replacing the

---

[1] The residuated lattices thus specified are sometimes called commutative (because the monoid is commutative), integral (because the unit of the monoid is a greatest element of the lattice), and zero-bounded (because there is a lowest element 0) [16].

spec RESIDUATEDLATTICES =
    sort Sat
    ops   0 : Sat, 1 : Sat
             _ $\vee$ _ : Sat $\times$ Sat $\longrightarrow$ Sat   [comm, assoc, unit 0, idem]
             _ $\wedge$ _ : Sat $\times$ Sat $\longrightarrow$ Sat   [comm, assoc, unit 1, idem]
             _ $*$ _ : Sat $\times$ Sat $\longrightarrow$ Sat   [comm, assoc, unit 1]
             _ $\rightarrow$ _ : Sat $\times$ Sat $\longrightarrow$ Sat
    pred _ $\leq$ _ : Sat $\times$ Sat
    $\forall$ a, b, c : Sat $\bullet$ a $\vee$ (a $\wedge$ b) = a
    $\bullet$ a $\wedge$ (a $\vee$ b) = a $\bullet$ a $\leq$ b iff a $\vee$ b = b
    $\bullet$ (a $*$ b) $\leq$ (a $*$ c) if b $\leq$ c $\bullet$ b $\leq$ (a $\rightarrow$ c) iff (a $*$ b) $\leq$ c

Fig. 1. The specification $(\Sigma_{\mathrm{RL}}, E_{\mathrm{RL}})$ of residuated lattices

'true'/'false' structure of truth values by a more complex kind of structures. In this paper, we consider that these structures are residuated lattices. The choice for residuated lattices is motivated by the fact that the addition of a residual operation to semirings and valuation structures has been shown in [3,7] to provide a unifying framework for soft CSP: residuated lattices generalise both commutative idempotent semirings and fair valuation structures, which are the structures usually employed with local consistency techniques [5].

We actually need for the lattices to be complete (i.e. that a supremum and an infimum exists for every set of degrees of satisfaction).

Definition 2 (Complete Residuated Lattices). *A* complete residuated lattice $\mathcal{L} = (L, \leq, \vee, \wedge, *, \rightarrow, 0, 1)$ *is a complete lattice (with supremum* $\vee$*, infimum* $\wedge$*, smallest element 0 and greatest element 1) equipped with a monoidal structure (a commutative and associative binary operation* $*$ *having 1 as identity) such that, for all elements* $x, y, z \in L$*,* $(x * y) \leq (x * z)$ *if* $y \leq z$*, and* $y \leq (x \rightarrow z)$ *iff* $x * y \leq z$*.*

A morphism $\lambda \colon \mathcal{L} \rightarrow \mathcal{L}'$ *is a function* $\lambda \colon L \rightarrow L'$ *that is simultaneously a morphism of complete lattices and of commutative monoids, and is compatible with the residual* $\rightarrow$*. We denote the corresponding category by* $\mathbb{RL}$*.*

Intuitively, the set L provides the degrees of satisfaction (with 0 as dissatisfaction and 1 as total satisfaction) which are ordered according to $\vee$ or, equivalently, to $\wedge$: $a \leq b$ iff $a \vee b = b$. The operation $*$ captures the accumulation of truth values that result from successive inferences, and $\rightarrow$ corresponds to the entailment between two degrees of satisfaction. To capture soft CSP as a many-valued logical system, we therefore extend the notion of institution in keeping with [10]:

Definition 3 (RL-institution). *An* $\mathbb{RL}$*-institution* $\mathcal{I}$ *is defined as a tuple* $(\mathrm{Sig}^{\mathcal{I}}, \mathrm{Sen}^{\mathcal{I}}, \mathrm{Mod}^{\mathcal{I}}, \mathcal{RL}^{\mathcal{I}}, \models^{\mathcal{I}})$ *consisting of*

- *a category* $\mathrm{Sig}^{\mathcal{I}}$*, a functor* $\mathrm{Sen}^{\mathcal{I}}$*, and a functor* $\mathrm{Mod}^{\mathcal{I}}$ *as for an institution,*
- *a truth space functor* $\mathcal{RL}^{\mathcal{I}} \colon (\mathrm{Sig}^{\mathcal{I}})^{\mathrm{op}} \rightarrow \mathbb{RL}$ *giving for every signature a complete residuated lattice, and*

– a *many-valued* satisfaction relation $\models_\Sigma^{\mathcal{I}} \colon |\mathrm{Mod}^{\mathcal{I}}(\Sigma)| \times \mathrm{Sen}^{\mathcal{I}}(\Sigma) \to \mathcal{RL}^{\mathcal{I}}(\Sigma)$
for every signature Σ,

such that the equality $\bigl(\mathrm{Mod}^{\mathcal{I}}(\varphi)(M') \models_\Sigma^{\mathcal{I}} \rho\bigr) = \mathcal{RL}^{\mathcal{I}}(\varphi)\bigl(M' \models_{\Sigma'}^{\mathcal{I}} \mathrm{Sen}^{\mathcal{I}}(\varphi)(\rho)\bigr)$
holds for any signature morphism $\varphi \colon \Sigma \to \Sigma'$, Σ'-model M' and Σ-sentence ρ.
The satisfaction relation extends to a consequence relation over $E, \Gamma \subseteq \mathrm{Sen}(\Sigma)$
as follows: $E \models_\Sigma^{\mathcal{I}} \Gamma = \bigwedge\{(M \models_\Sigma^{\mathcal{I}} E) \to (M \models_\Sigma^{\mathcal{I}} \Gamma) \mid M \in |\mathrm{Mod}(\Sigma)|\}$.

The rest of this section is dedicated to showing how, starting from an institution $\mathcal{I}$ that satisfies some structural properties, we can define an $\mathbb{RL}$-institution $\mathrm{CSP}(\mathcal{I})$ of soft-constraint satisfaction problems based on $\mathcal{I}$.

2.3   The First-Order Soft-Constraint $\mathbb{RL}$-institution

To specify systems using constraints, which we evaluate over residuated lattices, we consider only those presentations that extend $(\Sigma_{\mathrm{RL}}, E_{\mathrm{RL}})$, that is presentations (Σ, E) with $\Sigma_{\mathrm{RL}} \subseteq \Sigma$ and $E \models E_{\mathrm{RL}}$. This means that, on the one hand, every (Σ, E)-model has an underlying residuated lattice (its reduct as a Σ_{RL}-model) and that, on the other hand, we can make use of the symbols in Σ_{RL} when writing the sentences of E. Moreover, we admit only morphisms of presentations $\varphi \colon (\Sigma, E) \to (\Sigma', E')$ that do not change the symbols of Σ_{RL}.

Example 4. Figure 2 depicts the specification of a customer's book-buying preferences. CUSTOMER extends the specification BOOKDATA, which concerns a book trader that stores a number of books and offers three kinds of delivery: standard, express and online; for every book, two operations return the language in which the book is written and the number of days associated with each delivery mode.

```
 spec BOOKDATA = NAT
then sorts  Book, Language, Delivery
      ops   en, fr, de, pt, ro, es : Language
            standard, express, online : Delivery
            language : Book ⟶ Language
            deliveryTime : Book × Delivery ⟶ Nat

 spec CUSTOMER = BOOKDATA and RESIDUATEDLATTICES
then ops    languagePref : Language ⟶ Sat
            deliveryPref : Delivery × Book × Nat ⟶ Sat
      ∀ b : Book; n, n' : Nat
      • languagePref(en) ≤ languagePref(de)
      • languagePref(de) ≤ languagePref(fr)
      • deliveryPref(express, b, n) ≤ deliveryPref(online, b, n')
      • deliveryPref(standard, b, n) ≤ deliveryPref(online, b, n')
      • deliveryPref(express, b, n) ≤ deliveryPref(standard, b, n') iff n ≥ 3 ∧ n' ≤ 7
```

Fig. 2. The specifications BOOKDATA and CUSTOMER

CUSTOMER also extends the specification of residuated lattices given in Fig. 1 and adds two new function symbols – languagePref and deliveryPref – both of sort Sat. Because every model of Sat is a residuated lattice, the two new function symbols can be used to express preferences through axioms of the specification: German is preferred to English and French to German; regardless of the book and delivery time, online delivery is preferred to express and to standard; standard delivery is preferred to express when express delivery takes three days or more and standard takes seven days or less.

In order to include constraints in specifications, we need a new syntactic category through which we can declare *constraint variables*, and we need *constraint sentences* through which we can express preferences over those variables that we wish to be optimised. For example, in the case of CUSTOMER, we could specify the following constraint variables and sentences:

> **cvars** book : Book; delivery : Delivery
> - languagePref(language(book))
> - deliveryPref(delivery, book, deliveryTime(delivery, book))

A constraint sentence (or constraint for short) is a term of sort Sat. The specified constraints express the existence of preferences on the language in which the book is written, and the wish to optimise the method of delivery relatively to the expected delivery period. This optimisation is made relative to the axiomatisation of the preferences in CUSTOMER: given a model of CUSTOMER and a valuation χ of the constraint variables (i.e. a choice of a book and of a delivery mode), every constraint is assigned a value (degree of satisfaction) in the residuated lattice; the degree of satisfaction of a constraint in a model can then be defined as the supremum of all the degrees of satisfaction obtained by varying χ, i.e. for all possible combinations of books and delivery modes, which in soft CSP is known as *the best level of consistency* [5].

The extension of first-order logic with constraint sentences is best accommodated in what are called stratified institutions [1], which provide an elegant way of capturing the valuations of constraint variables through *states* of models:

Definition 5 (Stratified Institution). *A stratified institution $\mathcal{I}$ is defined as a tuple* $(\mathrm{Sig}^{\mathcal{I}}, \mathrm{Sen}^{\mathcal{I}}, \mathrm{Mod}^{\mathcal{I}}, \llbracket\_\rrbracket^{\mathcal{I}}, \models^{\mathcal{I}})^2$ *where*

- $\mathrm{Sig}^{\mathcal{I}}$, $\mathrm{Sen}^{\mathcal{I}}$ *and* $\mathrm{Mod}^{\mathcal{I}}$ *are as for an institution,*
- $\llbracket\_\rrbracket^{\mathcal{I}}$ *is a stratification, i.e. a collection of*
  - *functors* $\llbracket\_\rrbracket^{\mathcal{I}}_{\Sigma}\colon \mathrm{Mod}^{\mathcal{I}}(\Sigma) \to \mathbb{Set}$ *for every signature* Σ, *and*
  - *surjective[3] natural transformations* $\llbracket\_\rrbracket^{\mathcal{I}}_{\phi}\colon \llbracket\_\rrbracket^{\mathcal{I}}_{\Sigma'} \Rightarrow \mathrm{Mod}^{\mathcal{I}}(\phi) \, ; \llbracket\_\rrbracket^{\mathcal{I}}_{\Sigma}$ *for every signature morphism* $\phi\colon \Sigma \to \Sigma'$,
- *the satisfaction relation* $M \models^m_{\Sigma} \rho$ *is parameterised by model states,*

---

[2] In order to simplify the notation, we will omit the stratified institution in the superscript of the satisfaction relation.

[3] By the surjectivity of the natural transformations we understand that for every morphism $\phi\colon \Sigma \to \Sigma'$ and every $M' \in |\mathrm{Mod}^{\mathcal{I}}(\Sigma')|$, $\llbracket M'\rrbracket^{\mathcal{I}}_{\phi}$ is surjective.

such that, for every $\phi\colon \Sigma \to \Sigma'$, $M' \in |\mathrm{Mod}^{\mathcal{I}}(\Sigma')|$, $m' \in [\![M']\!]^{\mathcal{I}}_{\Sigma'}$, $\rho \in \mathrm{Sen}^{\mathcal{I}}(\Sigma)$:

$$\mathrm{Mod}^{\mathcal{I}}(\phi)(M') \models_{\Sigma}^{[\![M']\!]^{\mathcal{I}}_{\phi}(m')} \rho \quad \textit{iff} \quad M' \models_{\Sigma'}^{m'} \mathrm{Sen}^{\mathcal{I}}(\phi)(\rho).$$

The stratified version of the institution of first-order logic that we adopt, which will be denoted by <u>FOL</u>, has as signatures pairs $\langle \Sigma, V \rangle$ of a first-order signature Σ and a set of sorted constraint variables V. The $\langle \Sigma, V \rangle$-sentences are simply sentences over Σ with the constraint variables V as constants (nullary operation symbols). The models of a signature $\langle \Sigma, V \rangle$ are the Σ-models, while the states of a model M are the valuations $\chi\colon V \to M$, i.e., sorted functions from V to the many-sorted carrier set of M. The satisfaction of a $\langle \Sigma, V \rangle$-sentence ρ by a $\langle \Sigma, V \rangle$-model M in a state $\chi \in [\![M]\!]_{\langle \Sigma, V \rangle}$ is defined as the satisfaction of ρ in (M, χ), i.e. in the extension of M with the interpretation χ of variables.

Notice that every specification in the institution of first-order logic defines a specification in <u>FOL</u> by choosing an empty set of constraint variables, i.e. we identify a first-order specification such as $(\Sigma_{\mathrm{RL}}, E_{\mathrm{RL}})$ with $(\langle \Sigma_{\mathrm{RL}}, \emptyset \rangle, E_{\mathrm{RL}})$.

We can now summarise the construction of the $\mathbb{RL}$-institution $\mathrm{CSP}(\underline{\mathrm{FOL}})$ of first-order soft-constraint satisfaction problems:

Signatures. A signature is a pair $(\mathcal{L}, \Delta)$ of a complete residuated lattice $\mathcal{L}$ and an extension $\Delta\colon (\Sigma_{\mathrm{RL}}, E_{\mathrm{RL}}) \to (\langle \Sigma, V \rangle, E)$ of the specification of residuated lattices. We include a residuated lattice as part of a signature in order to let specifiers decide on which space of degrees of satisfaction they want to work with. For simplicity we may denote $(\mathcal{L}, \Delta\colon (\Sigma_{\mathrm{RL}}, E_{\mathrm{RL}}) \to (\langle \Sigma, V \rangle, E))$ by $(\mathcal{L}, \Sigma, V, E)$.

Constraint Sentences. A constraint sentence (or constraint for short) for a signature $(\mathcal{L}, \Sigma, V, E)$ is a $\langle \Sigma, V \rangle$-term of sort Sat.

Models. The models of $(\mathcal{L}, \Sigma, V, E)$ are the models of $(\langle \Sigma, V \rangle, E)$ whose reducts along Δ are complete and admit a morphism into $\mathcal{L}$. Notice that it would be too restrictive to choose only those models of $(\langle \Sigma, V \rangle, E)$ whose reducts over Σ_{RL} are $\mathcal{L}$ because we wish to support mappings between specifications that use different residuated lattices as their spaces of degrees of satisfaction. Formally, a model of $(\mathcal{L}, \Delta\colon (\Sigma_{\mathrm{RL}}, E_{\mathrm{RL}}) \to (\langle \Sigma, V \rangle, E))$ is a pair (M, f) consisting of a model M of $(\langle \Sigma, V \rangle, E)$ together with a morphism $f\colon M\!\restriction_{\Delta} \to \mathcal{L}$.

Satisfaction Relation. For every constraint signature $(\mathcal{L}, \Sigma, V, E)$ and every model M, we define the value of c over M as the *best level of consistency*:

$$((M, f) \models_{(\mathcal{L}, \Sigma, V, E)} c) = f\Big(\bigvee_{\chi \in [\![M]\!]_{\Sigma}} \mathrm{eval}_{(M, \chi)}(c)\Big),$$

where $\mathrm{eval}_{(M, \chi)}(c)$ is the usual (inductively defined) interpretation of the first-order $\langle \Sigma, V \rangle$-term c in (M, χ). Note that f translates the supremum to the residuated lattice $\mathcal{L}$ chosen by the specifier.

2.4 The $\mathrm{CSP}(\mathcal{I})$ $\mathbb{RL}$-institution of Soft CSP over $\mathcal{I}$

We now generalise the construction $\mathrm{CSP}(\underline{\mathrm{FOL}})$ to an arbitrary stratified institution $\mathcal{I} = (\mathbb{Sig}^{\mathcal{I}}, \mathrm{Sen}^{\mathcal{I}}, \mathrm{Mod}^{\mathcal{I}}, [\![\_]\!]^{\mathcal{I}}, \models^{\mathcal{I}})$ that satisfies the following conditions:

C1. To make residuated lattices available to the specifier, we require the existence of an $\mathcal{I}$-presentation $(\varSigma_{\mathrm{RL}}, E_{\mathrm{RL}})$ such that $\mathbb{RL} \subseteq \mathrm{Mod}^{\mathcal{I}}(\varSigma_{\mathrm{RL}}, E_{\mathrm{RL}})$. This does not restrict applicability as most institutions suitable for the domains where soft constraints are useful will provide the ability to specify data structures.

C2. In order to be able to express constraints, we require the existence of a functor $\mathrm{C}\colon \mathbb{Sig}^{\mathcal{I}} \to \mathbb{Set}$ that provides the set of constraints for each signature. In addition, we assume that for every object $\varDelta\colon (\varSigma_{\mathrm{RL}}, E_{\mathrm{RL}}) \to (\varSigma, E)$ of the comma category $(\varSigma_{\mathrm{RL}}, E_{\mathrm{RL}})/\mathbb{Pres}^{\mathcal{I}}$ there exists a family of functors $\lfloor\_\rfloor_{\varSigma}\colon \lfloor\_\rfloor_{\varSigma} \to [\mathrm{C}(\varSigma) \to \mathrm{Mod}^{\mathcal{I}}(\varDelta)]$ such that, for any signature morphism $\varphi\colon \varSigma \to \varSigma'$, $\varSigma'$-model M', state $\chi' \in [\![M']\!]_{\varSigma'}$, and constraint $c \in \mathrm{C}(\varSigma)$, $|M'{\restriction_\varphi}|_{\varSigma}([\![M']\!]_\varphi(\chi'))(c) = |M'|_{\varSigma'}(\chi')(\varphi(c))$.

On this basis, we define the logical system $\mathrm{CSP}(\mathcal{I})$ as follows:

- The category $\mathbb{Sig}^{\mathrm{CSP}(\mathcal{I})}$ of constraint signatures is the product category of $\mathbb{RL}^{\mathrm{op}}$ and the comma category $(\varSigma_{\mathrm{RL}}, E_{\mathrm{RL}})/\mathbb{Pres}^{\mathcal{I}}$.
- $\mathrm{Sen}^{\mathrm{CSP}(\mathcal{I})}((\mathcal{L}, \varDelta\colon (\varSigma_{\mathrm{RL}}, E_{\mathrm{RL}}) \to (\varSigma, E)) = \mathrm{C}(\varSigma)$.
- $\mathrm{Mod}^{\mathrm{CSP}(\mathcal{I})}(\mathcal{L}, \varDelta) = \mathrm{Mod}^{\mathcal{I}}(\varDelta)/\mathcal{L}$, with $\mathrm{Mod}^{\mathcal{I}}(\varDelta)\colon \mathrm{Mod}^{\mathcal{I}}(\varDelta)^{-1}(\mathbb{RL}) \to \mathbb{RL}$.
- Given an $(\mathcal{L}, \varDelta)$-model $(M, f\colon M{\restriction_\varDelta} \to \mathcal{L})$ and a sentence $\rho \in \mathrm{Sen}(\mathcal{L}, \varDelta)$, the satisfaction of ρ by (M, f) is defined as:

$$((M, f) \models_{(\mathcal{L}, \varDelta)} \rho) = f\big(\textstyle\bigvee_{\chi \in [\![M]\!]_{\varSigma}} |M|_{\varSigma}(\chi)(\rho)\big)$$

Theorem 6. *For any stratified institution $\mathcal{I}$ satisfying the conditions C1 and C2 above, $\mathrm{CSP}(\mathcal{I})$ is an $\mathbb{RL}$-institution.*

The following results are important for Sect. 3.

Proposition 7. $\mathrm{CSP}(\mathcal{I})$ *inherits the following properties of $\mathcal{I}$:*

1. *If $\mathbb{Sig}^{\mathcal{I}}$ is finitely cocomplete so is $\mathbb{Sig}^{\mathrm{CSP}(\mathcal{I})}$.*
2. *If $\mathcal{I}$ has (weak) model amalgamation, so does $\mathrm{CSP}(\mathcal{I})$.*
3. *Given factorisation systems [19] (E, M) for $\mathbb{Sig}^{\mathcal{I}}$ and $(\mathrm{E}_{\mathrm{RL}}, \mathrm{M}_{\mathrm{RL}})$ for $\mathbb{RL}$, we obtain a factorisation system for $\mathbb{Sig}^{\mathrm{CSP}(\mathcal{I})}$ by taking the epimorphisms to be the pairs of arrows in M_{RL} and $(\varSigma_{\mathrm{RL}}, E_{\mathrm{RL}})/\mathrm{E}^{\mathrm{pres}}$, and the monomorphisms to be the pairs of arrows in E_{RL} and $(\varSigma_{\mathrm{RL}}, E_{\mathrm{RL}})/\mathrm{M}^{\mathrm{pres}}$.*

3 Soft Constraints for Service-Oriented Computing

As an application of our approach, we study how soft-constraint institutions can be used for formalising structures and processes specific to service-oriented computing: we describe service applications and modules by means of constraint specifications, and define the requirements of applications and the properties guaranteed by service modules as constraint sentences. Consequently, we obtain a series of new results on the way in which service applications evolve through the processes of service discovery, selection, and binding.

We fix an arbitrary $\mathbb{RL}$-institution $(\mathbb{Sig}^{\mathcal{I}}, \mathrm{Sen}^{\mathcal{I}}, \mathrm{Mod}^{\mathcal{I}}, \mathcal{RL}^{\mathcal{I}}, \models^{\mathcal{I}})$ – see Definition 3 – for which the category of signatures has pushouts, is equipped with a factorisation system, and for which the functor $\mathcal{RL}^{\mathcal{I}}$ preserves pullbacks. In particular, for a soft constraint institution $\mathrm{CSP}(\mathcal{I})$, it suffices that $\mathbb{Sig}^{\mathcal{I}}$ has pushouts and admits a factorisation system (see Proposition 7). We use $\bar{n}$ to denote the set $\{1, \ldots, n\}$.

In our framework of service-oriented computing, for simplicity, we consider that we have two kinds of units, *service applications* and *service modules*. Service applications can be seen as units that require some services. We may consider that they have an orchestration part, describing what the unit intends to do, and some interfaces describing the services required. In particular, interfaces are subspecifications of the given orchestration together with some property that describes the preferences of the unit to use a given service.

Definition 8 (Service Application). *A service application* (Σ, I, R) *consists of a signature* $\Sigma \in |\mathbb{Sig}|$, *called* orchestration, *together with a finite family* $I = \{i_x\}_{x \in \bar{n}}$ *of interfaces, that is, a family of monic signature morphisms* $i_x \colon \Sigma_x \to \Sigma$ *such that* $\mathcal{RL}(\Sigma_x) = \mathcal{RL}(\Sigma)$, *and their associated* requirements $R = \{r_x \in \mathrm{Sen}(\Sigma_x)\}_{x \in \bar{n}}$. *We will refer to a pair* (Σ_x, r_x) *consisting of the domain of an interface and its corresponding requirement as a* requires-specification.

Example 9. As part of our running example, we consider a service application $\mathcal{C} = (\Sigma, I, R)$ whose orchestration Σ is CUSTOMER (as in Fig. 2), and whose single interface consists of the identity and the requirement

$$R = \mathsf{languagePref}(\mathsf{language}(\mathsf{book})) \wedge$$
$$\mathsf{deliveryPref}(\mathsf{delivery}, \mathsf{book}, \mathsf{deliveryTime}(\mathsf{delivery}, \mathsf{book})).$$

Service modules are like service applications but, in addition, they provide functionalities or resources. In this sense, they have an orchestration part and some interfaces for the services required, as well as a provides interface.

Definition 10 (Service Module). *A service module* (Ω, P, J, Q) *consists of an orchestration* $\Omega \in |\mathbb{Sig}|$, *a provides-property* $P \in \mathrm{Sen}(\Omega)$, *a finite family* $J = \{j_y\}_{y \in \bar{m}}$ *of interfaces* $j_y \colon \Omega_y \to \Omega$, *and a family of associated* requirements $Q = \{q_y \in \mathrm{Sen}(\Omega_y)\}_{y \in \bar{m}}$.

$$
\begin{array}{ccc}
& i_1 \quad \Sigma_1 \longmapsto r_1 & \\
\Sigma \Big\langle \quad \vdots & \qquad P \longmapsto \Omega \Big\langle \quad \vdots \\
& i_n \quad \Sigma_n \longmapsto r_n & \qquad j_n \quad \Omega_m \longmapsto q_m
\end{array}
$$

Example 11 We define a service module $\mathcal{S} = (\Omega, P, J, Q)$ for the application $\mathcal{C}$ given in Example 9 by taking Ω as the specification SUPPLIER in Fig. 3, the provides-property $P = \mathsf{available}(\mathsf{book}, \mathsf{delivery})$, and the requirement

spec SUPPLIER = BOOKDATA **and** RESIDUATEDLATTICES
then ops   Schiele : Book
                available : Book × Delivery ⟶ Sat
                deliverable : Book × Delivery × Nat ⟶ Sat
        cvars book : Book; delivery : Delivery; days : Nat
        ∀ b : Book; d : Delivery; n, n' : Nat
        • deliverable(b, d, n) = 0 if n > deliveryTime(b, d)
        • deliverable(b, d, n) ≤ deliverable(b, d, n') if n ≤ n'
        • available(b, d) = 1 ⇔ (b, d) belongs to the following table

id	book	language	delivery	deliveryTime
1.1			standard	6
1.2	Schiele	de	express	3
1.3			online	0

Fig. 3. The specification SUPPLIER (The table is only a convenient abbreviation for a set of sentences that specify, for example, that the book "Schiele" is available in German with 3-day express delivery. The column "id" is just an annotation that we use to reference the rows.)

$Q = $ deliverable(book, delivery, days) defined over Ω (i.e. J consists of an identity). The module guarantees the delivery of a book b for a method d within deliveryTime(b, d) days, but in turn it depends on another external delivery-service provider.

Definition 12 (α-Satisfiability of an Application). *A service application (Σ, I, R) is α-satisfiable if all of its requirements can be satisfied at once with a value greater than α, i.e. there exists a model of its orchestration that satisfies R with at least the value α:* $\bigvee_{M \in |\mathrm{Mod}(\Sigma)|} (\bigwedge_{x \in \overline{n}} M \models i_x(r_x)) \geq \alpha$.

Definition 13 (β-Correctness of a Service Module). *A service module $\mathcal{M} = (\Omega, P, J, Q)$ is said to be β-correct if P is a consequence of Q with a value $\beta_\mathcal{M}$ greater than β. Formally, this means that $\beta_\mathcal{M} = (\{j_y(q_y)\}_{y \in \overline{m}} \models_\Omega P) \geq \beta$.*

We now focus on the execution of service applications in the context of a fixed set *Rep* of service modules – a *service repository*. Each execution step is triggered by the need to fulfil a requirement of the current application, which in the context of our work corresponds to a requires-specification. Similarly to conventional soft-constraint satisfaction problems, the goal is to maximize the satisfaction of the requirement. To this end, we distinguish three elementary processes: discovery, selection and binding.

Service Discovery. Let $\mathcal{A} = (\Sigma, I, R)$ be a service application and (Σ_k, r_k) one of its requires-specifications. Unlike the selection and binding processes, we model the discovery of new service modules to be bound to $\mathcal{A}$ in a minimal way: all we assume is that it provides a set of possible matches – pairs $(\mathcal{M}, \phi)$ of service modules $\mathcal{M} = (\Omega, P, J, Q)$ from *Rep* and *attachment morphisms* $\phi \colon \Sigma_k \to \Omega$.

Note that the output of the discovery process only depends on the repository and the selected requires-specification, and not on the application itself.

Service Selection. In order to *select* from the set of discovered service modules the best module that satisfies the requirement, we compute for each match $(\mathcal{M}, \phi)$ provided by the discovery process the compatibility score between the provides-property P guaranteed by the correctness of the service module $\mathcal{M}$ and of the requirement r_k of the application. To this end, we first compute the pushout (i, j) of the signature morphisms i_k and ϕ linking the requires-specification (Σ_k, r_k) to the orchestrations of the application and of the service module (see the diagram below), and then translate both the requirement and the provides-property to the vertex Σ' of the pushout:

$$(j(P) \models \mathrm{Sen}(i_k; i)(r_k)) = \bigwedge_{M \in |\mathrm{Mod}(\Sigma')|} (M \models_{\Sigma'} j(P)) \to (M \models_{\Sigma'} \mathrm{Sen}(i_k; i)(r_k)).$$

These values belong to different lattices (of different service providers), hence we have to further translate them to the lattice of the service application via the morphisms $\mathcal{RL}(\phi; j)$ in order to be able to compare them. Here it is useful to note that $\mathcal{RL}(\phi; j) = \mathcal{RL}(\phi)$ because $\mathcal{RL}(j)$ is an identity.

However, computing such compatibility scores is not enough: the selection of a best module for the distinguished requirement of the application must also take into account the correctness of the modules. Thus, for every match $(\mathcal{M}, \phi)$, we have to multiply the score $\mathcal{RL}(\phi)(j(P) \models \mathrm{Sen}(i_k; i)(r_k))$ obtained as above with $\beta_{\mathcal{M}}$, the correctness of $\mathcal{M}$. Finally, we will select those service modules for which this product is maximal.

$$sel(Rep, \mathcal{A}, \Sigma_k, r_k) = \underset{(\mathcal{M}, \phi)}{\arg \max} \{\beta_{\mathcal{M}} * \mathcal{RL}(\phi)(j(P) \models \mathrm{Sen}(i_k; i)(r_k))\}$$

Example 14. Consider the repository $Rep = \{\mathcal{S}, \mathcal{S}'\}$ where the new service module $\mathcal{S}' = (\Omega', P', J', Q')$ is such that Ω' is as in Fig. 4, $P' = P$, and $Q' = Q$. When selecting a best supplier for the service application $\mathcal{C}$ from Example 9, the books that best fit the preferences are the online version of "Schiele" (1.3) for $\mathcal{S}$ and "Chagall – Ma vie" with an express delivery (2.2) for $\mathcal{S}'$. In principle, we would need to compute the compatibility scores between CUSTOMER and SUP-PLIER and OTHERSUPPLIER, respectively, using all possible models. However,

spec OTHERSUPPLIER = BOOKDATA **and** RESIDUATEDLATTICES
then ops   ChagallMaVie, Munch : Book
available : Book × Delivery ⟶ Sat
deliverable : Book × Delivery × Nat ⟶ Sat
cvars book : Book; delivery : Delivery; days : Nat
∀ b : Book; d : Delivery; n, n' : Nat
- deliverable(b, d, n) = 0 if n > deliveryTime(b, d)
- deliverable(b, d, n) ≤ deliverable(b, d, n') if n ≤ n'
- available(b, d) = 1 ⇔ (b, d) belongs to the following table

id	book	language	delivery	dTime
2.1	ChagallMaVie	fr	standard	14
2.2			express	8
3.1			standard	6
3.2	Munch	en	online	0

Fig. 4. The specification OTHERSUPPLIER

due to the way the specifications are written, the choice of the best book for each supplier can be calculated directly from the axioms. First, the constraint variables book and delivery are limited to the interpretations defined by the tables. Second, the axioms of CUSTOMER that express specific preferences, such as for a language, make it feasible to determine the best books provided by each supplier for any model. With respect to language, Book 3 is the least preferred, while 2.1 and 2.2 are the most preferred because languagePref(en) ≤ languagePref(de) ≤ languagePref(fr). In order to determine the best buying option, it suffices now to decide which variant of 2.1 and 2.2 is the most suitable for our constraints, which we do by comparing their delivery options: since express delivery is preferred to standard when the latter does not guarantee a delivery within seven days, the best choice is 2.2, and thus the selection process chooses $\mathcal{S}'$ as the best supplier.

Service Binding. After selecting a service module (non-deterministically from the set $sel(Rep, \mathcal{A}, \Sigma_k, r_k)$), the application will commit to the chosen provider through a *binding process* which changes the application as follows:

- The new orchestration is the vertex Σ' of the pushout (i, j).
- Apart from the interface i_k corresponding to the distinguished requirement, the interfaces of the application are preserved via a factorisation of the composition of the old interfaces and the morphism of orchestrations i: for $x \in \overline{n} \setminus \{k\}$, we obtain the interface $m_x^\Sigma : \Sigma_x' \to \Sigma'$ by taking the factorisation $e_x^\Sigma ; m_x^\Sigma$ of the composed morphism $i_x ; i$.
- The interface i_k is replaced by the interfaces of the selected service module: for $y \in \overline{m}$, $m_y^\Omega : \Omega_y' \to \Sigma'$ is the monic in the factorisation of $j_y ; j$.
- The distinguished requirement r_k is replaced by the requirements $\{e_y^\Omega(q_y)\}_{y \in \overline{m}}$ of the selected module, while the other requirements of the application are kept: for $x \in \overline{n} \setminus \{k\}$, r_x is translated to $e_x^\Sigma(r_x)$.

The final goal of binding a service application to different service modules is to obtain an application with all the requirements fulfilled. It is thus natural to be interested in determining a lower bound for the satisfiability of a service application based on the satisfiability of the application that results from the process of binding to a service module with a certain degree of correctness.

Proposition 15 (Correctness of Service Binding). *Let* $\mathcal{M} = (\Omega, P, J, Q)$ *be a β-correct module that matches a service application $\mathcal{A} = (\Sigma, I, R)$ through a morphism $\phi\colon \Sigma_k \to \Omega$. If the selection process guarantees that the compatibility score of the requirement r_k of $\mathcal{A}$ and the provides-property P of $\mathcal{M}$ is at least δ, and if the resulting application $\mathcal{A}' = (\Sigma', I', R')$ of their binding is α-satisfiable, then $\mathcal{A}$ is ζ-satisfiable with $\zeta = \mathcal{RL}(\phi)(\beta * \delta * \alpha)$.*

4   History and Value Systems

In this section, we analyse two distinguishing features of our method of selecting a best service module: unlike previous boolean approaches [13,14], it relies on arbitrary residuated lattices that may change through binding; moreover, it takes into account not only the properties of the supplier, but also the information encoded in the orchestration of the application. Each of these features raises new challenges in predicting which service modules will be bound to the application.

4.1   History Matters

The choice of a best supplier is usually not invariant to the change of the orchestration of an application. In this section, we identify those situations in which the information contained by the orchestration of a service application becomes irrelevant to the selection of a best service module.

Example 16. Consider the service application $\mathcal{C}' = (\Sigma', I', R)$ with the orchestration Σ' defined as the specification CUSTOMER of the application $\mathcal{C}$ from Example 9 to which we add the sentence

$$\forall b\colon \mathsf{Book}, d\colon \mathsf{Delivery}, n\colon \mathsf{Nat}.\ \mathsf{deliveryPref}(d, b, n) = 0 \text{ if } n > 7,$$

and having the same requirement R as $\mathcal{C}$. If we repeat the selection process for $\mathcal{C}'$ and the repository $Rep = \{\mathcal{S}, \mathcal{S}'\}$, the supplier $\mathcal{S}$ will be chosen instead of $\mathcal{S}'$. This is due to the fact that the delivery time for Book 2 is greater than seven days, and thus it does not meet the time-limit imposed by the new application.

Proposition 17. *Let* $\mathcal{A} = (\Sigma, I, R)$ *be a service application and (Σ_k, r_k) a requires-specification written over an $\mathbb{RL}$-institution having the model-amalgamation property. If the interface $i_k\colon \Sigma_k \to \Sigma \in I$ is a signature morphism that admits model expansions, the compatibility score between the requirement r_k of $\mathcal{A}$ and the provides-property of a service module $\mathcal{M} = (\Omega, P, J, Q)$ can be evaluated directly with respect to the orchestration Ω of $\mathcal{M}$, rather than having to first compute the pushout of the application and the module.*

Fact 18. *For a* CSP($\mathcal{I}$) *institution having the model-amalgamation property, a constraint signature morphism* $\varphi\colon (\Delta, \mathcal{L}) \to (\Delta', \mathcal{L}')$ *in* $\mathrm{Sig}^{\mathrm{CSP}(\mathcal{I})}$*, with underlying morphisms* $\varphi_{pr}\colon (\Sigma, E) \to (\Sigma', E')$ *and* $\varphi_{rl}\colon \mathcal{L}' \to \mathcal{L}$*, admits model expansions whenever the morphism of presentations* φ_{pr} *admits model expansions and the reduct* $M{\restriction}_\Delta$ *of any* (Σ, E)*-model* M *is projective with respect to* φ_{rl}*.*

4.2 Changing the Truth Space

The choice of a residuated lattice affects both the compatibility score (between a requirement and a provides-property) and the correctness of a service module.

Example 19. Consider once again the service application $\mathcal{C}$ from Example 9 and two suppliers $\mathcal{S}_1$ and $\mathcal{S}_2$ whose orchestrations have the same underlying signature – SIMPLESUPPLIER as in Fig. 5. Moreover, they have the same provides-property

$$P_1 = \mathsf{available}(\mathsf{book}, \mathsf{delivery}) \wedge (\mathsf{available}(\mathsf{book}, \mathsf{delivery}) \to$$
$$\mathsf{deliverable}(\mathsf{book}, \mathsf{delivery}, \mathsf{deliveryTime}(\mathsf{book}, \mathsf{delivery})))$$

and no requirements. The residuated lattices of the orchestrations of $\mathcal{S}_1$ and $\mathcal{S}_2$ differ: both $\mathcal{S}_1$ and $\mathcal{C}$ are based on the same Heyting algebra $\mathcal{L}$ with the underlying set of truth values $[0, 1]$, while $\mathcal{S}_2$ is based on the real-valued Łukasiewicz lattice $= ([0, 1], \min, \max, *, \to, 0, 1)$, with $x * y = \max\{0, x + y - 1\}$ and $x \to y = \min\{1, 1 - x + y\}$, for any $x, y \in [0, 1]$. The compatibility scores between the requirement $R = \mathsf{deliveryTime}(\mathsf{book}, \mathsf{delivery}, \mathsf{deliveryTime}(\mathsf{book}, \mathsf{delivery}))$ of the service application $\mathcal{C}$ and the provides-property P_1 of $\mathcal{S}_1$ and $\mathcal{S}_2$ will be 1 and 0.5, respectively. Consequently, for any match ϕ between $\mathcal{C}$ and $\mathcal{S}_2$ such that the morphism of residuated lattices $\mathcal{RL}(\phi)\colon \to \mathcal{L}$ does not map 0.5 to 1, the selection process will only determine $\mathcal{S}_1$ as a best service module. Notice that, even when $\mathcal{S}_1$ and $\mathcal{S}_2$ have the same underlying residuated lattices, the selection process may still depend on the matches between $\mathcal{C}$ and the two modules.

> **spec** SIMPLESUPPLIER = BOOKDATA **and** RESIDUATEDLATTICES
> **then ops** available : Book × Delivery $\longrightarrow$ Sat
> deliverable : Book × Delivery × Nat $\longrightarrow$ Sat

Fig. 5. The specification SIMPLESUPPLIER

Similarly, the correctness of a service module depends on its associated lattice.

Example 20. Let $\mathcal{S}_3$ be a service module based on the extension of SIMPLESUPPLIER with the sentence

$$\forall b\colon \mathsf{Book}, d\colon \mathsf{Delivery}.\ (\mathsf{deliverable}(b, d, \mathsf{deliveryTime}(b, d)) \to \mathsf{available}(b, d)) = 1.$$

Its provides-property is $P = \mathsf{available}(\mathsf{book}, \mathsf{delivery})$, and it has only one requirement, $\mathsf{deliverable}(\mathsf{book}, \mathsf{delivery}, \mathsf{deliveryTime}(\mathsf{book}, \mathsf{delivery}))$. The correctness of the module $\mathcal{S}_3$ will depend on the residuated lattice of its orchestration: for any Heyting algebra, the module will be correct with the value 1, while for the real-valued Łukasiewicz lattice, the module will only be 0.5-correct. Of course, these values cannot be compared, as they belong to different lattices. Still, the first one is absolute, while the second is not.

5   Conclusions and Future Work

We have developed a general technique for extending arbitrary institutions with soft constraints that formalises and generalises the results presented in [15]. Our approach consists in adding constraints to specifications written over a base stratified institution that provides functional requirements. The proposed technique requires that the underlying stratified institution $\mathcal{I}$ is expressive enough to capture residuated lattices, which provide the space of degrees of satisfaction in which constraints are expressed, and that every signature of $\mathcal{I}$ provides constraint variables, constraint sentences, and mappings through which each valuation of the constraint variables determines an interpretation of the constraints as elements of the residuated lattice. Building on this formalisation, we have shown how the selection of a best supplier in the context of service discovery and binding can be defined in terms of graded semantic consequence, and we have studied the unpredictability of the evolution of service applications that originates from the change of the truth structures that underlie the service components.

In order to facilitate an implementation of our model-theoretical approach to choosing a best supplier, we intend to further examine sound and complete proof systems defined in terms of many-valued rules as in [10]. These could be used in the development of operational semantics for the execution of such service-oriented applications (i.e. of a model for dynamic reconfiguration of systems in the style of [14]) with evolving preferences and truth spaces. Towards that end, the logic-programming semantics of services recently proposed in [26] provides a starting point. Besides the obvious need to adapt the theory presented therein to our many-valued setting (which means replacing linear temporal sentences with soft constraint specifications), the main open question is how to generalise the orchestrations of client applications and service modules in order to capture the way in which the satisfaction of constraint sentences changes upon iterations of the processes of service discovery, selection and binding.

We also consider worthwhile investigating how a graded variant of institution-independent logic programming, which generalises service-oriented logic programming, can be defined in relation to the developments presented in [25]. This would necessitate adapting the institution-independent abstractions of the concepts of Herbrand model, unification, resolution and computed answer (with a given degree of confidence) to the many-valued nature of our setting.

Acknowledgements. The authors would like to thank the anonymous referees for their very useful comments and suggestions. These have lead to an improved overall readability of the paper and to a more accurate presentation of the completeness requirement of the residuated lattices.

References

1. Aiguier, M., Diaconescu, R.: Stratified institutions and elementary homomorphisms. Inf. Process. Lett. **103**(1), 5–13 (2007)
2. Benavides, D., Trinidad, P., Ruiz-Cortés, A.: Automated reasoning on feature models. In: Pastor, Ó., e Cunha, J.F. (eds.) CAiSE 2005. LNCS, vol. 3520, pp. 491–503. Springer, Heidelberg (2005)
3. Bistarelli, S., Gadducci, F.: Enhancing constraints manipulation in semiring-based formalisms. In: Brewka, G., Coradeschi, S., Perini, A., Traverso, P. (eds.) ECAI, vol. 141, pp. 63–67. IOS Press (2006)
4. Bistarelli, S., Montanari, U., Rossi, F.: Semiring-based constraint satisfaction and optimization. J. ACM **44**(2), 201–236 (1997)
5. Bistarelli, S., Montanari, U., Rossi, F., Schiex, T., Verfaillie, G., Fargier, H.: Semiring-based CSPs and valued CSPs: frameworks, properties, and comparison. Constraints **4**(3), 199–240 (1999)
6. Bistarelli, S., Santini, F.: A nonmonotonic soft concurrent constraint language for SLA negotiation. Electr. Notes Theor. Comput. Sci. **236**, 147–162 (2009)
7. Bova, S.: Soft constraints processing over divisible residuated lattices. In: Sossai, C., Chemello, G. (eds.) ECSQARU 2009. LNCS, vol. 5590, pp. 887–898. Springer, Heidelberg (2009)
8. Mosses, P.D.: CASL Reference Manual, The Complete Documentation of the Common Algebraic Specification Language. LNCS, vol. 2960. Springer, Berlin (2004). doi:10.1007/b96103
9. Cohen, D.A., Cooper, M., Jeavons, P.G., Krokhin, A.A.: Soft constraints: complexity and multimorphisms. In: Rossi, F. (ed.) CP 2003. LNCS, vol. 2833, pp. 244–258. Springer, Heidelberg (2003)
10. Diaconescu, R.: Graded consequence: an institution theoretic study. Soft Comput. **18**(7), 1247–1267 (2014)
11. Fiadeiro, J.L.: Categories for Software Engineering. Springer, Heidelberg (2005)
12. Fiadeiro, J.L.: The many faces of complexity in software design. In: Hinchey, M., Coyle, L. (eds.) Conquering Complexity, pp. 3–47. Springer, Heidelberg (2012)
13. Fiadeiro, J.L., Lopes, A.: An interface theory for service-oriented design. Theor. Comput. Sci. **503**, 1–30 (2013)
14. Fiadeiro, J.L., Lopes, A.: A model for dynamic reconfiguration in service-oriented architectures. Softw. Syst. Model. **12**(2), 349–367 (2013)
15. Fiadeiro, J.L., Orejas, F.: Abstract constraint data types. In: De Nicola, R., Hennicker, R. (eds.) Wirsing Festschrift. LNCS, vol. 8950, pp. 155–170. Springer, Heidelberg (2015)
16. Galatos, N., Jipsen, P., Kowalski, T., Ono, H.: Residuated Lattices: An Algebraic Glimpse at Substructural Logics. Studies in Logic and the Foundations of Mathematics. Elsevier Science, New York (2007)
17. Goguen, J.A., Burstall, R.M.: Institutions: abstract model theory for specification and programming. J. ACM **39**(1), 95–146 (1992)
18. Harman, M., Jia, Y., Krinke, J., Langdon, W.B., Petke, J., Zhang, Y.: Search based software engineering for software product lineengineering: a survey and directions for future work. In: Gnesi, S., Fantechi, A., Heymans, P., Rubin, J., Czarnecki, K., Dhungana, D. (eds.) Software Product Line, pp. 5–18. ACM (2014)
19. Herrlich, H., Strecker, G.: Category Theory: An Introduction. Allyn and Bacon Series in Advanced Mathematics. Allyn and Bacon, Boston (1973)

20. Hölzl, M.M., Meier, M., Wirsing, M.: Which soft constraints do you prefer? Electr. Notes Theor. Comput. Sci. **238**(3), 189–205 (2009)
21. Mossakowski, T., Maeder, C., Lüttich, K.: The heterogeneous tool set, HETS. In: Grumberg, O., Huth, M. (eds.) TACAS 2007. LNCS, vol. 4424, pp. 519–522. Springer, Heidelberg (2007)
22. Pierce, B.C.: Basic Category Theory for Computer Scientists. Foundations of Computing. MIT Press, Cambridge (1991)
23. Sannella, D., Tarlecki, A.: Foundations of Algebraic Specification and Formal Software Development. Springer, Heidelberg (2012)
24. Schiex, T., Fargier, H., Verfaillie, G.: Valued constraint satisfaction problems: hard and easy problems. IJCAI **1**(95), 631–639 (1995)
25. Ţuţu, I., Fiadeiro, J.L.: From conventional to institution-independent logic programming. J. Logic Comput. (2015). http://logcom.oxfordjournals.org/content/early/2015/06/04/logcom.exv021.abstract
26. Ţuţu, I., Fiadeiro, J.L.: Service-oriented logic programming. Log. Meth. Comput. Sci. **11**(3), 1–38 (2015)
27. Wirsing, M., Clark, A., Gilmore, S., Hölzl, M., Knapp, A., Koch, N., Schroeder, A.: Semantic-based development of service-oriented systems. In: Najm, E., Pradat-Peyre, J.-F., Donzeau-Gouge, V.V. (eds.) FORTE 2006. LNCS, vol. 4229, pp. 24–45. Springer, Heidelberg (2006)

CafeInMaude: A CafeOBJ Interpreter in Maude

Adrián Riesco[1(✉)], Kazuhiro Ogata[2,3], and Kokichi Futatsugi[3]

[1] Facultad de Informática, Universidad Complutense de Madrid, Madrid, Spain
ariesco@fdi.ucm.es
[2] School of Information Science, JAIST, Nomi, Japan
[3] Research Center for Software Verification, JAIST, Nomi, Japan
{ogata,futatsugi}@jaist.ac.jp

Abstract. We present in this paper CafeInMaude, an interpreter for non-behavioral CafeOBJ specifications. The interpreter has been implemented in Maude. This alternative implementation combines CafeOBJ specification and theorem proving capabilities with efficient and extensible Maude commands and tools. Hence, it makes it possible to use both CafeOBJ proof scores and reduction commands and Maude model checking, narrowing, or theorem proving capabilities with the same tool.

Keywords: CafeOBJ · Full maude · Model checking · Theorem proving

1 Introduction

CafeOBJ [4] is a language for writing formal specifications for a wide variety of software and/or hardware systems, and verifying properties of them. CafeOBJ implements equational logic by rewriting and can be used as a powerful interactive theorem proving system. Specifiers can write proof scores [5] also in CafeOBJ and perform proofs by executing these proof scores. CafeOBJ, implemented in Lisp, provides several features to ease the specification of systems. These features include a flexible mix-fix syntax, powerful and clear typing system with ordered sorts, parameterized modules and views for instantiating the parameters, module expressions, operators for defining terms, equations for defining the (possibly conditional) equalities between terms, and (possibly conditional) transitions for specifying how a system evolves, among others.

CafeOBJ and Maude [1] are sister languages of the OBJ family. Maude modules are executable rewriting logic specifications and its C++ implementation shares many features with CafeOBJ. However, while the CafeOBJ community has focused on proofs via proof scores, the Maude community has focused on (i) verification of properties via model checking and exhaustive search, efficiently implemented in Maude, and (ii) tools implemented in Maude itself, thanks to the reflective capabilities of Maude [1], which allows users to extend Maude with new

Research partially supported by Japanese project Kakenhi 23220002, MICINN Spanish project *StrongSoft* (TIN2012-39391-C04-04), Comunidad de Madrid project N-Greens Software-CM (S2013/ICE-2731), and UCM-Santander grant GR3/14.

P. Stevens and A. Wąsowski (Eds.): FASE 2016, LNCS 9633, pp. 377–380, 2016.
DOI: 10.1007/978-3-662-49665-7_22

syntax and commands.[1] Among these tools we have the Maude Formal Environment (MFE) [3], which includes tools for proving termination, confluence, and coherence, the Constructor-based Inductive Theorem Prover (CITP) [6], a tool for proving inductive properties of systems specified with constructor-based logics, and the declarative debugger and test-case generator [8].

Taking into account the similarities between both languages, using Maude reflective capabilities, and using the translation in [7] we have implemented CafeInMaude, a CafeOBJ interpreter implemented in Maude. It defines both the parsing mechanisms required to introduce CafeOBJ specifications into the Maude database (hence allowing other Maude tools to be used with these specifications) and the execution strategies for faithfully executing proof scores. In this way it is possible to combine both Maude and CafeOBJ features. For example, it is now possible to first prove the termination and confluence of a theory using the MFE and then prove properties on it by using proof scores.

Moreover, CafeInMaude provides a simple framework where new features and commands can be added and tested just by using Maude code (much more familiar to CafeOBJ programmers than the Lisp implementation of CafeOBJ or the C++ implementation of Maude). Once these new features become mature they can be added to the standard Lisp implementation. In fact, we have easily added new features like the `metadata` and the `nonexec` attributes, which are used to indicate extra information and to prevent the engine from using these statements when executing, respectively.

We outline in the next section how to use the tool, explaining how to parse and execute standard CafeOBJ specifications in Sect. 2.1, how to use Maude tools with these specifications in Sect. 2.2, and how to extend CafeOBJ syntax in Sect. 2.3, while the limitations of the tool are presented in Sect. 2.4. Section 3 concludes and outlines some lines of future work. The tool and several case studies are available at https://github.com/ariesco/CafeInMaude.

2   Using CafeInMaude

We present in this section how to execute CafeOBJ specifications, how to combine them with Maude tools, and how to extend CafeOBJ syntax and commands. Finally, we summarize the limitations of the tool with respect to the standard Lisp implementation.

2.1   Executing CafeOBJ Specifications

Although Maude requires some constraints to allow input/output with the user, being the most important of them that modules and commands must be enclosed in parentheses, standard CafeOBJ specifications can be easily loaded by CafeInMaude by using the script provided in the webpage above. It executes a Java pre-parser to the files and introduces these modified files into Maude.

---

[1] Actually, we extend Full Maude [1, Part II], an extension of Maude written in Maude itself that is used as base for any further extension.

CafeInMaude supports any non-behavioral CafeOBJ specification and open-close environment, including those using the search predicates available in the latest releases of CafeOBJ [9]. As an interesting case study, we have used our tool for the falsification of the NSPK protocol, which finds a state in which NSPK does not enjoy the authentication property by combining bounded model checking by means of search and induction by using proof scores. More details are available at http://www.jaist.ac.jp/~kokichi/class/i613-1312 and https://github.com/ariesco/CafeInMaude.

2.2 Using Maude Commands

CafeInMaude considers both CafeOBJ and Maude specifications first-order citizens, so it is possible to import Maude modules into CafeOBJ modules and vice versa. Hence, it is possible to import, for example, the MODEL-CHECKER module. Once this module is imported, it is possible to define, *using CafeOBJ syntax*, the type for the states and the atomic formulas to be used in our LTL formulas. Then, it is possible to verify whether some initial CafeOBJ configurations fulfill these formulas by using the predefined modelCheck predicate.

In the same way, any command can be applied to CafeOBJ specifications. Therefore, it is possible to use Maude commands such as narrowing [2], which allows the user to perform symbolic search starting with non-ground terms.

Finally, additional tools extending Maude can also be used. In order to use these tools the user must indicate that the grammar used by the tool is an extension of the CafeOBJ grammar: CafeGrammar. Using this idea, we have already integrated the Maude Formal Environment (MFE) [3], the Constructor-based Inductive Theorem Prover (CITP) [6], and the declarative debugger and test-case generator [8].

2.3 Extending CafeOBJ

Since the implementation of CafeInMaude depends on a grammar defined in Maude, it is easy for Maude and CafeOBJ programmers to extend it. Extensions just require two steps: (i) defining the type (if it does not exist yet) and the syntax of the new feature and (ii) define how to parse it, which includes its translation into Maude. The former is straightforward and just requires to define some operators in the grammar module, while the latter, though complex, is greatly eased by the parsing functions that we provide for parsing and translating any CafeOBJ term. Using these ideas we have added the metadata, nonexec, and owise attributes to add information, prevent from executing, and apply only when it is the only applicable equation, respectively.

2.4 Limitations

Since CafeInMaude is based in a translation from CafeOBJ to Maude, it is constrained by the constructions available in CafeOBJ that are not available in

Maude. These limitations mainly affect the modules with loose semantics: in Maude these modules cannot be parameterized and can only be imported by other modules with loose semantics, and only in `including` mode (indicating that junk and confusion are allowed). We deal with these restriction in a conservative way: if the user allows a non-strict translation (which is enough for the tools currently integrated in CafeInMaude), they are translated as modules with tight semantics, while a warning message indicates the changes performed in the modules; otherwise, the translation fails.

Moreover, Maude does not allow modules with free parameters to be used to instantiate parameterized modules. In this case the tool cannot translate the module and it displays an error message.

3   Concluding Remarks and Ongoing Work

We have presented in this paper CafeInMaude, a tool to introduce CafeOBJ specifications into the Maude database. This tool provides an alternative implementation of CafeOBJ that allows us to use Maude modules and commands with CafeOBJ specifications, improves the performance of some of its commands, and eases the task of connecting CafeOBJ specifications with tools implemented on top of Full Maude. As future work we plan to use the narrowing techniques implemented in Maude [2] to analyze protocols previously defined in CafeOBJ.

References

1. Clavel, M., Durán, F., Eker, S., Lincoln, P., Martí-Oliet, N., Meseguer, J., Talcott, C.: Reflection, metalevel computation, and strategies. In: Clavel, M., Durán, F., Eker, S., Lincoln, P., Martí-Oliet, N., Meseguer, J., Talcott, C. (eds.) All About Maude - A High-Performance Logical Framework. LNCS, vol. 4350, pp. 419–458. Springer, Heidelberg (2007)
2. Clavel, M., Durán, F., Escobar, S., Eker, S., Lincoln, P., Martí-Oliet, N., Meseguer,J., Talcott, C.: Maude Manual (Version 2.7), March 2015. http://maude. cs.uiuc.edu/maude2-manual
3. Durán, F., Rocha, C., Álvarez, J.M.: Towards a maude formal environment. In: Agha, G., Danvy, O., Meseguer, J. (eds.) Formal Modeling: Actors, Open Systems, Biological Systems. LNCS, vol. 7000, pp. 329–351. Springer, Heidelberg (2011)
4. Futatsugi, K., Diaconescu, R.: CafeOBJ report. World Scientific, AMAST Series (1998)
5. Futatsugi, K., Găină, D., Ogata, K.: Principles of proof scores in CafeOBJ. Theor. Comput. Sci. **464**, 90–112 (2012)
6. Găină, D., Zhang, M., Chiba, Y., Arimoto, Y.: Constructor-based inductive theorem prover. In: Heckel, R., Milius, S. (eds.) CALCO 2013. LNCS, vol. 8089, pp. 328–333. Springer, Heidelberg (2013)
7. Riesco, A.: An integration of CafeOBJ into full maude. In: Escobar, S. (ed.) WRLA 2014. LNCS, vol. 8663, pp. 230–246. Springer, Heidelberg (2014)
8. Riesco, A., Verdejo, A., Martí-Oliet, N., Caballero, R.: Declarative debugging of rewriting logic specifications. JLAP **81**(7–8), 851–897 (2012)
9. Sawada, T., Futatsugi, K., Preining, N.: CafeOBJ Reference Manual (version 1.5.3), February 2015

Verification

Verifying a Verifier: On the Formal Correctness of an LTS Transformation Verification Technique

Sander de Putter and Anton Wijs[✉]

Eindhoven University of Technology, Eindhoven, The Netherlands
{s.m.j.d.putter,a.j.wijs}@tue.nl

Abstract. Over the years, various formal methods have been proposed and further developed to determine the functional correctness of models of concurrent systems. Some of these have been designed for application in a model-driven development workflow, in which model transformations are used to incrementally transform initial abstract models into concrete models containing all relevant details. In this paper, we consider an existing formal verification technique to determine that formalisations of such transformations are guaranteed to preserve functional properties, regardless of the models they are applied on. We present our findings after having formally verified this technique using the Coq theorem prover. It turns out that in some cases the technique is not correct. We explain why, and propose an updated technique in which these issues have been fixed.

1 Introduction

It is a well-known fact that concurrent systems are very hard to develop correctly. In order to support the development process, over the years, a whole range of formal methods techniques have been constructed to determine the functional correctness of system models [3]. Over time, these techniques have greatly improved, but the analysis of complex models is still time-consuming, and often beyond what is currently possible.

To get a stronger grip on the development process, model-driven development has been proposed [6]. In this approach, models are constructed iteratively, by defining *model transformations* that can be viewed as functions applicable on models: they are applied on models, producing new models. Using such transformations, an abstract initial model can be gradually transformed into a very detailed model describing all aspects of the system. If one can determine that the transformations are correct, then it is guaranteed that a correct initial model will be transformed into a correct final model.

Many model transformation verification techniques are focussed on determining that a given transformation applied on a given model produces a correct new model, but in order to show that a transformation is correct in general, one would

S. de Putter—This work is supported by ARTEMIS Joint Undertaking project EMC2 (grant nr. 621429).

P. Stevens and A. Wąsowski (Eds.): FASE 2016, LNCS 9633, pp. 383–400, 2016.
DOI: 10.1007/978-3-662-49665-7_23

have to determine this for *all possible input models*. There are some techniques that can do this [1,11], but it is often far from trivial to show that these are correct.

In this work, we formally prove the correctness of such a formal transformation verification technique proposed in [17,19] and implemented in the tool REFINER [20]. It is applicable on models with a semantics that can be captured by Labelled Transition Systems (LTSs). Transformations are formally defined as *LTS transformation rules*. Correctness of transformations is interpreted as the *preservation of properties*. Given a property φ written in a fragment of the μ-calculus [9], and a system of transformation rules Σ, REFINER checks whether Σ preserves φ for all possible input. This is done by first hiding all behaviour irrelevant for φ [9] and then checking whether the rules replace parts of the input LTSs by new parts that are *branching bisimilar* to the old ones. Branching bisimilarity preserves safety properties and a subset of liveness properties involving inevitable reachability [5]. When no property is considered, the technique checks for full semantics preservation, useful, for instance, when refactoring models.

The technique has been successfully applied to reason very efficiently about model transformations; speedups of five orders of magnitude have been measured w.r.t. traditional model checking of the models the transformations are applied on [17]. However, the correctness of the transformation verification technique, i.e. whether it returns **true** iff a given transformation is property preserving for all possible input models, has been an open question until now. With this paper we address that issue.

Contributions. We address the formal correctness of the transformation verification technique from [19]. We have fully verified the correctness of this technique using the Coq proof assistant[1], and therefore present proofs in this paper that have been rigorously checked. The full proof is available at [10]. We have identified situations in which the technique is in fact not correct for certain cases. We propose two alterations to repair the identified issues: one involves a more rigorous comparison of combinations of glue-states (the states in the LTS patterns that need to be matched, but will not be transformed), and one means determining whether a rule system has a particular property which we call *cascading*.

Structure of the Paper. Related work is discussed in Sect. 2. Section 3 presents the notions for and analysis of the application of a single transformation rule. Next, in Sect. 4, the discussion is continued by considering networks of concurrent process LTSs, and systems of transformation rules. Two issues with the correctness of the technique in this setting are presented and solutions are proposed. Furthermore, we present a proof sketch along the lines of the Coq proof for the repaired technique. Finally, Sect. 5 contains our conclusions and pointers to future work.

2   Related Work

Papers on incremental model checking (IMC) propose how to reuse model checking results of safety properties for a given input model after it has been

---

[1] http://coq.inria.fr.

altered [14,16]. We also consider verifying models that are subject to changes. However, we focus on analysing transformation specifications, i.e. the changes, themselves, allowing us to determine whether a change always preserves correctness, independent of the input model. Furthermore, our technique can also check the preservation of liveness properties.

In [12], an incremental algorithm is presented for updating bisimulation relations based on changes applied on a graph. Their goal is to efficiently maintain a bisimulation, whereas our goal is to assess whether bisimulations are guaranteed to remain after a transformation has been applied without considering the whole relation. As is the case for the IMC techniques, this algorithm works only for a given input graph, while we aim to prove correctness of the transformation specification itself regardless of the input.

In some works, e.g. [4,15], theorem proving is used to verify the preservation of behavioural semantics. The use of theorem provers requires expert knowledge and high effort [15]. In contrast, our equivalence checking approach is more lightweight, automated, and allows the construction of counter-examples which help developers identify issues with the transformations.

In [2], transformation rules for Open Nets are verified on the preservation of dynamic semantics. Open Nets are a reactive extension of Petri Nets. The technique is comparable to the technique that we verify with two main exceptions. First, they consider weak bisimilarity for the comparison of rule patterns, which preserves a strictly smaller fragment of the μ-calculus than branching bisimilarity [9]. Second, their technique does not allow transforming the communication interfaces between components. Our approach allows this, and checks whether the components remain 'compatible'.

Finally, in [13], transformations expressed in the DSLTrans language are checked for correspondence between source and target models. DSLTrans uses a symbolic model checker to verify properties that can be derived from the metamodels. The state space captures the evolution of the input model. In contrast, our approach considers the state spaces of combinations of transformation rules, which represent the potential behaviour described by those rules. An interesting pointer for future work is whether those two approaches can be combined.

3   Verifying Single LTS Transformations

This section introduces the main concepts related to the transformation of LTSs, and explains how a single transformation rule can be analysed to guarantee that it preserves the branching structure of all LTSs it can be applied on.

3.1   LTS Transformation and LTS Equivalence

We use *LTSs* as in Definition 1 to reason about the potential behaviour of processes.

Definition 1 (Labelled Transition System). *An LTS $\mathcal{G}$ is a tuple $(\mathcal{S}_{\mathcal{G}}, \mathcal{A}_{\mathcal{G}}, \mathcal{T}_{\mathcal{G}}, \mathcal{I}_{\mathcal{G}})$, with*

- $\mathcal{S}_\mathcal{G}$ a finite set of states;
- $\mathcal{A}_\mathcal{G}$ a set of action labels;
- $\mathcal{T}_\mathcal{G} \subseteq \mathcal{S}_\mathcal{G} \times \mathcal{A}_\mathcal{G} \times \mathcal{S}_\mathcal{G}$ a transition relation;
- $\mathcal{I}_\mathcal{G} \subseteq \mathcal{S}_\mathcal{G}$ a (non-empty) set of initial states.

Action labels in $\mathcal{A}_\mathcal{G}$ are denoted by a, b, c, etc. In addition, there is the special action label τ to represent internal, or hidden, system steps. A transition $(s, a, s') \in \mathcal{T}_\mathcal{G}$, or $s \xrightarrow{a}_\mathcal{G} s'$ for short, denotes that LTS $\mathcal{G}$ can move from state s to state s' by performing the a-action. For the transitive reflexive closure of $\xrightarrow{a}_\mathcal{G}$, we use $\xrightarrow{a}{}^*_\mathcal{G}$. Note that transitions are uniquely identifiable by the combination of their source state, action label, and target state. This property is sometimes called the *extensionality* of LTSs [21].

We allow LTSs to be transformed by means of formally defined transformation rules. Transformation rules are defined as shown in Definition 2.

Definition 2 (Transformation Rule). *A transformation rule* $r = \langle \mathcal{L}, \mathcal{R} \rangle$ *consists of a left pattern LTS* $\mathcal{L} = \langle \mathcal{S}_\mathcal{L}, \mathcal{A}_\mathcal{L}, \mathcal{T}_\mathcal{L}, \mathcal{I}_\mathcal{L} \rangle$ *and a right pattern LTS* $\mathcal{R} = \langle \mathcal{S}_\mathcal{R}, \mathcal{A}_\mathcal{R}, \mathcal{T}_\mathcal{R}, \mathcal{I}_\mathcal{R} \rangle$, *with* $\mathcal{I}_\mathcal{L} = \mathcal{I}_\mathcal{R} = \mathcal{S}_\mathcal{L} \cap \mathcal{S}_\mathcal{R}$.

The states in $\mathcal{S}_\mathcal{L} \cap \mathcal{S}_\mathcal{R}$ are called the glue-states. When applying a transformation rule to an LTS, the changes are applied relative to these glue-states. For the verification we consider glue-states as initial states, i.e. $\mathcal{I}_\mathcal{L} = \mathcal{I}_\mathcal{R} = \mathcal{S}_\mathcal{L} \cap \mathcal{S}_\mathcal{R}$. A transformation rule $r = (\mathcal{L}, \mathcal{R})$ is *applicable* on an LTS $\mathcal{G}$ iff a match $m : \mathcal{L} \to \mathcal{G}$ exists according to Definition 3.

Definition 3 (Match). *A pattern LTS* $\mathcal{P} = (\mathcal{S}_\mathcal{P}, \mathcal{A}_\mathcal{P}, \mathcal{T}_\mathcal{P}, \mathcal{I}_\mathcal{P})$ *has a* match $m : \mathcal{P} \to \mathcal{G}$ *on an LTS* $\mathcal{G} = (\mathcal{S}_\mathcal{G}, \mathcal{A}_\mathcal{G}, \mathcal{T}_\mathcal{G}, \mathcal{I}_\mathcal{G})$ *iff* m *is injective and* $\forall s \in \mathcal{S}_\mathcal{P} \setminus \mathcal{I}_\mathcal{P}, p \in \mathcal{S}_\mathcal{G}$:

- $m(s) \xrightarrow{a}_\mathcal{G} p \implies (\exists s' \in \mathcal{S}_\mathcal{P}.\ s \xrightarrow{a}_\mathcal{P} s' \wedge m(s') = p)$;
- $p \xrightarrow{a}_\mathcal{G} m(s) \implies (\exists s' \in \mathcal{S}_\mathcal{P}.\ s' \xrightarrow{a}_\mathcal{P} s \wedge m(s') = p)$.

A match is a behaviour preserving embedding of a pattern LTS $\mathcal{P}$ in an LTS $\mathcal{G}$ defined via a category of LTSs [21]. Moreover, a match may not cause removal of transitions that are not explicitly present in $\mathcal{P}$. The set $m(S) = \{m(s) \in \mathcal{S}_\mathcal{G} \mid s \in S\}$ is the image of a set of states S through match m on an LTS $\mathcal{G}$.

An LTS $\mathcal{G}$ is transformed to an LTS $T(\mathcal{G})$ according to Definition 4.

Definition 4 (LTS Transformation). *Let* $\mathcal{G} = \langle \mathcal{S}_\mathcal{G}, \mathcal{A}_\mathcal{G}, \mathcal{T}_\mathcal{G}, \mathcal{I}_\mathcal{G} \rangle$ *be an LTS and let* $r = \langle \mathcal{L}, \mathcal{R} \rangle$ *be a transformation rule with match* $m : \mathcal{L} \to \mathcal{G}$. *Moreover, consider match* $\hat{m} : \mathcal{R} \to T(\mathcal{G})$, *with* $\forall q \in \mathcal{S}_\mathcal{L} \cap \mathcal{S}_\mathcal{R}.\ \hat{m}(q) = m(q)$ *and* $\forall q \in \mathcal{S}_\mathcal{R} \setminus \mathcal{S}_\mathcal{L}.\ \hat{m}(q) \notin \mathcal{S}_\mathcal{G}$, *defining the new states being introduced by the transformation. The transformation of LTS* $\mathcal{G}$, *via rule* r *with match* m, *is defined as* $T(\mathcal{G}) = \langle \mathcal{S}_{T(\mathcal{G})}, \mathcal{A}_{T(\mathcal{G})}, \mathcal{T}_{T(\mathcal{G})}, \mathcal{I}_\mathcal{G} \rangle$ *where*

- $\mathcal{S}_{T(\mathcal{G})} = \mathcal{S}_\mathcal{G} \setminus m_\mathcal{L}(\mathcal{S}_\mathcal{L}) \cup m_\mathcal{R}(\mathcal{S}_\mathcal{R})$;
- $\mathcal{T}_{T(\mathcal{G})} = (\mathcal{T}_\mathcal{G} \setminus \{m_\mathcal{L}(s) \xrightarrow{a} m_\mathcal{L}(s') \mid s \xrightarrow{a}_\mathcal{L} s'\}) \cup \{m_\mathcal{R}(s) \xrightarrow{a} m_\mathcal{R}(s') \mid s \xrightarrow{a}_\mathcal{R} s'\}$
- $\mathcal{A}_{T(\mathcal{G})} = \{a \mid \exists s \xrightarrow{a} s' \in \mathcal{T}_{T(\mathcal{G})}\}$

Given a match, an LTS transformation replaces states and transitions matched by $\mathcal{L}$ by a copy of $\mathcal{R}$ yielding LTS $T(\mathcal{G})$. Since in general, $\mathcal{L}$ may have several matches on $\mathcal{G}$, we assume that transformations are *confluent*, i.e. they are guaranteed to terminate and lead to a unique $T(\mathcal{G})$. Confluence of LTS transformations can be checked efficiently [18]. Assuming confluence means that when verifying transformation rules, we can focus on having a single match, since the transformations of

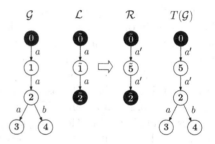

Fig. 1. Application of a transformation rule

individual matches do not influence each other. An application of a transformation rule is shown in Fig. 1. The initial and glue-states are coloured black. In the middle of Fig. 1, a transformation rule $r = (\mathcal{L}, \mathcal{R})$ is shown, which is applied on LTS $\mathcal{G}$ resulting in LTS $T(\mathcal{G})$. The states are numbered such that matches can be identified by the state label, i.e. a state $\tilde{i}$ is matched onto state i. The left-pattern of r does not match on states $\langle 1 \rangle$, $\langle 2 \rangle$, and $\langle 3 \rangle$ as this would remove the b-transition.

To compare LTSs, we use the *branching bisimulation* equivalence relation [5] as presented in Definition 5. Branching bisimulation supports abstraction from actions and is sensitive to internal actions and the branching structure of an LTS. Abstraction from actions is required for verification of abstraction and refinement transformations such that input and output models can be compared on the same abstraction level.

Definition 5 (Branching bisimulation). *A binary relation B between two LTSs $\mathcal{G}_1$ and $\mathcal{G}_2$ is a* branching bisimulation *iff $s \, B \, t$ implies*

1. $s \xrightarrow{a}_{\mathcal{G}_1} s' \implies (a = \tau \wedge s' \, B \, t) \vee (t \xrightarrow{\tau}{}^{*}_{\mathcal{G}_2} \hat{t} \xrightarrow{a}_{\mathcal{G}_2} t' \wedge s \, B \, \hat{t} \wedge s' \, B \, t')$,
2. $t \xrightarrow{a}_{\mathcal{G}_2} t' \implies (a = \tau \wedge s \, B \, t') \vee (s \xrightarrow{\tau}{}^{*}_{\mathcal{G}_1} \hat{s} \xrightarrow{a}_{\mathcal{G}_1} s' \wedge \hat{s} \, B \, t \wedge s' \, B \, t')$

Two states $s, t \in S$ are *branching bisimilar*, denoted $s \leftrightarrow_b t$, iff there is a branching bisimulation B such that $s \, B \, t$. Two sets of states S_1 and S_2 are called branching bisimilar, denoted $S_1 \leftrightarrow_b S_2$, iff $\forall s_1 \in S_1. \exists s_2 \in S_2. s_1 \leftrightarrow_b s_2$ and vice versa. We say that two LTSs $\mathcal{G}_1$ and $\mathcal{G}_2$ are branching bisimilar, denoted $\mathcal{G}_1 \leftrightarrow_b \mathcal{G}_2$, iff $\mathcal{I}_{\mathcal{G}_1} \leftrightarrow_b \mathcal{I}_{\mathcal{G}_2}$.

3.2 Analysing a Transformation Rule

The basis of the transformation verification procedure is to check whether the two patterns making up a rule are equivalent, while respecting that the patterns share initial states. That is, given a rule $r = \langle \mathcal{L}, \mathcal{R} \rangle$, we are looking for a branching bisimulation relation R such that for all $s \in \mathcal{S}_\mathcal{L} \cap \mathcal{S}_\mathcal{R}$, we have $s \, R \, s$.

Directly applying bisimilarity checking on a pair of LTSs, however, will not
necessarily produce a suitable bisimulation relation. For instance, consider the
rule in Fig. 2 which swaps a and b transitions. Without the κ-loops, explained
in the next paragraph, the LTS patterns
are branching bisimilar. However, the patterns should be interpreted as possible

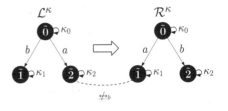

Fig. 2. κ-loops ensure $\langle \tilde{2} \rangle \not\leftrightarrow_b \langle \tilde{1} \rangle$

embeddings in larger LTSs. These larger LTSs may not be branching bisimilar,
because glue-states $\langle \tilde{1} \rangle$ and $\langle \tilde{2} \rangle$ could be mapped to states with different in- and
outgoing transitions, apart from the behaviour described in the LTS patterns.

To restrict bisimilarity checking to exactly those bisimulations that adhere
to relating glue-states to themselves, we introduce a so-called κ-transition-loop
for each glue-state, as defined in Definition 6. The resulting κ-extended trans-
formation rule can now be defined as $r^\kappa = (\mathcal{L}^\kappa, \mathcal{R}^\kappa)$, and is specifically used for
the purpose of analysing r, it does not replace r. The κ-loop of a glue-state s is
labelled with a unique label $\kappa_s \notin \mathcal{A}_\mathcal{L} \cup \mathcal{A}_\mathcal{R}$. If we add κ-loops to the rule in Fig. 2,
the analysis is able to determine that the rule does not guarantee bisimilarity
between input and output LTSs.

Definition 6 (κ-extension of an LTS). *The LTS $\mathcal{P}$ extended with κ-loops is
defined as:* $\mathcal{P}^\kappa = (\mathcal{S}_\mathcal{P}, \mathcal{A}_\mathcal{P} \cup \{\kappa_s \mid s \in \mathcal{I}_\mathcal{P}\}, \mathcal{T}_\mathcal{P} \cup \{(s, \kappa_s, s) \mid s \in \mathcal{I}_\mathcal{P}\}, \mathcal{I}_\mathcal{P})$.

The Analysis. A transformation rule preserves the branching structure of all
LTSs it is applicable on if the patterns of a transformation rule extended with
κ-loops are branching bisimilar. This is expressed in Proposition 1.

Proposition 1. *Let $\mathcal{G}$ be an LTS, let r be a transformation rule with matches
$m : \mathcal{L} \rightarrow \mathcal{G}$ and $\hat{m} : \mathcal{R} \rightarrow T(\mathcal{G})$ with $m(s) = \hat{m}(s)$ for all $s \in \mathcal{S}_\mathcal{L} \cap \mathcal{S}_\mathcal{R}$. Then,*

$$\mathcal{L}^\kappa \leftrightarrow_b \mathcal{R}^\kappa \implies \mathcal{G} \leftrightarrow_b T(\mathcal{G})$$

Intuition. A match of pattern $\mathcal{L}$ is replaced with an instance of pattern $\mathcal{R}$.
If $\mathcal{L}^\kappa \leftrightarrow_b \mathcal{R}^\kappa$, then these two patterns exhibit branching bisimilar behaviour.
Therefore, the behaviour of the original and transformed systems ($\mathcal{G}$ and $T_\mathcal{G}$
respectively) are branching bisimilar.

4   Verifying Sets of Dependent LTS Transformations

In this section, we extend the setting by considering sets of interacting process
LTSs in so-called *networks of LTSs* [7] or *LTS networks*. Transformations can
now affect multiple LTSs in an input network, and the analysis of transformations
is more involved, since changes to process-local behaviour may affect system-
global properties. We address two complications that arose while trying to prove
the correctness of the technique using Coq and propose how to fix the technique
to overcome these problems. Finally, we provide a proof-sketch of the correctness
of the fixed technique based on the complete Coq proof.

4.1   LTS Networks and Their Transformation

An LTS network (Definition 7) describes a system consisting of a finite number of concurrent process LTSs and a set of synchronisation laws which define the possible interaction between the processes. The explicit behaviour of an LTS network is defined by its *system LTS* (Definition 8). We write $1..n$ for the set of integers ranging from 1 to n. A vector $\bar{v}$ of size n contains n elements indexed from 1 to n. For all $i \in 1..n$, $\bar{v}_i$ represents the ith element of vector $\bar{v}$.

Definition 7 (LTS network). *An LTS network $\mathcal{M}$ of size n is a pair $(\Pi, \mathcal{V})$, where*

- *Π is a vector of n concurrent LTSs. For each $i \in 1..n$, we write $\Pi_i = (\mathcal{S}_i, \mathcal{A}_i, \mathcal{T}_i, \mathcal{I}_i)$.*
- *$\mathcal{V}$ is a finite set of synchronisation laws. A synchronisation law is a tuple $(\bar{t}, a)$, where $\bar{t}$ is a vector of size n, called the synchronisation vector, describing synchronising action labels, and a is an action label representing the result of successful synchronisation. We have $\forall i \in 1..n.$ $\bar{t}_i \in \mathcal{A}_i \cup \{\bullet\}$, where $\bullet$ is a special symbol denoting that Π_i performs no action.*

Definition 8 (System LTS). *Given an LTS network $\mathcal{M} = (\Pi, \mathcal{V})$, its system LTS is defined by $\mathcal{G}_\mathcal{M} = (\mathcal{S}_\mathcal{M}, \mathcal{A}_\mathcal{M}, \mathcal{T}_\mathcal{M}, \mathcal{I}_\mathcal{M})$, with*

- *$\mathcal{S}_\mathcal{M} = \mathcal{S}_1 \times \cdots \times \mathcal{S}_n$;*
- *$\mathcal{A}_\mathcal{M} = \{a \mid (\bar{t}, a) \in \mathcal{V}\}$;*
- *$\mathcal{I}_\mathcal{M} = \{\langle s_1, \ldots, s_n \rangle \mid s_i \in \mathcal{I}_i\}$, and*
- *$\mathcal{T}_\mathcal{M}$ is the smallest relation satisfying:*

$$(\bar{t}, a) \in \mathcal{V} \wedge \forall i \in 1..n. \quad \begin{pmatrix} (\bar{t}_i = \bullet \wedge \bar{s}_i = \bar{s}'_i \wedge \bar{s}_i \in \mathcal{S}_i) \\ \vee (\bar{t}_i \neq \bullet \wedge \bar{s}_i \xrightarrow{\bar{t}_i}_i \bar{s}'_i) \end{pmatrix} \implies \bar{s} \xrightarrow{a}_\mathcal{M} \bar{s}'$$

The system LTS is obtained by combining the processes in Π according to the synchronisation laws in $\mathcal{V}$. The LTS network model subsumes most hiding, renaming, cutting, and parallel composition operators present in process algebras, but also more expressive operators such as m among n synchronisation [8]. For instance, hiding can be applied by replacing the a component in a law by τ. A transition of a process LTS is *cut* if it is blocked with respect to the behaviour of the whole system (system LTS), i.e. there is no synchronization law involving the transition's action label on the process LTS.

Figure 3 shows an LTS network $\mathcal{M} = (\Pi, \mathcal{V})$ with two processes and three synchronisation laws (left) and its system LTS (right). To construct the system LTS, first, the initial states of Π_1 and Π_2 are combined to form the initial state of $\mathcal{G}_\mathcal{M}$. Then, the outgoing transitions of the initial states of Π_1 and Π_2 are combined using the synchronisation laws, leading to new states in $\mathcal{G}_\mathcal{M}$, and so on. For simplicity, we do not show unreachable states.

Law $(\langle a, a \rangle, a)$ specifies that the process LTSs can synchronise on their a-transitions, resulting in a-transitions in the system LTS. The other laws specify that b- and d-transitions can synchronise, resulting in e-transitions, and that c-transitions can be fired independently. Note that in fact, b- and d-transitions in Π_1 and Π_2 are never able to synchronise.

The set of indices of processes participating in a synchronisation law $(\bar{t}, a)$ is formally defined as $Ac(\bar{t}) = \{i \mid i \in 1..n \land \bar{t}_i \neq \bullet\}$; e.g. $Ac(\langle c, b, \bullet \rangle) = \{1, 2\}$.

Branching bisimilarity is a congruence for construction of the system LTS of

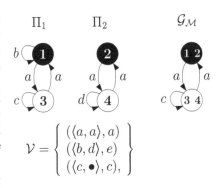

$$\mathcal{V} = \left\{ \begin{array}{l} (\langle a, a \rangle, a) \\ (\langle b, d \rangle, e) \\ (\langle c, \bullet \rangle, c), \end{array} \right\}$$

Fig. 3. An LTS network $\mathcal{M} = (\Pi, \mathcal{V})$ (left) and its system LTS $\mathcal{G}_\mathcal{M}$ (right)

LTS networks if the synchronisation laws do not synchronise, rename, or cut τ-transitions [7]. Given an LTS network $\mathcal{M} = (\Pi, \mathcal{V})$, these properties are formalised as follows:

1. $\forall (\bar{t}, a) \in \mathcal{V}, i \in 1..n. \; \bar{t}_i = \tau \implies Ac(\bar{t}) = \{i\}$ (no synchronisation of τ's);
2. $\forall (\bar{t}, a) \in \mathcal{V}, i \in 1..n. \; \bar{t}_i = \tau \implies a = \tau$ (no renaming of τ's);
3. $\forall i \in 1..n. \; \tau \in \mathcal{A}_i \implies \exists (\bar{t}, a) \in \mathcal{V}. \; \bar{t}_i = \tau$ (no cutting of τ's).

In this paper, we assume these properties hold.

Transformation of an LTS Network. A rule system is used to define transformations for LTS networks. A *rule system* Σ is a tuple $(R, \mathcal{V}', \hat{\mathcal{V}})$, where R is a vector of transformation rules, $\mathcal{V}'$ is a set of synchronisation laws that must be present in networks that Σ is applied on, and $\hat{\mathcal{V}}$ is a set of synchronisation laws introduced in the result of a transformation. A rule system $\Sigma = (R, \mathcal{V}', \hat{\mathcal{V}})$ is *applicable* on a given LTS network $\mathcal{M} = (\Pi, \mathcal{V})$ when for each synchronisation law in $\mathcal{V}'$ there is a synchronisation law in $\mathcal{V}$, and no other synchronisation laws in $\mathcal{V}$ involve behaviour described by the rules in R. As R is a vector, we identify transformation rules in R by an index. We write $\mathcal{L}_i$ and $\mathcal{R}_i$ for the left and right patterns, respectively, of rule r_i, where $i \in 1..|R|$.

Furthermore, the rule system must satisfy three *analysis conditions* related to transformation of synchronising behaviour in a network. The first condition concerns the applicability of a rule system on an LTS network. A rule transforming synchronising transitions must be applicable on all equivalent synchronising transitions:

$$\forall \Pi_i \in \mathcal{M}, r_j \in R, (\bar{t}, a) \in \mathcal{V}'. \; (\{j\} \subset Ac(\bar{t}) \land \exists m{:}\mathcal{L}_j \to \Pi_i) \tag{AC1}$$
$$\implies \forall (s, \bar{t}_j, s') \in \mathcal{T}_i. \; \exists m' : \mathcal{L}_j \to \Pi_i, p, p' \in \mathcal{S}_{\mathcal{L}_j}. \; m'(s) = p \land m'(s') = p'$$

Suppose Σ is applied on a network $\mathcal{M}$ and Σ contains a rule transforming synchronising a-transitions. If not all a-transitions are transformed it is unclear how this affects synchronisation between the processes, since the original and the transformed synchronising behaviour may coexist. The second and third conditions concern how a rule system is defined. The second condition requires that Σ is complete w.r.t. synchronising behaviour.

$$\forall(\bar{t}, a) \in \mathcal{V}', i \in 1..|R|. \ \bar{t}_i \in \mathcal{A}_{\mathcal{L}_i} \cup \{\bullet\} \tag{AC2}$$

For each action a synchronising with an action subjected to a rule there must be a rule also transforming a-transitions. This ensures that all the behaviour related to the synchronisation is captured in the rule system. Hence, the analysis considers a complete picture. For AC1 and AC2 the symmetric conditions involving the $\mathcal{R}$ and $\mathcal{V}' \cup \hat{\mathcal{V}}$ apply as well.

The third condition prevents that the new synchronisation laws in $\hat{\mathcal{V}}$ are defined over actions already present in the processes of an input network. Otherwise, a model could be altered without actually defining any transformation rules:

$$\forall(\bar{t}, a) \in \hat{\mathcal{V}}, i \in 1..|R|. \ \bar{t}_i \in (\mathcal{A}_{\mathcal{R}_i} \setminus \mathcal{A}_{\mathcal{L}_i}) \cup \{\bullet\} \tag{AC3}$$

When transforming an LTS network $\mathcal{M}$ by means of a rule system Σ, first, we check whether Σ is applicable on $\mathcal{M}$ and satisfies AC1. Then, for every Π_i ($i \in 1..n$) and every $r \in R$, the largest set of matches is calculated. For each match, the corresponding transformation rule is applied. We call the resulting network $T_\Sigma(\mathcal{M})$. In contrast, when verifying a rule system, we first check that it is confluent and satisfies both AC2 and AC3. Checking confluence, AC1, AC2 and AC3 can be done efficiently [17–20].

4.2 Analysing Transformations of an LTS Network

In a rule system, transformation rules can be dependent on each other regarding the behaviour they affect. In particular, the rules may refer to actions that require synchronisation according to some law, either in the network being transformed, or the network resulting from the transformation. Since in general, it is not known a-priori whether or not those synchronisations can actually happen (see Fig. 3, the a-transitions versus the b- and d-transitions), full analysis of such rules must consider both successful and unsuccessful synchronisation.

To this end, dependent rules must be analysed in all possible combinations. Potential synchronisation between the behaviour in transformation rules is characterised by the *direct dependency relation* $D = \{(i, j) \mid \exists(\bar{t}, a) \in \mathcal{V}' \cup \hat{\mathcal{V}}. \{i, j\} \subseteq Ac(\bar{t})\}$. Rule r_i is related via D to r_j iff both rules participate in a synchronisation law. The relation considering directly and indirectly dependent rules, called the *dependency relation*, is defined by the transitive closure of D, i.e. D^+. The D^+ relation can be used to construct a partition $\mathbb{D}$ of the transformation rules into classes of dependent rules. Each class can be analysed independently. We call these classes *dependency sets*.

For the analysis of combinations of LTS patterns, we define in Definition 9 LTS networks $\bar{\mathcal{L}}^\kappa$ and $\bar{\mathcal{R}}^\kappa$ of κ-extended patterns, or *pattern networks* in short, consisting of a combination of the κ-extended left and right LTS patterns of a rule system Σ, respectively.

Definition 9 ((κ-Extended) Pattern network). *Given a rule system* $\Sigma = (R, \mathcal{V}', \hat{\mathcal{V}})$, *its* left *and* right *pattern networks are* $\bar{\mathcal{L}}^{\kappa}$ *and* $\bar{\mathcal{R}}^{\kappa}$, *respectively, where*

$$\bar{\mathcal{L}}^{\kappa} = (\langle \mathcal{L}_1^{\kappa}, \ldots, \mathcal{L}_{|R|}^{\kappa} \rangle, \mathcal{V}' \cup \mathcal{V}^{\kappa}),$$
$$\bar{\mathcal{R}}^{\kappa} = (\langle \mathcal{R}_1^{\kappa}, \ldots, \mathcal{R}_{|R|}^{\kappa} \rangle, \mathcal{V}' \cup \hat{\mathcal{V}} \cup \mathcal{V}^{\kappa}), \text{ and}$$
$$\mathcal{V}^{\kappa} = \{(\bar{t}, \kappa_s) \mid \exists i \in 1..n. \; \kappa_s \in \mathcal{A}_{\mathcal{L}_i^{\kappa}} \wedge \bar{t}_i = \kappa_s \wedge \forall j \in 1..n \setminus i. \; \bar{t}_j = \bullet\}$$

In order to focus the analysis on combinations of *dependent* rules, we define how to *filter* an LTS network w.r.t. a given set I of indices. With the filtering operation, we can create *filtered κ-extended pattern networks* $\mathcal{L}_I^{\kappa}$, $\mathcal{R}_I^{\kappa}$ for any set I of indices of dependent rules.

Definition 10 (Filtered LTS network). *Given an LTS network* $\mathcal{M} = (\Pi, \mathcal{V})$ *of size* n *and a set of indices* $I \subseteq 1..n$, *the* filtered LTS network *is defined by* $\mathcal{M}_I = (\Phi, \mathcal{V}_\Phi)$, *with*

$$\forall i \in 1..n. \; \Phi_i = \begin{cases} \Pi_i & \text{if } i \in I \\ (\{*\}, \emptyset, \emptyset, \{*\}) & \text{otherwise} \end{cases}$$

$$\mathcal{V}_\Phi = \{(\bar{t}, a) \in \mathcal{V} \mid \forall i \in 1..n. \; \bar{t}_i \in \mathcal{A}_{\Phi_i} \cup \{\bullet\}\}$$

where $*$ *is a dummy state.*

Next, we discuss the analysis of networks with focus on two areas in which the analysis technique as presented in [17,19] was not correct. Firstly, the work did not consider the synchronisation of κ-transitions. Secondly, the consistency of synchronising behaviour across pattern networks was not considered.

Analysis of Pattern Networks and Synchronisation of κ-Transitions. Figure 4a shows a rule system Σ, in which the two rules are dependent. The example demonstrates that the verification technique may produce incorrect results, since it does not consider synchronisations between κ-transitions. The corresponding pattern networks for Σ are presented in Fig. 4b, if we ignore the last synchronisation law in $\mathcal{V}^{\kappa}$. The resulting bisimulation checks are given in Fig. 4c, if we ignore the κ_{12}-transitions. Unsuccessful synchronisation is considered in the checks between $\mathcal{L}_{\{1\}}^{\kappa}$ and $\mathcal{R}_{\{1\}}^{\kappa}$, and $\mathcal{L}_{\{2\}}^{\kappa}$ and $\mathcal{R}_{\{2\}}^{\kappa}$. In those, synchronisations are not possible (for instance between the z-transitions). The check between pattern networks $\mathcal{L}_{\{1,2\}}^{\kappa}$ and $\mathcal{R}_{\{1,2\}}^{\kappa}$ considers successful synchronisation. In the original verification technique [17,19] the κ_{12}-loops in pattern networks $\mathcal{L}_{\{1,2\}}^{\kappa}$ and $\mathcal{R}_{\{1,2\}}^{\kappa}$ were not introduced. Without those loops, the pattern networks are branching bisimilar. However, as pattern networks may appear as an embedding in a larger network, all possible in- and outgoing transitions must be considered. Hence, synchronising transitions which enter and leave the pattern network must be considered as well. The κ_{12}-transitions in Fig. 4c are the result of synchronising κ_1 and κ_2-transitions, and therefore represent these synchronising transitions. Observe that in $\mathcal{R}_{\{1,2\}}^{\kappa}$ the possibility to perform κ_{12}-transitions is lost once the

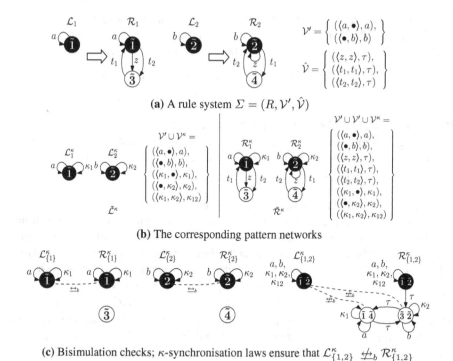

(a) A rule system $\Sigma = (R, \mathcal{V}', \hat{\mathcal{V}})$

(b) The corresponding pattern networks

(c) Bisimulation checks; κ-synchronisation laws ensure that $\mathcal{L}_{\{1,2\}}^{\kappa} \not\leftrightarrow_b \mathcal{R}_{\{1,2\}}^{\kappa}$

Fig. 4. A rule system and its pattern networks and bisimulation checks

τ-transition at state $\langle \tilde{1}, \tilde{2} \rangle$ has been taken, while in $\mathcal{L}_{\{1,2\}}^{\kappa}$ it is always possible to perform the κ_{12}-transition. Hence, the left and right networks are not branching bisimilar. These bisimulation checks show that Σ does not guarantee preservation of the branching structure in all cases; e.g. take $(\Pi, \mathcal{V}')$ as input network, with $\forall i \in 1..n.\ \Pi_i = \mathcal{L}_i$.

Fixing the Technique. To overcome the above mentioned shortcoming, we need to allow κ-transitions to synchronise. For this, additional κ-synchronisation laws must be introduced in the pattern networks by redefining $\mathcal{V}^{\kappa}$ in Definition 9 as follows:

$$\mathcal{V}^{\kappa} = \{(\bar{t}, \kappa_{\bar{s}}) \mid \exists I \subseteq 1..n.\ \bar{s} \in \mathcal{I}_{\mathcal{L}_I} \wedge (\forall i \in I.\ \bar{t}_i = \kappa_{\bar{s}_i}) \wedge (\forall i \in 1..n \setminus I.\ \bar{t}_i = \bullet)\}$$

For each vector glue-state $\bar{s} \in \mathcal{I}_{\mathcal{L}_I}$ ($I \subseteq 1..n$) there is now an enabled κ-synchronisation law. These κ-laws ensure that each vector of glue-states is at least related to itself.

Due to the κ-laws, groups of glue-states can be uniquely identified. This gives rise to Lemma 1 that states: if a state vector $\bar{s} \in \mathcal{S}_{\mathcal{L}_I}$, containing a group of glue-states, is related to a state vector $\bar{p} \in \mathcal{S}_{\mathcal{R}_I}$, then there must be a be a τ-path from $\bar{p}$ to a state $\hat{\bar{p}} \in \mathcal{S}_{\mathcal{R}_I}$ such that $\hat{\bar{p}}$ and $\bar{s}$ are related, and $\hat{\bar{p}}$ contains the same group of glue-states as $\bar{s}$.

Lemma 1. *Consider a rule system* $\Sigma = (R, \mathcal{V}', \hat{\mathcal{V}})$ *and sets of indices* $I \subseteq 1..n$ *and* $J \subseteq I$. *Let* $\mathcal{L}_I$ *and* $\mathcal{R}_I$ *be the corresponding pattern networks. Furthermore, let* B_I *be a branching bisimulation relation such that* $\mathcal{L}_I^\kappa \leftrightarrow_b \mathcal{R}_I^\kappa$, *then*

$$\forall \bar{s} \in \mathcal{S}_{\mathcal{L}_I}, \bar{p} \in \mathcal{S}_{\mathcal{R}_I} . \ \bar{s} \ B_I \ \bar{p} \wedge (\forall i \in J. \ \bar{s}_i \in \mathcal{I}_{\mathcal{L}_i}) \implies$$

$$\exists \hat{p} \in \mathcal{S}_{\mathcal{R}_I} . \ \bar{p} \xrightarrow{\tau}{}^*_{\mathcal{R}_I} \hat{p} \wedge \bar{s} \ B_I \ \hat{p} \wedge \forall i \in J. \ \hat{p}_i = \bar{s}_i$$

Proof. Follows from the fact that $\bar{s}$ has a loop with a unique label, say $\kappa_{\bar{s}_J}$, identifying the group of glue-states. Hence, if $\bar{s} \ B_I \ \bar{p}$, then $\bar{p}$ must be able to perform a $\kappa_{\bar{s}_J}$-transition directly (i.e. $\forall i \in J. \ \bar{s}_i = \bar{p}_i$) or be able to reach such a transition via a τ-path. $\qquad\square$

Consistency of Synchronising Behaviour. Formal verification of the analysis technique in Coq furthermore showed that in one other case, the technique also incorrectly concludes that a rule system is correct for all possible input. This happens when a rule system is not *behaviourally consistent* across pattern networks. Consider a rule system Σ with two transformation rules such that $\mathcal{L}_{\{1,2\}}^\kappa \leftrightarrow_b \mathcal{R}_{\{1,2\}}^\kappa$, $\mathcal{L}_{\{1\}}^\kappa \leftrightarrow_b \mathcal{R}_{\{1\}}^\kappa$, and $\mathcal{L}_{\{2\}}^\kappa \leftrightarrow_b \mathcal{L}_{\{2\}}^\kappa$. Furthermore, consider vector states $\langle t_{\mathcal{L}}, g \rangle \in \mathcal{S}_{\mathcal{L}_{\{1,2\}}^\kappa}$ and $\langle t_{\mathcal{R}}, g \rangle \in \mathcal{S}_{\mathcal{R}_{\{1,2\}}^\kappa}$ such that $\langle t_{\mathcal{L}}, g \rangle \leftrightarrow_b \langle t_{\mathcal{R}}, g \rangle$, where g is a glue-state. When we also have $t_{\mathcal{L}} \leftrightarrow_b t_{\mathcal{R}}$ we say that this relation *cascades* from the relation between $\langle t_{\mathcal{L}}, g \rangle$ and $\langle t_{\mathcal{R}}, g \rangle$. If such a cascading effect holds for all states across different combinations of pattern networks, then the rule system is said to be *cascading*, i.e. it is behaviourally consistent across the pattern networks. A formal definition is given in Definition 11.

Definition 11 (Cascading rule system). *A rule system* $\Sigma = (R, \hat{\mathcal{V}})$ *with synchronisation vectors of size* n *is called* cascading, *iff for all sets of indices* $I, J \subseteq 1..n$ *with* $I \cap J = \emptyset$:

$$\forall \bar{s} \in \mathcal{S}_{\mathcal{L}_I}, \bar{p} \in \mathcal{S}_{\mathcal{R}_I}, \bar{q} \in \mathcal{I}_{\mathcal{L}_J} . \ \bar{s} \leftrightarrow_b \bar{p} \iff \bar{s} \parallel \bar{q} \leftrightarrow_b \bar{p} \parallel \bar{q}$$

where $\bar{x} \parallel \bar{y}$ *is the merging of states* $\bar{x}$ *and* $\bar{y}$ *via vector addition with dummy state* $*$ *as the zero element. Intuitively, this operation constructs a state for the system LTS considering LTS patterns indexed by* $I \cup J$, *i.e. the parallel composition of* $\bar{x}$ *and* $\bar{y}$.

It may be the case that Σ is not cascading, i.e. we have $\langle t_{\mathcal{L}}, g \rangle \leftrightarrow_b \langle t_{\mathcal{R}}, g \rangle$, but not $t_{\mathcal{L}} \not\leftrightarrow_b t_{\mathcal{R}}$. In such a case it is *always* possible to construct an input LTS network $\mathcal{M}$ such that $\mathcal{M} \not\leftrightarrow_b T_\Sigma(\mathcal{M})$. To construct $\mathcal{M}$ take a copy of $\mathcal{L}_{\{1,2\}}$ and add a transition $g \xrightarrow{d}_2 s$, where s is a state that is not matched by $\mathcal{L}_1$ and the d-transition signifies departure from the pattern network. We have $\langle t_{\mathcal{L}}, g \rangle \xrightarrow{d}_{\mathcal{M}} \langle t_{\mathcal{L}}, s \rangle$ and $\langle t_{\mathcal{R}}, g \rangle \xrightarrow{d}_{T_\Sigma(\mathcal{M})} \langle t_{\mathcal{R}}, s \rangle$. To represent continuing behaviour in Π_1 (copy of $\mathcal{L}_1$) we add a selfloop $t_{\mathcal{L}} \xrightarrow{a}_1 t_{\mathcal{L}}$ where a is a unique action. Since state s is not matched and $t_{\mathcal{L}} \not\leftrightarrow_b t_{\mathcal{R}}$, it follows that $\langle t_{\mathcal{L}}, s \rangle$ can perform the a-loop while $\langle t_{\mathcal{R}}, s \rangle$ cannot. Hence, we have $\mathcal{M} \not\leftrightarrow_b T_\Sigma(\mathcal{M})$.

Figure 5a presents a transformation of an LTS network $\mathcal{M}$ using a non-cascading rule system Σ. The corresponding bisimulation checks are shown in

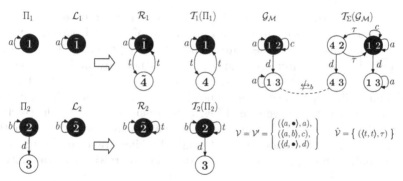

(a) Transforming an LTS network $\mathcal{M} = (\Pi, \mathcal{V})$ using a non-cascading rule system $\Sigma = (R, \mathcal{V}', \hat{\mathcal{V}})$

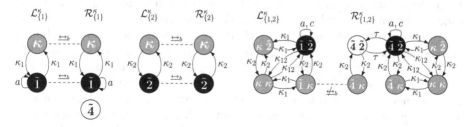

(b) The checks fail to detect that Σ does not guarantee bisimilarity between input and output LTS networks

Fig. 5. A transformation using a non-cascading rule system does not preserve the branching structure of LTS network $\mathcal{M}$

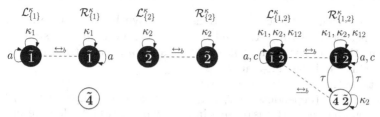

Fig. 6. The revised check recognises that the non-cascading rule system does not preserve the branching structure of input networks: $\langle \tilde{1}, \kappa \rangle \not\leftrightarrow_b \langle \tilde{4}, \kappa \rangle$

Fig. 5b. The rule system is not cascading since state $\langle \tilde{1} \rangle$ is not related to state $\langle \tilde{4} \rangle$, while $\langle \tilde{1}, \tilde{2} \rangle \leftrightarrow_b \langle \tilde{4}, \tilde{2} \rangle$. The matches of the latter states (i.e. $\langle 1, 2 \rangle$ and $\langle 4, 2 \rangle$) can perform a d-transition to states $\langle 1, 3 \rangle$ and $\langle 4, 3 \rangle$, respectively. However, state $\langle 1, 3 \rangle$ can perform an a-loop while state $\langle 4, 3 \rangle$ cannot. In other words, states $\langle \tilde{1}, \tilde{2} \rangle$ and $\langle \tilde{4}, \tilde{2} \rangle$ are branching bisimilar, but their matched states $\langle 1, 2 \rangle$ and $\langle 4, 2 \rangle$ are clearly not. Hence, the bisimulation checks fail to establish that Σ does not guarantee $\mathcal{M} \leftrightarrow_b T_\Sigma(\mathcal{M})$ for arbitrary $\mathcal{M}$.

Fixing the Technique. To overcome this shortcoming, we propose, instead of κ-loops, to introduce a κ-*state* in the κ-extension of an LTS pattern with κ-transitions from and to all glue-states. The κ-state represents all states that have transitions to and from (but are themselves not present in) matches of LTS patterns. This captures the possibility of leaving a match of a pattern network and ending up in a sub-state which is not related through the cascading effect. The κ-state extended version of Fig. 5b is presented in Fig. 6. The (vector) states containing κ-states are coloured grey. In the new situation, the lack of the cascading effect in Σ becomes visible through checking branching bisimilarity. We implemented this approach in REFINER, and observed no extra runtime overhead.

The Analysis. Checking a rule system $\Sigma = (R, \mathcal{V}', \hat{\mathcal{V}})$ now proceeds as follows:

1. Check whether in Σ, no τ-transitions can be synchronised, renamed, or cut, and whether Σ satisfies AC2 and AC3. If not, report this and stop.
2. Extend the patterns of each rule in R with a κ-state and κ-transitions between the κ-state and the glue-states.
3. Construct the set of dependency sets $\mathbb{D}$.
4. For each class (dependency set) $P \in \mathbb{D}$, and each non-empty subset $P' \subseteq P$:
   (a) Combine the patterns of rules in P' into networks $\mathcal{L}_{P'}^{\kappa}$, $\mathcal{R}_{P'}^{\kappa}$, respectively.
   (b) Determine whether $\mathcal{L}_{P'}^{\kappa} \underset{b}{\leftrightarrow} \mathcal{R}_{P'}^{\kappa}$ holds.

If 4b only gives positive results, then Σ is branching-structure preserving for all inputs it is applicable on. At step 4, all non-empty *subsets* of dependency sets are considered. Proper subsets represent unsuccessful synchronisation situations. Proposition 2 formally describes the technique. The full proof in the form of Coq code can be found at [10]. Here we present a proof sketch.

To show the correctness of Proposition 2, we have to define a branching bisimulation relation relating the original and transformed LTS networks. To simplify the proof, we assume that Σ has n rules, and that a rule r with index i, denoted as r_i, matches on Π_i in the LTS network that Σ is applied on. For confluent rule systems, the result can be lifted to the general case where rules can match arbitrary process LTSs. Moreover, we want to relate the matched elements of vector states via their corresponding pattern networks. For this we define a set of indices of elements in vector state $\bar{s}$ matched on by the corresponding transformation rule, i.e. $M(\bar{s}) = \{i \mid \bar{s}_i \in m_i(\mathcal{S}_{\mathcal{L}_i}) \cup \hat{m}_i(\mathcal{S}_{\mathcal{R}_i})\}$. With this set the elements of a vector state with transformed behaviour can be selected.

Furthermore, we introduce a mapping of state vectors. Similar to matches for a single rule, the mapping of a state vector of a pattern network defines how it is mapped to a state vector of an LTS network. By referring to matches of the individual vector elements, a state vector is mapped on to another state vector. Consider an LTS network $\mathcal{M} = (\Pi, \mathcal{V})$ of size n and a pattern network $\mathcal{M}_I = (\Pi_I, \mathcal{V}_I)$ with $I \subseteq 1..n$. We say a vector state $\bar{q} \in \mathcal{S}_{\mathcal{M}_I}$ is *mapped* to a state $\bar{s} \in \mathcal{S}_{\mathcal{M}}$, denoted by $\bar{q} \vdash_I \bar{s}$, iff $\forall i \in I. \, m(\bar{q}_i) = \bar{s}_i$. Mapping $\bar{q} \vdash_I \bar{s}$ amounts to a simulation relation between the state vectors: the group of states $\bar{s}_i$ indexed by $i \in I$ can simulate the behaviour of state vector $\bar{q}$.

Proposition 2. *Let* $\mathcal{M} = (\Pi, \mathcal{V})$ *be an LTS network of size* n *and let* $\Sigma = (R, \mathcal{V}', \hat{\mathcal{V}})$ *be a cascading rule system satisfying AC2 and AC3. Let* $\bar{r}$ *be a vector of size* n *such that for all* $i \in 1..n$, $\bar{r}_i \in R$ *with corresponding matches* $m_i : \mathcal{L}_i \to \Pi_i$ *and* $\hat{m}_i : \mathcal{R}_i \to T(\Pi_i)$. *Then,*

$$(\forall P \in \mathbb{D}, I \subseteq P.\ \mathcal{L}_I^\kappa \leftrightarrow_b \mathcal{R}_I^\kappa) \implies \mathcal{M} \leftrightarrow_b T_\Sigma(\mathcal{M})$$

Proof Sketch. By definition, we have $\mathcal{M} \leftrightarrow_b T_\Sigma(\mathcal{M})$ iff there exists a branching bisimulation relation C with $\mathcal{I}_\mathcal{M} \leftrightarrow_b \mathcal{I}_{T_\Sigma(\mathcal{M})}$. Branching bisimilarity is a congruence for the construction of system LTSs from LTS networks, i.e. two pairs of pattern networks $\mathcal{L}_I$ and $\mathcal{R}_I$, $\mathcal{L}_J$ and $\mathcal{R}_J$, with $\mathcal{L}_I \leftrightarrow_b \mathcal{R}_I$ and $\mathcal{L}_J \leftrightarrow_b \mathcal{R}_J$, can be combined to form pattern networks $\mathcal{L}_{I \cup J}$ and $\mathcal{R}_{I \cup J}$ such that $\mathcal{L}_{I \cup J} \leftrightarrow_b \mathcal{R}_{I \cup J}$. Therefore, we have $\forall I \subseteq 1..n.\ \mathcal{L}_I^\kappa \leftrightarrow_b \mathcal{R}_I^\kappa$ and we can avoid reasoning about the dependency sets in $\mathbb{D}$. As a consequence, for any $I \subseteq 1..n$ there exists a branching bisimulation relation B_I with $\mathcal{I}_{\mathcal{L}_I^\kappa} \leftrightarrow_b \mathcal{I}_{\mathcal{R}_I^\kappa}$. We define C as follows:

$$C = \{(\bar{s}, \bar{p}) \mid \forall i \in 1..n.\ (i \notin M(\bar{s}) \cup M(\bar{p}) \implies \bar{s}_i \in \mathcal{S}_i \wedge \bar{s}_i = \bar{p}_i)$$
$$\wedge\ (i \in M(\bar{s}) \cup M(\bar{p}) \implies \exists \bar{s}_m \in \mathcal{S}_{\mathcal{L}_{M(\bar{s}) \cup M(\bar{p})}}, \bar{p}_m \in \mathcal{S}_{\mathcal{R}_{M(\bar{s}) \cup M(\bar{p})}}.$$
$$\bar{s}_m\ B_{M(\bar{s}) \cup M(\bar{p})}\ \bar{p}_m \wedge \bar{s}_m \vdash_{M(\bar{s}) \cup M(\bar{p})} \bar{s} \wedge \bar{p}_m \vdash_{M(\bar{s}) \cup M(\bar{p})} \bar{p})\}$$

The first case in the relation, $i \notin M(\bar{s}) \cup M(\bar{p})$, relates the sub-states of a state vector that are not matched by transformation rules. The second case, $i \in M(\bar{s}) \cup M(\bar{p})$, relates the matched sub-states of a state vector. Because of the way that C is constructed we have that if $s\ C\ p$, then $M(\bar{s}) = M(\bar{p})$. For brevity, we will write $M(\bar{s})$ instead of $M(\bar{s}) \cup M(\bar{p})$.

To prove the proposition we have to show that C is a bisimulation relation. This requires proving that C relates the initial states of $\mathcal{M}$ and $T_\Sigma(\mathcal{M})$ and that C satisfies Definition 5 as presented below.

- C *relates the initial states of* $\mathcal{M}$ *and* $T_\Sigma(\mathcal{M})$, i.e. $\mathcal{I}_\mathcal{M}\ C\ \mathcal{I}_{T_\Sigma(\mathcal{M})}$. We have $\mathcal{I}_\mathcal{M} = \mathcal{I}_{T_\Sigma(\mathcal{M})}$. Initial states are not removed by the transformation. Furthermore, if states are matched on initial states, then the matching states are glue-states according to Definition 3. For $i \in M(\bar{s})$ glue-states are related to themselves. Furthermore, for $i \notin M(\bar{s})$ the sub-state is not touched by the transformation. Hence, C relates the initial states.

- *If* $\bar{s}\ C\ \bar{p}$ *and* $\bar{s} \xrightarrow{a}_\mathcal{M} \bar{s}'$ *then either* $a = \tau \wedge \bar{s}'\ C\ \bar{p}$, *or* $\bar{p} \Rightarrow_{T_\Sigma(\mathcal{M})} \hat{\bar{p}} \xrightarrow{a}_{T_\Sigma(\mathcal{M})}$ $\bar{p}' \wedge \bar{s}\ C\ \hat{\bar{p}} \wedge \bar{s}'\ C\ \bar{p}'$. Consider synchronisation law $(\bar{t}, a) \in \mathcal{V}$ enabling the transition $\bar{s} \xrightarrow{a}_\mathcal{M} \bar{s}'$. We distinguish two cases:

1. *There exists* $i \in Ac(\bar{t})$ *such that transition* $\bar{s} \xrightarrow{\bar{t}_i}_{\Pi_i} \bar{s}'$ *is matched. By analysis conditions* (AC1) *and* (AC2), *for all* $i \in Ac(\bar{t})$ *there must be a transition matching* $\bar{s} \xrightarrow{\bar{t}_i}_{\Pi_i} \bar{s}'$. Hence, we have $Ac(\bar{t}) \subseteq M(\bar{s})$ and a transition matching $\bar{s} \xrightarrow{a}_\mathcal{M} \bar{s}'$. Since the transition is matched there exists $\bar{s}_m, \bar{s}'_m \in \mathcal{S}_{\mathcal{L}_{M(\bar{s})}}$ and $\bar{p}_m \in \mathcal{S}_{\mathcal{R}_{M(\bar{s})}}$ with $\bar{s}_m \vdash_{M(\bar{s})} \bar{s}$, $\bar{p}_m \vdash_{M(\bar{s})} \bar{p}$, $\bar{s}_m\ B_{M(\bar{s})}\ \bar{p}_m$ and $\bar{s} \xrightarrow{a}_{\mathcal{L}_{M(\bar{s})}} \bar{s}'$ (by Definition of C). Since $\bar{s}_m\ B_{M(\bar{s})}\ \bar{p}_m$, by Definition 5, we have:

- $a = \tau$ with $\bar{s}'_m \ B_{M(\bar{s})} \ \bar{p}_m$. We have to show $\bar{s}' \ C \ \bar{p}$, which follows from def. of C and Definition 8 (system LTS).
- $\bar{p}_m \xrightarrow{\tau}{}^*_{\mathcal{R}_M(\bar{s})} \hat{\bar{p}}_m \xrightarrow{a}_{\mathcal{R}_M(\bar{s})} \bar{p}'$ with $\bar{s}_m \ B_{M(\bar{s})} \ \hat{\bar{p}}_m$ and $\bar{s}'_m \ B_{M(\bar{s})} \ \bar{p}'_m$. We construct states $\hat{\bar{p}}$ and $\bar{p}'$ such that $\bar{p} \xrightarrow{\tau}{}^*_{T_\Sigma(\mathcal{M})} \hat{\bar{p}} \xrightarrow{a}_{T_\Sigma(\mathcal{M})} \bar{p}'$ and $\bar{s} \ C \ \hat{\bar{p}}$. Finally, $\bar{s}' \ C \ \bar{p}'$ follows from def. of C and Definition 8 (system LTS).

2. *There is no transition matching $\bar{s} \xrightarrow{a}_{\mathcal{M}} \bar{s}'$.* We distinguish two cases:

   (a) *One or more active sub-states of $\bar{s}$ are matched on, i.e. $Ac(\bar{t}) \cap M(\bar{s}) \neq \emptyset$.* Since the transition is not matched the active sub-states of $\bar{s}$ must be matches of glue-states. By Lemma 1, we have states $\hat{\bar{p}}$ and $\bar{p}'$ such that $\bar{p} \xrightarrow{\tau}{}^*_{T_\Sigma(\mathcal{M})} \hat{\bar{p}} \xrightarrow{a}_{T_\Sigma(\mathcal{M})} \bar{p}'$ and $\bar{s} \ C \ \hat{\bar{p}}$. Left to show is $\bar{s}' \ C \ \bar{p}'$. Let $i \in 1..n$:

   - $i \notin M(\bar{s})$. By construction of $\bar{p}'$ it follows that $\bar{s}'_i = \bar{p}'_i$.
   - $i \in M(\bar{s})$. Only sub-states index by $Ac(\bar{t})$ change. Sub-states index by $Ac(\bar{t})$ may have a transition from a matched sub-state to another matched sub-state, or such a matched sub-state may transition to a sub-state that is not matched (or vice versa). We construct states $\bar{s}' \in \mathcal{S}_{\mathcal{L}_{M(\bar{s}')}}$ and $\bar{p}' \in \mathcal{S}_{\mathcal{R}_{M(\bar{s}')}}$ by considering the two disjoint sets $M(\bar{s}') \setminus Ac(\bar{t})$ and $M(\bar{s}') \cap Ac(\bar{t})$. For the first set we can construct two states $\bar{s}_{mJ}$ and $\bar{p}_{mJ}$ that, because of Definition 11 (cascading rule system), are related by $B_{M(\bar{s}') \setminus Ac(\bar{t})}$. From sub-states of $\bar{s}_m$ indexed by the second set we can construct a state $\bar{q} \in \mathcal{I}_{\mathcal{L}_{M(\bar{s}') \cap Ac(\bar{t})}}$. Because glue-state are related to themselves we have $\bar{q} \ B_{M(\bar{s}') \cap Ac(\bar{t})} \ \bar{q}$. From $\bar{s}_{mJ}$, $\bar{p}_{mJ}$, and $\bar{q}$ we can construct states $\bar{s}'_m$ and $\bar{p}'_m$ such that $\bar{s}'_m \ B_{M(\bar{s}')} \ \bar{p}'_m$ (by Definition 11).

   (b) *No active sub-states of $\bar{s}$ are matched on, i.e. $Ac(\bar{t}) \cap M(\bar{s}) = \emptyset$.* We construct a state $\bar{p}' \in \mathcal{S}_{T_\Sigma(\mathcal{M})}$ from $\bar{p}$ and the active sub-states of $\bar{s}'$ such that $\bar{p} \xrightarrow{a}_{T_\Sigma(\mathcal{M})} \bar{p}'$. Left to show $\bar{s}' \ C \ \bar{p}'$. Considering an $i \in 1..n$ we have to distinguish the following cases:

   - $i \notin M(\bar{s})$. We have to show that $\bar{s}'_i = \bar{p}'_i$, this can be derived from, $\bar{s} \ C \ \bar{p}$, Definition 8 (system LTS), and construction of $\bar{p}'$.
   - $i \in M(\bar{s})$. To relate $\bar{s}'$ and $\bar{p}'$ we need to find a relation $B_{M(\bar{s}')}$ relating two states that map on $\bar{s}'$ and $\bar{p}'$ respectively. If only active sub-states of $\bar{s}'$ are matched we can use the property that initial states are related to themselves in $B_{M(\bar{s}')}$. In the opposite case, there is a $j \in 1..n \setminus Ac(\bar{t})$ and we can use $\bar{s} \ C \ \bar{p}$ to construct the required relation.

- *The symmetric case: if $\bar{s} \ C \ \bar{p}$ and $\bar{p} \xrightarrow{a}_{\mathcal{M}} \bar{p}'$ then either $a = \tau \wedge \bar{s}' \ C \ \bar{p}$, or $\bar{s} \Rightarrow_{\mathcal{M}} \hat{\bar{s}} \xrightarrow{a}_{\mathcal{M}} \bar{s}' \wedge \bar{s} \ C \ \hat{\bar{p}} \wedge \bar{s}' \ C \ \bar{p}'.*

  This case is symmetric to the previous case with the exception that $\bar{p} \xrightarrow{a}_{T(\mathcal{M})} \bar{p}'$ is enabled by some $(\bar{t}, a) \in \mathcal{V} \cup \hat{\mathcal{V}}$. Therefore, when transition $\bar{p} \xrightarrow{a}_{T(\mathcal{M})} \bar{p}'$ is not matched on, we have to show that $(\bar{t}, a) \in \mathcal{V}$. Let $\bar{p}, \bar{p}' \in \mathcal{S}_{T_\Sigma(\mathcal{M})}$ such that $\bar{p} \xrightarrow{a}_{T(\mathcal{M})} \bar{p}'$ is enabled by some $(\bar{t}, a) \in \mathcal{V} \cup \hat{\mathcal{V}}$. Furthermore, transition $\bar{p} \xrightarrow{a}_{T(\mathcal{M})} \bar{p}'$ is not matched on. Assume for a contradiction that $(\bar{t}, a) \in \hat{\mathcal{V}}$. Since $(\bar{t}, a) \in \hat{\mathcal{V}}$ is introduced by the transformation , by (AC3), there must be an i such that $\bar{t}_i \in \mathcal{A}_{\mathcal{R}_i} \setminus \mathcal{A}_{\mathcal{L}_i}$. It follows that there is a transition matching $\bar{p} \xrightarrow{a}_{T(\mathcal{M})} \bar{p}'$ contradicting our earlier assumption. Hence, we must have $(\bar{t}, a) \in \mathcal{V}$. $\square$

5 Conclusions

We discussed the correctness of an LTS transformation verification technique. The aim of the technique is to verify whether a given LTS transformation system Σ preserves a property φ, written in a fragment of the μ-calculus, for all possible input models formalised as LTS networks. It does this by determining whether Σ is guaranteed to transform an input network into one that is branching bisimilar, ignoring the behaviour not relevant for φ.

It turned out that the technique was not correct for two reasons: (1) it ignored potentially synchronising behaviour connected to the glue-states of rules, but not part of the rule patterns, and (2) it did not check whether the rule system is cascading. We proposed how to repair the technique and presented a proof-sketch of its correctness. A complete proof has been carried out in Coq.

Future Work. Originally *divergence-sensitive* branching bisimulation was used [19], which preserves τ-loops and therefore liveness properties. In future work, we would like to prove that for this flavour of bisimulation the technique is also correct. Moreover, we would like to investigate what the practical limitations of the pre-conditions of the technique are in industrial sized transformation systems.

Finally, in [17], the technique from [19] has been extended to explicitly consider the communication interfaces between components, thereby removing the completeness condition AC2 regarding synchronising behaviour being transformed (see Sect. 4.1). We wish to prove that also this extension is correct.

References

1. Amrani, M., Combemale, B., Lúcio, L., Selim, G.M.K., Dingel, J., Le Traon, Y., Vangheluwe, H., Cordy, J.R.: Formal verification techniques for model transformations: a tridimensional classification. JOT **14**(3), 1–43 (2015)
2. Baldan, P., Corradini, A., Ehrig, H., Heckel, R., König, B.: Bisimilarity and behaviour-preserving reconfigurations of open petri nets. In: Mossakowski, T., Montanari, U., Haveraaen, M. (eds.) CALCO 2007. LNCS, vol. 4624, pp. 126–142. Springer, Heidelberg (2007)
3. Bowen, J., Hinchey, M.: Formal methods. In: Tucker, A.B. (ed.) Computer Science Handbook Chap. 106, pp. 106-1–106-25. ACM, New York (2004)
4. Giese, H., Glesner, S., Leitner, J., Schäfer, W., Wagner, R.: Towards verified model transformations. In: MoDeVVa 2006, pp. 78–93 (2006)
5. van Glabbeek, R.J., Weijland, W.P.: Branching time and abstraction in bisimulation semantics. J. ACM **43**(3), 555–600 (1996)
6. Kleppe, A., Warmer, J., Bast, W.: MDA Explained: The Model Driven Architecture(TM): Practice and Promise. Addison-Wesley Professional, Boston (2005)
7. Lang, F.: Refined interfaces for compositional verification. In: Najm, E., Pradat-Peyre, J.-F., Donzeau-Gouge, V.V. (eds.) FORTE 2006. LNCS, vol. 4229, pp. 159–174. Springer, Heidelberg (2006)
8. Lang, F., Mateescu, R.: partial model checking using networks of labelled transition systems and boolean equation systems. Log. Methods Comput. Sci. **9**(4), 1–32 (2013)

9. Mateescu, R., Wijs, A.: Property-dependent reductions adequate with divergence-sensitive branching bisimilarity. Sci. Comput. Prog. **96**(3), 354–376 (2014)

10. de Putter, S.: Coq code proving the correctness of the LTS transformation verification technique (2015). http://www.mdsetechnology.org/attachments/article/2/FASE16_property_preservation.zip

11. Rahim, L.A., Whittle, J.: A survey of approaches for verifying model transformations. Softw. Syst. Model. **14**, 1–26 (2013). http://dx.doi.org/10.1007/s10270-013-0358-0

12. Saha, D.: An incremental bisimulation algorithm. In: Arvind, V., Prasad, S. (eds.) FSTTCS 2007. LNCS, vol. 4855, pp. 204–215. Springer, Heidelberg (2007)

13. Selim, G.M.K., Lúcio, L., Cordy, J.R., Dingel, J., Oakes, B.J.: Specification and verification of graph-based model transformation properties. In: Giese, H., König, B. (eds.) ICGT 2014. LNCS, vol. 8571, pp. 113–129. Springer, Heidelberg (2014)

14. Sokolsky, O., Smolka, S.: Incremental model checking in the modal mu-calculus. In: Dill, D.L. (ed.) Computer Aided Verification. LNCS, vol. 818, pp. 351–363. Springer, Heidelberg (1994)

15. Stenzel, K., Moebius, N., Reif, W.: Formal verification of QVT transformations for code generation. In: Whittle, J., Clark, T., Kühne, T. (eds.) MODELS 2011. LNCS, vol. 6981, pp. 533–547. Springer, Heidelberg (2011)

16. Swamy, G.: Incremental methods for formal verification and logic synthesis. Ph.D. thesis, University of California (1996)

17. Wijs, A.: Define, verify, refine: correct composition and transformation of concurrent system semantics. In: Fiadeiro, J.L., Liu, Z., Xue, J. (eds.) FACS 2013. LNCS, vol. 8348, pp. 348–368. Springer, Heidelberg (2014)

18. Wijs, A.J.: Confluence detection for transformations of labelled transition systems. In: GaM 2015. EPTCS, vol. 181, pp. 1–15. Open Publishing Association (2015)

19. Wijs, A., Engelen, L.: Efficient property preservation checking of model refinements. In: Piterman, N., Smolka, S.A. (eds.) TACAS 2013 (ETAPS 2013). LNCS, vol. 7795, pp. 565–579. Springer, Heidelberg (2013)

20. Wijs, A., Engelen, L.: REFINER: towards formal verification of model transformations. In: Badger, J.M., Rozier, K.Y. (eds.) NFM 2014. LNCS, vol. 8430, pp. 258–263. Springer, Heidelberg (2014)

21. Winskel, G.: A Compositional proof system on a category of labelled transition systems. Inf. Comput. **87**(1–2), 2–57 (1990)

Hybrid Session Verification Through Endpoint API Generation

Raymond Hu[✉] and Nobuko Yoshida

Imperial College London, London, UK
{Raymond.Hu05,n.yoshida}@imperial.ac.uk

Abstract. This paper proposes a new hybrid session verification methodology for applying session types directly to mainstream languages, based on generating protocol-specific endpoint APIs from multiparty session types. The API generation promotes static type checking of the behavioural aspect of the source protocol by mapping the state space of an endpoint in the protocol to a family of channel types in the target language. This is supplemented by very light run-time checks in the generated API that enforce a linear usage discipline on instances of the channel types. The resulting hybrid verification guarantees the absence of protocol violation errors during the execution of the session. We implement our methodology for Java as an extension to the Scribble framework, and use it to specify and implement compliant clients and servers for real-world protocols such as HTTP and SMTP.

1 Introduction

Application of Session Types to Practice. Session types [4,14,15] are a type theory for communications programming which can guarantee the absence of communication errors in the execution of a session, such as sending an unexpected message or failing to handle an incoming message, and deadlocks due to mutual input dependencies between the participants. One direction of applying session types to practice has investigated extending existing languages with the necessary features, following the theory, to support static session typing. This includes extensions of Java [17,39] with first-class channel I/O primitives and mechanisms for restricting the aliasing of channel objects, that perform static session type checking as a preprocessor step alongside standard Java compilation. New languages have also been developed from session type concepts. The design of SILL [33,40] is based on a Curry-Howard isomorphism between propositions in linear logic and session types, giving a language with powerful linear and session typing features, but that requires programmers to shape their data structures and algorithms according to this paradigm.

To apply session types more directly to existing languages, another direction has investigated dynamic verification of sessions. In [8], multiparty session types (MPST) are used as a protocol specification language from which run-time endpoint monitors can be automatically generated. The framework guarantees that each monitor will allow its endpoint to perform only the I/O actions permitted according to the source protocol [1]. Although flexible, dynamic verification loses

© Springer-Verlag Berlin Heidelberg 2016
P. Stevens and A. Wąsowski (Eds.): FASE 2016, LNCS 9633, pp. 401–418, 2016.
DOI: 10.1007/978-3-662-49665-7_24

benefits of static type checking such as compile-time error detection and IDE support. Session types have been also applied through code generation to specific target contexts. Ng, et al. [30] develops a framework for MPI programming in C that uses MPST as a language for specifying parallel processing topologies, from which a skeleton implementation of the communication structure using MPI operations is generated. The skeleton is then merged with user supplied functions for the computations around the communicated messages to obtain the final program.

This Paper presents a new methodology for applying session types directly to mainstream statically typed languages. There are two main novel elements:

Hybrid Session Verification. A trend in recent works [2,6,7,12,41] has involved the study of explicit relationships between session types and linear types. In this work, we continue in the direction of developing session types as a system for tracking correct communication behaviour, in terms of I/O channel actions, built on top of a linear usage discipline for channel resources (every instance of a channel should be used exactly once). We apply this formulation practically as *hybrid* session verification: we statically verify the behavioural aspect through the native type system of the target language, supplemented by very light runtime checks on linear channel usage.

Endpoint API Generation. In this work, we use multiparty session types as a protocol specification language from which we can generate APIs for implementing the endpoints in a statically typed target language. Taking a finite state machine (FSM) representation of the endpoint behaviour in the protocol [10,20], the API generation (i.e. type generation) reifies each state as a distinct channel type in the target language that permits only the exact I/O operations in that state according to the source protocol. These *state channels* are linked up as a call-chaining API for the endpoint that returns a new instance of the successor state channel for the action performed. Our hybrid form of session type safety is thus ensured by static typing of I/O behaviour on each state channel, in conjunction with run-time checks that every instance of a state channel is used linearly.

Our methodology is a practical compromise that combines benefits from static session type systems with the utility of code generation approaches. First, this methodology allows protocol conformance to be statically checked in mainstream languages like Java, up to the linear channel usage contract of the generated API, by constraining outputs to the specified message types and promoting exhaustive handling of inputs. Second, by directly targetting existing languages, user implementations of session endpoints using generated APIs can be readily integrated with native language features, existing libraries and IDE support.

We present the implementation of our methodology for Java as an extension to Scribble [37], a practical protocol description language based on MPST. Beyond the core safety benefits of regulating session type behaviour through endpoint FSMs, we take advantage of hybrid verification and API generation to support additional practically motivated features for session programming in Java, and to apply further features from session type theory. The former includes value-switched session branching and the abstraction of nominal state channel types as I/O interfaces. Examples of the latter are the generation of state-specific input futures to support aspects of non-blocking inputs [16], safe permutations of I/O actions [3,25] and affine inputs [24,33]; and the generation of Java subtype hierarchies for I/O interfaces to reflect session subtyping [11]. We have tested our framework by using our API generation to implement compliant clients and servers for real-world protocols such as HTTP and SMTP.

Outline. Section 2 describes the Scribble toolchain that this paper builds on, and gives an overview of the proposed methodology for hybrid session verification through API generation. Section 3 presents our implementation that generates Java endpoint APIs from Scribble protocol specifications. Section 4 discusses SMTP as a use case, and practically motivated extensions to the core API generation related to session programming in Java and more advanced session type features. Section 5 discusses related work. An extended version of this paper and other resources can be found at http://www.doc.ic.ac.uk/~rhu/scribble.

2   Overview

The Scribble Toolchain. The Scribble [37,43] framework starts from specifying a *global protocol*, a description of the full protocol of interaction in a multiparty communication session from a neutral perspective, i.e. all potential and necessary message exchanges between all participants from the start of a session until completion. The communication model for Scribble protocols is designed for asynchronous but reliable message transports with ordered delivery between each pair of participants, which encompasses standard Internet applications and Web services that use TCP, HTTP, etc.

Global Protocol Specification. We use as the first running example a simple client-server protocol for a service that adds two integers, written in Scribble in Fig. 1(a). The main elements of the protocol specification are as follows.

The *protocol signature* (line 3) declares the name of the protocol (**Adder**) and the abstraction of each participant as a named **role** (C and S). *Payload format types* (line 1) give an alias (e.g. **Int**) to data type definitions from an external

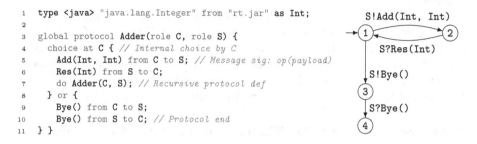

```
1   type <java> "java.lang.Integer" from "rt.jar" as Int;
2
3   global protocol Adder(role C, role S) {
4     choice at C { // Internal choice by C
5       Add(Int, Int) from C to S; // Message sig: op(payload)
6       Res(Int) from S to C;
7       do Adder(C, S); // Recursive protocol def
8     } or {
9       Bye() from C to S;
10      Bye() from S to C; // Protocol end
11  } }
```

Fig. 1. (a) A scribble global protocol. (b) The endpoint FSM for C.

language (`java.lang.Integer`) used to define the wire protocols for message formatting. A *message signature* (e.g. `Add(Int, Int)`) declares an *operator* name (`Add`) as an abstract message identifier (which may correspond concretely to, e.g., a header field value), and some number of payload types (a pair of `Int`). *Message passing* (e.g. line 5) is output-asynchronous: dispatching the message is non-blocking for the sender (`C`), but the message input is blocking for the receiver (`S`). *Located choice* (e.g. line 4) states the subject role (`C`) for which selecting one of the listed protocol blocks to follow is a mutually exclusive internal choice. This decision is an external choice to all other roles involved in each block, which must be appropriately coordinated by explicit messages. *Recursive protocol definitions* (line 7) describe recursive interactions between the roles involved. Non-recursive `do` statements can be used to factor out common subprotocols.

Scribble performs an initial validation on global protocols to assert that the protocol can indeed be soundly realised by a system of independent endpoint processes. For instance, in this example, the validation ensures that the two choice cases are communicated by `C` to `S` unambiguously (a simple error would be, e.g., if `C` firstly sends a `Bye` to `S` in both cases).

Local Protocol Projection and Endpoint FSMs. Following a top-down interpretation of formal MPST systems, Scribble syntactically *projects* a valid source global protocol to a *local protocol* for each role. Projection essentially extracts the parts of the global protocol in which the target role is directly involved, giving the localised behaviour required of each role in order for a session to execute correctly as a whole. Projecting `Adder` for `C` gives: `rec X { choice at C { Add(Int, Int) to S;` `Res(Int) from S; continue X; } or { Bye() to S; Bye() from S; } }` . A further validation step is performed on each projection of the source protocol for role-sensitive properties, such as reachability of all relevant protocol states per role. The validation also restricts recursive protocols to tail recursion. A valid global protocol with valid projections for each role is a *well-formed protocol*.

Building on a formal correspondence between syntactic local MPST and communicating FSMs, Scribble can transform the projection of any well-formed protocol for each of its roles to an equivalent *Endpoint FSM* (EFSM). Figure 1 (b) depicts the EFSM of the projection for `C`. The nodes delineate the state space of the endpoint in the protocol, and the transitions the explicit I/O actions between protocol states. The notation, e.g., `S!Bye()` means output of message `Bye()` to `S`; `?` dually denotes input.

The core features of the Scribble protocol language are based on and extend those of [5], to which we refer the reader for formal definitions of global and local protocols (i.e. multiparty session types). The global-local projection [4,5] and EFSM transformation [9,20] performed by the Scribble toolchain implement and extend those formalised in the afore-cited works to support the additional features of Scribble (such as located choice, sequencing and subprotocols).

Hybrid Session Verification Through Endpoint API Generation. This paper proposes a methodology for applying session types to practice that confers communication safety through a hybrid verification approach.

Static Type Checking of I/O Behaviour. We consider the EFSMs derived from a source global protocol to represent the *behavioural* aspect of the session type. Our methodology is to generate a protocol-specific endpoint implementation API for a target role by capturing its EFSM via the native type system of a statically typed target language. The key points of the Endpoint API generation are:

- The Scribble toolchain is used to validate the source global protocol, project to the local protocol, and generate the EFSM for the target role.
- Each state in the EFSM is reified as a distinct channel type in the type system of the target language. We refer to channels of these generated types as *state channels*.
- The only I/O operations permitted by a generated channel type are safe actions according to the corresponding EFSM state in the protocol.
- The return type of each generated I/O operation is the channel type for the next state following the corresponding transition from the current state. Performing an I/O operation on a state channel returns a new instance of the successor channel type.

Starting from a state channel of the initial protocol state and performing an I/O operation on each state channel returned by the previous operation, the generated API statically ensures that an endpoint implementation conforms to the encapsulated EFSM and thus observes the protocol. Consequently, the implicit usage contract of the generated API is to use every state channel returned by an API call exactly once up to the end of the session, to respect EFSM semantics in terms of following state transitions linearly up to the terminal state.

Run-time Checking of Linear State Channel Usage. Due to the lack of support for statically verifying linear usage of values or objects in most mainstream languages, we take the practical approach of checking linear usage of state channel instances at run-time. These checks are inlined into the Endpoint API as part of the API generation. There are two cases for state channel linearity to be violated.

Repeat Use. Every state channel instance maintains a boolean state value indicating whether an I/O operation has been performed. The generated API guards each I/O operation permitted by the channel type with a run-time check on this boolean to ensure the state channel is not used more than once.

Unused. All state channels for a given session instance share a boolean state value indicating whether the session is complete for the local endpoint. The generated API sets this flag when a *terminal operation*, i.e. an I/O action leading to the terminal EFSM state, is performed. In conjunction with a language mechanism for delimiting the scope of a session implementation, such as standard exception handling constructs, the generated API checks session completion when program execution leaves the scope of the session.

If any state channel remains unused (possibly discarded, e.g. garbage collected) on leaving the scope of a session implementation, then it is not possible for the completion flag to be set.

Hybrid Session Safety. Together, a statically typed Endpoint API with run-time state channel linearity checking satisfies the following properties. (1) If state channel linearity is respected by session endpoint implementations, then communication safety (in the sense of e.g. [15, error-freedom]) is statically ensured by the generated API types. (2) Regardless of state channel linearity, any statically type-safe endpoint implementation will never perform a message passing action whose execution trace is not accepted by the EFSM of the generated API.

The latter is because an implementation using an Endpoint API can only attempt a non-conformant messaging action by violating state channel linearity, which the API is generated to guard against. This hybrid form of session verification thus guarantees the absence of protocol violation errors during the execution of a session, up to premature termination (which is always a possibility in practice due to program errors outside of the session code or failures).

3   Hybrid Endpoint API Generation for Java

Our implementation of Endpoint API generation for Java takes an Endpoint FSM derived from a Java-based Scribble protocol specification (i.e. a well-formed global protocol with Java-defined payload format types), and outputs two main protocol-specific components, the *Session API* and the *State Channel API*.

Endpoint FSMs. (EFSMs) serve as an interface between source protocol validation and projection, and the subsequent API generation. Formally, an EFSM is a tuple $(\mathbb{R}, \mathbb{L}, \mathbb{T}, \Sigma, \mathbb{S}, \delta)$. $\mathbb{R}$ and $\mathbb{L}$ are the sets of role names (ranging over $r, r', ..$) and message operator names ($l, l', ..$) occurring in the source local protocol, and $\mathbb{T}$ is the set of payload format types ($T, T', ..$) that it declares. The *alphabet* Σ is a finite set of *actions* $\{\alpha_i\}_{i \in I}$, where α is either an *output* $r!l(\vec{T})$ or an *input* $r?l(\vec{T})$ with $r \in \mathbb{R}, l \in \mathbb{L}$ and each $T_i \in \mathbb{T}$. The set of *states* $\mathbb{S}$ is a finite non-empty set of state identifiers ranging over $S, S', ...$ The *transition function* δ is a partial function $\mathbb{S} \times \Sigma \rightarrow \mathbb{S}$. We additionally define $\delta(S) = \{\alpha \mid \exists S' \in \mathbb{S}.\delta(S, \alpha) = S'\}$.

Certain properties are guaranteed for any EFSM derived from a well-formed protocol by the Scribble toolchain. (1) There is exactly one initial state $S_{init} \in \mathbb{S}$ such that $\nexists S' \in \mathbb{S}, \alpha \in \Sigma.\delta(S', \alpha) = S_{init}$. (2) There is at most one terminal state $S_{term} \in \mathbb{S}$ such that $\delta(S_{term}) = \emptyset$. (3) Every $S \in \mathbb{S}$ is one of three kinds: an *output state* $S^!$, *input state* $S^?$, or S_{term}. An output state means $\delta(S) = \{\alpha_i\}_{i \in I}, |I| > 0$ and every $\alpha_{i \in I}$ is an output; similarly for input states. (4) For each $S^?$ with $\delta(S^?) = \{\alpha_i\}_{i \in I}$, every $\alpha_{i \in I}$ specifies the same r.

Session API. The generated Endpoint APIs make use of a small collection of protocol-independent base Java classes: `Role`, `Op`, `Session`, `SessionEndpoint` and `Buf`. The first three are abstract classes. We explain them below.

The main class of the Session API (referred to as the Session Class) is a generated final subclass of the base `Session` class with the same name as the source protocol, e.g. `Adder` (Fig. 1 (a)). Its two main purposes are as follows.

Reification of Abstract Names. Session types make use of abstract names as role and message identifiers in types, that the type system expects to be present in the program to drive the type checking. The Session API reifies these names as singleton Java types. For each role or operator name $n \in \mathbb{R} \cup \mathbb{L}$, we generate the following. (1) A final Java class named n that extends the relevant base class (`Role` or `Op`). The n class has a single private constructor, and a public static final field of type n and with name n, initialised to a singleton instance of this class (i.e. an eagerly initialised singleton pattern). E.g. `public static final C C = new C();`. (2) In the Session Class, a public static final field of type n and with name n that refers to the corresponding field constant in the n class.

The Session API is the Session Class with the role and message name classes.

Session Instantiation. As a distributed computing abstraction, a run-time session can be considered a unit of interaction that is an instance of a session type. Following this intuition, the API user starts an endpoint implementation by creating a new instance of the Session Class. The Session object is used by the API to encapsulate static information, such as the source protocol, and run-time state related to the execution of this session, such as the session ID.

A Session object is used to create a `SessionEndpoint<S, R>`, parameterised on the parent Session and target role types, as on lines 2–3 in Fig. 3 (a). The first two constructor arguments are the Session object and the singleton generated for the target role, from which the type parameters are inferred, and the third is an implementation of the Scribble `MessageFormatter` interface for this endpoint using the declared format types for message serialization and deserialization. The `SessionEndpoint` object encapsulates the state specific to this endpoint in the session, such as the local role and networking state.

State Channel API. Based on the aforementioned properties of EFSMs, the core State Channel API is given by generating the channel classes for each EFSM state according to Fig. 2 (a). In the following, we use r, l, etc. to denote both a session type name and its generated Java type (as described above); similarly, we use S for an EFSM state and its generated Java channel type.

An output state is generated as a `SendSocket` with one **send** method for each outgoing transition action α: the first two parameters are the role r and operator l singleton types, followed by the sequence of Java payload format types (ϵ means the empty sequence). The return type is `EndSocket` (which supports no session I/O operations) if the successor state is the terminal state, or else the channel class generated for the successor state. Unary and non-unary input states are treated differently. Channel class generation for unary inputs is similar to that for outputs. The main difference is that each payload format type is generated as a Scribble `Buf` type with a supertype of the payload type as a type parameter. A Scribble `Buf` is a simple parameterised buffer for a single payload value, which is written by the generated **receive** API code when the message is received. Non-unary inputs are explained later (Session branches).

State kind	Java state channel base class and session operation method signatures
$S^!$	SendSocket
	For each $\alpha = r!l(\vec{T}) \in \delta(S^!)$: T_{ret} send(r role, l op $[\![\vec{T}]\!]^!$)
Unary $S^?$	ReceiveSocket ($|\delta(S^?)| = 1$)
	For $\alpha = r?l(\vec{T}) \in \delta(S^?)$: T_{ret} receive(r role, l op $[\![\vec{T}]\!]^?$)
$S^?$	BranchSocket ($|\delta(S^?)| > 1$)
	For $\alpha = r?l(\vec{T}) \in \delta(S^?)$: $C_{S^?}$ branch(r role)
	where $C_{S^?}$ is the following CaseSocket class
	CaseSocket
	For each $\alpha = r?l(\vec{T}) \in \delta(S^?)$: T_{ret} receive(l op, $[\![\vec{T}]\!]^?$)

where $[\![\vec{T}]\!]^! = \epsilon$ if $|\vec{T}| = 0$, else ', T_1 pay$_1$, ...,T_n pay$_n$'

$\quad\quad [\![\vec{T}]\!]^? = \epsilon$ if $|\vec{T}| = 0$, else ', Buf<? super T_1> pay$_1$,.., Buf<? super T_n> pay$_n$'

$\quad\quad T_{ret} = \delta(S, \alpha)$ if $S \neq S_{\text{term}}$, else EndSocket

Gen. class	Session operation methods
Adder_C_1	Adder_C_2 send(S role, Add op, Integer pay1, Integer pay2)
	Adder_C_3 send(S role, Bye op)
Adder_C_2	Adder_C_1 receive(S role, Res op, Buf<? super Integer> pay1)
Adder_C_3	EndSocket receive(S role, Bye op)
Adder_S_1	Adder_S_1_Cases branch(C role)
Adder_S_1_Cases	Adder_S_2 receive(Add op, Buf<? super Integer> pay1,
	Buf<? super Integer> pay2)
	Adder_S_3 receive(Bye op)
	Adder_S_1 send(C role, Res op, Integer pay1)
Adder_S_3	EndSocket send(C role, Bye op)

Fig. 2. (a) Java state channel class generation. (b) Generated state channel API for the C and S roles of Adder (using the default channel class naming scheme).

Only the channel class corresponding to the initial EFSM state has a public constructor (taking a single argument of type SessionEndpoint<S, R>). Every other state channel class is only instantiated internally by the method-chaining API: each session method is generated to return a new instance of the successor state channel. Figure 2 (b) summarises the channel classes and session I/O methods generated for the C and S roles of the Adder example (Fig. 1). The API generation promotes the use of the generated utility types to direct implementations as much as possible. E.g. in Adder_C_1, the two output options are distinguished as **send** methods overloaded on the operator type (as well as the payload types).

Hybrid Verification of Endpoint Implementations. Figure 3 (a) lists an example implementation of C using the generated API in Fig. 2 (b).

Session Initiation and State Channel Chaining. Lines 1–5 are a typical preamble. We create a new Adder session instance and a SessionEndpoint for role C.

```
1  Adder adder = new Adder(); // New session object
2  try (SessionEndpoint<Adder, C> se =
3              new SessionEndpoint<>(adder, C, new AdderFormatter())) {
4    se.connect(S, SocketChannel::new, hostS, portS); // TCP channel
5    Adder_C_1 s1 = new Adder_C_1(se);
6    // State channel implementation of C starting from s1 of state type C_1
7    Buf<Integer> i = new Buf<>(1); // Field i.val stores the buffer value (Integer)
8    for (int j = 0; j < N; j++)
9      s1 = s1.send(S, Add, i.val, i.val).receive(S, Res, i); // C_1 -> C_2 -> C_1
10   s1.send(S, Bye).receive(S, Bye); // C_1 -> C_3 -> EndSocket
11 } // Session completion checked at run-time when se is (auto) closed
```

```
1  Adder_S_3 add(Adder_S_1 s1, Buf<Integer> i1, Buf<Integer> i2) throws ... {
2    Adder_S_1_Cases cases = s1.branch(C); // Receives message: S_1 -> S_1_Cases
3    switch (cases.op) { // op enum field set by API according to the received message
4      case Add: return add(cases.receive(Add, i2) // S_1_Cases -> S_1
5                               .send(C, Res, i1.val+i2.val), i1, i2); // .. -> S_1
6      case Bye: return cases.receive(Bye); // S_1_Cases -> S_3
7  } } // Exhaustive handling of enum cases can be generated or checked by an IDE
```

Fig. 3. Examples using the generated APIs from Fig. 2 (b): (a) session initiation and endpoint implementation for C, and (b) the main loop and branch of S.

The SessionEndpoint se is used to perform the client-side connect to S (first argument) as a standard TCP channel (second). The session connection phase is concluded when se is given as a constructor argument to create an initial state channel of type Adder_C_1, to commence the implementation of the C endpoint.

Lines 7–10 give a simple imperative style implementation of C that repeatedly adds an integer, stored in the Buf<Integer> i, to itself. In each protocol state, given by the channel class, the generated API ensures that any session operation performed is indeed permitted by the protocol, e.g. state channel s1 permits only a send(S, Add, int, int) or a send(S, Bye). The method-chaining API is used as a fluent interface (the implicit state transitions are in comments), chaining the receive onto the send Add, which returns a new instance of C_1 following the recursive protocol. The recursion is enacted N times by the for-loop, linearly assigning the new C_1 to the existing s1 variable in each iteration, before the final Bye exchange after the loop terminates. Naturally, the API also allows the equivalent safe implementation for a fixed N, unfolding the recursion:

```
s1.send(S, Add, i.val, i.val).receive(S, Res, i)..Add/Res chained N − 1 more times..
  .send(S, Bye).receive(S, Bye);
```

The flexibility of the Endpoint API as a native language API is demonstrated by the following Fibonacci client using Adder in a different recursive method style.

```
Adder_C_3 fib(Adder_C_1 s1, Buf<Integer> i1, Buf<Integer> i2, int i) throws ... {
  return (i < N) ? fib(s1.send(S, Add, i1.val, i1.val=i2.val) // C_1 -> C_2..
                      .receive(S, Res, i2), i1, i2, i+1) // .. -> C_1
                : s1.send(S, Bye); } // C_1 -> C_3
```

While the structure of the session code in (a) corresponds quite directly to that of the source protocol, the more obfuscated session control flow here demonstrates the value of the session type based Endpoint API in guiding the implementation and promoting safe protocol conformance. The Java API ensures that the nested send - receive argument expression safely returns the endpoint to the S_1 state for each recursive method call, and that the recursion terminates according to the S_3 return state.

State Channel Linearity. Linear usage of every session channel object in an endpoint implementation is enforced by inlining run-time checks into the generated Java API following the two cases of the basic approach outlined in Sect. 2.

Repeat Use of a state channel raises a `LinearityException`. The boolean state indicating linear object consumption, and the associated guard method called by every generated session operation method, are inherited from the `LinearSocket` superclass of all the base channel classes in Fig. 2 (a) (except `EndSocket`).

Session Completion is treated by generating the `SessionEndpoint` object to implement the Java `AutoCloseable` interface. The Endpoint API requires the user to declare the `SessionEndpoint` in a try-with-resource statement (as in Fig. 3 (a), line 2), allowing the API to check that a terminal session operation has been performed when control flow leaves the try-statement; if not, then an exception is raised. Java IDEs, such as Eclipse, support compile-time warnings when `AutoCloseable` resources are not safely handled in an appropriate try statement.

We observe that certain implementation styles using a generated API, taking advantage of fluent method-chaining (e.g. as above), can help avoid linearity bugs by reducing the use of intermediate protocol state variables and state channel aliasing due to assignments.

Session Branches. The theoretical languages for which session types were developed typically feature a special-purpose *input branching* primitive, e.g. $c\&(r, \{l_i : P_i\}_{i \in I})$ [5], that atomically inputs a message on a channel c from role r and, according to the received message label l_i, reduces to the corresponding process continuation P_i. For languages like Java that lack such I/O primitives, the API generation approach enables some different options.

The basic option, intended for use in standard `switch` patterns (or `if-else` cases, etc.), separates the branch input action from the subsequent case analysis on the received message operator by generating a pair of `BranchSocket` and `CaseSocket` classes (non-unary inputs in Fig. 2 (a)). To delimit the cases of a branch state in a type-directed manner, the API generation creates an enum covering the permitted operators in each `BranchSocket` class, e.g. for S in `Adder`:

    enum Adder_S_1_Enum implements OpEnum { Add, Bye }   // Generated in Adder_S_1

Figure 3 (b) lists the main loop and branch in an implementation of S in `Adder`. The `branch` operation of the `BranchSocket` s1 blocks until the message is received, and returns the corresponding `CaseSocket` with the op field, of the enum type `Adder_S_1_Enum`, set according to the received operator. Using a switch statement on the op enum, the user calls the appropriate `receive` method on the `CaseSocket` to obtain the corresponding state channel continuation. The API raises an exception if the wrong `receive` is used (like a cast error) thus introducing an additional run-time check to maintain this hybrid form of session type safety. Java IDEs are, however, able to statically check exhaustive enum handling, which could be supplemented by developing, e.g., an Eclipse plugin to statically check that the `receive` methods are correctly matched up in basic switch (etc.) patterns.

The alternative option supported by our implementation is the generation of *callback interfaces* for branch states. These confer fully static safety for branch handling, but require the user to program in an event-driven callback style.

4   Use Case and Further Endpoint API Generation Features

We have used Scribble and our Java API generation to specify and implement standardised Internet applications, such as HTTP and SMTP, as real-world use cases. Using examples from the SMTP use case, we discuss practically motivated extensions to the core Endpoint API generation methodology presented so far.

SMTP [18] is an Internet standard for email transmission. We have specified a subset of the protocol in Scribble [38] that includes authenticating a secure connection and conducting the main mail transaction. Using the generated Endpoint API, it is straightforward to implement a compliant Java client (e.g. [38]) that is interoperable with existing SMTP servers.

For this section, we use the simplified excerpt from the opening stages of `Smtp` in Fig. 4. On a plain TCP connection, the client (`C`) receives the `220` welcome message from the Server (`S`) and the initiation exchange (client `EHLO`, and the server `250-`/`250` list of service extensions) is performed. The client then starts the negotiation to secure the channel by `StartTls`. Once secured, the client and server perform the initiation exchange again (different service extensions may now be valid), and the remainder of the session is conducted over the secure channel. In this running example, we omit payload types for brevity.

```
global protocol Smtp(role C, role S) { // Main protocol decl (start of SMTP)
  220 from S to C; // "220 smtp2.cc.ic.ac.uk ESMTP Exim 4.85 ..."
  do Init(C, S); // First init exchange on plain TCP connection
  do StartTls(C, S); // Negotiate secure connection
  do Init(C, S); // Second init exchange on secure connection
  ... // Remainder of SMTP session over secure connection
}
global protocol Init(role C, role S) { // "Initiation exchange" subprotocol
  Ehlo from C to S; // "EHLO user.test.com"
  rec X { choice at S { 250d from S to C; // "250-smtp2.cc.ic.ac.uk Hello ..."
                        continue X; } // "250-SIZE 26214400", "250-8BITMIME", etc.
           or { 250 from S to C; } } // "250 HELP" (no dash after 250)
}
global protocol StartTls(role C, role S) {
  StartTls from C to S; // "STARTTLS"
  220 from S to C; // "220 TLS go ahead"
}
```

Fig. 4. Simplified excerpt from a Scribble specification of SMTP.

State-Specific Input Futures. There are many works on extending session type theory to support more advanced communication patterns while retaining the desired safety properties. The API generation approach offers a platform for exploring the application of some of these features in practice.

One extension we have implemented to the core API generation is the generation of *state-specific input futures*. For each unary input state, we generate: (1) a subclass of a base `InputFuture` class that performs the input when forced; and (2) an additional `async` method for the `ReceiveSocket` (Fig. 2 (a)) of this state.

$$T_{ret} \; \texttt{async(} \; r \; \texttt{role,} \; l \; \texttt{op, Buf<?} \; \texttt{super} \; F_{S?} \; \texttt{> fut)}$$

The r, l and T_{ret} types are as for the corresponding `receive` method, and $F_{S?}$ is the generated input future class type. In contrast to `receive`, `async` is generated to return immediately, regardless of whether the expected message has arrived, returning instead a new input future for this state (via the supplied `Buf`) and the successor state channel. The future is forced, i.e. the input is performed, by a `sync` method, which blocks the caller until the message is received and writes the received payload values to generated fields (e.g. `pay1`) of the future.

Consider the `Ehlo` message in `Init` (Fig. 4) from `C` to `S`, which, in this example, is necessarily preceded by a `220` from `S` to `C` for both occurrences of `Init`. Assuming an initial state channel `s1` of type `Smtp_C_1`, we can implement this exchange at `C` using the input future generated for the `220` (`Smtp_C_1_Future`) by:

```
Buf<Smtp_C_1_Future> buf = new Buf<>(); // For the generated Smtp_C_1 InputFuture
s1.async(S, _220, buf).send(S, Ehlo); // S?220 "postponed"; S!Ehlo done first
String pay1 = buf.val.sync().pay1; // Postponed input done via the Smtp_C_1_Future
```

Calling `sync` on an input future implicitly forces all pending prior futures, in order, for the same peer role. This safely preserves the FIFO messaging semantics between each pair of roles in a session, and endpoint implementations using generated input futures thus retain the same safety properties as implementations using only blocking receives. (With this extension, `receive` is simply generated as `async` and `sync` in one step.) Repeat forcing of an input future has no effect.

Generating input futures captures aspects of several advanced session type features, which we explain by the above example. (1) `async` enables safe *non-blocking input* in session implementations (the key element towards event-driven sessions [16]). `async` essentially allows the input *transition* in the local EFSM to be decoupled in the user program from the actual message input *action* in safe situations. (2) Postponing input actions supports natural communication patterns that exploit asynchronous messaging for *safe permutations* of I/O actions at an endpoint [3,25]. In the example, the input future allows `C` to safely permute the actions: send `Ehlo` first, then receive `220`. (Note the reverse permutation at `S` is unsafe, due to the potential for deadlock by mutual inputs.) (3) Input futures are not linear objects (cf. state channels), so may be discarded unused, treating the input as an *affine* action [24,33]. In session types, input actions are traditionally (e.g. [14,15]) treated linearly to prevent unread messages in input queues corrupting later inputs. Here, safety is preserved by the implicit completion of pending futures, clearing any potential garbage preceding the current future.

Interfaces for Abstract I/O States. The SMTP use case raised a practical issue in generating Java State Channel APIs from session types. While formal syntactic session types offer a structural abstraction of communication behaviour by focusing on the I/O actions between implicit protocol states, the API generation reifies these states explicitly as nominal Java types. Nominal channel types can be good for protocol documentation (the default numbering scheme for states can be replaced by a user-supplied mapping to more meaningful class names); this example, however, shows a situation where the nominal types limit code reuse within a session implementation using Endpoint APIs as generated so far. The repeated initiation exchange is factored out in the Scribble as a subprotocol (`Init`), but the two exchanges correspond to distinct parts of the resulting EFSM as a whole, and are thus generated as distinct "unrelated" channel types, preventing this pattern from being factored out in the implementation code.

To address this issue, our approach is to supplement the nominal Java channel types by generating *interfaces for abstract I/O states*, which we explain through the current example. There are four main elements:

(1) For every I/O action, we generate an *Action Interface* named according to its session type characterisation. E.g. In_S$250 means input of 250 from S:

```
interface In_S$250<_S1 extends Succ_In_S$250> { _S1 receive(S role, _250 op); }
```

Each Action Interface is parameterised on a corresponding Successor Interface.

(2) For every I/O action, we generate a *Successor Interface*, to be implemented by every I/O State Interface (explained next) that succeeds the action. E.g.

```
interface Succ_Out_S$Ehlo { // For all I/O States that may succeed an S!Ehlo..
  default Branch_S$250$_250d<?, ?> to(Branch_S$250$_250d<?, ?> c) {
    return (Branch_S$250$_250d<?, ?>) this; // Generated cast
} } // ..i.e. the input branch between 250 and 250d
```

Every Successor Interface is generated with a default to "cast" method for each I/O state that implements it: in the above, only Branch_S250_250d (see next).

(3) For every state, we generate a `Send`, `Receive` or `Branch/Case` *I/O State Interface* named according to its session type characterisation, e.g. Branch_S250_250d is a branch state for the cases of 250 and 250d from S (the action suffixes are ordered lexically). This interface: (a) extends all the Successor Interfaces for the actions that lead to a state with this I/O characterisation; (b) extends all the Action Interfaces permitted by this state; and (c) is parameterised on each of its possible successors, passed through to the corresponding Action Interface.

```
interface Branch_S$250$_250d<_S1 extends Succ_In_S$250,_S2 extends Succ_In_S$250d>
    extends Succ_Out_S$Ehlo, Succ_In_S$250d { // (a) Can succeed S!Ehlo or S?250d
  public static final Branch_S$250$d$_250<?, ?> cast = null; // Used for "to" casts
  Case_S$250d$_250<_S1, _S2> branch(S role);
} // Branch states are generated as a pair of Branch/Case I/O State Interfaces
interface Case_S$250$_250d<_S1 extends Succ_In_S$250, _S2 extends Succ_In_S$250d>
    extends In_S$250<_S1>, In_S$250d<_S2> { ... } // (b) Can do S?250 or S?250d
```

(4) Finally, each concrete channel class (e.g. Smtp_C_3) implements its characterising I/O State Interface, instantiating the generic parameters to its concrete successors. The other contents of the channel class are generated as previously.

```
1  Succ_In_S$250 doInit(Send_S$Ehlo<?> s) { // Take a S!Ehlo chan; return succ(S?250)
2    Branch_S$250$_250d<?, ?> b = s.send(S, Ehlo).to(Branch_S$250$_250d.cast);
3    for (Cases_S$250$_250d<?, ?> c = b.branch(S); true; c = b.branch(S))
4      switch (c.getOp()) {
5        case _250: return c.receive(S, _250);
6        case _250d: { b = c.receive(S, _250d).to(Branch_S$250$_250d.cast); break; }
7  } } // (Message payloads omitted in this running example for brevity)
```

Fig. 5. Using the generated I/O interfaces to factor out the initiation exchange.

```
class Smtp_C_3 implements Branch_S$250$_250d<Smtp_C_4, Smtp_C_3> {..} // Init #1
class Smtp_C_7 implements Branch_S$250$_250d<Smtp_C_8, Smtp_C_7> {..} // Init #2
```

The naming scheme for these generated I/O interfaces is not dissimilar to formal notations for session types, but restricted to the current state and immediate actions, with the continuations captured in the successor type parameters.

Using the State Channel API generated for C, including the I/O interfaces as above, we factor out one method to implement both initiation exchanges in Fig. 5. The method accepts any state channel with the Send_S$Ehlo I/O State Interface and performs the send . This returns the Successor Interface Succ_Out_S$Ehlo, for which the only I/O State Interface (in this example) is Branch_S250_250d. Hence the call to the generated to on line 2, although operationally a run-time type cast on the state channel reference, is a *safe* cast as it is guaranteed to be valid for all possible successor states at this point. The cast returns a state channel with this interface, and the branch is implemented using a switch according to the relevant I/O State Interfaces. We directly return the Succ_In_S$250 Successor Interface after receiving the 250 in the first case.

```
doInit( // Second init exchange on secure channel
  doInit(new Smtp_C_1(se).async(S, _220) // First init exchange on plain TCP
    .to(Send_S$StartTls.cast).send(S,StartTls).to(Receive_S$220.cast).async(S,_220)
    .to(Send_S$Ehlo.cast).wrapClient(S, SSLSocketChannelWrapper::new) // SSL/TLS
)....; // Remainder of session
```

As doInit is implemented using I/O State Interfaces only, it can be reused to perform both initiation exchanges as above. Unfortunately, because the return type of doInit is just Succ_In_S$250, which may concretely be the state after the first initiation exchange (send StartTls) or the second (remainder of session), safety of the immediately subsequent to casts relies on the run-time check. However, all to casts can in fact be eliminated from both doInit and the above by reimplementing doInit, leveraging type inference for generics, with the signature:

```
<S1 extends Branch_S$250$_250d<S2, S1>, S2 extends Succ_In_S$250>     // S2 is bound..
  S2 doInit(Send_S$Ehlo<S1> s) throws ... //..as the successor of the 250 case
```

5   Related Work

Much programming languages research based on session types has been developed in the past decade: see [42] for a comprehensive survey. Some of the most closely related work was mentioned in Sect. 1; here we give additional discussions.

Static Session Type Checking. A static MPST system uses local types to type check programs (binary session types are the special case of two-party MPST). An implementation of static session type checking, following standard presentations [4,14,15], typically requires two key elements: (1) a syntactic correspondence between local type constructors and I/O language primitives, and (2) a mechanism, such as linear or uniqueness typing, or restrictions on pointer/reference aliasing, that enables precise tracking of channel endpoints through the control flow of the program. Hu, et al. [17] is an extension of Java for binary session types, and [39] for multiparty session types, along these lines. Both introduce new syntax for declaring session types and special session constructs to facilitate typing, with an additional analysis to deal with aliasing of channels. Without such extensions, it is difficult to perform static session type checking in a language like Java without being extremely conservative in the programs that pass type checking. Our API generation approach confers benefits of session types directly to native Java programming, and can be readily generalised for other existing languages.

Other session-based systems that would also require syntax extensions or annotations to be implemented as static typing for most mainstream languages include: Mungo [26] and Bica [13] based on typestates in Java; Links [21,22] and Jolie [19] for Web services; Pabble [31] and ParTypes [23] based on indexed dependent types for parallel programs. We believe our hybrid API generation approach is a practical alternative for applying various forms of behavioural types. Implementations of static session typing in Haskell [34,35] are able to benefit from rich typing features (here, indexed parameterised monads) to ensure session linearity without language extensions, but with various usability tradeoffs. In [27], session code is restricted to a single channel to simplify the treatment of linearity. Outside of API generation, combining static and run-time mechanisms for session safety is being explored in other settings: [32] is an ML library for binary sessions with a focus on type inference, and [36] for actors in Scala.

Dynamic Session Verification and Code Generation From Session Types. Runtime monitoring of I/O actions [8,28,29] is the primary verification method in Scribble [37], and is subject to the common tradeoffs of dynamic verification (Sect. 1). Monitoring can be applied directly to existing languages, but endpoint implementations must still use a specific API or be instrumented with appropriate hooks for the monitor to intercept the actions. Monitoring also verifies only the observed execution trace, not the implementation itself. Our lightweight hybrid verification approach allows certain benefits of static typing to be reclaimed for free, including static protocol error detection, up to the linearity condition on state channels, and other IDE assistance for session programming, such as code generation (e.g. session method completion, branch case enumeration) and partial static checking of linearity (e.g. unused state channel variables).

The code generation framework in [30] (Sect. 1) works by targetting a specific context, that is, parallel MPI programs in C. In contrast, our API generation approach uses session types for lighter-weight generation of types, rather than final programs. Programming using a generated Endpoint API is amenable to varied user implementations in terms of local control flow style (e.g. imperative or functional) and concurrency (e.g. multithreaded or event-driven) via standard Java language features and existing libraries.

We thank Gary Brown and Matthew Arrott for collaborations, and Julien Lange for comments. This work is partially supported by EPSRC EP/K034413/1, EP/K011715/1, and EP/L00058X/1; and by EU FP7 612985 (UPSCALE).

References

1. Bocchi, L., Chen, T.-C., Demangeon, R., Honda, K., Yoshida, N.: Monitoring networks through multiparty session types. In: Beyer, D., Boreale, M. (eds.) FORTE 2013 and FMOODS 2013. LNCS, vol. 7892, pp. 50–65. Springer, Heidelberg (2013)
2. Caires, L., Pfenning, F.: Session types as intuitionistic linear propositions. In: Gastin, P., Laroussinie, F. (eds.) CONCUR 2010. LNCS, vol. 6269, pp. 222–236. Springer, Heidelberg (2010)
3. Chen, T., Dezani-Ciancaglini, M., Yoshida, N.: On the preciseness of subtyping in session types. In: PPDP 2014, pp. 135–146. ACM (2014)
4. Coppo, M., Dezani-Ciancaglini, M., Padovani, L., Yoshida, N.: A gentle introduction to multiparty asynchronous session types. In: Bernardo, M., Johnsen, E.B. (eds.) Formal Methods for Multicore Programming. Lecture Notes in Computer Science, vol. 9104, pp. 146–178. Springer, Switzerland (2015)
5. Coppo, M., Dezani-Ciancaglini, M., Yoshida, N., Padovani, L.: Global progress for dynamically interleaved multiparty sessions. Math. Struct. Comput. Sci. **760**, 1–65 (2015)
6. Dardha, O., Giachino, E., Sangiorgi, D.: Session types revisited. In: PPDP 2012, pp. 139–150. ACM Press (2012)
7. Demangeon, R., Honda, K.: Full abstraction in a subtyped pi-Calculus with linear types. In: Katoen, J.-P., König, B. (eds.) CONCUR 2011. LNCS, vol. 6901, pp. 280–296. Springer, Heidelberg (2011)
8. Demangeon, R., Honda, K., Hu, R., Neykova, R., Yoshida, N.: Practical interruptible conversations: distributed dynamic verification with multiparty session types and Python. In: Formal Methods in System Design, pp. 1–29 (2015)
9. Deniélou, P.-M., Yoshida, N.: Multiparty session types meet communicating automata. In: Seidl, H. (ed.) Programming Languages and Systems. LNCS, vol. 7211, pp. 194–213. Springer, Heidelberg (2012)
10. Deniélou, P.-M., Yoshida, N.: Multiparty compatibility in communicating automata: characterisation and synthesis of global session types. In: Fomin, F.V., Freivalds, R., Kwiatkowska, M., Peleg, D. (eds.) ICALP 2013, Part II. LNCS, vol. 7966, pp. 174–186. Springer, Heidelberg (2013)
11. Gay, S., Hole, M.: Subtyping for session types in the Pi-Calculus. Acta Informatica **42**(2/3), 191–225 (2005)
12. Gay, S., Vasconcelos, V.T.: Linear type theory for asynchronous session types. J. Funct. Program. **20**(1), 19–50 (2010)
13. Gay, S., Vasconcelos, V.T., Ravara, A., Gesbert, N., Caldeira, A.Z.: Modular session types for distributed object-oriented programming. In: POPL 2010, pp. 299–312. ACM (2010)
14. Honda, K., Vasconcelos, V.T., Kubo, M.: Language primitives and type discipline for structured communication-based programming. In: Hankin, C. (ed.) ESOP 1998. LNCS, vol. 1381, p. 122. Springer, Heidelberg (1998)

15. Honda, K., Yoshida, N., Carbone, M.: Multiparty asynchronous session types. In: POPL 2008, pp. 273–284. ACM (2008). (Full version to appear in JACM)
16. Hu, R., Kouzapas, D., Pernet, O., Yoshida, N., Honda, K.: Type-safe eventful sessions in Java. In: D'Hondt, T. (ed.) ECOOP 2010. LNCS, vol. 6183, pp. 329–353. Springer, Heidelberg (2010)
17. Hu, R., Yoshida, N., Honda, K.: Session-based distributed programming in Java. In: Vitek, J. (ed.) ECOOP 2008. LNCS, vol. 5142, pp. 516–541. Springer, Heidelberg (2008)
18. IETF. Simple Mail Transfer Protocol. https://tools.ietf.org/html/rfc5321
19. Jolie homepage. http://www.jolie-lang.org/
20. Lange, J., Tuosto, E., Yoshida, N.: From communicating machines to graphical choreographies. In: POPL 2015, pp. 221–232. ACM Press (2015)
21. Lindley, S., Morris, J.G.: A semantics for propositions as sessions. In: Vitek, J. (ed.) ESOP 2015. LNCS, vol. 9032, pp. 560–584. Springer, Heidelberg (2015)
22. Links homepage. http://groups.inf.ed.ac.uk/links/
23. Lopez, H.A., Marques, E.R.B., Martins, F., Ng, N., Santos, C., Vasconcelos, V.T., Yoshida, N.: Protocol-based verification of message-passing parallel programs. In: OOPSLA 2015, pp. 280–298. ACM (2015)
24. Mostrous, D., Vasconcelos, V.T.: Affine sessions. In: Kühn, E., Pugliese, R. (eds.) COORDINATION 2014. LNCS, vol. 8459, pp. 115–130. Springer, Heidelberg (2014)
25. Mostrous, D., Yoshida, N.: Session typing and asynchronous subtyping for the higher-order π-calculus. Inf. Comput. **241**, 227–263 (2015)
26. Mungo homepage. http://www.dcs.gla.ac.uk/research/mungo/
27. Neubauer, M., Thiemann, P.: An implementation of session types. In: Jayaraman, B. (ed.) PADL 2004. LNCS, vol. 3057, pp. 56–70. Springer, Heidelberg (2004)
28. Neykova, R., Bocchi, L., Yoshida, N.: Timed runtime monitoring for multiparty conversations. In: BEAT 2014, EPTCS, vol. 162, pp. 19–26 (2014)
29. Neykova, R., Yoshida, N.: Multiparty session actors. In: Kühn, E., Pugliese, R. (eds.) COORDINATION 2014. LNCS, vol. 8459, pp. 131–146. Springer, Heidelberg (2014)
30. Ng, N., de Figueiredo Coutinho, J.G., Yoshida, N.: Protocols by default. In: Franke, B. (ed.) CC 2015. LNCS, vol. 9031, pp. 212–232. Springer, Heidelberg (2015)
31. Ng, N., Yoshida, N., Honda, K.: Multiparty session C: safe parallel programming with message optimisation. In: Furia, C.A., Nanz, S. (eds.) TOOLS 2012. LNCS, vol. 7304, pp. 202–218. Springer, Heidelberg (2012)
32. Padovani, L.: A Simple Library Implementation of Binary Sessions (Unpublished). https://hal.archives-ouvertes.fr/hal-01216310
33. Pfenning, F., Griffith, D.: Polarized substructural session types. In: Pitts, A. (ed.) FOSSACS 2015. LNCS, vol. 9034, pp. 3–22. Springer, Heidelberg (2015)
34. Pucella, R., Tov, J.A.: Haskell session types with (almost) no class. In: Haskell 2008, pp. 25–36. ACM (2008)
35. Sackman, M., Eisenbach, S.: Session types in haskell (Unpublished). http://pubs.doc.ic.ac.uk/session-types-in-haskell/
36. Scalas, A., Yoshida, N.: Lightweight session types in Scala (Unpublished). http://www.doc.ic.ac.uk/research/technicalreports/2015/#7
37. Scribble homepage. http://www.scribble.org
38. Session types use cases: SMTP (Scribble). https://github.com/epsrc-abcd/session-types-use-cases/tree/master/Simple%20Mail%20Tranfer%20Protocol/scribble

39. Sivaramakrishnan, K.C., Nagaraj, K., Ziarek, L., Eugster, P.: Efficient session type guided distributed interaction. In: Clarke, D., Agha, G. (eds.) COORDINATION 2010. LNCS, vol. 6116, pp. 152–167. Springer, Heidelberg (2010)

40. Toninho, B., Caires, L., Pfenning, F.: Higher-order processes, functions, and sessions: a monadic integration. In: Felleisen, M., Gardner, P. (eds.) ESOP 2013. LNCS, vol. 7792, pp. 350–369. Springer, Heidelberg (2013)

41. Wadler, P.: Proposition as sessions. In: ICFP 2012, pp. 273–286 (2012)

42. Survey on languages based on behavioural types. http://www.di.unito.it/~padovani/BETTY/BETTY_WG3_state_of_art.pdf

43. Yoshida, N., Hu, R., Neykova, R., Ng, N.: The scribble protocol language. In: Abadi, M., Lluch Lafuente, A. (eds.) TGC 2013. LNCS, vol. 8358, pp. 22–41. Springer, Heidelberg (2014)

PVAIR: Partial Variable Assignment InterpolatoR

Pavel Jančík[2], Leonardo Alt[1], Grigory Fedyukovich[1], Antti E.J. Hyvärinen[1], Jan Kofroň[2(✉)], and Natasha Sharygina[1]

[1] University of Lugano, Lugano, Switzerland
{leonardo.alt,grigory.fedyukovich,antti.hyvarinen,natasha.sharygina}@usi.ch
[2] Faculty of Mathematics and Physics Department of Distributed and Dependable Systems, Charles University in Prague, Prague, Czech Republic
{pavel.jancik,jan.kofron}@d3s.mff.cuni.cz

Abstract. Despite its recent popularity, program verification has to face practical limitations hindering its everyday use. One of these issues is scalability, both in terms of time and memory consumption. In this paper, we present Partial Variable Assignment InterpolatoR (PVAIR) – an interpolation tool exploiting partial variable assignments to significantly improve performance when computing several specialized Craig interpolants from a single proof. Subsequent interpolant processing during the verification process can thus be more efficient, improving scalability of the verification as such. We show with a wide range of experiments how our methods improve the interpolant computation in terms of their size. In particular, (i) we used benchmarks from the SAT competition and (ii) performed experiments in the domain of software upgrade checking.

1 Introduction

Symbolic model-checking algorithms rely on expressing a verification problem as a logical formula and determining whether the formula satisfies a given property. Many sub-tasks of model-checking, such as computing safe inductive invariants for programs and summarizing functionality with respect to properties critical to program correctness, rely on over-approximating parts of the formula. To keep the formal verification manageable and the run time low it is critical that the over-approximations are suitable for the model-checking task at hand. *Craig interpolation* [7] is a process for computing over-approximations of first-order formulas that has proven useful in both program verification and automatic approximation refinement [15]. The idea in applying Craig interpolation in model checking is to reduce the over-approximation process into finding a compact interpolant I such that I is satisfied by all models of the part being over-approximated but still entails the properties of interest with respect to the rest of the formula. The *Labeled Interpolation System* (LIS) [8] is a widely used

---

This work was partially supported by the Grant Agency of the Czech Republic project 14-11384S and by the SNF projects number 200020_163001 and 200021_153402.

P. Stevens and A. Wąsowski (Eds.): FASE 2016, LNCS 9633, pp. 419–434, 2016.
DOI: 10.1007/978-3-662-49665-7_25

framework for computing Craig interpolants in propositional logic from a resolution refutation. The flexibility of LIS allows it to be used in a variety of verification tasks that place additional requirements for the interpolants [18].

In some tasks, (e.g., when proving safety of certain types of program updates or speeding up model-checking with parallel computing) it is useful to compute over-approximations of the formula under assumptions which are specific to the particular application problem. However, the LIS framework in its original form does not allow for computing interpolants under assumptions. There are several reasons why such *focused interpolants* would be beneficial in particular in the LIS framework. Firstly, the focused interpolants are in general smaller and therefore more manageable for the model checker. Secondly, the properties of interpolants provided by the LIS framework, such as the path interpolation property [13], can be preserved in the focused interpolants. Thirdly, several focused interpolants can be computed from a single resolution refutation, while constructing a resolution refutation is computationally expensive. In [12], we introduced an interpolation system exploiting partial variable assignments to improve efficiency of interpolant computation. We proved that following a set of requirements put on labeling during interpolation results in interpolants with the path interpolation property, which is required by some verification tools, e.g. [1], to work.

This paper presents the *Partial Variable Assignment InterpolatoR* (PVAIR), the first implementation that is able to construct such focused interpolants. The implementation is based on the *Labeled Partial Assignment Interpolation System* (LPAIS) [12], an extension of LIS which supports focusing the interpolant in the manner required by the verification applications. The PVAIR solution is generic and can be used in various model checking-based scenarios. In this paper, in addition to providing the description of the tool architecture, we also report an initial experimental study on how the interpolants constructed with PVAIR behave in different example tasks. The results show a significant improvement in both interpolant size and the overall model checking time, suggesting that the approach is viable for constructing focused interpolants.

The general intuition behind the applications of PVAIR is that sometimes a symbolic model checker can provide a partial truth assignment for the formula being verified, coming from the knowledge of the program structure and meaning of the variables. As a result, some constraints of the formula can get satisfied; the LPAIS framework allows for removing such clauses during the interpolant computation. This improves the interpolation in two ways: the interpolation becomes faster, and the resulting interpolant can be significantly smaller. Because of the latter the interpolants can be handled in a more efficient way during the subsequent computation. PVAIR is built on top of the open-source tool PERIPLO [18], which provides resolution proofs and is able to optimize the proofs for interpolation through transformations. PERIPLO has been used in various verification projects, including function summarization in EVOLCHECK [10] and FUNFROG [22], both as an interpolation engine and as a SAT solver.

We experimentally studied the performance of PVAIR on a set of its potential applications. We compared it to PERIPLO during computation of a summary for a particular function using EVOLCHECK. In this experiment, PVAIR was used to rule out the program paths that do not call the function. We also applied PVAIR in more generic settings, when constructing interpolation problems from a subset of the SAT Competition benchmarks. This experiment resembles closely the scenario of computing focused interpolants for a divide-and-conquer approach for parallel model checking. In both types of benchmarks, we report a substantial reduction in interpolant sizes. As shown in the EVOLCHECK use case, smaller interpolants also result in considerably faster upgrade-checking steps.

2 Preliminaries and Background Theory

A *literal* is a Boolean variable l or its negation $\bar{l}$. A *clause* is a disjunction over a set of literals. We use angle brackets $\langle \Theta \rangle$ to denote the clause built from the literals in set Θ. A propositional formula in Conjunctive Normal Form (CNF) is a conjunction (or equivalently set) of clauses. A *resolution proof* for a set of clauses Φ is a rooted DAG with each node having either no antecedents (*leaf node*) or exactly two antecedents (*inner node*). Each node in the resolution proof is associated with node clause; from now on we use proof node and corresponding node clause equivalently. A leaf node corresponds to an input clause from Φ. Each inner node with two antecedents $\langle \Theta_1, p \rangle$ and $\langle \Theta_2, \bar{p} \rangle$ has node clause $\langle \Theta_1, \Theta_2 \rangle$, thus representing a resolution where p is the *pivot* variable.

Given an unsatisfiable CNF formula Φ and its (A,B)-partitioning into $A \wedge B$ parts, a Craig interpolant [7] is a formula I such that I is implied by A ($\models A \Rightarrow I$), unsatisfiable with B ($\models B \wedge I \Rightarrow \bot$), and defined over common symbols (variables) of A and B. An interpolant can be seen as an over-approximation of A still being strong enough to be unsatisfiable with B.

Example 1: Figure 1 shows a resolution refutation proof for CNF formula $\Phi = \langle l_1 \vee l_2 \rangle \wedge \langle \bar{l}_3 \vee l_6 \rangle \wedge \langle \bar{l}_1 \vee l_5 \rangle \wedge \langle l_1 \vee l_3 \rangle \wedge \langle \bar{l}_2 \vee \bar{l}_6 \rangle \wedge \langle \bar{l}_4 \vee l_5 \rangle \wedge \langle \bar{l}_2 \vee l_4 \rangle \wedge \langle \bar{l}_1 \vee l_2 \rangle$. Assume a (A,B)-partitioning with A consisting of the conjunction of the first three clauses and B of the remaining five clauses. There might not be just a single interpolant for an unsatisfiable formula; many different ones of various strengths can exist. Formula $I_1 \equiv (l_1 \vee [(l_6 \vee \bar{l}_3) \wedge (\bar{l}_6 \vee l_2)]) \wedge (\bar{l}_1 \vee l_5)$ is one of the possible interpolants which can be computed from the proof in Fig. 1 using LIS. Figure 2 shows how McMillan's interpolant $I_2 \equiv (l_1 \vee l_2) \wedge (\bar{l}_3 \vee l_6) \wedge (\bar{l}_1 \vee l_5)$ can be derived (after constant propagation) from the proof in Fig. 1, e.g., by LIS or LPAIS with an empty assignment. Note that for convenience we write the partial interpolant associated to a particular node of the proof into brackets.

As an over-approximation, Craig interpolants express properties for all models of the formula. However, this might be unnecessarily strong for some applications. For example, while constructing a function summary through interpolation, it is possible to consider only the models corresponding to the paths going via the summarized function. Based on the encoding of the function body,

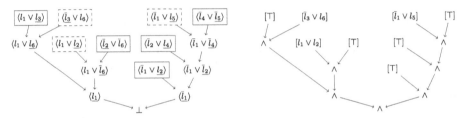

Fig. 1. Refutation resolution proof; the clauses from A-part and B-part are in dashed and full boxes, respectively.

Fig. 2. McMillan's interpolant.

a variable assignment blocking all the other paths can be derived. This applies also for the case of Abstract Reachability Graphs (ARGs). The label of a particular ARG node is an over-approximation of reachable states at that node. Since the paths in ARG which do not go via the node cannot influence the reachable states at that node, for each node it is possible to compute variable assignment blocking these paths; in other words, the assignment permits only the models corresponding to paths via the node. The node labels are computed by interpolation, however it is actually enough to compute a formula that is an interpolant for the models consistent with the assignment.

Focused Interpolants. A *Partial Variable Assignment* (PVA) π assigns value *True* resp. *False* to some variables from formula Φ; alternatively, PVA can be seen as a conjunction of literals. Given a partial variable assignment π, a set of clauses A can be partitioned into A_π – a subset of clauses from A satisfied by the assignment, and the remaining clauses $A_{\overline{\pi}}$ which are not satisfied by π. For a given unsatisfiable formula Φ, its partitioning into $A \wedge B$ and a partial variable assignment π, a *Partial Variable Assignment Interpolant* [12], shortly *focused interpolant*, is a formula I such that $\pi \models A \Rightarrow I$ and $\pi \models B \wedge I \Rightarrow \bot$ and I is defined over unassigned shared variables between $A_{\overline{\pi}}$ and $B_{\overline{\pi}}$, i.e., the symbols common to the π-unsatisfied parts of A and B. In other words, it is an interpolant, but only for models which agree on the values of variables assigned by π. Due to the weakened requirements, the focused interpolants can be of a smaller size compared to the Craig interpolants. The focused interpolants can be alternatively seen as Craig interpolants for the unsatisfied parts of the input – *sub-problem*, i.e., for $A_{\overline{\pi}} \wedge B_{\overline{\pi}}$ where literals falsified by the assignment are removed.

Example 1 (cont.): Let us assume assignment $\pi \equiv \overline{l}_2$ (i.e., assigning *False* to variable l_2) and the set of clauses from our previous example. Given the assignment, B can be split into $B_\pi \equiv \langle \overline{l}_2 \vee \overline{l}_6 \rangle \wedge \langle \overline{l}_2 \vee l_4 \rangle$ and $B_{\overline{\pi}} \equiv \langle \overline{l}_4 \vee \overline{l}_5 \rangle \wedge \langle \overline{l}_1 \vee l_2 \rangle$. A_π is empty thus $A_\pi \equiv \top$ and $A_{\overline{\pi}} \equiv A$.

Craig and focused interpolants differ in the variables which could occur in the interpolant. The shared variables between A and B (i.e., those that can appear in a Craig interpolant) are l_1, l_2, l_5 and l_6. Since focused interpolants consider for the shared variables only unsatisfied parts of A resp. B (i.e., $A_{\overline{\pi}}$ and

$B_{\overline{\pi}}$), fewer variables are shared; in our example only l_1 and l_5 could appear in a focused interpolant, which are those which can appear in a Craig interpolant for the sub-problem.

Given an assignment and a Craig interpolant, an alternative way to reduce the interpolant size is to assign the values inside the interpolant formula and propagate the Boolean constants. In this case the interpolants from the above example result in $I_1[\pi] \equiv (l_1 \vee [(l_6 \vee \overline{l}_3) \wedge \overline{l}_6]) \wedge (\overline{l}_1 \vee l_5)$ and $I_2[\pi] \equiv l_1 \wedge (\overline{l}_3 \vee l_6) \wedge (\overline{l}_1 \vee l_5)$. None of them is a valid focused interpolant since both contain variable l_6. Note that $I_2[\pi]$ can be equivalently rewritten as $l_1 \wedge l_5 \wedge (\overline{l}_3 \vee l_6)$x; in general, such a transformation requires a complex analysis and not all interpolants can be transformed into focused interpolants as I_1 shows. This means that the aforementioned techniques can be used to reduce the size of the formula, however not to compute focused interpolants. Below we introduce a method to compute focused interpolants for propositional logic which produces interpolants smaller than the approach above.

Table 1. Labeled Partial Assignment Interpolation System

Leaf v:		$\langle \Theta \rangle, [I]$	
$I = \begin{cases} -\langle \Theta \rangle\|_{b,\pi} \\ \neg\langle \Theta \rangle\|_{a,\pi} \\ \top \end{cases}$		if $\langle \Theta \rangle \in A_{\overline{\pi}}$ if $\langle \Theta \rangle \in B_{\overline{\pi}}$ if $\langle \Theta \rangle \in A_\pi \cup B_\pi$	Hyp-$A_{\overline{\pi}}$ Hyp-$B_{\overline{\pi}}$ Hyp-A_π, Hyp-B_π

Inner vertex v:	$v_1 : \langle p, \Theta_1 \rangle, [I_1]$	$v_2 : \langle \overline{p}, \Theta_2 \rangle, [I_2]$	
		$\langle \Theta_1, \Theta_2 \rangle, [I]$	
$I = \begin{cases} I_1 \vee I_2 \\ I_1 \wedge I_2 \\ (I_1 \vee p) \wedge (I_2 \vee \overline{p}) \\ I_2 \\ I_1 \end{cases}$	if $\mathsf{Lab}(v_1, p) \sqcup \mathsf{Lab}(v_2, \overline{p}) = a$ if $\mathsf{Lab}(v_1, p) \sqcup \mathsf{Lab}(v_2, \overline{p}) = b$ if $\mathsf{Lab}(v_1, p) \sqcup \mathsf{Lab}(v_2, \overline{p}) = ab$ if $\mathsf{Lab}(v_1, p) = d^+$ if $\mathsf{Lab}(v_2, \overline{p}) = d^+$		Res-a Res-b Res-ab Res-d^+ Res-d^+

Labeled Partial Assignment Interpolation System (LPAIS) — an extension of the Labeled Interpolation System [8] — yields focused interpolants from the resolution refutation of $A \wedge B$.

In LPAIS, each literal in the clauses of the resolution proof is assigned a label a, b, ab, or d^+. Labels a, b, and ab have the same meaning as in LIS, while the label d^+ is used for the literals from the assignment π. The lattice of labels is defined by the Hasse diagram in Fig. 3. The labels are specified via a *labeling function* Lab; e.g., $\mathsf{Lab}(v_2, \overline{p})$ is the label of literal $\overline{p}$ at node v_2 of the proof. The label of a literal in an inner node v is computed using join operator $\sqcup$ (defined by Fig. 3) from the labels of the literal in the antecedent nodes ($\mathsf{Lab}(v, l) = \mathsf{Lab}(v_1, l) \sqcup \mathsf{Lab}(v_2, l)$, where v_1 and v_2 are the antecedent nodes of v). Formal definition of labeling function as well as the requirements that labels must satisfy are described in [12].

Example 1 (cont.): Figure 4 shows how LPAIS assigns labels to literals; the label of a literal is shown as superscript. When choosing the strongest possible labeling,

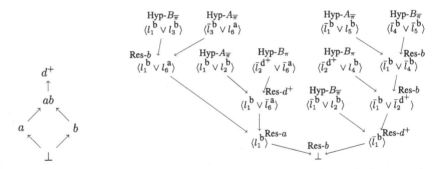

Fig. 3. Lattice of labels (⊔). **Fig. 4.** Labeled proof and rules to be applied at proof nodes.

LPAIS yields, for empty assignments, McMillan's interpolants; in particular, only variables occurring in $A_{\overline{\pi}}$ but not in $B_{\overline{\pi}}$ are labeled a (i.e., l_6), all the others (except for the literals from the assignment) re-labeled b.

The labeled partial assignment interpolation system assigns a *partial interpolant* $[I]$ to each proof node according to the rules described in Table 1. The partial interpolants of the leaf nodes are directly constructed from the node clauses (it means those forming $A \wedge B$) using the rules in the upper part of Table 1. The applied Hyp-* rule is determined by the set inclusion check in the middle column; in particular by occurrence of the node clause in $A_{\overline{\pi}}$, A_π, B_π and $B_{\overline{\pi}}$. A partial interpolant for the Hyp-$A_{\overline{\pi}}$ rule, defined as $\langle \Theta \rangle|_{b,\pi}$, represents a clause which is created from the node clause $\langle \Theta \rangle$ by omitting the literals over the π-assigned variables and those whose label differs from b. In particular node clause $\langle \bar{l}_3^{\,b} \vee l_6^{\,a} \rangle$ yields partial interpolant $\langle \bar{l}_3^{\,b} \vee l_6^{\,a} \rangle|_{b,\pi} \equiv [l_3]$. The leaf nodes with clauses satisfied by π have the partial interpolant $\top$.

For inner nodes, the rule from Table 1 is chosen based on the labels of the pivot in the antecedents (denoted by v_1 and v_2). Note the Res-d^+ rules, which correspond to the case where the pivot is satisfied by the assignment in one of the antecedents. In these cases, the partial interpolant is the same as the partial interpolant in the antecedent not being satisfied by the assignment; due

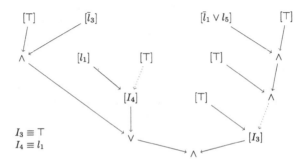

Fig. 5. Focused interpolant I_π, using labeling of Fig. 4.

to such nodes the size of the LPAIS interpolant is smaller compared to the LIS interpolant.

Example 1 (cont.): Figure 5 shows how focused interpolant $I_\pi \equiv l_1 \vee \bar{l}_3$ for our example can be derived. Note the dotted arrows at nodes corresponding to Res-d^+ resolutions; they highlight the antecedents whose partial interpolants are ignored and their sub-trees do not contribute to final focused interpolant. Also note that the focused interpolant I_π is smaller compared to both $I_1[\pi]$ and $I_2[\pi]$ from the examples above.

An assignment applied onto (interpolant) formula (i.e., if $I[\pi]$ is computed) can reduce the size of the formula only if the assigned variable appears in the (interpolant) formula (i.e., the variable has to be shared). However, LPAIS reduce the size of the interpolants even if the assigned variable does not appear in the interpolant, since the reduction is done as a part of interpolant computation and not as a post-processing step.

PVAIR implements the LPAIS framework. The tool can generate the McMillan's [16], Pudlák's [17], and McMillan's' [8] interpolants and their equivalents in presence of assignments. Additionally, PVAIR supports constructing different interpolants by providing different labelings for the literals in the leaves. The relative logical strength of interpolants constructed with LPAIS from the same resolution refutation is determined by the labeling function used. For instance, the McMillan's focused interpolants are sufficiently strong to have the path-interpolation property.

3   The Tool Architecture

The PVAIR architecture is shown in Fig. 6. It takes a propositional formula, its (A, B)-partitioning, and a partial variable assignment as input and produces focused interpolants if the input formula is unsatisfiable. The input can be provided either in a file in the SMT-LIB 2.0 format or via a C++ API.

When a verification tool decides to compute interpolants (e.g., to obtain either function summaries in the case of upgrade-checking and over-approximations of reachable states for covering checks) it constructs an input formula Φ which encodes the program being verified. Further, based on the way the input formula is constructed, the verification tool decides how to partition it (e.g., to obtain a summary of a given function) and which partial variable assignment to use (e.g., depending on the changes detected in the new version of the program). These inputs are then passed to the PVAIR tool.

The workflow of the PVAIR tool is as follows. First, the input formula is passed to the PERIPLO-based preprocessing module. Since the formula can be in an arbitrary form, it is transformed into CNF (the top box in Fig. 6) using an efficient, structure-sharing version of the Tseitin encoding [25]. Its satisfiability is then determined using the MiniSAT 2.2.0 solver [9].

In the case of an unsatisfiable input, an initial refutation is extracted from the solver in the compact MiniSAT internal proof format. The format is then transformed into a resolution DAG to allow more efficient handling of the proof (Proof

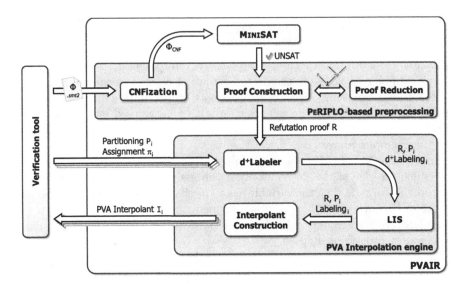

Fig. 6. PVAIR architecture.

Construction). In particular, using the resolution DAG form, the proof can be compressed using well-known proof reduction techniques such as structural hashing or pivot recycling [19,20] available in PERIPLO (Proof Reduction). The proof reduction techniques can be enabled/disabled via a configuration file or API.

Once the resolution proof R is computed, it is passed together with the partitionings and variable assignments to the interpolation engine (the bottom box in Fig. 6). From this point on, any number of partial variable assignments π_i and partitionings P_i (into $A_i \wedge B_i$) can be given as input to the tool and used to construct the corresponding interpolants I_i. Note that in any case only one SAT-solver call will be made during the entire execution. The first step inside the PVA interpolation engine is labeling all the literals in $A \wedge B$. The d^+Labeler will distribute d^+ labels among the literals according to the assigned variables, whereas the LIS will label the remaining literals according to the partitioning and the selected LIS-based interpolation algorithm (which can be chosen in the configuration file or via API). When the labeling is complete, it is used together with the partitioning and resolution proof R to compute interpolants (Interpolant Construction).

The construction starts by computing partial interpolants (according to the upper part of Table 1) for the leaf nodes of the refutation. The computation then proceeds from the leaves to the root node. In each inner node, depending on the label of the pivot, a partial interpolant of the node is computed by combining the partial interpolants from the antecedent nodes (the bottom part of Table 1). During the interpolant construction partial interpolants are optimized using Boolean constant propagation and structural sharing (hashing). The final interpolant is computed in the root node.

For the details on PVAIR usage, we refer the reader to the Tutorial section of the tool web page available at http://verify.inf.usi.ch/pvair.

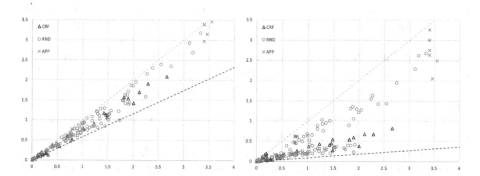

Fig. 7. Comparison of interpolant sizes computed without variable assignment [x] and with one variable assigned [y] (left) and five variables assigned (right).

4   Experiments

We ran PVAIR on two types of experiments: (1) SAT Competition benchmarks and (2) computational problems generated by the EVOLCHECK tool during verification procedure. To demonstrate the tool performance, we measured the size of produced interpolants and its effect on the total verification time.

4.1   SAT Competition

From the way focused interpolants are computed by PVAIR it is obvious that they are smaller compared to the Craig interpolants. In this part we illustrate the actual difference. Compared to experiments on functions summaries in the latter part, SAT Competition provides us with a larger set of more heterogeneous kinds of benchmarks. This helps one to see how the reduction of the size varies among inputs from different domains.

For experiments, we chose 47 unsatisfiable benchmarks from the SAT Competition[1] from all categories – 12 from the *Application* (APP), 11 from the *Crafted* (CRF), and 24 from the *Random* (RND) sets. Since the benchmarks are not partitioned, we generated six partitionings for each benchmark; we simulated the typical way the path interpolants are computed, i.e., we randomly chose n, first n clauses of the benchmark belonged to the A-part, the remaining clauses to the B-part. No assignment is given by authors of the benchmarks, thus for each partitioning we generated five random variable assignments consisting of a

---

[1] http://www.satcompetition.org/.

single, five, resp. twenty assigned variables. Assignments of various sizes indicate how the reduction scales w.r.t. the number of assigned variables.

Since focused interpolants can be seen as Craig interpolants for a sub-problem, for each pair of partitioning and assignment, we created the sub-problem instance and used PVAIR to computed the Craig interpolant. Sub-problems are simpler compared to the benchmark from which they were generated, so interpolants for sub-problems are typically smaller compared to Craig interpolants of the benchmark. However, the interpolant for each sub-problem is computed from a different refutation proof; in contrast to focused interpolants which, for a particular benchmark, are all computed from the same proof. The path interpolation property [13], which is often exploited during program model checking, might be missing in this case.

As to the interpretation of the results: *No assignment* reflects the state-of-the-art approaches, where Craig interpolants are used directly. Focused interpolants show how the size of the interpolants can be reduced if the model checker (i.e., a tool generation the input) provides a reasonable assignment together with a partitioning. The interpolants for a sub-problem can be seen as an alternative to focused interpolants because of their similar meaning, however these interpolants lack the properties of the focused ones.

For comparison, we use McMillan's interpolants – a widely used approach. The proof reduction techniques were disabled; we used the default PERIPLO settings. All benchmarks were run on a Linux blade server with Xeon X5687 CPU using the timeout of 60 min and the memory limit of 20GB using the Parallel environment [24].

Figure 7 compares the sizes of the computed interpolants. Each point in the graph corresponds to a single partitioning of a benchmark; the x-axis represents the interpolant size if no assignment is provided (Craig interpolant) while the y-axis represents the size of the focused interpolants with a single (resp. five) assigned variable(s). For presentation clarity, the y-axis is the average size of all five random assignments generated for a given partitioning. The values on axes represent millions of nodes if an interpolant is represented as DAG (counting literals and Boolean operators). The orange dashed line shows the average size of Craig interpolants for sub-problems. This illustrates what price is paid by focused interpolants for the path interpolation property and a single SAT solver call. Both graphs show interesting reduction in size for focused interpolants as well as substantially larger reduction in case of five assigned variables. In both graphs the same partition of the same benchmark share the same x-value, thus it is possible, especially for the larger ones, to compare their reductions.

Table 2. Average interpolant sizes by category and number of assigned variables.

Focused Itp.	APP	RND	CRF	All	Itp. from sub-prob.	APP	RND	CRF	All
No Assignment	344 298.7	1 308 750.1	489 469.1	776 573.9	No Assignment	344 298.7	1 308 750.1	489 469.1	776 573.9
1 var	92.8 %	83.0 %	78.1 %	83.7 %	1 var	69.5 %	55.0 %	65.5 %	58.8 %
5 vars	76.2 %	45.2 %	31.5 %	47.6 %	5 vars	24.4 %	5.7 %	9.7 %	9.1 %
20 vars	48.3 %	10.1 %	4.8 %	15.0 %	20 vars	0.12 %	0.01%	0.39%	0.09%

Table 2 summarizes the results shown in the graphs above, reporting precise numbers. The table on the left-hand side compares the sizes of focused interpolants to Craig interpolants (in the *No assignment* row). The *No assignment* row shows the average size of Craig interpolants for a given benchmark type. The remaining rows show the relative sizes of focused interpolants w.r.t. the *No assignment* row. The application benchmarks exhibit a smaller reduction compared to the other types, and even for twenty assigned variables, the interpolants are half in the size of the Craig interpolants. The table on the right-hand side compares the sizes of Craig interpolants for the benchmark with the Craig interpolants for sub-problems (corresponding to the assignments used in the left table). The table shows that these interpolants are on average smaller compared to the focused ones. The more variables are assigned, the bigger the difference is. While the sizes are comparable for a few assigned variables, the price paid for the path interpolation property of focused interpolants is high for larger assignments (e.g., twenty variables).

Time and memory demands are crucial properties of each interpolation tool. The reduction in overall running time and required memory roughly correspond to the reduction of interpolant sizes; e.g., PVAIR is 11 % faster and requires 9 % less memory on average if a single variable is assigned. The time and memory savings occur as well during the interpolant computation phase due to smaller interpolants being handled.

4.2   Applying PVAIR for Checking Software Upgrades

The usefulness of PVAIR is motivated by the tremendous role of interpolation in model checking. One of the possible applications of PVAIR is checking software upgrades by means of function summarization [23] implemented in the tool EVOLCHECK. Given a program S and an assertion a, EVOLCHECK verifies S with respect to a (i.e., proves that $S \wedge \neg a$ is unsatisfiable) and, for each function call in S, it constructs the interpolant and treats it as a *function summary*. In [21] we show that even if the constructed function summary is an over-approximation of the function behavior of S, it preserves the safety of the assertion a in S.

EVOLCHECK *validates* the computed function summaries to over-approximate the behavior of the corresponding functions of a program upgrade, U. In that context, programs S and U must have a non-empty set of common function calls. EVOLCHECK traverses this set starting from the deepest level of the (unwound during preprocessing) function call-tree and checks whether each original function summary still over-approximates the new behavior of the corresponding function. If there is a function call, the original summary of which does not over-approximate the new behavior, EVOLCHECK propagates the check to the caller function. If there is no function to propagate then U is unsafe. If at some depth of the unwound call-tree all the function summaries are proven to be valid, then U is safe, and EVOLCHECK reconstructs the summaries for the modified function calls.

Applying PVAIR *to* EVOLCHECK. Consider the case when U is obtained from S by *removing some functionality*. Then by construction, the original summaries of S are still valid over-approximation of the new function behavior in U. But at the same time, they might be unnecessarily general and consume excessive memory. While the use of the original summaries does not break soundness of the further upgrade checking, it is practical to refresh (and possibly shrink) the summaries to become more accurate with respect to U.

The *refreshed* summaries may be used to verify a further updated program W that additionally may *introduce new functionality* with respect to U. On the other hand, the summaries may be also used to speed up verification of a new assertion b, implanted in the code of U [21]. To enable both scenarios, the constructed summaries need to be externally stored and further migrated across the verification runs. Thus, the size of the summary also becomes important.

While EVOLCHECK does not provide a way to refresh summaries except of complete re-verification of U from scratch, PVAIR becomes particularly useful. Let $\Delta_{S,U}$ denote the behavioral difference of S and U, i.e., the set of behaviors of S not present in U. If the set $\Delta_{S,U}$ is non-empty, it could be exploited by PVAIR to generate the partial interpolants that represent new summaries for each function in U. These updated summaries are still guaranteed to preserve safety of the assertion a in U.

Experiments. We experimented with PVAIR on a set of 10 pairs of different benchmarks written in C. Notably, all benchmarks used non-linear arithmetic operations. After the required propositional encoding (i.e., bit-blasting), the resulting large-size formulae have been a bottleneck for solving and interpolation using the original EVOLCHECK approach.

In our experiments, for each pair of programs, S and U, we obtained U from the corresponding S by assigning guards in some conditional expressions. In particular, we replaced `if P do A else do B` by `assume(P); A`. This is equivalent to assigning `P = true`, and $\Delta_{S,U}$ consists of the behaviors specified by `assume(¬ P); B`. For simplicity, in our experiments, we assumed that $\Delta_{S,U}$ affected only a single function f.

The results of our experiments are shown in Table 3. For each S and U, we identified $\Delta_{S,U}$ and obtained the set of conditional expressions to be assigned in S (column *#var. assigned*). Then we performed two steps: (1) *constructed* the summary of f without/with $\Delta_{S,U}$; and (2) *validated* the corresponding summaries of f with respect to the new code in U. This experiment illustrates to what extent:

- the use of PVAIR yields smaller summaries compared to the ones by PERIPLO,
- the use of smaller summaries improves the overall performance of EVOL-CHECK.

We collected the size of the resulting interpolants and total verification time needed to perform steps (1) and (2). We used the Pudlák interpolation algorithm [17] to construct the "orig" interpolants (the ones constructed without $\Delta_{S,U}$).

As can be seen from the table, the use of PVAIR helped EVOLCHECK to make the function summaries up to 60 % smaller compared to the ones produced

Table 3. EVOLCHECK verification statistics.

C program		Interpolant (function summary) size				Verification time (sec)			
name	# var. assigned	# var. orig.	# var. PVAI	# cl. orig	# cl. PVAI	boot. orig.	boot. PVAI	upgr. orig.	upgr. PVAI
Test 0	3 vars	15227	62.61 %	45192	62.21 %	18.93	99.17 %	4.025	65.96 %
Test 1	1 var	23273	78.46 %	69330	78.31 %	10.36	99.24 %	4.034	77.79 %
Test 2	2 vars	31278	59.19 %	93345	58.98 %	8.71	100.32 %	3.878	57.61 %
Test 3	1 var	12236	63.80 %	36219	63.31 %	7.34	100.12 %	1.256	71.50 %
Test 4	2 vars	20447	74.57 %	60852	74.37 %	12.40	101.94 %	2.982	81.35 %
Test 5	3 vars	24716	32.50 %	73659	32.05 %	12.20	102.94 %	3.855	39.46 %
Test 6	3 vars	33076	37.89 %	98739	37.58 %	12.63	102.16 %	7.951	40.05 %
Test 7	1 var	12478	57.47 %	36945	56.91 %	8.88	100.29 %	2.350	57.96 %
Test 8	1 var	21201	50.42 %	63114	50.04 %	14.46	97.55 %	3.706	50.94 %
Test 9	2 vars	20314	39.71 %	60453	39.22 %	21.42	101.26 %	4.581	40.30 %

by PERIPLO (columns *#var. orig* vs. *#var. PVAI*, and *#cl. orig* vs. *#cl. PVAI*), while taking almost no additional time (columns *boot. orig.* vs. *boot. PVAI*). Furthermore, EVOLCHECK spent up to 60 % less effort in the validating step (columns *upgr. orig.* vs. *upgr. PVAI*), in which the model checker finally confirmed that the new code is safe. In other words, in the considered verification scenario and driven by PVAIR, EVOLCHECK improved both, the size of the summaries and the overall verification time, without sacrificing soundness of the entire model checking procedure.

5   Related Work

This section compares the PVAIR approach with various techniques for reducing the size of an interpolant based on variable assignments, proof compression, and interpolant post-processing.

Variable Assignments. Given a variable assignment, the most straightforward way to reduce the interpolant size is to apply the assignment directly onto the interpolant formula and propagate Boolean constants. This idea is used in the UFO [1] tool. Due to the tight integration into the interpolation process, LPAIS yields smaller interpolants compared to this simple approach. Since the assignment is considered by LPAIS already during the interpolant construction, this results in larger parts of the interpolant being cut away.

Proof Compression. Interpolants are often derived from a resolution proof and therefore their size is roughly proportional to the size of the proof. Several methods for compressing a resolution proof exist [2,4,6,11,19]. Different variants of these techniques are applied in PdTRAV [5] verification framework, the PERIPLO tool, and the Skeptik [3] proof transformer, just to name a few examples. In this work, the reduction of the interpolant size is based on the fact that only a proof of the unsatisfied part of the input formula is needed. Since the omitted (i.e., satisfied) parts can be important w.r.t. other assignments, the proof compression techniques cannot remove these parts from the proof. As a result, these techniques are orthogonal and PVAIR can benefit from proof compression if applied.

Interpolant Post-processing. Once an interpolant is computed, various techniques can be used to reduce its size. Such techniques include constant propagation, structural sharing, and various equivalence and subsumption checks. PdTRAV, for example, internally uses BDD-based sweeping to detect the equivalences and balancing/rewriting over And-Inverter Graphs [14] representation to further reduce the size of an interpolant. Any such post-processing technique producing smaller equivalent formulae can be applied to the interpolants produced by the PVAIR tool.

6   Conclusions

In this paper we presented the PVAIR interpolation tool, which exploits partial variable assignments obtained from an application-specific source to compute focused interpolants. The tool uses the extension of the labeled interpolation system, LPAIS, to construct the interpolants from a resolution refutation. We presented a potential application for the focused interpolants, in particular in software upgrade checking where we require the path interpolation property. We performed an initial study using a wide range of experiments varying the size of the partial variable assignment. The results show a good improvement compared to the baseline and suggest that the approach taken for computing focused interpolants has significant potential in reducing the interpolant size and model checking time. In the future we plan to integrate the PVAIR tool into a concrete implementation of a parallel model checker as well as to study other applications of model checking where partial assignments arise naturally.

References

1. Albarghouthi, A., Gurfinkel, A., Chechik, M.: From under-approximations to over-approximations and back. In: Flanagan, C., König, B. (eds.) TACAS 2012. LNCS, vol. 7214, pp. 157–172. Springer, Heidelberg (2012)
2. Bar-Ilan, O., Fuhrmann, O., Hoory, S., Shacham, O., Strichman, O.: Linear-time reductions of resolution proofs. In: Chockler, H., Hu, A.J. (eds.) HVC 2008. LNCS, vol. 5394, pp. 114–128. Springer, Heidelberg (2009)
3. Boudou, J., Fellner, A., Woltzenlogel Paleo, B.: Skeptik: a proof compression system. In: Demri, S., Kapur, D., Weidenbach, C. (eds.) IJCAR 2014. LNCS, vol. 8562, pp. 374–380. Springer, Heidelberg (2014)
4. Boudou, J., Woltzenlogel Paleo, B.: Compression of propositional resolution proofs by lowering subproofs. In: Galmiche, D., Larchey-Wendling, D. (eds.) TABLEAUX 2013. LNCS, vol. 8123, pp. 59–73. Springer, Heidelberg (2013)

5. Cabodi, G., Loiacono, C., Vendraminetto, D.: Optimization techniques for craig interpolant compaction in unbounded model checking. In: DATE, pp. 1417–1422 (2013)
6. Cotton, S.: Two techniques for minimizing resolution proofs. In: Strichman, O., Szeider, S. (eds.) SAT 2010. LNCS, vol. 6175, pp. 306–312. Springer, Heidelberg (2010)
7. Craig, W.: Three uses of the Herbrand-Gentzen theorem in relating model theory and proof theory. Symbol. Logic 22, 269–285 (1957)
8. D'Silva, V., Kroening, D., Purandare, M., Weissenbacher, G.: Interpolant strength. In: Barthe, G., Hermenegildo, M. (eds.) VMCAI 2010. LNCS, vol. 5944, pp. 129–145. Springer, Heidelberg (2010)
9. Eén, N., Biere, A.: Effective preprocessing in SAT through variable and clause elimination. In: Bacchus, F., Walsh, T. (eds.) SAT 2005. LNCS, vol. 3569, pp. 61–75. Springer, Heidelberg (2005)
10. Fedyukovich, G., Sery, O., Sharygina, N.: eVolCheck: incremental upgrade checker for C. In: Piterman, N., Smolka, S.A. (eds.) TACAS 2013 (ETAPS 2013). LNCS, vol. 7795, pp. 292–307. Springer, Heidelberg (2013)
11. Fontaine, P., Merz, S., Woltzenlogel Paleo, B.: Compression of propositional resolution proofs via partial regularization. In: Bjørner, N., Sofronie-Stokkermans, V. (eds.) CADE 2011. LNCS, vol. 6803, pp. 237–251. Springer, Heidelberg (2011)
12. Jancik, P., Kofroň, J., Rollini, S.F., Sharygina, N.: On interpolants and variable assignments. In: FMCAD, pp. 123–130 (2014)
13. Jhala, R., McMillan, K.L.: A practical and complete approach to predicate refinement. In: Hermanns, H., Palsberg, J. (eds.) TACAS 2006. LNCS, vol. 3920, pp. 459–473. Springer, Heidelberg (2006)
14. Kuehlmann, A., Ganai, M.K., Paruthi, V.: Circuit-based Boolean reasoning. In: DAC, pp. 232–237 (2001)
15. McMillan, K.L.: Interpolation and SAT-based model checking. In: Hunt Jr., W.A., Somenzi, F. (eds.) CAV 2003. LNCS, vol. 2725, pp. 1–13. Springer, Heidelberg (2003)
16. McMillan, K.L.: An interpolating theorem prover. In: Jensen, K., Podelski, A. (eds.) TACAS 2004. LNCS, vol. 2988, pp. 16–30. Springer, Heidelberg (2004)
17. Pudlák, P.: Lower bounds for resolution and cutting plane proofs and monotone computations. Symbol. Logic 62, 981–998 (1997)
18. Rollini, S.F., Alt, L., Fedyukovich, G., Hyvärinen, A.E.J., Sharygina, N.: PeRIPLO: a framework for producing effective interpolants in SAT-based software verification. In: McMillan, K., Middeldorp, A., Voronkov, A. (eds.) LPAR-19 2013. LNCS, vol. 8312, pp. 683–693. Springer, Heidelberg (2013)
19. Rollini, S.F., Bruttomesso, R., Sharygina, N., Tsitovich, A.: Resolution proof transformation for compression and interpolation. Formal Methods Syst. Des. 45, 1–41 (2014)
20. Rollini, S.F., Sery, O., Sharygina, N.: Leveraging interpolant strength in model checking. In: Madhusudan, P., Seshia, S.A. (eds.) CAV 2012. LNCS, vol. 7358, pp. 193–209. Springer, Heidelberg (2012)
21. Sery, O., Fedyukovich, G., Sharygina, N.: Interpolation-based function summaries in bounded model checking. In: Eder, K., Lourenço, J., Shehory, O. (eds.) HVC 2011. LNCS, vol. 7261, pp. 160–175. Springer, Heidelberg (2012)
22. Sery, O., Fedyukovich, G., Sharygina, N.: FunFrog: bounded model checking with interpolation-based function summarization. In: Chakraborty, S., Mukund, M. (eds.) ATVA 2012. LNCS, vol. 7561, pp. 203–207. Springer, Heidelberg (2012)

23. Sery, O., Fedyukovich, G., Sharygina, N.: Incremental upgrade checking by means of interpolation-based function summaries. In: FMCAD, pp. 114–121 (2012)
24. Tange, O.: GNU parallel - the command-line power tool. In: The USENIX Magazine, pp. 42–47 (2011)
25. Tseitin, G.S.: On the complexity of derivation in propositional calculus. In: Slisenko, A.O. (ed.) Studies in Constructive Mathematics and Mathematical Logic, pp. 115–125. Plenum, New York (1969)

Author Index

Printed in the United States
By Bookmasters